Environmental design

CIBSE Guide A

Typeset and printed in Great Britain by by The Yale Press Ltd, Norwood, London SE25 5LY

CHARTERED INSTITUTION OF BUILDING SERVICES ENGINEERS

CIBSE Guide A: *Environmental design*

CORRIGENDA

(1) Page 2-56: Table 2.28(*i*): wrong data in table; replacement provided on self-adhesive label.

(2) Pages 2-52 to 2-57: Table 2.28: dates at top of each table should read as follows:

Table 2.28(*a*): January 29
Table 2.28(*b*): February 26
Table 2.28(*c*): March 29
Table 2.28(*d*): April 28
Table 2.28(*e*): May 29
Table 2.28(*f*): June 21
Table 2.28(*g*): July 4
Table 2.28(*h*): August 4
Table 2.28(*i*): September 4
Table 2.28(*j*): October 4
Table 2.28(*k*): November 4
Table 2.28(*l*): December 4

(3) Page 2-59: example following equation 2.3 should read as follows:

For $v = 5$ m·s^{-1}, equation 2.2 gives $f(v) = 0.130$, i.e. the wind speed will be between 4.5 and 5.5 m·s^{-1} for 13% of the time.

(4) Page 3-20: equation 3.31 should read as follows:

$$U_f = \frac{2\,\lambda_g}{\pi\,L_f + d_{ef}}\, \log_e\left[(\pi\,L_f\,/\,d_{ef}) + 1)\right]$$

(5) Page 3-20: equation 3.32 should read as follows:

$$U_f = \lambda_g\,/\,(0.457\,L_f + d_{ef})$$

(6) Page 3-24: right hand column, first paragraph should read as follows:

"U_f may be determined ..... both sides of the floor as 0.17 m^2·K·W^{-1}."

(7) Page 3-37: equation 3.52 should read as follows:

$$\frac{1}{E\,A_1} = \frac{1}{A_1} + \frac{1 - \varepsilon_1}{A_1\,\varepsilon_1} + \frac{1 - \varepsilon_2}{A_2\,\varepsilon_2}$$

(8) Page 3-38: equation 3.62 should read as follows:

$$R_{se} = \frac{1}{E\,h_r + h_c}$$

continued .../

(9) Page 5-61: section 5.A2.2: add symbol definition as follows:

  f Decrement factor

(10) Corrections to computer disk:

  (a) Table of sol-air temperatures for London area (Bracknell) [filename: solairLo] (see item (1) above) has been corrected on disks marked "v1.2".

  (b) Dates for monthly sol-air data for all locations [filenames: solairEd, solairLo and solairMa] (see item (2) above) have been corrected on disks marked "v1.2".

Ref: GVA/04: 17/03/00

Preface

The production of this Guide is the culmination of considerable effort by a number of dedicated members who have selflessly given their own time that the membership at large may avail themselves of updated technological and intellectual data.

This Guide also provides a landmark in the CIBSE publications process as it marks the start of a policy whereby the Guide will be revised on a more regular schedule. This change in policy reflects the more rapidly changing world and the Institution's recognition of the necessity to keep members abreast of technical and legislative developments and the demands associated with European and international standards.

Preparation of the next edition is already in hand and this work will be facilitated if members communicate suggestions for amendments, modifications and revisions to the Institution's publications secretariat. Meaningful feedback from members is an essential ingredient of the publications process.

My personal thanks go to all those who contributed to the various sections of this Guide; particularly to the members of the Guide Steering Committee, its chairman, David Lush OBE, and secretary, Ken Butcher.

James E Fretwell
President

Note from the publisher

This publication is primarily intended to provide guidance to those responsible for the design, installation, commissioning, operation and maintenance of building services. It is not intended to be exhaustive or definitive and it will be necessary for users of the guidance given to exercise their own professional judgement when deciding whether to abide by or depart from it.

Foreword

This sixth edition of Guide A contains significant changes from the previous edition. The review of the whole range of topics covered by the volume, during a period when traditional design criteria and calculation methods were being reconsidered, resulted in an iterative process of revision, the consequence of which was a series of sectional drafts which were not always compatible. The task of bringing these together into a coherent single volume has contributed to the delayed publication of this Guide. The Institution has recently reviewed and amended its publications strategy to ensure that this and other major Guides are updated on a rolling programme, so that similar delays will not occur in future.

I would like to take this opportunity of thanking Institution members for their forbearance with the delay and commend this new edition to them. It provides the basis for selecting comfort criteria, along with the data and calculation methods required for good practice design. As a learned society, the Institution is recognised as the authoritative body in the theory and practice of building services engineering and the CIBSE Guide is often used in litigation as the foundation for resolving disputes concerning professional practice.

The changes made in the sixth edition, compared to the fifth, can be briefly summarised, as follows:

— Section 1: *Environmental criteria for design* covers the same basic topics of temperature, humidity, lighting and acoustics, as did the previous edition, but each has been extensively revised to provide more comprehensive data and recommendations for particular situations. The most significant change has been to replace the notion of a single 'comfort' temperature by summertime and wintertime temperature ranges, based on percentage mean vote (PMV). Also, new sections have been added dealing with indoor air quality, air filtration strategy and the electromagnetic and electrostatic environment.

— Section 2: *External design data* replaces the former section A2: Weather and solar data. The cold and warm weather data for the UK have been fully revised using meteorological provided by the Meteorological Office for the period 1976-1995, with detailed data for eight locations being included. The information is provided in a form that allows the external design limit conditions to be selected by the designer to meet the client's requirements regarding design risk. A selection of international heating and cooling design temperatures is included, drawn from data published by ASHRAE. These data are reproduced by kind permission of ASHRAE. Detailed solar data have been included for three UK locations, London area (Bracknell), Manchester (Aughton) and Edinburgh (Mylnefield). Tables of predicted irradiances for latitudes 0–60°N/S, based on computer algorithms, are also included. For reasons of space, some of these data are located on the computer disk that accompanies this Guide.

— Section 3: *Thermal properties of building structures*. This section is cited in Part L of the Building Regulations as one of the accepted means of complying with the regulatory requirements concerning the conservation of fuel and power. It has been fully revised and expanded and now includes more detailed calculation procedures to deal with the various types of window frame and glazing. Many of the relevant national, European and international standards have been, or are currently being revised and great efforts have been made to ensure that the calculation procedures given in the Guide are consistent with these standards. The tables of thermal properties of materials have been substantially increased, drawing from research undertaken by the Building Environmental Performance Analysis Club.

— Section 4: *Air infiltration and natural ventilation* explores the mechanisms of infiltration and natural ventilation, the forces creating these phenomena and methods for calculating infiltration and ventilation rates. A computer program listing is provided for calculating air change rates in single zone enclosures. This is reproduced by the kind permission of the Air Infiltration and Ventilation Centre. This section takes account of guidance contained in CIBSE Applications Manual AM10: Natural ventilation in non-domestic buildings.

— Section 5: *Thermal response and plant sizing* brings together the subject areas formerly covered in three separate Guide sections, i.e. A5: *Thermal response of buildings*, A8: *Summertime temperatures in buildings* and A9: *Estimation of plant capacity*, and provides a more coherent exploration of these topics. The new section considers a range of calculation procedures, from simple steady-state heat losses and the estimation of summertime temperatures through to computer-based dynamic modelling. The admittance procedure is retained as a simple dynamic model, suitable for application at an early stage in the design process. Guidance is provided on which methods are suitable for particular applications and examples of their use are given. This section also includes the data and equations necessary to apply the various models.

Cooling load tables are provided for three UK locations, London, Manchester and Edinburgh. These are based on the measured solar irradiances given in Section 2. Similar tables provide estimated cooling loads for latitudes 0–60°N/S, based on the predicted solar irradiances given in Section 2. These are included on the computer disk that accompanies this Guide. Various appendices provide detailed derivations of the equations and calculation techniques presented in the section.

— Section 6: *Internal heat gains* replaces section A7 of the fifth edition, which had the same title. The section has been comprehensively revised and includes data for a much wider range of equipment and systems, including computers and office machines. Guidance is given on diversity factors and on the division of heat gains into their radiant and convective components.

— Section 7: *Moisture transfer and condensation*. This replaces section A10 of the previous edition of Guide A. While the calculation procedures have been retained largely unchanged, the explanatory text has been revised and expanded and new example calculations have been added. Tables of resistivities for common building materials are now contained in Section 3.

The Institution appreciates the importance of its publications to its members' day-to-day activities. Guide A is accepted as the foundation for professional practice and applications in building services engineering and it is therefore in all our interests that it is kept up-to-date. In order to do this, the Institution needs the help of CIBSE members and other users of the Guide to identify areas where the present guidance is inadequate or needs to be improved. The Institution will shortly start work on the seventh edition of Guide A and members' input is essential to its success. A time scale of three to five years is envisaged for its preparation and the CIBSE Publications Department would be pleased to hear from users of the Guide, both members and non-members, who feel that they can contribute to this work.

Finally, having mentioned the importance of members' views for future editions, I must express my sincere thanks to the authors and contributors to this sixth edition of Guide A. They include CIBSE members, some non-members and the staff at CIBSE, to all of whom the Institution and I are extremely grateful.

David Lush
Chairman, CIBSE Guide A Steering Committee

Guide A Steering Committee

David Lush (Chairman) (consultant to Ove Arup & Partners)
Paul Appleby (Building Health and Safety Division, Thorburn Colquhoun Consulting Engineers)
Angus Gait (Ove Arup & Partners)
Michael Holmes (Ove Arup & Partners)
Geoff Levermore (UMIST)
Martin Liddament (Air Infiltration and Ventilation Centre)
Peter Owens (consultant)
Derek Tuddenham (former Chairman) (Roger Preston & Partners)
Ken Butcher (Secretary)

Task Groups, principal authors, contributors and acknowledgements

Section 1: *Environmental criteria for design*

Section Task Group/principal authors:
Paul Appleby (Chairman) (Building Health and Safety Division, Thorburn Colquhoun Consulting Engineers)
Vic Crisp (BRE)
Les Fothergill (Department of the Environment)
Ian Griffiths (deceased) (University of Surrey)
Peter Jackman (BSRIA)
Bjärne Olesen (VELTA, Germany)

Contributors:
Farshad Alamdari (BSRIA)
Geoff Leventhall (consultant)
Tony Mulhall (Health and Safety Executive)
Nigel Oseland (formerly BRE)
Gary Raw (BRE)
Paul R Ruffles (Lighting Design & Technology)

Acknowledgements:
David Handley (Healthy Buildings International)
Phil Haves (Loughborough University of Technology)
Rev. Michael Humphreys (Regents Park College)
David Lush (consultant)
Fergus Nichol (Oxford Brookes University)

Section 2: *External design data*

The text and data contained in this section are largely abstracted from CIBSE Guide: *Weather and solar data* (in preparation) the principal authors of which are given below. UK weather data were supplied by The Meteorological Office. The project was supported by the Department of the Environment, Transport and the Regions under its Partners in Innovation programme.

Principal authors:
Geoff Levermore (Chairman) (UMIST)
Eric Keeble (UMIST)
Tariq Muneer (Napier University)
John Page (consultant)
Chris Sanders (BRE Scottish Laboratory)
Andrew Wright (EA Technology)

Contributors:
Ken Butcher (CIBSE)
Ben Keeble (UMIST)
David Wood (Gibb Ltd)

Acknowledgements:
Department of the Environment, Transport and the Regions
The Meteorological Office
American Society of Heating, Refrigerating and Air-conditioning Engineers

Section 3: Thermal properties of buildings and components

Section Task Group/principal authors:
Peter Owens (Chairman) (consultant)
Brian Anderson (BRE Scottish Laboratory)
Jack Siviour
David Spooner

Contributors:
Joe Clarke (University of Strathclyde)
Alan Guy (Pilkington UK Ltd)
Ted King (DETR Building Regulations Division)

Acknowledgements:
Her Majesty's Stationery Office
British Standards Institution

Section 4: Air infiltration and natural ventilation

Principal authors:
Peter Jackman (BSRIA, retired)
Martin Liddament (Air Infiltration and Ventilation Centre)

Contributor:
Chris Sanders (BRE Scottish Laboratory)

Acknowledgements:
Air Infiltration and Ventilation Centre

Section 5: Thermal response and plant sizing

Principal authors:
Michael Holmes (Ove Arup & Partners)
Alexandra Wilson (Ove Arup & Partners)

Contributors:
Eric Keeble (UMIST)
Angus Gait (Ove Arup & Partners)
Tariq Muneer (Napier University)
John Page (consultant)

Acknowledgements:
David Lush (consultant to Ove Arup & Partners)
Morris Davies (University of Liverpool)
John Harrington-Lynn (HL Research)
Geoff Levermore (UMIST)
Geoff Spitler (Oklahoma State University)
Simon Rees (University of Loughborough)

Section 6: Internal heat gains

Principle author:
Greg Hayden (formerly BSRIA)

Contributor:
Martin Ratcliffe (South Bank University)

Acknowledgements:
American Society of Heating, Refrigerating and Air-conditioning Engineers

Section 7: Moisture transfer and condensation

Principal authors:
Angus Gait (Ove Arup & Partners)
John Moss (Ove Arup & Partners)

Editor

Ken Butcher

CIBSE Editorial Manager

Ken Butcher

Acknowledgement

Extracts from British Standards are reproduced with the permission of BSI under licence number PD/1999-1061. Complete copies of standards may be obtained by post from BSI Customer Services, 389 Chiswick High Road, London W4 4AL.

Contents

1 Environmental criteria for design

1.1 Introduction

1.1.1 Comfort

Comfort has been defined as 'that condition of mind that expresses satisfaction with the ... environment'[1].

The indoor environment should be designed and controlled so that occupants' comfort and health are assured. There are individual differences in perception and subjective evaluation, resulting in a base level of dissatisfaction within the building population. This dissatisfaction may be with a specific aspect of the environment or may be general and non-specific. The aim of design should be to minimise this dissatisfaction as far as is reasonably practicable.

The environmental factors considered here include the thermal, visual and acoustic conditions, indoor air quality, electromagnetic fields and static electricity. Currently, it is not possible to formulate a single index that quantifies the individual's response to all these factors, although there may be additive or synergistic effects resulting from interactions among a number of them. For example irritant contaminants, such as formaldehyde, become more noticeable at low air humidity.

Therefore, it is necessary to specify measurable limits or ranges for each of the environmental factors, making allowance, where possible, for any interactions that might occur.

1.1.2 Health aspects

The constitution of the World Health Organisation defines good health as '... a state of complete physical, mental and social well-being, not merely the absence of disease and infirmity'. While for most people this may be an ideal rather than reality, it indicates that the indoor environment should be managed in such a way as to promote health, not merely to avoid illness.

In some cases occupants experience symptoms, which may not be obviously related to a particular cause, but which become less severe or disappear when they leave a particular environment. These symptoms, such as nausea, mucosal dryness or irritation, runny nose, eye problems, headaches, skin problems, heavy head and flu-like symptoms, may be quite severe and lead to reduced productivity or absenteeism. If a significant proportion of occupants experience these symptoms then, by definition[2], the occupants are suffering from 'sick building syndrome'.

It is likely that the cause of sick building syndrome is multi-factorial. Researchers have identified a statistically significant correlation between symptom prevalence and many different and unrelated factors. It would appear that if environmental conditions are within the comfort limits set out in this Guide then the risk of occupant dissatisfaction and sick building syndrome is reduced, though not eliminated.

1.2 Notation

1.2.1 Symbols

The symbols used within this section are defined as follows.

A	Total area of internal surfaces (ceiling, floor, windows and walls) (m^2)
A_w	Net glazed area of window (m^2)
C	Heat loss by convection from surface of clothed body
$C_p,$	Concentration of pollutant (ppm)
C_p	Concentration of pollutant by volume (mg·m^{-3})
C_{pi}	Limit of concentration of pollutant in indoor air (ppm)
C_{po}	Concentration of pollutant in outdoor air (ppm)
C_{res}	Heat exchange by convection in respiratory tract
DF	Average daylight factor (%)
DR	Draught rating (%)
E	Heat loss by evaporation from surface of clothed body
E_{res}	Heat exchange by evaporation in respiratory tract
E_v	Ventilation effectiveness
f_{cl}	Ratio of the area of clothed human body to that of unclothed human body
h_c	Convective heat transfer coefficient at body surface (W·m^{-2}·K^{-1})
I_{cl}	Thermal resistance of clothing (m^2·K·W^{-1})
K	Heat flow by conduction from surface of clothed body
M	Metabolic rate (W·m^{-2} of body surface)
M_a	Activity level (met)
M_p	Molar mass of pollutant (kg·mole^{-1})
P	Pollutant emission rate (L·s^{-1})
p_s	Partial water vapour pressure in air surrounding the body (Pa)
Q	Outdoor air supply rate (L·s^{-1})
Q_c	Outdoor air supply rate to account for total contaminant load (L·s^{-1})
Q'	Reduced outdoor air supply rate to control intermittent pollution (L·s^{-1})
PMV	Predicted mean vote
PPD	Predicted percentage dissatisfied
R	Heat loss by radiation from surface of clothed body
R_a	Area-weighted average reflectance of interior surfaces (ceiling, floor, windows and walls)
S	Body heat storage
T	Diffuse transmittance of glazing material including effects of dirt

t_{ai}	Inside air temperature (°C)
t_c	Dry resultant temperature (°C)
t_{cl}	Surface temperature of clothing (°C)
t_p	Plane radiant temperature (°C)
t_r	Mean radiant temperature (°C)
T_u	Turbulence intensity (%)
V	Volume of space (m³)
v	Air speed (m·s⁻¹)
v_r	Relative air speed (m·s⁻¹)
v_{SD}	Standard deviation of air speed (m·s⁻¹)
W	Rate of performance of external work
θ	Angle in degrees subtended, in the vertical plane normal to the window, by sky visible from centre of window (degree)
θ_p	Duration of release of pollutant(s)

Note: in compound units, the abbreviation 'L' has been used to denote 'litre'.

1.2.2 Definitions of main thermal parameters

For the purposes of this Guide, the following terminology is adopted.

Indoor air temperature (t_{ai})

The dry bulb temperature of the air in the space.

Mean radiant temperature (t_r)

The uniform surface temperature of a radiantly black enclosure in which an occupant would exchange the same amount of radiant heat as in the actual non-uniform space. (See *ISO 7726*[3] for derivation.) Mean radiant temperature varies throughout the enclosure unless the surface temperatures of all the internal surfaces of the enclosure are equal.

Relative air speed (v_r)

The net mean air speed across the body. For sedentary occupancy, v_r is taken as the room air movement only (v). For people in motion it will be approximately equal to the speed of their movement plus the mean room air speed.

Humidity

The humidity of room air expressed in absolute terms, i.e. moisture content (mass of water vapour per unit mass of dry air (kg·kg⁻¹)) or vapour pressure (partial pressure of water vapour (Pa)).

Relative humidity

The ratio of vapour pressure to saturation vapour pressure at same dry bulb temperature, expressed as a percentage (% RH).

Percentage saturation

The ratio of moisture content to moisture content of saturated air at same dry bulb temperature, expressed as a percentage (% sat). (*Note:* at ambient temperatures and humidities the difference between relative humidity and percentage saturation is small and may be ignored.)

Clo

The unit for thermal insulation of clothing[4], where 1 clo = 0.155 m²·K·W⁻¹. A clothing ensemble that approximates to 1 clo consists of underwear, blouse/shirt, slacks/trousers, jacket, socks and shoes.

Met

The unit used to express the physical activity of humans is the met[5], where 1 met = 58.2 W·m⁻². One met is an average metabolic rate for a person seated at rest. The average body surface area for adults is about 1.8 m², therefore 1 met is equivalent to approximately 100 W of total heat emission.

1.3 Design criteria

Table 1.1 gives general guidance and recommendations on suitable winter and summer temperature ranges, outdoor air supply rates, filtration grades, maintained illuminances and noise ratings for a range of room and building types. The dry resultant temperature ranges, based on the assumed clothing insulation and metabolic rates indicated, correspond to a predicted mean vote (PMV) of ±0.25, see section 1.4.2.2. These are intended to give a base level from which corrections can be made for non-standard situations.

The summer comfort temperatures given in Table 1.1 apply to air conditioned buildings. Higher temperatures may be acceptable if air conditioning is not present, e.g. if for sedentary areas such as offices an inside dry resultant temperature of 25°C is not exceeded for more than 5% of the annual occupied period[6] (typically 125 hours). Note that for control purposes, thermostats are usually based on air temperature (t_{ai}).

The *Fuel and Electricity (Heating) (Control) Order 1974*[7] and the *Fuel and Electricity (Heating) (Control) (Amendment) Order 1980*[8] prohibit the use of fuels or electricity to heat premises above 19°C. This does not mean that the temperature in buildings must be kept below 19°C but only that fuel or electricity must not be used to raise the temperature above this level. In Table 1.1, for some applications, the recommended minimum winter design temperatures exceed 19°C. In these cases, it is assumed that the recommended temperatures can be maintained by contributions from heat sources other than the heating system. These may include solar radiation, heat gains from lighting, equipment and machinery and heat gains from the occupants themselves.

Guidance on adapting these general recommendations to other situations is given in subsequent sections and Table 1.2 indicates which section should be consulted for further guidance on any given design parameter. For example, if clothing insulation is expected to be outside that given in Table 1.1, guidance on the appropriate correction to the design dry resultant temperature may be found in section 1.4.3.2. The corrections suggested are made on the basis of comfort equations developed by Fanger[9].

Table 1.1 Recommended comfort criteria for specific applications

Building/room type	Winter dry resultant temperature range for stated activity and clothing levels*			Summer dry resultant temperature range† for stated activity and clothing levels*			Suggested air supply rate (L·s⁻¹·person⁻¹) except where stated otherwise	Filtration grade‡	Maintained illuminance (lux)§	Noise rating (NR)¶
	Temp. (°C)	Activity (met)	Clothing (clo)	Temp. (°C)	Activity (met)	Clothing (clo)				
Airport terminals:										
— baggage reclaim	12–19[1]	1.8	1.15	21–25[1]	1.8	0.65	8[2]	F6–F7	200	45
— check–in areas[3]	18–20	1.4	1.15	21–23	1.4	0.65	8[2]	F6–F7	500[4]	45
— concourse (no seats)	12–19[1]	1.8	1.15	21–25[1]	1.8	0.65	8[2]	F6–F7	200	45
— customs area	18–20	1.4	1.15	21–23	1.4	0.65	8[2]	F6–F7	500	45
— departure lounge	19–21	1.3	1.15	22–24	1.3	0.65	8[2]	F6–F7	200	40
Art galleries — see *Museums and art galleries*										
Banks, building societies, post offices:										
— counters	19–21	1.4	1.0	21–23	1.4	0.65	8[2]	F6–F7	500	35–40
— public areas	19–21	1.4	1.0	21–23	1.4	0.65	8[2]	F5–F7	300	35–45
Bars/lounges	20–22	1.3	1.0	22–24	1.3	0.65	8[2]	F5–F7	100–200[5]	30–40
Bus/coach stations — see *Railway/coach stations*										
Churches	19–21	1.3	1.15	22–24	1.3	0.65	8[2]	G4–F6	100–200	25–30
Computer rooms[6]	19–21	1.4	1.0	21–23	1.4	0.65	8[2]	F7–F9	300	35–45
Conference/board rooms	22–23	1.1	1.0	23–25	1.1	0.65	8[2]	F6–F7	300/500[7]	25–30
Drawing offices	19–21	1.4	1.0	21–23	1.4	0.65	8[2]	F7	750	35–45
Dwellings:										
— bathrooms	26–27	1.2	0.25	26–27	1.2	0.25	15 L·s⁻¹	G2–G4 (extract)[8]	100[4]	—
— bedrooms	17–19	0.9	2.5	23–25	0.9	1.2	0.4–1 ACH to control moisture[8]	G2–G4	100[4]	25
— hall/stairs/landings	19–24[1]	1.8	0.75	21–25[1]	1.8	0.65	—	—	100	—
— kitchen	17–19	1.6	1.0	21–23	1.6	0.65	60 L·s⁻¹	G2–G4 (extract)[8]	300	40–45
— living rooms	22–23	1.1	1.0	23–25	1.1	0.65	0.4–1 ACH to control moisture[8]	G2–G4	50–200	30
— toilets	19–21	1.4	1.0	21–23	1.4	0.65	>5 ACH	G2–G4	100[4]	—
Educational buildings:										
— lecture halls[9]	19–21	1.4	1.0	21–23	1.4	0.65	8[2]	G4–G5	300[10]	25–35
— seminar rooms	19–21	1.4	1.0	21–23	1.4	0.65	8[2]	G4–G5	300[10]	25–35
— teaching spaces[9]	19–21	1.4	1.0	21–23	1.4	0.65	8[2]	G4–G5	300[10]	25–35
Exhibition halls	19-21	1.4	1.0	21–23	1.4	0.65	8[2]	G3–G4	300	40
Factories:										
— heavy work	11–14[11]	2.5	0.85	—[12]	—	—	—[13]	Depends on use	—[14,15]	50–65
— light work	16–19	1.8	0.85	—[12]	—	—	—[13]	Depends on use	—[14,15]	45–55
— sedentary work	19–21	1.4	1.0	21–23	1.4	0.65	—[13]	Depends on use	—[14,15]	45
Fire/ambulance stations:										
— recreation rooms	20–22	1.3	1.0	22–24	1.3	0.65	8[2]	F5	300	35–40
— watchroom	22–23	1.1	1.0	24–26	1.1	0.65	8[2]	F5	200	35–40
Garages:										
— parking	—	—	—	—	—	—	6 ACH (extract)	—	100	55
— servicing	16–19	1.8	0.85	—	—	—	—	G2–G3	300/500	45–50
General building areas:										
— corridors	19–21	1.4	1.0	21–23	1.4	0.65	8[2]	—[16]	100	40
— entrance halls/lobbies	19–21	1.4	1.0	21–23	1.4	0.65	8[2]	—[16]	200[4]	35–40
— kitchens (commercial)	15–18	1.8	1.0	18–21	1.8	0.65	—[17]	G2–G4	500	40–45
— toilets	19–21	1.4	1.0	21–23	1.4	0.65	>5 ACH	G4–G5	100[4]	35–45
— waiting areas/rooms	19–21	1.4	1.0	21–23	1.44	0.65	8[2]	—[16]	200	30–35
Hospitals and health care buildings:										
— bedheads/wards	22–24	0.9	1.4	23–25	0.9	1.2	8[2]	F7–F9	—[18]	30
— circulation spaces (wards)[19]	19–24[1]	1.8	0.75	21–25[1]	1.8	0.65	8[2]	F7–F9	—[18]	35

Table 1.1 Recommended comfort criteria for specific applications — *continued*

Building/room type	Winter dry resultant temperature range for stated activity and clothing levels*			Summer dry resultant temperature range† for stated activity and clothing levels*			Suggested air supply rate (L·s⁻¹·person⁻¹ except where stated otherwise)	Filtration grade‡	Maintained illuminance (lux)§	Noise rating (NR)¶
	Temp. (°C)	Activity (met)	Clothing (clo)	Temp. (°C)	Activity (met)	Clothing (clo)				
Hospitals and health care buildings: *(contd.)*										
— consulting/treatment rooms	22–24	1.4	0.55	23–25	1.4	0.45	8[2]	F7–F9	—[18]	30
— nurses' station[19]	19–22	1.4	0.9	21–23	1.4	0.65	8[2]	F7–F9	—[18]	35
— operating theatres	17–19	1.8	0.8	17–19	1.8	0.8	0.65–1.0 m³·s⁻¹	F9	—[18]	30–35
Hotels:										
— bathrooms	26–27	1.2	0.25	25–27	1.2	0.25	12[2]	F5–F7	150	40
— bedrooms	19–21	1.0	1.0	21–23	1.0	1.2	8[2]	F5–F7	50/100	20–30
Ice rinks	12	—	—	—	—	—	3 ACH	G3	200[20]	40–50
Laundries:										
— commercial	16–19	1.8	0.85	—[12]	—	—	—[21]	G3–G4	300/500	45
— launderettes	16–18	1.6	1.15	20–22	1.6	0.65	—[21]	G2–G3	300	45–50
Law courts	19–21	1.4	1.0	21–23	1.4	0.65	8[2]	F5–F7	300	25–30
Libraries:										
— lending/reference areas[22]	19–21	1.4	1.0	21–23	1.4	0.65	8[2]	F5–F7	300	30–35
— reading rooms	22–23	1.1	1.0	24–25	1.1	0.65	8[2]	F5–F7	300[23]	30–35
— store rooms	15	—	—	—	—	—	—	F6–F8	200	—
Museums and art galleries:										
— display[24]	19–21	1.4	1.0	21–23	1.4	0.65	8[2]	F7–F8	200[25]	30–35
— storage[24]	19–21	1.4	1.0	21–23	1.4	0.65	8[2]	F7–F8	50[25]	30–35
Offices:										
— executive	21–23	1.2	0.85	22–24	1.2	0.7	8[2]	F7	500[7]	30
— general	21–23	1.2	0.85	22–24	1.2	0.7	8[2]	F6–F7	500[7]	35
— open–plan	21–23	1.2	0.85	22–24	1.2	0.7	8[2]	F6–F7	500[7]	35
Places of public assembly:										
— auditoria[26]	22–23[1]	1.0	1.0	24–25	1.1	0.65	8[2]	F5–F7	100–150[5]	20–30
— changing/dressing rooms	23–24	1.4	0.5	23–25	1.4	0.4	8[2]	F5–F7	100	35
— circulation spaces	13–20[1]	1.8	1.0	21–25[1]	1.8	0.65	8[2]	G4–G5	100	40
— foyers[27]	13–20[1]	1.8	1.0	21–25[1]	1.8	0.65	8[2]	F5–F7	200	40
— multi-purpose halls[28]	—	—	—	—	—	—	8[2]	G4–G5	300	—
Prison cells	19–21	1.0	1.7	21–23	1.0	1.2	8[2]	F5	100[4]	25–30
Railway/coach stations:										
— concourse (no seats)	12–19[1]	1.8	1.15	21–25[1]	1.8	0.65	8[2]	G4–G5	200	45
— ticket office	18–20	1.4	1.15	21–23	1.4	0.65	8[2]	G4–G5	500	40
— waiting room	21–22	1.1	1.15	24–25	1.1	0.65	8[2]	G4–G5	200	40
Restaurants/dining rooms	22–24	1.1	0.9	24–25	1.1	0.65	8[2]	F5–F7	50–200[5]	35–40
Retailing:										
— shopping malls	19–24[1]	1.8	0.75	21–25[1]	1.8	0.65	8[2]	G4–G5	50–300	40–50
— small shops, department stores[22]	19–21	1.4	1.0	21–23	1.4	0.65	8[2]	F5–F7	500/750	35–40
— supermarkets[29]	19–21	1.4	1.0	21–23	1.4	0.65	8[2]	F5–F7	750/1000	40–45
Sports halls[30]:										
— changing rooms	22–24	1.4	0.55	24–25	1.4	0.35	6–10 ACH	G3	100[20]	35–45
— hall	13–16	3.0	0.4	14–16	3.0	0.35	8[2]	G3–F5	300[20]	40–50
Squash courts[30]	10–12	4.0	0.25	—	—	—	4 ACH	G3	300[20]	50
Swimming pools:										
— changing rooms	23–24	1.4	0.5	24–25	1.4	0.35	10 ACH	G3	100[20]	35–45
— pool halls	23–26	1.6	<0.1	23–26	1.6	<0.1	0–15 L·s⁻¹·m⁻² (of wet area)	G3	300[20]	40–50
Television studios[26]	19–21	1.4	1.0	21–23	1.4	0.65	8[2]	F5–F7	—[31]	25

Notes: Except where indicated[1], temperature ranges based on stated values of met and clo and a PMV of ±0.25. Upper temperature of stated range may be increased and lower temperature decreased by approximately 1°C if PMV of ±0.5 (i.e. 90 PPD) is acceptable (see section 1.3.3.2. Calculation assumes RH = 50% and v_r = 0.15 m·s⁻¹. Insulation value of chair assumed to be 0.15 clo for all applications except dwellings, for which 0.3 has been assumed.

Footnotes to Table 1.1:

* See section 1.4.3. for additional data and variations due to different activities and levels of clothing.

† Higher temperatures may be acceptable if air conditioning not present, see section 1.3.

‡ See also Table 1.8, which gives requirements for specific pollutants

¶ See also Table 1.18

§ Illumination levels given thus: 200–500 indicate that the required level varies through the space depending on function and/or task. Illumination levels given thus: 300/500, indicate that one or the other level is appropriate depending on exact function. Illumination levels in this table give only a general indication of requirements. Reference must be made to the table of recommended illuminances in the *Code for Interior Lighting*[10] and CIBSE Lighting Guides for design guidance on specific applications (see notes to individual entries).

[1]   Based on PMV of ±0.5

[2]   Assumes no smoking; for spaces where smoking is permitted see Table 1.10

[3]   Based on comfort requirements for check-in staff

[4]   Local illumination may be required for specific tasks

[5]   Dimming normally required

[6]   Follow computer manufacturers' recommendations if necessary, otherwise design for occupant comfort

[7]   Refer to Lighting Guides *LG7: Lighting for offices*[11] and *LG3: Lighting for visual display screen use*[12]

[8]   Refer to *The Building Regulations: Part F1: Means of ventilation*[13]

[9]   Podium may require special consideration to cater for higher activity level

[10] Refer to Lighting Guide *LG5: The visual environment in lecture, conference and teaching spaces*[14]

[11] *The Workplace (Health, Safety and Welfare) Regulations 1992*[15] require 13°C where there is severe physical effort

[12] In the UK, air conditioning is not normally appropriate for this application. Cooling may be provided by local air jets. Some applications (e.g. steel mills, foundries) require special attention to reduce risk of heat stress

[13] As required for industrial process, if any, otherwise based on occupants' requirements

[14] Depends on difficulty of task

[15] Refer to Lighting Guide *LG1: The industrial environment*[16]

[16] Filtration should be suitable for the areas to which these spaces are connected

[17] See CIBSE *Guide B2*[17], Table B2.11

[18] Refer to Lighting Guide *LG2: Hospitals and health care buildings*[18]

[19] Design for clothing and activity levels appropriate to nurses

[20] Refer to Lighting Guide *LG4: Sports*[19]

[21] As required for removal of heat and moisture

[22] Based on comfort requirements of staff

[23] Study tables and carrels require 500 lux

[24] Conditions required for preservation/conservation of exhibits may override criteria for human comfort; abrupt changes in temperature and humidity should be avoided.

[25] Critical conservation levels may apply, refer to Lighting Guide *LG8: Lighting in museums and art galleries*[20]

[26] Performers may have wider range of met and clo values than audience, along with higher radiant component, necessitating special provision

[27] Dependent on use

[28] Design for most critical requirement for each parameter

[29] Special provision required for check-out staff to provide conditions as for small shops

[30] Audience may require special consideration depending on likely clothing levels

[31] Depends on production requirements

Table 1.2 Location of detailed guidance to environmental criteria

Parameter	Application and conditions	Section or table reference
Temperature	Known application, normal conditions	Table 1.1
	Non-typical conditions	Section 1.4.3
Humidity	Relating to temperature	Section 1.4.3.1
	Relating to comfort	Section 1.5
	Relating to static electricity	Sections 1.5.2 and 1.11.3
Outdoor air supply	Known application, odour sources unknown	Table 1.1 and section 1.7.2
	Specific pollutants, exposure limits	Section 1.6.2
	Specific pollutants, known emission rates, design exposure limits	Section 1.7.3
Filter selection	—	Table 1.1 and section 1.6.5
Visual criteria	—	Table 1.1 and section 1.8
Noise	—	Table 1.1 and section 1.9
Vibration	—	Section 1.10
Electromagnetic fields	—	Section 1.11.1
Ionisation	—	Section 1.11.2
Static electricity	—	Section 1.1.1.3

1.4 Thermal environment

1.4.1 Thermo-regulation and heat balance

Heat is continually being produced in the body and results, essentially, from the assimilation and utilisation of food. In the long term, if bodily heat storage or cooling is to be avoided, and thus a more or less constant deep-body temperature maintained, the amount of heat lost to the environment by a person must equal the amount produced. The rate of heat produced, expressed in $W \cdot m^{-2}$ of body surface or 'mets' (see section 1.2.2), varies with the physical activity and can range from 40 $W \cdot m^{-2}$ (sleeping) to about 500 $W \cdot m^{-2}$ (competitive wrestling). In temperate climates, under normal conditions, little heat is lost by sweating.

The human thermo-regulatory system attempts to maintain a constant deep-body temperature of about 37°C. When this temperature is exceeded, the body initiates heat control mechanisms, e.g. dilation of peripheral blood vessels and sweating. In response to perceptions of coldness, the brain instigates constriction of peripheral blood vessels, changes in muscular tone, erection of body hair and shivering.

The thermo-regulatory system can maintain a constant body temperature in a wide range of combinations of activity level and environmental variables. However, the range of conditions that are compatible with comfort is much narrower[9,21].

The heat balance of the human body may be written as:

$$M - W = C_{res} + E_{res} + K + R + C + E + S \qquad (1.1)$$

where M is the metabolic rate, W is the rate of performance of external work, C_{res} is the heat exchange by convection in the respiratory tract, E_{res} is the heat exchange by evaporation in the respiratory tract, K is the heat flow by conduction from the surface of the clothed body, R is the heat loss by radiation from the surface of the clothed body, C is the heat loss by convection from the surface of the clothed body, E is the heat loss by evaporation from the surface of the clothed body and S is the body heat storage.

In steady state conditions S would be zero but this does not necessarily mean that a comfortable thermal state is achieved. It is also necessary for skin temperatures to be neither too high nor too low, and for the sweat rate to be neither too high nor too low[9,21].

A person's heat balance, as described by equation 1.1, and thermal sensation are influenced by the following main physical parameters, which constitute the thermal environment:

— air temperature

— mean radiant temperature

— relative air speed

— humidity

Besides these environmental factors, metabolic rate is directly dependent upon activity level and body heat exchanges are modified by the thermal resistance of clothing and other materials in contact with the body (e.g. chair, if sitting).

1.4.2 Thermal indices

Many attempts have been made to devise indices which combine some or all of these variables into one value which can be used to evaluate how cool or warm people will feel in a given environment. For moderate thermal environments, a simple model can be used with a reasonable degree of accuracy, but under conditions of heat stress, cold stress or high air velocities, different indices are required.

1.4.2.1 Dry resultant temperature

This index has been adopted by the CIBSE as a thermal index for moderate thermal environments. In practice it is equivalent to the 'operative temperature' (t_o) which has been adopted for both ISO[22] and ANSI/ASHRAE[1] standards.

Dry resultant temperature combines air and mean radiant temperatures into a single index temperature, as follows:

$$t_c = \frac{t_{ai} \sqrt{(10v)} + t_r}{1 + \sqrt{(10v)}} \qquad (1.2)$$

where t_c is the dry resultant temperature (°C), t_{ai} is the inside air temperature (°C), t_r is the mean radiant temperature (°C) and v is the air speed ($m \cdot s^{-1}$).

At indoor air speeds below 0.1 $m \cdot s^{-1}$, equation 1.2 becomes:

$$t_c = 0.5 t_{ai} + 0.5 t_r \qquad (1.3)$$

In well-insulated buildings that are predominantly heated by convective means, the difference between the air and mean radiant temperatures (and hence between the air and dry resultant temperatures) is often very small. If the surface temperatures differ significantly from the air temperature the radiant asymmetry should be determined, see section 1.4.3.14. Where air movement may cause discomfort the draught rating should be determined, see section 1.4.3.10.

1.4.2.2 Predicted mean vote (PMV) and predicted percentage dissatisfied (PPD)

These indices combines the influence of air temperature, mean radiant temperature, air movement and humidity with that of clothing and activity level into one value on the thermal sensation scale, see Table 1.3.

The PMV index may be defined as the mean value of the votes of a large group of persons, exposed to the same environment with identical clothing and activity.

Appendix 1.A1 gives an equation for PMV derived by Fanger[9] and the listing (in BASIC) of a computer program for solution of the equation, based on that given in *ISO 7730*[22]. Solutions to this equation in tabular form, based on 50% saturation, are given in *ISO 7730*.

Except where stated otherwise the temperature ranges given in Table 1.1 are based on a PMV of ±0.25. These

Table 1.3 Thermal sensation scale

Index value	Thermal sensation
+3	Hot
+2	Warm
+1	Slightly warm
0	Neutral
−1	Slightly cool
−2	Cool
−3	Cold

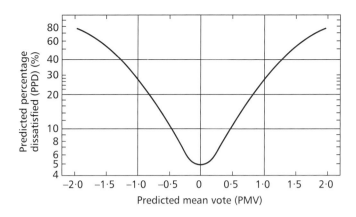

Figure 1.1 PPD as a function of PMV

temperature ranges may be widened by approximately 1°C at each end if a PMV of ±0.5 (i.e. PPD of 10%) is acceptable.

As individual thermal sensation votes will be scattered around the mean predicted value (i.e. PMV), it is useful also to predict the number of people who will be dissatisfied, i.e. feel uncomfortably cool or warm. The predicted percentage dissatisfied (PPD) can be obtained from the PMV using the following equation[22]:

$$PPD = 100 - 95 \exp\left[-(0.03353\,PMV^4 + 0.2179\,PMV^2)\right] \tag{1.4}$$

The predicted percentage dissatisfied (PPD) as a function of predicted mean vote (PMV) is shown in Figure 1.1.

1.4.3 Influences on thermal comfort

Thermal comfort has been defined as that state of mind in which satisfaction is expressed with the thermal environment[1]. This is usually taken to imply a state of overall thermal neutrality. In addition, it is a requirement that there be no local discomfort (either warm or cold) at any part of the human body due to, for example, asymmetric thermal radiation, draughts, warm or cold floors, or vertical air temperature differences.

People are thermally dissimilar. Ideally, each occupant should be able to control the thermal environment within his or her immediate locality. However, where a group of people is subject to the same environment, it will normally not be possible to satisfy everyone at the same time due to this variance. The aim, therefore, is to create optimum thermal comfort for the whole group, i.e. a condition in which the highest possible percentage of the group is thermally comfortable. Means should be provided to alleviate discomfort quickly if it should occur.

Thermal neutrality is defined as that situation in which people describe themselves as neither cool nor warm. It is therefore directly related to the optimal temperature for any combination of activity, clothing and environmental parameters. Figure 1.2[22] shows the optimal dry resultant temperature as a function of activity (expressed in mets and W·m⁻²) and clothing insulation (expressed in clo and m²·K·W⁻¹) at 50% saturation and for air velocities less than 0.1 m·s⁻¹.

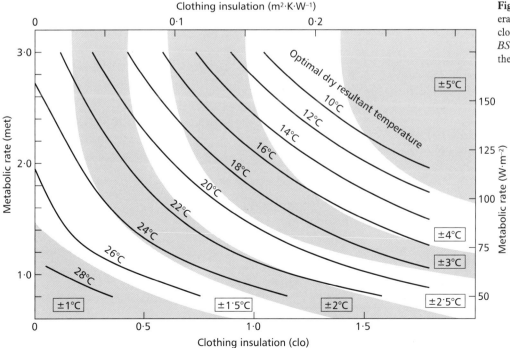

Figure 1.2 Dry resultant temperature as a function of activity and clothing insulation[22] (reproduced from *BS EN ISO 7730* by permission of the British Standards Institution)

The alternately shaded and plain areas represent regions within which the indicated temperature range corresponds to a PMV of ±0.25 at the optimal dry resultant temperature, obtained by plotting metabolic rate against clothing insulation. For example, the optimal dry resultant temperature in summer for occupants whose activity is equivalent to 1.5 met and who are wearing clothing providing insulation of 0.85 clo is 22°C. This falls within the ±2°C band, giving a temperature range of 21–23°C, equivalent to a PMV of ±0.25. This confirms the figures given in Table 1.1 for summer occupation of offices. The relative air movement due to body movement is taken to be zero for activity levels (M_a) less than 1 met and $0.3 \times (M_a - 1)$ for activity levels greater than 1 met.

1.4.3.1　Humidity

Humidity has little effect on feelings of warmth for sedentary, lightly clothed people at dry resultant temperatures of 23°C and below. Thus, for most practical purposes, the influence of humidity on warmth in moderate thermal environments may be ignored[23].

However, humidity may be important in the context of microbiological growth, the preservation of artefacts and the reduction of static electricity (see sections 1.5 and 1.11.3). The risk of condensation and microbiological growth will be reduced where room humidity is below, say, 70% saturation[24].

1.4.3.2　Clothing

Clothing worn by people indoors is modified greatly by the season and outdoor weather. During the summer months typical clothing ensembles in commercial premises may consist of lightweight dresses or trousers, short or long-sleeved shirts or blouses, and occasionally a suit jacket or sweater. Without jacket or sweater, these ensembles have clothing insulation values ranging from 0.35 to 0.6 clo.

During winter, people wear thicker, heavier ensembles, usually with more layers. A typical indoor winter ensemble would have an insulation value of 0.8 to 1.2 clo.

Table 1.4 Thermal insulation values for typical clothing ensembles for work and daily wear; these values were determined by measurement on a standard thermal mannequin (adapted from *ANSI/ASHRAE 55-1992*[1] and *BS ISO 9920*[4])

Description	Insulation level (clo)
Underpants plus:	
— shirt (short sleeves), lightweight trousers, light socks, shoes	0.5
— shirt, lightweight trousers, socks, shoes	0.6
— boiler suit, socks, shoes	0.7
— shirt, trousers, socks, shoes	0.75
— shirt, boiler suit, socks, shoes	0.8
— shirt, trousers, jacket, socks, shoes	0.85
— shirt, trousers, smock, socks, shoes	0.9
Underwear (short sleeves/legs) plus:	
— tracksuit (sweater and trousers), long socks, training shoes	0.75
— shirt, trousers, jacket or sweater, socks, shoes	1.0
— shirt, trousers, boiler suit, socks, shoes	1.1
— shirt, trousers, jacket, insulated jacket, socks, shoes	1.25
— boiler suit, insulated jacket and trousers, socks, shoes	1.4
— shirt, trousers, jacket, insulated jacket and trousers, socks, shoes	1.55
— shirt, trousers, jacket, quilted jacket and overalls, socks, shoes	1.85
— shirt, trousers, jacket, quilted jacket and overalls, socks, shoes, cap, gloves	2.0
Underwear (long sleeves/legs) plus:	
— shirt, trousers, pullover, jacket, socks, shoes	1.3
— insulated jacket and trousers, insulated jacket and trousers, socks, shoes	2.2
— insulated jacket and trousers, quilted parka, quilted overalls, socks, shoes, cap, gloves	2.55
Bra and pants plus:	
— T-shirt, shorts, light socks, sandals	0.30
— petticoat, stockings, lightweight dress (with sleeves), sandals	0.45
— stockings, blouse (short sleeves), skirt, sandals	0.55
— petticoat, stockings, dress, shoes	0.70
— petticoat, shirt, skirt, thick socks (long), shoes	0.80
— shirt, skirt, sweater, thick socks (long), shoes	0.90
— shirt, trousers, jacket, socks, shoes	1.00
— blouse (long sleeves), long skirt, jacket, stockings, shoes	1.10
Pyjamas (long sleeves/legs), bath robe, slippers (no socks)	0.96

Note: for sedentary persons, an allowance should be made for the insulating effect of the chair, i.e. 0.15 clo for office chair (corresponding to a temperature change of 0.9 K) and 0.3 clo for upholstered armchair (corresponding to a temperature change of 1.8 K)

Clothing insulation values for typical clothing ensembles are given in Table 1.4. The insulation provided by other clothing ensembles (I_{cl}) may be estimated by summing the insulation values for individual garments (I_{clu}), see Table 1.5.

At thermal equilibrium, the wearing or otherwise of an article of clothing is equivalent in its effect on subjective feelings of warmth to raising or lowering the resultant temperature. Table 1.5 shows these equivalencies, which may be used to modify the design temperature ranges given in Table 1.1.

The clothing insulation provided by an individual garment consists of the effective resistance of the material from which the garment is made plus the thermal resistance of the air layer trapped between the clothing and the skin. If the thickness of this layer is reduced, e.g. by air movement or change in posture, then the thermal resistance of the air layer is reduced leading to a reduction in the overall insulation provided by the clothing. In addition, body movement such as walking can lead to a pumping action in loose clothing that forces cool air between the skin and the surrounding clothing. Therefore, factors other than the thermal resistance of the clothing, e.g. looseness of fit, also affect the clo value.

For sedentary occupants, the insulating properties of the chair will affect comfort, see footnotes to Tables 1.4 and 1.5.

1.4.3.3 Activity

Table 1.6 gives metabolic rates for specific activities. For most people, daily activity consists of a mixture of specific activities and/or a combination of work and rest periods. A weighted-average metabolic rate may be used, provided that the activities frequently alternate, i.e. several times per hour.

For example, the average metabolic rate for a person typing for 50% of the time, filing while seated for 25% of the time and walking on the level for 25% of the time will be: $(0.5 \times 1.1) + (0.25 \times 1.2) + (0.25 \times 1.6) = 1.25$ met.

For people dressed in normal casual clothing ($I_{cl} = 0.5–1.0$ clo), a rise in activity of 0.1 met corresponds to a possible reduction of approximately 0.6 K in the design dry resultant temperatures given in Table 1.1. A greater reduction is possible for heavily clad people.

For example, a seated person with an activity level equivalent to 1.0 met who experiences optimum comfort at 24°C would find 22.8°C ideal when carrying out filing from a seated position (1.2 met).

Care must be used when applying Table 1.6 due to inaccuracies in measuring metabolic rate and in defining the tasks listed. It is reasonably accurate (i.e. $\pm$ 20%) for engineering purposes for well-defined activities with $M < 1.5$. However, for poorly defined activities with $M > 3.0$ the error may be as high as $\pm50\%$.

1.4.3.4 Temperature changes

Relatively slow changes in temperature produce results which are directly predictable at any time from the steady-state relationships between temperature and subjective

Table 1.5 Thermal insulation values for typical garments and corresponding reduction in acceptable dry resultant temperature for sedentary occupants[22] (reproduced from *BS EN ISO 7730* by permission of the British Standards Institution)

Description	Insulation level (clo)	Corresponding change in dry resultant temperature (K)
Underwear:		
— briefs/underpants	0.03	0.2
— underpants (long legs)	0.10	0.6
— singlet	0.04	0.2
— T-shirt	0.09	0.5
— vest (long sleeves)	0.12	0.7
— bra	0.01	0.06
Shirts/blouses:		
— short sleeve	0.15	0.9
— light blouse (long sleeves)	0.15	0.9
— lightweight (long sleeves)	0.20	1.2
— mediumweight (long sleeves)	0.25	1.5
— flannel shirt (long sleeves)	0.30	1.8
Trousers:		
— shorts	0.06	0.4
— lightweight	0.20	1.2
— mediumweight	0.25	1.5
— flannel	0.28	1.7
Skirts/dresses:		
— light skirt (summer)	0.15	0.2
— heavy skirt (winter)	0.25	1.5
— light dress (short sleeves)	0.20	1.2
— winter dress (long sleeves)	0.40	2.4
Boiler suit	0.55	3.3
Sweaters/pullovers:		
— sleeveless waistcoat	0.12	0.7
— thin	0.20	1.2
— medium	0.28	1.7
— thick	0.35	2.1
Jackets:		
— light (summer)	0.25	1.5
— medium	0.35	2.1
— smock	0.30	1.8
Highly insulative:		
— overall/ski suit	0.90	5.4
— trousers	0.35	2.1
— jacket	0.40	2.4
— sleeveless body-warmer	0.20	1.2
Outdoor clothing:		
— coat	0.60	3.6
— jacket	0.55	3.3
— parka	0.70	4.2
— heavyweight overalls	0.55	3.3
Miscellaneous:		
— ankle socks	0.02	0.1
— thick ankle socks	0.05	0.3
— thick long socks	0.10	0.6
— stockings	0.03	0.2
— shoes (thin soles)	0.02	0.1
— shoes (thick soles)	0.04	0.2
— boots	0.10	0.6
— gloves	0.05	0.3

Note: for sedentary persons, an allowance should be made for the insulating effect of the chair, i.e. 0.15 clo for office chair (corresponding to a temperature change of 0.9 K), and 0.3 clo for upholstered armchair (corresponding to a temperature change of 1.8 K)

sensations[25]. As long as changes in dry resultant temperature are within the ranges shown in Table 1.1, no significant discomfort should result.

Table 1.6 Typical metabolic rate and heat generation per unit area of body surface for various activities[1,5,22]

Activity	Metabolic rate (met)	Heat generation ($W \cdot m^{-2}$)
Resting:		
— sleeping	0.7	41
— reclining	0.8	46
— seated, quiet	1.0	58
— standing, relaxed	1.2	70
Walking (on level):		
— $0.9\ m \cdot s^{-1}$	1.0	58
— $1.3\ m \cdot s^{-1}$	1.6	93
— $1.8\ m \cdot s^{-1}$	3.8	221
Office work:		
— reading, seated	1.0	58
— writing	1.0	58
— typing	1.1	64
— filing, seated	1.2	70
— filing, standing	1.4	81
— lifting/packing	1.1	64
Occupational:		
— cooking	1.4–2.3	81–134
— house cleaning	1.7–3.4	99–198
— seated, heavy limb movement	1.2	70
— machine sawing	1.8	105
— light machine work	1.6–2.0	93–116
— heavy machine work	3.0	175
— handling 50 kg bags	4.0	233
Leisure:		
— dancing (social)	1.4–4.4	82–256
— callisthenics/exercise	3.0–4.0	175–233
— tennis (singles)	3.6–4.0	210–233
— basketball	5.0–7.6	291–442
— wrestling (competitive)	7.0–8.7	407–506

Note: average surface area of an adult human body is about 1.8 m^2

1.4.3.5   Adaptation and climate

Laboratory studies[9,26] have generally been unable to identify any change in comfort conditions attributable to adaptation to either high or low temperatures. Thermal comfort is not influenced by outdoor conditions except insofar as these influence clothing and mean radiant temperature, see section 1.2.2. Similarly, despite diurnal variations in internal body temperature, experiments[27–29] have found no variation in preferred temperature from one part of the day to another.

However, analysis of results from field studies[30,31] indicates that the PMV equation tends to over-estimate how warm the subjects felt when warmer conditions prevail. Field studies conducted in naturally ventilated buildings in warm climates[32,33] have also shown that PMV over-estimates people's feelings of warmth. It is probable that the differences are in part due to the cumulative effects of slight differences in posture, activity and clothing fabrics and styles (which are not easily captured by the PMV equation) and in part due to the changes in peoples' expectations.

Climate affects many aspects of building design, customary clothing and lifestyle, and thereby affects the temperature at which people are normally comfortable indoors[34].

1.4.3.6   Age

Studies[35–39] have revealed that at a given activity and clothing level the thermal environments preferred by older people do not differ from those preferred by younger ones. The lower metabolism in older people is compensated for by a lower evaporative loss[40]. Despite this, older people generally require higher temperatures because their activity level is usually lower.

1.4.3.7   Gender

Experiments[9,36,38] have shown that at the same activity and clothing levels men and women prefer almost the same thermal environments. Women's skin temperature and evaporative loss are slightly lower than those for men, and this balances the slightly lower metabolic rate of women. The reason that women often prefer higher ambient temperatures to those preferred by men may be explained by the lighter clothing normally worn by women and that women's ankles may be more exposed than those of men.

1.4.3.8   Colour of surfaces and lighting

Studies[41,42] have found no significant relationship between the colour of interior surfaces or lighting and perceptions of thermal comfort.

1.4.3.9   Occupants' state of health

Very little is known about the comfort requirements for people who are ill, disabled, undergoing treatments involving drugs etc. The comfort of immobilised people will depend on the insulation of the bedclothes along with clinical factors related to the nature of the illness and/or disability and the treatment regime (if any). However, bed-ridden or immobilised people will usually require higher temperatures than normal because of their lower activity level and lighter clothing.

1.4.3.10   Draughts

The cooling effect of air movement is well known. If excessive, this can give rise to complaints of draught. The temperature of the moving air is not necessarily that of the room air nor that of the incoming ventilation air but will generally lie between these values. The back of the neck is particularly sensitive to air movement and if the air stream is directed onto this part of the body, the maximum allowable air speed is reduced. It should also be noted that people are more tolerant of air movement if the direction of the air movement varies.

Where air speeds in a room are greater then 0.15 m·s^{-1} the resultant temperature should be increased from its 'still' air value to compensate for the cooling effect of the air movement. Suitable corrections are given in Figure 1.3. Note that air speeds greater than about 0.3 m·s^{-1} are probably unacceptable except in naturally ventilated buildings in summer when high air speeds may be desirable for their cooling effect.

The influence of mean relative air speed on the heat balance and general thermal comfort of humans is accounted for in the PMV index. However, even in thermally neutral conditions the air speed may be unacceptable for the

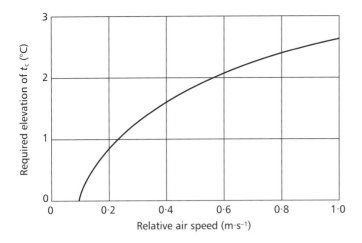

Figure 1.3 Correction to dry resultant temperature (t_c) to take account of air movement

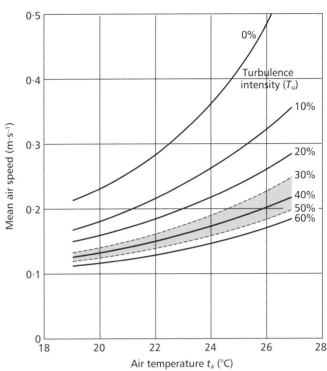

Figure 1.4 Combinations of mean air speed, air temperature and turbulence intensity for a draught rating of 15%[22] (reproduced from *BS EN ISO 7730* by permission of the British Standards Institution)

occupants. Studies[43] have shown that dissatisfaction due to draught is not only a function of mean air speed and local air temperature, but also fluctuations of air speed. It has been suggested that people are particularly sensitive if air speeds fluctuate at a frequency in the range of 0.3 to 0.6 Hz[42].

The relative air speed over the body surface increases with activity. A correction can be estimated where activity levels exceed 1 met by adding 0.3 $(M - 1)$ to the air speed relative to a stationary point. For example, for a person whose activity is equivalent to 1.8 met in a room in which the air speed is 0.1 m·s⁻¹, the relative air speed over that person's body is: $0.1 + 0.3 (1.8 - 1) = 0.34$ m·s⁻¹. This assumes that the direction of the airflow is at random. At higher air speeds, where airflow may be mono-directional, the relative air speed will depend on the direction of travel of the person.

Fluctuations in air speed may be described by the standard deviation of the air speed (v_{SD}), or the turbulence intensity (T_u) which is defined as the ratio of standard deviation of the air speed to the mean air speed, i.e.:

$$T_u = 100 \, (v_{SD}/v) \qquad (1.5)$$

where T_u is the turbulence intensity (%), v_{SD} is the standard deviation of the air speed (m·s⁻¹) and v is the mean air speed (m·s⁻¹).

For air conditioned and mechanically ventilated buildings, the draught rating (DR), expressed as a percentage, is given by[22]:

$$\text{DR} = (34 - t_{ai}) \, (v - 0.05)^{0.62} \, (0.37 \, v \, T_u + 3.14) \qquad (1.6)$$

where DR is the draught rating (%) and t_{ai} is the inside air temperature (°C). (For air speeds less than 0.05 m·s⁻¹, take v = 0.05 m·s⁻¹; for calculated DR values greater than 100%, use DR = 100%.)

A draught rating of more than 15% has been found to be unacceptable[43]. Figure 1.4[22] shows solutions for equation 1.6 for DR = 15% based on light, mainly sedentary, activity (i.e. 1.2 met). Each line on the graph shows the limits of acceptable temperature and velocity for a given turbulence intensity. For example, if the temperature of the air passing

over the body is 23°C and the turbulence intensity is 60%, the draught rating criterion of 15% corresponds to an air speed of 0.14 m·s⁻¹. However if the turbulence intensity is only 10%, the limiting velocity for comfort is 0.23 m·s⁻¹.

In the main body of most rooms, away from supply air jets, the turbulence intensity is usually between 30 and 50%.

1.4.3.11 Vertical air temperature differences[44–46]

The relationship between vertical air temperature differences and the percentage of occupants who are likely to be dissatisfied is given in Figure 1.5. Most studies have focused on a rise in temperature with distance from the floor. There is no evidence to suggest that people more readily accept temperature gradients in the other direction. However, it has been shown that ceilings cooled to temperatures up to 15°C lower than the walls and floor do not give rise to discomfort[9].

In general, it is recommended that the gradient in either direction should be not more than 3 K between head and feet[22]. If air velocities are higher at floor level than across the upper part of the body then a maximum gradient of 2 K·m⁻¹ is recommended.

1.4.3.12 Horizontal air temperature differences

The temperature at any given position within the occupied zone of a room should not be outside the ranges specified in Table 1.1

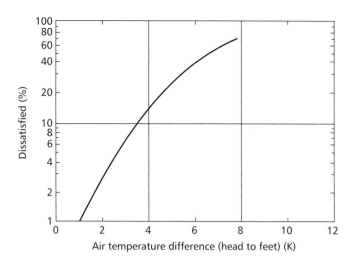

Figure 1.5 Percentage dissatisfied as a function only of vertical air temperature difference between head and ankles[44].

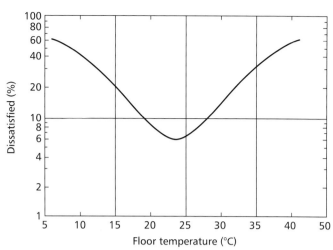

Figure 1.6 Percentage dissatisfied as a function of floor temperature only[44]

1.4.3.13   Warm or cold floors

Local discomfort of the feet can be caused by the floor temperature being too high or too low. If a floor is too cold and occupants feel discomfort in their feet, a common reaction is to increase the room air temperature, thus increasing energy consumption.

For rooms in which occupants spend much of their time with bare feet (e.g. swimming pools, bathrooms, dressing rooms etc.) or with their bodies in contact with the floor (e.g. gymnasia, kindergartens etc.), studies have found that the flooring material is important[47,48]. Comfort ranges for surface temperature of some typical flooring materials are given in Table 1.7.

Table 1.7 Comfortable temperature ranges for typical flooring materials

Material	Surface temperature range (°C)
Textiles	21–28
Pine wood	21.5–28
Oak wood	24.5–28
Hard thermoplastic floor covering	24–28
Concrete	26–28

For floors occupied by people wearing normal footwear, flooring material is unimportant. Studies have found an optimal surface temperature of 25°C for sedentary and 23°C for standing or walking persons[48]. Figure 1.6 shows percentage dissatisfied as a function of floor temperature for seated and standing people combined. In general, it is recommended that floor temperature should be in the range 19–26°C. (For the design of floor heating systems, *EN 1264*[49] suggests that a surface temperature of 29°C is appropriate.)

1.4.3.14   Asymmetric thermal radiation

There are three cases of asymmetric radiation that may lead to discomfort:

—   local cooling: radiation exchange with adjacent cold surfaces, such as single glazed windows

—   local heating: radiation from adjacent hot surfaces, such as overhead lighting or overhead radiant heaters

—   intrusion of short-wave radiation, such as solar radiation through glazing.

Radiant temperature asymmetry is defined as the difference between the plane radiant temperatures on opposite sides of the human body. The plane radiant temperature is the radiant temperature resulting from surfaces on one side of a notional plane passing through the point or body under consideration. The measurement and calculation of radiant temperature asymmetry are dealt with in *ISO 7726*[3]. The radiant temperature asymmetry in the vertical direction is calculated from the difference in plane radiant temperature between the upper and lower parts of the space with respect to a small horizontal plane, taken as 0.6 m above the floor for a seated person and 1.1 m above the floor for a standing person.

In the horizontal direction it is the difference between plane radiant temperatures in opposite directions from a small vertical plane with its centre located 0.6 m (seated) or 1.1 m (standing) above the floor.

Figure 1.7[50,51] can be used to predict dissatisfaction where surface temperatures are known and radiant temperature asymmetry can be calculated.

It is recommended that radiant temperature asymmetry should contribute no more than 5% dissatisfied. Hence, in the vertical direction radiant temperature asymmetry (warm ceiling) should be less than 5 K, and in the horizontal direction (cool wall) less than 10 K. Similarly, for a cool ceiling the maximum recommended radiant temperature asymmetry is 14 K and for a warm wall 23 K.

Cold windows

An example for a single glazed window is given in Figure 1.8 for radiant temperature asymmetry of 8 K (PPD = 3.5%), indicated by the 13°C plane radiant temperature contour

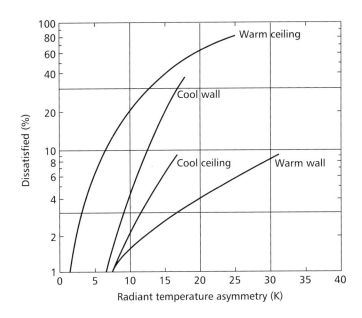

Figure 1.7 Percentage dissatisfied due to asymmetric radiation only[50,51]

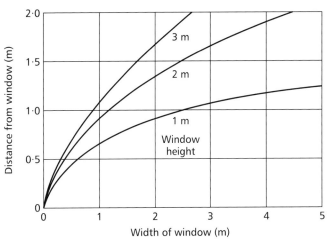

Figure 1.9 Minimum comfortable distances from the centre of a single-glazed window[52] for outside air temperature of –1°C

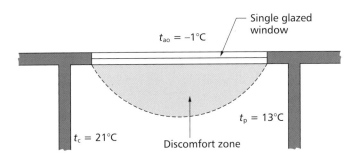

Figure 1.8 Discomfort zone produced by local cooling due to a single-glazed window

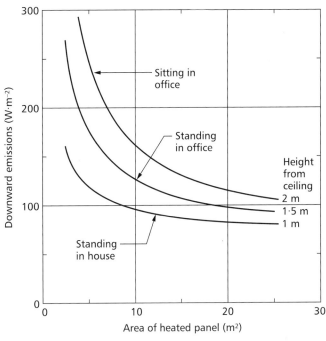

Figure 1.10 Downward heat emission from centre of a square low-temperature radiant panel

(t_p), assuming that all opposite surfaces are at the room temperature of 21°C and the outside air temperature is –1°C. Discomfort zones for various window sizes may be estimated from Figure 1.9.

Low-temperature radiant heating systems

It may not be possible to provide an economic ceiling-mounted radiant heating system while keeping the radiant temperature asymmetry within 5 K. For such systems it is permissible to design for a maximum radiant temperature asymmetry of 10 K, although this could lead to 20% dissatisfaction. Based on this criterion, Figure 1.10 suggests design limits of downward emission from horizontal panels for various head to panel distances.

Lighting

Another possible source of radiant heat is lighting. Fluorescent lamps are relatively cool. For example, for an illuminance of 1000 lux, fluorescent lighting would increase the mean radiant temperature such that it would be necessary to reduce the air temperature by 0.25–0.5 K, compared to the same room without lighting, in order to maintain the same dry resultant temperature. For the same illuminance provided by tungsten filament lamps, a reduction in the air temperature of about 1.5 K would be required. Radiant temperature asymmetry could be a problem in the latter case.

Short-wave radiation

When solar radiation falls on a window the transmitted short-wave radiation is almost all absorbed by the internal surfaces. This raises the temperature of these surfaces which, as well as contributing to the convective gain, augments the mean radiant temperature. In comfort terms, the most significant component is the direct radiation falling on occupants near the window. Internally-reflected radiation can normally be ignored[53].

Figure 1.11 shows the elevation of mean radiant temperature and dry resultant temperature due to incident short-wave radiation. Clothing absorptance of short-wave radiation will depend on the colour and the texture but can be taken as 0.7 for typical summer wear and 0.8 for the darker clothing typically worn in cold climates.

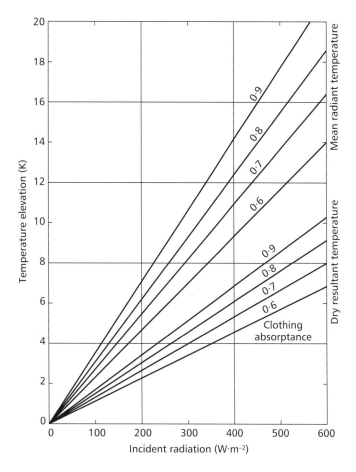

Figure 1.11 Effect of short-wave radiation on the mean radiant and dry resultant temperatures

People exposed to direct solar gain may also experience discomfort due to glare and veiling reflections. Where extensive glazed areas face south and west, it will be necessary to consider the provision of solar control devices.

1.5 Humidity

The nature of the role played by relative humidity in the environment is less well defined than is that for temperature. In normal circumstances, humidity in the range 40–70 % RH is acceptable[38].

As mentioned in section 1.4.3.1, humidity has a significant effect on thermal comfort only at high temperatures.

1.5.1 High humidity

Buildings in which there are prolonged periods of high air humidity are likely to experience problems such as airborne fungi[24] and house dust mites, particularly if room humidities exceed 70% RH for long periods. Fungi generally grow on damp organic material but they do not necessarily require either high air humidity or high air temperature for growth if the substrate conditions are suitable[54].

House dust mites require warm moist conditions for survival, such as those frequently found in mattresses and chair cushions[55]. These small arthropods have been found

in large numbers in homes and in office furniture and carpets. Their faeces become airborne and are known to provoke allergic reactions in many individuals.

High room humidity may occur through a combination of evaporation from moisture sources and poor ventilation, and/or high outdoor humidity, see Section 7: *Moisture transfer and condensation*. Bathrooms and kitchens are particularly prone.

For the purposes of designing air conditioning systems, a maximum room relative humidity of 60% within the recommended range of summer design dry resultant temperatures would provide acceptable comfort conditions for human occupancy and minimise the risk of mould growth and house dust mites. Condensation should be avoided within buildings on surfaces that could support microbial growth or be stained or otherwise damaged by moisture. This may be achieved by ensuring that, where possible, all surfaces are above the dew-point of the adjacent air.

1.5.2 Low humidity

There is some evidence from recent investigations into problem buildings[56,57] that there is a correlation between low room humidity and symptoms associated with dryness and irritation of the mucosa. It has been suggested[58] that low room moisture content increases evaporation from the mucosa and can produce micro-fissures in the upper respiratory tract which may act as sites for infection. The reduction in mucous flow inhibits the dilution and rejection of dust, micro-organisms and irritant chemicals such as formaldehyde. This is a particular problem for wearers of contact lenses.

If possible, at the design temperatures normally appropriate to sedentary occupancy, the room humidity should be above 40% RH. Lower humidity is often acceptable for short periods. Humidity of 30% RH or below may be acceptable but precautions should be taken to limit the generation of dust and airborne irritants, such as tobacco smoke, and to prevent static discharge from occupants. Note that for heated-only buildings in the UK, the humidity can remain below 40% RH during periods of sustained cold weather.

Shocks due to static electricity (see section 1.11.3) are unlikely with humidities above 40% RH or at lower humidities if precautions are taken in the specification of materials and equipment to prevent the build-up of static electricity.

1.6 Indoor air quality

1.6.1 General

Building occupants may be exposed to a mixture of hundreds, or thousands, of airborne contaminants. The air within a modern office may contain chemicals and micro-organisms which have originated from numerous sources, both inside and outside the building. Concentrations of individual contaminants are frequently in the order of one thousandth of published occupational exposure limits, or less, but may still be above odour detection thresholds[59].

For comfort, indoor air quality may be said to be acceptable if[60,61]:

(a)   not more than 50% of the occupants can detect any odour, and

(b)   not more than 20% experience discomfort, and

(c)   not more than 10% suffer from mucosal irritation, and

(d)   not more than 5% experience annoyance,

for less than 2% of the time.

These comfort-based criteria do not account for potential effects on health of the contaminants found in buildings. Some of these, e.g. radon and its progeny, are odourless and do not affect comfort but may have serious effects on the health of any individuals exposed to them.

The following measures, in sequential order, should be adopted to eliminate or reduce exposure of occupants to airborne contaminants in buildings:

(1)   eliminate contaminant(s) at source

(2)   substitute with sources that produce non-toxic or less malodorous contaminants

(3)   reduce emission rate of substance(s)

(4)   segregate occupants from potential sources of toxic or malodorous substances

(5)   improve ventilation, e.g. by local exhaust (if source of contamination is local), displacement or dilution

(6)   provide personal protection.

These measures are not mutually exclusive, and some combination will usually be necessary. Adequate ventilation will always be required, see Table 1.1.

Substantial improvements in indoor air quality can result if smoking is eliminated and low emission materials are used in the building fabric and furnishings, the ventilation plant and for cleaning. Regular cleaning and maintenance are also very important factors in reducing non-human odours.

All new buildings should be designed to minimise unacceptable odour, as far as is reasonably practicable and economically viable.

1.6.2   Human sensitivity to inhalation of pollutants

A substance that enters the nasal cavity may be sensed by two largely separate detection systems:

—   the olfactory sense: responsible for odour detection

—   the general chemical sense: sensitive to irritants.

The general chemical sense is located all over the mucous membranes, in the eyes as well as the nose.

The two senses may interact. For example, it is possible for an odour to be disguised by irritation and vice versa[62] or a single substance may evoke both odour and irritant sensations. Humans are known to adapt to odours with time, whereas irritation may increase with time[63,64].

There are two kinds of adaptation to odour. Over periods of about 30 minutes people become less sensitive to any odours present. Over much longer periods (i.e. weeks or months) people come to accept an odour as normal and harmless and therefore become less aware of it. Conversely, over a period of minutes or hours, the discomfort from exposure to irritants will normally increase. Over a longer period, adaptation is possible but this may be largely behavioural (e.g. by ceasing to wear contact lenses). The more likely outcome is to become sensitised so that the same concentration of an irritant has a greater effect. Sensitisation is also possible when a substance exerts its effect through the immune system (e.g. allergic reactions).

In the specific case of exposure to environmental tobacco smoke, one study[65] has found that irritation intensity increases by a factor of two during the first hour of exposure, after which steady state occurs. The same study found that perceived odour intensity declined by a factor of 50% and levelled out after only a few minutes.

Many everyday occurrences result in the release of odours, some of which may be perceived as pleasant and some unpleasant. Some evolve from the release of potentially harmful substances but the airborne contaminants likely to be encountered in non-industrial buildings do not usually result in irreversible health effects. However, the exceptions include radon gas, and lead and benzine from motor vehicle exhaust emissions.

Apart from the occupancy-dependent body odours and environmental tobacco smoke, modern buildings are likely to contain one or more of the following odorous substances:

—   organic compounds, used in the manufacture and cleaning of furniture, carpets, curtains and the building fabric

—   ozone, released from photocopiers, laser printers and electric motors

—   products of combustion

—   fumes from cooking

—   volatile organic compounds emitted from micro-organisms such as growing moulds

—   external pollutants

—   gases percolating through foundations from contaminated land-fill sites

—   emissions from industrial processes.

Many of these substances become irritants if concentrations are sufficiently high. Little is known about the possible additive or synergistic effects that may occur when a number of substances combine at low concentrations. This is particularly so in the case of ozone and VOCs.

Table 1.8 provides recommended guideline values for common pollutants found in indoor and outdoor air. It is based on guidelines[61] published by the World Health Organisation (WHO) and air quality objective levels (AQOLs) set by the Air Quality Regulations[66], which are to be achieved outdoors by local authorities by the year 2005. Designers should consult the references quoted in order to determine the rationales on which they are based. The WHO guidelines are not 'standards' but represent best scientific judgement at the time at which they were proposed.

The values given in Table 1.8 are based on exposure to single airborne chemicals through inhalation alone. They do not take account of additive, synergistic or antagonistic effects or exposure through routes other than inhalation. The basis for derivation is different for each chemical, hence they cannot be compared with each other within an overall hierarchy of exposure effects. For each chemical the WHO guidelines provide information on typical sources, occurrence in air, typical concentrations reported, routes of exposure, metabolic processes, proven and suspected health effects and an evaluation of human health risks.

1.6.3   Perception of odours

Odour perception is highly subjective and therefore extremely difficult to measure. Olfactometers have been developed for use by trained subjects[68,69] but the correlation between the responses of visiting researchers and those of adapted occupants is poor. Also, no automatic control sensor has yet been developed which accurately simulates the response of humans to airborne substances. Sensors are available which can give an approximate indication of air quality but it has been difficult to find a contaminant that is truly representative of perceived air quality. Currently carbon dioxide is the most commonly used surrogate for airborne contamination from humans.

Studies[26] have indicated that general perceptions of odour are at their lowest at humidities in the range of 45 to 65% saturation at normal comfort temperatures, although this varies with the nature of the contaminant. However the odour emission rate from many materials, such as paint, rubber, upholstery, floor coverings etc., tends to decline with falling humidity.

The adsorption of odours onto indoor surfaces, and their subsequent desorption as temperature, air speed and vapour pressures change, can lead to a considerable increase in odour levels as conditions become favourable for desorption. During one study[70] a panel of non-adapted people were asked to judge the odour intensity in bars during normal use and after all occupants had left. On average, odour intensities were judged to be higher in the bars once the occupants had left. This was thought to be primarily due to desorption of the gaseous components of tobacco smoke, which had been adsorbed onto internal surfaces, along with the particulate matter, during occupancy.

It has been suggested[71] that, in an air conditioned building, for every unit of odourous pollution perceived as arising from an individual there could be up to 6 or 7 units released from a combination of sources such as environmental tobacco smoke, building materials, furniture, mould spores and the internal components of the air handling system.

One study of eight existing air handling systems[72] found that perceived odour intensity increased considerably through the air handling units. Malodourous pollutants are released from the fungicides used to treat filter material and thermal wheels, as well as the lubricants and fan belts associated with motors and fans. Poorly maintained air handling systems release pollutants from dirt or mould accumulated in filters and other internal surfaces.

Microbiological contamination of cooling coils, sound-absorbing materials in ductwork, moisture eliminators and spray ponds may be a particular problem[73]. Malodorous chemicals are driven off during initial application of heat to dust-coated heat emitters.

1.6.4   Outdoor air constituents

The quality of outdoor air must be accounted for in the design of ventilation and air conditioning systems. An analysis of the most important pollutants should be carried out if there is any cause for concern about the quality of the air that can enter the building via windows or ventilation air intakes. The local environmental health department should be consulted to determine whether monitoring has already been carried out at a location with a similar environment close to the site under consideration. Data on atmospheric pollution in the UK are published annually[74,75]. Guidance on the design and positioning of ventilation air intakes is given in CIBSE Technical Memoranda TM21: *Minimising pollution at air intakes*[76].

The guideline values given in Table 1.8 apply to both indoor and outdoor pollutants. If a local survey indicates that these concentrations are likely to be exceeded in the incoming ventilation air on a regular basis then consideration should be given to specific filtration of the offending pollutants.

If external pollutant concentrations rise above the standards during a typical day, then it may be possible to reduce ventilation rates during peak times provided that such periods are sufficiently short that higher ventilation rates at other times will provide adequate compensation. This will require continuous sensing of a key indicator of outdoor air quality, such as carbon monoxide.

1.6.5   Filtration strategy

If the main form of outdoor pollution is particulates, the pollution concentration of the incoming air can be reduced by passing the air through fabric or electrostatic filters. Reducing the concentration of gases and vapours requires additional equipment, usually in the form of adsorption filters, see Guide B3[77].

The grade of filtration required depends on the following factors:

—   external pollution levels

—   exposure limits for the protection of occupants or processes within the building

—   degree of protection required for the internal surfaces of the building, air handling plant and air distribution system.

BS EN 779[78] gives a method of rating and specifying filters based on average arrestance and average efficiency. These terms are defined as follows:

—   average arrestance (A_m): the ratio of synthetic dust arrested by the filter to the weight of dust fed to the filter (%)

Table 1.8 Guideline values for individual substances

Substance	Averaging time	Guideline value concentration in air		Source/notes
		By mass	By volume	
Arsenic	Lifetime	—	—	Estimated 1500 deaths from cancer in population of 1 million through lifetime exposure of $1\,\mu g \cdot m^{-3}$ (WHO AQG: 1998; see note 1)
Benzene	1 year (running)	5 ppb	$16.0\,\mu g \cdot m^{-3}$	AQOL; see note 2
	Lifetime	—	—	Estimated 6 deaths from cancer in population of 1 million through lifetime exposure of $1\,\mu g \cdot m^{-3}$ (WHO AQG: 1998; see note 1)
1,3-butadiene	1 year (running)	1 ppb	$2.26\,\mu g \cdot m^{-3}$	AQOL; see note 2
Cadmium	Annual	—	$5\,ng \cdot m^{-3}$	WHO AQG: 1998; see note 1
Carbon monoxide	15 min	86 ppm	$100\,mg \cdot m^{-3}$	WHO AQG: 1998; see note 1
	30 min	52 ppm	$60\,mg \cdot m^{-3}$	WHO AQG: 1998; see note 1
	1 hour	26 ppm	$30\,mg \cdot m^{-3}$	WHO AQG: 1998; see note 1
	8 hour (running)	10 ppm	$11.6\,mg \cdot m^{-3}$	WHO AQG: 1998; see note 1
Chromium	Lifetime	—	—	Estimated 40,000 deaths from cancer in population of 1 million through lifetime exposure of $1\,\mu g \cdot m^{-3}$ (WHO AQG: 1998; see note 1)
1,2-dichloroethane	24 hours	168 ppb	$700\,\mu g \cdot m^{-3}$	WHO AQG: 1998; see note 1
Dichloromethane (methyl chloride)	24 hours	0.84 ppm	$3\,mg \cdot m^{-3}$	WHO AQG: 1998; see note 1
Formaldehyde	30 min	80 ppb	$100\,\mu g \cdot m^{-3}$	WHO AQG: 1998; see note 1
Hydrogen sulphide	30 min	5 ppb	$7\,\mu g \cdot m^{-3}$	WHO AQG: 1998; see note 1
Lead	1 year	—	$0.5\,\mu g \cdot m^{-3}$	Based on daily averages. AQOL; see note 2
MMVF–RC (man-made vitreous fibres; refractory ceramic fibres)	Lifetime	—	—	Estimated 40,000 deaths from cancer in population of 1 million through lifetime exposure of $1\,\mu g \cdot m^{-3}$ (WHO AQG: 1998; see note 1)
Manganese	1 year	—	$0.15\,\mu g \cdot m^{-3}$	WHO AQG: 1998; see note 1
Mercury	1 year	—	$1\,\mu g \cdot m^{-3}$	WHO AQG: 1998; see note 1
Nickel	Lifetime	—	—	Estimated 380 deaths from cancer in population of 1 million through lifetime exposure of $1\,\mu g \cdot m^{-3}$ (WHO AQG: 1998; see note 1)
Nitrogen dioxide	1 hour (mean)	150 ppb	$300\,\mu g \cdot m^{-3}$	AQOL; see note 2
	1 year	21 ppb	$42\,\mu g \cdot m^{-3}$	Based on hourly averages. AQOL; see note 2
Ozone	8 hour	60 ppb	$120\,\mu g \cdot m^{-3}$	WHO AQG: 1998; see note 1
PM_{10} (particulate matter $< 10\,\mu m$ diameter)	24 hour	—	$50\,\mu g \cdot m^{-3}$	99th. percentile (running). AQOL; see note 2
Radon	Lifetime	—	—	Estimated 36 deaths from cancer in population of 1 million through lifetime exposure of $1\,Bq \cdot m^{-3}$ (WHO AQG: 1998; see note 1)
Styrene	1 week	60 ppb	$260\,\mu g \cdot m^{-3}$	WHO AQG: 1998; see note 1
Sulphur dioxide	15 min	100 ppb	$270\,\mu g \cdot m^{-3}$	99.9th. percentile. AQOL; see note 2
	24 hour	46 ppb	$125\,\mu g \cdot m^{-3}$	WHO AQG: 1998; see note 1
	1 year	19 ppb	$50\,\mu g \cdot m^{-3}$	WHO AQG: 1998; see note 1
Tetrachloroethylene	24 hour	—	$250\,\mu g \cdot m^{-3}$	WHO AQG: 1998; see note 1
Toluene	1 week	68 ppb	$260\,\mu g \cdot m^{-3}$	WHO AQG: 1998; see note 1
Trichloroethylene	Lifetime	—	—	Estimated 4 deaths from cancer in population of 10 million through lifetime exposure of $1\,\mu g \cdot m^{-3}$ (WHO AQG: 1998; see note 1)

Notes:

(1) From WHO *Air Quality Guidelines for Europe* (1998), based on summary document of final consultation meeting held at WHO European Centre for Environment and Health, Bilthoven, Netherlands, 28–31 October 1996. These should be used along with the rationale given in the relevant chapters of the WHO publication[61].

(2) Air quality objective levels (AQOLS) are taken from the *Air Quality Regulations 1997*[66]. These levels are to be achieved outdoors throughout the UK by 2005. Local authorities have been tasked under Part IV of the *Environment Act 1995*[67] to review air quality within their areas to achieve these levels. The interpretation to the schedule in the *Regulations* defines how averaging should be achieved.

— average efficiency (E_m): the weighted average of the efficiencies for different specified dust loading levels (%).

At the time of writing (July 1999), *BS EN 779*[78] is under review with publication expected in late-1999. This standard will require that the average efficiency be determined by injecting an artificial dust of known size distribution into the air upstream of the filter and measuring the upstream and downstream concentrations at specified particle sizes using a particle counter. The classification will be based on particles of 0.4 μm diameter. Efficiencies should apply to the whole filter installation and not only to the filter media. EUROVENT publication 4/10[79] provides a method for in-situ testing of filter installations using a similar procedure to the proposed standard, which may be used to check the efficiency of the filter installation both during commissioning and as part of an on-going monitoring regime.

Table 1.9 gives the recommended classification for different applications. If high dust loadings are expected, it is wise to install coarse (i.e. G1 to G3) pre-filters upstream of the main filters. This will increase the replacement interval for the downstream higher efficiency (and therefore more costly) filters.

Table 1.9 Classification of filters as defined in BS EN 779[78]

Classification	Average arrestance, A_m (%)	Average efficiency, E_m (%)
G 1	$A_m < 65$	—
G 2	$65 \leq A_m < 80$	—
G 3	$80 \leq A_m < 90$	—
G 4	$A_m \geq 90$	—
F 5	—	$40 \leq E_m < 60$
F 6	—	$60 \leq E_m < 80$
F 7	—	$80 \leq E_m < 90$
F 8	—	$90 \leq E_m < 95$
F 9	—	$E_m \geq 95$

1.7 Determination of required outdoor air supply rate

1.7.1 General

Ventilation requirements for a wide range of building types are summarised in Table 1.1. Detailed information on specific applications is given in Guide B2[17]. For some industrial applications outdoor air may be required both to dilute specific pollutants and to make up the air exhausted through local extract ventilation systems (see Guide B3[77]). Specialist advice should be sought in dealing with toxic and/or high emission pollutants.

In the following sections three methods are described for determining the outdoor air supply rate required for particular applications.

The first method (see section 1.7.2) is prescriptive, providing either an outdoor air supply rate per person or an air change rate, depending on the application. These values are based primarily on chamber studies, in which all sources of odour other than body odour and/or cigarette smoke were excluded. Therefore these prescribed rates may underestimate the outdoor air supply requirements if odour sources other than body odour or smoking dominate. Examples of such situations are spaces having large areas of new floor covering, upholstery, curtains etc. or spaces in which the standards of cleaning and maintenance are less than excellent.

Method 2 (see section 1.7.3) should be used in situations where there are known pollutants being released into the space at a known rate and local extract ventilation (LEV) is not practicable. To apply method 2, it is necessary to know the appropriate concentration limits for the pollutants. Local extract should be used wherever source location permits and for all applications where risks to the health of the occupants are not acceptable. The ventilation strategy should be based on a risk assessment under the *Control of Substances Hazardous to Health Regulations 1994*[80]. Design guidance is given in *Guide B3*[77].

A further method has been suggested[81] which is intended for use where the pollution sources are known but (*a*) the emission rates of specific malodourous pollutants cannot be predicted, (*b*) their limiting concentrations are not known, or (*c*) odours are likely to result from complex mixtures of contaminants. Further research will be required to establish benchmark criteria. Ventilation rates calculated by this method will usually be higher than the prescribed rates determined using method 1. Details of this method are given in a report on ventilation requirements produced by the Commission for the European Community[82]. At the time of writing (July 1999) this method has not gained international acceptance.

1.7.2 Method 1: Prescribed outdoor air supply rates

For applications in which the main odorous pollutants arise due to human activities, e.g. body odour and environmental tobacco smoke, it is possible to supply a quantity of outdoor air based on the number of occupants in a given space. If smoking is prohibited, as is increasingly the case, then the ventilation rate for 'no smoking' applies. For a multi-occupancy space where smoking is allowed, an assessment of the likely overall level of smoking must be made, bearing in mind that smoking habits are changing.

Table 1.10 gives recommended outdoor air supply rates for sedentary occupation for populations in which the proportion of smokers varies from 0 to 75% of the occupants present. It is assumed that each smoker present smokes an average of 1.3 cigarettes per hour[83].

The category 'some smoking' corresponds to the situation where 25% of the occupants smoke, but not all at once. This rate may be applied to a typical open plan office space in which an average smoking rate might be expected. 'Heavy smoking' and 'very heavy smoking' are where 45% and 70% of the occupants are smokers respectively.

Table 1.10 Recommended outdoor air supply rates for sedentary occupants

Level of smoking	Proportion of occupants that smoke (%)	Outdoor air supply rate (L·s⁻¹·person⁻¹)
No smoking	0	8
Some smoking	25	16
Heavy smoking	45	24
Very heavy smoking	75	36

Adoption of the outdoor air supply rates given in Table 1.10 will not guarantee that non-smokers present will not be exposed to environmental tobacco smoke at levels at which they experience discomfort or possible health effects. The only way to ensure that this does not occur is to prevent smoking in areas where non-smokers are present and to ensure that there is no transfer of smoke from areas in which smoking is permitted.

The outdoor air supply rates given in Table 1.10 assume that the outdoor air supplied to the space is fully mixed with the room air. These rates should be adjusted if the ventilation effectiveness, see section 1.7.4, is expected to take a value other than 1.0.

1.7.3 Method 2: Specific pollutant control

1.7.3.1 Steady-state conditions

For pollutants emitted at a constant rate, the ventilation rate required to prevent the mean equilibrium concentration rising above a prescribed level may be calculated from the following equation:

$$Q = \frac{P\,(10^6 - C_{pi})}{E_v\,(C_{pi} - C_{po})} \qquad (1.7)$$

where Q is the outdoor air supply rate (L·s⁻¹), P is the pollutant emission rate (L·s⁻¹), C_{po} is the concentration of pollutant in the outdoor air (ppm), E_v is the ventilation effectiveness and C_{pi} is the limit of concentration of pollutant in the indoor air (ppm). Values for E_v are given in section 1.7.4, Table 1.11.

If the pollutant threshold is quoted in mg·m⁻³, the concentration in parts per million may be obtained from:

$$C_p = (C_p' \times 24.05526) / M_p \qquad (1.8)$$

where C_p is the concentration of pollutant (ppm), C_p' is the concentration of pollutant by volume (mg·m⁻³), M_p is the molar mass of the pollutant (kg·mole⁻¹). The numerical factor is the molar volume of an ideal gas (m³·mole⁻¹) at 20°C and pressure of 1 atmosphere. Molecular masses for pollutants are given in *EH40*[84] or from manufacturers' data.

If C_{pi} is small (i.e. $C_{pi} \ll 10^6$), equation 1.7 becomes:

$$Q = \frac{P \times 10^6}{E_v\,(C_{pi} - C_o)} \qquad (1.9)$$

If the incoming air is not contaminated by the pollutant in question, this equation simplifies to:

$$Q = (P \times 10^6) / E_v\,C_{pi} \qquad (1.10)$$

Where there is more than one known pollutant, the calculation should be performed for each pollutant separately. The outdoor air supply rate for ventilation is then highest of these calculated rates.

If E_v is equal to one in equations 1.7, 1.9 and 1.10, this indicates that a substantially uniform concentration exists throughout the space. If the ventilation results in a non-uniform concentration so that higher than average concentrations occur in the inhaled air, the outdoor air supply rate would need to be increased above the value calculated by these equations.

Example 1.1

Toluene is being released at a rate of 20 mL·h⁻¹; determine the rate of ventilation required to meet the WHO *Air Quality Guidelines for Europe*[61], assuming a ventilation effectiveness (E_v) of 1.0.

The release rate of the pollutant, $P = 20$ mL·h⁻¹ $= 5.56 \times 10^{-6}$ L·s⁻¹.

From Table 1.8 the WHO AQG threshold for toluene is 68 ppb (i.e. 0.068 ppm).

Assuming there is no toluene in the outdoor air, $C_o = 0$.

Therefore, using equation 1.10:

$$Q = (5.56 \times 10^{-6} \times 10^6) / (1 \times 0.068) = 81.7 \text{ L·s}^{-1}$$

1.7.3.2 Non-steady state conditions

The ventilation rate given by equation 1.10 is independent of the room or building volume. However the volume of the space affects the time taken for the equilibrium condition to be reached. This becomes important when the emission of a pollutant occurs for a limited duration only. In such cases the ventilation rate derived from equation 1.10 will exceed that required to maintain the concentration below the specified limit.

The ratio by which the steady-state ventilation rate may be reduced in these circumstances is given by:

$$Q'/Q = f(Q\,\theta_p / 1000\,V) \qquad (1.11)$$

where Q' is the reduced ventilation rate (L·s⁻¹), Q is the steady state ventilation rate (L·s⁻¹), θ_p is the duration of release of the pollutant (s) and V is the volume of the space (m³).

The form of the function $f(Q\,\theta_p / 1000\,V)$ is given by the solid curve in Figure 1.12. Although theoretically no ventilation is required when $(Q\,\theta / 1000\,V) < 1.0$, some ventilation should be provided because subsequent releases of pollutant are likely to occur.

Recurrent emissions can be taken into account by considering a regular intermittent emission where the releases occur for periods of θ_1 seconds at intervals of θ_2

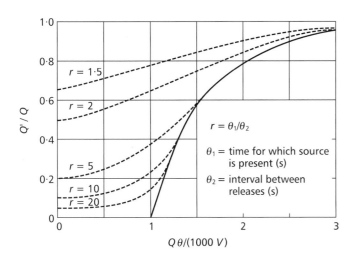

Figure 1.12 Reduction in fresh air rate for intermittent pollutant source

seconds. The ventilation rate ratio then becomes a function of $(Q \, \theta_1 / V)$ and the ratio of θ_1 to θ_2. The broken lines in Figure 1.12 may be used to determine (Q' / Q) where these parameters are known.

Example 1.2

If the toluene in Example 1.1 were released into a ventilated space of 160 m³ volume over a 40 minute period each day, determine the continuous outdoor air supply rate required to maintain the concentration of toluene at or below the WHO AQG value.

Initial data: $Q = 81.7$ L·s⁻¹, $\theta_p = 2400$ s, $V = 160$ m³.

Therefore:

$$(Q \, \theta_p / 1000 \, V) = (81.7 \times 2400) / (1000 \times 160) = 1.23$$

From Figure 1.12:

$$(Q' / Q) = 0.35$$

Therefore:

$$Q' = 0.35 \times 81.7 = 28.6 \text{ L·s}^{-1}$$

Example 1.3

If the toluene in Example 1.1 were periodically released for periods of 40 minutes with an interval of 20 minutes between releases, determine the appropriate outdoor air supply rate.

Initial data: $Q = 81.7$ L·s⁻¹, $\theta_p = 2400$ s, $V = 160$ m³.

As for Example 1.2:

$$(Q \, \theta_p / 1000 \, V) = 1.23$$

Ratio of source duration to return interval is given by:

$$r = \theta_1 / \theta_2 = 2400 / 1200 = 2$$

From Figure 1.12, for $r = 2$:

$$(Q' / Q) = 0.75$$

Therefore:

$$Q' = 0.75 \times 81.7 = 61.3 \text{ L·s}^{-1}$$

1.7.3.3   Indoor air pollutants: requirements

Published limits fall into two categories:

—   those that have been derived from studies of health effects

—   those based on comfort or sensory effects.

Exposure limits based on effects on health

Occupational exposure limits (OELs) for the UK are published annually by the Health and Safety Executive in *Occupational exposure limits (EH40)*[84]. These limits are levels used to demonstrate compliance with the *Health and Safety at Work etc. Act 1974*[85] and the *COSHH Regulations 1994*[80]. This legislation applies not just to industrial workplaces but equally to all workplaces including offices. In practice, in most circumstances the levels of exposure and the modes of exposure do not present a significant risk to the occupants of non-industrial workspaces such as offices.

The occupational exposure limits listed in *EH40* are not exclusive; absence from the list does not imply that a substance has no ill effects on health nor that it is safe to use without control. Where a particular substance does not have an OEL the employer, in carrying out a risk assessment, should also determine an adequate level of control for the substance and, in effect, set an 'in-house' OEL.

Evidence that the relevant OEL has been exceeded can be used in enforcement, including prosecutions, under this legislation the basic requirement of which is to prevent the exposure of employees to substances hazardous to health. Where it is not reasonably practicable to prevent exposure to such substances then the employer must adequately control exposure.

It is not appropriate to use OELs to calculate the required outside air supply. The provision of sufficient outside air is important but it is only one of a combination of measures required to provide adequate control of exposure. Such measures are outside the scope of this Guide and will often require specialist advice.

Exposure limits based on effects on senses

In practice, exposure of workers in non-industrial environments to the same concentrations of malodorous substances that occur in industry would not be acceptable. This is primarily because expectations are generally much higher amongst occupants of non-industrial buildings. Odour detection and hence comfort are not primary considerations in setting occupational exposure limits.

Sensory comfort guidelines[61] are available for only a small number of single substances. These are based on the odour detection threshold for given averaging times. These values can be used to calculate dilution rates when it is known that a specific substance may be responsible for odour annoyance.

The ideal solution is for the substance to be eliminated at source. For substances which do not appear in Table 1.8, an exposure limit for non-industrial applications can be estimated by multiplying the relevant occupational exposure limit from *EH40*[84] by a factor of 0.1.

1.7.4 Ventilation effectiveness

Guidance on the ventilation effectiveness for the ventilation arrangements shown in Figure 1.13 is given in Table 1.11. In each case, the space is considered as divided into two zones:

—   the zone into which air is supplied/exhausted

—   the remainder of the space, i.e. the 'breathing zone'.

In mixing ventilation (cases (a) and (b) in Figure 1.13), the outside air supply rates given in Table 1.10 assume that the supply zone is usually above the breathing zone. The best conditions are achieved when mixing is sufficiently effective that the two zones merge to form a single zone. In displacement ventilation (Figure 1.13(c)), the supply zone is usually at low level and occupied with people, and the exhaust zone is at a higher level. The best conditions are achieved when there is minimal mixing between the two zones. The values given in Table 1.11 consider the effects of air distribution and supply temperature but not the location of the pollutants, which are assumed to be evenly distributed throughout the ventilated space. For other types of displacement system, the ventilation effectiveness (E_v) may be assumed to be 1.0.

Table 1.11 Ventilation effectiveness for ventilation arrangements shown in Figure 1.13

Ventilation arrangement	Temperature difference between supply air and room air, $(t_s - t_{ai})$ (K)	Ventilation effectiveness, E_v
Mixing; high-level supply and exhaust (Figure 1.13(a))	< 0	0.9 – 1.0
	0 – 2	0.9
	2 – 5	0.8
	> 5	0.4 – 0.7
Mixing; high-level supply, low-level exhaust (Figure 1.13(b))	< –5	0.9
	(–5) – 0	0.9 – 1.0
	> 0	1.0
Displacement (Figure 1.13(c))	< 0	1.2 – 1.4
	0 – 2	0.7 – 0.9
	> 2	0.2 – 0.7

1.8 Visual environment

1.8.1 General

Lighting in a building has three purposes:

—   to enable the occupant to work and move about in safety

—   to enable tasks to be performed correctly and at an appropriate pace

—   to create a pleasing appearance.

A satisfactory visual environment can be achieved by electric lighting alone, but most people have a strong preference for some daylight. This is supported by the *Workplace (Health, Safety & Welfare) Regulations 1992*[86], which require access to daylight for all workers where reasonably practicable. Where daylight is available a good design will make use of it to save energy and enhance internal appearance without glare, distracting reflections, overheating or excessive heat loss.

Good lighting can aid the avoidance of hazards during normal use of a building and in emergencies by revealing obstacles and clearly indicating exits. It makes tasks easier to perform and it can contribute to an interior that is considered satisfactory and, even, inspiring by providing emphasis, colour and variety.

The balance between lighting for performance and for pleasantness is usually dependent upon the primary purpose for which the interior is intended. For example, in

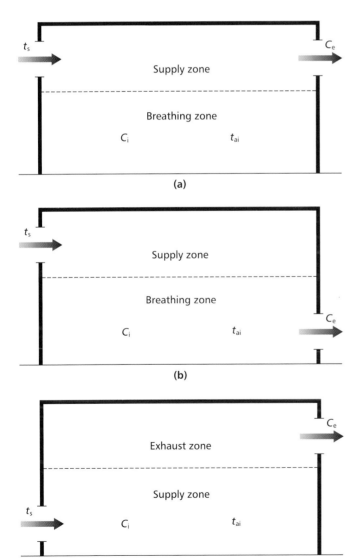

Figure 1.13 Supply/extract arrangements for ventilation; (*a*) mixing, supply and exhaust at high level, (*b*) mixing, supply at high level, exhaust at low level, (*c*) displacement

an engineering workshop the primary requirement of the lighting is to enable some product to be made quickly, easily and accurately. However, a cheerful but non-distracting atmosphere produced by careful lighting can be an aid to productivity. At the other extreme, the prime purpose of the lighting in restaurants is often to produce a particular atmosphere while ensuring that the food is not difficult to see. The lighting must be matched to the context and the operational requirements in order to be successful.

1.8.2   Lighting for safety

There are two aspects of lighting for safety. The first refers to the conditions prevailing in an interior when the normal lighting system is in operation. In these circumstances the main requirement is for the occupants to be able to move about the interior without tripping, or colliding with people or objects, and be able to operate machinery without risk of injury due to poor visibility. The second aspect becomes apparent when the normal lighting system fails, in which circumstances the alternative/standby lighting constitutes emergency lighting.

1.8.2.1   Lighting for safe normal use

Illuminance for safety while the normal lighting system is operating is usually satisfactory if the illuminance required for performance and/or pleasantness is maintained. Suitable values, for a wide range of applications, are given in the *Code for Interior Lighting*[10]. However, in many instances there are legally enforced minimum standards and the *Workplace (Health, Safety & Welfare) Regulations 1992*[86] and the *Provision and Use of Work Equipment Regulations 1998*[87] require that provision be made for 'suitable and sufficient lighting', with a preference for daylight, when available.

The Health and Safety Executive Guide, *Lighting at Work 1987*[88], indicates minimum lighting standards for safety in the workplace. These standards should not be confused with those given in the *Code for interior lighting*[10], which are the lighting levels required in order to perform tasks quickly and accurately.

Although the main purpose of legislation is to ensure safety, there are situations where health and welfare are the primary considerations. For locations where food is prepared (other than in agriculture), the *Food Hygiene (General) Regulations 1970*[89] require 'suitable and sufficient means of lighting' in order that proper cleanliness can be maintained and the local authority (which is responsible for enforcement of these regulations) should be consulted regarding the specific standards which apply.

The *Health and Safety (Display Screen Equipment) Regulations 1992*[90] provide protection for users of display screens and keyboards, and require that 'satisfactory lighting conditions' be provided, allowing for background conditions, glare, reflections and the visual requirements of users.

In the cases of schools and hospitals, minimum lighting standards are specified by the Department for Education and Employment and the Department of Health, respectively. Guidance is also provided in CIBSE Lighting Guides LG5[14] and LG2[18], respectively.

The above summary of mandatory requirements is not comprehensive and identifies only the most important legislation concerning the provision of lighting for safety. There may be other, more demanding requirements, specific to particular applications and it is essential that the relevant authorities (e.g. local authority, HM Factories Inspectorate etc.) be consulted at an early stage in the design process.

1.8.2.2   Emergency lighting

Emergency lighting can be divided into two classes:

(a)   standby lighting, which is intended to enable essential work to be carried out, e.g. hospital operating theatres

(b)   escape lighting which enables people to evacuate a building quickly and safely.

For general use an absolute minimum illuminance of 0.2 lux is required along the centre line of all escape routes and 1 lux average over open areas with no defined escape routes. The *Workplace Regulations 1992*[86] require that emergency lighting be 'suitable and sufficient'. Detailed guidance on the design of emergency lighting systems is given in *BS 5266*[91] and CIBSE Technical Memoranda TM12: *Emergency lighting*[92].

1.8.2.3   Layout of lighting

Escape routes

Emergency lighting must be located so as not to create glare and confusion. For example a 'headlight' style emergency light must not be positioned such that it throws light along an escape route towards the escapees. For emergency lighting, both *BS 5266*[91] and TM12[92] recommend that the ratio of maximum to minimum illuminance on escape routes should not exceed 40:1. It is particularly important that luminaires providing emergency lighting are arranged to draw attention to intersections and changes of direction or level. In addition to providing light for evacuation, an organised installation of luminaires serves to give a sense of orientation and direction. This is also true for normal lighting. Emergency lighting can be integrated into the normal lighting installation if required.

Staircases

The lighting of staircases must be given careful consideration, particularly if there are changes of direction at short intervals. Lighting schemes designed for appearance only may combine visual confusion with poor visibility. For example, uplighters that throw light into the faces of people descending a staircase must be avoided. Staircases constitute zones of potential hazard and the guiding principle should be to reveal clearly the stair treads (by locating sources so that each riser is shadowed) and to make evident the location and direction of the stairway.

Workplaces

In workplaces, reflections from shiny surfaces can make objects, machinery, controls or indicators difficult to see. This may be avoided by the use of matt surfaces or arranging the lighting to avoid specular reflections towards the subject. Another hazard with rotating machinery is the stroboscopic effect produced by discharge lamps operating from an AC supply. This can be reduced by wiring adjacent luminaires to different phases of the supply or by the use of high frequency control gear. Such hazards are considered in CIBSE Lighting Guide LG1[16].

1.8.3 Lighting for performance

1.8.3.1 General

The exact relationship between visual performance and illuminance or luminance has been the subject of many investigations[93–96]. All of these studies indicate that this relationship depends upon many factors, which vary with task, individual and environment.

Where tasks involve the observation of fine detail (i.e. requiring high acuity), if the contrast (i.e. the difference in appearance of two parts of a visual field seen simultaneously or successively) is low then no amount of increase in illuminance will raise the visual performance to the level which can be attained by providing high contrast. However, performance can be improved by higher contrast, even with very low values of illuminance.

For larger task detail (i.e. requiring low acuity), the visual performance does not decline with low contrast or luminance to the same extent.

Task performances also depends on other factors such as the visual complexity of the task, task movement, the age and eyesight of the workers and the significance to the worker of the visual component of the work.

The CIBSE *Code for interior lighting*[10] contains illuminance recommendations for many different working situations. Table 1.12, reproduced from the *Code*, summarises these in relation to different categories of visual task. It should be noted that these illuminances are intended to be measured on the appropriate working plane (i.e. horizontal, vertical or intermediate). Also, it is important to note that it is often more economic to improve performance by making the task easier through increase in apparent size of detail (e.g. by using optical aids) and improved contrast (e.g. by selecting a suitable task background) rather than by increasing illuminance.

Note that Table 1.12 is reproduced here for information purposes only. Reference should be made to the comprehensive tables of specific task illuminance values in

Table 1.12 Examples of activities/interiors appropriate for each maintained illuminance*[10]

Standard maintained illuminance (lux)	Characteristics of activity/interior	Representative activities/interiors
50	Interiors used rarely, with visual tasks confined to movement and casual seeing without perception of detail	Cable tunnels, indoor storage tanks, walkways
100	Interiors used occasionally, with visual tasks confined to movement, and casual seeing calling for only limited perception of detail	Corridors, changing rooms, bulk stores, auditoria
150	Interiors used occasionally, with visual tasks requiring some perception of detail or involving some risk to people, plant or product	Loading bays, medical stores, switchrooms plant rooms
200	Continuously occupied interiors, visual tasks not requiring perception of detail	Foyers and entrances, monitoring automatic processes, casting concrete, turbine halls, dining rooms
300	Continuously occupied interiors, visual tasks moderately easy, i.e. large details > 10 min. arc and/or high contrast	Libraries, sports and assembly halls, teaching spaces, lecture theatres, packing
500	Visual tasks moderately difficult, i.e. details to be seen are of moderate size (5–10 min. arc) and may be of low contrast; also colour judgement may be required	General offices, engine assembly, painting and spraying, kitchens, laboratories, retail shops
750	Visual tasks difficult, i.e. details to be seen are small (3–5 min. arc) and of low contrast; also good colour judgements may be required	Drawing offices, ceramic decoration, meat inspection, chain stores
1000	Visual tasks very difficult, i.e. details to be seen are very small (2–3 min. arc) and can be of very low contrast; also accurate colour judgements may be required	General inspection, electronic assembly, gauge and tool rooms, retouching paintwork, cabinet making, supermarkets
1500	Visual tasks extremely difficult, i.e. details to be seen extremely small (1–2 min. arc) and of low contrast; visual aids and local lighting may be of advantage	Fine work and inspection, hand tailoring, precision assembly
2000	Visual tasks exceptionally difficult, i.e. details to be seen exceptionally small (< 1 min. arc) with very low contrasts; visual aids and local lighting will be of advantage	Assembly of minute mechanisms, finished fabric inspection

* Maintained illuminance is defined as the average illuminance over the reference surface at the time maintenance has to be carried out by replacing lamps and/or cleaning the equipment and room surfaces

the *Code*, modified to take account of task contrast, age of operatives, consequences of error etc. as described in the *Code*.

These recommendations do not identify the source that is required to provide these illuminances and the recommended levels may be met using either daylight or electric light. However, when using daylight it is only possible to give the criteria in terms of daylight factor since the daylight illuminance varies continuously. Recommendations for interiors in which daylight is to be the dominant source are given in CIBSE Applications Manual AM2: *Window design*[97] and the *Code for Interior Lighting*[10].

1.8.3.2   Distribution of light

When considering the distribution of light in an interior, a decision must be made on the type of lighting to be used. Broadly, the alternatives are as follows:

—   an installation which provides a uniform illuminance across the notional working plane and hence complete flexibility of work layout in the space

—   a building lighting/task lighting approach where each task area has its own lighting and the general room lighting is used only as a background.

For the former, it is recommended that the ratio of minimum to average illuminance over the working plane should not be less than 0.8. Where a building lighting/task lighting approach is used, the ratio of the minimum to maximum illuminance over the working plane should not exceed 1:5.

1.8.3.3   Directional effects

Some directional effects of light make it easier to recognise the details of a task, others make recognition more difficult.

The contrasts perceived in a task depend on the reflection characteristics of its surface and on how the task is lit. Contrast is reduced if the images of bright sources, such as luminaires or the sky, are seen in shiny surfaces. This veiling effect, see section 1.8.3.4, is often most apparent when a bright source is reflected from glossy paper. Legibility of print is sometimes seriously impaired by veiling reflections.

A similar problem occurs when using display screen equipment where the screen tends to reflect back to the viewer images of bright objects in front of the screen. For this reason screens need to be positioned to avoid the images of windows and brightly lit areas of the room from being reflected in the screen. A full analysis of the problems involved and the solutions available is set out in CIBSE Lighting Guide LG3: *The visual environment for display screen use*[12].

In general terms loss of contrast due to veiling reflections can be minimised by careful positioning of the viewer, the task and the source. If a light source lies within a certain solid angle behind the viewer then veiling reflections will occur and bright sources should not be positioned in this region. For screens which are near flat, the size of the offending zone can be determined by extending the solid

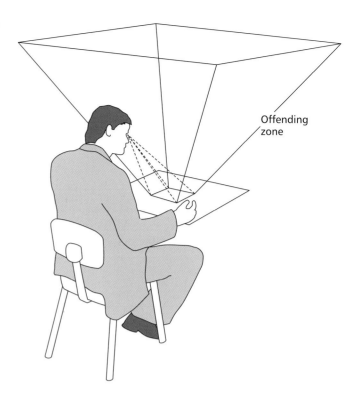

Figure 1.14 Avoidance of veiling reflections

angle created between the eyes and the screen as shown in Figure 1.14.

'Modelling' is the term used to describe ability of light to reveal solid form. Modelling may be harsh or flat depending on the strength of the light flow. Fairly strong and coherent modelling helps to reveal three-dimensional shapes.

Each task has special requirements and the extent to which modelling can assist perception should be determined from a combination of experience and practical trials. The details of some tasks may be revealed more clearly by careful adjustment of the direction of the light rather than by an increase in illuminance.

Surface texture and relief are normally emphasised if light is directed across the surface and subdued, or flat, if the surface is lit mainly from the front. Particular tasks should be lit to provide the maximum relevant visual information and the best arrangement is usually achieved through adjustable luminaires or by experiment.

1.8.3.4   Disability glare

Veiling reflections directly affect the visibility of the task by reflection from the task area. However, disability glare can influence the task visibility without reflection from the task. This effect is due to light entering the eye and then being scattered in such a way that it forms a veil over the retinal image of the task.

The effect is most noticeable when the source is close to the line of sight between the observer and the task. Therefore, disability glare caused by the reflection of light sources in areas adjacent to the work is particularly troublesome.

The only way of eliminating disability glare is to separate all areas of high luminance from areas immediately surrounding the task. This is usually a matter of avoiding the use of glossy surfaces close to the task or moving the task to another location. In practice, disability glare direct from luminaires is rare in interior lighting.

1.8.3.5 Health effects

There is evidence[98] that the 100 Hz light modulation from discharge lamps, including fluorescent tubes, is detected by the human visual system. This is not perceived as flicker, but studies have shown a correlation between this modulation and the reporting of headaches by susceptible individuals. Although such people probably form only a small minority of the population, the incidence of headaches has been found to be substantially reduced under lighting where this modulation was not present, e.g. by the use of fluorescent lamps controlled by electronic ballasts operating at high frequency (e.g. 1000 Hz). Susceptible individuals may therefore suffer fewer headaches if working under high frequency electric lighting or daylight.

1.8.4 Criteria for design using daylight

Table 1.13 gives recommended average and minimum daylight factors, at the positions indicated, for interiors where daylight from side windows is the chief source of light during the greater part of the year.

If the average daylight factor exceeds 5% on the horizontal plane, an interior will look cheerfully daylit, even in the absence of sunlight. If the average daylight factor is less than 2% the interior will not be perceived as well daylit and electric lighting may need to be in constant use.

The average daylight factor may be used as an initial design parameter. It is calculated as follows:

$$\mathrm{DF} = (T A_\mathrm{w}\, \theta) / A\, (1 - R_\mathrm{a}^2) \qquad (1.13)$$

where DF is the average daylight factor (%), T is the diffuse transmittance of the glazing material including effects of dirt (Table 1.14), A_w is the net glazed area of the window (m^2), θ is the angle in degrees subtended by sky which is visible from the centre of the window (degree) (see Figure 1.15), A is the total area of the internal surfaces (ceiling, floor, windows and walls) (m^2) and R_a is the area-weighted average reflectance of the interior surfaces (ceiling, floor windows and walls).

Light transmittances for clean glass are given in manufacturers' literature and CIBSE Applications Manual AM2: Window design[97]. These should be multiplied by an appropriate correction factor taken from Table 1.14.

Where different windows face different obstructions, see Figure 1.15(c), the average daylight factor for each window should be calculated separately and the results added together.

Equation 1.13 can also be used to provide a preliminary estimate of window size for design purposes.

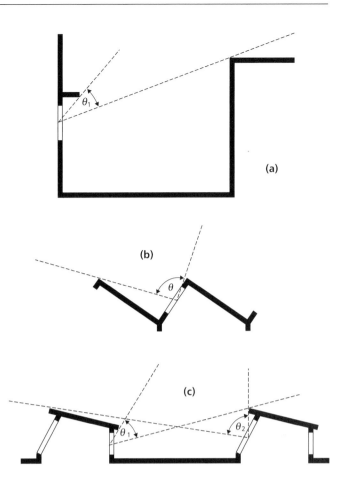

(a)

(b)

(c)

Figure 1.15 Angle of sky (θ) seen from centre of window; (a) window obstructed by overhang and nearby wall, (b) rooflight obstructed by roof construction, (c) different windows facing different obstructions

Table 1.14 Correction factors for dirt on glazing

Condition or location	Correction factor for given configuration		
	Vertical	Sloping	Horizontal
Clean	0.9	0.8	0.7
Very dirty	0.7	0.6	0.5
Industrial	0.8	0.7	0.6

The determination of daylight factor at specific points in a room is more complex. Several methods are described in CIBSE Applications Manual AM2: Window design[97].

1.8.5 Lighting for pleasantness

1.8.5.1 Quantity of light

It has been established that working environments lit uniformly to less than 200 lux tend to be rated as unsatisfactory for continuous occupation[99]. The CIBSE Code for interior lighting[10] recommends this value as a minimum amenity level in continuously occupied spaces, even though it may not be justified on performance grounds for occupations where the visual tasks are not demanding. Studies[100] have also shown that the preference for high lighting levels declines above 2000 lux.

Considerations of energy efficiency also affect the specification of a general preferred illuminance and energy

Table 1.13 Daylighting schedule[97]

Building type	Location	Daylight factor (%) Average	Daylight factor (%) Minimum*	Position of measurement
Airport buildings/coach stations	Reception areas	2	0.6	Desk
	Customs/immigration halls	2	0.6	Counter or desk
	Circulation areas, lounges	2	0.6	Working plane
Assembly and concert halls	Foyers, auditoria	1	0.6	Working plane
	Corridors	2	0.6	Floor
	Stairs	2	0.6	Stair treads
Banks	Counters, typing/accounting areas	5	2	Desk
	Public areas	2	0.6	Working plane
Churches	Body of church	5	1	Working plane
	Pulpit/lectern, chancel, choir	5	1.5	Desk
	Altar, communion table[1]	5	2	Table
Drawing offices	General	5	2.5	Drawing board
General building areas	Entrance halls, reception areas	2	0.6	Working plane
Hospitals[2]	Reception areas, waiting rooms	2	0.6	Working plane
	Wards	5	1[3]	Bedhead
	Pharmacies	5	3	Working plane
Libraries	Reading and reference rooms	5	1.5	Working plane
	Shelves/stacks	5	1.5	Vertical plane
Museums and art galleries[4]	General	5	1	Working plane
Offices	Business machines (manually operated)	5	2	Typing desk
	Computers[5]	5	2.5	Typing desk
Schools and colleges[6]	Assembly halls	1	0.3	Working plane
	Classrooms	5	2	Desk
	Art rooms	5	2	Easel
	Laboratories	5	2	Bench
	Staff rooms, common rooms	5	1.5	Working plane
Sports halls[7,8]	General	5	3.5	Working plane
Surgeries (medical and dental)[2]	Waiting rooms	2	0.6	Working plane
	Surgeries	5	2.5	Working plane
	Laboratories	5	2	Bench
Swimming pools[7,8]	Pool	5	2	Pool surface
	Surrounding areas	1	0.5	Working plane
Telephone exchanges (manual)[9]	General	—	2	Working plane
Dwellings	Lounges, multi-purpose rooms	1.5	0.5	
	Bedrooms	1	0.3	
	Kitchens	2	0.6	

* In general, all areas where daylight factor is less than 2% will require supplementary electric lighting. Minimum daylight factors are for side-lit rooms

Notes:

[1] Level depends on emphasis required; [2] See CIBSE Lighting Guide *LG2*[18]; [3] Refers to innermost bedheads; [4] See CIBSE Lighting Guide *LG8*[20]; [5] Visual display terminals must be treated separately, see CIBSE Lighting Guide LG3[12]; [6] See CIBSE Lighting Guide *LG5*[14]; [7] Top-lit; see CIBSE Lighting Guide *LG4*[15]; [8] Care must be taken to avoid glare and reflections from water surface; [9] Avoid specular reflections, limit daylight falling on internally-lit controls

savings may be achieved by separating the task lighting from the general building lighting. Daylight is often inappropriate as task lighting but even modest daylight admission can provide satisfactory building lighting for much of the working day. Furthermore, the provision of daylight is in itself a desirable amenity.

If a combination of general and task lighting is to be employed, utilising daylight where available, it is important to note that human reaction to sunlight is less predictable than to electric lighting[101,102] and effective sunlight control may be required for working environments.

For some interiors (e.g. circulation areas) there is no obvious visual task and reference to an illuminance on a working plane is not appropriate.

1.8.5.2 Distribution of light

Selective lighting may be used to make particular objects or spaces more conspicuous. In general, the brightest elements in the field of view should be those that it is wished to emphasise. If this is not so discomfort is experienced due to the visual conflict.

For working situations, the ratio of wall illuminance to working plane illuminance should be in the range 0.5–0.8 and ceiling/working plane illuminance ratio within the range 0.3–0.9[10]. The upper limits are directed by the expectation that the working plane should appear to be more strongly illuminated than either the walls or the ceiling. The exception to this is uplighting, which creates a visual environment more akin to daylight outdoors. The provision of lighting that achieves these illuminance ratios will usually ensure an acceptable distribution of light onto the main room surfaces but will not necessarily ensure a satisfactory balance of lighting on objects within the room.

1.8.5.3 Directional effects

The directional characteristics of light may be defined by an 'illumination vector'[10]. The magnitude of the illumination vector is the difference in illuminance on opposite sides of a flat surface that is so orientated to maximise this difference. Its direction is normal to this surface, the positive direction being from the higher illuminance to the lower.

Studies of the appearance of the human face show that a flow of light from above and to one side of the face gives the most natural appearance. This flow should not be too dominant or hard shadows below the brow and nose make faces appear harsh. A dominant flow of light across the space with general light to soften shadows is recommended, especially in areas where eye to eye contact is normal, e.g. reception areas and meeting rooms.

1.8.5.4 Discomfort glare

When the brightness of a surface or luminaire is higher than recommended then people may experience visual discomfort. Discomfort glare does not directly affect the visual difficulty of tasks. The standard methods for glare calculation are contained in CIBSE Technical Memoranda TM10: *Calculation of glare indices*[103].

The *Code for Interior Lighting*[10] contains a schedule of values of limiting glare index LGI based on assessments of the acceptability of actual lighting installations. LGI values vary according to the situation and the recommended values should not be exceeded. Table 1.15 provides LGI values for various applications.

1.8.5.5 Colour of light

All sources of light, both natural and artificial, differ in their spectral composition. Surface colour is produced by a combination of the wavelengths of the incident light and the spectral reflectance of the surface. Therefore, different sources will produce changes of colour of the surface. For most purposes these changes are modified by chromatic adaption, whereby the observer adapts to the particular composition of the light. However, for some tasks, the perceived colour of the surface is important and a suitable light source must be chosen.

Natural light sources such as sunlight and daylight have visible spectra which approximate to that of a black-body radiator at the appropriate temperature. Non-incandescent electric lamps generally have discontinuous spectra, an extreme example being the low-pressure sodium lamp,

Table 1.15 Values of limiting glare index[10]

Application	Limiting glare index
Museums, art galleries, lecture theatres, control rooms, industrial inspection	16
Classrooms, libraries, laboratories, general offices, fine assembly work	19
Supermarkets, circulation areas, medium assembly work	22
Boiler houses, rough assembly work	25
Foundries, bulk storage areas	28

which is a monochromatic source. Lamps of this type are widely used for street lighting. They have very poor colour properties, particularly colour rendering. Light sources having much better colour rendering properties are required for interior lighting.

The general colour rendering index (CRI) adopted by the Commission Internationale de l'Eclairage (CIE), R_a, specifies the accuracy with which lamps reproduce colours relative to a standard source. The CRI takes values up to a maximum of 100. Table 1.16 gives the colour rendering groups adopted in the CIBSE *Code for Interior Lighting*[10] and corresponding ranges for the CIE colour rendering index and their application.

In general, the higher the CRI the more accurately colours are reproduced with respect to the standard, and the greater is the enhancement of differences between colours. The *Code*[10] recommends sources appropriate in various situations using the international classification of sources into groups according to CRI value. The advice of the lamp manufacturer should be sought when selecting lamps for applications where colour judgement is particularly important.

The colour rendering index is not the only parameter that needs to be considered. The colour appearance of the source is also important. For almost all interiors, the recommended light sources are nominally white in appearance with varying degrees of warmth. This degree of warmth is quantified by the correlated colour temperature (CCT) of the lamp. This is the temperature of the black-body radiator which most closely approximates to the colour appearance of the lamp.

The commonly used light sources are classified as follows:

— warm (CCT < 3300 K)

— intermediate (3300 K < CCT < 5300 K)

— cold (CCT > 5300 K).

Having selected a source with the required CCT, a source having a high colour rendering index should be chosen to ensure that surface colours are rendered to an accuracy appropriate to the application. Detailed guidance is given in the *Code for Interior Lighting*[10].

For daylight, this variation is catered for naturally when bright, blue-sky conditions give way to warm tints of sunset. Where electric lighting is being used in a daylit

Table 1.16 Colour rendering groups and corresponding CRI values

Colour rendering group	CIE general colour rendering index, R_a	Application
1A	Ra ≥ 90	Where accurate colour matching is required, e.g. colour printing inspection
1B	80 ≤ Ra < 90	Where accurate colour judgements are necessary and/or good colour rendering is required for reasons of appearance, e.g. shop displays and other commercial applications
2	60 ≤ Ra < 80	Where moderate colour rendering is required
3	40 < Ra < 60	Where colour rendering is of little significance but marked distortion of colour is unacceptable
4	20 ≤ Ra < 40	Where colour rendering is of no importance and distortion of colour is acceptable

space, lamps with a cool colour appearance give a good blend with daylight.

Refer to the *Code*[10] for advice on the selection of warm or cool source colour appearance. Satisfaction with the appearance of surface colours is likely to be increased by selecting a source having a high colour rendering index. The *Code*[10] should also be referred to for guidance on allowances to be made for maintenance.

1.9 Acoustic environment

Noise affects people in different ways depending on its level and may cause annoyance, interference to speech intelligibility or hearing damage. The acoustic environment must be designed, as far as possible, to avoid such detrimental effects.

1.9.1 Sound level in a room

The sound energy emitted by a source can be quantified by its sound power level. This is a property of the source and is not affected by the characteristics of the room in which it is located. The effects of a noise source are assessed in terms of sound pressure level. The sound power level of a source may be used to calculate the resulting sound pressure level in a room, which depends on the volume of the room and the amount of absorbing material it contains. These acoustic characteristics of a room contribute to its reverberation time, i.e. the time taken for a sound to decay by 60 dB.

For a constant sound power input, the sound pressure level within a room will vary from place to place. The highest level is experienced near the noise source(s), it then decreases roughly with the square of the distance from the source until it reaches an approximately constant level. This constant level depends on the reverberation time of the room.

The calculation of noise levels within a space due to individual noise sources has been investigated by Beranek[104]. Noise from heating, ventilating and air conditioning plant is considered in CIBSE Guide B12[105].

1.9.2 Human hearing response

The human hearing system responds to frequencies in the range 20 Hz to 20,000 Hz. The precise range differs from person to person and hearing acuity at high frequencies tends to diminish with age due to deterioration in the receptor cells in the ear.

The response of the hearing system is non-linear and it is less sensitive to low and high frequencies than to mid-range frequencies. The sensitivity of the ear is represented by the curves of equal loudness shown in Figure 1.16. These curves have been derived by subjective experiments and show that the sensitivity of the ear varies with both sound pressure level and frequency.

The unit of loudness level is the phon. For example, the curve representing a loudness of 60 phon illustrates that a 1000 Hz note at a sound pressure level of 60 dB is perceived as being of equal loudness to a 100 Hz note at 66 dB. However, this method of assessing loudness is too complicated for everyday use.

When sound levels are measured, the variation in the sensitivity of the ear can be taken into account by incorporating frequency-weighting networks in the measuring instrument. The most widely used of these is the

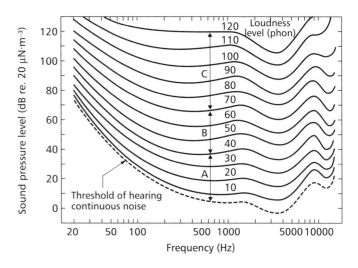

Figure 1.16 Equal loudness level contours and ranges of operation of A-, B- and C-weightings

A-weighting network. Other networks are known as B- and C-weightings. The B-weighting has fallen into disuse so the main measurement curves are the A- and C-weighting curves, see Figure 1.17. The C-weighting gives more prominence to lower frequencies than does the A-weighting, having an approximately level response above 31.5 Hz. In contrast, the A-weighting rises gradually to 1000 Hz, thus discriminating against lower frequencies. The reason for these differences arises from the different equal loudness responses of the human ear over a range of sound pressure levels, see Figure 1.16.

A-weighting was proposed in the 1930s for low sound pressure levels and C-weighting for high sound pressure levels, see Figure 1.16. This distinction has since been lost with the result that the A-weighting is now employed at sound levels for which it was not originally intended. Problems may arise if there is an excess of low frequency noise, since this will not register its full subjective impact when measured using the A-weighting.

At the time that the weighting networks were devised, the complexities of the human hearing system were not fully understood. Methods of loudness evaluation were developed in the 1970s which take account of frequency and sound level in far more detail than do the simple A- and C-weighting networks.

1.9.3   Noise assessment

The dBA measure is often used as an indicator of human subjective reactions to noise across the full range of frequencies audible to humans. This index is simple to measure using a sound level meter incorporating an A-weighting network. In addition, the measured noise spectrum can be compared with reference curves such as the NR or NC curves which aid identification of any tonal frequency components. This is the usual method of assessment for mechanical services installations[106].

Noise rating (NR) curves, see Figure 1.18, are commonly used in Europe for specifying noise levels from mechanical services in order to control the character of the noise.

However, it should be noted that NR is not recognised by the International Standards Organisation or similar standardisation bodies. Noise criteria (NC) curves, see Figure 1.19, are similar to NR but less stringent at high frequencies and more stringent at low frequencies. The curves are very close at middle frequencies and, as long as there are no spectrum irregularities at low and high frequencies, they may be regarded as reasonably interchangeable. More recent developments in North America have lead to the introduction of room criterion (RC) curves[107], see section 1.8.7.

The relationship between NR and dBA is not constant because it depends upon the spectral characteristics of the noise. However, for ordinary intrusive noise found in buildings, dBA is usually between 4 and 8 dB greater than the corresponding NR. If in doubt, both should be determined for the specific noise spectrum under consideration.

Noise from many sources, such as road traffic and aircraft, varies with time and the human response to the noise depends on its amplitude and temporal characteristics. Single number indices, such as $L_{A10,T}$, $L_{A90,T}$ and $L_{Aeq,T}$ may be used to describe these types of noise.

$L_{A10,T}$ is the A-weighted sound pressure level exceeded for 10% of the measurement period, T, which must be stated.

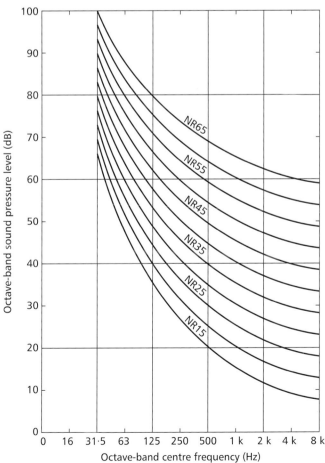

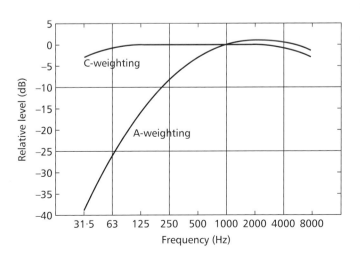

Figure 1.17 A- and C-weighting curves

Figure 1.18 Noise rating (NR) curves

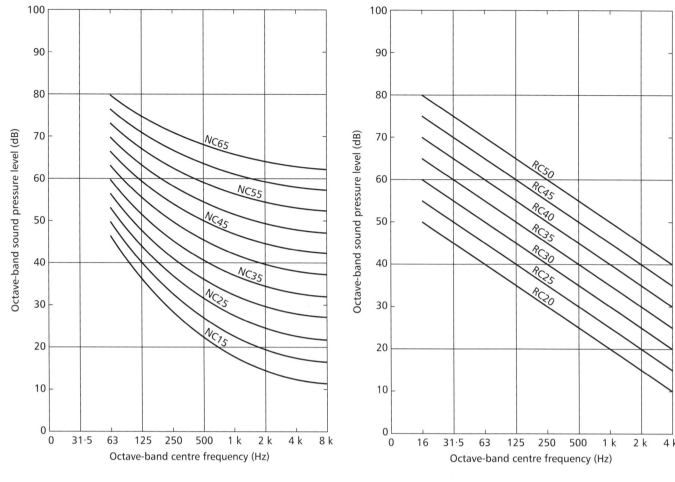

Figure 1.19 Noise criterion (NC) curves

Figure 1.20 Room criterion (RC) curves

Similarly, $L_{A90,T}$ denotes the level exceeded for 90% of the measurement period. It is often used to measure background noise levels. $L_{Aeq,T}$ is the A-weighted sound pressure level of a continuous steady sound having the same energy as the variable noise over the same time period. It is found to correlate well with subjective response to noises having different characteristics, and is used with *BS 8233*[108], which recommends appropriate design limits for common situations see Table 1.17.

Noise from plant may be audible outside the building and control measures may be necessary to avoid complaints. Noise limits may also be set by the local authority. Noise emanating from industrial premises in mixed industrial and residential areas is usually assessed according to *BS 4142*[109].

The past 15–20 years has seen significant developments in North American usage of noise criteria but these have not yet made an impact in Europe. NR was never adopted in the US and ASHRAE no longer recommends NC as a design criterion. For some time the preferred assessment method has been room criterion (RC) curves, see Figure 1.20, as proposed by Blazier[110] in the early 1980s.

RC curves are based on actual measurements in air conditioned buildings in which the occupants are judged to have good acoustical environments. The result is a set of parallel lines falling from low to high frequencies at –5 dB/octave. Noise spectra following these slopes are acoustically 'neutral'. The use of the curves is explained in

ASHRAE *Applications Handbook*[107], where it is shown how to determine whether a noise has 'rumble', 'neutral' or 'hiss' characteristics, and the frequency regions where improvement is required. More recent work by Blazier[111] has aimed at using the RC curves to determine the acoustical 'quality' of a noise by separating its low frequency (rumble), middle frequency (roar) and high frequency (hiss) characteristics and comparing these with subjective acceptability ratings.

RC curves provide a more detailed description of the noise than is available from NR. In addition, room criteria are more prescriptive at low frequencies than NR. At 31.5 Hz, permitted NR35 levels are 19 dB higher than RC35 levels. A noise which follows the NR curve will be unpleasantly 'rumbly' compared with the neutral sound of a noise that follows the RC curve. Therefore NR continues to be adequate only where low frequency noise levels are well below the NR limit. The potential drawback of NRs is that they permit unacceptable noises that would have been rejected if RC had been applied.

1.9.4   Noise due to building services and other sources

In specifying noise design goals for a building, a balance must be sought between noise from the building services and noise from the activities taking place within the building. The acceptability of noise from building services does not depend only upon its absolute level and frequency content, but also on its relationship with noise from other sources. It is important that the designer considers the likely activity-related and extraneous noise level and frequency content at an early stage of design. However, while noise from the building services is controlled by the building services engineer, activity noise is a function of the office or other equipment in the space and is therefore under the control of the office management. Noise from outside the building, e.g. traffic noise, is controlled mainly by the fabric of the building, which is the responsibility of the architect. The building services engineer must work to an agreed specification for the noise level from the building services and may be able to influence the level set down in the specification.

Reasonable design limits to minimise annoyance from broadband continuous noise from building services installations are given in Table 1.17. If the noise contains recognisable tones or is intermittent or impulsive it will be more annoying and the appropriate NR value from Table 1.17 should be corrected using the factors given in Table 1.18.

Noise levels for building services are often specified for the unoccupied space. Noise from the building services becomes more noticeable when other noise is at its minimum level, as is usually the case outside the occupied period. The building services designer cannot rely on external or activity noise in order to permit noise levels from services higher than those given in Table 1.17. Indeed, it may be necessary to control noise from these other sources to achieve an acceptable acoustical environment.

In the absence of noise from other sources, noise from building services may become noticeable. If so, the aim should be to reduce the services noise rather than to attempt to mask it by noise from other sources. However, provided that it is within the limits required by the specification, a steady level of services noise can sometimes help to improve acoustical privacy in open plan offices.

In modern offices, a prominent source of noise at workstations is the cooling fans in office equipment, such as personal computers. The characteristic of this noise is different from that of services noise, tending to have a tonal spectrum with peaks at about 250 Hz and associated harmonics, depending on the design of the fan. Clearly, this source of noise is not under the control of the building services engineer.

1.9.5 Speech intelligibility

Speech intelligibility is dependent upon the ambient noise and the distance between listener and speaker. Table 1.19 gives an indication of the distance at which normal speech will be intelligible for various ambient noise levels[108].

Ambient noise may also interfere with the intelligibility of telephone conversations. However, conversation can be carried out in reasonable comfort if the ambient level is below 60 dBA, which should be the case in well-designed offices where the maximum levels are not likely to exceed 45 dBA.

Table 1.17 Suggested maximum permissible background noise levels generated by building services installations[108] (reproduced from *BS 8233* by permission of the British Standards Institution)

Situation	Noise rating (NR)
Studios and auditoria:	
— sound broadcasting (drama)	15
— sound broadcasting (general), television (general), sound recording	20
— television (audience studio)	25
— concert hall, theatre	20–25
— lecture theatre, cinema	25–30
Hospitals:	
— audiometric room	20–25
— operating theatre, single bed ward	30–35
— multi–bed ward, waiting room	35
— corridor, laboratory	35–40
— wash room, toilet, kitchen	35–40
— staff room, recreation room	30–40
Hotels:	
— individual room, suite	20–30
— ballroom, banquet room	30–35
— corridor, lobby	35–40
— kitchen, laundry	40–45
Restaurants, shops and stores:	
— restaurant, department store (upper floors)	35–40
— night club, public house, cafeteria, canteen, department store (main floors)	40–45
Offices:	
— boardroom, large conference room	25–30
— small conference room, executive office, reception room	30–35
— open plan office	35
— drawing office, computer suite	35–45
Public buildings:	
— law court	25–30
— assembly hall	25–35
— library, bank, museum	30–35
— washroom, toilet	35–45
— swimming pool, sports arena	40–50
— garage, car park	55
Ecclesiastical and academic buildings:	
— church	25–30
— classroom, lecture theatre	25–35
— laboratory, workshop	35–40
— corridor, gymnasium	35–45
Industrial:	
— warehouse, garage	45–50
— light engineering workshop	45–55
— heavy engineering workshop	50–65
Dwellings (urban):	
— bedroom	25
— living room	30

Note: dBA $\approx$ NR + 6

Table 1.18 Corrections to noise rating for certain types of noise

Type of noise	NR correction
Pure tone easily perceptible	+5
Impulsive and/or intermittent noise	+3

1.9.6 Hearing damage

Exposure to high noise levels, such as may occur in a plant room, can cause temporary or permanent hearing damage. Where employees are exposed to high noise levels, the *Noise at Work Regulations 1989*[112] require that the noise levels are

Table 1.19 Maximum noise levels and speech communication[108] (reproduced from *BS 8233* by permission of the British Standards Institution)

Distance between talker and listener (m)	Noise level, L_{Aeq} (dB)	
	Normal voice	Raised voice
1	57	62
2	51	56
4	45	50
8	39	44

assessed by a 'competent person'. The regulations identify two levels of 'daily personal noise exposure' (measured in a manner similar to $L_{Aeq,T}$) at which actions become necessary. These levels are 85 dBA and 90 dBA, corresponding to advisory and compulsory requirements. In addition, there is a sound pressure 'peak action level' of 200 pascals which is intended to limit exposure to extreme impulse noise. Suppliers of machinery must provide noise data for machines likely to cause exposure to noise above the action levels.

1.10 Vibration

1.10.1 General

In the context of building services installations, vibrations arise from reciprocating machines or from unbalanced forces in rotating machines. The vibration is often most noticeable during machine start-up (i.e. low-frequency movement), during which some machines pass through a critical (resonant) speed before reaching their normal operating condition. Vibration associated with start-up may not be important if the machine operates for long periods, since that condition occurs only infrequently. However, machines which switch on and off under thermostatic control, for example, may require special precautions.

Vibrations transmitted from machines through their bases to the building structure may be felt and heard at considerable distances from the plant and, in extreme cases, even in neighbouring buildings. Therefore, adequate isolation is important in those cases where vibration is expected. Vibration isolators must be chosen to withstand the static load of the machine as well as isolate it from the structure. Efficient vibration isolation is the preferred way of controlling structure-borne noise, which occurs when vibration transmitted to building surfaces is re-radiated as noise. Structure-borne noise is enhanced when the excitation frequency corresponds with a structural resonance frequency, which may cause unexpected noise problems.

1.10.2 Response of the human body to vibration

Vibrating motion of the human body can produce both physical and biological effects. The physical effect is the excitation of parts of the body and under extreme conditions physical damage may result. Building vibration may affect the occupants by reducing both quality of life and working efficiency. Complaints about continuous vibration in residential situations are likely to arise from occupants when the vibration levels are only slightly greater than the threshold of perception.

The levels of complaint resulting from vibration and acceptable limits for building vibration depend upon the characteristics of the vibration and the building environment, as well as individual response. These factors are incorporated in guidance given in *BS 6472*[113] which gives magnitudes of vibrations below which the probability of complaints is low. This guidance takes the form of base curves of RMS acceleration against frequency over the range 1–80 Hz, for vibration along x-, y-, and z-axes. The axes of vibration with respect to the human body are shown in Figure 1.21. The values for the x- and y-axis curves are more severe than that for the z-axis curve, reflecting the greater sensitivity of the human body to x- and y-axis motion at low frequencies.

The base curves (not shown here) are modified by factors appropriate to the building environment, time of day and type of vibration (see Table 1.20) to produce curves of design maximum vibration magnitude, Figure 1.22. The curves are labelled to correspond to the multiplying factors appropriate to the situations listed in Table 1.20.

1.10.3 Effect on structure

Vibration can damage building structures. The degree of damage depends largely on the magnitude and frequency of vibration. In general, the level of vibration likely to cause cosmetic damage, such as plaster cracking, is significantly greater than that which would be easily perceptible to the occupants. Therefore, the occupants provide early warning of vibration levels likely to cause damage to the fabric.

Although vibrations in buildings are often noticeable, there is little documented evidence to show that they produced even cosmetic damage[113–115].

1.11 Electromagnetic and electrostatic environment

1.11.1 Electromagnetic fields

Since the 1960s concern has been expressed regarding the possible effects on health of extremely low frequency electromagnetic fields (i.e. below 300 Hz). Some reports have suggested that exposure to these fields, such as might be experienced by those living near high voltage overhead power lines, increases the risk of cancer, particularly leukaemia, especially amongst children. Other studies have raised the possibility that 'electrical' occupations, such as those that entail prolonged proximity to visual display terminals, result in an increased risk of illness.

A review of these studies[116] reveals that all suffer from methodological or other shortcomings but it is not clear whether these are sufficient to explain the results. Experiments with animals have produced conflicting and

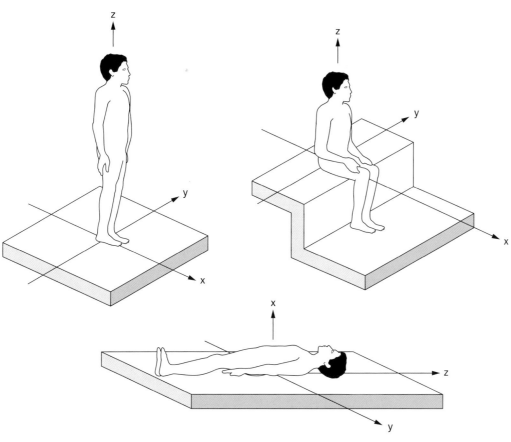

Figure 1.21 Definition of axes of vibration with respect to the human body[113]; x-axis = back to chest, y-axis = right side to left side, z-axis = foot to head (reproduced from *BS 6472* by permission of the British Standards Institution)

Table 1.20 Multiplying factors used to specify satisfactory magnitudes of building vibration with respect to human response[113] (reproduced from *BS 8233* by permission of the British Standards Institution)

Situation	Multiplying factor for stated vibration[1,5]	
	Exposure to continuous vibration (16 hour day, 8 hour night)[2]	Intermittent vibration with up to 3 occurrences
Critical working areas, e.g. hospital operating theatre, precision laboratory[3,9]		
— daytime	1	1
— night	1	1
Residential buildings:		
— daytime	2–4 [4]	60–90 [4,8]
— night	1.4	20
Offices:		
— daytime	4	128 [6]
— night	4	128
Workshops:		
— daytime	8[7]	128 [6,7]
— night	8	128

Notes:

[1] Magnitude of vibration below which the probability of adverse comments is low (any acoustical noise caused by structural vibration is not considered); [2] Doubling of suggested vibration magnitudes may result in adverse comment and this may increase significantly if magnitudes are quadrupled (where available, dose/response curves may be consulted); [3] Magnitudes of vibration in hospital operating theatres and critical working places pertain to periods of time when operations are in progress or critical work is being performed; at other times magnitudes as high as those for residences are satisfactory provided there is due agreement and warning; [4] In residential areas people exhibit wide variations of vibration tolerance; specific values dependent upon social and cultural factors, psychological attitudes and expected degree of intrusion; [5] Vibration to be measured at point of entry of the vibration to the subject; where this is not possible it is essential that transfer functions be evaluated; [6] Magnitudes for vibration in offices and workshop areas should not be increased without considering the possibility of significant disruption of work activity; [7] Vibration acting on operators in certain processes such as drop forges or crushers, which cause the working place to vibrate, may be in a separate category from the workshop areas considered in the table. Vibration magnitudes specified in relevant standards apply to the operators of these processes; [8] When short term works such as piling, demolition and construction give rise to impulsive vibrations, undue restriction on vibration levels can significantly prolong these operations resulting in greater annoyance. In certain circumstances higher magnitudes can be used; [9] Where sensitive equipment or delicate tasks impose more stringent criteria than human comfort, the corresponding more stringent values should be applied

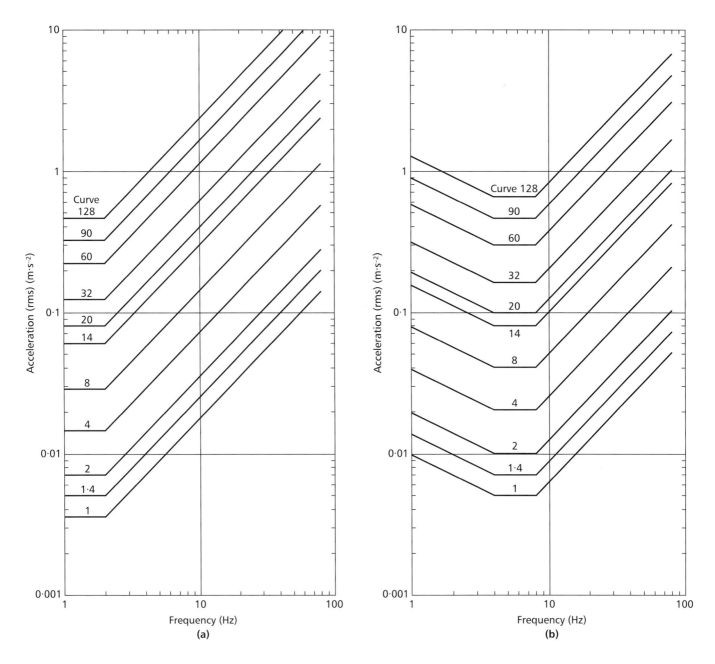

Figure 1.22 Design maximum vibration curves[113] corresponding to multiplying factors for the situations given in Table 1.20; (*a*) for *x*- and *y*-axes, (*b*) for *z*-axis (reproduced from *BS 6472* by permission of the British Standards Institution)

confusing results, and their relevance to the effect on humans is difficult to assess. No plausible mechanism for carcinogenesis due to exposure to electrical or magnetic fields has yet been deduced. It has been established that such fields affect the function of cardiac pacemakers but this is unlikely to be a hazard at the field strengths normally encountered and most modern pacemakers are designed to cope with high field strengths.

Therefore, current evidence does not permit firm conclusions to be drawn on the relationship between electromagnetic fields and physiological or psychological effects on humans. Until the situation is clarified by further research and provided that no significant cost penalties result, it is suggested that potential fields be minimised. Often this can be achieved by ensuring that line and return cables are in close proximity, as is usual practice for mains wiring.

1.11.2   Air ionisation

It has been suggested that the ion balance of the air is an important factor in human comfort in that negative ions tend to produce sensations of freshness and well-being and positive ions cause headache, nausea and general malaise. Present evidence on the effects of air ions and, in particular, the effectiveness of air ionisers is inconclusive and hence no design criteria can be established[117,118].

1.11.3   Static electricity

Static electricity can lead to shocks when occupants are not adequately earthed via the floor covering. The incidence of electrostatic shocks depends on the electrical resistance of the floor covering. The resistance is a function of the material itself and its moisture content. The highest electrical resistance is produced by fibrous carpets with an insulating backing when low in moisture content.

At low room humidity, some types of carpet can become highly charged and electrostatic shocks may be experienced. Typical body voltages are shown in Figure 1.23 as a function of room percentage saturation. Extreme values, as reported, and the shock voltage threshold are also shown. In general, shocks are unlikely above 40% saturation. Carpeted buildings with underfloor heating have particularly dry carpets and require humidity to be above 55% saturation to avoid electrostatic shocks.

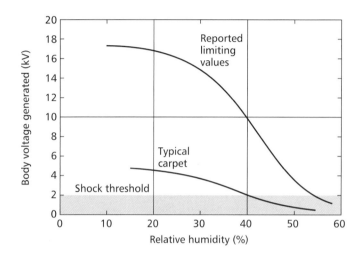

Figure 1.23 Relationship between relative humidity and electrostatic shocks

References

1   *Thermal environmental conditions for human occupancy* ANSI/ASHRAE Standard 55-1992 (Atlanta GA: American Society of Heating, Refrigerating and Air-Conditioning Engineers) (1992)

2   *Indoor air pollutants: Exposure and Health Effects* Report of a WHO meeting, Norlinger, 8–11 June 1982 (Copenhagen: World Health Organisation Regional Office for Europe) (1982)

3   *BS EN ISO 7726:1994: Thermal environments. Instruments and methods for measuring physical quantities* (London: British Standards Institution) (1994)

4   *BS ISO 9920: 1995: Ergonomics of the thermal environment. Estimation of the thermal insulation and evaporative resistance of a clothing ensemble* (London: British Standards Institution) (1995)

5   *BS EN 28996: 1994: Ergonomics. Determination of metabolic heat production* (London: British Standards Institution) (1994)

6   *NEN 1068: Thermal insulation of buildings: Terminology and methods of calculation for steady state situations* (Delft, Netherlands: Nederlands Normalisatie Instituut) (1981)

7   *Control of Fuel and Electricity. The Fuel and Electricity (Heating) (Control) Order 1974* Statutory Instrument 1974 No. 2160 (London: The Stationery Office) (1974)

8   *Control of Fuel and Electricity. The Fuel and Electricity (Heating) (Control) (Amendment) Order 1980* Statutory Instrument 1980 No. 1013 (London: The Stationery Office) (1980)

9   Fanger P O *Thermal comfort* (Malabar, FL, USA: Krieger) (1982)

10   *Code for interior lighting* (London: Chartered Institution of Building Services Engineers) (1994)

11   *Lighting for offices* CIBSE Lighting Guide LG7 (London: Chartered Institution of Building Services Engineers) (1993)

12   *The visual environment for visual display screen use* CIBSE Lighting Guide LG3 (London: Chartered Institution of Building Services Engineers) (1996)

13   *Building and Buildings. The Building Regulations 1991* (London: The Stationery Office) (1991)

14   *The visual environment in lecture, teaching and conference rooms* CIBSE Lighting Guide LG5 (London: Chartered Institution of Building Services Engineers) (1991)

15   *The Workplace (Health, Safety and Welfare) Regulations 1992* (London: The Stationery Office) (1992)

16   *The industrial environment* CIBSE Lighting Guide LG1 (London: Chartered Institution of Building Services Engineers) (1989)

17   *Ventilation and air conditioning (requirements)* CIBSE Guide B2 (London: Chartered Institution of Building Services Engineers) (1986)

18   *Hospitals and health care buildings* CIBSE Lighting Guide LG2 (London: Chartered Institution of Building Services Engineers) (1989)

19   *Sports* CIBSE Lighting Guide LG4 (London: Chartered Institution of Building Services Engineers) (1990)

20   *Lighting for museums and art galleries* CIBSE Lighting Guide LG8 (London: Chartered Institution of Building Services Engineers) (1994)

21   Hensel H *Thermoreception and temperature regulation* Physiological Society Monograph No. 38 (London: Academic Press) (1981)

22   *BS EN ISO 7730: Moderate thermal environments. Determination of the PMV and PPD indices and specification of the conditions for thermal comfort* (London: British Standards Institution) (1995)

23   McIntyre D A Response to atmospheric humidity: a comparison of three experiments *Ann. Occupational Hygiene* **21** 177–190 (1978)

24   Morey P R, Hodgson M J, Sorenson W G, Kullman G J, Rhodes W W and Visvesvara G S Environmental studies in mouldy office buildings: biological agents, sources and preventive measures *Ann. American Conference Governmental Industrial Hygienists — Evaluating Office Environmental Problems* **10** (1984).

25   Griffiths I D and McIntyre D A Sensitivity to temporal changes in thermal conditions *Ergonomics* **17** 499–507 (1974)

26   McIntyre D A *Indoor Climate* (London: Applied Science Publishers) (1980)

27   Fanger P O, Hojbjerre J and Thomsen J O Man's preferred ambient temperature during the day *Arch. Science Physiology* **27** (4) A395–A402 (1973)

28   Ostberg O and McNicholl A G The preferred thermal conditions for 'morning' and 'evening' types of subject during day and night — preliminary results *Build Internat.* **6** (1) 147–157 (1973)

29   Fanger P O, Hojbjerre J and Thomsen J O Thermal comfort conditions in the morning and evening *Internat. J. Biometeorology* **18** (1) 16 (1974)

30   Humphreys M A Thermal comfort requirements, climate and energy in *Renewable Energy — Technology and the Environment* (ed. Sayligh A A M) 1725–1734 (London: Pergamon Press) (1992)

31   Humphreys M A Field studies and climate chamber experiments in thermal comfort research in *Thermal Comfort: past, present and future* (eds. Oseland N A and Humphreys M A) 52–72 (Garston: Building Research Establishment) (1994)

32   de Dear R Outdoor climate influences on indoor thermal comfort requirements in *Thermal Comfort: past, present and future*

(eds. Oseland N A and Humphreys M A) 106–133 (Garston: Building Research Establishment) (1994)

33   de Dear R Thermal comfort in air-conditioned office buildings in the tropics in *Standards for Thermal Comfort* (eds. Nicol F, Humphreys M A, Sykes O and Roaf S) 122–131 (London: Chapman & Hall) (1995)

34   Humphreys M A Outdoor temperatures and comfort indoors *Building Res. and Practice* **6** 82–105 (1978)]

35   Griffiths I D and McIntyre D A The balance of radiant and air temperature for warmth in older women *Environmental Res.* **6** (4) 382–388 (1973)

36   Fanger P O and Langkilde G Inter-individual differences in ambient temperature preferred by seated persons *ASHRAE Trans.* **81** (2) 140–147 (1975)

37   Langkilde G Thermal comfort for people of high age *Comfort thermique: Aspects Physiologiques et Psychologiques (INSERM)* **75** 187–193 (1979)

38   Nevins R G, Rohles F H, Springer W E and Feyerherm A M Temperature–humidity chart for thermal comfort of seated persons *ASHRAE Trans.* **72** (1) 283 (1966)

39   Rohles F H and Johnson M A Thermal comfort in the elderly *ASHRAE Trans.* **78** (1) 131 (1972)

40   Collins K J and Hoinville E Temperature requirements in old age *Building Serv. Eng. Res. Technol.* **1** (4) 165–172 (1980)

41   Berry P C The effect of coloured illumination on perceived temperature *J. Applied Psychol.* **45** 248–250 (1961)

42   Fanger P O and Pedersen C J Discomfort due to air velocities in spaces *Proc. IIR Commissions B1/B2/E1, Belgrade, 1977* (1977)

43   Fanger P O, Melikov A, Hanzawa H and Ring J Air turbulence and sensation of draught *Energy and Buildings* **12** 21–39 (1988)

44   Olesen B W, Schøler M and Fanger P O Vertical air temperature differences and comfort in Fanger and Valbjørn (eds.) *Indoor Climate* (Copenhagen: Danish Building Research Institute) (1979)

45   McNair H P *A preliminary study of the subjective effects of vertical air temperature gradients* British Gas Corporation Reports WH/T/R and D/73/94 (London: British Gas Corporation) (1973)

46   McNair H P and Fishman D S *A further study of the subjective effects of vertical air temperature gradients* British Gas Corporation Reports WH/T/R and D/74/2 (London: British Gas Corporation) (1974)

47   Olesen B W Thermal comfort requirements for floors *Proc. IIR Commissions B1/B2/E1 Belgrade* 337–343 (1977)

48   Olesen B W Thermal comfort requirements for floors occupied by people with bare feet *ASHRAE Trans.* **83** (2) (1977)

49   *BS EN 1264: Floor heating. Systems and components* (London: British Standards Institution) (1998)

50   Fanger P O, Banhidi L, Olesen B W and Langkilde G Comfort limits for heated ceilings *ASHRAE Trans.* **86** (1980)

51   Fanger P O, Ipsen G, Langkilde G, Olesen B W, Christiansen N K and Tanabe S Comfort limits for asymmetric thermal radiation *Energy and Buildings* **8** 225–236 (1985)

52   McIntyre D A Radiation draughts *Building Services Eng.* **43** 136–139 (1975)

53   Owens P G T Air conditioned comfort and sunshine *JIHVE* **37** 92–96 (July 1969)

54   Rytkonen A-L, Pasanen P, Kalliokoski P, Nevalainen A and Jantunen M The effect of air temperature and humidity on the growth of some fungi *Healthy Buildings 88* (eds. Berglund B and Lindvall T) **2** 345–349 (Stockholm: Swedish Council for Building Research) (1988)

55   Raw G, Leinster P, Thomson N, Leaman A and Whitehead C A new approach to the investigation of sick building syndrome *Proc. CIBSE National Conf. 1991, University of Kent* 339–344 (London: Chartered Institution of Building Services Engineers) (1991)

56   Abritti G, Accattoli M P, Colangeli C, Fabbri T, Muzi G, Fiordi T, Dell'Omo M and Gabrielli A R Sick building syndrome: High prevalence in a new air conditioned building *Indoor Air 90* **1** 513–518 (Ottawa: Canada Mortgage and Housing Corporation) (1990)

57   Reinikainen L, Jaakkola J J K and Heinonen O P The effect of air humidification on different symptoms in an office building, an epidemiological study *Healthy Buildings 88* (eds. Berglund B and Lindvall T) **3** 207–215 (Stockholm: Swedish Council for Building Research) (1988)

58   Green G H The health implications of the level of indoor air humidity *Indoor Air 84* **1** (Stockholm: Swedish Council for Building Research) (1984)

59   Berglund B The role of sensory reactions as guides for non-industrial indoor air quality (preprint) *American Industrial Hygiene Conf. St Louis, USA* (May 1989)

60   *Ventilation for acceptable indoor air quality* ANSI/ASHRAE Standard 62-1989 (Atlanta: American Society of Heating, Refrigerating and Air-Conditioning Engineers) (1989)

61   *Air quality guidelines for Europe* (Copenhagen: World Health Organisation) (1987)

62   Cain W S *Perceptual characteristics of nasal irritation* (New Haven: John B Pierce Foundation Laboratory) (1989)

63   Cain W S, See L C and Tosun T Irritation and odour from formaldehyde: chamber studies *Proc. ASHRAE Conf. IAQ 86: Managing the Indoor Air for Health and Energy Conservation, Atlanta, USA* (1986)

64   Gunnarsen L and Fanger P O Adaptation to indoor air pollution *Healthy Buildings 88* (ed. Berglund B and Lindvall T) **3** 157–167 (Stockholm: Swedish Council for Building Research) (1988)

65   Clausen G H, Nielsen K S, Sahin F and Fanger P O Sensory irritation from exposure to environmental tobacco smoke *Indoor Air 87* (ed. Seifert B *et al.*) **2** 52–56 (1987)

66   *Air Quality Regulations 1997* (London: The Stationary Office) (1997)

67   *Environment Act 1995* (London: The Stationery Office) (1995)

68   *Odors* ASHRAE Handbook: Fundamentals (Atlanta: American Society of Heating, Refrigerating and Air-Conditioning Engineers) (1993)

69   Bluyssen P *Olfbar* (Lyngby, Denmark: Technical University of Denmark) (1989)

70   Pejtersen J, Clausen G H and Fanger P O Olf-values of spaces previously exposed to tobacco smoking *Healthy Buildings 88* (ed. Berglund B and Lindvall T) **3** 197–205 (Stockholm: Swedish Council for Building Research) (1988)

71   Fanger P O, Lauridsen J and Clausen G H Air pollution sources in offices and assembly halls, quantified by the olf unit *Energy and Buildings* **12** 7–19 (1988)

72   Pejtersen J, Bluyssen P, Kondo H, Clausen G H and Fanger P O *Air pollution sources in ventilation systems* (Lyngby, Denmark: Technical University of Denmark) (1989)

73   *Minimising the risk of Legionnaires' disease* CIBSE Technical Memoranda TM13 (London: Chartered Institution of Building Services Engineers) (1991)

74   Broughton *et.al. Air pollution in the UK 1995* (Abingdon: AEA Technology) (1997)

75   *Annual digest of environmental statistics* (London: The Stationery Office) (published annually)

76   *Minimising pollution at air intakes* CIBSE Technical Memoranda TM21 (London: Chartered Institution of Building Services Engineers) (1999)

77   *Ventilation and air conditioning (systems and equipment)* CIBSE Guide B3 (London: Chartered Institution of Building Services Engineers) (1986)

78   *BS EN 779: 1993: Particulate air filters for general ventilation. Requirements, testing, marking* (London: British Standards Institution) (1993)

79   *In-situ determination of fractional efficiency of general ventilation filters* Eurovent 4/10 (Paris: EUROVENT/CECOMAF) (1996)

80   *The Control of Substances Hazardous to Health Regulations 1988* (London: The Stationery Office) (1988)

81   Fanger P O The new comfort equation for indoor air quality *Proc. ASHRAE Conf. IAQ '89: The Human Equation — Health and Comfort, San Diego CA, USA* (April 1989)

82   Guidelines for Ventilation Requirements in Buildings *European Concerted Action: Indoor Air Quality and its Impact on Man* Report No. 11 (Luxembourg: CEC Directorate General Information Market and Innovation) (1992)

83   Cain W S, Leaderer B P, Isseroff R, Berglund L G, Huey R G, Lipsitt E D and Perlman D   Ventilation requirements in buildings: I — Control of occupancy odor and tobacco smoke odor *Atmospheric Environment* **17**(6) 1183–1197 (1983)

84   *Occupational Exposure Limits* EH40 (London: The Stationery Office) (published annually)

85   *The Health and Safety at Work etc. Act 1974* (London: The Stationery Office) (1994)

86   *The Workplace (Health, Safety and Welfare) Regulations 1998* (London: The Stationery Office) (1998)

87   *The Provision and Use of Work Equipment Regulations 1992* (London: The Stationery Office) (1992)

88   *Lighting at Work* **HS(G)38** (Bootle: Health and Safety Executive) (1987)

89   *Food Hygiene (General) Regulations 1970* (London: The Stationery Office) (1970)

90   *The Health and Safety (Display Screen Equipment) Regulations 1992* (London: The Stationery Office) (1992)

91   *BS 5266: Emergency lighting: Part 1: 1988: Code of practice for the emergency lighting of premises other than cinemas and certain other specified premises used for entertainment* (London: British Standards Institution) (1988)

92   *Emergency Lighting* CIBSE Technical Memoranda TM12 (London: Chartered Institution of Building Services Engineers) (1986)

93   Weston H C The relation between illumination and visual performance *Industrial Health Research Board Report* **87** (London: The Stationery Office) (1945)

94   Stenzel A G and Sommer J The effect of illumination on tasks which are independent of vision *Lichttechnik* **21** 143–146 (1969)

95   Boyce P R Age, illuminance, visual performance and preference *Lighting Res. Technol.* **5**(3) 125–144 (1973)

96   Rea M S and Ouellette M J Visual performance using reaction times *Lighting Res. Technol.* **20**(4) 139–153 (1988)

97   *Window Design* CIBSE Applications Manual AM2 (London: Chartered Institution of Building Services Engineers) (1987)

98   Wilkins A J, Nimmo-Smith I, Slater A I and Bedocs L Fluorescent lighting, headaches and eyestrain *Lighting Res. Technol.* **21**(1) 11–18 (1989)

99   Saunders J E The role of the level and diversity of horizontal illumination in an appraisal of a simple office task *Lighting Res. Technol.* **1**(1) 37–46 (1969)

100   Fischer D The European approach to the integration of *lighting and air-conditioning Lighting Res. Technol.* **2**(3) 174–185 (1970)

101   Bitter C and Van Ireland J F A A Appreciation of sunlight in the home *Proc. CIE Int. Conf.* Newcastle-on-Tyne (April 1965)

102   Ne'eman E Visual aspects of sunlight in buildings *Lighting Res. Technol.* **6**(3) 159–164 (1974)

103   *Calculation of glare indices* CIBSE Technical Memoranda TM10 (London: Chartered Institution of Building Services Engineers) (1985)

104   Beranek L L *Noise and vibration control* (Washington DC: Institute of Noise Control Engineering) (1988)

105   *Sound control* CIBSE Guide B12 (London: Chartered Institution of Building Services Engineers) (1986)

106   *Noise Control in Building Services* (London: Pergamon Press) (1988)

107   *Sound and Vibration Control* ASHRAE Handbook: Applications (Atlanta GA: American Society of Heating, Ventilating and Air-conditioning Engineers) (1995)

108   *BS 8233: 1987: Sound insulation and noise reduction for buildings* (London: British Standards Institution) (1987)

109   *BS 4142: 1990: Method for rating industrial noise affecting mixed residential and industrial areas* (London: British Standards Institution) (1990)

110   Blazier W E Revised noise quality criteria for application in the acoustic design and control of HVAC systems *Noise Control Eng.* **16**(2) 64–73 (1981)

111   Blazier W E Sound quality criteria in rating noise from heating, ventilating and air-conditioning (HVAC) systems in buildings *Noise Control Eng.* **43**(3) 53–63 (1995)

112   *The Noise at Work Regulations 1989* (London: The Stationery Office) (1989)

113   *BS 6472: 1992: Guide to evaluation of human exposure to vibration in buildings (1 Hz to 80 Hz)* (London: British Standards Institution) (1992)

114   *Damage to structures from ground-borne vibration* BRE Digest 353 (Garston: Building Research Establishment) (1990)

115   *BS 7385: Evaluation and measurements for vibration in buildings: Part 1: 1990: Guide for measurement of vibration and evaluation of their effects on buildings* (London: British Standards Institution) (1990)

116   Naismith O F *Electromagnetic fields: A Review of the evidence for effects on health* BR 206 (Garston: Building Research Establishment) (1991)

117   Hamilton G and Kew J *Negative air ionisation in buildings* Technical Note TN 4/85 (Bracknell: Building Services Research and Information Association) (1985)

118   Raw G *Sick Building Syndrome: a review of the evidence* HSE CRR 42/1992 (Bootle: Health and Safety Executive) (1992)

Appendix 1.A1: Determination of predicted mean vote (PMV)

1.A1.1 Equation for determination of pmv

The predicted mean vote (PMV) is given by the equation:

$$\begin{aligned}
\text{PMV} = (0.303\,e^{-0.036M} + 0.028)\,\{(M-W)\\
- 0.00305\,[5733 - 6.99\,(M-W) - p_s]\\
- 0.42\,[M-W-58.15]\\
- (1.7 \times 10^{-5})\,M\,(5867 - p_s)\\
- 0.0014\,M\,(34 - t_{ai})\\
- (3.96 \times 10^{-8})\,f_{cl}\,[(t_{cl} + 273)^4\\
- (t_r + 273)^4] - [f_{cl}\,(h_c\,(t_{cl} - t_{ai}))]\}\quad (1.14)
\end{aligned}$$

where PMV is the predicted mean vote, M is metabolic rate (W·m^{-2} of body surface), W is external work (W·m^{-2} of body surface) (0 for most activities), f_{cl} is the ratio of the area of the clothed human body to that of the unclothed human body, t_{ai} is the average air temperature surrounding the body (°C), t_r is the mean radiant temperature (°C), p_s is the partial water vapour pressure in the air surrounding the body (Pa), h_c is the convective heat transfer coefficient at the body surface ($\text{W·m}^{-2}\text{·K}^{-1}$) and t_{cl} is the surface temperature of clothing (°C).

The surface temperature of clothing (t_{cl}) is given by:

$$\begin{aligned}
t_{cl} = 35.7 - 0.028\,(M-W) - I_{cl}\,\{(3.96 \times 10^{-8})\\
\times f_{cl}\,[(t_{cl} + 273)^4 - t_r + 273)^4] + f_{cl}\,h_c\,(t_{cl} - t_{ai})\}
\end{aligned}$$

(1.15)

where I_{cl} is the thermal resistance of clothing ($\text{m}^2\text{·K·W}^{-1}$).

For $\{2.38\,(t_{cl} - t_{ai})^{0.25}\} > 12.1\,\sqrt{v_r}$, h_c is given by:

$$h_c = 2.38\,(t_{cl} - t_{ai})^{0.25} \quad (1.16)$$

and for $\{2.38\,(t_{cl} - t_{ai})^{0.25}\} < 12.1\sqrt{v_r}$, by:

$$h_c = 12.1\,\sqrt{v_r} \quad (1.17)$$

For $I_{cl} \le 0.078\ \text{m}^2\text{·K·W}^{-1}$:

$$f_{cl} = 1 + 1.29\,I_{cl} \quad (1.18)$$

and for $I_{cl} > 0.078\ \text{m}^2\text{·K·W}^{-1}$:

$$f_{cl} = 1.05 + 0.645\,I_{cl} \quad (1.19)$$

1.A1.2 Computer program for determination of PMV

The following BASIC program computes the PMV for a given set of input variables, as follows:

CLO   Clothing (clo)
MET   Metabolic rate (met)
WME   External work (met)
TAI   Air temperature (°C)
TR   Mean radiant temperature (°C)
VEL   Relative air velocity (m·s^{-1})
SAT   Percentage saturation (%)
PS   Partial vapour pressure (Pa)

```
10     'Computer program (BASIC) for calculation of
20     'Predicted Mean Vote (PMV) in accordance with
30     'CIBSE Guide A1: Environmental criteria for design (1999)
40     CLS:PRINT "DATA ENTRY":'data entry
50     INPUT " Clothing                        (clo)"; CLO
60     INPUT " Metabolic rate                  (met)"; MET
70     INPUT " External work, normally around 0 (met)"; WME
80     INPUT " Air temperature                 (C)"; TA
90     INPUT " Mean radiant temperature        (C)"; TR
100    INPUT "Relative air velocity            (m/s)"; VEL
110    PRINT "ENTER EITHER %SAT OR VAPOUR PRESSURE BUT NOT BOTH"
120    INPUT "Percentage saturation            (%)"; SAT
130    INPUT "Vapour pressure                  (Pa)"; PS
140    DEF FNPS(T)=EXP(16.6536-4030.183/(T+235)):'saturated vapour pressure,KPa
150    IF PS=0 THEN PS=SAT*10*FNPS(TAI) :'vapour pressure,Pa
160    ICL = .155 * CLO          :'thermal insulation of the clothing in m2K/W
170    M = MET * 58.15           :'metabolic rate in W/m2
180    W = WME * 58.15           :'external work in W/m2
190    MW = M - W                :'internal heat production in W/m2
200    IF ICL < .078 THEN FCL = 1 + 1.29 * ICL ELSE FCL=1.05+.645*ICL:'clothing area factor
210    HCF=12.1*SQR(VEL)
220    TAA = TA + 273            :'air temperature in kelvin
230    TRA = TR + 273            :'mean radiant temperature in kelvin
240    '————CALCULATE SURFACE TEMPERATURE OF CLOTHING BY ITERATION————
```

```
250        TCLA = TAA + (35.5-TA)/(3.5*(6.45*ICL+.1):'first guess for surface temp of clothing
260        P1 = ICL * FCL              :'calculation term
270        P2 = P1 * 3.96              :'calculation term
280        P3 = P1 + 100              :'calculation term
290        P4 = P1 * TAA              :'calculation term
300        P5 = 308.7 - .028 * MW + P2 * (TRA/100) ^ 4 :'calculation term
310        XN = TCLA / 100
320        XF = XN
330        N = 0                       :'N: number of iterations
340        EPS = .00015               :'stop criterion in iteration
350        XF = (XF+XN)/2
360        HCN=2.38*ABS(100*XF-TAA) ^ .25 :'heat trans coeff by nat convection
370        IF HCF>HCN THEN HC=HCF ELSE HC=HCN
380        XN=(P5+P4*HC-P2*XF ^ 4)/(100+P3*HC)
390        N = N+1
400        IF N > 150 THEN GOTO 550
410        IF ABS(XN-XF) > EPS GOTO 350
420        TCL=100*XN-273  : 'surface temperature of the clothing
430        '——————————————HEAT LOSS COMPONENTS——————————————
440        HL1 = 3.05*.001*(5733-6.99*MW-PA)           :'heat loss diff. through skin
450        IF MW > 58.15 THEN HL2 = .42*(MW-58.15) ELSE HL2 = 0!:'heat loss by sweating (comfort)
460        HL3 = 1.7*.00001*M*(5867-PA)               :'latent respiration heat loss
470        HL4 = .0014*M*(34-TA)                       :'dry respiration heat loss
480        HL5 = 3.96*FCL*(XN ^ 4-(TRA/100) ^ 4)       :'heat loss by radiation
490        HL6 = FCL*HC*(TCL-TA)                       :'heat loss by convection
500        '——————————————CALCULATE PMV——————————————
510        TS = .303*EXP(-.036*M)+.028                 :'thermal sensation trans coeff
520        PMV = TS*(MW-HL1-HL2-HL3-HL4-HL5-HL6) :'predicted mean vote
530        GOTO 570
520        PMV = 999999!
530        PRINT:PRINT "OUTPUT"                        :'output
540        PRINT " Predicted mean vote   (PMV): ";:PRINT USING "##.#; PMV
550        PRINT: INPUT "NEXT RUN (Y/N)" ; RS
560        IF (RS="Y" OR RS="y") THEN RUN
570        END
```

1.A1.3   Example

DATA ENTRY:
Clothing (clo)? 1.0
Metabolic rate (met)? 1.2
External work, normally around 0 (met)? 0
Air temperature (C)? 19.0
Mean radiant temperature (C)? 18.0
Relative air velocity (m/s)? 0.1
ENTER EITHER %SAT OR WATER VAPOUR PRESSURE BUT NOT BOTH
Percentage saturation (%)? 40

Water vapour pressure (Pa)?

OUTPUT:

Predicted mean vote (PMV): -0.7.

2 External design data

2.1 Introduction

2.1.1 General

The intention of this section is to provide the basic weather and solar data required for manual calculation of heating and cooling loads in the UK and Europe. More extensive data are contained in CIBSE Guide: *Weather and solar data*[1], which deals in detail with meteorological and solar data and provides the basis for the data presented in this section.

2.1.2 Scope of data

Cold and warm weather data for eight locations in the UK are given in sections 2.3 and 2.4. The locations considered are:

— Belfast (Aldergrove)

— Birmingham (Elmdon)

— Cardiff (Rhoose)

— Edinburgh (Turnhouse)

— Glasgow (Abbotsinch)

— London (Heathrow)

— Manchester (Ringway)

— Plymouth (Mount Batten)

Heating and cooling design temperatures for a range of world-wide locations are given in section 2.6. These data have been selected from the extensive tables of design temperatures for world-wide locations contained in ASHRAE Handbook: *Fundamentals*[2] and are reproduced here by kind permission of ASHRAE.

Measured solar radiation data and sol-air temperatures are given for three UK locations, as follows:

— London area (Bracknell)

— Manchester (Aughton) (on computer disk only)

— Edinburgh (Mylnefield) (on computer disk only)

Tables of data for Bracknell are included within this section. Tables for all three sites are included on the computer disk that accompanies this Guide. The computer disk also contains tables of theoretical solar irradiances, based on computer algorithms, for all latitudes. The theoretical basis for these tables is fully explained in CIBSE Guide: *Weather and solar data*[1].

2.1.3 Time differences

With the exception of solar radiation data, climatological data for the UK are referred to mean time, i.e. Greenwich Mean Time (GMT). Solar radiation data are referred to sun time, i.e. local apparent time (LAT), on which scale the sun is due south at noon. The difference between the two scales leads to GMT being slow relative to sun time by a maximum of 16 minutes in early November and fast by a maximum of 14 minutes in mid-February. There is a further difference at longitudes other than 0° (the reference longitude for GMT), GMT being slow/fast on sun time by 4 minutes for every degree east/west of 0° longitude, respectively.

In other countries, local mean time (LAT) is that given by the corresponding time zone, which usually differs by an integer number of hours from GMT. LAT in these other countries differs from LAT in the same manner that LAT differs from GMT in the UK. Care must be taken in design to account for daylight saving time where applicable.

2.2 Notation

A — Weibull coefficient

C — Proportion of the year (%)

$C_R(z)$ — Roughness coefficient at height z (for wind speed calculations)

C_T — Topography coefficient (for wind speed calculations)

DF — Daylight factor (%)

E_v — Diffuse illuminance received on the horizontal plane (klux)

$E_{vd}(c)$ — Diffuse horizontal irradiance available for proportion c (%) of the year (klux)

f_o — Orientation factor

$F(v)$ — Probability that wind speed v will be exceeded

$f(v)$ — Frequency of occurrence of wind speed v

H — Effective height of topographical feature (for wind speed calculations) (m)

k — Weibull coefficient

K_R — Terrain factor (for wind speed calculations)

L_d — Length of the downwind slope in the wind direction (m)

L_e — Effective length of upwind slope (for wind speed calculations) (m)

L_u — Length of the upwind slope in the wind direction (m)

s — Slope factor (for wind speed calculations)

v — Wind speed to nearest metre per second (m·s^{-1})

v_{ref} — Reference regional wind speed (m·s^{-1})

v_z — Wind speed at height z (m·s^{-1})

x — Horizontal distance of site from the top of crest (for wind speed calculations) (m)

z — Vertical distance from ground level of site (for wind speed calculations) (m)

z_{min} — Minimum height (for wind speed calculations) (m)

z_0 Roughness length (for wind speed calculations) (m)
Φ Upwind slope (H/L_u) in wind direction

2.3   UK cold weather data

2.3.1   Winter design temperatures

2.3.1.1   General

Outside design temperatures are near-extreme values of dry-bulb temperature used to determine the sizes of central plant, distribution systems and room terminals. Design temperature has a large influence on the capital cost of building services systems, and some influence on running costs.

The selection method described in this Guide is founded in that first expressed by Jamieson[3]. This method reflects the thermal response of the building by defining two different averaging times. For most buildings, a 24-hour mean temperature is appropriate. However, a 48-hour mean temperature is more suitable for buildings with high thermal inertia (i.e. high thermal mass, low heat losses), with a response factor $f_r \geq 6$. Response factor is defined in Section A5: *Thermal response and plant sizing*.

It is important to choose the correct temperature for the type of building and the level of performance needed. This edition of Guide A introduces selection based on variable risk, so that different design temperatures may be chosen for different risks of exceedence. This choice needs to be agreed between designer and client, taking account of the consequences for the building, its users and contents of the severity and duration of periods when external design temperatures are surpassed. For buildings with low thermal inertia, the previous edition of Guide A[4] recommended design temperatures such that, on average, only one day in each heating season had a lower mean temperature. Similarly, for buildings with high inertia, a design temperature was recommended such that only one two-day period in each heating season had a lower mean temperature.

Selection of an external winter design temperature should be based upon meteorological data from the nearest recording station to the site of the subject building.

2.3.1.2   Average frequency of occurrence of low temperatures

Data for eight sites are presented to provide an indicative guide to the selection of an external winter design temperature, based on 24-hour and 48-hour means. The data are presented in graphical form in Figures 2.1 to 2.8. The graphs show the average number of times per year that 24-hour and 48-hour mean temperatures fall below a given value. Overlapping 48-hour periods have been eliminated to avoid giving undue weight to several consecutive days of cold weather. Note that two different vertical scales are used for frequency: 0 to 12 for the colder sites (Glasgow, Birmingham and Edinburgh), and 0 to 6 for the remaining sites. The numerical data on which these graphs are based are given in Table 2.1.

2.3.1.3   Design temperatures corresponding to given frequencies of occurrence

An alternative approach is to determine the temperature that is not exceeded for a given frequency of occurrence. Table 2.2 provides temperatures for eight sites, for a range of frequencies of occurrence. For example, for Glasgow, the first entry shows that, on average, the 24-hour temperature is below –15.2°C, and the 48-hour temperature is below –9.6°C, 0.1 times per year (i.e. once in ten years). Again, overlapping 48-hour periods have been eliminated.

These design temperatures should be reduced by 0.6°C for every complete 100 m by which the altitude of the design site exceeds that of the recording station indicated.

2.3.2   Occurrence of condensation

Condensation may occur when the weather changes at the end of a cold spell, if a cold air-mass is replaced within a few hours by a warm, moist air-mass. For heavyweight structures, the atmospheric dew-point may rise more quickly than the surface temperature, producing temporary condensation on such surfaces exposed to outside air. This is most likely to happen internally on surfaces in poorly heated or unheated buildings such as warehouses and storage buildings. Condensation may also occur on the contents of the building. In such conditions, unheated buildings should, as far as possible, be closed to exclude humid external air. For further detail, see Section 7: *Moisture transfer and condensation*.

Table 2.3 shows the frequency of such conditions for eight UK locations. These values are based on positive differences between the dew-point temperature in the middle of the day (mean of values at 09, 12 and 15 GMT) and the mean dry-bulb temperature of the previous day (mean of hourly values from 01 to 24 GMT). Almost all days with a risk of condensation from external air occur during the cold half of the year. The values given in Table 2.3 indicate the likely frequency of condensation following a rapid rise in atmospheric dew-point. This assumes that the surface temperature of an unheated, heavyweight building at the end of cold spell is equal to mean outside dry-bulb temperature.

For a typical heavyweight structure that has approached thermal equilibrium during a cold spell and is ventilated at 1 air change per hour, the surface temperature of the inside walls will increase by only one-quarter of the rise in outside air temperature during the first 12 hours. Condensation will occur on the walls but at only about 20% of the possible rate because the low ventilation rate limits the amount of water vapour available. Increasing the rate of ventilation causes a corresponding increase in condensation.

Sensitivity to condensation varies with the thermal characteristics and ventilation strategy of the building. Most unheated heavyweight buildings are liable to suffer condensation from this cause at least once per year. Condensation may also occur in buildings held at a steady temperature other than that of the outside air. The values in Table 2.3 may be adapted for this purpose by adding to, or subtracting from, the temperature difference values in the left-hand column. For example, for a building in Glasgow, Table 2.3 shows there are on average 0.15 occasions per year (i.e. 3 occasions in 20 years) when the temperature

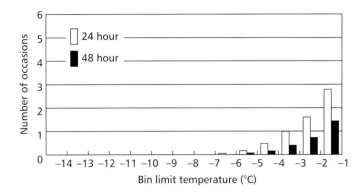

Figure 2.1 Winter temperature distribution: Belfast (Aldergrove) (1976–1995)

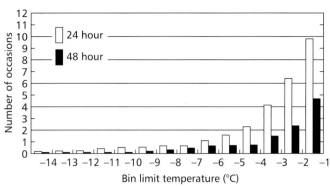

Figure 2.5 Winter temperature distribution: Glasgow (Abbotsinch) (1976–1995)

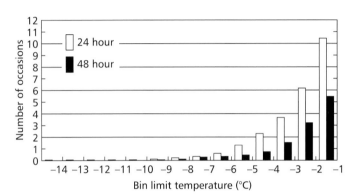

Figure 2.2 Winter temperature distribution: Birmingham (Elmdon) (1976–1995)

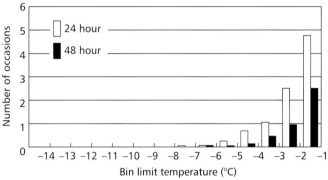

Figure 2.6 Winter temperature distribution: London (Heathrow) (1976–1995)

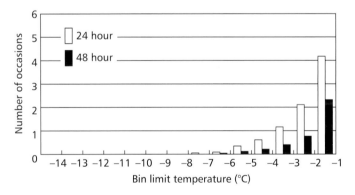

Figure 2.3 Winter temperature distribution: Cardiff (Rhoose) (1976–1995)

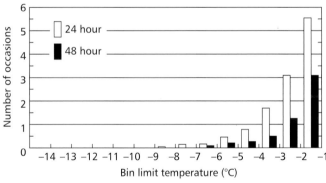

Figure 2.7 Winter temperature distribution: Manchester (Ringway) (1976–1995)

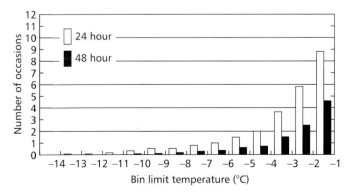

Figure 2.4 Winter temperature distribution: Edinburgh (Turnhouse) (1976–1995)

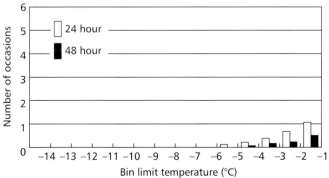

Figure 2.8 Winter temperature distribution: Plymouth (Mount Batten) (1976–1995)

difference is in the range 9.0 to 9.9°C. If the initial temperature of the building were 3°C above mean outside dry-bulb temperature, there would be 0.15 occasions per year when the temperature difference is 6.0 to 6.9°C.

2.3.3 Coincidence of wind speed and low temperature

The coincidence of low external temperatures and significant wind speeds can help to assess the infiltration heat loss of a building under design conditions. Figures 2.9 to 2.11 show cold, windy spells of various duration for three locations for the following combinations of wind speed and temperature:

— dry-bulb < 2.5°C, wind speed > 2.5 m/s

— dry-bulb < 2.5°C, wind speed > 5.0 m/s

— dry-bulb < 0°C, wind speed > 2.5 m/s

— dry-bulb < 0°C, wind speed > 5.0 m/s

Table 2.1 Binned frequencies of occurrence of low 24-hour and 48-hour average temperatures

Bin limit temperatures		Binned frequency of occurrence of low 24-hour and 48-hour average temperatures							
Lower	Upper*	Belfast (Aldergrove) (altitude: 68 m)		Birmingham (Elmdon) (altitude: 96 m)		Cardiff (Rhoose) (altitude: 67 m)		Edinburgh (Turnhouse) (altitude: 35 m)	
		24-hour	48-hour	24-hour	48-hour	24-hour	48-hour	24-hour	48-hour
−14	−13	0	0	0.05	0	0	0	0.05	0
−13	−12	0	0	0.05	0	0	0	0.05	0
−12	−11	0	0	0.05	0	0	0	0.15	0
−11	−10	0	0	0.05	0.05	0	0	0.35	0.05
−10	−9	0	0	0.10	0.05	0	0	0.55	0.10
−9	−8	0	0	0.20	0.05	0	0	0.55	0.15
−8	−7	0	0	0.30	0.25	0.05	0	0.80	0.25
−7	−6	0.05	0	0.60	0.30	0.10	0.05	1.05	0.35
−6	−5	0.15	0.05	1.30	0.45	0.35	0.10	1.50	0.60
−5	−4	0.45	0.15	2.30	0.65	0.60	0.20	2.00	0.75
−4	−3	1.00	0.35	3.70	1.50	1.15	0.40	3.60	1.45
−3	−2	1.60	0.70	6.15	3.20	2.10	0.75	5.85	2.50
−2	−1	2.80	1.40	10.40	5.45	4.20	2.30	8.80	4.60

* Temperature equal to or less than stated bin limit temperature

Note: single zero indicates no occurrence

Table 2.1 — *continued*

Bin limit temperatures		Binned frequency of occurrence of low 24-hour and 48-hour average temperatures							
Lower	Upper*	Glasgow (Abbotsinch) (altitude: 68 m)		London (Heathrow) (altitude: 96 m)		Manchester (Ringway) (altitude: 67 m)		Plymouth (Mount Batten) (altitude: 35 m)	
		24-hour	48-hour	24-hour	48-hour	24-hour	48-hour	24-hour	48-hour
−14	−13	0.20	0.10	0	0	0	0	0	0
−13	−12	0.25	0.10	0	0	0	0	0	0
−12	−11	0.40	0.10	0	0	0	0	0	0
−11	−10	0.50	0.10	0	0	0	0	0	0
−10	−9	0.55	0.20	0	0	0	0	0	0
−9	−8	0.65	0.25	0	0	0	0	0	0
−8	−7	0.70	0.45	0.05	0	0.15	0	0	0
−7	−6	1.00	0.60	0.05	0.05	0.15	0.10	0	0
−6	−5	1.60	0.65	0.25	0.05	0.45	0.20	0.10	0
−5	−4	2.30	0.70	0.65	0.10	0.80	0.25	0.20	0.05
−4	−3	4.15	1.45	1.00	0.45	1.70	0.50	0.35	0.15
−3	−2	6.40	2.30	2.45	0.90	3.10	1.25	0.65	0.20
−2	−1	9.85	4.70	4.65	2.45	5.55	3.10	1.05	0.50

* Temperature equal to or less than stated bin limit temperature

Note: single zero indicates no occurrence

Table 2.2 Temperature below which the mean temperature over 24-hour and non-overlapping 48-hour periods falls on indicated average number of occasions per year (1976–1995)

| Average number of occasions | Temperature (°C) below which mean temperature falls during stated period | | | | | | | |
| | Belfast (Aldergrove) (altitude: 68 m) | | Birmingham (Elmdon) (altitude: 96 m) | | Cardiff (Rhoose) (altitude: 67 m) | | Edinburgh (Turnhouse) (altitude: 35 m) | |
	24-hour	48-hour	24-hour	48-hour	24-hour	48-hour	24-hour	48-hour
0.1	−5.5	−4.1	−9.0	−7.2	−6.0	−4.4	−11.1	−8.2
0.2	−4.5	−3.9	−8.0	−7.1	−5.3	−3.7	−10.2	−7.0
0.33	−4.4	−2.9	−6.6	−5.7	−4.9	−3.2	−9.8	−5.9
0.5	−4.0	−2.2	−6.3	−4.6	−4.3	−2.5	−9.0	−5.5
1	−2.9	−1.5	−5.5	−3.5	−3.4	−1.9	−6.1	−3.5
2	−1.5	−0.8	−4.1	−2.6	−2.2	−1.1	−4.0	−2.4
3	−0.9	−0.2	−3.4	−2.0	−1.4	−0.7	−3.4	−1.6
5	−0.3	0.2	−2.3	−1.1	−0.7	−0.2	−2.3	−0.9
10	0.6	1.0	−1.1	0.1	0.3	0.8	−0.7	0.1
15	1.3	1.6	0.0	0.6	1.1	1.5	0.2	0.7

Note: 0.1 occasions per year is equivalent to one occasion in ten years

Table 2.2 — *continued*

| Average number of occasions | Temperature (°C) below which mean temperature falls during stated period | | | | | | | |
| | Glasgow (Abbotsinch) (altitude: 5 m) | | London (Heathrow) (altitude: 25 m) | | Manchester (Ringway) (altitude 75 m) | | Plymouth (Mount Batten) (altitude: 27 m) | |
	24-hour	48-hour	24-hour	48-hour	24-hour	48-hour	24-hour	48-hour
0.1	−15.2	−9.6	−5.2	−3.7	−7.0	−5.3	−4.5	−3.3
0.2	−12.1	−8.4	−5.0	−3.6	−5.4	−4.2	−3.9	−1.8
0.33	−11.1	−7.8	−4.5	−3.1	−5.0	−3.3	−2.7	−1.2
0.5	−9.7	−6.1	−4.3	−2.9	−4.7	−2.7	−2.3	−1.0
1	−5.9	−3.5	−3.0	−1.9	−3.7	−2.2	−1.0	−0.7
2	−4.1	−2.2	−2.2	−1.2	−2.7	−1.5	−0.5	−0.1
3	−3.4	−1.7	−1.7	−0.8	−2.0	−1.0	0.1	0.6
5	−2.6	−0.9	−0.9	−0.2	−1.1	−0.5	1.0	1.3
10	−1.0	0.1	0.4	1.0	−0.2	0.4	2.2	2.5
15	0.0	0.6	1.3	1.6	0.6	1.0	3.0	3.3

Note: 0.1 occasions per year is equivalent to one occasion in ten years

Table 2.3 Average number of occasions per year when the dew-point temperature exceeds the preceding day's dry bulb temperature by the amount indicated (1976–1995)

| Amount by which dry bulb temperature is exceeded (K) | Average number of occasions per year | | | | | | | |
	Belfast	Birmingham	Cardiff	Edinburgh	Glasgow	London	Manchester	Plymouth
0.0–0.9	21.65	18.00	22.80	20.15	19.10	16.85	14.90	21.00
1.0–1.9	13.30	10.15	12.70	10.45	12.05	10.50	8.20	11.05
2.0–2.9	6.15	6.15	6.40	5.40	6.65	5.20	5.25	5.90
3.0–3.9	3.65	3.20	3.15	2.75	3.05	2.85	2.60	2.45
4.0–4.9	1.70	2.10	1.85	1.80	2.10	1.65	1.25	1.05
5.0–5.9	0.85	0.90	0.60	0.70	1.10	0.75	0.40	0.75
6.0–6.9	0.30	0.30	0.15	0.30	0.55	0.20	0.15	0.20
7.0–7.9	0	0.35	0.10	0.20	0.45	0.25	0.30	0.10
8.0–8.9	0.10	0.10	0.05	0.10	0.15	0.05	0	0.00
9.0–9.9	0	0	0	0.10	0.15	0	0	0.10
10.0–10.9	0	0.05	0	0	0.05	0	0	0
11.0–11.9	0	0	0	0	0.00	0	0	0
>12	0	0	0	0	0.05	0	0	0

Notes: single zero indicates no occurrences; calculated using 24-hour average daily dry and wet bulb temperatures and standard pressure.

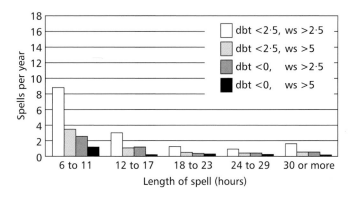

Figure 2.9 Cold spells with significant wind: London (Heathrow) (1976–1995)

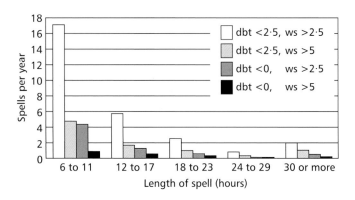

Figure 2.10 Cold spells with significant wind: Manchester (Ringway) (1976–1995)

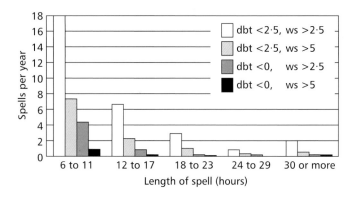

Figure 2.11 Cold spells with significant wind: Edinburgh (Turnhouse) (1976–1995)

2.4   UK warm weather data

2.4.1   Coincidence of wet and dry bulb temperatures

The frequency of coincidence of wet and dry bulb temperatures is important for air conditioning design. Tables 2.4 to 2.11 give these data for eight sites, over 24 hours, for the four months from June to September. Tables 2.12 and 2.13 show the percentage frequency with which the dry bulb and wet bulb temperatures respectively exceed

given values for eight UK locations. These are simply the cumulative frequencies for wet and dry bulb temperature derived from the totals given in Tables 2.4 to 2.11.

The data in Tables 2.4 to 2.11 may be used to plot the percentage frequencies of combinations of hourly dry bulb and wet bulb temperatures on a psychrometric chart. This enables the frequency with which the specific enthalpy exceeds given values to be determined, from which summer design conditions may be established. Figure 2.12 shows the data for London (Heathrow) plotted on a psychrometric chart.

Meteorological Office Climatological Memoranda[5] contain coincident wet- and dry-bulb data for other locations which enable similar analyses to be carried out. The Memoranda provide data for each month, quarter and year for various locations.

2.4.2   Design temperatures — approximate method

Where wet and dry bulb temperature data for the required locality are not sufficiently comprehensive to enable the analysis illustrated in Figure 2.12, the following method may be employed. This uses only general information available from the UK Meteorological Office or other sources. Note that this is *not* the basis of the world-wide cooling design temperatures given in section 2.6.2.

The method requires the following data:

—   average monthly maximum dry bulb temperature (e.g. for July, the average over a period of years of the highest temperature in each July within that period)

—   average daily maximum dry bulb temperature (e.g. for July, the average over a period of years of the highest temperatures for each July day within that period; i.e. for a 30-year period, the average of the maximum temperatures on all 930 July days within that period)

—   average daily minimum relative humidity (e.g. for July, the average over a period of years of the lowest relative humidity for each July day in that period).

The design temperature is obtained as follows:

(1)   The month having the highest average *monthly* maximum dry bulb temperature is selected; this highest average *monthly* maximum dry bulb temperature is taken as the design dry bulb temperature.

(2)   For the month selected in step 1, using psychrometric charts or tables[6], a moisture content, dew-point temperature or vapour pressure is determined for the average *daily* maximum dry bulb temperature and average *daily* minimum relative humidity.

(3)   The moisture content, dew-point temperature or vapour pressure determined in step 2 is combined with the highest average *monthly* maximum dry bulb temperature determined in step 1 to give a screen wet bulb temperature, which is taken as the design wet bulb temperature.

Note that if the CIBSE psychrometric chart is used, step 3 yields the sling wet bulb temperature rather than the screen wet-bulb. The difference between screen and sling wet bulb temperatures varies with position on the chart.

Example 2.1

For Berlin, meteorological data indicate July as the month having the highest average monthly maximum dry bulb temperature (31.8°C). For July, the average daily maximum dry bulb temperature is 23.5°C, the average daily minimum relative humidity (at 1400 h) is 60%.

Step 1: the design dry bulb temperature is 31.8°C (rounded to 32°C).

Step 2: from psychrometric tables(6), for relative humidity of 61% and dry bulb temperature of 23.5°C:

— moisture content = 0.01102 kg·kg^{-1}

— dew-point temperature = 15.5°C

— vapour pressure = 1.757 kPa

Step 3: from psychrometric tables, for dry bulb temperature of 32°C and moisture content of 0.01102 kg·kg^{-1} (or equivalent dew-point temperature or vapour pressure), the screen wet bulb temperature is 21.7°C. Therefore, the design wet bulb temperature is 21.7°C (rounded to 22°C)

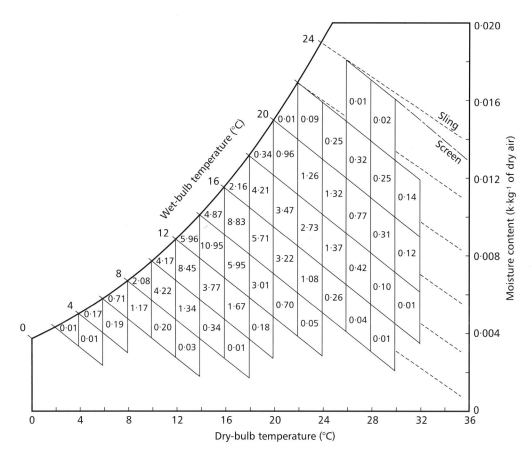

Figure 2.12 Percentage frequencies of wet and dry bulb temperatures plotted on a psychrometric chart: London (Heathrow) (1976–1995)

Table 2.4 Percentage frequency of combinations of hourly dry bulb and wet bulb temperatures for June to September: Belfast (Aldergrove) (1976–1995)

Dry bulb temperature (°C)	Wet bulb temperature (°C)													Total
	−2 to 0	0 to 2	2 to 4	4 to 6	6 to 8	8 to 10	10 to 12	12 to 14	14 to 16	16 to 18	18 to 20	20 to 22	22 to 24	
−2 to 0														
0 to 2		0.01												0.01
2 to 4		0.02	0.20											0.22
4 to 6			0.15	0.69										0.84
6 to 8				0.69	1.94									2.63
8 to 10				0.03	3.30	5.32								8.65
10 to 12					0.57	9.34	9.57							19.48
12 to 14					0.04	2.24	14.42	9.02						25.72
14 to 16						0.24	4.27	11.64	4.79					20.94
16 to 18						0.01	0.49	4.22	5.85	1.35				11.92
18 to 20							0.03	0.65	2.74	1.89	0.13			5.44
20 to 22							0.01	0.08	0.72	1.33	0.25			2.39
22 to 24								0.01	0.20	0.65	0.30			1.16
24 to 26									0.03	0.13	0.25	0.03		0.44
26 to 28										0.01	0.07	0.03		0.11
28 to 30														
30 to 32														
Total		0.03	0.35	1.41	5.85	17.15	28.79	25.62	14.33	5.36	1.00	0.06		

Table 2.5 Percentage frequency of combinations of hourly dry bulb and wet bulb temperatures for June to September: Birmingham (Elmdon) (1976–1995)

Dry bulb temperature (°C)	Wet bulb temperature (°C)													Total
	−2 to 0	0 to 2	2 to 4	4 to 6	6 to 8	8 to 10	10 to 12	12 to 14	14 to 16	16 to 18	18 to 20	20 to 22	22 to 24	
−2 to 0	0.01													0.01
0 to 2		0.09												0.09
2 to 4		0.01	0.27											0.28
4 to 6			0.09	0.64										0.73
6 to 8				0.59	1.82									2.41
8 to 10				0.06	2.60	4.14								6.80
10 to 12					0.53	6.94	6.22							13.69
12 to 14					0.12	2.60	10.79	6.8						20.31
14 to 16					0.01	0.71	5.23	10.12	3.69					19.76
16 to 18					0.04	1.87	6.00	5.81	1.33					15.05
18 to 20							0.27	2.58	4.02	2.22	0.12			9.21
20 to 22							0.01	0.59	2.34	2.11	0.48	0.01		5.54
22 to 24								0.07	0.91	1.63	0.62	0.03		3.26
24 to 26								0.03	0.26	0.72	0.59	0.07		1.67
26 to 28									0.06	0.26	0.34	0.06		0.72
28 to 30									0.02	0.10	0.19	0.06	0.01	0.38
30 to 32										0.02	0.09	0.03		0.14
Total	0.01	0.10	0.36	1.29	5.08	14.43	24.39	26.19	17.11	8.39	2.43	0.26	0.01	

Table 2.6 Percentage frequency of combinations of hourly dry bulb and wet bulb temperatures for June to September: Cardiff (Rhoose) (1976–1995)

Dry bulb temperature (°C)	Wet bulb temperature (°C)													Total
	−2 to 0	0 to 2	2 to 4	4 to 6	6 to 8	8 to 10	10 to 12	12 to 14	14 to 16	16 to 18	18 to 20	20 to 22	22 to 24	
−2 to 0														0
0 to 2														0
2 to 4		0.01	0.03											0.04
4 to 6			0.06	0.28										0.34
6 to 8				0.38	1.33									1.71
8 to 10				0.01	1.78	3.15								4.94
10 to 12					0.21	4.96	6.24							11.41
12 to 14					0.02	1.43	10.54	9.49						21.48
14 to 16						0.16	3.54	13.82	8.19					25.71
16 to 18						0.01	0.60	4.98	9.33	3.03				17.95
18 to 20							0.06	0.99	4.05	3.26	0.17			8.53
20 to 22								0.13	1.23	2.27	0.54			4.17
22 to 24								0.03	0.29	0.97	0.73	0.03		2.05
24 to 26									0.09	0.36	0.40	0.12		0.97
26 to 28									0.03	0.14	0.22	0.07	0.01	0.47
28 to 30									0.01	0.03	0.09	0.06	0.01	0.20
30 to 32											0.02	0.04		0.06
Total		0.01	0.09	0.67	3.34	9.71	20.98	29.44	23.22	10.06	2.17	0.32	0.02	

Table 2.7 Percentage frequency of combinations of hourly dry bulb and wet bulb temperatures for June to September: Edinburgh (Turnhouse) (1976–1995)

Dry bulb temperature (°C)	Wet bulb temperature (°C)													Total
	−2 to 0	0 to 2	2 to 4	4 to 6	6 to 8	8 to 10	10 to 12	12 to 14	14 to 16	16 to 18	18 to 20	20 to 22	22 to 24	
−2 to 0	0.04													0.04
0 to 2	0.02	0.13												0.15
2 to 4		0.04	0.32											0.36
4 to 6			0.23	1.07										1.30
6 to 8				1.02	2.38									3.40
8 to 10				0.10	4.02	5.46								9.58
10 to 12					0.85	9.91	8.13							18.89
12 to 14					0.09	3.00	13.54	7.73						24.36
14 to 16						0.51	5.60	10.29	3.33					19.73
16 to 18						0.01	1.37	5.17	5.31	0.72				12.58
18 to 20						0.01	0.08	1.41	2.86	1.43	0.04			5.83
20 to 22							0.01	0.13	0.92	1.20	0.19			2.45
22 to 24								0.02	0.22	0.48	0.23	0.01		0.96
24 to 26								0.01	0.03	0.13	0.11	0.02		0.30
26 to 28										0.02	0.04	0.02		0.08
28 to 30										0.01	0.03	0.01		0.05
30 to 32														
Total	0.06	0.17	0.55	2.19	7.34	18.90	28.73	24.76	12.67	3.99	0.64	0.06		

Table 2.8 Percentage frequency of combinations of hourly dry bulb and wet bulb temperatures for June to September: Glasgow (Abbotsinch) (1976–1995)

Dry bulb temperature (°C)	Wet bulb temperature (°C)													Total
	−2 to 0	0 to 2	2 to 4	4 to 6	6 to 8	8 to 10	10 to 12	12 to 14	14 to 16	16 to 18	18 to 20	20 to 22	22 to 24	
−2 to 0	0.04													0.04
0 to 2	0.01	0.22												0.23
2 to 4		0.05	0.47											0.52
4 to 6			0.24	1.11										1.35
6 to 8			0.01	0.9	2.53									3.44
8 to 10				0.10	3.56	5.22								8.88
10 to 12					0.63	9.22	8.26							18.11
12 to 14					0.12	2.80	13.63	8.02						24.57
14 to 16						0.55	5.15	11.22	4.13					21.05
16 to 18						0.02	1.12	4.81	5.08	0.85				11.88
18 to 20							0.06	1.14	2.67	1.25	0.04			5.16
20 to 22							0.01	0.17	0.90	1.13	0.15			2.36
22 to 24								0.05	0.24	0.71	0.30	0.01		1.31
24 to 26									0.06	0.31	0.36	0.03		0.76
26 to 28										0.09	0.16	0.07		0.32
28 to 30										0.02	0.03	0.01		0.06
30 to 32														
Total	0.05	0.27	0.72	2.11	6.84	17.81	28.23	25.41	13.08	4.36	1.04	0.12		

Table 2.9 Percentage frequency of combinations of hourly dry bulb and wet bulb temperatures for June to September: London (Heathrow) (1976–1995)

Dry bulb temperature (°C)	Wet bulb temperature (°C)													Total
	−2 to 0	0 to 2	2 to 4	4 to 6	6 to 8	8 to 10	10 to 12	12 to 14	14 to 16	16 to 18	18 to 20	20 to 22	22 to 24	
−2 to 0														
0 to 2														
2 to 4			0.01											0.01
4 to 6			0.01	0.17										0.18
6 to 8				0.19	0.71									0.90
8 to 10					1.17	2.08								3.25
10 to 12					0.20	4.22	4.17							8.59
12 to 14					0.03	1.34	8.45	5.96						15.78
14 to 16						0.34	3.77	10.95	4.87					19.93
16 to 18						0.01	1.67	5.95	8.83	2.16				18.62
18 to 20							0.18	3.01	5.71	4.21	0.34			13.45
20 to 22								0.70	3.22	3.47	0.94	0.01		8.34
22 to 24								0.05	1.08	2.73	1.26	0.09		5.21
24 to 26									0.26	1.37	1.32	0.25		3.20
26 to 28									0.04	0.42	0.77	0.32		1.55
28 to 30									0.01	0.10	0.31	0.25	0.01	0.68
30 to 32									0	0.01	0.12	0.14	0.02	0.29
Total			0.02	0.36	2.11	7.99	18.24	26.62	24.02	14.47	5.06	1.06	0.03	

Table 2.10 Percentage frequency of combinations of hourly dry bulb and wet bulb temperatures for June to September: Manchester (Ringway) (1976–1995)

Dry bulb temperature (°C)	Wet bulb temperature (°C)													Total
	−2 to 0	0 to 2	2 to 4	4 to 6	6 to 8	8 to 10	10 to 12	12 to 14	14 to 16	16 to 18	18 to 20	20 to 22	22 to 24	
−2 to 0														
0 to 2		0.01												0.01
2 to 4		0.01	0.11											0.12
4 to 6			0.07	0.33										0.40
6 to 8				0.51	1.31									1.82
8 to 10				0.05	2.44	3.69								6.18
10 to 12				0.01	0.69	7.59	6.52							14.81
12 to 14					0.11	2.81	12.74	6.90						22.56
14 to 16					0.01	0.61	5.87	11.45	3.85					21.79
16 to 18						0.03	1.53	6.16	6.16	1.12				15.00
18 to 20							0.07	1.81	3.72	2.28	0.13			8.01
20 to 22							0.02	0.32	1.83	2.05	0.36			4.58
22 to 24								0.05	0.61	1.29	0.51	0.02		2.48
24 to 26								0.01	0.15	0.55	0.47	0.06		1.24
26 to 28									0.05	0.22	0.35	0.07		0.69
28 to 30									0.01	0.04	0.18	0.03		0.26
30 to 32											0.05	0.01		0.06
Total		0.02	0.18	0.90	4.56	14.73	26.75	26.7	16.38	7.55	2.05	0.19		

Table 2.11 Percentage frequency of combinations of hourly dry bulb and wet bulb temperatures for June to September: Plymouth (Mount Batten) (1976–1995)

Dry bulb temperature (°C)	Wet bulb temperature (°C)													Total
	−2 to 0	0 to 2	2 to 4	4 to 6	6 to 8	8 to 10	10 to 12	12 to 14	14 to 16	16 to 18	18 to 20	20 to 22	22 to 24	
−2 to 0														
0 to 2														0
2 to 4														0
4 to 6				0.09										0.09
6 to 8				0.12	0.62									0.74
8 to 10					0.80	2.03	0.02							2.85
10 to 12					0.09	3.33	4.82							8.24
12 to 14					0.01	0.89	10.05	9.81						20.76
14 to 16						0.15	3.43	15.40	11.83					30.81
16 to 18							0.55	4.62	11.07	4.28				20.52
18 to 20							0.02	0.92	3.80	4.34	0.20			9.28
20 to 22								0.10	1.12	2.12	0.59			3.93
22 to 24								0.02	0.22	0.93	0.56	0.03		1.76
24 to 26									0.05	0.20	0.34	0.09		0.68
26 to 28										0.03	0.17	0.05		0.25
28 to 30										0.01	0.03	0.03		0.07
30 to 32												0.02		0.02
Total				0.21	1.52	6.40	18.89	30.87	28.09	11.91	1.89	0.22		

Table 2.12 Percentage frequency for which the hourly dry bulb temperatures exceeds the stated values in the period June to September (1976–1995)

Dry bulb temperature (°C)	Frequency (%)							
	Belfast	Birmingham	Cardiff	Edinburgh	Glasgow	London	Manchester	Plymouth
12	68.17	75.99	81.58	66.30	67.44	87.07	76.65	88.08
13	55.24	66.37	72.21	53.80	55.38	80.13	66.08	79.62
14	42.44	55.68	60.09	41.95	42.86	71.30	54.10	67.32
15	30.87	45.46	46.87	31.32	31.29	61.38	42.50	52.13
16	21.49	35.93	34.39	22.22	21.82	51.38	32.31	36.50
17	14.36	27.68	24.36	14.91	14.77	41.44	23.83	24.43
18	9.58	20.89	16.44	9.64	9.94	32.76	17.32	15.98
19	6.30	15.68	11.29	6.06	6.79	25.33	12.66	10.20
20	4.13	11.68	7.91	3.81	4.79	19.30	9.31	6.72
21	2.73	8.61	5.43	2.35	3.42	14.69	6.72	4.28
22	1.74	6.16	3.74	1.37	2.43	10.95	4.74	2.78
23	1.10	4.29	2.55	0.78	1.71	8.00	3.22	1.76
24	0.57	2.90	1.69	0.42	1.13	5.73	2.25	1.01
25	0.29	1.89	1.12	0.20	0.70	3.88	1.56	0.63
26	0.12	1.23	0.71	0.11	0.37	2.53	1.00	0.33
27	0.04	0.79	0.39	0.07	0.16	1.60	0.59	0.16
28	0.01	0.51	0.24	0.04	0.06	0.98	0.32	0.09
29		0.29	0.11	0.01	0.00+	0.62	0.15	0.04
30		0.13	0.06			0.29	0.06	0.02
31		0.04	0.02			0.12	0.02	0.01

Note: 0.00+ indicates a value greater than zero but less than 0.005.

Table 2.13 Percentage frequency for which the hourly wet bulb temperatures exceed the stated values in the period June to September (1976–1995)

Wet bulb temperature (°C)	Frequency (%)							
	Belfast	Birmingham	Cardiff	Edinburgh	Glasgow	London	Manchester	Plymouth
12	46.42	54.35	65.22	42.10	43.98	71.28	52.87	72.98
13	32.10	40.58	50.52	27.86	29.84	58.44	38.57	58.37
14	20.79	28.17	35.78	17.34	18.57	44.66	26.17	42.11
15	12.35	18.63	22.66	9.65	10.47	31.52	16.68	26.14
16	6.44	11.07	12.56	4.67	5.51	20.64	9.80	14.02
17	3.04	5.78	5.93	1.95	2.70	12.03	5.02	5.93
18	1.07	2.68	2.50	0.69	1.15	6.16	2.25	2.11
19	0.35	1.02	1.03	0.20	0.43	2.89	0.78	0.78
20	0.06	0.26	0.33	0.05	0.12	1.09	0.19	0.23
21	0.02	0.05	0.07		0.02	0.19	0.03	0.05
22	0.00+	0.01	0.02		0.01	0.03	0.00+	0.00+
23								0.00+

Note: 0.00+ indicates a value greater than zero but less than 0.005.

2.5 Accumulated temperature difference (degree-days and degree-hours)

Accumulated temperature differences are relatively simple forms of climatic data, useful as an index of climatic severity as it affects energy use for space heating or cooling. Accumulated temperature differences are calculated as the difference between the prevailing external, dry-bulb temperature and a 'base temperature'. This is the external temperature at which, in theory, no artificial heating (or cooling) is required to maintain an acceptable internal temperature.

Two types of degree-day are used in building services engineering. Heating degree-days (K·day) indicate the severity of the heating season and therefore heating energy requirements. Cooling degree-days (K·day), or cooling degree-hours (K·h), indicate the warmth of the summer and hence cooling requirements. The most widely used form of accumulated temperature difference is heating degree-days, which have proved particularly useful in monitoring heating energy consumption in buildings from year to year.

Table 2.14 gives 20-year averages of monthly and annual heating degree-day totals for all 18 degree-day regions, referred to the traditional standard base temperature of 15.5°C. These data are standard degree-day totals[7], calculated from daily maximum and minimum temperature.

Tables 2.15 to 2.17 give heating degree-day and cooling degree-hour totals for a range of base temperatures for London (Heathrow), Manchester (Ringway) and Edinburgh (Turnhouse), respectively. Cooling degree-hours are calculated when the external dry-bulb temperature exceeds the stated base temperature.

Table 2.14 Mean monthly and annual heating degree-day totals (base temperature 15.5°C) for 18 UK degree-day regions (1976–1995)

Degree-day region		Mean total degree-days (K·day)												
		Jan	Feb	Mar	Apr	May	Jun	Jul	Aug	Sep	Oct	Nov	Dec	Year
1	Thames Valley (Heathrow)	340	309	261	197	111	49	20	23	53	128	234	308	2033
2	South-eastern (Gatwick)	351	327	283	218	135	68	32	38	75	158	254	324	2255
3	Southern (Hurn)	338	312	279	222	135	70	37	42	77	157	246	311	2224
4	South-western (Plymouth)	286	270	249	198	120	58	23	26	52	123	200	253	1858
5	Severn Valley (Filton)	312	286	253	189	110˙	46	17	20	48	129	217	285	1835
6	Midland (Elmdon)	365	338	291	232	153	77	39	45	85	186	271	344	2425
7	W Pennines (Ringway)	360	328	292	220	136	73	34	42	81	170	259	331	2228
8	North-western (Carlisle)	370	329	309	237	159	89	45	54	101	182	271	342	2388
9	Borders (Boulmer)	364	328	312	259	197	112	58	60	102	186	270	335	2483
10	North-eastern (Leeming)	379	339	304	235	159	83	40	46	87	182	272	345	2370
11	E Pennines (Finningley)	371	339	294	228	150	79	39	45	82	174	266	342	2307
12	E Anglia (Honington)	371	338	294	228	143	74	35	37	70	158	264	342	2254
13	W Scotland (Abbotsinch)	380	336	317	240	159	93	54	64	107	206	286	358	2494
14	E Scotland (Leuchars)	390	339	320	253	185	104	57	65	113	204	290	362	2577
15	NE Scotland (Dyce)	394	345	331	264	194	116	62	72	122	216	295	365	2668
16	Wales (Aberporth)	328	310	289	231	156	89	44	44	77	156	234	294	2161
17	N Ireland (Aldergrove)	362	321	304	234	158	88	47	56	102	189	269	330	2360
18	NW Scotland (Stornoway)	336	296	332	260	207	124	85	88	135	214	254	330	2671

Table 2.15 Heating degree-day and cooling degree-hour totals to various base temperatures: London (Heathrow) (1976–1995)

Month	Heating degree-day total (K·day) for stated base temperature (°C)								Cooling degree-hours (K·h) for stated base temperature (°C)		
	10.0	12.0	14.0	15.5	16.0	18.0	18.5	20.0	5.0	12.0	18.0
January	165	224	286	332	348	410	425	472	1132	7	0
February	153	207	263	305	319	376	390	432	1070	14	0
March	104	158	217	263	278	340	355	402	2015	88	9
April	66	109	160	202	216	274	288	333	3031	402	38
May	19	43	78	112	124	176	190	233	5720	1509	252
June	2	9	27	48	57	97	109	145	7671	2857	641
July	0	2	7	17	22	48	57	87	9855	4682	1342
August	0	3	9	21	26	55	65	97	9416	4269	1071
September	4	13	31	53	62	106	119	159	7100	2361	285
October	26	52	91	129	143	201	216	262	4942	919	43
November	87	132	186	229	244	304	319	364	2507	188	0
December	138	193	254	300	316	378	393	440	1559	˙47	0
Year	764	1145	1609	2011	2155	2765	2926	3426	56018	17343	3681

Table 2.16 Heating degree-day and cooling degree-hour totals to various base temperatures: Manchester (Ringway) (1976–1995)

Month	Heating degree-day total (K·day) for stated base temperature (°C)								Cooling degree-hours (K·h) for stated base temperature (°C)		
	10.0	12.0	14.0	15.5	16.0	18.0	18.5	20.0	5.0	12.0	18.0
January	190	250	312	359	374	436	452	498	761	4	0
February	169	224	280	323	337	393	408	450	750	7	0
March	127	185	246	293	308	370	385	432	1415	33	3
April	83	131	186	229	243	302	317	362	2415	230	26
May	29	60	103	141	154	211	225	270	4775	967	120
June	5	18	45	74	85	133	146	187	6484	1878	323
July	1	4	16	34	42	81	93	131	8357	3243	639
August	1	6	21	41	50	93	105	145	7921	2864	474
September	8	23	52	83	95	148	162	205	5902	1405	84
October	38	73	122	164	179	240	255	301	4035	486	18
November	105	156	214	259	273	333	348	393	1919	70	0
December	165	223	285	331	347	409	424	471	1081	26	0
Year	921	1353	1882	2331	2487	3149	3320	3845	45815	11213	1687

Table 2.17 Heating degree-day and cooling degree-hour totals to various base temperatures: Edinburgh (Turnhouse) (1976–1995)

Month	Heating degree-day total (K·day) for stated base temperature (°C)								Cooling degree-hours (K·h) for stated base temperature (°C)		
	10.0	12.0	14.0	15.5	16.0	18.0	18.5	20.0	5.0	12.0	18.0
January	210	271	333	380	395	457	473	519	599	2	0
February	182	237	294	336	350	407	421	463	606	3	0
March	149	208	269	316	331	393	409	455	1138	15	0
April	102	155	212	256	271	330	345	390	1875	102	15
May	46	86	136	178	192	252	267	313	3762	505	41
June	10	29	63	97	109	162	176	218	5618	1275	134
July	2	9	29	53	63	111	124	166	7254	2272	235
August	5	14	35	61	71	120	134	177	6983	2101	196
September	16	37	73	109	123	179	194	238	5132	940	28
October	54	95	148	192	207	268	284	330	3453	301	5
November	126	180	238	283	298	358	373	418	1594	43	0
December	188	248	310	356	372	434	449	496	884	9	0
	1090	1569	2140	2617	2782	3471	3649	4183	38898	7568	654

2.6   World-wide weather data

Tables 2.18 and 2.19 provide information on meteorological conditions for selected locations world-wide. These have been selected from the extensive tables of data contained in ASHRAE Handbook: *Fundamentals*[2] and are reproduced by permission of ASHRAE.

The locations are listed alphabetically by country. The purpose of these tables is to give general guidance on design temperatures. Where possible, before finally selecting design temperatures, reference should be made to local meteorological data since the design temperatures quoted may be appropriate to only a relatively small area around the meteorological station from which the data were obtained.

2.6.1   Heating design temperatures and wind speeds (world-wide)

External winter design temperatures for selected world-wide locations are given in Table 2.18. The information provided is as follows:

— Columns 1–7: name of observing station, World Meteorological Office (WMO) station number, latitude, longitude, elevation, standard pressure at stated elevation and the period analysed.

— Columns 8 and 9: dry bulb temperature (DB) corresponding to 99.6% and 99.0% annual cumulative frequency of occurrence (cold).

— Columns 10–12: extreme wind speed corresponding to 1.0%, 2.5% and 5.0% annual cumulative frequency of occurrence.

— Columns 13–16: wind speed (WS) corresponding to the 0.4% and 1.0% cumulative frequency of occurrence for the coldest month (i.e. lowest average dry bulb temperature) at the stated location, and the mean coincident dry bulb temperature (MDB).

— Columns 17–20: mean wind speed (MWS) coincident with the 99.6% dry bulb temperature (DB) (column 8) and 0.4% dry bulb temperature (Table 2.19, column 2), and wind direction (MWD)

most frequently occurring with the 99.6% and 0.4% dry bulb temperatures. (Wind direction is expressed in degrees true with 360° representing a north wind.)

— Columns 21–24: average of annual extreme maximum and minimum dry bulb temperatures (DB) and associated standard deviations (SD).

Values of ambient dry bulb temperature and wind speed corresponding to the various annual percentiles represent the value that is exceeded on average by the indicated percentage of the total number of hours in the year (8760). The 0.4%, 1.0%, 2.0% and 5.0% values are exceeded, on average, for 35, 88, 175 and 438 hours, respectively. The 99.0% and 99.6% values are defined in a similar way but are usually viewed as the values for which the corresponding weather element is less than the design condition for 88 and 35 hours respectively. Mean coincident values are the average of the stated weather element occurring concurrently with the corresponding design value.

The design conditions given in the table explicitly represent the same annual probability of occurrence in any location, regardless of country or general climatic conditions.

The 99.6% and 99% design conditions (columns 8 and 9) are often used in sizing heating equipment. In cold spells, dry bulb temperatures below the design conditions can last for a week or more. Columns 13–16 and 17–20 are useful in estimating peak heating loads allowing for infiltration. Columns 13–16 provides extreme wind speeds for the coldest month, with the mean coincident dry bulb temperature. Columns 17–20 provide the mean wind speed and direction coincident with the corresponding percentile design dry bulb temperature.

Columns 21 and 22 provide the means of the extreme maximum and minimum dry bulb temperatures. These are calculated from extremes of hourly observations and are therefore less extreme than the extreme temperature recorded by a 'max/min' thermometer by about 0.5 K. the standard deviation (columns 23 and 24) may be used to estimate the likely recurrence interval of the extremes, see ASHRAE *Fundamentals*[2] for details.

Table 2.18 Heating and wind design conditions for selected locations world-wide[2]

Station	WMO station number	Lat.(°)	Long.(°)	Elev. (m)	Std. press. (kPa)	Period	Heating DB 99.6%	Heating DB 99%	Extreme wind speed (m/s) 1%	2.5%	5%	Coldest month WS/MDB 0.4% WS	MDB	1% WS	MDB	MSW/MWD coincident with DB 99.6% MWS	MWD	0.4% MWS	MWD	Annual extreme daily Mean DB Max.	Min.	Std. dev. DB Max.	Min.
ALGERIA																							
Algiers	603900	36.72N	3.25E	25	101.03	82–93	2.0	3.1	11.0	9.5	8.3	11.8	12.9	9.8	13.0	0.7	200	5.2	60	40.8	−0.1	2.5	1.4
Constantine	604190	36.28N	6.62E	694	93.26	82–93	−0.6	0.4	10.5	9.0	7.6	11.8	7.6	9.8	8.0	0.8	320	5.2	240	39.7	−2.7	1.4	0.8
ARGENTINA																							
Buenos Aires	875760	34.82S	58.53W	20	101.08	82–93	−0.7	1.0	10.4	9.1	8.1	9.8	11.9	8.5	11.5	2.0	270	4.9	270	36.6	−2.9	1.4	1.1
San Juan	873110	31.57S	68.42W	598	94.34	82–93	−2.0	−0.5	14.3	12.4	10.5	12.7	11.3	10.5	11.1	0.3	360	5.0	180	41.5	−5.1	1.4	1.6
ARMENIA																							
Yerevan	377890	40.13N	44.47E	890	91.08	82–93	−14.1	−11.7	9.7	7.3	6.2	6.1	4.8	4.4	0.1	0.4	180	2.7	210	38.4	−15.9	3.5	3.8
ASCENSION ISLAND																							
Georgetown	619020	7.97S	14.40W	79	100.38	82–93	20.8	21.3	11.5	10.6	10.2	11.3	24.6	10.5	24.4	7.3	90	8.6	120	30.6	18.6	1.0	1.6
AUSTRALIA																							
Adelaide	946720	34.93S	138.52E	4	101.28	82–93	4.0	5.2	12.2	10.7	9.6	11.4	11.7	10.1	12.4	1.0	50	5.7	310	39.8	1.8	1.7	1.2
Brisbane	945780	27.38S	153.10E	5	101.26	82–93	6.6	7.8	9.6	8.6	7.7	9.6	15.5	8.3	16.0	1.8	220	5.0	20	35.0	3.8	2.1	1.1
Canberra	949260	35.30S	149.18E	577	94.58	82–93	−3.1	−1.8	10.5	9.3	8.2	10.9	7.9	9.8	8.7	0.0	310	5.3	310	36.1	−6.4	2.2	4.5
Darwin	941200	12.40S	130.87E	30	100.97	82–93	17.9	19.0	8.4	7.6	6.9	8.2	26.5	7.4	26.9	3.1	140	5.2	290	36.8	15.4	1.6	1.4
Perth	946100	31.93S	115.95E	29	100.98	82–93	4.8	6.1	10.6	9.5	8.4	10.1	14.4	8.7	14.4	0.3	50	4.3	270	41.5	2.2	1.9	1.2
Sydney	947670	33.95S	151.18E	3	101.29	82–93	5.8	6.8	11.3	9.9	8.8	11.1	14.2	9.1	13.4	1.1	320	5.3	300	39.3	3.1	2.9	1.9
AUSTRIA																							
Innsbruck	111200	47.27N	11.35E	593	94.40	82–93	−12.2	−10.2	8.3	6.8	5.5	8.2	5.4	6.5	3.9	0.5	260	3.5	70	32.8	−14.9	1.5	3.8
Salzburg	111500	47.80N	13.00E	450	96.03	82–93	−14.1	−11.1	7.8	6.7	5.9	8.9	5.5	7.6	3.6	1.4	130	3.0	330	33.2	−16.4	2.3	4.6
Vienna	110350	48.25N	16.37E	200	98.95	82–93	−11.1	−8.6	10.1	8.5	7.5	11.9	6.1	10.4	5.7	2.8	240	4.0	140	33.0	−12.8	1.8	3.7
AZORES																							
Lajes	85090	38.77N	27.10W	55	100.67	82–93	8.0	9.1	12.6	10.4	9.2	13.4	13.6	11.7	13.9	1.3	300	3.7	250	28.5	4.9	1.0	2.1
BAHAMAS																							
Nassau	780730	25.05N	77.47W	7	101.24	82–93	14.1	15.8	9.3	8.4	7.7	9.5	22.0	8.7	21.9	1.5	300	4.5	130	33.9	10.9	0.7	1.7
BAHRAIN																							
Al-Manamah	411500	26.27N	50.65E	2	101.30	82–93	11.0	12.2	11.3	10.3	9.4	11.5	13.5	10.7	14.2	5.8	290	5.0	340	42.9	8.1	1.4	3.1
BELARUS																							
Babruysk (Bobruysk)	269610	53.12N	29.25E	165	99.36	82–93	−23.0	−19.1	8.9	7.9	7.1	9.0	−2.8	8.1	−1.0	1.6	210	3.6	200	30.4	−26.4	2.2	11.7
Minsk	268500	53.87N	27.53E	234	98.55	82–93	−20.7	−17.6	7.4	6.4	5.9	7.8	−4.8	6.7	−4.4	2.1	300	4.0	70	29.7	−22.2	2.1	4.0
BELGIUM																							
Antwerp	64500	51.20N	4.47E	14	101.16	82–93	−8.7	−6.0	10.6	9.2	8.2	12.3	8.2	10.5	6.6	3.0	50	3.2	90	31.6	−9.4	2.3	4.0
Brussels	64510	50.90N	4.53E	58	100.63	82–93	−9.3	−6.2	12.0	10.4	9.2	13.8	7.7	11.8	7.0	3.1	50	3.6	60	31.5	−9.5	2.1	4.8
Oostende	64070	51.20N	2.87E	5	101.26	82–93	−7.8	−5.4	15.0	13.2	11.7	18.0	7.8	14.8	7.4	4.9	70	4.6	100	30.0	−9.2	1.8	3.6

Table 2.18 Heating and wind design conditions for selected locations world-wide[2]—*continued*

Station	WMO station number	Lat.(°)	Long.(°)	Elev. (m)	Std. press. (kPa)	Period	Heating DB 99.6%	Heating DB 99%	Extreme wind speed (m/s) 1%	2.5%	5%	Coldest month WS/MBD 0.4% WS	0.4% MDB	1% WS	1% MDB	MSW/MWD coincident with DB 99.6% MWS	99.6% MWD	0.4% MWS	0.4% MWD	0.4% DB	Annual extreme daily Mean DB Max.	Mean DB Min.	Std. dev. DB Max.	Std. dev. DB Min.
BENIN Parakou	653300	9.35N	2.62E	393	96.69	82–93	18.2	19.3	6.4	5.5	4.9	5.5	24.2	5.0	24.4	1.6	40	2.4	40	39.5	39.5	12.6	2.8	5.1
BERMUDA Hamilton	780160	32.37N	64.68W	3	101.29	82–93	12.9	13.9	13.0	11.4	10.2	13.4	18.3	12.6	18.0	7.2	310	4.8	190	32.1	32.1	8.3	0.7	4.2
BOLIVIA La Paz	852010	16.52S	68.18W	4014	61.53	82–93	−4.0	−3.0	8.5	7.7	6.4	9.6	11.1	8.4	11.0	0.9	330	3.4	60	20.8	20.8	−6.0	2.6	1.1
BOSNIA–HERZEGOVINA Banja Luka	132420	44.78N	17.22E	156	99.46	82–93	−12.0	−8.9	5.9	4.3	3.4	6.4	11.1	4.5	9.8	1.1	320	2.0	360	36.6	36.6	−14.5	2.2	4.2
BRAZIL Brasilia	833780	15.87S	47.93W	1061	89.21	82–93	9.1	10.8	7.6	6.3	5.4	8.0	21.5	6.5	22.3	0.2	90	3.2	90	34.4	34.4	6.7	1.8	3.2
Rio De Janeiro	837460	22.82S	43.25W	6	101.25	82–93	14.9	15.9	8.5	7.7	6.8	7.6	23.4	6.6	23.0	1.2	320	3.1	50	41.5	41.5	10.0	1.4	5.2
Sao Paulo	837800	23.62S	46.65W	803	92.04	82–93	8.8	9.9	6.9	5.9	5.2	6.4	19.0	5.4	18.0	2.0	160	2.6	330	34.3	34.3	5.9	1.5	2.1
BULGARIA Sofia	156140	42.65N	23.38E	595	94.38	82–93	−12.1	−9.9	9.3	7.6	6.4	9.8	0.4	8.2	−0.1	1.1	360	2.4	110	34.3	34.3	−16.3	2.7	4.7
BRUNEI Brunei	963150	4.93N	114.93E	15	101.14	82–93	21.4	22.0	7.3	6.3	5.5	8.1	28.0	7.2	27.8	0.0	220	3.7	320	35.4	35.4	19.3	1.4	2.6
CANADA Calgary	718770	51.12	114.02	1084	88.96	61–93	−30.0	−27.1	12.3	10.7	9.5	14.1	−1.5	12.4	−2.7	2.9	0	4.7	160	31.8	31.8	−33.2	1.5	3.1
Edmonton	711230	53.30	113.58	723	92.94	61–93	−33.4	−30.5	10.8	9.2	8.0	10.9	−11.3	9.4	−11.6	2.5	180	3.8	180	30.8	30.8	−38.0	1.7	4.5
Halifax	713950	44.88	63.50	145	99.60	69–93	−19.0	−16.7	12.1	10.3	9.1	13.4	−3.1	12.1	−3.6	5.1	320	5.2	200	30.4	30.4	−22.4	1.5	2.4
Montreal	716270	45.47	73.75	36	100.89	61–93	−24.4	−21.8	10.2	9.0	7.9	13.2	−7.4	11.5	−7.7	3.2	250	5.0	230	32.0	32.0	−28.3	1.3	2.5
Ottawa	716280	45.32	75.67	114	99.96	61–93	−24.8	−22.2	10.0	8.8	7.7	11.9	−8.5	10.3	−9.3	3.9	290	4.5	250	33.0	33.0	−28.4	1.5	2.8
Quebec	717140	46.80	71.38	73	100.45	61–93	−26.4	−24.0	10.8	9.4	8.3	13.2	−10.4	11.6	−11.5	4.3	250	5.2	250	31.7	31.7	−30.4	1.3	2.7
Toronto	716240	43.67	79.63	173	99.26	65–93	−19.9	−17.2	11.6	10.0	8.8	13.0	−5.8	11.4	−5.1	4.1	340	5.3	270	33.1	33.1	−24.0	1.6	3.1
Vancouver	718920	49.18	123.17	2	101.30	61–93	−7.8	−4.7	10.0	8.3	7.1	11.3	5.2	9.4	5.8	2.7	90	3.3	290	28.0	28.0	−10.0	1.6	3.5
Winnipeg	718520	49.90	97.23	239	98.49	61–93	−32.8	−30.6	12.9	11.3	10.1	13.3	−14.9	11.7	−15.0	3.2	320	5.7	180	34.5	34.5	−36.2	1.9	2.6
CANARY ISLANDS Las Palmas	600300	27.93N	15.38W	25	101.03	82–93	13.0	13.9	14.2	13.3	12.5	11.9	18.6	10.6	18.5	1.8	320	8.7	30	34.4	34.4	10.8	2.4	0.5
Santa Cruz De Tenerife	600250	28.05N	16.57W	72	100.46	82–93	13.8	14.1	13.1	11.9	10.9	12.6	20.1	11.3	19.8	3.4	360	8.5	60	38.4	38.4	10.3	3.0	3.6
CAPE VERDE Sal Island	85940	16.73N	22.95W	55	100.67	82–93	17.1	17.8	12.2	11.3	10.5	12.5	22.2	11.8	22.2	4.6	30	6.5	60	32.7	32.7	14.2	1.0	2.4
CHILE Concepcion	856820	36.77S	73.05W	16	101.13	82–93	1.8	2.8	13.2	11.5	10.3	16.1	12.2	13.0	11.9	1.8	140	8.5	240	33.2	33.2	−1.0	8.6	0.8
Santiago	855740	33.38S	70.78W	476	95.74	82–93	−1.4	−0.1	8.5	7.3	6.3	7.2	9.7	5.3	10.0	0.9	20	5.4	210	38.6	38.6	−3.7	5.1	1.3

Table 2.18 Heating and wind design conditions for selected locations world-wide[2] — *continued*

Station	WMO station number	Lat.(°)	Long.(°)	Elev. (m)	Std. press. (kPa)	Period	Heating DB 99.6%	Heating DB 99%	Extreme wind speed (m/s) 1%	2.5%	5%	Coldest month WS/MBD 0.4% WS	0.4% MDB	1% WS	1% MDB	MSW/MWD coincident with DB 99.6% MWS	99.6% MWD	0.4% MWS	0.4% MWD	Annual extreme daily Mean DB Max.	Mean DB Min.	Std. dev. DB Max.	Std. dev. DB Min.
Beijing	545110	39.93N	116.28E	55	100.67	82–93	−10.4	−9.2	9.2	7.6	6.3	9.4	−1.1	7.9	−2.4	2.0	340	3.1	200	38.1	−13.4	1.9	1.7
Dinghai	584770	30.03N	122.12E	37	100.88	82–93	−0.7	0.5	9.2	7.7	6.8	8.9	3.9	7.8	4.9	3.3	340	2.9	140	35.2	−2.7	0.9	1.4
Guangzhou	592870	23.13N	113.32E	8	101.23	82–93	5.3	6.7	6.8	5.7	5.0	6.7	11.7	5.6	11.7	2.7	360	2.3	270	36.4	2.9	0.8	1.5
Hangzhou	584570	30.23N	120.17E	43	100.81	82–93	−2.4	−1.1	7.4	6.4	5.5	7.4	4.7	6.3	4.7	1.9	340	3.6	160	37.5	−5.6	1.0	2.1
Jinan	548230	36.68N	116.98E	58	100.63	82–93	−8.0	−6.4	8.8	7.6	6.7	8.2	0.3	7.1	2.2	2.2	70	4.3	200	36.9	−10.6	1.1	2.3
Kowloon	450070	22.33N	114.18E	24	101.04	82–93	9.0	10.8	10.0	8.8	8.0	9.1	16.9	8.3	17.1	3.5	330	4.6	250	35.4	7.1	1.2	1.4
Macau	450110	22.20N	113.53E	59	100.62	82–93	6.9	8.3	8.4	7.4	6.6	8.3	9.9	7.6	10.6	6.0	360	3.0	200	34.6	5.3	0.9	1.5
Nanjing	582380	32.00N	118.80E	12	101.18	82–93	−5.2	−3.5	7.9	6.9	6.0	7.5	3.3	6.7	2.7	0.8	340	4.0	220	36.5	−8.0	1.4	2.0
Shanghai	583670	31.17N	121.43E	7	101.24	82–93	−3.1	−1.8	8.7	7.6	6.7	8.7	3.4	7.7	3.8	2.5	290	3.5	200	36.6	−6.0	1.1	1.5
Shenyang	543420	41.77N	123.43E	43	100.81	82–93	−21.0	−18.7	9.7	8.1	6.9	8.3	−5.5	7.0	−6.4	1.5	70	4.2	200	33.2	−24.6	1.3	2.8
Tianjin	545270	39.10N	117.17E	5	101.26	82–93	−10.0	−8.5	7.9	6.3	5.3	8.5	−3.7	7.1	−3.8	1.9	340	2.7	250	36.5	−13.6	1.3	2.3
Wuhan	574940	30.62N	114.13E	23	101.05	82–93	−2.8	−1.5	6.6	5.4	4.7	6.0	4.3	5.2	4.1	1.0	20	3.5	220	36.9	−6.2	1.4	3.2
Zhanjiang	596580	21.22N	110.40E	28	100.99	82–93	7.6	8.9	7.1	5.9	5.2	6.2	12.4	5.4	13.4	3.6	340	3.5	250	36.2	5.7	1.7	2.2
COLOMBIA																							
Bogota	802220	4.70N	74.13W	2548	74.23	82–93	2.2	3.9	9.4	8.0	6.4	10.3	17.6	8.5	17.4	0.2	320	4.5	90	28.0	−0.9	4.7	1.5
CROATIA																							
Split	133330	43.53N	16.30E	21	101.07	82–93	−1.9	−0.1	10.6	8.4	7.0	10.4	4.9	8.5	6.6	3.9	340	3.7	230	34.6	−7.1	3.9	9.3
Zagreb	131310	45.73N	16.07E	107	100.05	82–93	−13.2	−10.0	8.5	7.2	5.9	7.7	4.0	6.3	3.9	1.0	240	2.9	230	33.5	−16.5	3.2	4.6
CUBA																							
Guantanamo	783670	19.90N	75.15W	17	101.12	82–93	19.2	20.1	10.0	8.9	7.9	9.3	29.2	8.4	29.0	3.5	360	5.2	130	37.6	16.0	2.6	4.6
CYPRUS																							
Akrotiri	176010	34.58N	32.98E	23	101.05	82–93	4.6	6.0	11.1	10.0	9.0	12.9	11.4	11.5	12.3	2.3	350	4.3	260	35.2	2.4	1.7	2.4
Larnaca	176090	34.88N	33.63E	2	101.30	82–93	3.0	4.6	11.9	10.2	8.9	12.5	12.2	10.8	12.2	3.2	310	5.5	200	36.9	0.8	1.2	1.9
CZECH REPUBLIC																							
Brno	117230	49.15N	16.70E	246	98.40	82–93	−14.4	−10.9	10.6	9.2	8.2	11.5	−1.0	9.5	−0.7	3.4	60	4.5	180	32.6	−15.8	1.6	4.0
Prague	115180	50.10N	14.28E	366	97.00	82–93	−16.1	−12.4	12.4	10.4	9.0	13.9	4.0	11.9	2.3	1.9	10	3.5	160	32.8	−18.0	2.0	4.9
DENMARK																							
Alborg	60300	57.10N	9.87E	3	101.29	82–93	−13.1	−9.2	13.0	11.4	10.2	14.3	7.0	12.5	5.8	2.6	220	4.7	100	28.0	−14.1	2.2	6.9
Copenhagen	61800	55.63N	12.67E	5	101.26	82–93	−11.1	−8.0	13.0	11.6	10.5	13.2	4.3	12.0	3.1	5.1	360	4.7	160	27.5	−10.3	1.8	4.5
ECUADOR																							
Quito	840710	0.15S	78.48W	2812	71.80	82–93	7.0	7.9	7.8	6.6	5.9	6.6	17.6	6.0	17.8	0.3	350	4.1	150	28.8	4.7	4.3	1.8
EGYPT																							
Alexandria	623180	31.20N	29.95E	7	101.24	82–93	6.8	7.8	10.7	9.2	8.1	13.0	13.6	11.3	14.6	2.1	190	4.3	340	39.0	2.9	1.8	2.1
Cairo	623660	30.13N	31.40E	74	100.44	82–93	7.0	8.0	9.5	8.3	7.3	10.3	14.6	8.7	16.4	2.6	210	5.6	350	42.1	3.1	1.6	2.7
ESTONIA																							
Tallinn	260380	59.35N	24.80E	44	100.80	82–93	−19.8	−16.0	9.2	8.1	7.3	9.8	0.9	8.6	0.0	2.9	140	3.6	40	28.0	−19.6	2.4	4.8

Table 2.18 Heating and wind design conditions for selected locations world-wide[2] — continued

Station	WMO station number	Lat.(°)	Long.(°)	Elev. (m)	Std. press. (kPa)	Period	Heating DB 99.6%	Heating DB 99%	Extreme wind speed (m/s) 1%	2.5%	5%	Coldest month WS/MBD 0.4% WS	MDB	1% WS	MDB	MSW/MWD coincident with DB 99.6% MWS	MWD	0.4% MWS	MWD	Annual extreme daily Mean DB Max.	Min.	Std. dev. DB Max.	Min.
FAEROE ISLANDS																								
Torshavn	60110	62.02N	6.77W	39	100.86	82-93	-3.2	-2.3	18.2	15.3	13.7	21.5	5.7	19.2	6.2	5.8	320	4.8	210	18.1	-5.4	1.9	1.4
FIJI																								
Nadi	916800	17.75S	177.45E	18	101.11	82-93	16.0	17.1	8.9	7.8	7.0	8.7	25.8	7.7	26.0	1.6	120	5.8	350	34.9	13.1	2.0	3.3
FINLAND																								
Helsinki	29740	60.32N	24.97E	56	100.65	82-93	-23.7	-19.5	10.0	8.8	7.9	10.9	1.5	9.7	-0.1	2.4	340	4.8	210	28.4	-24.7	1.7	5.3
Pello	28440	66.80N	24.00E	84	100.32	82-93	-31.4	-29.1	6.4	5.6	5.0	6.3	-3.7	5.4	-4.4	0.4	300	3.0	340	27.6	-34.7	2.7	3.0
FRANCE																								
Bordeaux	75100	44.83N	0.70W	61	100.59	82-93	-5.8	-3.0	9.9	8.3	7.1	10.6	10.3	9.0	10.4	1.6	40	3.3	80	35.9	-7.4	1.5	4.1
Brest	71100	48.45N	4.42W	103	100.09	82-93	-2.8	-1.0	11.8	10.4	9.3	12.7	8.7	11.4	8.0	3.4	120	4.0	40	29.5	-4.4	2.2	2.4
Lyon	74810	45.73N	5.08E	240	98.47	82-93	-8.5	-5.1	11.4	9.6	8.2	11.8	6.6	10.0	7.2	1.4	20	5.2	180	34.8	-9.7	1.5	4.1
Marseille	76500	43.45N	5.23E	36	100.89	82-93	-3.9	-2.0	16.8	14.4	12.4	17.1	6.7	14.4	6.5	3.8	360	5.6	280	35.1	-5.6	1.8	3.1
Nice	76900	43.65N	7.20E	10	101.20	82-93	1.6	2.9	11.2	9.4	7.8	10.5	11.9	8.7	11.0	4.7	340	3.6	160	32.2	-0.4	1.5	2.7
Paris, Orly	71490	48.73N	2.40E	96	100.18	82-93	-7.1	-4.8	11.2	9.7	8.4	12.8	8.8	10.8	8.5	3.7	20	3.4	100	33.4	-8.2	2.0	4.2
Strasbourg	71900	48.55N	7.63E	154	99.49	82-93	-11.0	-8.2	9.8	8.3	7.2	11.7	8.7	9.5	4.9	2.9	340	3.4	20	34.1	-12.5	1.4	4.5
Toulouse	76300	43.63N	1.37E	153	99.50	82-93	-5.8	-3.0	9.8	8.5	7.5	10.0	8.9	8.7	9.1	2.2	280	3.3	140	37.0	-7.2	2.0	4.5
GERMANY																								
Berlin	103840	52.47N	13.40E	49	100.74	82-93	-11.8	-9.2	10.4	9.1	8.1	11.5	6.5	9.5	5.1	3.4	80	3.7	150	33.8	-12.2	2.1	4.9
Dresden	104880	51.13N	13.78E	226	98.64	82-93	-13.3	-10.3	9.6	8.3	7.3	10.2	5.3	8.8	4.8	1.9	320	3.0	990	33.6	-14.6	1.6	6.2
Dusseldorf	104000	51.28N	6.78E	44	100.80	82-93	-9.9	-6.9	10.4	9.2	8.1	11.8	7.0	10.1	6.4	2.8	60	3.8	130	33.4	-10.8	1.5	4.9
Frankfurt	106370	50.05N	8.60E	113	99.97	82-93	-11.0	-8.2	10.2	8.8	7.7	11.3	7.2	9.4	5.3	3.3	30	3.9	40	34.1	-12.1	1.7	4.3
Hamburg	101470	53.63N	10.00E	16	101.13	82-93	-11.6	-8.9	10.2	9.0	8.1	10.6	5.6	9.5	4.2	2.5	60	4.7	90	31.5	-12.5	2.5	5.0
Hannover	103380	52.47N	9.70E	54	100.68	82-93	-12.7	-9.8	10.2	8.9	8.0	11.1	6.0	9.6	5.0	2.5	80	4.2	110	32.5	-13.1	2.2	5.6
Koln	105130	50.87N	7.17E	99	100.14	82-93	-11.4	-8.1	9.2	8.1	7.2	11.0	7.4	9.2	6.2	1.9	110	3.5	130	33.4	-13.3	1.7	5.9
Leipzig	104690	51.42N	12.23E	133	99.74	82-93	-13.4	-10.4	12.5	10.8	9.4	13.4	5.5	11.3	4.8	2.8	70	4.0	190	33.6	-14.3	1.8	6.8
Munich	108660	48.13N	11.70E	529	95.13	82-93	-15.4	-12.5	11.9	9.6	7.9	12.9	5.3	10.6	4.5	1.6	80	3.6	30	32.5	-18.6	2.0	4.5
Stuttgart	107380	48.68N	9.22E	419	96.39	82-93	-12.7	-10.0	9.4	7.9	6.8	10.3	5.0	9.0	4.4	1.9	90	3.0	90	33.2	-15.4	2.2	5.7
GEORGIA																								
Batumi	374840	41.65N	41.63E	6	101.25	82-93	-1.7	-0.2	13.5	12.2	10.6	13.7	9.5	12.7	9.8	6.0	130	4.2	300	32.9	-6.3	5.0	6.8
Tbilisi	375490	41.68N	44.95E	467	95.84	82-93	-6.0	-4.7	21.7	18.8	16.6	22.6	2.1	20.1	2.1	2.6	320	4.5	180	36.2	-8.7	1.7	2.2
GIBRALTAR																								
North Front	84950	36.15N	5.35W	5	101.26	82-93	7.8	8.9	14.6	12.5	11.1	16.0	14.1	14.4	13.9	4.0	270	6.2	200	36.1	4.7	2.6	2.4
GREECE																								
Athens	167160	37.90N	23.73E	15	101.14	82-93	1.2	2.9	10.2	9.2	8.4	11.2	8.2	9.8	8.6	3.5	360	6.1	30	37.4	-0.4	2.4	1.7
Iraklion, Crete	167540	35.33N	25.18E	39	100.86	82-93	5.0	6.8	14.5	12.9	11.2	18.0	11.5	14.8	10.8	6.2	340	4.7	320	36.2	2.7	2.0	2.0
Rodhos	167490	36.40N	28.08E	11	101.19	82-93	5.0	6.6	10.6	9.7	9.0	12.5	9.3	10.4	9.5	6.0	360	6.4	270	35.3	3.5	2.0	2.0
Thessaloniki	166220	40.52N	22.97E	4	101.28	82-93	-3.8	-2.0	13.1	10.6	8.9	14.2	5.6	12.6	6.0	3.6	110	4.4	180	37.4	-7.2	2.5	1.8
GREENLAND																								
Godthab	42500	64.17N	51.75W	70	100.49	82-93	-24.5	-22.4	20.3	16.1	13.4	18.5	-7.0	14.8	-7.0	5.9	350	4.6	20	17.8	-22.4	2.9	3.4

Table 2.18 Heating and wind design conditions for selected locations world-wide[2] — *continued*

Station	WMO station number	Lat.(°)	Long.(°)	Elev. (m)	Std. press. (kPa)	Period	Heating DB 99.6%	Heating DB 99%	Extreme wind speed (m/s) 1%	2.5%	5%	Coldest month WS/MBD 0.4% WS	MDB	1% WS	MDB	MSW/MWD coincident with DB 99.6% MWS	MWD	0.4% MWS	MWD	Annual extreme daily Mean DB Max.	Min.	Std. dev. DB Max.	Min.
HUNGARY Budapest	128390	47.43N	19.27E	185	99.12	82–93	−13.2	−10.2	16.1	12.8	10.6	15.6	4.3	12.1	4.2	0.9	170	4.5	200	34.5	−16.5	1.2	4.4
ICELAND Reykjavik	40300	64.13N	21.90W	61	100.59	82–93	−9.8	−8.1	18.1	15.4	13.7	21.0	2.5	18.6	2.5	4.3	90	5.5	360	18.4	−12.1	1.9	1.4
INDIA Bangalore	432950	12.97N	77.58E	921	90.74	82–93	14.9	15.7	6.0	5.2	4.4	5.0	21.7	4.3	22.1	1.4	90	1.7	90	37.0	12.2	1.1	1.9
Bombay	430030	19.12N	72.85E	14	101.16	82–93	16.5	17.6	6.7	6.0	5.3	5.4	26.2	5.0	26.6	0.2	360	3.1	320	38.5	13.4	1.3	1.6
Calcutta	428090	22.65N	88.45E	6	101.25	82–93	12.0	13.1	5.6	4.7	3.8	3.3	22.9	3.0	22.6	0.2	360	2.0	180	39.2	10.2	1.1	0.8
Goa/Panaji	431920	15.48N	73.82E	60	100.61	82–93	19.6	20.3	7.5	6.4	5.5	5.2	28.6	4.4	28.6	2.2	50	2.7	320	37.2	16.4	1.5	3.0
Hyderabad	431280	17.45N	78.47E	545	94.95	82–93	14.5	15.8	9.2	8.3	7.7	5.6	24.5	5.1	25.0	0.4	50	3.7	320	41.6	11.5	1.1	2.0
Jaipur	423480	26.82N	75.80E	390	96.73	82–93	6.8	8.2	7.1	5.8	5.0	5.3	17.9	4.4	18.0	0.2	90	3.8	320	43.5	3.9	1.2	1.7
Madras	432790	13.00N	80.18E	16	101.13	82–93	19.9	20.5	7.4	6.4	5.7	5.6	26.8	4.8	26.8	0.9	290	3.7	270	41.2	18.3	1.2	1.0
New Delhi	421820	28.58N	77.20E	216	98.76	82–93	6.6	7.6	7.4	6.3	5.4	6.4	18.9	5.7	18.7	0.7	270	3.3	320	43.4	5.0	1.2	1.1
IRELAND Dublin	39690	53.43N	6.25W	85	100.31	82–93	−1.6	−0.4	13.8	12.3	10.9	15.6	6.9	13.5	6.8	4.2	250	4.9	230	24.9	−3.6	1.8	1.8
Kilkenny	39600	52.67N	7.27W	64	100.56	82–93	−3.7	−2.3	11.9	10.0	8.5	13.1	8.5	11.7	8.4	1.0	360	3.1	180	26.2	−6.6	2.2	2.3
Rosslare	39570	52.25N	6.33W	25	101.03	82–93	0.2	1.2	14.5	13.1	11.8	16.0	5.0	13.9	6.3	6.5	90	5.1	220	22.7	−1.1	1.9	1.3
Shannon	39620	52.70N	8.92W	20	101.08	82–93	−2.0	−0.6	13.9	12.0	10.4	16.3	7.2	14.0	7.6	2.9	70	4.1	110	25.7	−4.4	2.4	1.7
ISRAEL Jerusalem	401840	31.78N	35.22E	754	92.59	82–93	0.6	1.6	10.5	9.3	8.3	12.6	5.0	10.5	5.7	2.5	270	4.5	290	36.4	−0.8	3.0	1.3
Tel Aviv	401760	32.10N	34.78E	4	101.28	82–93	6.4	7.6	12.6	9.9	8.4	13.2	13.4	10.9	13.5	3.1	120	4.1	310	37.2	5.1	3.0	1.4
ITALY Bologna	161400	44.53N	11.30E	42	100.82	82–93	−5.5	−3.9	7.2	5.9	4.9	6.3	4.8	4.9	2.8	0.5	220	2.4	80	36.0	−8.0	1.9	3.3
Milan	160800	45.43N	9.28E	103	100.09	82–93	−6.0	−4.1	7.2	5.4	4.3	8.9	7.8	6.3	7.9	0.4	90	2.2	220	34.8	−7.7	3.3	2.8
Naples	162890	40.85N	14.30E	72	100.46	82–93	0.0	1.2	10.1	8.2	6.9	11.8	9.7	9.2	9.4	1.8	340	3.4	200	36.4	−2.3	2.1	1.6
Palermo	164050	38.18N	13.10E	34	100.92	82–93	6.9	7.9	13.5	11.6	9.9	14.1	13.8	12.7	13.0	4.8	210	5.1	250	37.9	3.6	2.9	2.6
Rome	162420	41.80N	12.23E	3	101.29	82–93	−0.9	0.1	12.3	10.5	9.2	12.7	8.7	10.3	10.1	3.8	60	5.2	270	34.4	−3.2	2.9	1.7
Venice	161050	45.50N	12.33E	6	101.25	82–93	−4.9	−3.1	9.8	7.5	5.9	12.5	2.2	9.4	0.5	1.8	60	2.7	160	33.6	−7.0	2.4	2.2
JAMAICA Kingston	783970	17.93N	76.78W	9	101.22	82–93	21.9	22.3	14.9	13.9	12.9	14.8	28.5	13.8	28.7	2.5	330	11.2	110	35.4	20.2	1.3	0.8
JAPAN Asahikawa	474070	43.77N	142.37E	116	99.94	82–93	−19.1	−16.4	5.6	5.1	4.4	5.4	−3.0	4.6	−3.7	0.7	80	2.9	270	32.5	−22.5	1.4	2.7
Fukuoka	478080	33.58N	130.45E	12	101.18	82–93	−1.0	0.0	9.2	8.2	7.3	9.4	4.2	8.6	5.0	3.4	10	5.0	10	35.3	−3.3	1.1	1.3
Hiroshima	477650	34.40N	132.47E	53	100.69	82–93	−1.3	−0.3	9.4	8.2	7.2	8.8	7.2	7.8	6.1	2.8	20	4.4	220	35.0	−2.8	1.8	1.5
Nagoya	476350	35.25N	136.93E	17	101.12	82–93	−3.0	−1.9	9.6	8.2	7.1	9.7	7.3	8.5	6.7	1.4	350	3.9	10	35.7	−5.1	1.5	1.3
Sapporo	474120	43.05N	141.33E	19	101.10	82–93	−11.0	−9.5	7.1	6.2	5.4	6.9	−0.2	5.7	−1.7	1.4	130	3.2	150	31.6	−13.6	1.5	2.0
Tokyo	476710	35.55N	139.78E	8	101.23	82–93	−0.8	0.2	12.3	10.8	9.5	11.9	9.9	10.5	7.4	3.3	280	6.4	10	34.4	−2.6	1.4	1.7
JORDAN Amman	402700	31.98N	35.98E	773	92.38	82–93	0.8	1.8	10.3	8.9	7.8	12.1	6.2	9.8	6.0	2.7	90	3.6	290	38.2	−3.3	1.6	6.7

Table 2.18 Heating and wind design conditions for selected locations world-wide[2] — *continued*

Station	WMO station number	Lat.(°)	Long.(°)	Elev. (m)	Std. press. (kPa)	Period	Heating DB 99.6%	Heating DB 99%	Extreme wind speed (m/s) 1%	Extreme wind speed (m/s) 2.5%	Extreme wind speed (m/s) 5%	Coldest month WS/MBD 0.4% WS	Coldest month WS/MBD 0.4% MDB	Coldest month WS/MBD 1% WS	Coldest month WS/MBD 1% MDB	MSW/MWD coincident with DB 99.6% MWS	MSW/MWD coincident with DB 99.6% MWD	MSW/MWD coincident with DB 0.4% MWS	MSW/MWD coincident with DB 0.4% MWD	Annual extreme daily Mean DB Max.	Annual extreme daily Mean DB Min.	Annual extreme daily Std. dev. DB Max.	Annual extreme daily Std. dev. DB Min.
Pavlodar	360030	52.28N	76.95E	123	99.86	82–93	−31.1	−28.5	9.6	8.5	7.5	10.1	−6.2	9.1	−6.7	2.4	60	3.2	230	36.2	−33.0	1.7	3.6
Zhambyl (Dzhambul)	383410	42.85N	71.38E	653	93.72	82–93	−20.6	−17.0	12.0	9.7	7.1	12.1	2.5	9.6	2.1	0.8	180	3.9	20	38.8	−21.4	1.7	3.9
KENYA																							
Kisumu	637080	0.10S	34.75E	1146	88.29	82–93	15.8	16.4	9.8	8.4	7.4	8.4	24.7	7.2	26.1	1.6	90	5.7	230	37.8	11.3	6.2	3.9
Nairobi	637400	1.32S	36.92E	1624	83.28	82–93	9.5	10.8	10.4	9.3	8.4	7.8	21.2	6.6	20.5	2.6	240	6.3	60	32.1	5.2	2.5	2.7
KOREA, NORTH																							
Ch'ongjin	470080	41.78N	129.82E	43	100.81	82–93	−14.0	−12.0	6.9	5.4	4.4	6.8	−8.5	5.6	−8.6	2.9	320	1.3	90	31.0	−15.9	1.7	2.8
Changjin	470310	40.37N	127.25E	1081	89.00	82–93	−28.2	−26.1	8.9	8.1	7.2	9.1	−15.8	8.2	−15.7	0.5	320	2.7	320	29.6	−31.9	2.6	1.9
P'yongyang	470580	39.03N	125.78E	38	100.87	82–93	−16.2	−14.1	6.4	5.4	4.5	6.5	−7.3	5.6	−7.3	1.1	110	1.8	270	32.9	−18.6	1.3	3.6
KOREA, SOUTH																							
Cheju	471820	33.50N	126.55E	27	101.00	82–93	−1.1	−0.1	12.2	10.7	9.6	12.4	3.0	11.2	4.6	6.2	40	6.3	230	33.8	−3.2	1.2	1.4
Inch'on	471120	37.48N	126.63E	70	100.49	82–93	−11.2	−9.5	9.9	8.5	7.3	10.1	−4.6	8.8	−5.3	4.7	320	3.1	230	33.5	−12.8	3.8	2.6
Seoul	471100	37.55N	126.80E	19	101.10	82–93	−14.1	−12.1	8.6	7.5	6.5	8.3	−4.5	7.2	−3.7	1.2	10	4.2	160	33.5	−16.8	0.9	3.4
KUWAIT																							
Kuwait	405820	29.22N	47.98E	55	100.67	82–93	3.2	5.0	11.5	10.4	9.5	10.5	16.0	9.3	15.3	1.7	300	6.1	340	49.4	0.7	1.3	1.3
KYRGYZSTAN																							
Bishkek (Frunze)	383530	42.85N	74.53E	635	93.93	82–93	−22.4	−18.8	9.2	7.7	6.5	8.3	0.0	6.8	0.5	1.2	150	3.4	220	38.4	−24.0	1.2	4.2
LATVIA																							
Riga	264220	56.97N	24.07E	3	101.29	82–93	−19.6	−15.5	10.8	9.2	8.2	10.3	2.6	9.2	2.1	2.0	40	4.1	150	29.5	−19.2	2.0	7.3
LIBYA																							
Banghazi	620530	32.08N	20.27E	132	99.75	82–93	6.7	7.5	13.5	12.2	10.3	13.1	12.8	10.4	13.7	2.3	90	6.6	350	41.1	3.9	1.0	1.6
Tripoli	620100	32.67N	13.15E	81	100.36	82–93	4.1	5.1	10.3	9.4	8.4	9.6	15.0	8.4	14.6	1.7	240	5.6	60	45.5	1.9	1.7	1.1
LIECHTENSTEIN																							
Vaduz	69900	47.13N	9.53E	463	95.89	82–93	−11.1	−8.6	10.0	7.6	6.0	9.7	9.9	8.1	9.0	1.2	180	4.5	320	31.7	−13.1	1.1	3.7
LITHUANIA																							
Vilnius	267300	54.63N	25.28E	156	99.46	82–93	−20.4	−16.7	11.3	10.1	9.0	11.2	−1.4	10.0	−1.5	2.2	70	4.7	140	30.2	−20.6	1.6	4.3
LUXEMBOURG																							
Luxembourg	65900	49.62N	6.22E	379	96.85	82–93	−10.5	−7.9	10.7	9.3	8.2	11.9	5.1	10.2	1.1	4.9	50	3.8	80	31.2	−11.3	2.0	4.0
MACEDONIA																							
Skopje	135860	41.97N	21.65E	239	98.49	82–93	−12.4	−9.3	9.0	7.7	6.2	8.3	2.2	6.7	1.1	0.4	50	2.0	270	38.0	−15.8	2.5	5.2
MADEIRA ISLANDS																							
Funchal	85210	32.68N	16.77W	55	100.67	82–93	11.9	12.8	13.5	11.9	10.4	15.0	16.3	12.8	16.5	3.6	310	4.9	30	30.7	10.0	2.9	1.0

Table 2.18 Heating and wind design conditions for selected locations world-wide[2]—continued

Station	WMO station number	Lat.(°)	Long.(°)	Elev. (m)	Std. press. (kPa)	Period	Heating DB 99.6%	Heating DB 99%	Extreme wind speed (m/s) 1%	2.5%	5%	Coldest month WS/MBD 0.4% WS	MDB	1% WS	MDB	MSW/MWD coincident with DB 99.6% MWS	MWD	0.4% MWS	MWD	Annual extreme daily Mean DB Max.	Min.	Std. dev. DB Max.	Min.
Kuala Lumpur	486470	3.12N	101.55E	22	101.06	82-93	21.6	22.0	7.0	6.1	5.3	5.9	29.5	5.1	29.4	0.5	340	3.4	270	36.6	19.9	1.7	1.9
MALI																							
Bamako	612910	12.53N	7.95W	381	96.83	82-93	15.1	16.8	8.9	7.6	6.7	8.2	25.2	7.3	25.0	3.0	40	4.0	80	43.1	9.8	3.4	3.7
MALTA																							
Luqa	165970	35.85N	14.48E	91	100.24	82-93	6.8	7.8	11.5	10.2	9.1	12.9	13.2	11.4	13.2	2.6	270	4.1	310	37.3	3.3	2.3	1.7
MAURITANIA																							
Nouadhibou	614150	20.93N	17.03W	3	101.29	82-93	12.9	13.9	14.4	13.4	12.5	13.4	17.2	12.3	17.4	6.3	360	6.3	20	38.3	8.9	1.6	3.5
MEXICO																							
Acapulco	768056	16.77N	99.75W	5	101.26	82-93	20.0	20.9	10.2	8.3	7.6	7.7	28.9	6.3	29.1	1.0	320	7.4	200	36.2	15.8	1.5	4.8
Mexico City	766790	19.43N	99.08W	2234	77.21	82-93	4.0	5.4	22.6	9.8	8.0	22.8	10.9	9.8	19.1	2.1	90	4.8	360	31.3	0.0	1.2	2.3
Veracruz	766910	19.20N	96.13W	14	101.16	82-93	14.0	15.2	20.6	15.2	12.9	20.8	20.9	15.5	20.0	2.0	330	9.6	90	38.4	9.8	2.2	2.5
MOLDOVA																							
Chisinau (Kishnev)	338150	47.02N	28.87E	180	99.18	82-93	-14.2	-12.0	6.8	5.9	5.2	7.4	-0.3	6.3	-1.9	2.1	300	2.8	200	32.9	-15.4	2.1	3.2
MONGOLIA																							
Ulaangom	442120	49.97N	92.08E	936	90.57	82-93	-40.2	-38.4	7.9	6.0	4.9	3.9	-34.0	3.2	-33.8	0.6	180	2.1	50	31.8	-41.6	2.8	2.2
MOROCCO																							
Casablanca	601550	33.57N	7.67W	62	100.58	82-93	5.7	6.7	9.4	8.0	7.1	10.4	14.4	8.4	14.5	2.3	180	3.4	360	35.2	2.8	3.3	1.3
Tanger	601010	35.73N	5.90W	21	101.07	82-93	4.8	5.9	19.3	16.7	14.2	18.5	13.1	15.0	14.0	1.8	100	10.6	80	37.2	2.1	2.1	1.8
NETHERLANDS																							
Amsterdam	62400	52.30N	4.77E	-2	101.35	82-93	-8.3	-6.0	13.8	12.1	10.7	15.5	8.4	13.7	6.7	5.0	70	4.9	70	30.0	-8.9	1.9	4.6
Eindhoven	63700	51.45N	5.42E	22	101.06	82-93	-9.0	-6.2	11.0	9.5	8.5	12.2	6.8	10.3	6.7	3.3	40	4.1	50	31.8	-10.3	2.0	4.4
Groningen	62800	53.13N	6.58E	4	101.28	82-93	-10.1	-7.6	12.4	10.9	9.6	13.8	7.1	12.2	6.5	3.0	50	3.9	100	30.8	-11.7	1.8	4.3
Rotterdam	63440	51.95N	4.45E	-4	101.37	82-93	-8.3	-5.9	13.3	11.9	10.6	14.9	6.8	13.1	6.9	4.1	50	4.4	90	30.2	-9.2	1.9	3.7
NEW ZEALAND																							
Auckland	931190	37.02S	174.80E	6	101.25	82-93	1.8	2.8	13.7	12.4	11.2	14.5	11.9	12.7	11.9	4.6	240	5.9	20	29.6	1.7	7.6	1.2
Christchurch	937800	43.48S	172.55E	34	100.92	82-93	-2.2	-1.2	12.0	10.4	9.4	10.9	8.7	9.4	8.7	0.6	280	7.0	300	33.2	-4.0	6.0	0.7
Wellington	934360	41.33S	174.80E	7	101.24	82-93	1.8	2.0	18.7	16.8	14.9	17.9	9.9	15.3	10.1	6.3	10	7.7	360	28.7	1.9	8.0	1.2
NIGER																							
Agadez	610240	16.97N	7.98E	502	95.44	82-93	10.3	11.7	14.3	12.2	10.4	15.7	21.5	14.3	21.9	3.1	100	4.8	120	45.2	4.5	2.4	4.4
NORWAY																							
Bergen	13110	60.30N	5.22E	50	100.73	82-93	-9.0	-6.8	11.7	10.2	8.9	13.3	5.1	12.1	4.3	1.5	60	3.5	240	25.7	-11.1	1.5	4.0
Oslo	13840	60.20N	11.08E	204	98.90	82-93	-22.0	-18.9	8.9	7.8	6.8	9.9	2.1	8.5	1.3	1.1	30	3.3	180	28.0	-23.5	2.5	5.7
Stavanger	14150	58.88N	5.63E	9	101.22	82-93	-10.3	-7.9	13.3	11.7	10.4	13.6	3.3	12.1	4.0	1.5	150	5.2	320	26.1	-11.8	1.9	4.1
Trondheim	12710	63.47N	10.93E	17	101.12	82-93	-18.1	-14.2	12.3	10.4	8.8	14.4	2.4	12.1	3.4	3.8	120	4.4	260	28.4	-19.1	1.8	4.5

Table 2.18 Heating and wind design conditions for selected locations world-wide[2]—*continued*

Station	WMO station number	Lat.(°)	Long.(°)	Elev. (m)	Std. press. (kPa)	Period	Heating DB 99.6%	Heating DB 99%	Extreme wind speed (m/s) 1%	Extreme wind speed (m/s) 2.5%	Extreme wind speed (m/s) 5%	Coldest month WS/MBD 0.4% WS	Coldest month WS/MBD 0.4% MDB	Coldest month WS/MBD 1% WS	Coldest month WS/MBD 1% MDB	MSW/MWD coincident with DB 99.6% MWS	MSW/MWD coincident with DB 99.6% MWD	MSW/MWD coincident with DB 0.4% MWS	MSW/MWD coincident with DB 0.4% MWD	Annual extreme daily Mean DB Max.	Annual extreme daily Mean DB Min.	Annual extreme daily Std. dev. DB Max.	Annual extreme daily Std. dev. DB Min.
OMAN																							
Masqat	412560	23.58N	58.28E	15	101.14	82–93	16.1	17.0	9.0	7.8	6.8	8.2	23.4	7.2	22.8	2.1	200	5.0	340	46.6	11.0	1.3	4.6
PANAMA																							
Panama	788060	8.92N	79.60W	16	101.13	82–93	22.8	22.9	7.5	6.5	5.7	6.8	27.0	5.3	27.8	0.8	10	5.2	10	37.0	19.7	2.5	5.4
PARAGUAY																							
Asuncion	862180	25.27S	57.63W	101	100.12	82–93	4.9	6.9	10.2	9.0	8.1	11.0	21.4	9.6	20.6	1.0	180	6.2	360	39.6	1.6	2.4	1.5
PERU																							
Lima	846280	12.00S	77.12W	13	101.17	82–93	13.9	14.5	10.6	9.1	8.0	9.4	16.9	8.2	17.3	1.9	170	5.9	170	30.5	9.9	1.2	3.4
PHILLIPINES																							
Manila	984290	14.52N	121.00E	21	101.07	82–93	20.4	21.5	18.2	16.1	14.1	17.8	28.4	15.9	28.5	0.7	90	9.5	90	37.0	6.2	1.0	7.9
POLAND																							
Gdansk	121500	54.38N	18.47E	138	99.68	82–93	−17.2	−12.9	13.7	11.7	10.1	14.2	4.9	12.1	2.5	0.8	130	5.1	10	30.2	−18.7	2.9	6.1
Krakow	125660	50.08N	19.80E	237	98.51	82–93	−18.2	−14.4	9.0	8.1	7.3	10.6	4.8	8.9	2.3	1.3	60	2.5	240	31.7	−19.6	1.8	5.2
Warsaw	123750	52.17N	20.97E	107	100.05	82–93	−17.5	−13.4	10.8	9.4	8.4	11.3	−0.4	10.0	0.9	2.1	90	3.9	150	32.7	−17.8	2.1	6.2
PORTUGAL																							
Lisbon	85360	38.78N	9.13W	123	99.86	82–93	4.0	5.1	10.2	9.1	8.2	9.9	12.8	8.4	12.9	2.0	50	4.9	330	38.6	1.4	1.7	1.4
Porto	85450	41.23N	8.68W	73	100.45	82–93	1.8	2.9	10.6	9.2	8.1	11.6	12.4	10.0	12.2	3.2	90	4.0	330	35.0	−1.0	1.3	1.4
PUERTO RICO																							
San Juan	785260	18.43N	66.00W	19	101.10	82–93	20.3	20.8	8.3	7.6	7.1	8.4	27.0	7.7	27.0	1.3	190	5.4	170	34.7	13.6	1.2	12.4
QATAR																							
Ad Dawhah	411700	25.25N	51.57E	10	101.20	82–93	10.3	11.6	11.2	9.9	8.8	9.5	18.5	8.5	18.0	3.2	290	6.9	350	46.2	6.1	1.0	3.9
ROMANIA																							
Bucharest	154200	44.50N	26.13E	91	100.24	82–93	−13.5	−10.2	9.0	7.8	6.9	8.8	−2.3	7.9	−1.7	1.3	250	2.2	230	36.1	−16.8	2.1	3.6
RUSSIA																							
Aldan	310040	58.62N	125.37E	682	93.40	82–93	−40.6	−38.1	6.3	5.4	4.8	6.3	−18.9	5.4	−18.3	0.7	200	2.3	180	29.8	−42.8	1.0	3.3
Groznyy	372350	43.35N	45.68E	162	99.39	82–93	−14.8	−12.4	10.5	9.2	8.0	11.2	−2.3	9.6	−1.9	1.3	270	4.2	90	35.6	−19.1	2.3	2.6
Moscow	276120	55.75N	37.63E	156	99.46	82–93	−23.1	−20.1	7.8	6.4	5.6	8.3	−3.5	7.3	−5.9	1.5	20	2.0	210	30.1	−25.8	1.8	3.0
Omsk	286980	54.93N	73.40E	123	99.86	82–93	−31.3	−27.9	11.2	9.4	8.2	11.7	−8.5	9.8	−8.8	3.0	210	4.5	120	33.7	−33.4	2.4	3.7
Rostov–Na–Donu	347310	47.25N	39.82E	77	100.40	82–93	−16.9	−14.9	13.7	11.9	10.2	15.8	−2.2	14.0	−6.6	4.8	80	5.1	110	34.1	−19.5	1.9	2.7
Smolensk	267810	54.75N	32.07E	241	98.46	82–93	−22.7	−19.8	7.9	6.7	5.9	7.5	0.6	6.7	−1.4	2.6	280	2.8	230	28.9	−24.6	1.8	3.5
St Petersburg	260630	59.97N	30.30E	4	101.28	82–93	−22.6	−18.9	8.3	7.0	6.2	10.3	0.0	8.4	−0.7	1.2	40	2.6	180	29.0	−24.0	2.0	4.7
Vladivostok	319600	43.12N	-131.90E	184	99.13	82–93	−22.1	−20.2	15.5	13.7	12.2	14.8	−15.7	13.5	−15.5	9.4	360	4.4	240	29.8	−24.5	1.3	3.1
Volgograd	345600	48.68N	44.35E	145	99.60	82–93	−21.2	−18.9	14.4	12.7	11.1	15.1	−6.0	13.1	−7.0	4.1	340	6.6	110	35.4	−24.1	2.1	2.8
SAMOA																							
Pago Pago	917650	14.33S	170.72W	3	101.29	82–93	22.0	23.0	11.3	10.3	9.6	11.4	25.5	10.7	25.8	2.4	310	5.1	80	33.6	14.5	1.8	8.9

Table 2.18 Heating and wind design conditions for selected locations world-wide[(2)] — *continued*

Station	WMO station number	Lat.(°)	Long.(°)	Elev. (m)	Std. press. (kPa)	Period	Heating DB 99.6%	Heating DB 99%	Extreme wind speed (m/s) 1%	2.5%	5%	Coldest month WS/MBD 0.4% WS	0.4% MDB	1% WS	1% MDB	MSW/MWD coincident with DB 99.6% MWS	99.6% MWD	0.4% MWS	0.4% MWD	Annual extreme daily Mean DB Max.	Mean DB Min.	Std. dev. DB Max.	Std. dev. DB Min.
SAUDI ARABIA																							
Jiddah	410240	21.67N	39.15E	12	101.18	82–93	14.8	15.9	10.2	9.2	8.3	10.2	25.3	9.3	24.8	2.8	30	5.9	330	45.3	12.0	2.5	1.9
Khamis Mushayt	411140	18.30N	42.80E	2054	78.96	82–93	4.3	6.1	9.2	8.2	7.2	9.7	16.1	8.9	16.1	0.8	150	4.5	30	36.2	1.8	3.8	2.3
Riyadh	404380	24.72N	46.72E	612	94.19	82–93	5.1	6.8	9.9	8.5	7.5	9.2	15.6	8.0	15.5	1.6	320	4.8	360	46.0	1.9	0.8	1.5
SENEGAL																							
Dakar	616410	14.73N	17.50W	24	101.04	82–93	16.2	16.8	10.3	9.4	8.5	10.3	20.8	9.4	20.8	4.5	360	4.3	360	37.9	12.3	2.2	4.3
SINGAPORE																							
Singapore	486980	1.37N	103.98E	16	101.13	82–93	22.8	23.1	8.0	7.2	6.3	8.2	28.5	7.6	28.7	2.0	330	4.7	30	33.9	18.3	1.1	6.7
SLOVAKIA																							
Bratislava	118160	48.20N	17.20E	130	99.77	82–93	−13.0	−10.0	9.2	8.0	7.1	10.1	1.4	8.6	2.5	1.5	50	3.5	160	34.3	−15.2	1.6	4.9
SOLVENIA																							
Ljubljana	130140	46.22N	14.48E	385	96.78	82–93	−13.0	−10.4	6.2	5.1	4.2	5.5	1.0	4.4	1.4	0.5	290	3.1	130	33.7	−16.2	2.5	3.2
SOUTH AFRICA																							
Cape Town	688160	33.98S	18.60E	42	100.82	82–93	3.6	4.9	14.5	13.0	11.8	13.7	14.1	12.4	14.2	0.1	40	5.2	170	34.5	1.3	1.6	0.8
Durban	685880	29.97S	30.95E	8	101.23	82–93	10.0	11.1	11.9	10.4	9.2	10.6	21.0	9.2	20.5	0.3	340	6.3	30	34.0	7.6	1.2	1.1
Johannesburg	683680	26.13S	28.23E	1700	82.50	82–93	1.0	2.8	9.6	8.5	7.6	8.7	12.7	7.9	12.3	4.1	210	4.1	300	31.6	−1.6	1.0	1.7
Pretoria	682620	25.73S	28.18E	1322	86.42	82–93	3.9	5.1	6.4	5.4	4.7	5.8	15.9	5.0	15.2	0.5	220	1.9	270	34.7	1.6	1.6	1.1
SPAIN																							
Barcelona	81810	41.28N	2.07E	6	101.25	82–93	0.1	1.6	9.2	7.8	6.9	9.5	10.0	8.2	9.1	3.7	350	4.0	210	32.0	−2.0	1.6	1.9
Madrid	82210	40.45N	3.55W	582	94.53	82–93	−4.5	−3.1	10.0	8.7	7.5	10.1	8.1	8.4	8.2	0.2	360	3.4	240	38.9	−6.8	1.0	1.7
Malaga	84820	36.67N	4.48W	7	101.24	82–93	3.8	4.9	12.1	10.3	9.0	14.4	12.9	12.6	13.1	4.4	320	5.6	320	39.5	0.7	1.8	1.7
Palma	83060	39.55N	2.73E	8	101.23	82–93	−0.5	0.8	10.2	9.1	8.1	10.6	12.1	9.3	12.3	0.2	60	4.6	60	37.2	−3.3	1.8	1.2
Santander	80230	43.47N	3.82W	65	100.55	82–93	2.3	4.0	10.6	8.4	7.0	12.3	10.6	10.2	10.6	2.1	110	3.1	40	33.0	1.2	2.2	1.4
Sevilla	83910	37.42N	5.90W	31	100.95	82–93	1.2	2.8	9.0	7.9	6.8	9.1	12.9	7.9	12.6	1.1	30	3.4	240	42.9	−1.2	1.5	1.7
Valencia	82840	39.50N	0.47W	62	100.58	82–93	0.9	2.2	12.2	10.1	8.4	14.6	14.1	12.0	13.5	1.9	280	5.3	120	37.6	−1.5	2.2	1.5
SWEDEN																							
Goteborg	25260	57.67N	12.30E	169	99.31	82–93	−16.2	−12.1	11.4	10.1	9.1	12.2	3.6	10.9	2.7	4.0	40	4.0	310	28.5	−16.4	2.3	5.4
Ostersund	22260	63.18N	14.50E	370	96.96	82–93	−25.8	−21.6	11.9	10.2	8.8	15.6	1.0	12.3	0.1	1.2	320	3.0	280	26.5	−27.4	1.7	5.2
Stockholm	24600	59.65N	17.95E	61	100.59	82–93	−18.9	−15.2	10.5	9.3	8.2	12.4	2.6	10.5	2.2	2.0	350	3.7	180	29.1	−18.5	1.9	5.7
SWITZERLAND																							
Geneva	67000	46.25N	6.13E	416	96.43	82–93	−8.0	−5.2	9.0	7.8	6.7	9.2	3.6	8.2	3.5	2.9	230	3.4	210	33.4	−10.0	1.1	3.8
Lugano	67700	46.00N	8.97E	276	98.05	82–93	−3.7	−2.0	7.9	6.3	5.0	7.5	7.4	5.7	7.4	1.5	360	2.8	190	32.2	−8.1	1.7	5.5
Zurich	66600	47.38N	8.57E	569	94.67	82–93	−10.4	−7.8	8.8	7.2	5.8	10.2	6.6	8.8	5.6	2.6	60	2.2	230	31.7	−11.5	1.5	4.4
SYRIA																							
Damascus	400800	33.42N	36.52E	605	94.27	82–93	−4.1	−2.2	11.4	10.1	8.9	11.3	10.2	9.6	9.3	1.3	30	3.3	210	40.8	−7.2	1.6	2.1
TAIWAN																							
Taipei	466960	25.07N	121.55E	6	101.25	82–93	8.8	10.0	9.0	8.0	7.3	8.5	17.2	7.9	17.2	1.8	110	5.1	290	36.7	5.7	1.5	2.1

Table 2.18 Heating and wind design conditions for selected locations world-wide[2] — *continued*

Station	WMO station number	Lat.(°)	Long.(°)	Elev. (m)	Std. press. (kPa)	Period	Heating DB 99.6%	Heating DB 99%	Extreme wind speed (m/s) 1%	2.5%	5%	Coldest month WS/MBD 0.4% WS	MDB	1% WS	MDB	MSW/MWD coincident with DB 99.6% MWS	MWD	0.4% MWS	MWD	Annual extreme daily Mean DB Max.	Min.	Std. dev. DB Max.	Min.
TAJIKISTAN																							
Dushanbe	388360	38.55N	68.78E	803	92.04	82-93	-7.3	-5.1	5.6	4.4	3.5	5.7	5.2	4.2	5.7	1.1	60	1.5	270	40.7	-10.6	3.5	3.2
THAILAND																							
Bangkok	484560	13.92N	100.60E	12	101.18	82-93	18.4	19.9	8.3	7.3	6.4	6.2	27.7	5.3	27.4	1.9	40	4.8	180	38.8	16.3	1.7	1.5
Tak	483760	16.88N	99.15E	124	99.84	82-93	14.0	15.5	8.1	6.3	5.2	3.6	26.8	3.1	26.8	0.0	270	2.1	270	40.9	11.3	0.7	1.6
TRINIDAD																							
Port of Spain	789700	10.62N	61.35W	15	101.14	82-93	20.1	20.9	8.4	7.8	7.2	9.0	28.9	8.2	28.8	0.1	90	5.2	90	34.4	15.8	1.1	6.5
TUNISIA																							
Tunis	607150	36.83N	10.23E	4	101.28	82-93	4.9	5.9	11.8	10.4	9.2	12.4	12.6	10.6	13.1	2.8	240	4.9	180	41.7	1.7	2.9	0.7
TURKEY																							
Ankara	171280	40.12N	32.98E	949	90.43	82-93	-16.9	-13.1	9.2	7.9	6.9	8.7	0.6	7.3	0.8	0.4	20	3.5	270	35.0	-19.0	2.7	5.3
Istanbul	170600	40.97N	28.82E	37	100.88	82-93	-3.2	-1.8	10.4	9.5	9.0	11.8	-0.1	10.1	2.8	6.2	360	5.9	60	34.9	-6.0	2.3	3.5
TURKMENISTAN																							
Dashhowuz (Tashauz)	383920	41.83N	59.98E	88	100.27	82-93	-14.9	-12.1	9.9	8.7	8.0	9.2	0.8	8.3	0.7	2.7	200	4.5	360	42.3	-18.2	1.0	3.3
UKRAINE																							
Kyyiv (Kiev)	333450	50.40N	30.45E	168	99.32	82-93	-19.0	-15.9	9.6	8.2	7.1	9.6	-8.5	8.2	-7.2	3.0	270	2.9	180	30.6	-19.4	1.9	5.1
Odesa	338370	46.48N	30.63E	35	100.91	82-93	-14.1	-11.2	12.2	10.3	9.2	13.2	-2.9	11.4	-2.6	5.0	360	4.4	180	33.2	-15.8	1.7	3.5
Poltava	335060	49.60N	34.55E	159	99.43	82-93	-19.4	-16.6	10.8	9.3	7.9	12.4	-6.6	10.4	-7.0	2.9	360	3.1	70	31.8	-21.2	1.6	4.6
UNITED ARAB EMIRATES																							
Abu Dhabi	412170	24.43N	54.65E	27	101.00	82-93	10.9	12.0	9.6	8.5	7.7	9.3	20.7	8.2	20.7	2.0	200	4.2	320	46.5	7.7	0.5	1.4
Dubai	411940	25.25N	55.33E	5	101.26	82-93	12.0	13.0	9.4	8.3	7.4	9.8	18.8	8.5	19.9	1.8	170	4.9	270	45.5	9.7	1.4	1.0
Sharjah	411960	25.33N	55.52E	33	100.93	82-93	9.2	10.7	8.6	7.5	6.7	8.9	19.8	7.5	20.4	2.1	120	4.5	270	46.2	5.3	1.2	2.3
UNITED KINGDOM																							
Aberdeen/Dyce	30910	57.20N	2.22W	65	100.55	82-93	-5.7	-3.0	12.8	11.1	9.9	14.8	4.8	13.0	5.4	1.4	360	4.7	170	25.1	-10.3	1.6	4.8
Aberporth	35020	52.13N	4.57W	134	99.73	82-93	-3.1	-1.5	18.3	15.9	14.4	20.8	6.7	18.6	7.5	6.4	90	5.6	130	26.6	-4.6	2.7	2.3
Aughton	33220	53.55N	2.92W	56	100.65	82-93	-3.5	-2.1	11.8	10.3	9.2	13.1	6.6	11.2	6.4	3.7	130	3.9	130	27.6	-4.7	2.2	2.3
Belfast	39170	54.65N	6.22W	81	100.36	82-93	-2.8	-1.4	12.7	11.0	9.7	14.5	5.9	12.8	6.9	1.8	180	3.9	110	25.0	-5.7	2.1	1.9
Birmingham	35340	52.45N	1.73W	99	100.14	82-93	-6.2	-4.2	10.2	9.0	8.1	11.7	6.5	10.3	6.1	1.9	70	3.9	100	28.9	-9.2	2.5	4.3
Bournemouth	38620	50.78N	1.83W	11	101.19	82-93	-5.4	-3.8	12.0	10.4	9.3	13.3	9.4	11.6	8.6	1.9	20	4.4	90	28.7	-8.0	2.3	2.2
Bristol	37260	51.47N	2.60W	11	101.19	82-93	-3.5	-1.7	10.5	9.2	8.0	11.9	8.4	10.2	8.3	3.4	70	3.9	90	29.2	-5.2	2.2	3.0
Cardiff	37150	51.40N	3.35W	67	100.52	82-93	-4.0	-2.2	14.0	12.3	10.9	16.9	6.9	14.6	6.6	6.2	60	4.0	60	28.5	-5.6	2.2	2.5
Edinburgh	31600	55.95N	3.35W	41	100.83	82-93	-5.9	-3.8	12.5	11.0	9.8	14.7	8.3	13.2	6.8	0.7	250	4.2	250	25.9	-9.1	2.1	3.3
Exeter	38390	50.73N	3.42W	30	100.97	82-93	-4.3	-2.7	12.2	10.5	9.3	14.7	8.3	12.7	7.5	3.0	40	4.4	150	27.9	-5.8	2.5	1.9
Glasgow	31400	55.87N	4.43W	8	101.23	82-93	-6.2	-4.2	13.4	11.8	10.3	17.6	7.8	15.0	7.0	1.1	270	4.2	230	26.8	-9.6	1.9	3.1
Jersey/Channel Islands	38950	49.22N	2.20W	84	100.32	82-93	-2.5	-0.7	14.7	12.9	11.4	17.6	8.1	14.9	8.0	5.6	100	4.6	70	28.3	-4.2	2.2	3.3

Table 2.18 Heating and wind design conditions for selected locations world-wide[2] —*continued*

Station	WMO station number	Lat.(°)	Long.(°)	Elev. (m)	Std. press. (kPa)	Period	Heating DB 99.6%	Heating DB 99%	Extreme wind speed (m/s) 1%	2.5%	5%	Coldest month WS/MBD 0.4% WS	MDB	1% WS	MDB	MSW/MWD coincident with DB 99.6% MWS	MWD	0.4% MWS	MWD	Annual extreme daily Mean DB Max.	Min.	Std. dev. DB Max.	Min.
Lerwick	30050	60.13N	1.18W	84	100.32	82–93	−2.2	−1.2	19.2	16.9	15.1	20.1	5.5	18.1	5.7	6.3	350	5.3	180	18.7	−4.4	1.9	1.1
London, Heathrow	37720	51.48N	0.45W	24	101.04	82–93	−4.0	−2.3	10.0	8.8	7.9	11.4	8.2	10.0	6.4	2.7	20	4.5	90	30.5	−6.3	2.3	2.3
Manchester	33340	53.35N	2.27W	78	100.39	82–93	−4.2	−2.7	11.2	10.0	8.9	12.7	5.5	11.2	6.3	2.5	90	3.9	130	28.3	−6.4	2.4	2.1
Nottingham	33540	53.00N	1.25W	117	99.93	82–93	−4.9	−3.2	10.7	9.5	8.4	12.4	5.0	11.0	6.2	3.5	20	3.6	210	29.1	−7.1	2.6	3.2
Plymouth	38270	50.35N	4.12W	27	101.00	82–93	−1.7	−0.3	15.2	13.4	11.8	17.6	9.5	14.9	8.8	3.7	80	4.5	80	27.0	−3.3	2.2	2.1
Stornoway	30260	58.22N	6.32W	13	101.17	82–93	−1.8	−0.4	16.7	14.5	13.0	18.8	7.2	16.4	6.1	2.8	300	4.4	160	21.3	−4.2	1.8	1.7
UNITED STATES OF AMERICA																							
Boston (MA)	725090	42.37N	71.03W	9	101.22	61–93	−13.7	−11.3	13.1	11.3	10.2	13.5	−1.3	12.2	−2.1	7.5	320	6.2	270	35.4	−17.6	1.5	2.6
Chicago (IL)	725300	41.98N	87.90W	205	98.89	61–93	−21.2	−18.1	11.7	10.4	9.2	12.0	−4.6	10.4	−4.9	4.6	270	5.4	230	35.4	−24.6	1.6	3.6
Cleveland (OH)	725240	41.42N	81.87W	245	98.42	61–93	−17.4	−14.7	11.5	10.2	9.1	12.0	−2.2	10.5	−2.5	5.5	230	5.3	230	33.9	−21.3	1.6	3.5
Dallas/Fort Worth (TX)	722590	32.90N	97.03W	182	99.16	82–93	−8.1	−4.4	11.4	10.3	9.4	11.8	7.7	10.5	8.1	5.6	350	4.6	170	39.4	−10.0	1.7	4.6
Denver (CO)	724699	39.75N	104.87W	1625	83.26	82–93	−19.7	−16.1	10.4	8.8	7.5	11.1	4.1	9.5	4.4	2.7	180	4.1	160	36.3	−23.7	1.3	3.9
Fairbanks (AK)	702610	64.82N	147.87W	138	99.68	61–93	−44.0	−40.7	7.8	6.7	5.8	7.1	−11.6	5.4	−11.9	0.7	10	3.7	220	30.3	−44.4	2.1	4.3
Honolulu (HI)	911820	21.35N	157.93W	5	101.26	61–93	16.0	17.2	10.4	9.5	8.7	10.4	23.5	9.3	23.9	2.3	320	6.6	60	32.5	14.2	1.1	1.2
Las Vegas (NV)	723860	36.08N	115.17W	664	93.60	61–93	−2.7	−0.9	13.3	11.5	10.2	11.2	8.9	9.9	9.6	3.3	250	5.5	230	44.1	−6.3	1.2	2.6
Los Angeles (CA)	722950	33.93N	118.40W	32	100.94	61–93	6.2	7.4	9.2	7.9	7.1	8.9	13.6	7.4	13.3	2.8	70	4.4	250	35.9	3.5	2.8	1.7
Memphis (TN)	723340	35.05N	90.00W	87	100.28	61–93	−8.9	−6.3	9.8	8.6	7.8	10.0	5.3	8.9	5.6	4.4	20	4.1	240	36.9	−12.6	1.6	4.0
Miami (FL)	722020	25.82N	80.28W	4	101.28	61–93	7.6	9.8	10.1	9.0	8.2	9.6	19.9	8.8	20.4	4.5	340	5.0	150	34.4	3.6	1.2	2.8
Minneapolis–St. Paul (MN)	726580	44.88N	93.22W	255	98.30	61–93	−26.5	−23.7	11.1	9.9	8.9	11.2	−11.2	9.9	−10.3	4.2	300	6.3	180	35.8	−30.2	1.9	3.0
Montgomery (AL)	722260	32.30N	86.40W	62	100.58	61–93	−4.7	−2.8	8.8	7.7	6.7	9.1	6.9	8.1	7.4	3.1	360	3.5	270	36.8	−9.6	1.6	3.5
New Orleans (LA)	722310	29.98N	90.25W	9	101.22	61–93	−1.3	0.8	9.4	8.3	7.5	9.4	8.8	8.4	9.2	3.3	340	3.5	360	35.6	−4.8	1.1	2.9
New York (NY)	744860	40.65N	73.78W	7	101.24	61–93	−11.4	−9.2	12.1	10.5	9.5	13.2	−1.4	11.9	−2.3	7.6	320	5.9	230	35.3	−14.7	1.4	2.6
Oklahoma City (OK)	723530	35.40N	97.60W	397	96.65	61–93	−12.6	−9.6	12.9	11.3	10.3	13.0	0.4	11.5	2.8	6.9	360	5.9	180	39.3	−15.7	1.9	2.7
Philadelphia (PA)	724080	39.88N	75.25W	9	101.22	61–93	−11.9	−9.7	10.9	9.6	8.5	11.7	−0.8	10.1	−1.4	5.2	290	4.8	230	35.7	−15.3	1.6	3.1
Phoenix (AZ)	722780	33.43N	112.02W	337	97.34	61–93	1.2	3.0	8.5	7.1	6.1	7.6	15.1	6.4	14.5	2.4	90	4.2	270	45.4	−1.2	1.2	2.6
Richmond (VA)	724010	37.50N	77.33W	54	100.68	61–93	−10.1	−7.6	8.8	7.9	7.0	9.2	4.2	8.2	4.1	3.1	340	4.4	230	36.4	−14.4	1.4	3.2
Sacramento (CA)	724839	38.70N	121.58W	7	101.24	61–93	−0.8	0.6	10.0	8.6	7.7	10.1	10.5	8.8	9.7	1.3	340	3.8	220	41.6	−2.9	3.7	1.7
Salt Lake City (UT)	725720	40.78N	111.97W	1288	86.78	61–93	−14.7	−11.7	12.0	10.1	8.8	11.9	5.7	9.6	4.2	2.9	160	5.0	340	37.9	−19.2	1.1	3.7
San Francisco (CA)	724940	37.62N	122.38W	5	101.26	61–93	2.7	3.9	13.0	11.5	10.4	11.9	11.4	9.9	11.2	2.4	160	5.6	300	34.7	0.8	2.4	1.7
Seattle (WA)	727930	47.45N	122.30W	137	99.69	61–93	−4.8	−2.2	9.8	8.6	7.6	10.6	6.9	9.5	6.7	4.4	10	4.5	350	33.4	−7.4	2.0	3.8
St. Louis (MO)	724340	38.75N	90.37W	172	99.28	61–93	−16.8	−13.6	11.4	10.0	8.8	11.7	−3.4	10.3	−2.8	5.4	290	4.8	240	37.4	−20.7	1.9	3.4
Washington DC	724050	38.85	77.03	20	101.08	8293	−9.3	−6.5	10.1	8.9	8.1	10.7	1.2	9.5	1.9	5.0	340	4.8	170	37.0	−13.5	1.4	3.8
URUGUAY																							
Montevideo	865800	34.83S	56.00W	32	100.94	82–93	1.8	3.1	14.5	12.5	10.7	13.5	11.4	12.0	12.8	3.5	330	6.4	360	36.1	−0.4	1.7	1.2
UZBEKISTAN																							
Tashkent	384570	41.27N	69.27E	489	95.59	82–93	−10.3	−7.8	6.0	5.1	4.4	6.1	7.0	5.1	5.7	0.9	90	1.7	300	40.7	−12.2	1.2	3.0
VANUATU																							
Luganville	915540	15.52S	167.22E	44	100.80	82–93	18.8	19.9	8.3	7.4	6.4	8.0	24.8	7.3	25.1	0.7	290	4.0	100	31.6	16.5	0.9	1.7

Table 2.18 Heating and wind design conditions for selected locations world-wide[2] — *continued*

Station	WMO station number	Lat.(°)	Long.(°)	Elev. (m)	Std. press. (kPa)	Period	Heating DB		Extreme wind speed (m/s)			Coldest month WS/MBD				MSW/MWD coincident with DB				Annual extreme daily			
							99.6%	99%	1%	2.5%	5%	0.4%		1%		99.6%		0.4%		Mean DB		Std. dev. DB	
												WS	MDB	WS	MDB	MWS	MWD	MWS	MWD	Max.	Min.	Max.	Min.
VENEZUELA Caracas	804150	10.60N	66.98W	48	100.75	82–93	20.9	21.6	5.5	4.7	4.1	5.4	27.2	4.8	27.4	0.3	140	2.7	340	36.1	15.2	1.2	7.8
VIETNAM Ho Chi Minh City (Saigon)	489000	10.82N	106.67E	19	101.10	82–93	20.0	21.0	17.2	11.4	7.7	11.2	28.2	7.3	27.5	1.9	360	4.1	160	38.5	13.1	2.8	11.4
YUGOSLAVIA Belgrade	132720	44.82N	20.28E	99	100.14	82–93	−11.5	−8.9	11.1	9.1	7.8	10.2	−0.4	8.9	0.1	2.5	10	2.7	120	36.2	−14.6	2.2	4.6
ZIMBABWE Harare	677750	17.92S	31.13E	1503	84.52	82–93	7.0	8.0	8.9	7.9	7.1	8.4	15.6	7.4	15.8	2.5	120	4.5	60	32.4	4.3	1.8	1.7

2.6.2 Cooling design temperatures (world-wide)

Cooling design temperatures for selected world-wide locations are given in Table 2.19. The information provided is as follows:

— Column 1: name of observing station (see Table 2.18 for WMO station number, latitude, longitude, elevation, standard pressure at stated elevation and the period analysed).

— Columns 2–7: dry bulb temperature (DB) corresponding to 0.4%, 1.0% and 2.0% annual cumulative frequency of occurrence and the mean coincident wet bulb temperature (warm) (MWB).

— Columns 8–13: wet bulb temperature (WB) corresponding to 0.4%, 1.0% and 2.0% annual cumulative frequency of occurrence and the mean coincident dry bulb temperature (MDB).

— Columns 14–22: dew point temperature (DP) corresponding to 0.4%, 1.0% and 2.0% annual cumulative frequency of occurrence and the mean coincident dry bulb temperature (MDB) and humidity ratio (HR). (HR is calculated for dew point temperature at standard atmospheric pressure at the elevation of the station, see Table 2.18.)

— Column 23: mean daily range of dry bulb temperature (i.e. mean of difference between daily maximum and daily minimum temperatures for the month with the highest average dry bulb temperature).

Values of ambient dry bulb temperature and wind speed corresponding to the various annual percentiles represent the value that is exceeded on average by the indicated percentage of the total number of hours in the year (8760). The 0.4%, 1.0% and 2.0% values are exceeded, on average, for 35, 88 and 175 hours, respectively. Mean coincident values are the average of the stated weather element occurring concurrently with the corresponding design value.

The design conditions given in the table explicitly represent the same annual probability of occurrence in any location, regardless of country or general climatic conditions.

The 0.4%, 1% and 2% dry bulb and mean coincident wet bulb temperatures in columns 2–7 often represent conditions. on hot, mostly sunny days. They are useful for cooling applications, especially air conditioning. Design conditions based on wet bulb temperatures (columns 8–13) represent extremes of the total sensible plus latent heat of outdoor air. This information is useful for cooling towers, evaporative coolers, and fresh air ventilation systems design.

The design conditions based on dew-point temperatures (columns 14–22) are directly related to extremes of humidity ratio, which represent peak moisture loads from the weather. Extreme dew-point conditions may occur on days with moderate dry bulb temperatures resulting in high relative humidity. The values are especially useful for applications involving humidity control, such as desiccant cooling and dehumidification, cooling-based dehumidification, and fresh air ventilation systems.

The humidity ratio values (columns 15, 18 and 21) correspond to the combination of dew-point temperature and the mean coincident dry bulb temperature calculated at the standard pressure for the elevation of the location (given in Table 2.18).

Table 2.19 Cooling and dehumidification design conditions for selected locations world-wide[2]

Station	Cooling dry-bulb (DB) and mean wet-bulb (MWB) 0.4% DB	MWB	1% DB	MWB	2% DB	MWB	Wet-bulb (WB) and mean dry-bulb (MDB) 0.4% WB	MDB	1% WB	MDB	2% WB	MDB	Dew-point (DP), humidity ratio (HR) and mean dry-bulb (MDB) 0.4% DP	HR	MDB	1% DP	HR	MDB	2% DP	HR	MDB	Range of daily mean dry-bulb
ALGERIA																						
Algiers	35.2	21.7	33.2	21.8	31.7	22.0	25.0	30.3	24.4	29.4	23.8	28.6	23.5	18.4	27.5	23.0	17.8	27.1	22.2	16.9	26.6	11.6
Constantine	37.5	18.9	35.8	19.3	34.0	19.1	21.8	31.3	21.0	30.6	20.3	29.8	19.1	15.1	24.7	18.2	14.3	24.4	17.2	13.4	23.8	15.0
ARGENTINA																						
Buenos Aires	33.9	22.8	32.1	22.3	30.7	21.6	24.7	30.1	23.8	28.9	23.1	28.2	23.2	18.0	26.9	22.4	17.1	26.2	21.7	16.4	25.3	12.0
San Juan	37.6	20.8	36.1	20.1	34.7	19.9	23.0	33.8	22.2	32.6	21.5	31.7	19.9	15.7	27.9	18.8	14.6	27.5	18.0	13.9	27.0	13.2
ARMENIA																						
Yerevan	35.6	20.5	34.2	20.4	32.8	19.6	22.2	33.0	21.1	32.5	20.3	31.3	18.4	14.8	29.5	17.1	13.6	27.6	16.1	12.8	27.0	13.6
ASCENSION ISLAND																						
Georgetown	30.0	24.1	29.6	23.9	29.2	23.7	25.0	28.7	24.6	28.4	24.3	28.0	23.9	18.9	27.3	23.5	18.5	26.9	23.1	18.0	26.9	4.3
AUSTRALIA																						
Adelaide	35.2	18.0	33.1	17.8	31.1	17.3	21.0	28.5	20.0	27.4	19.1	26.8	19.0	13.8	23.4	17.7	12.7	22.7	16.3	11.6	22.3	10.8
Brisbane	31.2	22.5	30.0	22.4	29.1	22.1	25.1	28.7	24.4	27.9	23.7	27.3	24.1	19.0	27.3	23.2	18.0	26.5	22.6	17.3	26.1	7.6
Canberra	32.5	17.1	30.3	17.1	28.3	16.6	19.7	26.2	18.8	25.6	18.1	24.9	17.8	13.7	21.7	16.7	12.8	21.2	15.8	12.0	20.0	13.3
Darwin	34.0	23.8	33.2	24.2	33.0	24.4	27.7	31.4	27.3	31.0	27.0	30.8	27.0	22.8	30.2	26.2	21.7	29.4	26.1	21.6	29.2	7.2
Perth	37.2	19.2	35.1	19.0	32.9	18.6	22.0	30.5	21.2	29.7	20.5	28.2	19.6	14.4	24.1	18.7	13.6	23.4	18.0	13.0	23.1	12.5
Sydney	32.2	20.0	29.5	19.7	27.9	20.1	23.0	28.0	22.3	26.2	21.7	25.3	21.7	16.4	24.8	21.1	15.8	24.3	20.6	15.3	23.9	6.7
AUSTRIA																						
Innsbruck	29.2	18.1	27.8	17.5	26.1	16.6	19.1	27.1	18.3	25.5	17.6	23.6	16.9	13.0	20.3	16.1	12.3	19.5	15.2	11.6	19.4	11.4
Salzburg	29.8	19.3	27.9	18.5	26.1	17.5	19.9	28.0	19.1	26.9	18.2	24.8	17.2	13.0	22.4	16.2	12.2	21.4	15.8	11.8	21.3	10.5
Vienna	30.1	20.1	28.5	19.3	26.8	18.7	21.1	28.4	20.3	26.8	19.6	25.0	18.9	14.0	23.3	18.2	13.4	23.0	17.5	12.8	22.4	9.3
AZORES																						
Lajes	26.5	21.9	25.8	21.4	24.9	20.8	22.5	25.4	22.0	24.9	21.5	23.7	21.6	16.4	24.0	21.0	15.8	23.7	20.3	15.1	23.3	6.3
BAHAMAS																						
Nassau	33.0	25.9	32.2	25.7	31.9	25.6	27.2	30.6	26.7	30.4	26.4	30.3	26.2	21.6	28.6	26.0	21.4	28.5	25.4	20.6	28.3	6.9
BAHRAIN																						
Al-Manamah	39.2	25.1	38.2	25.5	37.2	26.2	30.7	34.7	30.2	34.2	29.7	33.8	29.9	27.0	33.7	29.1	25.8	33.4	28.7	25.2	33.4	6.9
BELARUS																						
Babruysk (Bobruysk)	27.8	18.6	26.1	18.4	24.5	17.2	20.1	25.8	19.2	24.4	18.2	23.1	18.3	13.5	23.0	17.2	12.5	21.4	16.3	11.8	20.4	11.5
Minsk	27.3	18.3	25.8	18.0	24.1	16.9	19.6	25.4	18.7	24.1	17.8	22.8	17.6	13.0	21.7	16.7	12.2	20.7	15.8	11.5	20.4	9.6
BELGIUM																						
Antwerp	28.0	20.2	26.3	19.1	24.6	18.4	21.1	26.5	20.1	25.2	19.0	23.4	19.1	13.9	24.0	18.1	13.0	22.6	17.1	12.2	21.4	9.0
Brussels	27.9	19.6	26.2	18.9	24.5	18.2	20.7	26.5	19.8	24.9	18.7	23.3	18.7	13.6	23.2	17.8	12.9	22.2	16.9	12.1	21.4	9.4
Oostende	25.2	18.9	23.0	18.2	21.3	17.4	19.7	23.6	18.8	22.2	18.0	20.9	18.2	13.1	21.4	17.5	12.5	20.7	16.7	11.9	19.6	7.8
BENIN																						
Parakou	36.8	21.6	36.0	21.4	35.2	21.4	25.7	32.8	25.3	32.1	25.0	31.5	23.9	19.7	29.1	23.6	19.3	28.8	23.2	18.9	28.4	11.5

Note: WMO station number, latitude, longitude, elevation, standard atmospheric pressure and period analysed are given in Table 2.18

Table 2.19 Cooling and dehumidification design conditions for selected locations world-wide[2]—*continued*

Station	Cooling dry-bulb (DB) and mean wet-bulb (MWB)						Wet-bulb (WB) and mean dry-bulb (MDB)						Dew-point (DP), humidity ratio (HR) and mean dry-bulb (MDB)									Range of daily mean dry-bulb
	0.4%		1%		2%		0.4%		1%		2%		0.4%			1%			2%			
	DB	MWB	DB	MWB	DB	MWB	WB	MDB	WB	MDB	WB	MDB	DP	HR	MDB	DP	HR	MDB	DP	HR	MDB	
BERMUDA																						
Hamilton	31.2	25.5	30.9	25.4	30.1	25.0	26.8	29.7	26.4	29.3	26.0	29.0	26.1	21.5	28.9	25.4	20.6	28.5	25.0	20.1	28.1	4.6
BOLIVIA																						
La Paz	17.3	6.6	16.7	6.4	15.9	6.1	9.2	14.2	8.7	13.8	8.2	13.1	7.2	10.4	10.6	6.8	10.2	10.0	6.2	9.7	9.4	12.6
BOSNIA-HERZEGOVINA																						
Banja Luka	33.1	20.4	31.0	20.3	29.2	19.6	22.3	29.2	21.4	28.4	20.4	27.4	20.1	15.1	26.1	19.0	14.1	24.3	18.2	13.4	23.0	12.7
BRAZIL																						
Brasilia	31.8	18.3	30.9	18.2	30.0	18.5	21.7	26.6	21.3	26.2	21.0	26.1	20.4	17.2	22.6	20.1	16.9	22.3	19.9	16.6	22.1	13.0
Rio De Janeiro	38.9	26.1	37.1	25.2	35.9	24.9	27.7	35.2	27.0	34.2	26.4	32.6	26.1	21.5	30.1	25.2	20.3	28.9	25.0	20.1	28.9	10.7
Sao Paulo	31.9	20.3	30.9	20.3	29.9	20.4	22.9	27.4	22.3	27.1	21.9	26.8	21.8	18.2	24.9	21.1	17.4	24.4	20.8	17.1	23.8	8.3
BULGARIA																						
Sofia	31.3	18.7	29.5	18.4	27.9	17.7	20.1	28.2	19.2	27.6	18.5	26.4	17.1	13.1	23.5	16.2	12.4	22.5	15.5	11.8	22.0	12.1
BRUNEI																						
Brunei	33.6	26.1	33.1	26.3	32.6	26.3	27.7	31.4	27.5	31.2	27.2	30.9	26.9	22.6	30.0	26.5	22.1	29.7	26.2	21.7	29.4	7.8
CANADA																						
Calgary	28.5	15.4	26.4	14.7	24.7	14.1	16.9	25.3	15.9	24.1	15.0	23.0	13.9	11.3	19.6	12.9	10.6	18.4	11.7	9.8	17.8	12.2
Edmonton	27.6	17.1	25.6	16.5	24.0	15.7	18.9	25.0	17.7	23.9	16.5	22.5	16.4	12.7	22.5	15.2	11.8	20.7	14.1	11.0	19.1	12.1
Halifax	26.9	19.7	25.3	18.8	23.8	17.9	21.2	24.9	20.3	23.3	19.3	22.0	20.1	15.1	22.7	19.2	14.2	21.6	18.4	13.5	20.5	9.3
Montreal	29.5	21.9	28.1	20.9	26.5	20.1	23.1	27.9	22.0	26.5	21.1	25.2	21.3	16.0	26.1	20.4	15.1	24.9	19.6	14.4	23.8	9.8
Ottawa	30.1	21.3	28.5	20.5	26.8	19.5	22.8	28.0	21.8	26.4	20.8	25.3	21.1	16.0	25.5	20.2	15.1	24.6	19.2	14.2	23.7	10.3
Quebec	28.7	20.9	26.9	19.9	25.3	18.8	22.5	26.7	21.2	25.2	20.2	23.8	21.0	15.8	24.9	19.9	14.7	23.6	18.7	13.6	22.5	10.6
Toronto	30.3	21.8	28.7	20.9	27.1	20.1	23.3	28.5	22.2	26.9	21.3	25.5	21.6	16.6	26.1	20.7	15.7	25.0	19.8	14.8	23.8	11.2
Vancouver	24.6	18.2	23.2	17.6	21.8	16.9	18.8	23.8	18.0	22.4	17.2	21.3	16.6	11.8	21.7	15.9	11.3	20.9	15.3	10.9	19.9	7.8
Winnipeg	30.8	19.9	29.0	19.6	27.0	18.7	22.1	28.0	20.9	26.8	19.8	25.3	20.2	15.3	25.4	18.9	14.1	23.9	17.9	13.2	22.9	11.4
CANARY ISLANDS																						
Las Palmas	30.2	19.9	28.8	20.1	27.2	20.4	24.7	26.6	23.7	25.8	23.0	25.5	24.0	18.9	25.9	23.0	17.8	25.2	22.1	16.8	24.6	5.5
Santa Cruz De Tenerife	32.9	20.1	30.5	20.1	28.9	20.4	23.8	27.9	23.2	27.2	22.6	26.7	22.2	17.0	26.4	21.9	16.7	26.2	21.1	15.9	25.4	6.9
CAPE VERDE																						
Sal Island	30.1	23.9	29.6	24.0	29.0	23.7	25.7	28.0	25.2	27.6	24.8	27.3	25.0	20.2	27.0	24.4	19.5	27.0	24.0	19.0	26.5	4.9
CHILE																						
Concepcion	24.3	17.3	23.2	16.7	22.2	16.3	18.5	22.5	17.7	21.7	17.1	21.0	17.0	12.2	19.7	16.1	11.5	18.9	15.7	11.2	18.6	11.2
Santiago	31.9	18.4	30.9	18.2	29.9	18.0	19.9	29.3	19.2	28.8	18.7	28.0	16.1	12.1	24.3	15.4	11.6	23.8	14.9	11.2	23.2	17.5
CHINA																						
Beijing	34.2	21.9	32.9	21.8	31.5	21.9	26.2	30.5	25.4	29.0	24.7	28.3	25.1	20.3	28.4	24.2	19.2	27.6	23.6	18.5	27.1	8.7
Dinghai	32.2	27.2	31.1	26.7	30.1	26.2	27.6	31.5	27.1	30.6	26.6	29.6	26.6	22.3	30.4	26.1	21.6	29.5	25.7	21.1	28.7	5.4
Guangzhou	34.6	26.4	33.9	26.3	33.0	26.2	27.7	31.9	27.4	31.5	27.1	31.1	26.7	22.3	29.5	26.4	21.9	29.1	26.1	21.5	29.0	6.9
Hangzhou	35.8	27.2	34.4	26.6	33.1	26.6	28.2	33.4	27.6	32.8	27.0	31.9	27.0	22.8	31.4	26.2	21.7	30.0	25.9	21.3	29.7	7.5

Note: WMO station number, latitude, longitude, elevation, standard atmospheric pressure and period analysed are given in Table 2.18

Table 2.19 Cooling and dehumidification design conditions for selected locations world-wide[2] — *continued*

Station	Cooling dry-bulb (DB) and mean wet-bulb (MWB) 0.4% DB	MWB	1% DB	MWB	2% DB	MWB	Wet-bulb (WB) and mean dry-bulb (MDB) 0.4% WB	MDB	1% WB	MDB	2% WB	MDB	Dew-point (DP), humidity ratio (HR) and mean dry-bulb (MDB) 0.4% DP	HR	MDB	1% DP	HR	MDB	2% DP	HR	MDB	Range of daily mean dry-bulb
Jinan	34.8	22.9	33.5	23.1	32.3	22.9	26.7	31.5	26.1	30.8	25.4	29.6	25.4	20.7	29.5	24.7	19.9	29.0	24.1	19.1	28.3	7.3
Kowloon	33.2	26.1	32.8	26.1	32.0	26.1	27.6	31.1	27.3	30.7	27.0	30.6	27.0	22.8	29.7	26.2	21.7	29.3	26.1	21.5	29.3	4.5
Macau	33.1	27.3	32.4	27.2	31.7	26.9	28.1	32.0	27.7	31.3	27.4	30.9	27.1	23.0	30.4	26.7	22.4	30.0	26.6	22.3	29.8	4.2
Nanjing	34.6	27.1	33.2	26.8	31.9	26.0	28.1	32.4	27.6	31.9	27.1	31.1	27.1	22.9	30.8	26.5	22.0	30.3	26.0	21.4	29.8	6.2
Shanghai	34.4	27.4	33.1	27.4	31.8	26.7	28.4	33.0	27.7	31.9	27.1	31.0	27.2	23.0	31.0	26.8	22.4	30.6	26.1	21.5	29.6	6.4
Shenyang	31.1	23.2	29.9	22.7	28.8	22.0	25.3	29.6	24.5	28.3	23.8	27.1	24.0	19.0	27.9	23.4	18.3	27.1	22.6	17.4	26.3	8.0
Tianjin	33.5	23.1	32.2	23.0	31.1	22.8	26.6	30.1	25.8	29.5	25.2	28.7	25.5	20.7	29.0	24.8	19.8	28.2	24.1	19.0	27.7	7.2
Wuhan	35.1	27.3	34.0	26.9	32.9	26.5	28.3	32.9	27.9	32.5	27.4	31.8	27.2	23.0	30.8	26.7	22.3	30.7	26.2	21.7	30.4	6.1
Zhanjiang	33.9	26.5	33.1	26.6	32.3	26.6	28.0	31.4	27.7	30.9	27.4	30.6	27.2	23.1	29.8	26.9	22.6	29.5	26.6	22.2	29.4	4.7
COLOMBIA																						
Bogota	21.1	13.3	20.2	13.5	20.0	13.5	15.3	18.9	14.9	18.6	14.6	18.2	14.1	13.8	17.5	13.8	13.5	17.0	13.1	12.9	16.5	11.5
CROATIA																						
Split	32.8	21.2	31.7	20.4	30.2	20.0	22.5	29.9	21.7	29.3	21.1	28.7	20.1	14.8	25.9	19.1	13.9	25.3	18.2	13.1	24.7	10.3
Zagreb	31.1	21.3	29.5	21.0	28.1	20.1	22.5	29.4	21.6	28.1	20.8	26.9	20.2	15.1	25.6	19.2	14.2	24.9	18.5	13.5	23.6	12.3
CUBA																						
Guantanamo	34.2	25.8	34.0	25.7	33.2	25.4	27.6	32.8	27.1	32.6	26.7	32.3	26.1	21.5	31.5	25.6	20.9	31.3	25.1	20.2	30.8	8.5
CYPRUS																						
Akrotiri	32.7	21.7	31.4	22.2	30.3	22.6	25.6	29.2	25.1	28.7	24.6	28.1	24.6	19.6	27.7	24.0	18.9	27.6	23.4	18.2	27.3	7.2
Larnaca	33.8	21.7	32.7	22.1	31.6	22.4	25.7	29.9	25.1	29.5	24.6	29.1	24.2	19.1	28.5	23.8	18.7	28.2	23.1	17.9	27.7	9.9
CZECH REPUBLIC																						
Brno	29.5	19.1	27.7	18.5	26.1	17.6	20.2	27.5	19.3	26.2	18.5	24.3	17.7	13.1	23.2	17.0	12.5	21.9	16.2	11.9	21.3	10.8
Prague	28.8	18.4	26.8	17.8	25.0	17.1	19.7	26.2	18.7	24.7	17.8	23.4	17.3	12.9	22.1	16.4	12.2	20.6	15.8	11.7	20.3	11.1
DENMARK																						
Alborg	25.0	17.1	23.1	16.3	21.5	15.5	18.1	23.7	17.2	21.8	16.2	20.3	16.0	11.4	20.2	15.1	10.7	19.3	14.2	10.1	18.1	8.4
Copenhagen	25.0	17.2	23.2	16.4	21.9	15.8	18.2	23.2	17.4	21.7	16.5	20.4	16.2	11.5	20.0	15.5	11.0	19.4	14.8	10.5	18.9	8.1
ECUADOR																						
Quito	22.0	12.5	21.2	12.3	20.8	12.1	14.6	19.4	14.1	19.0	13.7	18.4	13.0	13.3	16.1	12.2	12.6	15.1	12.1	12.5	14.8	10.2
EGYPT																						
Alexandria	32.5	21.6	30.9	22.9	29.9	23.1	25.0	29.7	24.4	28.8	24.0	28.5	23.5	18.3	27.9	23.0	17.8	27.5	22.5	17.2	27.4	6.3
Cairo	38.0	20.3	36.2	20.5	35.1	20.8	24.1	31.5	23.6	30.4	23.1	30.1	22.2	17.0	26.0	21.9	16.7	25.8	21.2	16.0	25.6	13.3
ESTONIA																						
Tallinn	24.9	17.6	23.3	16.9	21.6	16.0	19.0	23.0	17.9	21.9	16.9	20.6	17.4	12.5	20.8	16.3	11.7	20.0	15.2	10.8	18.7	8.2
FAEROE ISLANDS																						
Torshavn	14.3	12.4	13.5	11.8	12.7	11.5	13.0	13.9	12.4	13.1	11.9	12.5	12.6	9.1	13.3	12.0	8.8	12.7	11.5	8.5	12.2	3.0
FIJI																						
Nadi	32.3	25.0	31.7	25.0	31.2	24.8	26.6	30.4	26.2	30.0	25.9	29.7	25.6	20.9	28.5	25.2	20.4	28.2	24.9	20.0	28.0	7.9

Note: WMO station number, latitude, longitude, elevation, standard atmospheric pressure and period analysed are given in Table 2.18

Table 2.19 Cooling and dehumidification design conditions for selected locations world-wide[2] — *continued*

Station	Cooling dry-bulb (DB) and mean wet-bulb (MWB)						Wet-bulb (WB) and mean dry-bulb (MDB)						Dew-point (DP), humidity ratio (HR) and mean dry-bulb (MDB)									Range of daily mean dry-bulb
	0.4%		1%		2%		0.4%		1%		2%		0.4%			1%			2%			
	DB	MWB	DB	MWB	DB	MWB	WB	MDB	WB	MDB	WB	MDB	DP	HR	MDB	DP	HR	MDB	DP	HR	MDB	
FINLAND																						
Helsinki	25.9	17.6	24.1	16.3	22.7	15.9	18.7	23.6	17.6	22.4	16.7	20.8	17.0	12.2	19.6	15.9	11.4	19.2	14.9	10.7	18.4	9.8
Pello	24.2	16.0	22.2	15.4	20.3	14.3	17.4	22.0	16.2	20.4	15.1	18.8	15.5	11.1	19.1	14.4	10.3	17.9	13.3	9.6	16.8	8.8
FRANCE																						
Bordeaux	32.1	21.2	30.0	20.8	28.1	20.0	23.0	29.6	21.8	27.5	20.9	26.1	21.1	15.9	25.9	20.0	14.8	24.0	19.1	14.0	23.1	11.3
Brest	25.8	18.5	23.5	18.3	21.7	17.2	19.7	24.4	18.6	22.1	17.7	20.1	18.2	13.3	20.6	17.5	12.7	19.5	16.9	12.2	18.9	7.6
Lyon	32.0	20.7	30.0	20.3	28.1	19.6	22.2	29.1	21.1	27.9	20.2	26.5	19.9	15.0	25.7	18.9	14.1	24.1	18.0	13.3	22.9	11.9
Marseille	32.0	21.6	30.7	21.2	29.2	20.6	23.7	28.7	22.8	27.9	21.9	27.0	22.1	16.8	26.2	21.1	15.8	25.8	20.1	14.9	24.9	10.4
Nice	29.1	23.2	28.1	22.8	27.2	22.5	25.3	27.7	24.5	26.9	23.7	26.2	24.4	19.4	27.0	23.8	18.7	26.6	22.8	17.5	25.9	6.8
Paris, Orly	29.9	20.3	28.0	19.4	26.1	18.6	21.4	27.9	20.3	25.9	19.5	24.4	19.2	14.1	23.7	18.2	13.3	22.9	17.4	12.6	21.9	10.2
Strasbourg	30.5	20.9	28.8	20.0	27.0	19.2	21.9	27.9	20.9	26.8	20.0	25.5	19.9	14.9	24.7	18.9	14.0	23.8	18.0	13.2	22.5	11.5
Toulouse	33.0	21.1	31.0	20.7	29.1	20.0	23.0	30.2	21.9	28.0	21.0	27.2	20.9	15.8	26.3	19.9	14.9	25.2	19.0	14.0	23.8	11.9
GERMANY																						
Berlin	29.9	18.8	27.9	18.1	26.1	17.5	20.1	27.0	19.2	25.9	18.3	24.1	17.9	12.9	22.3	16.9	12.1	21.2	15.9	11.4	20.8	9.3
Dresden	29.7	18.8	27.5	18.2	25.8	17.4	20.1	27.4	19.1	25.3	18.2	24.2	17.6	13.0	22.4	16.8	12.3	21.6	15.9	11.6	20.5	9.8
Dusseldorf	29.6	19.6	27.8	18.6	26.0	17.8	20.5	27.4	19.6	26.0	18.7	24.3	18.2	13.2	22.9	17.4	12.5	22.0	16.5	11.8	21.4	9.7
Frankfurt	30.3	19.4	28.5	18.8	26.7	17.9	20.5	27.8	19.6	26.6	18.7	24.8	18.2	13.3	22.6	17.4	12.6	21.5	16.5	11.9	20.9	11.0
Hamburg	27.8	18.9	25.9	18.0	24.0	17.1	19.9	25.7	18.8	24.3	17.9	22.6	17.8	12.8	22.1	16.9	12.1	21.0	16.0	11.4	20.1	9.3
Hannover	28.8	19.3	26.9	18.4	25.1	17.6	20.3	26.5	19.3	25.3	18.4	23.4	18.3	13.3	22.5	17.3	12.4	21.4	16.3	11.7	20.8	10.4
Koln	29.6	19.2	27.7	18.3	25.9	17.5	20.3	27.1	19.4	25.9	18.6	24.4	18.1	13.2	22.7	17.2	12.4	21.5	16.4	11.8	20.8	11.0
Leipzig	29.7	19.0	27.6	18.4	25.8	17.6	20.2	27.0	19.2	25.7	18.4	24.3	17.8	13.0	22.9	17.0	12.3	21.7	16.1	11.6	21.1	10.3
Munich	29.0	18.7	27.1	18.0	25.5	17.4	19.6	26.7	18.8	25.6	18.1	24.3	17.1	13.0	22.2	16.4	12.4	21.4	15.7	11.9	20.7	11.2
Stuttgart	29.1	18.9	27.3	18.3	25.6	17.4	19.9	27.3	19.0	25.7	18.2	24.3	17.3	13.0	23.1	16.5	12.4	21.9	15.8	11.8	21.1	10.8
GEORGIA																						
Batumi	27.7	22.8	26.9	22.2	26.1	21.7	23.8	26.8	23.1	26.0	22.4	25.2	22.8	17.5	26.1	22.1	16.8	25.3	21.4	16.1	24.5	5.8
Tbilisi	33.5	21.2	31.9	21.2	30.4	20.7	22.9	31.3	22.1	30.2	21.2	28.8	20.2	15.8	27.2	19.4	15.0	26.2	18.6	14.2	25.6	10.2
GIBRALTAR																						
North Front	31.1	20.4	29.2	20.1	27.9	20.1	23.4	26.2	22.9	25.6	22.3	25.0	22.5	17.2	24.6	22.0	16.7	24.6	21.4	16.1	23.7	7.0
GREECE																						
Athens	34.1	20.6	33.0	20.1	31.8	20.1	23.8	29.7	22.9	29.2	22.1	28.5	21.9	16.6	28.2	20.8	15.5	27.5	19.8	14.5	26.7	9.4
Iraklion, Crete	31.2	18.9	29.9	19.5	28.8	19.9	23.2	27.5	22.6	27.3	22.0	26.5	21.8	16.5	26.7	21.0	15.7	26.3	20.1	14.9	25.9	5.9
Rodhos	32.0	21.5	30.8	21.4	29.8	21.3	24.3	27.7	23.8	27.6	23.3	27.3	23.2	18.0	26.1	22.7	17.4	26.1	22.0	16.7	25.9	5.6
Thessaloniki	33.2	21.2	32.1	20.7	30.9	20.5	22.9	30.4	22.2	29.0	21.5	28.9	20.8	15.5	27.0	19.9	14.6	26.3	19.0	13.8	25.4	11.6
GREENLAND																						
Godthab	14.0	9.4	12.1	8.4	10.5	8.0	10.1	13.0	9.1	11.5	8.2	10.1	8.7	7.0	10.2	7.6	6.5	9.3	6.8	6.2	8.6	5.8
HUNGARY																						
Budapest	32.1	20.4	30.2	19.9	28.8	19.0	21.4	30.5	20.6	29.2	19.7	26.9	18.2	13.4	21.6	17.9	13.1	23.4	17.0	12.4	23.5	12.2
ICELAND																						
Reykjavik	15.6	11.5	14.2	10.9	13.3	10.4	12.5	14.5	11.7	13.6	11.0	12.9	11.4	8.4	13.4	10.6	8.0	12.5	10.0	7.7	11.7	4.7

Note: WMO station number, latitude, longitude, elevation, standard atmospheric pressure and period analysed are given in Table 2.18

Table 2.19 Cooling and dehumidification design conditions for selected locations world-wide[2] — *continued*

Station	Cooling dry-bulb (DB) and mean wet-bulb (MWB)						Wet-bulb (WB) and mean dry-bulb (MDB)						Dew-point (DP), humidity ratio (HR) and mean dry-bulb (MDB)									Range of daily mean dry-bulb
	0.4%		1%		2%		0.4%		1%		2%		0.4%			1%			2%			
	DB	MWB	DB	MWB	DB	MWB	WB	MDB	WB	MDB	WB	MDB	DP	HR	MDB	DP	HR	MDB	DP	HR	MDB	
INDIA																						
Bangalore	34.4	19.5	33.6	19.4	32.8	19.5	23.4	28.8	22.8	28.0	22.4	27.4	22.2	18.9	25.1	21.6	18.2	24.6	21.2	17.8	24.3	10.7
Bombay	35.0	22.8	34.0	23.3	33.2	24.0	27.7	31.6	27.4	31.3	27.1	30.9	26.7	22.3	30.2	26.4	21.9	29.9	26.1	21.5	29.6	5.2
Calcutta	37.0	25.7	35.9	26.0	35.0	26.3	29.3	34.2	28.9	33.3	28.5	32.7	28.2	24.4	32.2	27.8	23.8	31.6	27.5	23.4	31.1	10.0
Goa/Panaji	33.7	25.1	33.2	25.2	32.7	25.1	28.2	31.3	27.6	31.1	27.2	30.6	27.3	23.3	30.5	26.7	22.5	29.8	26.3	21.9	29.3	5.8
Hyderabad	40.3	21.6	39.2	21.5	38.1	21.5	25.2	32.0	24.7	31.2	24.4	30.5	23.7	19.8	27.3	23.3	19.3	26.8	23.0	19.0	26.4	10.5
Jaipur	42.2	20.7	40.8	20.5	39.5	20.8	26.9	31.3	26.5	30.7	26.1	30.3	26.0	22.4	28.7	25.6	21.9	28.3	25.2	21.3	28.0	12.4
Madras	38.1	25.1	37.0	25.2	36.0	25.2	28.3	32.6	27.9	32.0	27.5	31.4	27.3	23.2	30.6	27.0	22.7	30.2	26.6	22.2	29.8	8.1
New Delhi	41.7	22.0	40.5	22.4	39.2	22.6	28.0	33.2	27.6	32.6	27.2	32.0	26.9	23.2	30.4	26.5	22.6	30.0	26.1	22.1	29.8	12.0
IRELAND																						
Dublin	22.0	17.0	20.6	16.3	19.4	15.6	17.9	20.5	17.1	19.7	16.3	18.8	16.8	12.1	19.5	15.9	11.4	18.5	15.1	10.8	17.6	7.0
Kilkenny	24.3	17.7	22.5	16.8	20.9	16.3	18.6	22.5	17.7	21.2	16.9	20.0	17.2	12.4	20.2	16.3	11.7	19.1	15.5	11.1	18.3	8.8
Rosslare	20.0	16.6	18.9	15.9	18.0	15.4	17.3	19.1	16.6	18.2	16.0	17.5	16.5	11.8	18.3	15.9	11.3	17.5	15.2	10.8	16.8	4.9
Shannon	23.8	17.9	21.9	17.0	20.2	16.1	18.6	22.2	17.7	20.9	16.9	19.6	17.1	12.2	20.0	16.3	11.6	19.4	15.6	11.1	18.6	6.7
ISRAEL																						
Jerusalem	31.6	18.1	30.2	17.7	29.1	17.4	21.3	27.4	20.5	26.3	19.8	25.6	19.6	15.7	23.6	18.7	14.8	22.4	18.1	14.3	21.9	10.2
Tel Aviv	31.2	20.6	30.0	23.6	29.3	23.5	25.7	29.1	25.1	28.5	24.6	28.2	24.6	19.6	28.2	24.0	18.9	27.9	23.4	18.2	27.6	5.5
ITALY																						
Bologna	33.8	23.7	32.2	22.9	31.0	22.4	24.9	31.6	24.1	30.3	23.2	29.4	23.0	17.8	28.2	22.1	16.9	27.4	21.2	15.9	27.0	11.3
Milan	31.6	22.8	30.3	22.3	29.2	21.7	24.2	29.7	23.5	28.7	22.6	27.7	22.7	17.6	27.4	21.8	16.7	26.4	21.0	15.9	25.8	10.1
Naples	33.2	22.8	31.9	22.6	30.8	22.8	26.0	29.5	25.1	29.1	24.3	28.1	25.0	20.3	28.6	24.0	19.0	27.5	23.0	17.9	26.7	11.0
Palermo	33.2	21.8	31.1	22.8	30.0	23.9	26.6	29.5	26.1	28.9	25.5	28.5	25.9	21.3	29.2	25.1	20.3	28.5	24.5	19.6	27.9	5.3
Rome	30.8	23.3	29.8	23.2	28.9	23.4	26.1	28.6	25.4	27.9	24.6	27.2	25.2	20.3	28.1	24.5	19.5	27.3	23.8	18.7	26.8	9.9
Venice	30.8	23.3	29.5	22.6	28.2	21.8	25.1	28.4	24.1	27.8	23.1	27.0	24.0	18.9	27.4	22.9	17.6	26.8	21.9	16.6	25.8	9.1
JAMAICA																						
Kingston	33.2	25.6	32.9	25.6	32.2	25.4	27.1	31.5	26.6	31.4	26.2	30.9	26.0	21.4	29.5	25.2	20.4	29.3	25.0	20.1	29.2	6.5
JAPAN																						
Asahikawa	29.9	22.7	28.0	21.3	26.4	20.2	23.6	28.7	22.7	27.0	21.6	25.1	22.0	16.9	27.5	21.1	16.0	25.6	20.2	15.1	24.6	8.7
Fukuoka	33.8	24.9	32.7	25.6	31.2	24.9	26.3	31.5	25.9	30.6	25.5	29.8	25.1	20.2	28.5	24.2	19.1	27.6	24.1	19.0	27.9	7.3
Hiroshima	32.6	25.3	31.6	25.1	30.6	24.8	26.3	30.9	25.8	30.3	25.4	29.5	25.1	20.3	29.0	24.6	19.7	28.3	24.2	19.2	27.9	6.5
Nagoya	33.8	25.2	32.2	24.5	31.1	24.0	26.1	31.0	25.6	30.0	25.1	29.7	25.0	20.1	28.0	24.1	19.0	27.4	23.8	18.7	27.5	7.8
Sapporo	29.1	22.7	27.3	21.9	25.7	20.5	23.6	28.0	22.6	26.5	21.6	25.0	22.1	16.8	26.6	21.2	15.9	25.8	20.3	15.0	24.5	6.5
Tokyo	32.8	25.6	31.2	25.1	30.2	24.8	26.6	31.3	26.1	30.1	25.7	29.1	25.2	20.4	28.6	25.0	20.1	28.6	24.2	19.1	27.8	6.2
JORDAN																						
Amman	34.9	18.6	33.2	18.1	31.9	17.8	21.9	28.5	20.9	28.0	20.2	27.4	20.2	16.4	24.4	19.0	15.2	23.2	18.1	14.3	22.5	11.3
KAZAKHSTAN																						
Pavlodar	32.2	18.6	30.4	18.1	28.7	17.2	20.2	27.9	19.5	26.8	18.7	26.2	18.1	13.2	22.5	17.0	12.3	21.8	16.0	11.5	21.5	11.2
Zhambyl (Dzhambul)	35.6	17.6	33.9	17.5	32.5	17.0	19.3	31.4	18.6	31.0	17.9	29.9	15.4	11.8	22.2	14.4	11.1	22.2	13.4	10.4	22.3	13.9

Note: WMO station number, latitude, longitude, elevation, standard atmospheric pressure and period analysed are given in Table 2.18

Table 2.19 Cooling and dehumidification design conditions for selected locations world-wide[2] —continued

Station	Cooling dry-bulb (DB) and mean wet-bulb (MWB)						Wet-bulb (WB) and mean dry-bulb (MDB)						Dew-point (DP), humidity ratio (HR) and mean dry-bulb (MDB)									Range of daily mean dry-bulb
	0.4%		1%		2%		0.4%		1%		2%		0.4%			1%			2%			
	DB	MWB	DB	MWB	DB	MWB	WB	MDB	WB	MDB	WB	MDB	DP	HR	MDB	DP	HR	MDB	DP	HR	MDB	
KENYA																						
Kisumu	32.5	18.7	31.5	19.0	30.7	19.2	22.2	28.0	21.7	27.6	21.4	27.2	20.5	17.5	24.7	20.1	17.0	24.2	19.7	16.6	23.8	11.0
Nairobi	29.0	15.8	28.2	15.8	27.3	15.8	18.7	23.9	18.2	23.2	17.9	22.7	17.4	15.2	19.6	17.1	14.9	19.0	16.8	14.6	18.7	13.5
KOREA, NORTH																						
Ch'ongjin	27.4	21.9	25.7	21.0	24.5	20.8	23.5	26.1	22.6	24.6	21.7	23.6	22.7	17.5	25.2	21.8	16.5	24.6	21.0	15.7	23.2	5.2
Changjin	25.1	18.5	23.6	17.4	22.2	16.8	20.5	23.6	19.5	21.9	18.6	21.0	19.6	16.4	21.9	18.7	15.5	20.9	17.8	14.6	20.1	9.0
P'yongyang	30.7	23.7	29.5	23.1	28.4	22.5	25.3	29.0	24.6	27.9	24.0	26.7	24.3	19.3	27.0	23.7	18.6	26.5	23.1	17.9	26.0	7.6
KOREA, SOUTH																						
Cheju	31.8	25.8	30.2	25.9	29.2	25.7	27.5	30.0	26.8	29.3	26.2	28.8	27.0	22.8	29.1	26.1	21.6	28.4	25.8	21.2	28.2	5.4
Inch'on	30.5	24.4	29.1	23.4	27.8	22.8	25.2	28.8	24.6	27.6	24.0	26.6	24.3	19.4	27.2	23.7	18.7	26.4	23.2	18.1	26.0	5.8
Seoul	31.8	24.8	30.1	24.0	29.0	23.1	26.5	30.2	25.8	28.1	25.0	26.7	26.0	21.4	28.0	25.1	20.3	27.1	24.2	19.2	26.3	8.0
KUWAIT																						
Kuwait	47.2	20.6	46.2	20.4	45.2	19.8	28.0	34.7	25.8	33.0	24.1	33.4	26.2	21.8	33.3	23.8	18.8	30.5	21.2	16.0	29.3	15.4
KYRGYZSTAN																						
Bishkek (Frunze)	35.1	19.3	33.7	18.6	32.2	18.1	20.7	32.2	19.9	30.8	19.1	29.6	17.1	13.2	25.1	16.2	12.4	23.4	15.4	11.8	23.1	14.2
LATVIA																						
Riga	26.1	18.2	24.3	17.6	22.7	16.6	19.6	23.7	18.7	22.7	17.7	21.4	18.1	13.0	21.8	17.1	12.2	20.5	16.0	11.4	19.9	7.9
LIBYA																						
Banghazi	37.2	22.1	35.2	21.6	33.6	21.3	25.5	31.7	24.6	30.2	24.0	29.2	24.0	19.2	28.1	23.1	18.1	27.0	22.5	17.5	26.5	9.3
Tripoli	41.4	24.3	39.6	23.6	37.7	23.0	27.0	37.2	25.7	34.2	24.7	32.5	24.7	19.9	30.9	23.6	18.6	29.1	22.7	17.6	28.3	13.8
LIECHTENSTEIN																						
Vaduz	28.3	19.2	26.8	18.3	25.3	17.7	20.1	26.8	19.3	25.5	18.5	24.0	17.7	13.4	23.4	17.0	12.8	22.2	16.2	12.2	21.4	9.2
LITHUANIA																						
Vilnius	27.1	18.1	25.3	17.7	23.8	16.7	19.8	25.3	18.7	23.6	17.7	22.2	17.8	13.0	21.9	16.8	12.2	21.0	15.9	11.5	19.9	9.0
LUXEMBOURG																						
Luxembourg	28.0	18.1	26.1	17.4	24.5	16.6	19.5	25.4	18.5	24.2	17.6	22.5	17.5	13.1	21.8	16.6	12.4	20.2	15.7	11.7	19.7	9.5
MACEDONIA																						
Skopje	35.2	20.2	33.3	19.8	31.8	19.4	21.7	32.3	21.0	31.1	20.1	30.0	18.1	13.4	25.5	17.2	12.6	24.4	16.8	12.3	24.0	15.2
MADEIRA ISLANDS																						
Funchal	27.1	20.3	26.1	20.3	25.2	20.1	22.1	25.4	21.5	24.6	21.0	24.4	21.0	15.8	24.2	20.2	15.0	23.8	19.8	14.6	23.6	4.7
MALAYSIA																						
Kuala Lumpur	34.2	25.4	33.8	25.5	33.2	25.5	27.3	32.1	26.9	31.9	26.7	31.5	26.2	21.7	29.4	25.9	21.3	29.0	25.5	20.8	28.7	9.0
MALI																						
Bamako	40.0	20.3	39.2	20.3	38.3	20.3	26.2	32.6	25.7	31.9	25.4	31.2	25.0	21.0	28.6	24.2	20.0	27.9	24.0	19.8	27.7	12.3

Note: WMO station number, latitude, longitude, elevation, standard atmospheric pressure and period analysed are given in Table 2.18

Table 2.19 Cooling and dehumidification design conditions for selected locations world-wide[2] — *continued*

| Station | Cooling dry-bulb (DB) and mean wet-bulb (MWB) | | | | | | Wet-bulb (WB) and mean dry-bulb (MDB) | | | | | | Dew-point (DP), humidity ratio (HR) and mean dry-bulb (MDB) | | | | | | | | | Range of daily mean dry-bulb |
| | 0.4% | | 1% | | 2% | | 0.4% | | 1% | | 2% | | 0.4% | | | 1% | | | 2% | | | |
	DB	MWB	DB	MWB	DB	MWB	WB	MDB	WB	MDB	WB	MDB	DP	HR	MDB	DP	HR	MDB	DP	HR	MDB	
MALTA Luqa	33.2	21.7	31.3	22.4	30.1	22.2	25.1	28.8	24.5	27.9	24.0	27.7	24.1	19.2	26.8	23.2	18.2	26.4	22.9	17.8	26.2	8.0
MAURITANIA Nouadhibou	33.1	20.6	31.2	20.5	29.8	20.3	24.4	28.4	23.5	27.2	22.7	27.0	23.2	18.0	26.1	22.1	16.8	25.8	21.3	16.0	24.8	8.8
MEXICO Acapulco	33.2	26.5	33.1	26.5	32.9	26.5	27.7	32.2	27.3	31.9	27.0	31.7	26.2	21.6	30.4	26.1	21.5	30.2	26.0	21.4	29.8	7.2
Mexico City	29.0	13.8	27.9	13.7	26.9	13.5	16.6	23.2	16.1	23.0	15.7	22.0	14.9	14.0	18.4	14.1	13.2	17.8	13.9	13.1	17.3	13.8
Veracruz	34.2	26.6	33.2	26.7	32.8	26.6	27.7	32.8	27.2	32.1	26.8	31.7	26.2	21.7	29.7	26.1	21.5	29.6	25.8	21.1	29.4	8.3
MOLDOVA Chisinau (Kishinev)	30.2	19.6	28.7	19.1	27.3	18.4	21.1	27.4	20.1	26.6	19.3	25.6	18.9	14.0	24.2	17.9	13.1	23.1	17.0	12.4	22.1	9.1
MONGOLIA Ulaangom	27.9	16.1	26.3	15.5	24.8	14.9	17.3	25.5	16.4	24.4	15.7	23.0	14.4	11.5	20.2	13.3	10.7	20.2	12.4	10.0	19.1	10.7
MOROCCO Casablanca	29.6	22.0	27.3	22.0	26.0	22.0	24.0	26.7	23.3	25.9	22.8	25.2	23.1	18.0	25.3	22.6	17.4	24.8	22.0	16.8	24.3	5.1
Tanger	33.1	21.4	31.5	21.5	30.0	21.2	23.4	29.9	22.7	28.8	22.2	27.4	21.6	16.3	26.1	21.0	15.7	25.3	20.2	14.9	24.9	9.3
NETHERLANDS Amsterdam	26.6	19.0	24.8	18.1	23.1	17.7	20.3	24.8	19.2	23.5	18.4	22.0	18.7	13.5	22.2	17.8	12.8	20.8	17.0	12.1	19.8	8.2
Eindhoven	28.3	19.2	26.6	18.3	24.8	17.7	20.3	26.5	19.3	25.0	18.4	23.4	18.2	13.1	22.7	17.3	12.4	21.0	16.5	11.8	20.3	9.9
Groningen	27.1	19.3	25.0	18.3	23.1	17.6	20.6	25.2	19.4	23.3	18.3	21.8	18.8	13.6	23.1	17.9	12.9	21.1	17.0	12.1	20.0	9.7
Rotterdam	26.9	19.6	25.1	18.5	23.4	17.9	20.6	25.4	19.5	23.8	18.6	22.3	18.9	13.7	22.7	18.0	12.9	21.5	17.1	12.2	20.2	8.1
NEW ZEALAND Auckland	25.2	19.1	24.2	19.1	23.3	18.8	21.2	23.9	20.4	22.9	19.7	22.3	20.2	14.9	22.3	19.4	14.2	21.8	18.7	13.5	21.1	6.3
Christchurch	28.1	16.9	26.1	16.2	24.2	15.5	18.5	25.1	17.6	23.6	16.8	21.6	16.5	11.8	19.4	15.7	11.2	19.3	14.9	10.6	18.4	9.7
Wellington	23.1	17.6	21.9	17.4	20.9	16.7	19.0	21.7	18.3	20.7	17.6	19.9	18.0	12.9	20.3	17.2	12.3	19.7	16.5	11.8	19.3	5.4
NIGER Agadez	42.1	19.4	41.4	19.4	40.7	19.1	24.0	33.3	23.5	33.2	23.0	32.9	21.7	17.4	27.4	21.0	16.6	27.5	20.2	15.8	27.9	12.5
NORWAY Bergen	22.6	14.8	20.2	13.8	18.2	12.9	15.9	19.8	15.1	17.9	14.3	17.0	14.9	10.6	16.0	14.0	10.0	15.4	13.1	9.5	14.8	6.4
Oslo	25.5	15.6	23.7	14.7	21.8	13.7	16.6	22.7	15.6	20.9	14.8	19.7	14.8	10.8	17.1	13.8	10.1	16.8	12.8	9.4	15.9	10.0
Stavanger	22.9	15.2	20.9	14.7	18.9	14.1	16.8	20.6	15.7	18.9	15.1	17.5	15.5	11.0	17.5	14.7	10.5	16.8	13.9	9.9	16.0	6.3
Trondheim	24.0	15.6	21.9	15.2	20.0	14.3	17.4	21.3	16.3	19.9	15.4	18.6	16.0	11.4	18.7	15.0	10.7	17.5	14.0	10.0	16.3	6.9
OMAN Masqat	43.0	22.8	41.8	22.8	40.5	22.8	30.1	34.0	29.5	33.8	29.1	33.6	29.1	25.8	32.8	28.5	24.9	32.6	28.0	24.2	32.4	8.3
PANAMA Panama	34.8	24.7	34.0	25.0	33.2	24.8	27.7	31.8	27.3	31.4	27.0	31.0	26.9	22.6	30.1	26.2	21.7	29.4	26.1	21.5	29.6	8.8

Note: WMO station number, latitude, longitude, elevation, standard atmospheric pressure and period analysed are given in Table 2.18

Table 2.19 Cooling and dehumidification design conditions for selected locations world-wide[2] — continued

Station	Cooling dry-bulb (DB) and mean wet-bulb (MWB)						Wet-bulb (WB) and mean dry-bulb (MDB)						Dew-point (DP), humidity ratio (HR) and mean dry-bulb (MDB)									Range of daily mean dry-bulb
	0.4%		1%		2%		0.4%		1%		2%		0.4%			1%			2%			
	DB	MWB	DB	MWB	DB	MWB	WB	MDB	WB	MDB	WB	MDB	DP	HR	MDB	DP	HR	MDB	DP	HR	MDB	
PARAGUAY																						
Asuncion	36.5	23.9	35.2	24.1	34.2	24.1	26.6	32.9	26.1	32.3	25.7	31.6	25.1	20.5	30.0	24.2	19.4	28.6	24.1	19.2	28.5	10.3
PERU																						
Lima	29.9	24.1	28.8	23.2	27.8	22.6	24.6	28.6	24.0	27.4	23.4	26.6	23.2	18.0	26.8	22.9	17.7	26.8	22.1	16.8	26.3	6.4
PHILLIPPINES																						
Manila	35.0	27.0	34.1	26.5	33.4	26.3	28.4	32.8	27.9	32.3	27.5	31.9	27.2	23.0	31.5	26.8	22.5	31.1	26.2	21.7	30.4	8.8
POLAND																						
Gdansk	26.8	18.6	24.8	17.4	22.9	16.5	19.5	24.9	18.3	22.8	17.2	21.6	17.8	13.0	21.0	16.2	11.7	20.1	15.2	11.0	19.3	9.7
Krakow	29.2	20.4	27.2	19.3	25.2	18.2	21.2	27.9	20.1	26.0	19.2	24.4	18.9	14.1	24.2	18.0	13.3	22.8	17.1	12.6	21.6	10.9
Warsaw	29.0	19.7	27.0	19.0	25.2	17.9	21.0	27.6	19.9	25.3	18.9	24.3	18.9	13.9	24.2	17.9	13.0	22.5	17.0	12.3	21.4	11.0
PORTUGAL																						
Lisbon	34.1	20.7	32.0	20.2	29.9	19.8	22.7	30.8	21.7	28.4	20.9	27.4	20.2	15.1	24.4	19.8	14.7	24.5	18.9	13.9	23.7	10.5
Porto	30.1	19.4	28.0	19.1	25.9	18.3	20.8	27.2	20.1	25.6	19.4	23.8	19.1	14.0	22.0	18.3	13.3	20.9	18.0	13.1	20.6	9.6
PUERTO RICO																						
San Juan	33.2	25.0	32.2	25.4	31.7	25.4	27.0	30.9	26.6	30.5	26.3	30.3	25.7	21.0	29.3	25.5	20.8	29.1	25.2	20.4	28.8	6.8
QATAR																						
Ad Dawhah	43.0	21.9	41.9	22.1	40.8	22.3	30.5	34.7	29.9	34.1	29.4	33.8	29.4	26.3	33.2	29.0	25.7	33.0	28.2	24.4	33.1	10.8
ROMANIA																						
Bucharest	33.0	22.0	31.2	21.2	29.9	20.7	23.6	30.5	22.6	29.4	21.7	28.3	21.9	16.8	25.7	20.8	15.6	24.8	19.9	14.8	23.7	13.3
RUSSIA																						
Aldan	27.2	16.3	25.2	15.5	23.3	14.9	17.6	24.9	16.7	23.1	15.8	21.5	15.3	11.8	19.7	14.3	11.0	18.9	13.3	10.3	18.6	10.2
Groznyy	32.9	21.4	31.3	20.7	29.8	20.1	22.7	30.6	21.9	28.9	21.1	27.7	20.4	15.4	25.9	19.6	14.6	25.0	19.0	14.1	24.1	10.3
Moscow	27.6	19.3	26.0	18.6	24.5	17.8	20.5	25.6	19.5	24.6	18.6	22.9	18.6	13.7	22.9	17.7	12.9	22.1	16.8	12.2	21.2	8.2
Omsk	30.7	18.9	28.9	18.0	27.2	17.5	20.3	27.7	19.4	26.8	18.5	25.3	17.7	12.9	23.1	16.8	12.2	22.3	15.9	11.5	21.3	10.7
Rostov-Na-Donu	31.4	20.8	29.9	20.2	28.5	19.7	22.3	29.2	21.5	27.6	20.7	26.4	20.1	14.9	25.3	19.3	14.2	24.4	18.6	13.6	24.0	10.3
St Petersburg	26.3	18.4	24.6	17.6	23.0	16.7	19.7	24.4	18.7	23.1	17.7	21.8	17.9	12.9	22.1	16.8	12.0	20.8	15.9	11.3	19.8	7.5
Vladivostok	25.8	20.4	24.0	19.4	22.4	19.0	22.2	24.0	21.2	22.6	20.3	21.5	21.6	16.6	23.0	20.7	15.7	22.0	19.8	14.8	21.0	4.8
Volgograd	32.5	18.6	30.9	18.4	29.3	18.0	20.7	29.1	19.9	27.5	19.1	26.4	18.1	13.3	23.0	17.4	12.7	23.0	16.5	12.0	22.5	10.5
SAMOA																						
Pago Pago	31.3	26.7	31.0	26.7	30.7	26.5	27.6	30.5	27.2	30.2	27.1	30.1	26.6	22.2	29.8	26.3	21.8	29.5	26.1	21.5	29.3	5.2
SAUDI ARABIA																						
Jiddah	40.2	22.0	39.0	22.9	38.0	23.6	28.2	34.2	27.9	34.2	27.3	33.5	27.0	22.7	31.5	26.2	21.6	31.5	26.0	21.4	31.2	12.2
Khamis Mushayt	31.1	13.8	30.6	13.7	30.0	13.4	19.0	24.1	18.2	23.3	17.6	23.1	17.2	15.9	21.8	16.6	15.2	21.5	15.9	14.6	21.0	12.3
Riyadh	44.0	18.0	43.1	17.8	42.2	17.7	20.6	35.6	19.7	36.3	19.0	35.6	16.9	13.0	22.9	15.6	11.9	22.1	14.1	10.8	22.2	14.0
SENEGAL																						
Dakar	31.8	23.4	31.0	24.9	30.2	25.1	27.0	30.2	26.6	29.5	26.2	29.0	26.2	21.7	28.8	26.0	21.4	28.6	25.5	20.8	28.4	5.4

Note: WMO station number, latitude, longitude, elevation, standard atmospheric pressure and period analysed are given in Table 2.18

Table 2.19 Cooling and dehumidification design conditions for selected locations world-wide[2] — *continued*

Station	Cooling dry-bulb (DB) and mean wet-bulb (MWB)						Wet-bulb (WB) and mean dry-bulb (MDB)						Dew-point (DP), humidity ratio (HR) and mean dry-bulb (MDB)									Range of daily mean dry-bulb
	0.4%		1%		2%		0.4%		1%		2%		0.4%			1%			2%			
	DB	MWB	DB	MWB	DB	MWB	WB	MDB	WB	MDB	WB	MDB	DP	HR	MDB	DP	HR	MDB	DP	HR	MDB	
SINGAPORE																						
Singapore	33.0	25.9	32.2	25.9	32.0	25.9	27.2	30.9	27.1	30.7	26.8	30.3	26.2	21.7	28.9	26.2	21.7	28.8	26.1	21.5	28.7	6.3
SLOVAKIA																						
Bratislava	31.8	20.4	30.0	20.0	28.2	19.3	21.6	29.5	20.8	28.6	19.9	26.7	19.0	14.0	25.2	18.1	13.2	24.1	17.2	12.5	23.2	12.3
SOLVENIA																						
Ljubljana	30.1	20.0	28.3	19.2	26.9	18.5	20.9	28.4	20.0	26.8	19.2	25.8	18.2	13.7	23.2	17.6	13.2	22.5	16.9	12.6	22.3	12.4
SOUTH AFRICA																						
Cape Town	30.3	19.7	28.6	19.3	27.0	18.6	21.2	27.7	20.5	26.4	19.9	24.9	19.3	14.1	22.7	18.6	13.5	22.4	18.1	13.1	22.2	8.8
Durban	30.3	23.7	29.3	23.7	28.5	23.4	25.5	28.7	24.9	28.1	24.5	27.4	24.5	19.5	27.4	24.0	18.9	27.1	23.5	18.3	26.7	5.5
Johannesburg	29.0	15.6	27.9	15.6	26.9	15.5	18.6	24.9	18.1	24.2	17.6	23.7	16.8	14.8	20.4	16.2	14.2	19.9	15.7	13.7	19.6	10.4
Pretoria	31.9	17.6	30.9	17.1	30.0	17.1	20.5	26.8	19.9	26.6	19.4	26.2	18.7	15.9	22.8	18.0	15.2	22.5	17.4	14.6	22.2	9.8
SPAIN																						
Barcelona	29.3	23.4	28.8	23.5	27.9	22.9	25.2	28.1	24.4	27.5	23.6	26.8	24.1	19.0	27.5	23.2	18.0	26.7	22.6	17.3	26.3	8.4
Madrid	36.0	20.7	34.7	20.0	33.1	19.6	21.9	34.4	21.0	33.0	20.1	31.6	17.8	13.7	27.5	16.8	12.9	26.6	15.8	12.0	26.0	16.2
Malaga	34.1	20.2	32.0	19.8	30.1	19.8	23.9	27.5	23.4	27.0	22.7	26.7	22.9	17.6	26.1	22.1	16.8	25.8	21.3	16.0	25.1	9.1
Palma	33.0	23.1	31.4	22.9	30.2	22.9	25.8	29.2	25.0	28.9	24.3	28.5	24.8	19.9	28.4	23.9	18.8	27.6	23.0	17.8	27.0	12.4
Santander	26.5	19.5	24.7	19.4	23.7	19.0	21.5	24.4	20.7	23.3	20.1	22.8	20.5	15.3	22.7	19.7	14.5	22.4	19.0	13.9	21.9	5.2
Sevilla	39.8	23.7	38.0	22.2	36.1	21.7	24.6	36.4	23.3	35.3	22.4	33.3	21.0	15.7	29.1	20.0	14.8	26.7	19.1	13.9	25.5	16.7
Valencia	32.2	21.9	31.0	22.1	30.0	22.1	24.7	29.2	24.1	28.5	23.6	27.8	23.2	18.1	27.1	22.9	17.8	26.9	22.1	16.9	26.4	9.2
SWEDEN																						
Goteborg	25.8	16.6	23.9	15.8	22.0	14.8	17.7	23.5	16.7	21.6	15.8	19.9	15.9	11.5	18.7	15.0	10.9	17.7	14.1	10.2	16.7	8.3
Ostersund	23.2	14.6	21.2	13.9	19.3	13.0	15.9	21.7	14.7	19.7	13.7	18.2	13.4	10.0	17.1	12.4	9.4	16.0	11.5	8.8	15.4	7.5
Stockholm	26.8	17.1	24.8	16.1	22.8	15.2	18.4	23.6	17.4	21.9	16.4	20.8	17.0	12.2	19.2	15.9	11.4	18.3	14.9	10.7	17.6	9.0
SWITZERLAND																						
Geneva	30.1	19.1	28.5	18.4	26.9	18.0	20.0	27.8	19.4	26.6	18.6	25.2	17.6	13.3	22.2	16.9	12.7	21.6	16.1	12.0	21.1	12.3
Lugano	29.7	21.4	28.2	20.8	27.0	20.0	22.6	27.9	21.7	26.9	20.9	26.0	20.8	16.0	25.9	19.9	15.1	25.2	19.0	14.3	24.3	9.8
Zurich	28.1	18.8	26.4	18.1	24.8	17.3	19.7	26.5	18.9	25.0	18.1	23.3	17.5	13.4	21.8	16.8	12.8	21.1	16.1	12.3	20.5	8.9
SYRIA																						
Damascus	38.1	17.9	36.9	17.8	35.8	17.6	20.6	29.6	20.0	29.4	19.4	28.9	18.8	14.7	22.3	17.9	13.8	22.0	16.9	13.0	21.6	18.8
TAIWAN																						
Taipei	34.6	26.8	33.9	26.7	33.1	26.6	27.7	32.9	27.4	32.4	27.0	32.0	26.4	21.9	30.1	26.1	21.5	29.9	25.9	21.2	29.8	7.4
TAJIKISTAN																						
Dushanbe	37.1	19.6	36.0	19.3	34.8	19.0	21.7	33.7	20.7	32.8	20.0	32.0	17.7	14.0	28.6	16.5	13.0	27.4	15.5	12.1	26.5	14.2
THAILAND																						
Bangkok	37.1	26.5	36.1	26.1	35.2	25.7	28.8	34.3	28.1	32.7	27.6	31.9	27.5	23.4	31.3	27.1	22.9	30.6	26.7	22.3	30.3	9.3
Tak	39.1	23.2	38.1	23.5	37.1	23.3	26.7	32.2	26.3	31.7	26.1	31.3	25.4	20.9	28.6	25.1	20.5	28.5	24.7	20.0	28.2	10.4

Note: WMO station number, latitude, longitude, elevation, standard atmospheric pressure and period analysed are given in Table 2.18

Table 2.19 Cooling and dehumidification design conditions for selected locations world-wide[2]—continued

Station	Cooling dry-bulb (DB) and mean wet-bulb (MWB)						Wet-bulb (WB) and mean dry-bulb (MDB)						Dew-point (DP), humidity ratio (HR) and mean dry-bulb (MDB)									Range of daily mean dry-bulb
	0.4%		1%		2%		0.4%		1%		2%		0.4%			1%			2%			
	DB	MWB	DB	MWB	DB	MWB	WB	MDB	WB	MDB	WB	MDB	DP	HR	MDB	DP	HR	MDB	DP	HR	MDB	
TRINIDAD																						
Port of Spain	33.0	25.1	32.2	25.0	32.0	24.9	26.6	30.6	26.3	30.3	26.1	30.1	25.7	21.0	28.5	25.2	20.4	27.9	25.1	20.2	27.8	7.9
TUNISIA																						
Tunis	36.7	22.6	34.2	23.0	32.9	22.6	25.8	31.0	25.0	30.1	24.2	29.4	24.2	19.1	28.0	23.5	18.3	27.5	22.8	17.5	27.2	12.1
TURKEY																						
Ankara	32.0	17.3	30.2	17.1	28.8	16.4	18.6	29.0	17.8	28.1	17.0	27.4	14.8	11.8	23.0	13.9	11.1	22.0	13.0	10.5	21.3	15.8
Istanbul	30.2	21.0	29.1	20.8	28.1	20.3	23.2	27.6	22.5	26.7	21.8	25.8	22.0	16.7	25.3	21.1	15.8	24.7	20.2	15.0	24.4	8.5
TURKMENISTAN																						
Dashhowuz (Tashauz)	39.2	23.3	37.4	22.6	35.8	21.9	25.1	36.4	24.1	35.1	23.1	33.9	21.2	16.0	33.5	20.2	15.0	32.3	19.1	14.0	31.1	13.5
UKRAINE																						
Kyyiv (Kiev)	28.2	19.7	26.7	18.9	25.2	18.1	20.8	26.3	19.9	25.0	19.1	23.9	19.0	14.1	23.5	18.1	13.3	22.6	17.2	12.5	21.6	9.2
Odesa	30.1	19.6	28.8	19.4	27.2	19.0	22.2	26.1	21.2	26.0	20.3	25.1	20.9	15.6	24.5	19.7	14.5	23.6	18.8	13.7	22.6	10.2
Poltava	29.4	19.0	27.8	18.7	26.4	18.1	20.8	26.3	19.9	25.6	19.1	24.6	18.9	14.0	23.7	17.9	13.1	22.6	17.0	12.4	21.7	9.8
UNITED ARAB EMIRATES																						
Abu Dhabi	43.8	23.6	42.5	23.4	41.1	23.8	30.3	35.0	29.7	34.3	29.2	34.1	29.2	26.0	32.9	28.8	25.4	32.8	28.0	24.2	32.5	12.8
Dubai	41.9	23.8	40.7	24.0	39.3	24.5	30.2	34.6	29.7	34.2	29.2	34.1	29.2	25.9	33.0	28.8	25.3	32.8	28.0	24.1	32.7	9.7
Sharjah	43.1	24.9	41.9	25.2	40.9	25.2	30.1	37.1	29.4	36.1	28.8	35.6	28.8	25.4	33.5	28.0	24.2	33.0	27.1	22.9	32.7	13.3
UNITED KINGDOM and NORTHERN IRELAND																						
Aberdeen/Dyce	21.7	16.8	20.0	15.8	18.5	14.7	17.5	21.0	16.3	19.4	15.3	17.9	15.8	11.3	19.6	14.9	10.7	18.0	14.0	10.0	16.9	7.2
Aberporth	22.3	16.9	20.2	16.0	18.5	15.4	17.7	20.8	16.8	19.0	16.0	17.9	16.6	12.0	18.6	15.9	11.5	17.8	15.2	11.0	16.9	5.2
Aughton	23.9	17.6	22.0	16.6	20.3	15.8	18.3	22.7	17.4	20.8	16.5	19.5	16.7	12.0	19.8	16.0	11.4	18.9	15.2	10.9	17.9	6.0
Belfast	22.5	16.7	20.7	15.9	19.2	15.3	17.7	21.1	16.8	19.7	16.0	18.4	16.3	11.7	19.0	15.5	11.1	18.1	14.7	10.5	17.5	7.1
Birmingham	25.7	17.5	23.9	16.5	22.3	16.1	18.5	23.8	17.6	22.4	16.7	20.9	16.7	12.0	20.1	15.9	11.4	19.3	15.0	10.8	18.5	9.4
Bournemouth	25.7	18.2	23.8	17.2	22.3	16.5	19.1	24.3	18.1	22.2	17.3	20.7	17.2	12.3	20.5	16.6	11.8	19.4	16.0	11.4	18.9	10.0
Bristol	26.3	18.2	24.5	17.4	22.8	16.6	19.2	24.6	18.2	22.8	17.3	21.2	17.1	12.2	21.4	16.4	11.7	20.0	15.7	11.2	19.1	7.1
Cardiff	25.0	17.8	23.1	17.2	21.4	16.4	18.8	23.3	17.8	21.5	17.0	20.2	17.2	12.4	20.3	16.5	11.8	19.1	15.8	11.3	18.4	8.2
Edinburgh	22.1	16.3	20.4	15.6	19.0	14.8	17.2	20.8	16.3	19.5	15.5	18.2	15.7	11.2	18.8	14.9	10.6	17.6	14.1	10.1	17.1	8.1
Exeter	25.5	18.2	23.7	17.7	22.2	16.8	19.4	24.3	18.4	22.7	17.6	20.9	17.5	12.6	21.2	16.8	12.0	20.0	16.2	11.6	19.3	8.8
Glasgow	23.7	17.0	21.6	16.0	19.6	15.0	17.7	22.4	16.7	20.5	15.7	18.7	15.9	11.3	19.5	15.0	10.7	18.4	14.2	10.1	17.3	8.1
Jersey/Channel Islands	24.7	18.1	22.8	17.0	21.1	16.5	18.7	23.4	17.8	21.4	17.2	19.9	17.2	12.4	19.5	16.6	11.9	18.6	16.1	11.6	18.2	6.1
Lerwick	15.8	13.5	14.7	12.8	13.9	12.4	14.1	15.1	13.4	14.2	12.8	13.5	13.6	9.8	14.5	13.0	9.4	13.8	12.4	9.1	13.1	3.8
London, Heathrow	27.4	18.7	25.7	17.7	24.1	17.2	19.6	26.0	18.7	23.8	17.8	22.4	17.4	12.5	21.3	16.7	11.9	20.7	16.0	11.4	20.0	9.2
Manchester	25.2	17.3	23.1	16.4	21.5	15.6	18.3	23.2	17.4	21.7	16.6	20.3	16.5	11.9	20.0	15.7	11.3	19.2	14.8	10.6	18.3	7.6
Nottingham	25.5	18.0	23.6	17.2	21.9	16.3	19.0	24.0	17.9	22.3	16.9	20.8	17.1	12.4	21.3	16.1	11.6	19.8	15.3	11.0	18.6	8.9
Plymouth	23.8	17.3	22.1	16.6	20.6	16.1	18.4	22.3	17.6	20.4	17.0	19.4	17.1	12.2	19.5	16.6	11.9	18.7	16.0	11.4	18.0	6.1
Stornoway	18.3	15.1	16.8	14.2	15.7	13.4	15.7	17.6	14.7	16.1	14.0	15.3	14.7	10.5	16.4	14.1	10.1	15.5	13.4	9.6	14.8	4.8

Note: WMO station number, latitude, longitude, elevation, standard atmospheric pressure and period analysed are given in Table 2.18

Table 2.19 Cooling and dehumidification design conditions for selected locations world-wide[2] — *continued*

Station	Cooling dry-bulb (DB) and mean wet-bulb (MWB)						Wet-bulb (WB) and mean dry-bulb (MDB)						Dew-point (DP), humidity ratio (HR) and mean dry-bulb (MDB)									Range of daily mean dry-bulb
	0.4%		1%		2%		0.4%		1%		2%		0.4%			1%			2%			
	DB	MWB	DB	MWB	DB	MWB	WB	MDB	WB	MDB	WB	MDB	DP	HR	MDB	DP	HR	MDB	DP	HR	MDB	
UNITED STATES of AMERICA																						
Boston (MA)	32.5	22.6	30.7	21.9	28.9	21.1	24.1	30.3	23.2	28.4	22.3	26.9	22.3	17.0	26.7	21.5	16.2	25.9	20.7	15.4	25.4	8.5
Chicago (IL)	32.8	23.6	31.3	22.8	29.7	21.9	25.1	31.0	24.1	29.5	23.1	28.1	23.3	18.6	28.9	22.4	17.5	27.8	21.4	16.4	26.6	10.9
Cleveland (OH)	31.4	22.9	30.0	22.1	28.6	21.4	24.2	29.7	23.3	28.3	22.4	27.1	22.6	17.8	27.6	21.7	16.9	26.4	20.9	16.0	25.4	10.3
Dallas/Fort Worth (TX)	37.8	23.6	36.4	23.5	35.3	23.5	25.4	33.2	25.0	32.6	24.6	32.2	23.7	18.9	28.0	23.3	18.5	27.5	22.9	18.0	27.3	11.3
Denver (CO)	33.8	15.3	32.3	15.2	30.8	15.1	18.1	27.2	17.3	26.6	16.7	25.8	15.6	13.7	20.4	14.6	12.8	20.1	13.7	12.1	20.1	14.9
Fairbanks (AK)	27.1	15.8	25.2	15.1	23.4	14.6	17.0	24.8	16.1	23.4	15.2	21.6	14.2	10.3	18.2	13.3	9.7	17.7	12.4	9.1	17.3	10.3
Honolulu (HI)	31.8	22.9	31.3	22.7	30.7	22.6	24.4	29.1	23.9	28.9	23.5	28.6	23.1	17.8	26.6	22.4	17.2	26.4	21.9	16.6	26.2	6.8
Las Vegas (NV)	42.2	18.9	40.9	18.6	39.6	18.2	21.9	34.8	21.2	33.9	20.6	33.7	18.6	14.5	26.2	17.1	13.2	27.4	15.6	12.0	29.4	13.8
Los Angeles (CA)	29.2	17.7	27.0	17.6	25.4	17.9	21.0	25.8	20.3	24.7	19.8	23.8	19.4	14.2	26.2	18.7	13.6	27.4	18.1	13.1	22.1	6.1
Memphis (TN)	35.4	25.3	34.2	25.1	33.2	24.7	26.7	33.1	26.2	32.5	25.6	31.6	25.1	20.4	30.3	24.4	19.6	29.8	23.9	19.0	29.0	9.3
Miami (FL)	32.8	25.2	32.2	25.1	31.6	24.9	26.4	30.4	26.1	30.3	25.8	29.9	25.4	20.6	28.3	25.0	20.1	28.1	24.7	19.7	28.0	6.3
Minneapolis-St. Paul (MN)	32.8	22.7	31.1	21.9	29.4	21.1	24.4	30.8	23.4	29.1	22.3	27.8	22.5	17.7	28.5	21.4	16.6	27.2	20.4	15.6	26.0	10.6
Montgomery (AL)	35.1	24.6	34.0	24.4	32.9	24.3	26.3	32.6	25.8	31.8	25.3	31.1	24.6	19.8	29.3	24.1	19.2	28.7	23.7	18.6	28.3	10.4
New Orleans (LA)	33.9	26.1	33.1	25.7	32.3	25.6	27.3	31.9	26.8	31.3	26.4	30.7	26.1	21.5	30.2	25.6	20.9	29.4	25.2	20.3	29.0	8.6
New York (NY)	32.5	23.1	30.9	22.4	29.5	21.7	24.6	29.9	23.8	28.8	23.1	27.6	23.1	17.8	26.8	22.4	17.1	26.5	21.7	16.3	25.9	7.7
Oklahoma City (OK)	37.3	23.2	35.7	23.1	34.2	22.9	24.9	32.8	24.4	32.4	23.9	31.8	22.8	18.4	28.4	22.3	17.8	27.8	21.7	17.2	27.4	11.7
Philadelphia (PA)	33.4	23.9	31.9	23.3	30.6	22.6	25.4	31.1	24.7	29.7	23.9	28.7	23.9	18.8	28.2	23.2	18.0	27.3	22.6	17.3	26.6	9.8
Phoenix (AZ)	43.2	20.9	42.0	20.9	40.9	20.8	24.2	35.8	23.7	35.4	23.2	35.0	21.5	16.8	27.8	20.6	15.9	28.6	19.6	14.9	29.6	12.8
Richmond (VA)	34.5	24.6	33.1	24.1	31.8	23.5	26.0	32.1	25.3	31.1	24.7	30.0	24.4	19.5	28.9	23.8	18.7	28.0	23.2	18.0	27.2	10.6
Sacramento (CA)	37.8	20.8	36.0	20.3	34.2	19.7	22.0	35.7	21.1	34.3	20.3	32.8	16.8	12.0	27.9	15.9	11.3	26.4	15.2	10.8	25.4	18.5
Salt Lake City (UT)	35.8	16.7	34.6	16.5	33.2	16.2	18.9	29.6	18.2	29.2	17.5	29.2	15.8	13.1	22.5	14.4	12.0	22.5	13.2	11.0	22.8	15.4
San Francisco (CA)	28.4	17.0	25.6	16.4	23.3	15.8	18.0	25.9	17.2	23.8	16.6	22.1	15.2	10.8	19.4	14.6	10.4	18.9	14.1	10.1	18.5	9.3
Seattle (WA)	29.4	18.3	27.4	17.6	25.4	16.8	19.1	28.3	18.1	26.3	17.2	24.5	15.4	11.1	21.6	14.7	10.6	20.5	14.1	10.2	19.8	10.2
St. Louis (MO)	35.1	24.6	33.6	24.1	32.2	23.6	26.1	32.3	25.3	31.3	24.6	30.4	24.3	19.7	29.3	23.7	18.9	28.5	22.9	18.1	27.8	10.2
Washington DC	34.8	24.7	33.6	24.2	31.7	23.4	26.0	31.8	25.3	30.9	24.7	30.0	24.6	19.6	28.5	24.0	18.9	28.2	23.4	18.2	27.4	9.2
URUGUAY																						
Montevideo	31.9	22.1	30.0	21.6	28.2	21.1	24.2	28.6	23.5	27.1	22.7	26.3	23.1	17.9	26.2	22.2	16.9	25.0	21.8	16.5	24.7	9.3
UZBEKISTAN																						
Tashkent	38.0	21.4	36.7	20.1	35.2	20.1	24.0	35.0	22.5	33.5	21.2	32.2	20.2	15.8	31.5	18.5	14.2	28.7	17.1	13.0	28.0	14.9
VANUATU																						
Luganville	30.3	25.3	30.0	25.3	29.6	25.2	26.6	29.2	26.2	28.9	26.0	28.7	25.7	21.1	28.3	25.5	20.8	28.0	25.2	20.4	27.7	5.8
VENEZUELA																						
Caracas	33.2	28.7	32.7	28.5	32.0	28.2	30.2	32.0	29.6	31.6	29.1	31.0	29.9	27.2	31.7	29.1	25.9	31.1	28.7	25.3	30.6	7.0
VIETNAM																						
Ho Chi Minh City (Saigon)	35.1	25.2	33.9	25.2	32.7	25.2	27.2	32.2	26.9	31.9	26.6	31.6	26.1	21.5	29.8	25.7	21.0	29.3	25.2	20.4	28.7	8.2
YUGOSLAVIA																						
Belgrade	33.4	21.8	31.8	21.1	29.9	20.5	22.7	30.3	21.8	29.6	21.1	28.6	20.1	15.0	26.8	19.2	14.1	25.4	18.4	13.4	24.4	12.3
ZIMBABWE																						
Harare	30.1	16.6	29.1	16.3	28.3	16.2	20.0	24.7	19.6	24.2	19.2	23.6	18.9	16.5	21.0	18.4	16.0	20.6	18.1	15.7	20.5	11.7

Note: WMO station number, latitude, longitude, elevation, standard atmospheric pressure and period analysed are given in Table 2.18

2.7 Solar and illuminance data

2.7.1 Solar geometry

Two angles are used to define the angular position of the sun as seen from a given point on the surface of the earth, see Figure 2.13. These are:

— Solar altitude, γ_s: the angular elevation of the centre of the solar disk above the horizontal plane.

— Solar azimuth, α_s: the horizontal angle between the vertical plane containing the centre of the solar disk and the vertical plane running in a true N–S direction. Solar azimuth is measured clockwise from due south in the northern hemisphere and anti-clockwise measured from due north in the southern hemisphere. Values are negative before solar noon and positive after solar noon.

Other important angles for solar geometry are:

— Wall azimuth, α: the orientation of the wall, measured clockwise from due south in the northern hemisphere and anti-clockwise measured from due north in the southern hemisphere.

— Wall–solar azimuth angle, sometimes called the horizontal shadow angle, α_f: the angle between the vertical plane containing the normal to the surface and the vertical plane passing through the centre of the solar disk, i.e. the resolved angle on the horizontal plane between the direction of the sun and the direction of the normal to the surface.

Table 2.20 provides numerical values of altitude angle and bearings to the nearest degree. These tables have been calculated at 10-degree intervals of latitude from 0° to 60° with an additional table for latitude 55°. Linear interpolation can be used for intermediate latitudes. The solar bearings in the table, which is structured for the northern hemisphere, are measured from true north. The table is applicable in both hemispheres but care must be taken to use the correct dates for the hemisphere concerned, as given in the table heading. Also, when considering the southern hemisphere, the bearings must be adjusted as explained in the footnote to the table.

Except for the sunrise and sunset hours, the angles have been calculated on the half-hour using local apparent time (LAT). In the sunrise hours, the solar geometry has been calculated for the solar time midway between sunrise and the end of the first sunlit hour of the day. In the sunset hours, the time midway between the beginning of the last hour and sunset has been used. These values are indicated by italic type to distinguish them from the normal mid-hour values.

2.7.2 Sun position

Data on sun position may be presented in graphical or tabular forms. Sun-path diagrams are useful for visualising the course of the sun across the year and can be used in various graphical methods for analysing the effects of solar shading, whether due to external obstructions, building features or window position. Various projections can be used but the simplest presentation for any given latitude is to plot the hourly solar altitude as a function of the hourly

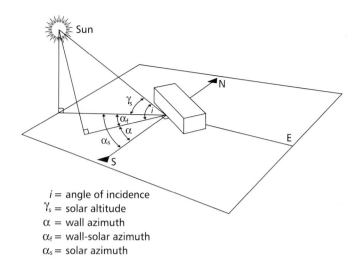

i = angle of incidence
γ_s = solar altitude
α = wall azimuth
α_f = wall–solar azimuth
α_s = solar azimuth

Figure 2.13 Solar geometry

solar bearing for a range of declinations covering the year. Figure 2.14 shows an example sun-path diagram for latitude 52°N.

2.7.3 Solar irradiation

2.7.3.1 Monthly mean daily irradiation on inclined planes (UK)

Tables 2.21 to 2.23 provide values of monthly mean daily irradiation on a range of inclined planes are provided for three sites in the UK: London area (Bracknell) (51° 23′N), Manchester (Aughton) (53° 34′N) and Edinburgh (Mylnefield) (56° 27′N). For Tables 2.22 and 2.23, refer to the computer disk that accompanies this Guide.

These tables were calculated from data tapes using observed hourly global and diffuse horizontal irradiation values for the 12-year period 1981 to 1992 (inclusive), using a ground albedo (i.e. ground reflectance for entire solar radiation spectrum) of 0.2. See CIBSE Guide: *Weather and solar data*[1] for further details.

2.7.3.2 Near-extreme global irradiation with associated diffuse irradiation (UK)

Tables 2.24 to 2.26 provide values of near-extreme hourly irradiation (formerly termed 'design maxima') for three UK sites: London area (Bracknell), Manchester (Aughton) and Edinburgh (Mylnefield), respectively. For Tables 2.25 and 2.26, refer to the computer disk that accompanies this Guide.

The tables provide mean hourly irradiation values associated with a known exceedence of daily global irradiation and are intended for use in risk-based design applications. They provide the basis for the tables of solar cooling load provided in Section 5: *Thermal response and plant sizing.*

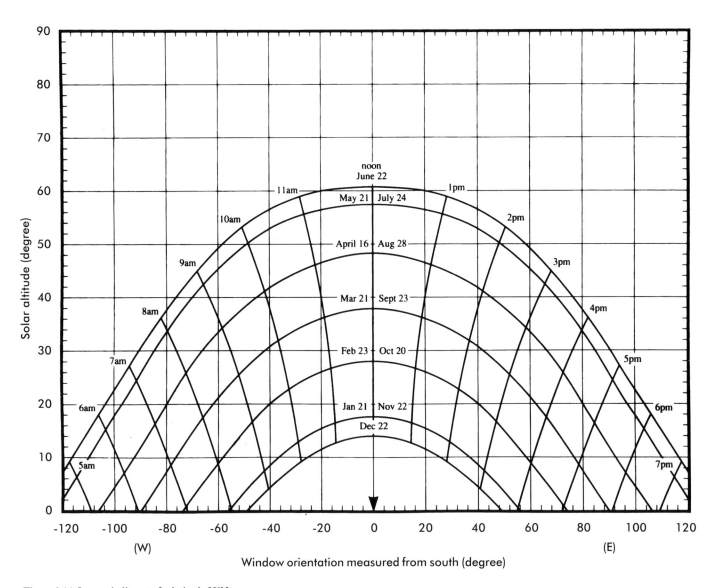

Figure 2.14 Sun-path diagram for latitude 52°N

In the case of Bracknell and Aughton, the input data sets include the observed hourly horizontal diffuse irradiation measured during the same hour as the corresponding hourly global irradiation. The diffuse data for Mylnefield have been estimated using the observed hourly global irradiation. The clear sky model used for this purpose is described in CIBSE Guide: *Weather and solar data*[1]. In all cases, the horizontal beam irradiation is the difference between the horizontal global and horizontal diffuse irradiation.

Monthly mean hourly near-extreme values of global and diffuse horizontal irradiation have been established using the hourly data for all days when the daily horizontal global daily irradiation data on that day fell into the category of the highest 5% of the days in each long-term monthly daily series. As the hourly mean horizontal values tabulated are based on taking hourly averages for all the days in a month with a daily global irradiation above 95% level, the tables may be considered to be representative of the 97.5 percentile daily global horizontal irradiation conditions month-by-month. Details of the quality control procedures used in the generation of these data have been published by Page[8].

The corresponding hourly slope irradiation values were calculated, hour-by-hour, using the monthly mean hourly

values of the observed hourly global and diffuse horizontal observations for each of the selected monthly extreme-day data series. The declination values needed to generate the underlying solar geometry were set at the standard clear day design values, see CIBSE Guide: *Weather and solar data*. A ground albedo of 0.2 was assumed.

2.7.3.3 Daily mean and hourly solar irradiance (latitudes 0–60°)

In many design situations, observed hourly global and diffuse irradiation data for horizontal surfaces are not available and a theoretical approach has to be adopted. For building services engineering design, maximum or near maximum cooling loads are associated with cloudless or near cloudless days, particularly in the case of heavily glazed buildings. Table 2.27 provides daily mean and hourly values of clear sky short-wave irradiance for latitudes from 60°N to 60°S. This table is included on the computer disk that accompanies this Guide.

Details of the computer algorithms used to generate Table 2.27 and notes on how the values may be adapted to local conditions of climate and geography are given in CIBSE Guide: *Weather and solar data*[1].

Table 2.20 Solar altitude angles and bearings from true north for northern hemisphere sites; bearings must be corrected for the southern hemisphere, see footnote (© J K Page; used with permission)

Solar altitude angle and bearing for stated date in northern (N) and southern (S) hemispheres

Latitude 0°

Solar time	(N) Jan 29 / (S) Jul 3		Feb 26 / Aug 3		Mar 29 / Sep 3		Apr 28 / Oct 3		May 29 / Nov 3		Jun 21 / Dec 21		Jul 4 / Jan 28		Aug 4 / Feb 25		Sep 4 / Mar 28		Oct 4 / Apr 28		Nov 4 / May 29		Dec 4 / Jun 3	
	Alt.	Bear.	Alt.	Bear.	Alt.	Bear.	Alt.	Bear.	Alt.	Bear.	Alt.	Bear.	Alt.	Bear.	Alt.	Bear.	Alt.	Bear.	Alt.	Bear.	Alt.	Bear.	Alt.	Bear.
06:30	7	108	7	99	7	87	7	76	7	68	7	66	7	67	7	73	7	83	7	94	7	106	7	112
07:30	21	110	22	100	22	86	22	75	21	67	21	65	21	66	21	72	22	82	22	95	22	107	21	114
08:30	35	113	37	101	37	86	36	72	34	63	34	61	34	62	36	69	37	81	37	96	36	109	34	117
09:30	49	118	52	105	52	84	50	67	48	57	47	55	47	55	49	63	52	78	52	97	50	114	47	124
10:30	61	131	66	113	67	81	64	57	59	44	58	42	58	42	62	51	66	72	67	101	63	126	59	137
11:30	70	158	78	141	82	65	74	27	67	18	65	17	66	17	71	23	80	46	81	121	73	155	67	162
12:30	70	202	78	219	82	295	74	333	67	342	65	343	66	343	71	337	80	314	81	240	73	205	67	198
13:30	61	229	66	247	67	279	64	304	59	316	58	319	58	318	62	309	66	288	67	259	63	234	59	223
14:30	49	242	52	255	52	276	50	293	48	303	47	306	47	305	49	297	52	282	52	263	50	246	47	236
15:30	35	248	37	259	37	274	36	288	34	297	34	299	34	298	36	291	37	279	37	265	36	251	34	243
16:30	21	251	22	260	22	274	22	285	21	293	21	295	21	295	21	289	22	278	22	265	22	253	21	246
17:30	7	252	7	261	7	274	7	284	7	292	7	294	7	293	7	287	7	277	7	266	7	255	7	248
Sunrise:	06:13		06:06		05:58		05:50		05:44		05:42		05:43		05:47		05:55		06:03		06:11		06:17	
Sunset:	17:47		17:54		18:02		18:10		18:16		18:18		18:17		18:13		18:05		17:57		17:49		17:43	

Latitude 10°

Solar time	(N) Jan 29 / (S) Jul 3		Feb 26 / Aug 3		Mar 29 / Sep 3		Apr 28 / Oct 3		May 29 / Nov 3		Jun 21 / Dec 21		Jul 4 / Jan 28		Aug 4 / Feb 25		Sep 4 / Mar 28		Oct 4 / Apr 28		Nov 4 / May 29		Dec 4 / Jun 3	
	Alt.	Bear.	Alt.	Bear.	Alt.	Bear.	Alt.	Bear.	Alt.	Bear.	Alt.	Bear.	Alt.	Bear.	Alt.	Bear.	Alt.	Bear.	Alt.	Bear.	Alt.	Bear.	Alt.	Bear.
05:30							*1*	*76*	*2*	*68*	*2*	*67*	*2*	*67*	*1*	*73*	*1*	*83*						
06:30	*5*	*110*	*7*	*100*	8	88	10	77	11	70	11	68	11	68	10	74	9	84	7	96	*6*	*107*	*5*	*114*
07:30	18	113	20	104	23	91	24	79	24	71	25	69	25	69	24	76	23	87	21	99	18	110	16	117
08:30	31	118	34	108	38	93	39	80	38	70	38	68	38	69	39	76	38	89	36	103	32	115	29	123
09:30	43	127	48	116	52	97	53	80	52	67	52	65	52	66	53	75	53	91	50	109	45	124	41	132
10:30	54	142	61	130	67	105	68	77	65	59	65	55	65	56	67	69	68	96	63	122	56	139	51	146
11:30	61	165	70	158	80	131	82	60	76	31	75	27	75	28	80	45	82	110	74	152	64	164	57	167
12:30	61	195	70	202	80	229	82	301	76	329	75	333	75	332	80	316	82	250	74	208	64	196	57	193
13:30	54	218	61	230	67	255	68	283	65	301	65	305	65	304	67	291	68	265	63	238	56	222	51	214
14:30	43	233	48	244	52	263	53	280	52	293	52	295	52	295	53	285	53	269	50	251	45	236	41	228
15:30	31	242	34	252	38	267	39	280	38	290	38	292	38	291	39	284	38	271	36	257	32	245	29	237
16:30	18	247	20	256	23	270	24	281	24	289	25	291	25	291	24	285	23	274	21	261	18	250	16	243
17:30	*5*	*251*	*7*	*260*	8	272	10	283	11	290	11	292	11	292	10	286	9	276	7	264	*6*	*253*	*5*	*246*
18:30							*1*	*284*	*2*	*292*	*2*	*294*	*2*	*293*	*1*	*287*	*1*	*277*						
Sunrise:	06:13		06:06		05:58		05:50		05:44		05:42		05:43		05:47		05:55		06:03		06:11		06:17	
Sunset:	17:47		17:54		18:02		18:10		18:16		18:18		18:17		18:13		18:05		17:57		17:49		17:43	

Note: bearings measured from true north and must be corrected for the southern hemisphere by subtracting the tabulated value from 180° if the tabulated value is less than 180° and from 540° if the tabulated value is greater than 180°.

Table 2.20 Solar altitude angles and bearings from true north for northern hemisphere sites — *continued*

Solar altitude angle and bearing for stated date in northern (N) and southern (S) hemispheres

Latitude	Solar time	(N) Jan 29 (S) Jul 3		Feb 26 Aug 3		Mar 29 Sep 3		Apr 28 Oct 3		May 29 Nov 3		Jun 21 Dec 21		Jul 4 Jan 28		Aug 4 Feb 25		Sep 4 Mar 28		Oct 4 Apr 28		Nov 4 May 29		Dec 4 Jun 3	
		Alt.	Bear.	Alt.	Bear.	Alt.	Bear.	Alt.	Bear.	Alt.	Bear.	Alt.	Bear.	Alt.	Bear.	Alt.	Bear.	Alt.	Bear.	Alt.	Bear.	Alt.	Bear.	Alt.	Bear.
20°	*05:30*					*1*	*87*	*2*	*76*	*4*	*68*	*4*	*67*	*4*	*67*	*3*	*73*	*1*	*83*						
	06:30	4	*111*	5	102	8	89	12	79	14	72	14	70	14	71	13	76	9	86	6	97	4	*108*	3	*115*
	07:30	14	*115*	18	107	22	95	26	83	27	75	28	73	28	74	26	80	24	91	19	102	15	*113*	12	*119*
	08:30	26	*123*	31	114	36	101	40	88	41	78	41	76	41	77	40	84	38	97	33	110	27	*121*	24	*127*
	09:30	37	*134*	43	125	50	110	54	93	55	81	55	77	55	78	54	88	51	104	46	119	39	*131*	34	*137*
	10:30	46	*149*	53	141	63	124	68	102	69	82	69	77	69	78	69	94	65	117	57	135	48	*146*	42	*151*
	11:30	51	*169*	60	165	72	155	81	128	83	285	82	62	82	66	82	110	75	150	65	162	54	*168*	47	*170*
	12:30	51	*191*	60	195	72	205	81	232	83	285	82	298	82	294	82	250	75	211	65	198	54	*192*	47	*190*
	13:30	46	*212*	53	219	63	236	68	258	69	279	69	283	69	282	69	266	65	243	57	225	48	*214*	42	*209*
	14:30	37	*226*	43	235	50	251	54	267	55	280	55	283	55	282	54	272	51	256	46	241	39	*229*	34	*223*
	15:30	26	*237*	31	246	36	259	40	272	41	282	41	284	41	283	40	276	38	264	33	251	27	*240*	24	*233*
	16:30	14	*245*	18	253	22	265	26	277	27	285	28	287	28	286	26	280	24	269	19	258	15	*247*	12	*241*
	17:30	4	*249*	5	258	8	271	12	281	14	288	14	290	14	290	13	284	9	274	6	263	4	*252*	3	*245*
	18:30					*1*	*273*	*2*	*284*	*4*	*292*	*4*	*294*	*4*	*293*	*3*	*287*	*1*	*277*						
	Sunrise:	06:27		06:13		05:55		05:39		05:27		05:24		05:25		05:34		05:50		06:06		06:23		06:34	
	Sunset:	17:33		17:47		18:05		18:21		18:33		18:36		18:35		18:26		18:10		17:54		17:37		17:26	
30°	*05:30*					*1*	*87*	*4*	*76*	*5*	*68*	*6*	*66*	*6*	*67*	*4*	*73*	*2*	*83*						
	06:30	2	*112*	4	*103*	8	91	13	81	17	74	18	73	17	73	15	78	10	88	5	98	2	*109*	1	*116*
	07:30	9	*117*	14	110	21	99	26	88	30	81	30	79	30	79	28	85	23	95	17	106	11	*115*	7	*121*
	08:30	20	*127*	26	119	34	108	39	96	42	87	43	85	43	86	41	93	36	104	29	115	22	*124*	17	*130*
	09:30	30	*138*	37	131	46	120	52	106	55	95	56	92	56	93	54	102	48	115	40	127	32	*136*	27	*141*
	10:30	37	*153*	45	148	56	137	64	122	68	107	69	103	69	104	66	117	59	133	49	144	40	*151*	33	*155*
	11:30	41	*171*	50	168	63	164	73	155	79	139	81	133	80	135	76	150	66	161	55	167	44	*170*	37	*171*
	12:30	41	*190*	50	192	63	196	73	205	79	221	81	227	80	225	76	210	66	199	55	193	44	*190*	37	*189*
	13:30	37	*207*	45	213	56	223	64	238	68	253	69	257	69	256	66	243	59	227	49	216	40	*209*	33	*205*
	14:30	30	*222*	37	229	46	241	52	254	55	265	56	268	56	267	54	258	48	245	40	233	32	*224*	27	*219*
	15:30	20	*233*	26	241	34	252	39	264	42	273	43	275	43	274	41	267	36	256	29	245	22	*236*	17	*230*
	16:30	9	*243*	14	250	21	261	26	272	30	279	30	281	30	281	28	275	23	265	17	254	11	*245*	7	*239*
	17:30	2	*248*	4	257	8	269	13	279	17	286	18	287	17	287	15	282	10	273	5	262	2	*251*	1	*244*
	18:30					*1*	*274*	*4*	*284*	*5*	*292*	*6*	*294*	*6*	*293*	*4*	*288*	*2*	*277*						
	Sunrise:	06:44		06:21		05:52		05:26		05:07		05:02		05:04		05:19		05:43		06:10		06:37		06:55	
	Sunset:	17:16		17:39		18:08		18:34		18:53		18:58		18:56		18:41		18:17		17:50		17:23		17:05	

Note: bearings measured from true north and must be corrected for the southern hemisphere by subtracting the tabulated value from 180° if the tabulated value is less than 180° and from 540° if the tabulated value is greater than 180°.

Table 2.20 Solar altitude angles and bearings from true north for northern hemisphere sites — *continued*

Solar altitude angle and bearing for stated date in northern (N) and southern (S) hemispheres

Latitude	Solar time	(N) Jan 29 (S) Jul 3 Alt	Bear	Feb 26 Aug 3 Alt	Bear	Mar 29 Sep 3 Alt	Bear	Apr 28 Oct 3 Alt	Bear	May 29 Nov 3 Alt	Bear	Jun 21 Dec 21 Alt	Bear	Jul 4 Jan 28 Alt	Bear	Aug 4 Feb 25 Alt	Bear	Sep 4 Mar 28 Alt	Bear	Oct 4 Apr 28 Alt	Bear	Nov 4 May 29 Alt	Bear	Dec 4 Jun 3 Alt	Bear
40°	04:30									2	63	2	61	2	61										
	05:30					1	87	4	75	8	69	9	67	9	68	5	72	2	83						
	06:30	3	104	8	92	8	94	15	84	20	76	20	76	17	81	17	81	10	89	1	111				
	07:30	5	119	11	112	19	102	26	93	31	86	32	85	31	85	28	91	22	99	14	108	6	116	3	123
	08:30	14	129	21	123	30	114	38	104	42	96	43	94	43	95	39	101	33	110	25	120	16	127	11	132
	09:30	22	141	30	136	40	127	48	118	53	109	54	106	54	107	50	114	43	124	34	133	25	140	19	144
	10:30	28	156	37	152	48	145	58	136	63	127	65	124	64	125	60	133	51	143	41	150	31	155	24	157
	11:30	31	172	40	170	53	168	63	164	71	159	72	157	72	157	66	162	56	166	45	169	34	171	27	172
	12:30	31	188	40	190	53	193	63	196	71	201	72	203	72	203	66	198	56	194	45	191	34	189	27	188
	13:30	28	204	37	208	48	215	58	224	63	233	65	236	64	235	60	227	51	218	41	210	31	205	24	203
	14:30	22	219	30	224	40	233	48	243	53	251	54	254	54	253	50	246	43	236	34	227	25	220	19	217
	15:30	14	231	21	237	30	247	38	256	42	264	43	266	43	265	39	259	33	250	25	240	16	233	11	228
	16:30	5	241	11	248	19	258	26	267	31	274	32	275	31	275	28	270	22	261	14	252	6	244	3	237
	17:30			3	256	8	268	15	276	19	283	20	284	20	284	17	279	10	271	4	261	1	249		
	18:30					1	274	4	285	8	291	9	293	9	292	5	288	2	277						
	19:30									2	297	2	299	2	299										
	Sunrise:	07:04		06:31		05:48		05:11		04:42		04:35		04:37		05:00		05:36		06:15		06:54		07:20	
	Sunset:	16:56		17:29		18:12		18:49		19:18		19:25		19:23		19:00		18:24		17:45		17:06		16:40	
50°	04:30							1	69	4	60	5	58	4	59	2	65								
	05:30					1	86	6	75	12	70	13	69	13	70	8	73	3	82						
	06:30			1	106	7	94	16	86	21	81	22	80	22	80	18	84	10	91	3	101				
	07:30	1	122	7	113	17	105	25	98	31	92	32	91	32	91	28	96	20	103	11	110	3	119		
	08:30	8	131	15	126	26	118	35	111	40	105	42	103	41	104	37	109	29	116	19	123	10	129	4	133
	09:30	14	143	23	139	34	133	43	126	49	120	51	118	50	119	46	124	37	131	27	137	17	142	10	145
	10:30	19	157	28	155	40	150	50	145	57	140	58	138	58	139	53	143	43	149	32	153	22	157	15	159
	11:30	21	172	31	171	43	170	54	168	61	166	63	165	62	165	57	167	47	169	35	171	24	172	17	173
	12:30	21	188	31	189	43	190	54	192	61	195	63	195	62	195	57	193	47	191	35	189	24	188	17	187
	13:30	19	203	28	205	40	210	50	215	57	220	58	222	58	221	53	217	43	211	32	207	22	203	15	202
	14:30	14	217	23	221	34	227	43	234	49	240	51	242	50	241	46	236	37	229	27	223	17	218	10	215
	15:30	8	230	15	234	26	242	35	249	40	255	42	257	41	256	37	251	29	244	19	237	10	231	4	227
	16:30	1	238	7	247	17	255	25	262	31	268	32	269	32	269	28	264	20	257	11	250	3	241		
	17:30			1	254	7	267	16	274	21	279	22	280	22	280	18	276	10	269	3	259				
	18:30					1	274	6	285	12	290	13	291	13	291	8	287	3	278						
	19:30							1	292	4	300	5	302	4	301	2	295								
	Sunrise:	07:32		06:44		05:44		04:50		04:07		03:56		03:59		04:33		05:26		06:21		07:17		07:57	
	Sunset:	16:28		17:16		18:16		19:10		19:53		20:04		20:01		19:27		18:34		17:39		16:43		16:03	

Note: bearings measured from true north and must be corrected for the southern hemisphere by subtracting the tabulated value from 180° if the tabulated value is less than 180° and from 540° if the tabulated value is greater than 180°.

Table 2.20 Solar altitude angles and bearings from true north for northern hemisphere sites — *continued*

Solar altitude angle and bearing for stated date in northern (N) and southern (S) hemispheres

Latitude	Solar time	(N) Jan 29 (S) Jul 3 Alt.	Bear.	Feb 26 Aug 3 Alt.	Bear.	Mar 29 Sep 3 Alt.	Bear.	Apr 28 Oct 3 Alt.	Bear.	May 29 Nov 3 Alt.	Bear.	Jun 21 Dec 21 Alt.	Bear.	Jul 4 Jan 28 Alt.	Bear.	Aug 4 Feb 25 Alt.	Bear.	Sep 4 Mar 28 Alt.	Bear.	Oct 4 Apr 28 Alt.	Bear.	Nov 4 May 29 Alt.	Bear.	Dec 4 Jun 3 Alt.	Bear.
55°	03:30									1	52	2	50	2	50										
	04:30							2	67	6	60	7	59	7	59	3	64								
	05:30					1	86	7	76	13	71	15	70	14	71	10	74	3	82						
	06:30			1	107	7	94	16	88	22	83	23	82	23	82	18	86	10	92	2	101				
	07:30			5	114	16	107	24	100	30	95	32	94	31	94	27	98	19	105	9	111	2	120		
	08:30	4	131	12	127	23	120	33	114	39	109	40	108	40	108	35	112	27	118	17	124	7	130	2	135
	09:30	10	144	19	142	30	135	40	130	46	125	48	123	48	124	43	128	34	134	23	139	13	143	6	146
	10:30	14	158	23	157	35	152	46	148	53	144	54	143	54	143	48	147	39	151	28	155	17	157	10	159
	11:30	17	173	26	172	38	171	49	169	56	167	58	167	57	167	52	168	42	170	30	171	19	172	12	173
	12:30	17	187	26	188	38	190	49	191	56	193	58	193	57	193	52	192	42	190	30	189	19	188	12	187
	13:30	14	202	23	204	35	208	46	212	53	216	54	217	54	217	48	214	39	209	28	206	17	203	10	201
	14:30	10	216	19	219	30	225	40	230	46	235	48	237	48	236	43	232	34	227	23	221	13	217	6	215
	15:30	4	229	12	233	23	240	33	246	39	251	40	253	40	252	35	248	27	242	17	236	7	230	2	225
	16:30			5	246	16	253	24	260	30	265	32	266	31	266	27	262	19	255	9	249	2	240		
	17:30			1	253	7	266	16	272	22	277	23	278	23	278	18	274	10	268	2	259				
	18:30					1	274	7	284	13	289	15	290	14	289	10	286	3	278						
	19:30							2	293	6	300	7	301	7	301	3	297								
	20:30									1	308	2	311	2	310										
	Sunrise:	07:52		06:53		05:40		04:35		03:42		03:27		03:32		04:15		05:19		06:25		07:33		08:23	
	Sunset:	16:08		17:07		18:20		19:25		20:18		20:33		20:28		19:45		18:41		17:35		16:27		15:37	
60°	02:30											1	39												
	03:30									2	48	4	47	3	47	1	55								
	04:30							2	65	8	60	10	59	9	60	4	62								
	05:30					1	86	9	76	15	73	17	72	16	72	11	75								
	06:30					7	95	16	89	22	85	24	84	23	84	19	88	3	81						
	07:30			3	114	14	108	23	103	30	98	31	97	31	97	26	101	10	93	2	102				
	08:30	2	133	9	127	21	122	30	117	37	113	39	111	38	112	33	115	17	106	7	112	4	130		
	09:30	6	144	15	142	27	137	37	133	43	129	45	128	45	128	39	131	24	120	14	126	9	144	2	146
	10:30	10	158	19	157	31	154	41	150	48	148	50	147	50	147	44	149	30	136	19	140	12	158	6	159
	11:30	12	173	21	172	33	171	44	170	51	169	53	169	53	169	47	170	34	153	23	156	14	173	8	173
	12:30	12	187	21	188	33	189	44	190	51	191	53	192	53	191	47	191	37	171	25	172	14	188	8	187
	13:30	10	202	19	204	31	206	41	210	48	213	50	213	50	213	44	211	37	189	25	188	12	202	6	201
	14:30	6	216	15	219	27	223	37	227	43	231	45	232	45	232	39	229	34	207	23	205	9	216	2	214
	15:30	2	227	9	233	21	238	30	243	37	248	39	249	38	248	33	245	30	224	19	220	4	230		
	16:30			3	246	14	252	23	258	30	262	31	263	31	263	26	259	24	240	14	235				
	17:30					7	265	16	271	22	275	24	276	23	276	19	272	17	254	7	248				
	18:30					1	274	9	284	15	287	17	288	16	288	11	285	10	267	2	258				
	19:30							2	295	8	300	10	301	9	300	4	298	3	279						
	20:30									2	312	4	313	3	313	1	305								
	21:30											1	321												
	Sunrise:	08:18		07:04		05:36		04:16		03:06		02:45		02:52		03:50		05:10		06:31		07:54		09:00	
	Sunset:	15:42		16:56		18:24		19:44		20:54		21:15		21:08		20:10		18:50		17:29		16:06		15:00	

Note: bearings measured from true north and must be corrected for the southern hemisphere by subtracting the tabulated value from 180° if the tabulated value is less than 180° and from 540° if the tabulated value is greater than 180°.

Table 2.21 Monthly mean daily irradiation on inclined planes: London area (Bracknell) (1981–1992)

| Month | Mean irradiation ($W \cdot h \cdot m^{-2}$) for stated inclination from horizontal (°) | | | | | | | | | | | | | | | | | | |
| | Beam | | | | | Diffuse | | | | | Total | | | | | Ground reflected | | | |
	0	30	45	60	90	0	30	45	60	90	0	30	45	60	90	30	45	60	90
West:																			
Jan	223	207	199	187	144	467	441	407	357	227	690	657	627	578	440	9	20	35	70
Feb	440	400	376	347	254	857	813	747	655	415	1298	1230	1161	1067	800	17	38	65	130
Mar	771	699	650	586	417	1428	1350	1243	1085	686	2199	2078	1957	1781	1323	29	64	110	220
Apr	1552	1371	1245	1101	753	2093	1981	1836	1618	1032	3644	3401	3188	2902	2149	49	107	182	365
May	2034	1808	1631	1428	951	2578	2446	2269	2002	1278	4612	4316	4035	3661	2690	62	135	231	462
Jun	1929	1681	1490	1281	813	2874	2698	2497	2187	1373	4802	4443	4129	3708	2667	64	141	241	481
Jul	2116	1870	1679	1460	952	2699	2546	2360	2074	1312	4815	4481	4180	3775	2746	65	141	241	482
Aug	1868	1633	1473	1295	867	2319	2194	2031	1792	1139	4187	3884	3627	3296	2425	56	123	210	419
Sep	1250	1124	1038	929	652	1626	1546	1436	1262	809	2877	2709	2558	2335	1749	39	84	144	288
Oct	637	568	529	484	352	1009	957	884	776	495	1646	1547	1461	1343	1012	22	48	82	165
Nov	309	290	277	260	199	575	545	502	440	281	884	847	806	745	569	12	26	44	89
Dec	155	147	145	136	107	377	356	328	287	182	532	510	488	450	343	7	16	27	54
Mean	1107	983	894	791	539	1575	1489	1378	1211	769	2682	2508	2351	2137	1576	36	79	134	269
South-west:																			
Jan	223	463	539	579	541	467	496	482	449	337	690	968	1042	1062	948	9	21	34	70
Feb	440	721	792	810	695	857	880	843	771	557	1298	1618	1673	1646	1382	17	38	65	130
Mar	771	1028	1068	1037	801	1428	1419	1337	1202	826	2199	2476	2470	2349	1847	29	65	110	220
Apr	1552	1742	1700	1557	1062	2093	2053	1928	1724	1147	3644	3844	3735	3463	2574	49	107	182	365
May	2034	2086	1954	1720	1064	2578	2496	2325	2063	1347	4612	4643	4414	4014	2873	61	135	231	462
Jun	1929	1879	1717	1473	844	2874	2745	2538	2233	1431	4802	4688	4395	3947	2756	64	140	241	481
Jul	2116	2114	1957	1705	1018	2699	2597	2411	2130	1376	4815	4775	4510	4076	2877	64	142	241	483
Aug	1868	2006	1921	1730	1138	2319	2263	2119	1889	1247	4187	4325	4163	3829	2804	56	123	210	419
Sep	1250	1553	1576	1497	1105	1626	1627	1540	1390	951	2877	3218	3201	3031	2344	38	85	144	288
Oct	637	954	1024	1026	845	1009	1031	984	897	642	1646	2007	2056	2005	1652	22	48	82	165
Nov	309	594	679	719	656	575	605	587	544	405	884	1211	1292	1307	1150	12	26	44	89
Dec	155	356	424	462	444	377	403	394	368	280	532	767	833	857	778	8	15	27	54
Mean	1107	1291	1279	1193	851	1575	1551	1457	1305	879	2682	2878	2815	2632	1999	36	79	134	269
South:																			
Jan	223	580	705	782	774	467	521	518	495	391	690	1111	1244	1311	1234	10	21	34	69
Feb	440	875	1009	1075	987	857	914	891	834	630	1298	1806	1938	1973	1747	17	38	64	130
Mar	771	1188	1281	1286	1040	1428	1454	1387	1269	909	2199	2671	2732	2665	2168	29	64	110	219
Apr	1552	1920	1914	1777	1164	2093	2085	1965	1772	1204	3644	4054	3986	3732	2734	49	107	183	366
May	2034	2184	2054	1785	950	2578	2501	2327	2066	1341	4612	4747	4516	4082	2753	62	135	231	462
Jun	1929	1956	1786	1501	703	2874	2748	2540	2238	1431	4802	4769	4467	3980	2616	65	141	241	482
Jul	2116	2196	2031	1733	862	2699	2600	2414	2136	1376	4815	4861	4586	4110	2720	65	141	241	482
Aug	1868	2183	2128	1927	1172	2319	2291	2150	1928	1286	4187	4530	4400	4065	2877	56	122	210	419
Sep	1250	1756	1836	1791	1347	1626	1665	1591	1456	1034	2877	3460	3511	3391	2669	39	84	144	288
Oct	637	1146	1291	1348	1189	1009	1068	1037	966	720	1646	2235	2376	2396	2074	21	48	82	165
Nov	309	733	877	960	930	575	634	628	597	467	884	1379	1531	1602	1486	12	26	45	89
Dec	155	449	554	622	629	377	425	424	407	325	532	881	994	1056	1007	7	16	27	53
Mean	1107	1430	1455	1382	979	1575	1576	1489	1347	926	2682	3042	3023	2864	2174	36	79	135	269
South-east:																			
Jan	223	471	550	592	556	467	497	484	451	340	690	977	1055	1078	966	9	21	35	70
Feb	440	742	821	846	735	857	881	844	772	558	1298	1640	1704	1683	1423	17	39	65	130
Mar	771	1056	1107	1084	849	1428	1424	1344	1210	836	2199	2509	2516	2404	1906	29	65	110	221
Apr	1552	1813	1795	1668	1171	2093	2060	1937	1734	1157	3644	3922	3839	3585	2693	49	107	183	365
May	2034	2128	2012	1790	1128	2578	2493	2322	2057	1337	4612	4682	4469	4077	2927	61	135	230	462
Jun	1929	1938	1796	1564	919	2874	2754	2550	2244	1442	4802	4757	4487	4049	2842	65	141	241	481
Jul	2116	2157	2014	1770	1073	2699	2601	2417	2136	1380	4815	4822	4572	4146	2936	64	141	240	483
Aug	1868	2102	2048	1874	1265	2319	2272	2130	1900	1257	4187	4430	4301	3984	2941	56	123	210	419
Sep	1250	1593	1630	1559	1164	1626	1628	1542	1392	952	2877	3260	3256	3094	2404	39	84	143	288
Oct	637	996	1083	1096	922	1009	1033	987	901	645	1646	2051	2118	2080	1733	22	48	83	166
Nov	309	600	689	731	670	575	606	588	545	406	884	1218	1302	1320	1165	12	25	44	89
Dec	155	357	425	463	445	377	404	394	369	281	532	768	835	859	780	7	16	27	54
Mean	1107	1329	1331	1253	908	1575	1554	1462	1309	883	2682	2920	2871	2696	2059	37	78	134	268

Table 2.21 Monthly mean daily irradiation on inclined planes: London area (Bracknell) (1981–1992)

Month	Beam					Diffuse					Total					Ground reflected			
	0	30	45	60	90	0	30	45	60	90	0	30	45	60	90	30	45	60	90
East:																			
Jan	223	216	212	200	156	467	443	408	358	228	690	668	640	592	453	9	20	34	69
Feb	440	424	406	380	284	857	813	748	656	417	1298	1255	1191	1101	832	18	37	65	131
Mar	771	733	692	632	458	1428	1355	1250	1093	696	2199	2117	2007	1836	1374	29	65	111	220
Apr	1552	1464	1362	1227	858	2093	1989	1845	1627	1039	3644	3502	3314	3036	2263	49	107	182	366
May	2034	1866	1709	1512	1010	2578	2442	2263	1992	1262	4612	4370	4107	3734	2733	62	135	230	461
Jun	1929	1763	1596	1392	897	2874	2711	2508	2198	1380	4802	4538	4245	3831	2758	64	141	241	481
Jul	2116	1930	1757	1542	1013	2699	2553	2365	2078	1312	4815	4547	4263	3861	2807	64	141	241	482
Aug	1868	1765	1636	1465	1016	2319	2206	2043	1804	1153	4187	4026	3801	3479	2588	55	122	210	419
Sep	1250	1176	1101	996	712	1626	1548	1438	1264	811	2877	2763	2623	2404	1811	39	84	144	288
Oct	637	621	596	556	413	1009	960	886	779	498	1646	1603	1531	1417	1076	22	49	82	165
Nov	309	299	289	272	209	575	546	503	441	281	884	857	818	758	579	12	26	45	89
Dec	155	147	146	136	108	377	356	328	287	182	532	510	489	450	344	7	15	27	54
Mean	1107	1034	958	859	594	1575	1493	1382	1215	772	2682	2563	2419	2208	1635	36	79	134	269

The header also includes: Mean irradiation ($W{\cdot}h{\cdot}m^{-2}$) for stated inclination from horizontal (°)

Table 2.22 Monthly mean daily irradiation on inclined planes: Manchester (Aughton) (1981–1992): refer to computer disk

Table 2.23 Monthly mean daily irradiation on inclined planes: Edinburgh (Mylnefield) (1981–1992): refer to computer disk

Table 2.24 Design 97.5 percentile of beam and diffuse irradiance on vertical and horizontal surfaces: London area (Bracknell) (1981–1992)

Date and times of sunrise/sunset	Orient-ation	Type	Mean	0330	0430	0530	0630	0730	0830	0930	1030	1130	1230	1330	1430	1530	1630	1730	1830	1930	2030
Jan 29	Beam normal		156	—	—	—	—	*104*	288	466	593	617	612	507	363	224	*81*	—	—	—	—
	N	Beam	0	—	—	—	—	*0*	0	0	0	0	**0**	0	0	0	*0*	—	—	—	—
Sunrise: 07:37		Diffuse	15	—	—	—	—	*9*	23	40	53	61	**62**	57	42	24	*10*	—	—	—	—
Sunset: 16:23	NE	Beam	1	—	—	—	—	*23*	22	0	0	0	**0**	0	0	0	*0*	—	—	—	—
		Diffuse	16	—	—	—	—	*25*	29	45	53	61	**62**	57	42	24	*10*	—	—	—	—
	E	Beam	34	—	—	—	—	*88*	217	**269**	215	77	0	0	0	0	*0*	—	—	—	—
		Diffuse	23	—	—	—	—	*34*	80	**99**	94	72	71	57	42	24	*10*	—	—	—	—
	SE	Beam	98	—	—	—	—	*101*	285	449	**521**	460	349	186	53	0	*0*	—	—	—	—
		Diffuse	36	—	—	—	—	*37*	97	135	**149**	146	128	101	57	27	*10*	—	—	—	—
	S	Beam	130	—	—	—	—	*55*	186	365	522	**574**	569	447	285	145	*43*	—	—	—	—
		Diffuse	43	—	—	—	—	*28*	72	118	150	**166**	169	157	114	70	*32*	—	—	—	—
	SW	Beam	89	—	—	—	—	*0*	0	68	217	352	**456**	446	350	222	*79*	—	—	—	—
		Diffuse	35	—	—	—	—	*9*	26	54	95	126	**148**	157	129	92	*42*	—	—	—	—
	W	Beam	28	—	—	—	—	*0*	0	0	0	0	76	184	**210**	169	*69*	—	—	—	—
		Diffuse	23	—	—	—	—	*9*	23	40	53	70	73	101	**97**	77	*39*	—	—	—	—
	NW	Beam	1	—	—	—	—	*0*	0	0	0	0	**0**	0	0	17	*18*	—	—	—	—
		Diffuse	16	—	—	—	—	*9*	23	40	53	61	**62**	57	47	30	*29*	—	—	—	—
	Horiz.	Beam	42	—	—	—	—	*3*	34	106	180	213	211	154	82	26	*2*	—	—	—	—
	Horiz.	Diffuse	24	—	—	—	—	*19*	41	65	77	87	89	91	74	47	*22*	—	—	—	—
	Horiz.	Global	66	—	—	—	—	*22*	75	171	257	300	300	245	156	73	*24*	—	—	—	—
Feb 26	Beam normal		201	—	—	—	*67*	210	375	503	605	647	636	603	552	426	238	*77*	—	—	—
	N	Beam	0	—	—	—	*0*	0	0	0	0	**0**	0	0	0	0	0	*0*	—	—	—
Sunrise: 06:46		Diffuse	26	—	—	—	*9*	23	44	68	82	**92**	90	82	66	44	22	*9*	—	—	—
Sunset: 17:14	NE	Beam	6	—	—	—	*32*	**77**	57	0	0	0	0	0	0	0	0	*0*	—	—	—
		Diffuse	28	—	—	—	*26*	**49**	59	79	82	92	90	82	66	44	22	*8*	—	—	—
	E	Beam	46	—	—	—	*64*	192	294	**302**	229	83	0	0	0	0	0	*0*	—	—	—
		Diffuse	37	—	—	—	*34*	81	115	**138**	130	103	102	82	66	44	22	*8*	—	—	—
	SE	Beam	106	—	—	—	*59*	194	358	466	**509**	454	330	185	42	0	0	*0*	—	—	—
		Diffuse	49	—	—	—	*32*	81	129	173	**184**	181	155	121	71	49	22	*8*	—	—	—
	S	Beam	145	—	—	—	*18*	83	213	358	491	558	549	489	392	242	94	*21*	—	—	—
		Diffuse	57	—	—	—	*24*	50	97	150	181	**201**	196	179	146	99	51	*24*	—	—	—
	SW	Beam	111	—	—	—	*0*	0	0	39	185	336	446	**507**	512	407	220	*67*	—	—	—
		Diffuse	49	—	—	—	*8*	23	49	74	121	158	177	**183**	170	133	85	*32*	—	—	—
	W	Beam	50	—	—	—	*0*	0	0	0	0	0	82	228	**332**	334	217	*74*	—	—	—
		Diffuse	37	—	—	—	*8*	23	44	68	82	104	101	129	**135**	118	84	*34*	—	—	—
	NW	Beam	7	—	—	—	*0*	0	0	0	0	0	0	0	0	65	**87**	*37*	—	—	—
		Diffuse	30	—	—	—	*8*	23	44	68	82	92	90	129	77	59	**49**	*26*	—	—	—
	Horiz.	Beam	75	—	—	—	*1*	24	95	184	270	316	311	269	202	108	27	*1*	—	—	—
	Horiz.	Diffuse	40	—	—	—	*18*	44	77	109	121	131	129	120	100	73	42	*18*	—	—	—
	Horiz.	Global	115	—	—	—	*19*	68	172	293	391	447	440	389	302	181	69	*19*	—	—	—
Mar 29	Beam normal		263	—	—	*70*	221	385	524	610	649	696	683	663	631	552	415	238	*76*	—	—
	N	Beam	0	—	—	*5*	0	0	0	0	0	0	**0**	0	0	0	0	0	*5*	—	—
Sunrise: 05:43		Diffuse	41	—	—	*27*	30	53	77	96	112	119	**120**	112	96	75	51	28	*24*	—	—
Sunset: 18:17	NE	Beam	20	—	—	*53*	145	**180**	131	12	0	0	0	0	0	0	0	0	*0*	—	—
		Diffuse	45	—	—	*35*	72	**97**	107	90	118	119	120	112	96	75	49	24	*9*	—	—
	E	Beam	72	—	—	*70*	219	355	**415**	371	248	90	0	0	0	0	0	0	*0*	—	—
		Diffuse	57	—	—	*41*	93	136	**167**	169	160	128	135	112	96	75	49	24	*9*	—	—
	SE	Beam	117	—	—	*46*	165	322	455	**513**	489	426	293	141	0	0	0	0	*0*	—	—
		Diffuse	65	—	—	*33*	78	129	176	**196**	205	194	173	136	117	79	49	24	*9*	—	—
	S	Beam	139	—	—	*0*	14	100	229	354	443	**512**	503	453	367	241	108	15	*0*	—	—
		Diffuse	67	—	—	*11*	32	78	129	166	196	**210**	210	196	165	126	75	30	*10*	—	—
	SW	Beam	121	—	—	*0*	0	0	0	0	138	298	418	499	**531**	480	347	177	*50*	—	—
		Diffuse	65	—	—	*9*	26	51	80	118	137	172	195	204	**195**	172	126	75	*30*	—	—
	W	Beam	75	—	—	*0*	0	0	0	0	0	0	89	253	384	**437**	383	236	*76*	—	—
		Diffuse	56	—	—	*9*	26	51	77	96	112	134	129	159	168	**164**	134	91	*37*	—	—
	NW	Beam	22	—	—	*0*	0	0	0	0	0	0	0	0	12	138	**194**	156	*57*	—	—
		Diffuse	45	—	—	*9*	26	51	77	96	112	119	120	118	89	104	**94**	70	*32*	—	—
	Horiz.	Beam	131	—	—	*2*	28	110	223	330	404	462	454	413	341	235	118	30	*2*	—	—
	Horiz.	Diffuse	59	—	—	*21*	50	87	120	139	158	161	163	155	135	113	81	46	*19*	—	—
	Horiz.	Global	190	—	—	*23*	78	197	343	469	562	623	617	568	476	348	199	76	*21*	—	—

* Mean over hour centred at stated solar time

Note: italicised values are calculated for time halfway between sunrise and the end of the sunrise hour or halfway between the beginning of the sunset hour and sunset; the figures shown in bold type, when added together, give the peak total irradiance (i.e. beam plus diffuse) for the stated orientation.

Table 2.24 Design 97.5 percentile of beam and diffuse irradiance on vertical and horizontal surfaces: London area (Bracknell) (1981–1992) — *continued*

Date and times of sunrise/sunset	Orient-ation	Type	Mean	0330	0430	0530	0630	0730	0830	0930	1030	1130	1230	1330	1430	1530	1630	1730	1830	1930	2030
Apr 28 Sunrise: 04:46 Sunset: 19:14		Beam normal	343	—	*74*	235	440	555	674	707	744	765	761	740	724	655	568	408	218	*69*	—
	N	Beam	7	—	*27*	59	24	0	0	0	0	0	**0**	0	0	0	0	22	55	*26*	—
		Diffuse	56	—	*25*	43	53	87	101	117	130	139	**141**	131	120	100	88	52	41	*25*	—
	NE	Beam	47	—	*68*	202	316	**298**	220	71	0	0	0	0	0	0	0	0	0	*0*	—
		Diffuse	64	—	*33*	86	123	**142**	142	119	145	139	141	131	120	100	77	47	22	*8*	—
	E	Beam	103	—	*69*	226	423	497	**519**	417	276	96	0	0	0	0	0	0	0	*0*	—
		Diffuse	74	—	*34*	93	146	183	**196**	185	171	143	155	131	120	100	77	47	22	*8*	—
	SE	Beam	128	—	*29*	118	282	405	513	**519**	483	392	253	92	0	0	0	0	0	*0*	—
		Diffuse	77	—	*25*	61	115	164	195	**202**	205	196	179	136	138	100	77	47	22	*8*	—
	S	Beam	122	—	*0*	0	0	76	207	317	407	458	**455**	404	324	202	78	0	0	*0*	—
		Diffuse	74	—	*8*	24	57	90	139	168	192	207	**212**	194	174	138	91	56	23	*8*	—
	SW	Beam	127	—	*0*	0	0	0	0	0	92	255	390	480	**531**	499	415	262	109	*27*	—
		Diffuse	77	—	*8*	23	48	77	101	134	135	175	201	207	**210**	192	165	110	58	*25*	—
	W	Beam	101	—	*0*	0	0	0	0	0	0	0	97	275	427	**504**	509	392	210	*64*	—
		Diffuse	74	—	*8*	23	48	77	101	117	130	152	146	173	192	**193**	184	139	86	*34*	—
	NW	Beam	45	—	*0*	0	0	0	0	0	0	0	0	0	73	214	**305**	293	187	*63*	—
		Diffuse	64	—	*8*	23	48	77	101	117	130	139	141	146	122	140	**143**	117	80	*33*	—
	Horiz.	Beam	199	—	*1*	26	119	235	377	475	558	605	602	555	486	367	240	110	25	*1*	—
	Horiz.	Diffuse	73	—	*18*	44	80	117	138	151	163	170	177	166	157	138	116	80	43	*18*	—
	Horiz.	Global	272	—	*19*	70	199	352	515	626	721	775	779	721	643	505	356	190	68	*19*	—
May 29 Sunrise: 04:01 Sunset: 19:59		Beam normal	386	—	*145*	350	482	580	685	753	787	794	793	787	758	693	623	511	371	*154*	—
	N	Beam	22	—	*73*	**114**	66	0	0	0	0	0	0	0	0	0	0	70	120	*78*	—
		Diffuse	68	—	*49*	**72**	77	108	116	126	137	143	142	134	125	113	104	73	68	*43*	—
	NE	Beam	63	—	*140*	308	**360**	333	255	117	0	0	0	0	0	0	0	0	0	*0*	—
		Diffuse	74	—	*64*	121	**144**	159	154	136	159	143	142	134	125	108	87	60	36	*15*	—
	E	Beam	112	—	*125*	323	444	498	**505**	426	280	96	0	0	0	0	0	0	0	*0*	—
		Diffuse	81	—	*59*	124	162	191	**197**	188	170	145	153	134	125	108	87	60	36	*14*	—
	SE	Beam	117	—	*36*	148	268	372	460	**486**	443	343	207	47	0	0	0	0	0	*0*	—
		Diffuse	80	—	*44*	81	125	167	189	**197**	194	184	165	126	134	108	87	60	36	*14*	—
	S	Beam	98	—	*0*	0	0	28	145	261	347	389	388	347	262	147	30	0	0	*0*	—
		Diffuse	72	—	*16*	39	72	89	133	163	180	**191**	190	177	159	128	85	68	37	*14*	—
	SW	Beam	120	—	*0*	0	0	0	0	0	47	207	343	443	**489**	465	399	284	157	*38*	—
		Diffuse	79	—	*16*	39	64	90	111	137	128	165	184	190	**193**	183	160	118	76	*39*	—
	W	Beam	116	—	*0*	0	0	0	0	0	0	0	96	280	429	511	**535**	471	342	*132*	—
		Diffuse	80	—	*16*	39	64	90	111	126	137	153	145	168	184	**191**	184	153	117	*53*	—
	NW	Beam	66	—	*0*	0	0	0	0	0	0	0	0	0	118	258	357	**382**	327	*149*	—
		Diffuse	74	—	*17*	39	64	90	111	126	137	143	142	157	134	149	153	**136**	114	*56*	—
	Horiz.	Beam	243	—	*10*	74	175	296	439	564	649	685	685	649	567	444	318	186	79	*10*	—
	Horiz.	Diffuse	77	—	*33*	70	101	133	146	153	156	162	161	153	148	140	121	91	63	*29*	—
	Horiz.	Global	320	—	*43*	144	276	429	585	717	805	847	846	802	715	584	439	277	142	*39*	—
Jun 21 Sunrise: 03:49 Sunset: 20:11		Beam normal	414	*64*	191	387	554	683	747	797	826	837	840	809	771	705	639	531	390	192	*65*
	N	Beam	27	*40*	100	**132**	85	0	0	0	0	0	0	0	0	0	0	82	133	100	*40*
		Diffuse	71	*25*	55	**76**	85	111	117	125	134	139	140	135	127	121	114	85	77	58	*25*
	NE	Beam	74	*64*	185	342	**417**	397	285	134	0	0	0	0	0	0	0	0	0	0	*0*
		Diffuse	77	*32*	72	124	**157**	158	150	134	158	139	140	135	127	113	94	69	42	21	*9*
	E	Beam	124	*50*	162	352	504	**579**	544	445	290	100	0	0	0	0	0	0	0	0	*0*
		Diffuse	83	*27*	66	126	175	**189**	189	180	163	140	149	135	127	113	94	69	42	20	*8*
	SE	Beam	122	*7*	44	155	296	422	484	**496**	447	345	204	36	0	0	0	0	0	0	*0*
		Diffuse	79	*21*	50	82	133	163	180	**187**	183	173	157	123	134	113	94	69	42	20	*8*
	S	Beam	94	*0*	0	0	0	18	141	256	342	387	**389**	335	247	133	17	0	0	0	*0*
		Diffuse	72	*8*	18	41	77	83	125	154	170	179	**180**	172	158	130	87	77	42	20	*8*
	SW	Beam	118	*0*	0	0	0	0	0	0	37	203	346	438	**479**	457	395	284	157	44	*7*
		Diffuse	80	*8*	18	41	69	91	110	132	122	156	175	185	**193**	188	169	133	83	52	*21*
	W	Beam	120	*0*	0	0	0	0	0	0	0	0	101	284	431	513	**542**	483	355	163	*51*
		Diffuse	83	*8*	18	41	69	91	110	125	134	148	140	165	185	197	**196**	175	128	69	*27*
	NW	Beam	71	*0*	0	0	0	0	0	0	0	0	0	130	269	371	**399**	345	186	65	
		Diffuse	77	*9*	19	41	69	91	110	125	134	139	140	159	138	156	164	**157**	126	75	*32*
	Horiz.	Beam	264	*1*	17	91	214	362	493	610	694	735	738	679	590	465	339	205	92	18	*1*
	Horiz.	Diffuse	76	*16*	37	71	104	120	132	140	141	144	146	146	149	146	131	107	72	38	*16*
	Horiz.	Global	341	*17*	54	162	318	482	625	750	835	879	884	825	739	611	470	312	164	56	*17*

Daily mean irradiance (W·m⁻²) and mean hourly irradiance (W·m⁻²) for stated solar time*

* Mean over hour centred at stated solar time

Note: italicised values are calculated for time halfway between sunrise and the end of the sunrise hour or halfway between the beginning of the sunset hour and sunset; the figures shown in bold type, when added together, give the peak total irradiance (i.e. beam plus diffuse) for the stated orientation.

Table 2.24 Design 97.5 percentile of beam and diffuse irradiance on vertical and horizontal surfaces: London area (Bracknell) (1981–1992) — *continued*

Date and times of sunrise/sunset	Orient-ation	Type	Mean	0330	0430	0530	0630	0730	0830	0930	1030	1130	1230	1330	1430	1530	1630	1730	1830	1930	2030
Jul 4	Beam normal		381	57	170	362	505	610	687	729	751	753	765	750	717	672	616	502	360	169	57
	N	Beam	24	35	88	**122**	75	0	0	0	0	0	0	0	0	0	0	74	121	87	35
Sunrise: 03:53		Diffuse	66	20	47	**64**	73	103	110	121	133	140	141	132	123	113	102	78	62	43	18
Sunset: 20:08	NE	Beam	67	57	165	320	**379**	353	260	119	0	0	0	0	0	0	0	0	0	0	0
		Diffuse	71	25	61	103	**132**	146	143	132	156	140	141	132	123	107	85	64	35	15	6
	E	Beam	114	45	145	331	461	**519**	502	409	265	90	0	0	0	0	0	0	0	0	0
		Diffuse	77	22	57	106	147	**174**	179	176	166	144	150	132	123	107	85	64	35	14	5
	SE	Beam	113	7	40	148	273	381	450	**459**	412	315	190	37	0	0	0	0	0	0	0
		Diffuse	76	16	43	69	113	151	171	**183**	186	179	162	124	131	107	85	64	35	14	5
	S	Beam	89	0	0	0	0	20	135	240	318	355	**361**	317	236	132	20	0	0	0	0
		Diffuse	70	6	16	35	67	81	121	152	173	185	**186**	172	156	124	80	71	35	14	5
	SW	Beam	112	0	0	0	0	0	0	0	37	187	320	411	**451**	440	385	272	147	40	7
		Diffuse	76	6	16	35	60	85	104	129	124	161	180	185	**188**	176	150	121	67	39	15
	W	Beam	113	0	0	0	0	0	0	0	0	0	92	264	402	491	**524**	459	329	144	45
		Diffuse	78	6	16	35	60	85	104	121	133	149	144	165	181	184	**173**	157	102	52	20
	NW	Beam	66	0	0	0	0	0	0	0	0	0	0	0	117	254	357	**377**	318	164	57
		Diffuse	72	6	17	35	60	85	104	121	133	140	141	155	135	147	145	**141**	100	56	23
	Horiz.	Beam	241	0	14	83	191	319	449	554	627	658	668	626	545	439	323	190	82	14	0
	Horiz.	Diffuse	75	13	31	60	90	116	130	143	154	162	162	153	150	137	114	97	58	29	12
	Horiz.	Global	315	13	45	143	281	435	579	697	781	820	830	779	695	576	437	287	140	43	12
Aug 4	Beam normal		333	—	93	259	411	551	644	698	755	744	727	706	705	609	496	361	227	82	—
	N	Beam	10	—	40	73	36	0	0	0	0	**0**	0	0	0	0	0	32	64	35	—
Sunrise: 04:29		Diffuse	57	—	33	50	58	89	101	116	127	134	**135**	131	116	100	87	56	47	32	—
Sunset: 19:31	NE	Beam	49	—	87	225	301	**305**	222	86	0	0	0	0	0	0	0	0	0	0	—
		Diffuse	64	—	44	88	118	**137**	140	122	143	134	135	131	116	100	75	48	27	11	—
	E	Beam	101	—	84	245	389	486	**488**	406	276	93	0	0	0	0	0	0	0	0	—
		Diffuse	72	—	43	93	136	171	**186**	179	162	138	147	131	116	100	75	48	27	11	—
	SE	Beam	118	—	31	122	250	383	468	**488**	465	358	221	70	0	0	0	0	0	0	—
		Diffuse	74	—	32	62	107	152	182	**192**	189	182	166	133	130	100	75	48	27	11	—
	S	Beam	107	—	0	0	0	55	174	284	381	**413**	404	356	287	164	50	0	0	0	—
		Diffuse	70	—	11	28	59	84	131	160	177	**190**	193	187	159	131	83	55	28	11	—
	SW	Beam	113	—	0	0	0	0	0	0	74	226	350	434	**493**	442	345	219	107	28	—
		Diffuse	73	—	11	27	51	77	100	130	126	163	185	200	**191**	181	146	98	58	31	—
	W	Beam	94	—	0	0	0	0	0	0	0	0	91	258	410	**461**	438	342	215	74	—
		Diffuse	72	—	11	27	51	77	100	116	127	145	141	171	178	**184**	164	123	85	41	—
	NW	Beam	45	—	0	0	0	0	0	0	0	0	0	87	210	**274**	264	197	77	—	—
		Diffuse	64	—	11	27	51	77	100	116	127	134	135	149	121	140	**133**	107	80	42	—
	Horiz.	Beam	204	—	4	40	127	253	383	492	590	612	598	552	497	362	228	112	35	3	—
	Horiz.	Diffuse	72	—	23	51	84	113	136	147	148	159	166	167	146	140	116	82	50	22	—
	Horiz.	Global	276	—	27	91	211	366	519	639	738	771	764	719	643	502	344	194	85	25	—
Sep 4	Beam normal		302	—	—	139	371	551	654	683	678	688	720	716	683	604	452	304	114	—	—
	N	Beam	1	—	—	19	0	0	0	0	0	**0**	**0**	0	0	0	0	0	16	—	—
Sunrise: 05:24		Diffuse	43	—	—	30	36	58	76	99	115	**118**	118	109	95	77	59	37	33	—	—
Sunset: 18:36	NE	Beam	34	—	—	111	252	**272**	182	32	0	0	0	0	0	0	0	0	0	—	—
		Diffuse	48	—	—	40	88	**105**	104	94	123	118	118	109	95	77	55	31	12	—	—
	E	Beam	93	—	—	137	365	505	**515**	412	257	89	0	0	0	0	0	0	0	—	—
		Diffuse	58	—	—	45	112	146	**157**	165	158	126	131	109	95	77	55	31	12	—	—
	SE	Beam	132	—	—	84	264	442	546	**551**	488	399	286	131	0	0	0	0	0	—	—
		Diffuse	64	—	—	36	90	135	162	**188**	197	182	159	123	113	79	55	31	12	—	—
	S	Beam	139	—	—	0	9	120	258	367	433	475	**498**	457	367	238	99	7	0	—	—
		Diffuse	64	—	—	12	32	76	117	158	187	194	**191**	175	150	119	77	34	13	—	—
	SW	Beam	125	—	—	0	0	0	0	0	124	273	418	515	**551**	505	363	217	69	—	—
		Diffuse	64	—	—	11	30	54	78	118	132	162	179	184	**178**	164	131	88	39	—	—
	W	Beam	85	—	—	0	0	0	0	0	0	0	93	272	412	**475**	414	299	113	—	—
		Diffuse	57	—	—	11	30	54	76	99	115	132	124	148	157	**159**	141	107	49	—	—
	NW	Beam	28	—	—	0	0	0	0	0	0	0	0	32	168	**223**	206	91	—	—	—
		Diffuse	48	—	—	11	30	54	76	99	115	118	118	116	90	107	**104**	85	43	—	—
	Horiz.	Beam	158	—	—	7	66	184	310	402	454	489	512	479	402	286	151	54	6	—	—
	Horiz.	Diffuse	56	—	—	23	51	79	99	128	151	153	145	134	120	107	88	57	25	—	—
	Horiz.	Global	214	—	—	30	117	263	409	530	605	642	657	613	522	393	239	111	31	—	—

Daily mean irradiance (W·m⁻²) and mean hourly irradiance (W·m⁻²) for stated solar time*

* Mean over hour centred at stated solar time

Note: italicised values are calculated for time halfway between sunrise and the end of the sunrise hour or halfway between the beginning of the sunset hour and sunset; the figures shown in bold type, when added together, give the peak total irradiance (i.e. beam plus diffuse) for the stated orientation.

Table 2.24 Design 97.5 percentile of beam and diffuse irradiance on vertical and horizontal surfaces: London area (Bracknell) (1981–1992) — *continued*

Date and times of sunrise/sunset	Orient-ation	Type	Mean	0330	0430	0530	0630	0730	0830	0930	1030	1130	1230	1330	1430	1530	1630	1730	1830	1930	2030
Oct 4	Beam normal		237	—	—	—	*148*	381	551	679	700	644	632	605	568	451	312	*121*	—	—	—
	N	Beam	0	—	—	—	*0*	0	0	0	0	**0**	**0**	0	0	0	0	*0*	—	—	—
Sunrise: 06:22		Diffuse	29	—	—	—	*12*	30	52	71	84	**94**	**94**	90	76	53	31	*13*	—	—	—
Sunset: 17:38	NE	Beam	13	—	—	—	*83*	**155**	105	0	0	0	0	0	0	0	0	*0*	—	—	—
		Diffuse	32	—	—	—	*36*	**66**	71	85	86	94	94	90	76	53	31	*12*	—	—	—
	E	Beam	68	—	—	—	*145*	351	**436**	412	267	84	0	0	0	0	0	*0*	—	—	—
		Diffuse	41	—	—	—	*47*	107	**132**	135	124	104	106	90	76	53	31	*12*	—	—	—
	SE	Beam	127	—	—	—	*122*	341	512	**611**	569	433	308	165	23	0	0	*0*	—	—	—
		Diffuse	51	—	—	—	*42*	105	146	**165**	169	168	148	123	75	57	31	*12*	—	—	—
	S	Beam	153	—	—	—	*28*	132	287	452	537	**528**	518	465	378	235	108	*23*	—	—	—
		Diffuse	57	—	—	—	*32*	61	106	141	164	**184**	**184**	179	150	102	60	*33*	—	—	—
	SW	Beam	113	—	—	—	*0*	0	0	29	191	314	425	491	**511**	419	280	*100*	—	—	—
		Diffuse	51	—	—	—	*12*	30	57	69	112	148	168	184	**175**	137	98	*44*	—	—	—
	W	Beam	57	—	—	—	*0*	0	0	0	0	0	82	231	**345**	357	287	*119*	—	—	—
		Diffuse	41	—	—	—	*12*	30	52	71	84	106	104	136	**144**	125	100	*49*	—	—	—
	NW	Beam	11	—	—	—	*0*	0	0	0	0	0	0	0	0	86	**127**	*68*	—	—	—
		Diffuse	32	—	—	—	*12*	30	52	71	84	94	94	92	90	71	**64**	*38*	—	—	—
	Horiz.	Beam	99	—	—	—	*8*	68	176	295	361	359	352	312	246	144	56	*6*	—	—	—
	Horiz.	Diffuse	41	—	—	—	*24*	51	77	91	105	127	129	130	111	83	55	*25*	—	—	—
	Horiz.	Global	140	—	—	—	*32*	119	253	386	466	486	481	442	357	227	111	*31*	—	—	—
Nov 4	Beam normal		194	—	—	—	—	*173*	428	612	693	718	642	569	463	324	*130*	—	—	—	—
	N	Beam	0	—	—	—	—	*0*	0	0	0	0	**0**	0	0	0	*0*	—	—	—	—
Sunrise: 07:21		Diffuse	17	—	—	—	—	*10*	26	45	56	64	**66**	60	46	28	*12*	—	—	—	—
Sunset: 16:39	NE	Beam	3	—	—	—	—	*47*	**43**	0	0	0	0	0	0	0	*0*	—	—	—	—
		Diffuse	18	—	—	—	—	*29*	**35**	51	56	64	66	60	46	28	*12*	—	—	—	—
	E	Beam	47	—	—	—	—	*151*	327	**359**	256	90	0	0	0	0	*0*	—	—	—	—
		Diffuse	25	—	—	—	—	*39*	93	**106**	94	72	76	60	46	28	*12*	—	—	—	—
	SE	Beam	119	—	—	—	—	*166*	420	584	**603**	527	357	198	57	0	*0*	—	—	—	—
		Diffuse	37	—	—	—	—	*41*	111	143	**145**	139	128	99	57	32	*12*	—	—	—	—
	S	Beam	155	—	—	—	—	*84*	267	468	597	**655**	586	490	353	202	*63*	—	—	—	—
		Diffuse	44	—	—	—	—	*31*	81	124	144	**158**	166	152	119	79	*35*	—	—	—	—
	SW	Beam	105	—	—	—	—	*0*	0	77	241	400	472	**495**	442	318	*125*	—	—	—	—
		Diffuse	37	—	—	—	—	*11*	30	56	92	121	147	**153**	136	106	*46*	—	—	—	—
	W	Beam	37	—	—	—	—	*0*	0	0	0	0	81	210	**272**	248	*113*	—	—	—	—
		Diffuse	25	—	—	—	—	*10*	26	45	56	73	77	102	**103**	90	*44*	—	—	—	—
	NW	Beam	2	—	—	—	—	*0*	0	0	0	0	0	0	0	**32**	*36*	—	—	—	—
		Diffuse	18	—	—	—	—	*10*	26	45	56	64	66	60	52	**37**	*32*	—	—	—	—
	Horiz.	Beam	58	—	—	—	—	*8*	68	165	241	279	250	198	125	51	*6*	—	—	—	—
	Horiz.	Diffuse	24	—	—	—	—	*21*	43	62	71	78	91	88	73	51	*24*	—	—	—	—
	Horiz.	Global	82	—	—	—	—	*29*	111	227	312	357	341	286	198	102	*30*	—	—	—	—
Dec 4	Beam normal		149	—	—	—	—	—	208	456	592	624	591	533	410	*187*	—	—	—	—	—
	N	Beam	0	—	—	—	—	—	*0*	0	0	0	**0**	0	0	*0*	—	—	—	—	—
Sunrise: 08:03		Diffuse	11	—	—	—	—	—	*13*	29	42	49	**50**	41	29	*13*	—	—	—	—	—
Sunset: 15:57	NE	Beam	0	—	—	—	—	—	*7*	0	0	0	**0**	0	0	*0*	—	—	—	—	—
		Diffuse	12	—	—	—	—	—	*33*	32	42	49	**50**	41	29	*13*	—	—	—	—	—
	E	Beam	29	—	—	—	—	—	*152*	**257**	210	75	0	0	0	*0*	—	—	—	—	—
		Diffuse	17	—	—	—	—	—	*42*	**86**	84	60	57	41	29	*13*	—	—	—	—	—
	SE	Beam	94	—	—	—	—	—	*208*	443	**527**	474	348	207	72	*0*	—	—	—	—	—
		Diffuse	30	—	—	—	—	—	*50*	125	**144**	136	116	83	45	*15*	—	—	—	—	—
	S	Beam	130	—	—	—	—	—	*142*	369	535	**595**	563	482	332	*127*	—	—	—	—	—
		Diffuse	37	—	—	—	—	—	*41*	110	145	**157**	156	135	102	*41*	—	—	—	—	—
	SW	Beam	91	—	—	—	—	—	*0*	80	230	368	**449**	474	398	*187*	—	—	—	—	—
		Diffuse	29	—	—	—	—	—	*15*	47	88	117	**135**	134	116	*50*	—	—	—	—	—
	W	Beam	26	—	—	—	—	—	*0*	0	0	0	71	189	**231**	*137*	—	—	—	—	—
		Diffuse	17	—	—	—	—	—	*13*	29	42	56	61	80	**81**	*42*	—	—	—	—	—
	NW	Beam	0	—	—	—	—	—	*0*	0	0	0	**0**	0	0	*7*	—	—	—	—	—
		Diffuse	12	—	—	—	—	—	*13*	29	42	49	**50**	41	32	*33*	—	—	—	—	—
	Horiz.	Beam	32	—	—	—	—	—	*12*	74	141	173	164	127	67	*11*	—	—	—	—	—
	Horiz.	Diffuse	17	—	—	—	—	—	*25*	48	63	70	72	63	48	*25*	—	—	—	—	—
	Horiz.	Global	49	—	—	—	—	—	*37*	122	204	243	236	190	115	*36*	—	—	—	—	—

* Mean over hour centred at stated solar time

Note: italicised values are calculated for time halfway between sunrise and the end of the sunrise hour or halfway between the beginning of the sunset hour and sunset; the figures shown in bold type, when added together, give the peak total irradiance (i.e. beam plus diffuse) for the stated orientation.

Table 2.25 Design 97.5 percentile of beam and diffuse irradiance on vertical and horizontal surfaces: Manchester (Aughton) (1981–1992) — refer to CD-ROM

Table 2.26 Design 97.5 percentile of beam and diffuse irradiance on vertical and horizontal surfaces: Edinburgh (Mylnefield) (1981–1992) — refer to CD-ROM

Table 2.27 Predicted clear day beam and diffuse irradiances on vertical and horizontal surfaces on specified days for latitudes 0–60°N/S (©J K Page; used with permission): refer to CD-ROM

conditions of climate and geography are given in CIBSE Guide: *Weather and solar data*[1].

2.7.4   Sol-air temperatures for the UK

The procedure for estimating long-wave radiation loss and the calculation of sol-air temperatures are given in Appendix 2.A1. Tables 2.28 to 2.30 provide and hourly air and sol-air temperatures for three UK locations: London area (Bracknell), Manchester (Aughton) and Edinburgh (Mylnefield). For Tables 2.29 and 2.30, refer to the computer disk that accompanies this Guide.

These tables were derived from the 97.5 percentile daily global irradiation exceedence data, see Tables 2.24 to 2.26, in combination with the associated month by month mean hour ending synoptic data. The associated hourly means of the synoptic data were extracted for the same days used to determine the 97.5 percentile irradiation data sets. It was assumed that synoptic time and LAT were identical.

Standardised values for the various parameters were assumed, as follows:

— short-wave surface absorptance: $\alpha_{rad} = 0.9$ (dark coloured surface), 0.5 (light coloured surface)

— long-wave surface absorptance/emittance: $\alpha_l = \varepsilon_l = 0.9$

The long-wave radiation was calculated using sunshine data when the solar altitude was above 6° and cloud data when the solar altitude was 6° or less. The solar radiation was set to zero when the solar altitude was below 1°. For further details see CIBSE Guide: *Weather and solar data*[1].

2.7.5   Illuminance data

Quantitative daylight illuminance data are needed for daylighting design calculations including the sizing of windows, choice of glazing materials and the design of window shading systems. Daylighting and electric lighting systems must be designed to operate interactively. The quantitative estimation of the energy consumption of artificial lighting with different control systems needs knowledge of the statistical availability of the horizontal components of daylight, the global horizontal illuminance and the diffuse horizontal illuminance from the sky vault. A means of assessing the effect of orientation on vertical surface daylight availability is also required. These issues are considered in detail in the CIBSE Lighting Guide LG10: *Daylighting and window design*[9]. The required climatic data are discussed in detail in CIBSE Guide: *Weather and solar data*[1].

2.7.5.1   Cumulative frequency data

Cumulative frequency distributions of horizontal illuminance are required in order to assess lighting system design. New UK data have been recently derived using luminous efficacy algorithms for global and diffuse illumination estimation[10]. These algorithms have been based on short time series of simultaneously observed values of irradiation and illuminance[11]. The algorithms have been applied to the recent observed UK hourly irradiation time-series data sets to estimate the corresponding hourly illuminance time-series. These derived illuminance time-series were then analysed statistically to produce annual cumulative frequency illuminance data.

The cumulative frequency analysis must be based on defined working day lengths. Hunt[12] defined the standard UK working day for illumination design purposes as 09:00 to 17:30 LAT in winter and 08:00 to 16:30 LAT for the period between April and October to allow for British Summer Time. For practical purposes, the difference between LAT and GMT is negligible for the sites analysed. The cumulative data are based on the above standard working year.

Annual global cumulative frequency data[10] for a range of UK sites are given in Table 2.31 and the corresponding diffuse cumulative frequency data are given in Table 2.32. The tables are arranged in order of increasing latitude. In general, increase of latitude decreases the annual availability of daylight. However, because northern climates are much clearer, the impact on the horizontal beam illuminance of lower solar altitudes in mid-summer during cloudless clear hours is offset by greater mid-summer clarity.

The maximum diffuse illuminances are about 60 klux, except in central London where the illuminance is affected by pollution. Figure 2.15 shows the range of both the annual global and diffuse data for Aberporth and Stornoway. The influence of latitude is greater on annual global cumulative illuminance than on annual diffuse cumulative illuminance. This is because the high levels of cloud in summer in the north increases the diffuse illuminance which offsets the substantial reduction in diffuse illumination in winter. Values for other sites can be estimated from Tables 2.31 and 2.32 using linear interpolation based on latitude. However, the effects of urban pollution mean that the data for central London should not be used for latitude interpolation.

2.7.5.2   Orientation factor for UK

The effect of orientation on the availability of diffuse illuminance can be taken into account by means of an orientation factor, see Table 2.33.

The diffuse illuminance received on the horizontal plane in a room with CIE sky daylight factor DF (%) is given by:

$$E_v = E_{vd}(c)\,(DF/100)\,f_o \tag{2.1}$$

where E_v is the diffuse illuminance received on the horizontal plane (klux), $E_{vd}(c)$ is the diffuse horizontal irradiance available for proportion c (%) of the year (klux), DF is the daylight factor (%) and f_o is the orientation factor.

$E_{vd}(c)$ is obtained from Table 2.32 using linear interpolation based on latitude.

The orientation factor applies only to the annual cumulative diffuse illuminance values.

Table 2.28 Air and sol-air temperatures: London area (Bracknell) (1981–1992)

(a) January

Hour*	Air temp.	Horizontal Dark	Light	North Dark	Light	North-east Dark	Light	East Dark	Light	South-east Dark	Light	South Dark	Light	South-west Dark	Light	West Dark	Light	North-west Dark	Light
01	2.5	0.2	0.2	0.6	0.6	0.6	0.6	0.6	0.6	0.6	0.6	0.6	0.6	0.6	0.6	0.6	0.6	0.6	0.6
02	2.0	−0.2	−0.2	0.2	0.2	0.2	0.2	0.2	0.2	0.2	0.2	0.2	0.2	0.2	0.2	0.2	0.2	0.2	0.2
03	1.9	−0.4	−0.4	0.0	0.0	0.0	0.0	0.0	0.0	0.0	0.0	0.0	0.0	0.0	0.0	0.0	0.0	0.0	0.0
04	1.4	−1.1	−1.1	−0.6	−0.6	−0.6	−0.6	−0.6	−0.6	−0.6	−0.6	−0.6	−0.6	−0.6	−0.6	−0.6	−0.6	−0.6	−0.6
05	1.2	−1.4	−1.4	−0.8	−0.8	−0.8	−0.8	−0.8	−0.8	−0.8	−0.8	−0.8	−0.8	−0.8	−0.8	−0.8	−0.8	−0.8	−0.8
06	0.9	−1.6	−1.6	−1.1	−1.1	−1.1	−1.1	−1.1	−1.1	−1.1	−1.1	−1.1	−1.1	−1.1	−1.1	−1.1	−1.1	−1.1	−1.1
07	0.7	−1.9	−1.9	−1.4	−1.4	−1.4	−1.4	−1.4	−1.4	−1.4	−1.4	−1.4	−1.4	−1.4	−1.4	−1.4	−1.4	−1.4	−1.4
08	0.7	−2.0	−2.0	−1.4	−1.4	−1.4	−1.4	−1.4	−1.4	−1.4	−1.4	−1.4	−1.4	−1.4	−1.4	−1.4	−1.4	−1.4	−1.4
09	1.2	1.3	0.1	0.2	−0.3	1.8	0.6	13.9	7.4	17.9	9.7	11.9	6.3	0.2	−0.3	0.2	−0.3	0.2	−0.3
10	2.3	5.6	2.9	2.7	1.8	2.7	1.8	18.7	10.8	28.7	16.5	24.0	13.8	6.9	4.1	2.7	1.8	2.7	1.8
11	3.7	9.6	5.7	4.9	3.8	4.9	3.8	16.7	10.4	32.7	19.5	32.7	19.5	16.7	10.4	4.9	3.8	4.9	3.8
12	4.7	11.5	7.3	6.2	5.0	6.2	5.0	10.3	7.3	29.6	18.2	35.1	21.4	24.2	15.1	6.2	5.0	6.2	5.0
13	5.5	12.2	8.0	7.0	5.8	7.0	5.8	7.0	5.8	24.5	15.6	35.0	21.7	29.7	18.6	11.0	8.0	7.0	5.8
14	5.9	10.9	7.5	7.1	6.0	7.1	6.0	7.1	6.0	16.7	11.4	29.6	18.7	29.6	18.7	16.7	11.4	7.1	6.0
15	5.8	8.5	6.2	6.3	5.4	6.3	5.4	6.3	5.4	9.3	7.1	21.5	14.0	24.8	15.9	17.6	11.8	6.3	5.4
16	5.3	5.0	4.2	4.3	3.9	4.3	3.9	4.3	3.9	4.3	3.9	11.2	7.8	14.7	9.8	12.3	8.4	5.3	4.5
17	4.3	1.9	1.9	2.3	2.3	2.3	2.3	2.3	2.3	2.3	2.3	2.3	2.3	2.3	2.3	2.3	2.3	2.3	2.3
18	3.7	1.2	1.2	1.7	1.7	1.7	1.7	1.7	1.7	1.7	1.7	1.7	1.7	1.7	1.7	1.7	1.7	1.7	1.7
19	3.3	1.0	1.0	1.4	1.4	1.4	1.4	1.4	1.4	1.4	1.4	1.4	1.4	1.4	1.4	1.4	1.4	1.4	1.4
20	3.0	10.7	0.7	1.1	1.1	1.1	1.1	1.1	1.1	1.1	1.1	1.1	1.1	1.1	1.1	1.1	1.1	1.1	1.1
21	2.7	0.4	0.4	0.8	0.8	0.8	0.8	0.8	0.8	0.8	0.8	0.8	0.8	0.8	0.8	0.8	0.8	0.8	0.8
22	2.2	−0.2	−0.2	0.2	0.2	0.2	0.2	0.2	0.2	0.2	0.2	0.2	0.2	0.2	0.2	0.2	0.2	0.2	0.2
23	1.8	−0.6	−0.6	−0.1	−0.1	−0.1	−0.1	−0.1	−0.1	−0.1	−0.1	−0.1	−0.1	−0.1	−0.1	−0.1	−0.1	−0.1	−0.1
24	1.8	−0.6	−0.6	−0.2	−0.2	−0.2	−0.2	−0.2	−0.2	−0.2	−0.2	−0.2	−0.2	−0.2	−0.2	−0.2	−0.2	−0.2	−0.2
Mean:	2.9	2.5	1.6	1.7	1.4	1.8	1.5	3.6	2.5	6.9	4.4	8.5	5.2	6.2	4.0	3.1	2.2	1.8	1.4

* Hour ending

(b) February 3

Hour*	Air temp.	Horizontal Dark	Light	North Dark	Light	North-east Dark	Light	East Dark	Light	South-east Dark	Light	South Dark	Light	South-west Dark	Light	West Dark	Light	North-west Dark	Light
01	2.3	−0.2	−0.2	0.2	0.2	0.2	0.2	0.2	0.2	0.2	0.2	0.2	0.2	0.2	0.2	0.2	0.2	0.2	0.2
02	2.0	−0.6	−0.6	−0.1	−0.1	−0.1	−0.1	−0.1	−0.1	−0.1	−0.1	−0.1	−0.1	−0.1	−0.1	−0.1	−0.1	−0.1	−0.1
03	1.9	−0.8	−0.8	−0.3	−0.3	−0.3	−0.3	−0.3	−0.3	−0.3	−0.3	−0.3	−0.3	−0.3	−0.3	−0.3	−0.3	−0.3	−0.3
04	1.5	−1.2	−1.2	−0.6	−0.6	−0.6	−0.6	−0.6	−0.6	−0.6	−0.6	−0.6	−0.6	−0.6	−0.6	−0.6	−0.6	−0.6	−0.6
05	1.4	−1.2	−1.2	−0.7	−0.7	−0.7	−0.7	−0.7	−0.7	−0.7	−0.7	−0.7	−0.7	−0.7	−0.7	−0.7	−0.7	−0.7	−0.7
06	1.2	−1.4	−1.4	−0.9	−0.9	−0.9	−0.9	−0.9	−0.9	−0.9	−0.9	−0.9	−0.9	−0.9	−0.9	−0.9	−0.9	−0.9	−0.9
07	1.1	−1.5	−1.5	−1.0	−1.0	−1.0	−1.0	−1.0	−1.0	−1.0	−1.0	−1.0	−1.0	−1.0	−1.0	−1.0	−1.0	−1.0	−1.0
08	1.4	0.8	−0.2	0.2	−0.2	4.5	2.1	10.4	5.5	10.5	5.5	4.7	2.3	0.2	−0.2	0.2	−0.2	0.2	−0.2
09	2.5	6.3	3.4	3.3	2.3	7.2	4.4	21.2	12.3	24.9	14.5	16.4	9.6	3.3	2.3	3.3	2.3	3.3	2.3
10	3.8	10.9	6.6	5.9	4.5	5.9	4.5	22.6	13.9	31.1	18.7	25.4	15.5	8.2	5.8	5.9	4.5	5.9	4.5
11	5.2	14.7	9.3	7.9	6.3	7.9	6.3	19.7	12.9	33.3	20.7	32.4	20.2	17.4	11.7	7.9	6.3	7.9	6.3
12	6.3	17.3	11.2	9.5	7.8	9.5	7.8	13.8	10.2	32.0	20.4	36.9	23.3	26.3	17.2	9.5	7.8	9.5	7.8
13	7.1	17.5	11.7	10.1	8.5	10.1	8.5	10.1	8.5	26.0	17.4	36.1	23.1	31.4	20.5	14.2	10.8	10.1	8.5
14	7.7	16.5	11.4	10.1	8.6	10.1	8.6	10.1	8.6	19.1	13.7	33.4	21.8	34.3	22.3	21.3	14.9	10.1	8.6
15	7.7	14.0	10.0	9.3	8.1	9.3	8.1	9.3	8.1	11.4	9.3	27.9	18.5	33.4	21.7	25.2	17.0	9.3	8.1
16	7.2	10.0	7.6	7.5	6.7	7.5	6.7	7.5	6.7	7.5	6.7	19.2	13.3	27.0	17.7	23.6	15.8	11.0	8.6
17	6.1	5.6	4.8	5.1	4.7	5.1	4.7	5.1	4.7	5.1	4.7	8.4	6.6	12.7	9.0	12.7	9.0	8.3	6.5
18	5.0	2.6	2.6	3.1	3.1	3.1	3.1	3.1	3.1	3.1	3.1	3.1	3.1	3.1	3.1	3.1	3.1	3.1	3.1
19	4.4	1.8	1.8	2.3	2.3	2.3	2.3	2.3	2.3	2.3	2.3	2.3	2.3	2.3	2.3	2.3	2.3	2.3	2.3
20	3.8	1.2	1.2	1.7	1.7	1.7	1.7	1.7	1.7	1.7	1.7	1.7	1.7	1.7	1.7	1.7	1.7	1.7	1.7
21	3.3	0.6	0.6	1.2	1.2	1.2	1.2	1.2	1.2	1.2	1.2	1.2	1.2	1.2	1.2	1.2	1.2	1.2	1.2
22	3.0	0.2	0.2	0.7	0.7	0.7	0.7	0.7	0.7	0.7	0.7	0.7	0.7	0.7	0.7	0.7	0.7	0.7	0.7
23	2.7	−0.1	−0.1	0.4	0.4	0.4	0.4	0.4	0.4	0.4	0.4	0.4	0.4	0.4	0.4	0.4	0.4	0.4	0.4
24	2.5	−0.3	−0.3	0.3	0.3	0.3	0.3	0.3	0.3	0.3	0.3	0.3	0.3	0.3	0.3	0.3	0.3	0.3	0.3
Mean:	3.8	4.7	3.1	3.1	2.7	3.5	2.8	5.7	4.1	8.6	5.7	10.3	6.7	8.4	5.6	5.4	3.9	3.4	2.8

* Hour ending

Table 2.28 Air and sol-air temperatures: London area (Bracknell) (1981–1992) — *continued*

(c) March 3

Hour*	Air temp.	Horizontal		North		North-east		East		South-east		South		South-west		West		North-west	
		Dark	Light	Dark	Light	Dark	Light	Dark	Light	Dark	Light	Dark	Light	Dark	Light	Dark	Light	Dark	Light
01	4.8	1.7	1.7	2.4	2.4	2.4	2.4	2.4	2.4	2.4	2.4	2.4	2.4	2.4	2.4	2.4	2.4	2.4	2.4
02	4.3	1.4	1.4	2.0	2.0	2.0	2.0	2.0	2.0	2.0	2.0	2.0	2.0	2.0	2.0	2.0	2.0	2.0	2.0
03	4.1	1.1	1.1	1.7	1.7	1.7	1.7	1.7	1.7	1.7	1.7	1.7	1.7	1.7	1.7	1.7	1.7	1.7	1.7
04	3.5	0.2	0.2	0.9	0.9	0.9	0.9	0.9	0.9	0.9	0.9	0.9	0.9	0.9	0.9	0.9	0.9	0.9	0.9
05	3.2	−0.2	−0.2	0.6	0.6	0.6	0.6	0.6	0.6	0.6	0.6	0.6	0.6	0.6	0.6	0.6	0.6	0.6	0.6
06	3.0	−0.3	−0.3	0.5	0.5	0.5	0.5	0.5	0.5	0.5	0.5	0.5	0.5	0.5	0.5	0.5	0.5	0.5	0.5
07	3.2	3.1	1.7	2.0	1.4	12.4	7.3	17.5	10.2	13.9	8.1	3.3	2.1	2.0	1.4	2.0	1.4	2.0	1.4
08	4.6	10.6	6.6	6.3	4.9	19.8	12.5	32.1	19.6	29.9	18.3	14.1	9.3	6.3	4.9	6.3	4.9	6.3	4.9
09	6.6	17.0	11.0	9.7	7.8	18.4	12.7	36.0	22.8	38.5	24.2	24.7	16.3	9.7	7.8	9.7	7.8	9.7	7.8
10	8.2	22.4	14.7	12.5	10.3	13.3	10.8	34.4	22.7	42.4	27.3	33.5	22.2	12.5	10.3	12.5	10.3	12.5	10.3
11	9.7	26.5	17.7	15.0	12.5	15.0	12.5	29.1	20.5	42.2	28.0	39.8	26.6	23.0	17.0	15.0	12.5	15.0	12.5
12	11.1	29.6	20.0	16.8	14.3	16.8	14.3	21.9	17.1	40.0	27.4	44.5	30.0	33.2	23.5	16.8	14.3	16.8	14.3
13	12.1	30.0	20.7	17.7	15.2	17.7	15.2	17.7	15.2	33.5	24.1	44.5	30.4	40.1	27.9	22.6	17.9	17.7	15.2
14	12.6	28.6	20.2	17.6	15.2	17.6	15.2	17.6	15.2	25.3	19.6	41.7	28.9	44.1	30.3	31.3	23.0	17.6	15.2
15	12.7	26.2	18.8	16.7	14.7	16.7	14.7	16.7	14.7	16.7	14.7	37.0	26.2	45.7	31.1	37.9	26.7	17.5	15.1
16	12.6	21.6	16.2	15.1	13.4	15.1	13.4	15.1	13.4	15.1	13.4	28.9	21.2	41.9	28.7	39.6	27.3	23.2	18.0
17	12.1	16.1	12.9	12.8	11.7	12.8	11.7	12.8	11.7	12.8	11.7	19.5	15.4	33.2	23.2	35.1	24.3	24.4	18.3
18	10.9	10.3	9.3	9.6	9.2	9.6	9.2	9.6	9.2	9.6	9.2	10.6	9.7	18.2	14.0	20.8	15.5	17.2	13.4
19	9.7	6.6	6.6	7.3	7.3	7.3	7.3	7.3	7.3	7.3	7.3	7.3	7.3	7.3	7.3	7.3	7.3	7.3	7.3
20	8.6	5.6	5.6	6.2	6.2	6.2	6.2	6.2	6.2	6.2	6.2	6.2	6.2	6.2	6.2	6.2	6.2	6.2	6.2
21	7.7	4.6	4.6	5.3	5.3	5.3	5.3	5.3	5.3	5.3	5.3	5.3	5.3	5.3	5.3	5.3	5.3	5.3	5.3
22	6.8	3.4	3.4	4.2	4.2	4.2	4.2	4.2	4.2	4.2	4.2	4.2	4.2	4.2	4.2	4.2	4.2	4.2	4.2
23	5.8	2.4	2.4	3.2	3.2	3.2	3.2	3.2	3.2	3.2	3.2	3.2	3.2	3.2	3.2	3.2	3.2	3.2	3.2
24	5.6	2.2	2.2	3.0	3.0	3.0	3.0	3.0	3.0	3.0	3.0	3.0	3.0	3.0	3.0	3.0	3.0	3.0	3.0
Mean:	7.6	11.3	8.3	7.9	7.0	9.3	7.8	12.4	9.6	14.9	11.0	15.8	11.5	14.5	10.7	12.0	9.3	9.1	7.7

* Hour ending

(d) April 3

Hour*	Air temp.	Horizontal		North		North-east		East		South-east		South		South-west		West		North-west	
		Dark	Light	Dark	Light	Dark	Light	Dark	Light	Dark	Light	Dark	Light	Dark	Light	Dark	Light	Dark	Light
01	7.1	3.9	3.9	4.7	4.7	4.7	4.7	4.7	4.7	4.7	4.7	4.7	4.7	4.7	4.7	4.7	4.7	4.7	4.7
02	6.4	3.2	3.2	4.0	4.0	4.0	4.0	4.0	4.0	4.0	4.0	4.0	4.0	4.0	4.0	4.0	4.0	4.0	4.0
03	6.0	2.9	2.9	3.6	3.6	3.6	3.6	3.6	3.6	3.6	3.6	3.6	3.6	3.6	3.6	3.6	3.6	3.6	3.6
04	5.6	2.3	2.3	3.1	3.1	3.1	3.1	3.1	3.1	3.1	3.1	3.1	3.1	3.1	3.1	3.1	3.1	3.1	3.1
05	5.3	2.0	2.0	2.7	2.7	2.7	2.7	2.7	2.7	2.7	2.7	2.7	2.7	2.7	2.7	2.7	2.7	2.7	2.7
06	5.7	5.1	3.9	8.7	6.2	18.4	11.7	20.1	12.7	12.7	8.5	4.3	3.8	4.3	3.8	4.3	3.8	4.3	3.8
07	7.4	12.3	8.6	10.3	8.2	29.8	19.3	36.7	23.3	27.7	18.1	8.4	7.2	8.4	7.2	8.4	7.2	8.4	7.2
08	9.4	19.0	13.4	12.2	10.5	29.8	20.4	41.0	26.8	35.9	23.9	16.9	13.1	12.2	10.5	12.2	10.5	12.2	10.5
09	11.1	25.6	17.9	15.5	13.4	27.4	20.1	43.1	29.1	42.9	29.0	26.9	19.8	15.5	13.4	15.5	13.4	15.5	13.4
10	12.8	30.6	21.5	18.3	15.9	22.0	18.0	39.9	28.1	45.0	31.1	34.8	25.2	18.3	15.9	18.3	15.9	18.3	15.9
11	14.3	33.7	23.9	20.3	17.8	20.3	17.8	33.7	25.4	43.5	31.0	39.9	28.9	24.8	20.3	20.3	17.8	20.3	17.8
12	15.2	35.3	25.3	21.5	19.0	21.5	19.0	25.9	21.4	39.6	29.2	42.5	30.9	33.3	25.6	21.5	19.0	21.5	19.0
13	16.0	36.0	26.0	22.4	19.8	22.4	19.8	22.4	19.8	34.0	26.4	43.2	31.6	40.2	29.9	26.7	22.2	22.4	19.8
14	16.4	34.2	25.2	22.0	19.7	22.0	19.7	22.0	19.7	26.1	22.0	40.1	29.9	43.4	31.8	34.3	26.6	22.0	19.7
15	16.4	31.6	23.7	21.1	19.0	21.1	19.0	21.1	19.0	21.1	19.0	35.5	27.1	44.5	32.2	40.0	29.7	24.3	20.8
16	16.1	27.6	21.3	19.6	17.8	19.6	17.8	19.6	17.8	19.6	17.8	28.8	23.0	42.0	30.5	42.2	30.6	29.3	23.3
17	15.5	23.0	18.5	17.6	16.2	17.6	16.2	17.6	16.2	17.6	16.2	21.4	18.4	37.0	27.2	41.3	29.6	32.0	24.3
18	14.6	17.5	15.1	16.4	15.0	15.1	14.2	15.1	14.2	15.1	14.2	15.1	14.2	27.8	21.4	33.9	24.8	29.3	22.2
19	13.2	12.7	11.9	14.8	13.3	12.1	11.8	12.1	11.8	12.1	11.8	12.1	11.8	17.2	14.6	21.7	17.1	20.7	16.6
20	11.8	9.5	9.5	9.9	9.9	9.9	9.9	9.9	9.9	9.9	9.9	9.9	9.9	9.9	9.9	9.9	9.9	9.9	9.9
21	10.8	8.3	8.3	8.8	8.8	8.8	8.8	8.8	8.8	8.8	8.8	8.8	8.8	8.8	8.8	8.8	8.8	8.8	8.8
22	9.7	7.2	7.2	7.7	7.7	7.7	7.7	7.7	7.7	7.7	7.7	7.7	7.7	7.7	7.7	7.7	7.7	7.7	7.7
23	9.1	6.4	6.4	6.9	6.9	6.9	6.9	6.9	6.9	6.9	6.9	6.9	6.9	6.9	6.9	6.9	6.9	6.9	6.9
24	8.3	5.5	5.5	6.1	6.1	6.1	6.1	6.1	6.1	6.1	6.1	6.1	6.1	6.1	6.1	6.1	6.1	6.1	6.1
Mean:	11.0	16.5	12.8	12.4	11.2	14.9	12.6	17.8	14.3	18.8	14.8	17.8	14.3	17.8	14.2	16.6	13.6	14.1	12.2

* Hour ending

Table 2.28 Air and sol-air temperatures: London area (Bracknell) (1981–1992) — *continued*

(*e*) May 3

Hour*	Air temp.	Sol-air temperature (°C) for stated orientation and surface colour																
		Horizontal		North		North-east		East		South-east		South		South-west		West		North-west	
		Dark	Light	Dark	Light	Dark	Light	Dark	Light	Dark	Light	Dark	Light	Dark	Light	Dark	Light	Dark	Light
01	9.8	6.4	6.4	7.2	7.2	7.2	7.2	7.2	7.2	7.2	7.2	7.2	7.2	7.2	7.2	7.2	7.2	7.2	7.2
02	9.2	5.7	5.7	6.6	6.6	6.6	6.6	6.6	6.6	6.6	6.6	6.6	6.6	6.6	6.6	6.6	6.6	6.6	6.6
03	8.7	5.2	5.2	6.1	6.1	6.1	6.1	6.1	6.1	6.1	6.1	6.1	6.1	6.1	6.1	6.1	6.1	6.1	6.1
04	8.3	4.9	4.9	5.7	5.7	5.7	5.7	5.7	5.7	5.7	5.7	5.7	5.7	5.7	5.7	5.7	5.7	5.7	5.7
05	8.1	5.8	5.4	6.5	6.1	6.5	6.1	6.5	6.1	6.5	6.1	6.2	6.0	6.2	6.0	6.2	6.0	6.2	6.0
06	9.2	12.1	9.5	17.9	13.3	31.5	21.0	32.5	21.6	20.4	14.7	9.5	8.6	9.5	8.6	9.5	8.6	9.5	8.6
07	10.9	18.6	13.9	17.4	14.0	35.5	24.3	40.6	27.2	30.1	21.2	13.1	11.6	13.1	11.6	13.1	11.6	13.1	11.6
08	12.7	25.0	18.3	16.5	14.6	35.5	25.3	44.6	30.5	37.8	26.6	18.4	15.6	16.5	14.6	16.5	14.6	16.5	14.6
09	14.4	30.8	22.4	19.5	17.2	32.7	24.7	45.4	32.0	43.2	30.7	27.2	21.6	19.5	17.2	19.5	17.2	19.5	17.2
10	16.0	35.7	25.9	22.1	19.6	27.7	22.8	42.7	31.3	45.6	33.0	34.9	26.8	22.1	19.6	22.1	19.6	22.1	19.6
11	17.4	38.6	28.1	23.9	21.4	23.9	21.4	36.6	28.6	44.1	32.8	39.8	30.3	25.9	22.5	23.9	21.4	23.9	21.4
12	18.4	40.2	29.5	25.2	22.7	25.2	22.7	29.4	25.0	40.4	31.3	42.5	32.4	34.4	27.8	25.2	22.7	25.2	22.7
13	19.3	40.6	30.1	25.9	23.5	25.9	23.5	25.9	23.5	34.9	28.5	42.9	33.0	40.9	31.9	30.0	25.7	25.9	23.5
14	19.8	39.7	29.8	25.9	23.6	25.9	23.6	25.9	23.6	27.9	24.7	41.0	32.1	45.1	34.4	38.0	30.4	25.9	23.6
15	20.1	37.3	28.6	25.4	23.3	25.4	23.3	25.4	23.3	25.4	23.3	36.7	29.6	46.4	35.1	43.8	33.6	30.4	26.1
16	20.0	33.5	26.4	24.1	22.3	24.1	22.3	24.1	22.3	24.1	22.3	30.6	25.9	44.4	33.7	46.3	34.8	35.4	28.6
17	19.6	29.1	23.8	22.4	20.9	22.4	20.9	22.4	20.9	22.4	20.9	23.9	21.7	40.2	30.9	46.0	34.2	38.3	29.8
18	18.8	24.0	20.6	23.4	20.9	20.1	19.1	20.1	19.1	20.1	19.1	20.1	19.1	33.1	26.4	41.3	31.0	37.4	28.8
19	17.4	18.7	17.1	22.8	19.8	17.3	16.7	17.3	16.7	17.3	16.7	17.3	16.7	24.4	20.7	32.5	25.2	31.8	24.9
20	15.7	13.9	13.7	14.4	14.1	14.2	14.1	14.2	14.1	14.2	14.1	14.2	14.1	14.4	14.1	14.4	14.2	14.4	14.2
21	14.3	11.8	11.8	12.4	12.4	12.4	12.4	12.4	12.4	12.4	12.4	12.4	12.4	12.4	12.4	12.4	12.4	12.4	12.4
22	13.1	10.5	10.5	11.1	11.1	11.1	11.1	11.1	11.1	11.1	11.1	11.1	11.1	11.1	11.1	11.1	11.1	11.1	11.1
23	12.1	9.2	9.2	9.9	9.9	9.9	9.9	9.9	9.9	9.9	9.9	9.9	9.9	9.9	9.9	9.9	9.9	9.9	9.9
24	11.4	8.2	8.2	9.0	9.0	9.0	9.0	9.0	9.0	9.0	9.0	9.0	9.0	9.0	9.0	9.0	9.0	9.0	9.0
Mean:	14.4	21.1	16.9	16.7	15.2	19.2	16.7	21.7	18.1	21.8	18.1	20.3	17.2	21.0	17.6	20.7	17.5	18.5	16.2

* Hour ending

(*f*) june 3

Hour*	Air temp.	Sol-air temperature (°C) for stated orientation and surface colour																
		Horizontal		North		North-east		East		South-east		South		South-west		West		North-west	
		Dark	Light	Dark	Light	Dark	Light	Dark	Light	Dark	Light	Dark	Light	Dark	Light	Dark	Light	Dark	Light
01	13.9	10.5	10.5	11.4	11.4	11.4	11.4	11.4	11.4	11.4	11.4	11.4	11.4	11.4	11.4	11.4	11.4	11.4	11.4
02	13.1	9.4	9.4	10.4	10.4	10.4	10.4	10.4	10.4	10.4	10.4	10.4	10.4	10.4	10.4	10.4	10.4	10.4	10.4
03	12.4	8.8	8.8	9.6	9.6	9.6	9.6	9.6	9.6	9.6	9.6	9.6	9.6	9.6	9.6	9.6	9.6	9.6	9.6
04	12.0	8.5	8.5	9.3	9.3	9.3	9.3	9.3	9.3	9.3	9.3	9.3	9.3	9.3	9.3	9.3	9.3	9.3	9.3
05	12.2	10.3	9.6	11.0	10.3	11.2	10.4	11.1	10.4	11.0	10.3	10.6	10.1	10.6	10.1	10.6	10.1	10.6	10.1
06	13.3	17.8	14.3	24.9	19.0	40.7	28.1	41.4	28.5	26.7	20.0	14.1	12.9	14.1	12.9	14.1	12.9	14.1	12.9
07	15.0	25.7	19.4	24.3	19.7	46.9	32.7	52.5	36.0	38.8	28.0	18.0	16.1	18.0	16.1	18.0	16.1	18.0	16.1
08	16.8	33.4	24.6	21.5	19.2	46.5	33.5	57.3	39.8	48.0	34.4	22.7	19.9	21.5	19.2	21.5	19.2	21.5	19.2
09	18.5	39.8	29.0	24.7	22.1	41.6	31.7	56.3	40.2	53.0	38.3	33.1	26.8	24.7	22.1	24.7	22.1	24.7	22.1
10	20.1	44.9	32.6	27.4	24.6	34.8	28.7	51.8	38.5	54.5	40.1	41.5	32.6	27.4	24.6	27.4	24.6	27.4	24.6
11	21.5	47.8	35.0	29.3	26.5	29.3	26.5	44.3	34.9	52.3	39.5	47.0	36.5	31.0	27.4	29.3	26.5	29.3	26.5
12	22.7	49.3	36.3	30.6	27.8	30.6	27.8	35.4	30.4	47.6	37.4	49.7	38.6	40.6	33.4	30.6	27.8	30.6	27.8
13	23.6	49.3	36.8	31.3	28.5	31.3	28.5	31.3	28.5	41.0	34.0	49.9	39.0	47.9	37.9	35.9	31.1	31.3	28.5
14	24.4	48.1	36.4	31.5	28.8	31.5	28.8	31.5	28.8	33.0	29.7	47.6	37.9	52.4	40.7	45.1	36.5	31.5	28.8
15	24.5	44.8	34.7	30.8	28.3	30.8	28.3	30.8	28.3	30.8	28.3	42.5	34.9	53.3	41.1	51.1	39.8	36.9	31.7
16	24.4	40.5	32.2	29.4	27.2	29.4	27.2	29.4	27.2	29.4	27.2	35.8	30.8	51.3	39.6	53.9	41.1	42.4	34.6
17	24.2	36.1	29.6	27.8	26.0	27.8	26.0	27.8	26.0	27.8	26.0	28.7	26.5	47.4	37.1	54.4	41.1	46.3	36.4
18	23.5	30.8	26.4	30.1	26.7	25.6	24.2	25.6	24.2	25.6	24.2	25.6	24.2	40.6	32.7	50.7	38.4	46.5	36.0
19	22.5	25.2	22.8	30.4	26.2	22.8	22.0	22.8	22.0	22.8	22.0	22.8	22.0	31.6	26.9	42.2	32.9	41.7	32.6
20	20.9	19.5	19.0	19.9	19.4	19.6	19.3	19.6	19.3	19.6	19.3	19.6	19.3	19.9	19.4	19.9	19.4	19.9	19.5
21	19.3	16.6	16.6	17.1	17.1	17.1	17.1	17.1	17.1	17.1	17.1	17.1	17.1	17.1	17.1	17.1	17.1	17.1	17.1
22	17.9	15.1	15.1	15.7	15.7	15.7	15.7	15.7	15.7	15.7	15.7	15.7	15.7	15.7	15.7	15.7	15.7	15.7	15.7
23	16.8	13.7	13.7	14.4	14.4	14.4	14.4	14.4	14.4	14.4	14.4	14.4	14.4	14.4	14.4	14.4	14.4	14.4	14.4
24	15.7	12.5	12.5	13.2	13.2	13.2	13.2	13.2	13.2	13.2	13.2	13.2	13.2	13.2	13.2	13.2	13.2	13.2	13.2
Mean:	18.7	27.4	22.2	21.9	20.1	25.1	21.9	27.9	23.5	27.6	23.3	25.4	22.1	26.4	22.6	26.3	22.5	23.9	21.2

* Hour ending

Table 2.28 Air and sol-air temperatures: London area (Bracknell) (1981–1992) — *continued*

(g) July 3

Hour*	Air temp.	Horizontal		North		North-east		East		South-east		South		South-west		West		North-west	
		Dark	Light	Dark	Light	Dark	Light	Dark	Light	Dark	Light	Dark	Light	Dark	Light	Dark	Light	Dark	Light
01	14.8	11.5	11.5	12.3	12.3	12.3	12.3	12.3	12.3	12.3	12.3	12.3	12.3	12.3	12.3	12.3	12.3	12.3	12.3
02	14.2	10.7	10.7	11.5	11.5	11.5	11.5	11.5	11.5	11.5	11.5	11.5	11.5	11.5	11.5	11.5	11.5	11.5	11.5
03	13.6	10.1	10.1	10.9	10.9	10.9	10.9	10.9	10.9	10.9	10.9	10.9	10.9	10.9	10.9	10.9	10.9	10.9	10.9
04	13.2	9.6	9.6	10.4	10.4	10.4	10.4	10.4	10.4	10.4	10.4	10.4	10.4	10.4	10.4	10.4	10.4	10.4	10.4
05	13.3	11.1	10.6	11.8	11.3	11.9	11.3	11.9	11.3	11.8	11.3	11.5	11.1	11.5	11.1	11.5	11.1	11.5	11.1
06	14.3	18.1	15.0	24.5	19.2	39.1	27.6	39.9	28.0	26.4	20.3	14.8	13.8	14.8	13.8	14.8	13.8	14.8	13.8
07	15.9	25.3	19.7	23.9	19.9	44.3	31.6	49.6	34.6	37.4	27.5	18.4	16.8	18.4	16.8	18.4	16.8	18.4	16.8
08	17.7	32.5	24.6	22.1	20.0	44.1	32.5	53.9	38.2	45.8	33.5	23.5	20.7	22.1	20.0	22.1	20.0	22.1	20.0
09	19.5	38.5	28.8	25.2	22.8	40.2	31.3	53.6	39.0	50.8	37.4	33.0	27.2	25.2	22.8	25.2	22.8	25.2	22.8
10	21.0	42.7	31.9	27.6	25.0	34.0	28.6	49.2	37.3	51.7	38.7	40.4	32.2	27.6	25.0	27.6	25.0	27.6	25.0
11	22.5	45.5	34.2	29.6	27.0	29.6	27.0	42.8	34.4	50.0	38.5	45.4	35.9	31.4	27.9	29.6	27.0	29.6	27.0
12	23.4	46.7	35.3	30.8	28.0	30.8	28.0	35.0	30.4	45.8	36.6	47.7	37.6	39.7	33.1	30.8	28.0	30.8	28.0
13	24.2	48.0	36.4	31.7	29.0	31.7	29.0	31.7	29.0	40.8	34.1	49.0	38.8	47.1	37.7	36.1	31.4	31.7	29.0
14	24.8	46.8	35.9	31.7	29.1	31.7	29.1	31.7	29.1	33.3	30.0	46.8	37.7	51.2	40.2	44.3	36.2	31.7	29.1
15	25.3	44.4	34.8	31.3	29.0	31.3	29.0	31.3	29.0	31.3	29.0	42.7	35.3	52.8	41.1	50.5	39.8	37.0	32.1
16	25.4	40.5	32.7	30.1	28.1	30.1	28.1	30.1	28.1	30.1	28.1	36.5	31.7	51.1	40.0	53.4	41.3	42.4	35.0
17	25.0	35.8	29.9	28.2	26.6	28.2	26.6	28.2	26.6	28.2	26.6	29.2	27.2	46.7	37.0	53.1	40.7	45.3	36.3
18	24.4	30.6	26.7	30.0	27.1	26.1	24.9	26.1	24.9	26.1	24.9	26.1	24.9	39.6	32.5	48.5	37.6	44.7	35.4
19	23.3	25.2	23.3	29.5	26.2	23.3	22.7	23.3	22.7	23.3	22.7	23.3	22.7	30.8	26.9	39.6	31.9	39.1	31.6
20	21.7	20.1	19.8	20.6	20.2	20.4	20.1	20.4	20.1	20.4	20.1	20.4	20.1	20.5	20.2	20.6	20.3	20.6	20.3
21	20.1	17.6	17.6	18.1	18.1	18.1	18.1	18.1	18.1	18.1	18.1	18.1	18.1	18.1	18.1	18.1	18.1	18.1	18.1
22	18.9	16.1	16.1	16.7	16.7	16.7	16.7	16.7	16.7	16.7	16.7	16.7	16.7	16.7	16.7	16.7	16.7	16.7	16.7
23	17.5	14.4	14.4	15.2	15.2	15.2	15.2	15.2	15.2	15.2	15.2	15.2	15.2	15.2	15.2	15.2	15.2	15.2	15.2
24	16.7	13.4	13.4	14.2	14.2	14.2	14.2	14.2	14.2	14.2	14.2	14.2	14.2	14.2	14.2	14.2 ·	14.2	14.2	14.2
Mean:	19.6	27.3	22.6	22.4	20.7	25.3	22.4	27.8	23.8	27.6	23.7	25.8	22.6	26.7	23.1	26.5	23.0	24.2	21.8

* Hour ending

(h) August 3

Hour*	Air temp.	Horizontal		North		North-east		East		South-east		South		South-west		West		North-west	
		Dark	Light	Dark	Light	Dark	Light	Dark	Light	Dark	Light	Dark	Light	Dark	Light	Dark	Light	Dark	Light
01	15.7	12.5	12.5	13.2	13.2	13.2	13.2	13.2	13.2	13.2	13.2	13.2	13.2	13.2	13.2	13.2	13.2	13.2	13.2
02	15.0	11.6	11.6	12.4	12.4	12.4	12.4	12.4	12.4	12.4	12.4	12.4	12.4	12.4	12.4	12.4	12.4	12.4	12.4
03	14.4	10.9	10.9	11.7	11.7	11.7	11.7	11.7	11.7	11.7	11.7	11.7	11.7	11.7	11.7	11.7	11.7	11.7	11.7
04	13.9	10.3	10.3	11.1	11.1	11.1	11.1	11.1	11.1	11.1	11.1	11.1	11.1	11.1	11.1	11.1	11.1	11.1	11.1
05	13.4	10.4	10.2	11.1	10.9	11.1	11.0	11.1	11.0	11.1	10.9	11.0	10.9	11.0	10.9	11.0	10.9	11.0	10.9
06	14.0	15.1	13.3	19.1	16.0	29.4	21.8	30.7	22.6	22.4	17.9	13.7	12.9	13.7	12.9	13.7	12.9	13.7	12.9
07	15.6	22.3	17.8	20.3	17.5	39.5	28.4	45.5	32.0	35.9	26.3	17.2	15.8	17.2	15.8	17.2	15.8	17.2	15.8
08	17.4	30.4	23.3	21.3	19.2	42.0	31.0	53.6	37.8	47.0	33.9	25.3	21.5	21.3	19.2	21.3	19.2	21.3	19.2
09	19.4	37.6	28.2	25.0	22.5	39.1	30.5	55.1	39.7	53.9	39.0	36.0	28.7	25.0	22.5	25.0	22.5	25.0	2.5
10	21.2	42.2	31.7	27.7	25.1	32.7	27.9	50.7	38.1	55.2	40.7	44.0	34.3	27.7	25.1	27.7	25.1	27.7	25.1
11	22.6	45.7	34.3	29.7	27.0	29.7	27.0	44.2	35.2	53.9	40.8	49.7	38.3	33.5	29.1	29.7	27.0	29.7	27.0
12	23.9	46.8	35.6	31.2	28.4	31.2	28.4	35.8	31.0	49.2	38.6	51.9	40.2	42.6	34.9	31.2	28.4	31.2	28.4
13	24.8	47.0	36.0	31.9	29.2	31.9	29.2	31.9	29.2	43.0	35.5	52.0	40.6	49.4	39.1	36.5	31.8	31.9	29.2
14	25.4	45.9	35.6	32.0	29.4	32.0	29.4	32.0	29.4	35.5	31.3	49.8	39.5	53.6	41.7	45.0	36.7	32.0	29.4
15	25.8	43.2	34.3	31.2	29.0	31.2	29.0	31.2	29.0	31.2	29.0	45.1	36.8	54.9	42.4	51.0	40.1	35.4	31.3
16	25.7	38.8	31.8	29.8	27.9	29.8	27.9	29.8	27.9	29.8	27.9	38.2	32.6	51.7	40.3	52.6	40.8	40.4	33.8
17	25.2	33.6	28.7	27.7	26.2	27.7	26.2	27.7	26.2	27.7	26.2	30.5	27.8	45.6	36.3	50.2	38.9	42.0	34.3
18	24.3	28.0	25.2	27.0	25.2	25.1	24.1	25.1	24.1	25.1	24.1	25.1	24.1	37.0	30.8	43.3	34.4	39.3	32.1
19	23.0	23.1	22.1	25.3	23.6	22.4	22.0	22.4	22.0	22.4	22.0	22.4	22.0	27.0	24.6	31.5	27.0	30.8	26.6
20	21.3	19.0	18.9	19.4	19.3	19.4	19.3	19.4	19.3	19.4	19.3	19.4	19.3	19.4	19.3	19.4	19.4	19.4	19.4
21	20.0	17.4	17.4	17.9	17.9	17.9	17.9	17.9	17.9	17.9	17.9	17.9	17.9	17.9	17.9	17.9	17.9	17.9	17.9
22	18.9	16.2	16.2	16.7	16.7	16.7	16.7	16.7	16.7	16.7	16.7	16.7	16.7	16.7	16.7	16.7	16.7	16.7	16.7
23	18.0	15.1	15.1	15.7	15.7	15.7	15.7	15.7	15.7	15.7	15.7	15.7	15.7	15.7	15.7	15.7	15.7	15.7	15.7
24	17.1	14.1	14.1	14.7	14.7	14.7	14.7	14.7	14.7	14.7	14.7	14.7	14.7	14.7	14.7	14.7	14.7	14.7	14.7
Mean:	19.8	26.6	22.3	21.8	20.4	24.5	21.9	27.5	23.7	28.2	24.0	26.9	23.3	26.8	23.3	25.8	22.7	23.4	21.3

* Hour ending

CORRIGENDUM
The following replaces Table 2.28(*i*) at the top of page 2-56

Table 2.28 Air and sol-air temperatures: London area (Bracknell) (1981–1992) — *continued*

(*i*) September 3

Hour*	Air temp.	Horizontal		North		North-east		East		South-east		South		South-west		West		North-west	
		Dark	Light	Dark	Light	Dark	Light	Dark	Light	Dark	Light	Dark	Light	Dark	Light	Dark	Light	Dark	Light
01	11.6	8.1	8.1	9.0	9.0	9.0	9.0	9.0	9.0	9.0	9.0	9.0	9.0	9.0	9.0	9.0	9.0	9.0	9.0
02	11.1	7.4	7.4	8.3	8.3	8.3	8.3	8.3	8.3	8.3	8.3	8.3	8.3	8.3	8.3	8.3	8.3	8.3	8.3
03	10.4	6.7	6.7	7.7	7.7	7.7	7.7	7.7	7.7	7.7	7.7	7.7	7.7	7.7	7.7	7.7	7.7	7.7	7.7
04	9.9	6.0	6.0	7.1	7.1	7.1	7.1	7.1	7.1	7.1	7.1	7.1	7.1	7.1	7.1	7.1	7.1	7.1	7.1
05	9.6	5.7	5.7	6.7	6.7	6.7	6.7	6.7	6.7	6.7	6.7	6.7	6.7	6.7	6.7	6.7	6.7	6.7	6.7
06	9.6	6.3	6.0	7.2	7.0	7.2	7.0	7.3	7.0	7.2	7.0	7.1	6.9	7.1	6.9	7.1	6.9	7.1	6.9
07	10.6	13.5	10.8	10.8	9.9	31.0	21.4	39.4	26.3	31.8	21.9	11.7	10.4	10.8	9.9	10.8	9.9	10.8	9.9
08	12.7	21.6	16.2	14.8	13.3	34.2	24.3	49.5	33.2	45.5	30.8	23.6	18.2	14.8	13.3	14.8	13.3	14.8	13.3
09	15.1	29.1	21.5	18.8	16.8	30.6	23.5	50.8	35.2	52.7	36.3	35.3	26.2	18.8	16.8	18.8	16.8	18.8	16.8
10	17.2	33.9	25.2	22.1	19.8	24.0	20.9	45.6	33.2	53.1	37.6	43.0	31.7	22.1	19.8	22.1	19.8	22.1	19.8
11	18.6	36.6	27.4	24.2	21.8	24.2	21.8	38.1	29.7	50.1	36.5	47.3	34.9	31.0	25.6	24.2	21.8	24.2	21.8
12	19.6	38.5	28.9	25.5	23.0	25.5	23.0	30.2	25.7	46.3	34.8	50.2	37.1	39.9	31.1	25.5	23.0	25.5	23.0
13	20.4	39.7	29.9	26.3	23.8	26.3	23.8	26.3	23.8	41.1	32.2	51.8	38.3	47.8	36.0	31.1	26.6	26.3	23.8
14	21.0	38.6	29.5	26.2	23.9	26.2	23.9	26.2	23.9	33.0	27.8	49.5	37.2	52.4	38.9	40.2	31.9	26.2	23.9
15	21.2	36.0	28.1	25.4	23.4	25.4	23.4	25.4	23.4	25.4	23.4	44.5	34.2	53.7	39.5	46.8	35.6	27.1	24.4
16	21.1	31.7	25.6	23.9	22.3	23.9	22.3	23.9	22.3	23.9	22.3	37.0	29.7	50.9	37.6	49.4	36.8	33.2	27.5
17	20.5	26.1	22.2	21.8	20.6	21.8	20.6	21.8	20.6	21.8	20.6	27.8	23.9	42.6	32.3	45.4	33.9	34.8	27.9
18	19.4	20.4	18.8	19.0	18.4	19.0	18.4	19.0	18.4	19.0	18.4	19.7	18.7	31.4	25.3	35.9	27.9	30.8	25.0
19	18.0	15.3	15.1	15.8	15.7	15.7	15.6	15.7	15.6	15.7	15.6	15.7	15.6	15.8	15.7	15.8	15.7	15.8	15.7
20	16.6	13.5	13.5	14.1	14.1	14.1	14.1	14.1	14.1	14.1	14.1	14.1	14.1	14.1	14.1	14.1	14.1	14.1	14.1
21	15.4	12.3	12.3	12.9	12.9	12.9	12.9	12.9	12.9	12.9	12.9	12.9	12.9	12.9	12.9	12.9	12.9	12.9	12.9
22	14.4	11.1	11.1	11.8	11.8	11.8	11.8	11.8	11.8	11.8	11.8	11.8	11.8	11.8	11.8	11.8	11.8	11.8	11.8
23	13.5	10.0	10.0	10.8	10.8	10.8	10.8	10.8	10.8	10.8	10.8	10.8	10.8	10.8	10.8	10.8	10.8	10.8	10.8
24	12.9	9.3	9.3	10.1	10.1	10.1	10.1	10.1	10.1	10.1	10.1	10.1	10.1	10.1	10.1	10.1	10.1	10.1	10.1
Mean:	15.4	19.9	16.5	15.8	14.9	18.1	16.2	21.6	18.2	23.5	19.3	23.4	19.2	22.4	18.6	20.3	17.4	17.3	15.8

* Hour ending

(*j*) October 3

Hour*	Air temp.	Horizontal		North		North-east		East		South-east		South		South-west		West		North-west	
		Dark	Light	Dark	Light	Dark	Light	Dark	Light	Dark	Light	Dark	Light	Dark	Light	Dark	Light	Dark	Light
01	9.0	5.7	5.7	6.4	6.4	6.4	6.4	6.4	6.4	6.4	6.4	6.4	6.4	6.4	6.4	6.4	6.4	6.4	6.4
02	8.6	5.3	5.3	6.1	6.1	6.1	6.1	6.1	6.1	6.1	6.1	6.1	6.1	6.1	6.1	6.1	6.1	6.1	6.1
03	8.2	5.0	5.0	5.7	5.7	5.7	5.7	5.7	5.7	5.7	5.7	5.7	5.7	5.7	5.7	5.7	5.7	5.7	5.7
04	7.8	4.5	4.5	5.2	5.2	5.2	5.2	5.2	5.2	5.2	5.2	5.2	5.2	5.2	5.2	5.2	5.2	5.2	5.2
05	7.5	4.1	4.1	4.9	4.9	4.9	4.9	4.9	4.9	4.9	4.9	4.9	4.9	4.9	4.9	4.9	4.9	4.9	4.9
06	7.4	4.2	4.2	4.9	4.9	4.9	4.9	4.9	4.9	4.9	4.9	4.9	4.9	4.9	4.9	4.9	4.9	4.9	4.9
07	7.8	5.1	4.9	5.6	5.5	5.8	5.6	5.8	5.6	5.8	5.6	5.8	5.6	5.6	5.5	5.6	5.5	5.6	5.5
08	9.2	11.5	9.1	9.1	8.3	20.3	14.6	33.4	22.1	32.8	21.8	18.6	13.6	9.1	8.3	9.1	8.3	9.1	8.3
09	11.4	19.0	14.2	13.0	11.6	20.3	15.7	41.7	28.0	46.3	30.7	32.3	22.5	13.0	11.6	13.0	11.6	13.0	11.6
10	13.4	25.0	18.5	16.3	14.6	16.3	14.6	40.2	28.2	51.1	34.6	42.4	29.5	18.0	15.5	16.3	14.6	16.3	14.6
11	14.8	28.3	21.0	18.4	16.6	18.4	16.6	32.9	24.8	48.6	33.8	47.0	32.9	28.8	22.5	18.4	16.6	18.4	16.6
12	15.9	29.2	22.1	19.8	17.8	19.8	17.8	24.3	20.4	42.2	30.6	47.0	33.3	36.2	27.1	19.8	17.8	19.8	17.8
13	16.4	29.4	22.4	20.2	18.3	20.2	18.3	20.2	18.3	36.3	27.4	46.9	33.4	42.2	30.7	24.6	20.8	20.2	18.3
14	16.6	28.4	21.9	20.1	18.3	20.1	18.3	20.1	18.3	29.1	23.3	44.5	32.1	45.9	32.9	32.5	25.3	20.1	18.3
15	16.8	25.6	20.5	19.2	17.7	19.2	17.7	19.2	17.7	20.7	18.5	39.0	28.9	45.7	32.7	37.3	27.9	19.2	17.7
16	15.9	21.0	17.5	17.1	16.0	17.1	16.0	17.1	16.0	17.1	16.0	30.3	23.4	40.1	29.0	36.8	27.1	22.1	18.8
17	14.9	16.2	14.5	14.7	14.0	14.7	14.0	14.7	14.0	14.7	14.0	21.0	17.5	30.3	22.8	30.7	23.1	22.0	18.1
18	13.6	11.2	11.0	11.6	11.4	11.6	11.4	11.6	11.4	11.6	11.4	11.7	11.5	11.7	11.5	11.7	11.5	11.7	11.5
19	12.8	9.7	9.7	10.3	10.3	10.3	10.3	10.3	10.3	10.3	10.3	10.3	10.3	10.3	10.3	10.3	10.3	10.3	10.3
20	11.9	8.9	8.9	9.5	9.5	9.5	9.5	9.5	9.5	9.5	9.5	9.5	9.5	9.5	9.5	9.5	9.5	9.5	9.5
21	11.1	8.0	8.0	8.6	8.6	8.6	8.6	8.6	8.6	8.6	8.6	8.6	8.6	8.6	8.6	8.6	8.6	8.6	8.6
22	10.5	7.3	7.3	8.0	8.0	8.0	8.0	8.0	8.0	8.0	8.0	8.0	8.0	8.0	8.0	8.0	8.0	8.0	8.0
23	9.8	6.6	6.6	7.3	7.3	7.3	7.3	7.3	7.3	7.3	7.3	7.3	7.3	7.3	7.3	7.3	7.3	7.3	7.3
24	9.5	6.3	6.3	6.9	6.9	6.9	6.9	6.9	6.9	6.9	6.9	6.9	6.9	6.9	6.9	6.9	6.9	6.9	6.9
Mean:	11.7	13.6	11.4	11.2	10.6	12.0	11.0	15.2	12.9	18.3	14.6	19.6	15.3	17.1	13.9	14.2	12.2	11.7	10.9

* Hour ending

Table 2.28 Air and sol-air temperatures: London area (Bracknell) (1981–1992) — *continued*

(*k*) November 3

Hour*	Air temp.	Sol-air temperature (°C) for stated orientation and surface colour																
		Horizontal		North		North-east		East		South-east		South		South-west		West		North-west	
		Dark	Light	Dark	Light	Dark	Light	Dark	Light	Dark	Light	Dark	Light	Dark	Light	Dark	Light	Dark	Light
01	5.2	2.6	2.6	3.2	3.2	3.2	3.2	3.2	3.2	3.2	3.2	3.2	3.2	3.2	3.2	3.2	3.2	3.2	3.2
02	5.0	2.3	2.3	2.8	2.8	2.8	2.8	2.8	2.8	2.8	2.8	2.8	2.8	2.8	2.8	2.8	2.8	2.8	2.8
03	4.5	2.0	2.0	2.5	2.5	2.5	2.5	2.5	2.5	2.5	2.5	2.5	2.5	2.5	2.5	2.5	2.5	2.5	2.5
04	4.3	1.5	1.5	2.1	2.1	2.1	2.1	2.1	2.1	2.1	2.1	2.1	2.1	2.1	2.1	2.1	2.1	2.1	2.1
05	3.9	1.0	1.0	1.7	1.7	1.7	1.7	1.7	1.7	1.7	1.7	1.7	1.7	1.7	1.7	1.7	1.7	1.7	1.7
06	3.7	0.7	0.7	1.4	1.4	1.4	1.4	1.4	1.4	1.4	1.4	1.4	1.4	1.4	1.4	1.4	1.4	1.4	1.4
07	3.7	0.6	0.6	1.3	1.3	1.3	1.3	1.3	1.3	1.3	1.3	1.3	1.3	1.3	1.3	1.3	1.3	1.3	1.3
08	3.9	1.5	1.3	2.0	1.8	2.1	1.9	2.1	1.9	2.2	1.9	2.1	1.9	2.0	1.8	2.0	1.8	2.0	1.8
09	5.4	7.1	5.0	5.0	4.4	8.1	6.1	26.9	16.7	32.8	20.1	23.0	14.5	5.0	4.4	5.0	4.4	5.0	4.4
10	7.0	12.6	8.7	7.8	6.7	7.8	6.7	29.3	18.9	42.0	26.2	35.4	22.4	12.5	9.4	7.8	6.7	7.8	6.7
11	8.4	16.3	11.5	9.9	8.7	9.9	8.7	23.8	16.5	41.9	26.9	41.6	26.7	23.1	16.1	9.9	8.7	9.9	8.7
12	9.5	18.7	13.3	11.4	10.1	11.4	10.1	16.3	12.8	38.8	25.6	45.1	29.3	32.4	21.9	11.4	10.1	11.4	10.1
13	9.9	18.4	13.3	11.9	10.6	11.9	10.6	11.9	10.6	30.7	21.1	42.1	27.7	36.4	24.4	16.3	13.0	11.9	10.6
14	10.2	16.8	12.6	11.6	10.4	11.6	10.4	11.6	10.4	22.4	16.4	37.5	25.0	37.7	25.2	23.0	16.8	11.6	10.4
15	10.0	13.9	10.9	10.6	9.6	10.6	9.6	10.6	9.6	14.0	11.5	30.0	20.6	34.7	23.3	25.7	18.1	10.6	9.6
16	9.1	9.7	8.3	8.6	8.0	8.6	8.0	8.6	8.0	8.6	8.0	18.8	13.8	24.4	16.9	21.0	15.0	10.4	9.1
17	7.9	5.5	5.3	5.9	5.8	5.9	5.8	5.9	5.8	5.9	5.8	6.0	5.9	6.0	5.9	6.0	5.9	6.0	5.9
18	7.3	4.6	4.6	5.1	5.1	5.1	5.1	5.1	5.1	5.1	5.1	5.1	5.1	5.1	5.1	5.1	5.1	5.1	5.1
19	6.7	4.2	4.2	4.6	4.6	4.6	4.6	4.6	4.6	4.6	4.6	4.6	4.6	4.6	4.6	4.6	4.6	4.6	4.6
20	6.3	3.8	3.8	4.2	4.2	4.2	4.2	4.2	4.2	4.2	4.2	4.2	4.2	4.2	4.2	4.2	4.2	4.2	4.2
21	5.9	3.4	3.4	3.8	3.8	3.8	3.8	3.8	3.8	3.8	3.8	3.8	3.8	3.8	3.8	3.8	3.8	3.8	3.8
22	5.7	3.1	3.1	3.6	3.6	3.6	3.6	3.6	3.6	3.6	3.6	3.6	3.6	3.6	3.6	3.6	3.6	3.6	3.6
23	5.4	2.7	2.7	3.2	3.2	3.2	3.2	3.2	3.2	3.2	3.2	3.2	3.2	3.2	3.2	3.2	3.2	3.2	3.2
24	5.0	2.5	2.5	2.9	2.9	2.9	2.9	2.9	2.9	2.9	2.9	2.9	2.9	2.9	2.9	2.9	2.9	2.9	2.9
Mean:	6.4	6.5	5.2	5.3	4.9	5.4	5.0	7.9	6.4	11.7	8.6	13.5	9.6	10.7	8.0	7.1	6.0	5.4	5.0

* Hour ending

(*l*) December 3

Hour*	Air temp.	Sol-air temperature (°C) for stated orientation and surface colour																
		Horizontal		North		North-east		East		South-east		South		South-west		West		North-west	
		Dark	Light	Dark	Light	Dark	Light	Dark	Light	Dark	Light	Dark	Light	Dark	Light	Dark	Light	Dark	Light
01	1.3	−1.9	−1.9	−1.1	−1.1	−1.1	−1.1	−1.1	−1.1	−1.1	−1.1	−1.1	−1.1	−1.1	−1.1	−1.1	−1.1	−1.1	−1.1
02	1.1	−2.1	−2.1	−1.3	−1.3	−1.3	−1.3	−1.3	−1.3	−1.3	−1.3	−1.3	−1.3	−1.3	−1.3	−1.3	−1.3	−1.3	−1.3
03	0.7	−2.5	−2.5	−1.7	−1.7	−1.7	−1.7	−1.7	−1.7	−1.7	−1.7	−1.7	−1.7	−1.7	−1.7	−1.7	−1.7	−1.7	−1.7
04	0.2	−3.2	−3.2	−2.4	−2.4	−2.4	−2.4	−2.4	−2.4	−2.4	−2.4	−2.4	−2.4	−2.4	−2.4	−2.4	−2.4	−2.4	−2.4
05	0.0	−3.7	−3.7	−2.7	−2.7	−2.7	−2.7	−2.7	−2.7	−2.7	−2.7	−2.7	−2.7	−2.7	−2.7	−2.7	−2.7	−2.7	−2.7
06	−0.2	−3.9	−3.9	−2.9	−2.9	−2.9	−2.9	−2.9	−2.9	−2.9	−2.9	−2.9	−2.9	−2.9	−2.9	−2.9	−2.9	−2.9	−2.9
07	−0.4	−3.8	−3.8	−3.0	−3.0	−3.0	−3.0	−3.0	−3.0	−3.0	−3.0	−3.0	−3.0	−3.0	−3.0	−3.0	−3.0	−3.0	−3.0
08	−0.3	−3.8	−3.8	−2.9	−2.9	−2.9	−2.9	−2.9	−2.9	−2.9	−2.9	−2.9	−2.9	−2.9	−2.9	−2.9	−2.9	−2.9	−2.9
09	−0.1	−2.5	−2.9	−2.0	−2.2	−1.7	−2.1	−1.7	−2.1	−1.6	−2.1	−1.7	−2.1	−2.0	−2.2	−2.0	−2.2	−2.0	−2.2
10	1.2	3.5	1.2	1.2	0.4	1.2	0.4	18.3	10.1	30.0	16.8	25.4	14.2	6.7	3.5	1.2	0.4	1.2	0.4
11	2.7	7.9	4.1	3.5	2.4	3.5	2.4	17.4	10.2	37.2	21.6	37.7	21.9	18.7	11.0	3.5	2.4	3.5	2.4
12	4.0	10.2	5.9	5.0	3.8	5.0	3.8	9.9	6.6	34.3	20.5	41.3	24.6	27.9	16.8	5.0	3.8	5.0	3.8
13	4.9	10.8	6.7	5.9	4.7	5.9	4.7	5.9	4.7	27.6	17.0	40.2	24.3	33.6	20.4	10.6	7.3	5.9	4.7
14	5.4	9.6	6.2	5.8	4.7	5.8	4.7	5.8	4.7	19.2	12.3	36.1	22.0	35.6	21.7	18.1	11.7	5.8	4.7
15	5.1	6.2	4.2	4.5	3.8	4.5	3.8	4.5	3.8	9.1	6.4	24.5	15.1	28.3	17.2	18.6	11.7	4.5	3.8
16	4.1	1.9	1.5	2.3	2.0	2.3	2.0	2.3	2.0	2.3	2.0	2.5	2.1	2.5	2.1	2.5	2.1	2.4	2.1
17	3.3	0.2	0.2	0.9	0.9	0.9	0.9	0.9	0.9	0.9	0.9	0.9	0.9	0.9	0.9	0.9	0.9	0.9	0.9
18	2.7	−0.5	−0.5	0.2	0.2	0.2	0.2	0.2	0.2	0.2	0.2	0.2	0.2	0.2	0.2	0.2	0.2	0.2	0.2
19	2.2	−0.8	−0.8	−0.2	−0.2	−0.2	−0.2	−0.2	−0.2	−0.2	−0.2	−0.2	−0.2	−0.2	−0.2	−0.2	−0.2	−0.2	−0.2
20	1.8	−1.2	−1.2	−0.6	−0.6	−0.6	−0.6	−0.6	−0.6	−0.6	−0.6	−0.6	−0.6	−0.6	−0.6	−0.6	−0.6	−0.6	−0.6
21	1.6	−1.5	−1.5	−0.8	−0.8	−0.8	−0.8	−0.8	−0.8	−0.8	−0.8	−0.8	−0.8	−0.8	−0.8	−0.8	−0.8	−0.8	−0.8
22	1.4	−1.8	−1.8	−1.1	−1.1	−1.1	−1.1	−1.1	−1.1	−1.1	−1.1	−1.1	−1.1	−1.1	−1.1	−1.1	−1.1	−1.1	−1.1
23	1.1	−1.8	−1.8	−1.2	−1.2	−1.2	−1.2	−1.2	−1.2	−1.2	−1.2	−1.2	−1.2	−1.2	−1.2	−1.2	−1.2	−1.2	−1.2
24	0.7	−2.5	−2.5	−1.8	−1.8	−1.8	−1.8	−1.8	−1.8	−1.8	−1.8	−1.8	−1.8	−1.8	−1.8	−1.8	−1.8	−1.8	−1.8
Mean:	1.9	0.5	−0.3	0.2	−0.1	0.2	−0.1	1.7	0.7	5.6	3.0	7.6	4.1	5.4	2.8	1.5	0.6	0.2	−0.1

* Hour ending

Table 2.29 Air and sol-air temperatures: Manchester (Aughton) (1981–1992): refer to computer disk

Table 2.30 Air and sol-air temperatures: Edinburgh (Mylnefield) (1981–1992): refer to computer disk

Table 2.31 Proportion of year for which stated global horizontal illuminance is exceeded (based on measured global horizontal irradiation and luminous efficacy algorithms)

Illuminance (klux)	London (51°52′N)	Aberporth (52°13′N)	Aughton (53°55′N)	Dunstaffanage (56°47′N)	Aberdeen (57°20′N)	Stornaway (58°52′N)
0.0 (axis)†	0.971	0.970	0.967	0.959	0.957	0.954
1.0	0.938	0.944	0.916	0.898	0.931	0.898
2.0	0.905	0.908	0.890	0.862	0.861	0.866
3.0	0.882	0.883	0.865	0.828	0.827	0.834
4.0	0.859	0.857	0.840	0.794	0.797	0.802
5.0	0.834	0.834	0.817	0.762	0.770	0.774
6.0	0.806	0.808	0.793	0.733	0.743	0.746
7.0	0.784	0.784	0.770	0.704	0.717	0.720
8.0	0.761	0.762	0.748	0.677	0.693	0.695
9.0	0.736	0.739	0.728	0.652	0.670	0.672
10.0	0.714	0.718	0.705	0.628	0.649	0.647
15.0	0.613	0.624	0.606	0.528	0.553	0.545
20.0	0.522	0.541	0.519	0.447	0.472	0.455
25.0	0.422	0.470	0.450	0.381	0.403	0.383
30.0	0.379	0.407	0.386	0.326	0.341	0.320
35.0	0.321	0.351	0.332	0.276	0.285	0.262
40.0	0.268	0.300	0.282	0.231	0.235	0.210
45.0	0.218	0.254	0.236	0.191	0.188	0.164
50.0	0.174	0.214	0.194	0.159	0.150	0.130
55.0	0.139	0.178	0.156	0.131	0.118	0.103
60.0	0.106	0.147	0.122	0.106	0.091	0.080
65.0	0.080	0.120	0.094	0.085	0.068	0.062
70.0	0.058	0.095	0.070	0.065	0.050	0.046
75.0	0.039	0.073	0.050	0.049	0.035	0.033
80.0	0.025	0.054	0.033	0.034	0.022	0.022
85.0	0.014	0.038	0.019	0.022	0.012	0.014
90.0	0.006	0.024	0.010	0.011	0.005	0.007
95.0	0.000	0.012	0.004	0.004	0.000	0.002
100.0	0.000	0.004	0.001	0.001	0.000	0.000
105.0	0.000	0.000	0.000	0.000	0.000	0.000

† Values at 0 klux estimated algorithmically

Note: measurement periods: London/Aberporth/Dunstaffanage/Aberdeen: 1975–1994; Aughton/Stornaway: 1982–1994

Table 2.32 Proportion of year for which stated diffuse horizontal illuminance is exceeded (based on measured diffuse irradiation and luminous efficacy algorithms)

Illuminance (klux)	London (51°52′N)	Aberporth (52°13′N)	Aughton (53°55′N)	Stornaway (58°52′N)
0.0 (axis)†	0.971	0.960	0.967	0.954
1.0	0.945	0.947	0.916	0.915
2.0	0.911	0.909	0.888	0.871
3.0	0.877	0.875	0.856	0.826
4.0	0.848	0.845	0.830	0.791
5.0	0.817	0.823	0.802	0.758
6.0	0.786	0.793	0.772	0.720
7.0	0.755	0.763	0.742	0.686
8.0	0.719	0.734	0.712	0.656
9.0	0.687	0.705	0.682	0.627
10.0	0.658	0.674	0.652	0.599
15.0	0.513	0.526	0.515	0.466
20.0	0.385	0.392	0.396	0.349
25.0	0.266	0.284	0.284	0.248
30.0	0.168	0.195	0.190	0.164
35.0	0.095	0.126	0.119	0.098
40.0	0.043	0.078	0.066	0.052
45.0	0.015	0.046	0.032	0.025
50.0	0.005	0.026	0.013	0.011
55.0	0.000	0.013	0.004	0.004
60.0	0.000	0.006	0.001	0.000
65.0	0.000	0.000	0.000	0.000

† Values at 0 klux estimated algorithmically

Note: measurement periods: London/Aberporth: 1975–1994; Aughton/Stornaway: 1982–1994

Table 2.33 Orientation factor for availability of diffuse illuminance (vertical apertures)

Orientation	Factor, f_o
North	0.97
East	1.15
South	1.55
West	1.21

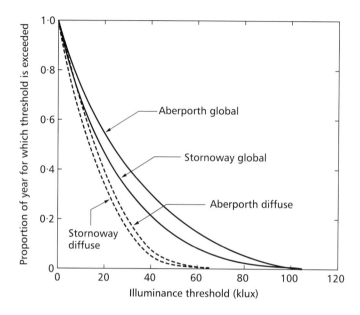

Figure 2.15 Proportion of year for which global and diffuse horizontal illuminances are exceeded for Aberporth and Stornoway

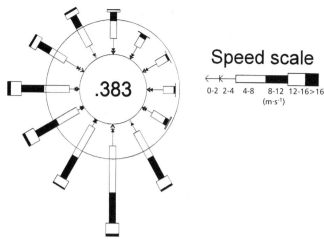

Figure 2.16 Example of a wind rose; the centre number is the percentage frequency of calms, other frequencies are drawn from the inner circle with the outer circle indicating 5% frequency

2.8 Wind data

2.8.1 Measurement of wind data

Wind data are measured with an anemometer and wind vane mounted, where possible, 10 m above ground level, or in some cases, above the roof of a building. Most sites are in exposed open situations such as airports; few or no data are available from city centres. The wind speed data in this Guide are derived from measurements from anemometers designed to record high wind speeds. However, as these have a relatively high starting speed, low speed data (i.e. below 2 m·s⁻¹) are less reliable.

The hourly values used to derive the statistics quoted in the tables are hourly mean speeds and median direction, derived either from anemograph charts or from a dedicated logging system which records data at 1-minute intervals.

2.8.2 Sources of published data

Comprehensive data on wind speed and direction for the UK are published by the Meteorological Office and include tabulated values for about 100 stations[13] and contour maps of hourly mean wind speeds exceeded for percentages of time between 0.1% and 75% of the time[14]. The *European Wind Atlas*[15] gives detailed wind statistics for 22 UK stations and a large number of European locations

2.8.3 Wind climate in the UK

Table 2.34 summarises the wind climate for 20 locations in the UK shown. The following information is given for each station:

— The name and location of the station and the terrain category of its surroundings (see Table 2.41).

— A wind rose, see Figure 2.16, summarising the distribution of wind speed and direction. The length of each symbol is proportional to the relative frequency of winds in each speed and direction band.

— The mean wind speed (m·s⁻¹).

— The parameters of the Weibull distribution fitted to the wind speeds. These can be used to calculate the frequency of occurrence, $f(v)$, of any wind speed, v, with a bandwidth of 1 m·s⁻¹, as follows:

$$f(v) = (k/A)(v/A)^{k-1} \exp\left[-(v/A)^k\right] \qquad (2.2)$$

where $f(v)$ is the frequency of occurrence of wind speed v, k and A are Weibull coefficients and v is the wind speed to the nearest metre per second (m·s⁻¹).

The probability of the wind speed exceeding v is given by:

$$F(v) = \exp\left[-(v/A)^k\right] \qquad (2.3)$$

For example, for Heathrow $A = 4.47$ and $k = 1.80$. For $v = 5$ m·s⁻¹, equation 2.2 gives $f(v) = 0.130$, i.e. the wind speed will be between 3.5 and 4.5 m·s⁻¹ for 13% of the time. Equation 2.3 gives $F(v) = 0.29$, i.e. the wind speed will exceed 5 m·s⁻¹ for 29% of the time.

— The percentiles of the distribution of wind speed. For example, at Heathrow the wind speed will be less than or equal to 1.54 m/s for 20% of the time and less than or equal to 6.17 m/s for 90% of the time.

Note that the percentiles given are derived directly from the data, whereas the Weibull coefficients are derived from a smoothed curve through the whole wind spectrum. Therefore, there will not be exact agreement between the two methods, especially at low wind speeds.

2.8.4 Wind speed, direction and external temperature

To aid ventilation design, frequency distributions of wind speed by direction and wind speed by external temperature are shown for the whole year for London (Heathrow), Manchester (Ringway) and Edinburgh (Turnhouse) in

Tables 2.35 to 2.40. The binned data are derived from the original observed data as follows:

— wind speed: recorded in whole knots, which have been converted to m·s^{-1} the bin labels therefore give only a guide to the values they contain

— wind direction: recorded to the nearest 10° with north represented by 360°; 'calm' (i.e. a wind speed of zero) and 'variable' (i.e. a wind speed of 2 knots or where no clear direction existed over the hour) have been combined

— dry bulb temperature: recorded to the nearest 0.1°C.

Frequencies greater than zero but less than 0.005% are shown as '0.00+'.

CIBSE Guide: *Weather and solar data*[1] provides the same data but divided into seasonal and daytime/night-time frequency distributions.

Table 2.34 Summary of wind climate at each station

Aberdeen (Dyce)		Aberporth, NW Wales		Belfast (Aldergrove)		Birmingham (Elmdon)	
Terrain category II		Terrain category I		Terrain category II		Terrain category III	
Mean speed = 4.50 m·s^{-1}		Mean speed = 6.78 m·s^{-1}		Mean speed = 4.83 m·s^{-1}		Mean speed = 3.91 m·s^{-1}	
$A = 5.82; k = 1.92$		$A = 8.38; k = 2.04$		$A = 6.09; k = 2.03$		$A = 5.14; k = 1.94$	
Percentile	Speed (m·s^{-1})	Percentile	Speed (m·s^{-1})	Percentile	Speed (m·s^{-1})	Percentile	Speed (m·s^{-1})
5	1.01	5	1.01	5	1.01	5	1.01
10	1.01	10	2.02	10	1.52	10	1.01
20	2.02	20	3.03	20	2.53	20	2.02
30	2.53	30	4.04	30	3.03	30	2.53
40	3.54	40	5.56	40	4.04	40	3.03
50	4.04	50	6.57	50	4.55	50	3.54
60	5.05	60	7.58	60	5.05	60	4.04
70	5.56	70	8.59	70	6.06	70	5.05
80	6.57	80	10.10	80	7.07	80	5.56
90	8.08	90	12.12	90	8.08	90	7.07
95	9.60	95	14.14	95	9.60	95	8.08

Table 2.34 Summary of wind climate at each station — *continued*

Bristol (Bristol Weather Centre)		Bournemouth (Hurn)		Cardiff (Rhoose)		Edinburgh (Turnhouse)	
Terrain category IV		Terrain category II		Terrain category II		Terrain category II	

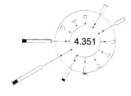  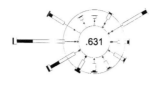 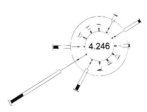

Mean speed = 3.59 m·s⁻¹		Mean speed = 4.01 m·s⁻¹		Mean speed = 5.06 m·s⁻¹		Mean speed = 4.45 m·s⁻¹	
$A = 4.75; k = 1.76$		$A = 5.26; k = 1.83$		$A = 6.49; k = 1.87$		$A = 5.78; k = 1.93$	
Percentile	Speed (m·s⁻¹)	Percentile	Speed (m·s⁻¹)	Percentile	Speed (m·s⁻¹)	Percentile	Speed (m·s⁻¹)
5	1.01	5	1.01	5	1.01	5	1.01
10	1.01	10	1.01	10	1.52	10	1.01
20	1.52	20	1.52	20	2.53	20	1.52
30	2.02	30	2.53	30	3.03	30	2.53
40	3.03	40	3.03	40	4.04	40	3.54
50	3.54	50	3.54	50	4.55	50	4.04
60	4.04	60	4.55	60	5.56	60	5.06
70	4.55	70	5.05	70	6.57	70	5.56
80	5.56	80	6.06	80	7.58	80	6.57
90	6.57	90	7.58	90	9.09	90	8.09
95	7.58	95	8.59	95	10.10	95	9.61

Finningley, South Yorkshire		Gatwick, Sussex		Glasgow (Abbotsinch)		Hemsby, Norfolk coast	
Terrain category II		Terrain category II		Terrain category II		Terrain category II	

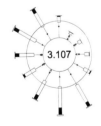  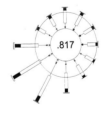 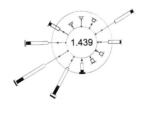

Mean speed = 3.91 m·s⁻¹		Mean speed = 3.67 m·s⁻¹		Mean speed = 4.39 m·s⁻¹		Mean speed = 6.78 m·s⁻¹	
$A = 5.14; k = 1.94$		$A = 4.87; k = 1.83$		$A = 5.65; k = 1.73$		$A = 8.38; k = 2.04$	
Percentile	Speed (m·s⁻¹)	Percentile	Speed (m·s⁻¹)	Percentile	Speed (m·s⁻¹)	Percentile	Speed (m·s⁻¹)
5	1.01	5	1.01	5	1.01	5	1.01
10	1.01	10	1.01	10	1.01	10	2.02
20	2.02	20	1.52	20	1.52	20	3.03
30	2.53	30	2.02	30	2.53	30	3.54
40	3.03	40	3.03	40	3.03	40	4.04
50	3.54	50	3.54	50	4.04	50	5.05
60	4.55	60	4.04	60	4.55	60	5.56
70	5.05	70	4.55	70	5.56	70	6.57
80	6.06	80	5.56	80	6.57	80	7.58
90	7.58	90	7.07	90	8.08	90	9.09
95	9.09	95	8.08	95	9.60	95	10.10

Table 2.34 Summary of wind climate at each station — *continued*

Herstmonceux, Sussex	Leuchars, East Fife	London (Heathrow)	London (London Weather Centre)
Terrain category II	Terrain category II	Terrain category III	Terrain category IV

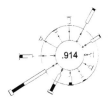
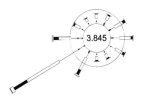
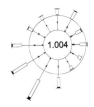
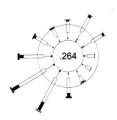

Mean speed = 4.23 m·s⁻¹		Mean speed = 4.97 m·s⁻¹		Mean speed = 3.46 m·s⁻¹		Mean speed = 5.08 m·s⁻¹	
A = 5.40; k = 1.59		A = 6.39; k = 1.89		A = 4.47; k = 1.80		A = 6.71; k = 2.35	
Percentile	Speed (m·s⁻¹)	Percentile	Speed (m·s⁻¹)	Percentile	Speed (m·s⁻¹)	Percentile	Speed (m·s⁻¹)
5	1.01	5	1.01	5	1.03	5	1.52
10	1.01	10	1.01	10	1.03	10	2.53
20	1.52	20	2.53	20	1.54	20	3.03
30	2.02	30	3.03	30	2.06	30	3.54
40	3.03	40	3.54	40	2.57	40	4.04
50	3.54	50	4.55	50	3.09	50	5.05
60	4.55	60	5.56	60	3.60	60	5.56
70	5.56	70	6.06	70	4.12	70	6.06
80	6.57	80	7.58	80	5.14	80	7.07
90	8.59	90	9.09	90	6.17	90	8.08
95	10.10	95	11.11	95	7.20	95	9.09

Manchester (Ringway)	Plymouth (Mountbatten)	St. Mawgan, Cornwall	Stornoway, Western Isles
Terrain category II	Terrain category I	Terrain category II	Terrain category II

Mean speed = 5.06 m·s⁻¹		Mean speed = 5.27 m·s⁻¹		Mean speed = 5.97 m·s⁻¹		Mean speed = 5.67 m·s⁻¹	
A = 6.49; k = 1.87		A = 6.72; k = 1.78		A = 7.66; k = 2.04		A = 7.16; k = 1.88	
Percentile	Speed m·s⁻¹	Percentile	Speed m·s⁻¹	Percentile	Speed m·s⁻¹	Percentile	Speed m·s⁻¹
5	1.01	5	1.01	5	1.52	5	1.01
10	1.01	10	1.01	10	2.02	10	1.52
20	2.02	20	2.53	20	3.03	20	2.53
30	2.53	30	3.03	30	4.04	30	3.54
40	3.54	40	4.04	40	4.55	40	4.04
50	4.04	50	5.05	50	5.56	50	5.05
60	4.55	60	5.56	60	6.57	60	6.06
70	5.06	70	6.57	70	7.58	70	7.07
80	6.07	80	7.58	80	8.59	80	8.59
90	7.58	90	9.60	90	10.10	90	10.61
95	8.59	95	11.62	95	12.12	95	12.63

Table 2.35 Annual average percentage frequency of wind speed by direction: London (Heathrow) (1975–1994)

Direction (°)	Percentage frequency for stated range of wind speed (m·s⁻¹)										All speeds
	0–2	2–4	4–6	6–8	8–10	10–12	12–14	14–16	16–18	18–20	
Calm/variable	1.06										1.06
350 to 010	2.74	2.80	1.48	0.49	0.11	0.02	0.01	0.00+	0.00+		7.65
020 to 040	1.99	3.28	2.16	0.86	0.20	0.03	0.00+				8.52
050 to 070	0.81	1.82	1.42	0.71	0.19	0.05	0.01				5.01
080 to 100	0.80	2.19	1.78	0.79	0.18	0.03	0.01				5.76
110 to 130	1.27	2.18	0.97	0.24	0.02						4.68
140 to 160	1.69	1.94	0.95	0.30	0.06	0.01	0.00+				4.96
170 to 190	2.54	3.96	2.40	1.01	0.30	0.09	0.02	0.00+		0.00+	10.32
200 to 220	3.43	5.71	4.57	2.43	0.72	0.19	0.04	0.01	0.00+		17.10
230 to 250	2.98	4.96	4.08	1.91	0.44	0.07	0.02	0.00+	0.00+	0.00+	14.46
260 to 280	3.28	4.66	2.47	1.01	0.32	0.07	0.02	0.00+			11.82
290 to 310	2.74	2.40	1.30	0.50	0.15	0.03	0.01				7.14
320 to 340	0.70	0.53	0.23	0.05	0.02	0.00+					1.53
All directions	26.03	36.42	23.80	10.29	2.71	0.59	0.13	0.01	0.00+	0.00+	100.00

Table 2.36 Annual average percentage frequency of wind speed by temperature: London (Heathrow) (1975–1994)

Temperature (°C)	Percentage frequency for stated range of wind speed (m·s⁻¹)										All speeds
	0–2	2–4	4–6	6–8	8–10	10–12	12–14	14–16	16–18	18–20	
−10.0 to −8.1	0.00+										0
−8.0 to −6.1	0.01	0.01	0.00+								0.02
−6.0 to −4.1	0.03	0.02	0.01	0.00+							0.06
−4.0 to −2.1	0.16	0.06	0.03	0.01	0.01	0.00+					0.27
−2.0 to −0.1	0.45	0.19	0.09	0.06	0.04	0.01	0.00+				0.85
0.0 to 1.9	2.64	1.97	0.91	0.40	0.13	0.04	0.01				6.10
2.0 to 3.9	2.36	2.25	1.32	0.58	0.14	0.03	0.01	0.00+			6.69
4.0 to 5.9	2.60	3.09	1.86	0.80	0.23	0.04	0.01	0.00+	0.00+		8.63
6.0 to 7.9	2.91	3.76	2.28	1.03	0.32	0.08	0.01	0.00+	0.00+		10.40
8.0 to 9.9	2.94	4.21	2.92	1.40	0.43	0.09	0.02	0.00+	0.00+	0.00+	12.03
10.0 to 11.9	2.91	4.36	2.99	1.54	0.47	0.12	0.03	0.00+	0.00+		12.42
12.0 to 13.9	2.99	4.25	2.58	1.21	0.37	0.08	0.02	0.00+		0.00+	11.50
14.0 to 15.9	2.55	4.05	2.43	0.91	0.19	0.03	0.01	0.00+			10.17
16.0 to 17.9	1.76	3.16	2.12	0.76	0.13	0.02					7.96
18.0 to 19.9	1.06	2.12	1.60	0.57	0.08	0.01					5.44
20.0 to 21.9	0.60	1.28	1.02	0.33	0.04	0.00+	0.00+				3.28
22.0 to 23.9	0.31	0.83	0.63	0.19	0.02						1.98
24.0 to 25.9	0.18	0.53	0.36	0.13	0.01	0.00+					1.21
26.0 to 27.9	0.07	0.25	0.18	0.08	0.01						0.59
28.0 to 29.9	0.01	0.10	0.08	0.04	0.01						0.24
30.0 to 31.9	0.00+	0.04	0.04	0.02	0.00+						0.11
32.0 to 33.9	0.00+	0.02	0.02	0.00+							0.04
34.0 to 35.9		0.01	0.00+								0.01
All temps.	26.58	36.54	23.47	10.07	2.62	0.57	0.13	0.01	0.00+	0.00+	100.00

Table 2.37 Annual average percentage frequency of wind speed by direction: Manchester (Ringway) (1975–1994)

Direction (°)	Percentage frequency for stated range of wind speed (m·s⁻¹)										All speeds
	0–2	2–4	4–6	6–8	8–10	10–12	12–14	14–16	16–18	18–20	
Calm/variable	1.30	0.09	0.00								1.39
350 to 010	0.61	1.02	0.60	0.29	0.10	0.02	0.01				2.64
020 to 040	0.55	1.58	1.36	0.74	0.20	0.04	0.00				4.48
050 to 070	1.15	1.93	1.70	1.11	0.37	0.13	0.02				6.41
080 to 100	1.45	1.87	1.51	0.93	0.33	0.10	0.03	0.01			6.22
110 to 130	1.28	1.89	1.26	0.62	0.18	0.04	0.01	0.00			5.27
140 to 160	1.54	2.85	2.16	1.08	0.35	0.10	0.01	0.00			8.10
170 to 190	2.62	5.66	5.61	3.13	1.18	0.37	0.07	0.01	0.00		18.65
200 to 220	2.15	3.15	3.49	2.55	0.95	0.33	0.08	0.01	0.00		12.70
230 to 250	1.83	2.41	2.38	1.59	0.62	0.21	0.04	0.01	0.00		9.10
260 to 280	1.67	2.80	2.75	1.90	0.93	0.37	0.10	0.02	0.01		10.56
290 to 310	1.13	2.94	3.15	1.55	0.45	0.12	0.02	0.00	0.00		9.37
320 to 340	1.23	2.09	1.21	0.45	0.09	0.03	0.00				5.10
All directions	18.51	30.29	27.18	15.94	5.74	1.86	0.40	0.07	0.01		100.00

Table 2.38 Annual average percentage frequency of wind speed by temperature: Manchester (Ringway) (1975–1994)

Temperature (°C)	Percentage frequency for stated range of wind speed (m·s⁻¹)										All speeds
	0–2	2–4	4–6	6–8	8–10	10–12	12–14	14–16	16–18	18–20	
−10.0 to −8.1	0.00+										0
−12.0 to −10.1	0.00+										0
−10.0 to −8.1	0.01	0.00+									0.01
−8.0 to −6.1	0.02	0.01									0.03
−6.0 to −4.1	0.08	0.02	0.01	0.00+							0.11
−4.0 to −2.1	0.18	0.06	0.02	0.02	0.01						0.29
−2.0 to −0.1	0.60	0.23	0.09	0.04	0.03	0.02	0.00+				1.01
0.0 to 1.9	2.48	2.62	1.27	0.65	0.32	0.11	0.03	0.00+			7.49
2.0 to 3.9	1.75	2.65	2.05	1.10	0.41	0.16	0.04	0.01			8.15
4.0 to 5.9	1.87	3.16	2.90	1.73	0.66	0.22	0.06	0.02	0.00+		10.63
6.0 to 7.9	2.00	3.32	3.33	2.21	0.90	0.31	0.08	0.02	0.00+		12.16
8.0 to 9.9	2.05	3.57	3.47	2.41	0.95	0.32	0.07	0.01	0.00+		12.86
10.0 to 11.9	2.19	3.77	3.44	2.17	0.92	0.33	0.06	0.00+	0.00+		12.87
12.0 to 13.9	1.94	3.75	3.49	1.96	0.65	0.21	0.04	0.01	0.00+		12.06
14.0 to 15.9	1.47	2.83	3.02	1.65	0.43	0.11	0.02	0.00+			9.53
16.0 to 17.9	0.89	1.85	2.00	1.08	0.23	0.04	0.00+	0.00+			6.08
18.0 to 19.9	0.48	1.10	0.97	0.47	0.12	0.02	0.01				3.16
20.0 to 21.9	0.24	0.64	0.58	0.22	0.06	0.01	0.00+				1.77
22.0 to 23.9	0.15	0.42	0.28	0.11	0.03	0.00+					0.99
24.0 to 25.9	0.06	0.18	0.14	0.07	0.01	0.00+					0.45
26.0 to 27.9	0.04	0.08	0.08	0.03	0.01						0.24
28.0 to 29.9	0.02	0.02	0.03	0.02	0.00+						0.09
30.0 to 31.9	0.00+	0.01	0.01	0.00+							0.02
32.0 to 33.9	0.00+	0.00+	0.01								0.01
All temps.	18.51	30.29	27.18	15.94	5.74	1.86	0.40	0.07	0.01		100.00+

Table 2.39 Annual average percentage frequency of wind speed by direction: Edinburgh (Turnhouse) (1975–1994)

Direction (°)	Percentage frequency for stated range of wind speed (m·s⁻¹)										All speeds
	0–2	2–4	4–6	6–8	8–10	10–12	12–14	14–16	16–18	18–20	
Calm/variable	4.25	0.00+									4.25
350 to 010	0.89	0.71	0.45	0.27	0.08	0.02	0.01	0.00+			2.42
020 to 040	1.79	2.67	1.66	0.60	0.17	0.04	0.02	0.00+			6.95
050 to 070	1.40	3.82	3.75	1.87	0.58	0.20	0.06	0.00+			11.68
080 to 100	0.83	1.69	1.71	0.94	0.29	0.10	0.03	0.00+			5.59
110 to 130	0.70	0.90	0.66	0.34	0.09	0.02	0.00+				2.72
140 to 160	0.61	0.70	0.44	0.18	0.05	0.01	0.01	0.00+			1.99
170 to 190	0.76	0.86	0.79	0.43	0.19	0.08	0.04	0.01	0.01		3.17
200 to 220	1.49	2.35	3.25	2.76	1.38	0.53	0.20	0.06	0.01	0.00+	12.04
230 to 250	3.64	7.35	8.31	7.14	3.52	1.38	0.46	0.12	0.02	0.01	31.95
260 to 280	2.32	2.75	2.22	2.19	1.26	0.57	0.18	0.04	0.01	0.00+	11.53
290 to 310	1.03	0.99	0.61	0.29	0.07	0.02	0.00+	0.00+			3.02
320 to 340	0.81	0.82	0.65	0.32	0.07	0.01	0.00+				2.69
All directions	20.51	25.62	24.48	17.33	7.77	2.99	1.01	0.24	0.04	0.01	100.00

Table 2.40 Annual average percentage frequency of wind speed by temperature: Edinburgh (Turnhouse) (1975–1994)

Temperature (°C)	Percentage frequency for stated range of wind speed (m·s⁻¹)										All speeds
	0–2	2–4	4–6	6–8	8–10	10–12	12–14	14–16	16–18	18–20	
−16.0 to −14.1	0.01	0.00+									0.01
−14.0 to −12.1	0.03	0.00+									0.03
−12.0 to −10.1	0.04	0.00+									0.04
−10.0 to −8.1	0.06	0.01									0.06
−8.0 to −6.1	0.11	0.02	0.00+								0.13
−6.0 to −4.1	0.22	0.04	0.00+								0.27
−4.0 to −2.1	0.45	0.10	0.01	0.01	0.00+	0.01	0.00+				0.59
−2.0 to −0.1	0.85	0.29	0.05	0.02	0.01	0.01	0.01				1.25
0.0 to 1.9	3.71	2.51	1.58	0.84	0.31	0.11	0.03	0.00+			9.09
2.0 to 3.9	2.43	2.45	2.15	1.59	0.72	0.29	0.11	0.01	0.01		9.77
4.0 to 5.9	2.44	2.79	2.76	1.92	0.90	0.35	0.12	0.03	0.01	0.01	11.32
6.0 to 7.9	2.15	3.05	3.08	2.38	1.17	0.46	0.13	0.04	0.01	0.00+	12.48
8.0 to 9.9	2.28	3.19	3.25	2.51	1.23	0.55	0.20	0.04	0.01	0.00+	13.26
10.0 to 11.9	2.23	3.43	3.35	2.37	1.23	0.53	0.23	0.07	0.01	0.00+	13.45
12.0 to 13.9	1.78	3.20	3.18	2.11	0.93	0.34	0.11	0.03	0.00+		11.69
14.0 to 15.9	1.02	2.19	2.37	1.64	0.67	0.19	0.05	0.00+			8.12
16.0 to 17.9	0.45	1.27	1.45	1.15	0.39	0.12	0.02	0.00+			4.86
18.0 to 19.9	0.16	0.61	0.70	0.54	0.14	0.03	0.01				2.18
20.0 to 21.9	0.06	0.29	0.34	0.17	0.04	0.00+					0.91
22.0 to 23.9	0.02	0.13	0.13	0.06	0.01	0.00+					0.36
24.0 to 25.9	0.01	0.05	0.04	0.02	0.00+						0.11
26.0 to 27.9	0.00+	0.01	0.01	0.01	0.00+						0.03
28.0 to 29.9	0.00+	0.00+	0.01	0.00+	0.00+						0.01
All temps.	20.51	25.62	24.48	17.33	7.77	2.99	1.01	0.24	0.04	0.01	100.00+

2.8.5   Influence of height and environment on mean wind speed

2.8.5.1   General

The mean wind speed is a function of the local environment (topography, ground roughness, nearby obstacles). Mean wind speeds, observed at two different sites of similar altitude within about ten kilometres, will not differ significantly if both sites have a similar local environment. In the opposite case, to obtain the reference regional wind, v_{ref}, from observations over a site, or to obtain an estimate of wind conditions over a site from the reference wind, the mean wind speed should be corrected using the following relationship (in the case where there are no near obstacles):

$$v_z = v_{ref} C_R(z) C_T \tag{2.4}$$

where v_z the wind speed at height z (m·s^{-1}), v_{ref} is the reference regional wind speed (m·s^{-1}), $C_R(z)$ is the roughness coefficient at height z and C_T is the topography coefficient.

2.8.5.2   Roughness coefficient

The roughness coefficient accounts for the variability of mean wind speed at the site due to:

—   height above the ground

—   roughness of the terrain over which the wind has passed.

The roughness coefficient at height z (where $z \geq z_{min}$) is given by:

$$C_R(z) = K_R \log_e (z / z_o) \tag{2.5}$$

where K_R is the terrain factor, z_o is the roughness length (m) and z_{min} is the minimum height (m), see Table 2.41.

It is not possible to make realistic estimates of wind speed at heights below z_{min}; locally measured data should be used wherever possible.

The parameters depend on the terrain category, see Table 2.41. If there is a change of roughness upwind of a site within a kilometre, the smoothest terrain category in the upwind direction should be used.

2.8.5.3   Topography coefficient

The topography coefficient accounts for the increase in mean wind speed over isolated hills and escarpments (not undulating and mountainous regions) and is related to the wind speed upwind to the hill. It should be taken into account for locations that are:

—   more than halfway up the slope of the hill

—   within 1.5 times the height of the cliff from the base of the cliff.

It is defined as follows:

$$C_T = 1 \text{ for } \Phi < 0.05 \tag{2.6}$$

$$C_T = (1 + 2 s \Phi) \text{ for } 0.05 < \Phi < 0.3 \tag{2.7}$$

$$C_T = (1 + 0.6 s) \text{ for } \Phi > 0.3 \tag{2.8}$$

where C_T is the topography coefficient, s is a slope factor (obtained from Figures 2.17 and 2.18) and Φ is the upwind slope in the wind direction (H / L_u).

The slope factor s must be scaled to the length of the upwind or downwind slopes, see Figure 2.19, where L_u is the actual length of the upwind slope in the wind direction (m), L_d is the actual length of the downwind slope (m), H is the effective height of the feature (m), Φ is the upwind slope (H / L_u) in the wind direction, L_e is the effective length of the upwind slope (m), as defined in Table 2.42, x is the horizontal distance of the site from the top of the crest (m) and z is the vertical distance from the ground level of the site (m).

Table 2.42 Values of L_e

Slope ($\Phi = H / L_u$)	L_e value
Shallow ($0.05 < \Phi < 0.3$)	L_u
Steep ($\Phi > 0.3$)	$H / 0.3$

Table 2.41 Terrain categories and related parameters

Terrain category	Description	K_R	z_o (m)	z_{min} (m)
I	Rough open sea; lake shore with at least 5 km fetch up-wind and smooth flat country without obstacles	0.17	0.01	2
II	Farm land with boundary hedges, occasional small farm structures, houses or trees	0.19	0.05	4
III	Suburban or industrial areas and permanent forests	0.22	0.3	8
IV	Urban areas in which at least 15% of surface is covered with buildings of average height exceeding 15 m	0.24	1	16

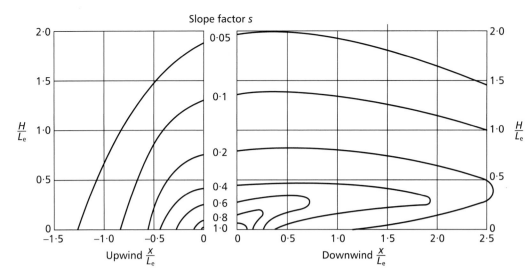

Figure 2.17 Slope factor *s* for cliffs and escarpments

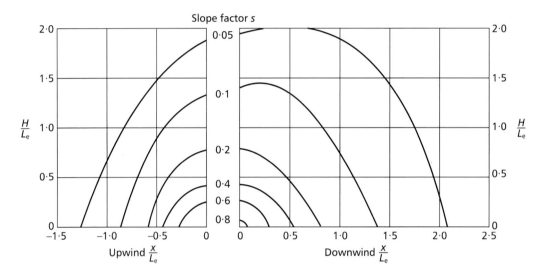

Figure 2.18 Slope factor *s* for hills and ridges

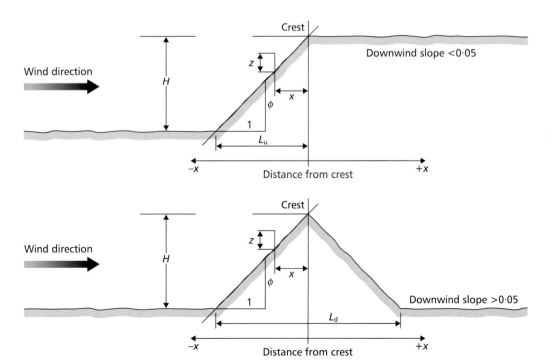

Figure 2.19 Definition of topographic features

Example 2.2

It is required to estimate the wind at 15 metres above ground in a suburban area, three quarters of the way up the slope of a hill that rises 120 m over 1 km in the direction of the prevailing wind, and is then flat. The mean wind measured at an adjacent airfield site is 4.5 m/s.

The roughness coefficient is given by equation 2.5, using the values given in Table 2.41 for terrain category III, i.e:

$$C_R(15) = 0.22 \log_e(15/0.3) = 0.861$$

From Figure 2.19, the parameters that define the topography coefficient are as follows:

— $L_u = 1000\,\mathrm{m}$

— $L_d = \infty$

— $H = 120\,\mathrm{m}$

— $\Phi = 120/1000 = 0.12$

— $L_e = L_u = 1000$ (see Table 2.42)

— $H/L_e = 120/1000 = 0.012$

— $x = -250\,\mathrm{m}$

— $x/L_e = -0.25$

Hence, from Figure 2.17, $s = 0.6$.

Therefore, from equation 2.7, the topography coefficient is:

$$C_T = 1 + (2 \times 0.6 \times 0.12) = 1.144$$

From equation 2.4, the desired wind speed is:

$$v_z = 4.5 \times 0.861 \times 1.144 = 4.43\,\mathrm{m/s}$$

References

1 *Weather and solar data* CIBSE Guide (London: Chartered Institution of Building Services Engineers) (in preparation)

2 *Fundamentals* ASHRAE Handbook (Atlanta GA: American Society of Heating, Refrigerating and Air-Conditioning Engineers) (1997)

3 Jamieson H Meteorological data and design temperatures *J. Inst. Heating Ventilating Eng.* **22** 465–495 (1955)

4 *Weather and solar data* CIBSE Guide A2 (London: Chartered Institution of Building Services Engineers) (1986)

5 *Percentage frequency of hourly values of dry-bulb and wet-bulb temperatures* Meteorological Office Climatological Memoranda (Bracknell) (Meteorological Office)

6 *Properties of humid air* CIBSE Guide C1 (London: Chartered Institution of Building Services Engineers) (1986)

7 *Degree days* Fuel Efficiency Booklet No. 7 (London: Department of Environment, Transport and the Regions) (1993)

8 Page J K Estimating cumulative illuminance data from month mean daily illumination and sunshine *Lighting Res. Technol.* (to be published)

9 *Daylighting and window design* CIBSE Lighting Guide LG10 (London: Chartered Institution of Building Services Engineers) (1999)

10 Kinghorn D and Muneer T Daylight illuminance frequency distribution; review of computational techniques and new data for UK locations *Lighting Res. Technol.* **30**(4) 139–150 (1998)

11 Muneer T and Kinghorn D Luminous efficacy of solar irradiance: improved models *Lighting Res. Technol.* **29**(4) 185–191 (1997)

12 Hunt D R G *Availability of daylight — designing for natural and artificial lighting* (Garston: Building Research Establishment) (1979)

13 Shellard H C *Tables of surface wind speed and direction over the United Kingdom* Met O 792 (Bracknell: Meteorological Office) (1968)

14 Caton P G F *Maps of hourly mean wind speed over the UK 1965–1973* Meteorological Office Climatological Memorandum 79 (Bracknell: Meteorological Office) (1976)

15 Troen I and Petersen E L *European Wind Atlas* (Roskilde, Denmark: Rise National Laboratory)

Appendix 2.A1: Long-wave radiation exchange and sol-air temperature

2.A1.1 Notation

Symbols used in this appendix are as follows.

F — Long-wave radiation flux emitted by a plane surface $(W \cdot m^{-2})$

$G(\beta,\alpha)$ — Global solar irradiation $(W \cdot m^{-2})$ for a plane of slope β (degree) and orientation α (degree)

k_3 — Factor related to inclination of surface

h_c — Convective heat transfer coefficient $(W \cdot m^{-2} \cdot K^{-1})$

L_g — Long-wave upward flux falling on a horizontal surface $(W \cdot m^{-2})$

$L_g(\beta)$ — Long-wave radiation received from the ground by surface of inclination β $(W \cdot m^{-2})$

L_{sky} — Daytime sky long-wave irradiance on a horizontal surface $(W \cdot m^{-2})$

$L_{sky}(\beta)$ — Long-wave radiation received from the sky by surface of inclination β $(W \cdot m^{-2})$

$L^*(\beta)$ — Long-wave radiation energy exchange for surface of inclination β $(W \cdot m^{-2})$

N — Cloud cover (okta)

p_w — Water vapour pressure (hPa)

r_g — Ground view factor for the inclined plane

r_{sky} — Sky view factor for the inclined plane

$R^*(\beta,\alpha)$ — Total radiative exchange for surface of inclination β and orientation α $(W \cdot m^{-2})$

S_h — Hourly sunshine fraction

T_a — (Absolute) ambient air temperature (K)

T_{eo} — (Absolute) temperature of surface (K)

t_{eo} — Sol-air temperature (°C)

v — Wind speed $(m \cdot s^{-1})$

α — Orientation of surface (degree)

α_{rad} — Short-wave surface absorptance

β — Inclination of surface (degree)

ε_l — Long-wave emittance of surface

ρ_g — Short-wave ground albedo

σ — Stephan-Boltzmann constant (5.6697×10^{-8}) $(W \cdot m^{-2} \cdot K^{-4})$

2.A1.2 Long-wave radiation

Long-wave radiation is thermal radiation emitted at temperatures at or close to those found at the earth's surface. The waveband range is from 4 µm and 100 µm. Long-wave radiation exchange at any surface involves a two-way process. Long-wave radiation is absorbed at the surface from the radiative environment seen by the surface while long-wave radiation is emitted simultaneously from the surface to that surrounding environment. The net long-wave energy balance on any surface is the difference between the incoming and the outgoing long-wave radiation.

Incoming long-wave radiation is received from the sky and from all other elements to which the surface is radiatively exposed as a consequence of its surface orientation. For inclined surfaces, this includes the ground, surrounding building elements, landscape elements etc. The exchange is also influenced by the long-wave surface emittance/absorptance properties of the surface. There is normally a net long-wave radiation loss from external building surfaces to the outdoor environment.

Under cold conditions, the adverse radiative balance found on clear nights is of particular concern. Then the incoming long-wave flux from the cloudless sky is low. Cloud cover increases the incoming downward radiative flux, thereby reducing the net loss of long-wave radiation. In hot weather such night-time cooling is advantageous.

The following is based on work undertaken for the purposes of the CEC *European Solar Radiation Atlas*[A1-1] funded by DGXII of the Commission of the European Communities. The key contributors to the improved scientific analysis of long-wave radiation for practical applications have been R. Aguiar (INETI, Portugal), G. Czeplak (DWD, Germany), R. Dognieux (IRMB, Belgium) and J.K.Page (University of Sheffield, England).

2.A1.2.1 Estimating long-wave radiation exchange

The incoming long-wave radiation falling on horizontal surfaces (L_{sky}) is not widely measured and so has to be estimated from other variables. The incoming long-wave radiation falling on an inclined surface consists of atmospheric long-wave radiation received directly from the sky $(L_{sky}(\beta))$ and long-wave radiation received from the ground $(L_g(\beta))$. This component includes radiation both emitted from and reflected from the ground and/or any other surrounding surfaces to which the surface is radiatively exposed. In this Guide, the long-wave radiation and sol-air temperatures have been computed on the assumption that the exposed surfaces are unobstructed. In this unobstructed site case, the two incoming long-wave components does not depend on the orientation of the surface but only on its inclination, β. Only plane surfaces are considered in the following analysis.

The long-wave radiation absorbed by any plane surface depends on the amount of incident long-wave radiation and on the long-wave absorptance of the surface. For a given wavelength, the absorptance and emittance are equal. However, because the overall radiative exchange involves both long-wave and short-wave radiation, a distinction must be made between the long-wave and short-wave radiation surface absorptance/emittance properties of the surface materials. With the exception of metallic surfaces, most building materials have long-wave emittances in the range 0.85–0.95, see Table 2.43. As the long-wave absorptance and the long-wave emittance are equal, the two absorbed long-wave radiation components are the sky component, $\varepsilon_l L_{sky}(\beta)$, and the ground component, $\varepsilon_l L_g(\beta)$.

The long-wave radiation flux emitted by a plane surface is calculated from the Stefan-Boltzmann law:

$$F = \varepsilon_l \sigma T_{eo}^{\ 4} \qquad (2.9)$$

where F is the long-wave radiation flux emitted by a plane surface $(W \cdot m^{-2})$, ε_l is the long-wave emittance of the surface, σ is the Stefan-Boltzmann constant (5.6697×10^{-8}) $(W \cdot m^{-2} \cdot K^{-4})$ and T_{eo} is the absolute temperature of the surface (K).

Table 2.43 Long-wave and short-wave absorptance/emittance for typical building materials at about 30°C[A1-2]

Material	Long-wave surface emittance	Short-wave surface emittance
Black non-metallic surfaces	0.90–0.98	0.85–0.98
Red brick, tile, concrete or stone; rusty steel; dark painted surfaces	0.85–0.95	0.65–0.80
Yellow or buff brick or stone	0.85–0.95	0.50–0.70
White or cream brick, tile or paint, plaster, whitewash	0.85–0.95	0.30–0.50
Window glass (ordinary)	0.90–0.95	—†
Bright aluminium paint	0.40–0.60	0.30–0.50
Dull brass, copper, aluminium or galvanised iron	0.20–0.30	0.40–0.65
Polished brass or copper	0.02–0.05	0.03–0.50
Highly polished aluminium, nickel or chromium	0.02–0.04	0.10–0.40

† Not a simple surface phenomemon

Table 2.44 Long-wave radiation flux from the sky on horizontal surfaces for cloudless and overcast sky conditions

Ambient temperature T_a (K)	Black body radiation (σT_a^4)	Long-wave radiation flux received by horizontal surface from sky, L_{sky} (W·m^{-2}), for cloudless and overcast conditions for stated vapour pressure, p_w (hPa)											
		0		5		10		15		20		25	
		C'less	O'cast	C'less	O'cast	C'less	O'cast	C'less	O'cast	C'less	O'cast	C'less	O'cast
313	544	326	492	395	486	423	483	444	481	463	480	478	478
308	510	306	461	370	456	396	453	417	451	434	450	449	449
303	478	287	432	347	427	371	424	390	423	406	421	421	420
298	447	268	404	324	399	347	397	365	396	380	394	393	393
293	418	251	378	303	373	325	371	341	370	355	368	*368*	*367*
288	390	234	353	283	348	303	346	319	345	*332*	*344*		
283	364	212	329	264	325	283	323	*297*	*322*				
278	339	203	306	246	302	*263*	*301*						
273	315	189	285	228	281								
268	292	175	264	*212*	*261*								
263	271	163	245										
258	251	150	227										
253	232	139	210										

The outgoing flux does not depend on the orientation of the emitting surface. Therefore, the consequent long-wave radiation energy exchange on a sloping plane may be written as a net balance:

$$L^*(\beta) = \varepsilon_1 [L_{sky}(\beta) + L_g(\beta) - \sigma T_{eo}^4] \qquad (2.10)$$

where $L^*(\beta)$ is the long-wave radiation energy exchange for surface of inclination β (W·m^{-2}), $L_{sky}(\beta)$ is the atmospheric long-wave radiation received directly from the sky by surface of inclination β (W·m^{-2}) and $L_g(\beta)$ is the long-wave radiation received from the ground by surface of inclination β (W·m^{-2}) and β is the inclination of the surface (°).

For the special case of the unobstructed horizontal ground surface, equation 2.10 simplifies to:

$$L^* = \varepsilon_1 (L_{sky} - \sigma T_{eo}^4) \qquad (2.11)$$

Various formulae have been proposed to estimate the long-wave radiation emitted by the atmosphere and from level ground. The following procedure is closely based on work by Page et al.[A1-3] which forms the basis of the *European Solar Radiation Atlas*[A1-1] on long-wave radiation. The daytime sky long-wave irradiance from the atmosphere falling on a horizontal surface may be estimated as:

$$L_{sky} = \sigma T_a^4 \{0.904 - (0.304 - 0.061 p_w^{1/2}) S_h$$
$$- 0.005 p_w^{1/2}\} \qquad (2.12)$$

where L_{sky} is the daytime sky long-wave irradiance on a horizontal surface (W·m^{-2}), T_a is the absolute ambient air temperature (K), p_w is the water vapour pressure (hPa) and S_h is the hourly sunshine fraction.

During the nocturnal period, S_h is replaced by $[1 - (N / 8)]$ where N is the hourly cloud cover in oktas. As the values of S_h are not very reliable during the first and last hour of daylight, it is best to treat these two hours as lying in the nocturnal period. Table 2.44 provides values of L_{sky} for cloudless and overcast conditions. Intermediate values can be estimated from Table 2.44 by linear interpolation using either the cloud fraction (okta / 8) or the sunshine fraction, or directly calculated using equation 2.12. Long-wave radiation emitted by a blackbody at different air temperatures (σT_a^4) is also provided. The figures printed in italic type in Table 2.44 lie above the saturated vapour pressure and are provided for interpolation procedures only.

The daytime ground long-wave upward flux is given by:

$$L_g = \sigma \{0.980 \, T_a + 0.037 \, (1 - \rho_g) \, G\}^4 \qquad (2.13)$$

where L_g is the long-wave upward flux falling on a horizontal surface (W·m^{-2}), T_a is the screen air temperature (K), ρ_g is the short-wave ground albedo and G is the global irradiance (W·m^{-2}).

Values for albedo (i.e. ground reflectance for entire solar radiation spectrum) are given in Table 2.45. An albedo of 0.2 is usually regarded as representative of typical conditions at higher latitudes.

During the night the term associated with G becomes zero. The introduction of the global irradiance allows the warming effect of the rays of the sun on the ground surface temperature to be taken into account in striking the long-wave radiative balance on inclined surfaces.

Example 2.3

Estimate the long-wave radiation balance for a black, non-metallic flat roof for a cloudless and an overcast night-time hour with both the screen air temperature and the roof surface temperature at 0°C (i.e. 273.15 K). The vapour pressure is 2.5 hPa. The long-wave emittance of the roof is 0.9.

From Table 2.44, for p_w = 2.5 hPa and T_a = 273.15K:

— by interpolation, incoming radiation for cloudless conditions, L_{sky} = 208 W·m^{-2}

— by interpolation, incoming radiation for overcast conditions, L_{sky} = 283 W·m^{-2}

— outgoing radiation for a black body, (σT^4) = 315 W·m^{-2}.

The long-wave radiation balance is obtained from equation 2.11.

Hence:

— cloudless sky : $L^*(\beta) = 0.9 \, (208 - 315) = -96 \, \text{W·m}^{-2}$

— overcast sky : $L^*(\beta) = 0.9 \, (283 - 315) = -29 \, \text{W·m}^{-2}$

The actual surface temperature, as explained below, depends on the energy balance of the surface. However, the example illustrates the large long-wave radiation losses from horizontal surfaces on clear nights.

The night-time long-wave radiation emitted from the ground is given by equation 2.13 as:

$$L_g = \sigma \{(0.98 \times 273.15) + 0\}^4 = 291 \, \text{W·m}^{-2}$$

Table 2.45 Typical abedo values for various ground types

Surface type	Albedo, ρ_a
Grass (UK, summertime)	0.25
Lawn	0.18–0.23
Dry grass	0.28–0.32
Uncultivated fields	0.26
Bare soil	0.17
Macadam	0.18
Ashpalt	0.15
Concrete:	
— new, before weathering	0.55
— weathered, industrial city	0.20
Snow:	
—fresh	0.80–0.90
— old	0.45–0.70
Water surface (for stated solar altitude angle γ_s):	
— $\gamma_s > 45°$	0.05
— $\gamma_s = 30°$	0.08
— $\gamma_s = 20°$	0.12
— $\gamma_s = 10°$	0.22

2.A1.2.2 Long-wave radiation exchange for inclined flat planes

The treatment of the long-wave radiation from the sky on inclined planes is based on Cole[A1-4]. For a sloping surface of inclination β, $L_{sky}(\beta)$ is estimated from L_{sky} and the cloud cover, N, as follows:

$$L_{sky}(\beta) = L_{sky} \, r_{sky} + 0.09 \, k_3 \{1 - (N/8) \, [0.7067 + 0.00822 \, (T_a - 273.15)]\} \, \sigma T_a^4 \qquad (2.14)$$

where $L_{sky}(\beta)$ is the atmospheric long-wave radiation received directly from the sky from surface of inclination β (W·m^{-2}), L_{sky} is the daytime sky long-wave irradiance on a horizontal surface (W·m^{-2}), r_{sky} is the sky view factor for the inclined plane, k_3 is a function of the inclination β, N is the cloud cover (okta), T_a is the screen air temperature (K), σ is the Stefan-Boltzmann constant (5.6697 $\times$ 10^{-8}) (W·m^{-2}·K^{-4}) and β is the inclination of the surface (°).

Function k_3 obtained from:

$$k_3 = 0.7629 \, (0.01 \, \beta)^4 - 2.2215 \, (0.01 \, \beta)^3 + 1.7483 \, (0.01 \, \beta)^2 + 0.054 \, (0.01 \, \beta) \qquad (2.15)$$

For vertical surfaces $k_3 = 0.3457$.

If only hourly sunshine data are available, then cloud cover can be estimated using the method given in CIBSE Guide: *Weather and solar data*[A1-5].

The ground reflected component is found by applying the ground view factor r_g to L_g, as follows:

$$L_g(\beta) = L_g \, r_g \qquad (2.16)$$

where L_g is the long-wave upward flux falling on a horizontal surface (W·m^{-2}), and r_g is ground view factor for the inclined plane.

The sky and ground view factors are functions of the inclination:

$$r_{sky} = \cos^2(\beta/2) \qquad (2.17)$$

$$r_g = \sin^2(\beta/2) \qquad (2.18)$$

where β is the inclination of the plane (°).

The total radiative exchange (i.e. absorbed short-wave plus long-wave) is given by:

$$R^*(\beta, \alpha) = \alpha_{rad} G(\beta, \alpha) + \varepsilon_1 [L_{sky}(\beta) + L_g(\beta) - \sigma T_{eo}{}^4]$$
$$(2.19)$$

where $R^*(\beta, \alpha)$ is the total radiative exchange for surface of inclination β and orientation α (W·m^{-2}), α_{rad} is the short-wave surface absorptance, $G(\beta, \alpha)$ is the global solar irradiance (W·m^{-2}) for a plane of slope β (degree) and orientation α (°) and T_{eo} is the (absolute) external surface temperature (K),

Meteorological records normally present hour-by-hour irradiation (W·h·m^{-2}). The mean irradiance during the hour (W·m^{-2}) is estimated as being numerically equal to the hourly irradiation, i.e. (W·h·m^{-2})/h, where $h = 1$ hour.

Example 2.4

Assuming the same input data as for Example 2.3, estimate the corresponding night-time long-wave radiation balance for vertical surfaces.

From Example 2.3:

— incoming long-wave radiation on horizontal surface for cloudless conditions: $L_{sky} = 208$ W·m^{-2}

— incoming long-wave radiation on horizontal surface for overcast conditions: $L_{sky} = 283$ W·m^{-2}

— outgoing (vertical) radiation from the ground: $L_g = 290$ W·m^{-2}.

From equation 2.16, the ground reflected component on a vertical surface is given by:

$$L_g(90) = 291 \sin^2(90/2) = 291 \times 0.5 = 145 \text{ W·m}^{-2}$$

For a vertical surface, $k_3 = 0.3457$ and for a cloudless sky, $N = 0$. Therefore, from equation 2.14, the sky component is given by:

$$L_{sky}(90) = 208 \cos^2(90/2) + (0.09 \times 0.3457) \sigma T_a{}^4$$

From Table 2.44, for a screen air temperature of 0°C (i.e. 273.15 K): $(\sigma T_a{}^4) = 316$ W·m^{-2}.

Hence:

$$L_{sky}(90) = (208 \times 0.5) + (0.09 \times 0.3457 \times 316)$$
$$= 114 \text{ W·m}^{-2}$$

The total incoming long-wave radiation (cloudless sky) is:

$$L_g(90) + L_{sky}(90) = 145 + 114 = 259 \text{ W·m}^{-2}$$

For overcast conditions, the ground component, $L_g(90)$, is unaltered at 145 W·m^{-2} but, for $N = 8$, with an incoming flux of 283 W·m^{-2}, equation 2.14 now gives the sky component as:

$$L_{sky}(90) = 283 \cos^2(90/2) + (0.09 \times 0.3457) \{1 - (N/8)$$
$$\times [0.7067 + 0.00822(T_a - 273.15)]\} \sigma T_a{}^4$$

Hence:

$$L_{sky}(90) = (283 \times 0.5) + (0.09 \times 0.3457) \{1 - [0.7067$$
$$+ 0.00822(273.15 - 273.15)]\} \sigma T_a{}^4$$

Again, from Table 2.44, $(\sigma T_a{}^4) = 315$ W·m^{-2}.

Therefore:

$$L_{sky}(90) = 141 + 2.9 = 144 \text{ W·m}^{-2}$$

The total incoming long-wave radiation (overcast sky) is:

$$L_g(90) + L_{sky}(90) = 145 + 144 = 289 \text{ W·m}^{-2}$$

Therefore from equation 2.10, for an emittance of 0.9, the net long-wave radiation balance for the vertical surface is as follows:

— cloudless sky: $L^*(90) = 0.9(259 - 315)$
   $= -50.4$ W·m^{-2}

— overcast sky: $L^*(90) = 0.9(289 - 315)$
   $= -23.4$ W·m^{-2}

This example shows the adverse long-wave radiative exposure of vertical surfaces in cold, clear weather is much less severe than is the case for the horizontal surface considered in Example 2.3.

2.A2.2.3 Calculation of sol-air temperature

The sol-air temperature, t_{eo}, for an exposed surface of slope β and orientation α may be obtained from the (absolute) external surface temperature by considering its energy balance, i.e:

$$T_{eo} = \{[\alpha_{rad} G(\beta, \alpha) + L^*(\beta)]/h_c\} + T_a \qquad (2.20)$$

where T_{eo} is the (absolute) external surface temperature (K), α_{rad} is the short-wave surface absorptance, $G(\beta, \alpha)$ is the global solar irradiace (W·m^{-2}) for a plane of slope β (°) and orientation α (°), $L^*(\beta)$ is the long-wave radiation balance, h_c is the convective heat transfer coefficient due to wind (W·m^{-2}·K^{-1}), and T_a is the (absolute) screen air temperature (K).

The long-wave radiation balance is obtained from equation 2.10, see section 2.A1.2.1.

The convective heat transfer coefficient is obtained from the empirical relationship[A1-6]:

$$h_c = 4.0 + 4.0v \qquad (2.21)$$

where h_c is the convective heat transfer coefficient ($\text{W·m}^{-2}\text{·K}^{-1}$) and v is the wind speed (m·s^{-1}).

Note that the sol-air tables presented in this section (Tables 2.28 to 2.30) were calculated using the older Jurges formula, i.e.: $h_c = 5.8 + 4.1\,v$, for estimating h_c. The value of h_c for vertical surfaces was reduced by $^2/_3$.

The above relationship for h_c is valid for horizontal surfaces but for vertical surfaces h_c is evaluated using a wind speed component set to two-thirds of the horizontal wind component.

Equation 2.20 is a 4th order, non-linear equation that may be solved for T_{eo} using an iterative procedure. The sol-air temperature (°C) is then obtained from:

$$t_{eo} = T_{eo} - 273.15 \qquad (2.22)$$

For further details, see CIBSE Guide: *Weather and solar data*[A1-5].

References for Appendix 2.A1

A1-1 *The European Solar Radiation Atlas* (4th Edition) (Paris: Presse de l'Ecole des Mines de Paris) (1999)

A1-2 Billington N S *Building Physics: Heat* (London: Pergamon) (1967)

A1-3 Page J K, Czeplak G and Dognieux R *Estimation of long-wave radiation exchanges between buildings and the sky and ground* European Solar Radiation Atlas Project, Internal Task II Report. 15 (Sheffield: J K Page) (1998)

A1-4 Cole R J The long-wave radiation incident upon inclined surfaces *Solar Energy* **22**(5) 459–462 (1979)

A1-5 *Weather and solar data* CIBSE Guide (London: Chartered Institution of Building Services Engineers) (in preparation)

A1-6 *BS EN ISO 6946: 1997: Building components and building elements. Thermal resistance and thermal transmittance. Calculation method* (London: British Standards Institution) (1997)

3 Thermal properties of building structures

3.1 Introduction

3.1.1 General

This is the first major revision of Guide A3 since 1980. Substantial changes have been made to those sections concerned with heat losses through thermally bridged constructions, through solid and suspended ground floors and through windows.

Since publication of the previous edition, *BS 874*[1] has been revised to include hot box determination of the thermal transmittances of building elements as well as guarded hot plate determination of the conductivity of building materials. In addition, a method for the calculation of the thermal transmittance of glazing has been published as *BS 6993*[2]. The tabular data contained herein are based on the methods given in that standard.

It should be noted that the European Committee for Standardization (CEN) is currently developing European standards dealing with both the calculation and measurement of thermal transmittance. These standards supersede the equivalent national standards within the member states of the European Union.

The tables of thermal properties of materials, see Appendix 3.A7, comprise data abstracted from a comprehensive review[3] of published datasets undertaken by the Building Environmental Performance Analysis Club (BEPAC). The data are reproduced here by permission of BEPAC. The original source of the data is indicated. The tables contain only a selection of the data given in the BEPAC report, these being regarded as broadly representative of the materials tested.

The tables of thermal transmittances for typical structures, see Appendix 3.A8, have been substantially revised. These tables represent generic construction types and give both bridged and unbridged data where applicable. The data are indicative of the U-values for the types of structure listed. Where the materials or dimensions of a particular structure deviate from those described the U-value should be calculated using the methods detailed within this document.

3.1.2 Calculation of heat losses/gains

The thermal transmittance (U-value) of the building envelope is the principal factor in the determination of the steady-state heat losses/gains. Hence, the capacity of the heating or cooling system required to maintain specified inside design conditions under design external conditions. Design internal temperatures are considered in Section 1: *Environmental design* and design external temperatures in Section 2: *External design data*.

There are many different calculation procedures for determining the dynamic thermal behaviour of building structures. The parameters required for one of these, the admittance procedure, are given in Appendix 3.A6. The mathematical basis of the admittance procedure is given in Section 5: *Thermal response and plant sizing*. The estimation of plant capacity, using both steady state and dynamic calculation procedures, is also dealt with in Section 5.

3.1.3 Building Regulations

Part L of schedule 1 to the *Building Regulations 1991*[4], which apply to England and Wales, requires that reasonable provision shall be made for the conservation of fuel and power in buildings. Ways of showing compliance with this requirement are given in *Approved Document L*[5], although designers may choose to show demonstrate compliance using other methods which are acceptable to the building control authority as providing equivalent performance. In terms of the thermal performance of the building structure, the aim of this part of the Regulations is to limit the heat loss and, where appropriate, maximise the heat gains through the fabric of the building.

In meeting this objective, *Approved Document L* conveys standards of fabric insulation which are set having regard to national standards of cost effectiveness, the need to avoid unacceptable technical risks and the need to provide flexibility for designers. However, for individual buildings, better standards of insulation can often be justified to clients using their own economic criteria and some guidance is given in *BS 8207*[6] and *BS 8211*[7].

In Scotland, the *Building Standards (Scotland) Regulations 1990*[8] apply and the relevant technical standard is given in *Part J*[9]. In Northern Ireland the *Building Regulations (Northern Ireland) 1994*[10] apply and the relevant technical standards are given in *Technical Booklet F*[11]. There are minor differences in terms of presentation and procedure between these regulations and those of the *Building Regulations 1991*[4] for England and Wales. However, the technical requirements are broadly similar and the technical guidance differs only in minor respects.

It is essential for designers to be fully conversant with current statutory requirements, and the various means of compliance, and be aware of any proposed amendments that may be relevant to design work already in hand. This is very important since the designer may be called upon to certify compliance with Building Regulations.

The standards of insulation conveyed by *Approved Document L*[5] take account of the effects of thermal bridging and the proportional area method has been adopted in the calculation of U-values. While this method still tends to underestimate U-values, the error is much less than that which resulted from ignoring thermal bridging.

This Guide recommends the combined method, see section 3.3.11.3, for greater accuracy.

The *Building Regulations* now include requirements for floors and the methods set out in section 3.5 provide procedures that can be used to demonstrate compliance.

With regard to windows, *Approved Document L* now conveys thermal performance standards that take account of the window frame and the thermal bridging at the edges of masonry openings. Indicative values for compliance with the *Building Regulations* are given in Table 3.35.

3.1.4 Prediction of moisture condensation

In addition to demonstrating compliance with the *Building Regulations*, accurate assessment of the thermal properties of the building structure is essential for the prediction of moisture condensation in the structure. Detailed guidance on methods of prediction of condensation is given in Section 7: *Moisture transfer and condensation*.

3.1.5 Calculation of energy demands

The energy demand of a building and its services is only partly determined by the thermal transmittance. Other considerations, such as ventilation and ventilation heat loss, the effect of solar radiation falling on the building, especially that falling on the windows, and fortuitous heat gains from people, electrical equipment and lights, must be taken into account.

3.2 Notation

The symbols used within this section are defined as follows.

A_f	Area of floor (m^2)
A_{fg}	Area of floor in contact with ground (m^2)
A_g	Projected area of glazing (m^2)
A_m, A_n	Areas of elements composed of materials m, n (m^2)
A_p, A_q	Areas of elements composed of materials p, q (m^2)
A_{wf}	Projected area of window frame or sash (m^2)
A_1	Area of exposed surface(s) (m^2)
A_2	Area of non-exposed surface(s) (m^2)
b_a	Breadth of air space (m)
C	Constant related to depth of spacer below edge of window frame
d	Thickness of material (m)
d_a	Thickness of air space (m)
d_{ef}	Total equivalent thickness of floor (m)
d_{eg}	Total equivalent thickness of ground (m)
d_{ei}'	Additional equivalent thickness of floor due to edge insulation (m)
d_{fi}	Thickness of (floor) edge insulation (or foundation) (m)
d_g	Total thickness of glass panes (m)
d_{gb}	Average thickness of bounding panes (m)
D_i	Depth of vertical (floor) edge insulation (m)
d_m, d_n	Thickness of elements composed of materials m, n (m)

d_p, d_q	Thickness of elements composed of materials p, q (m)
d_s	Thickness of window spacer (m)
d_w	Thickness of wall surrounding ground floor (m)
E	Emissivity factor
F	Surface factor
f	Decrement factor
F_w	Wind shielding factor
H_t	Transmission heat loss coefficient ($W \cdot K^{-1}$)
h_c	Convective heat transfer coefficient ($W \cdot m^{-2} \cdot K^{-1}$)
h_f	Height of floor above external ground level (m)
h_r	Radiative heat transfer coefficient ($W \cdot m^{-2} \cdot K^{-1}$)
K	Constant related to room geometry
L	Length of a thermal bridge (m)
L_f	Characteristic dimension of floor (m)
p_f	Exposed perimeter of floor (m)
P_m, P_n	Proportions of total surface area occupied by elements composed of materials m, n
P_p, P_q	Proportions of total surface area occupied by elements composed of materials p, q
p_{wf}	Length of inner perimeter of window frame or sash (m)
q_s	Rate of heat transfer to/from surface ($W \cdot m^{-2}$)
Q_f	Rate of heat loss through floor (W)
R	Thermal resistance ($m^2 \cdot K \cdot W^{-1}$)
R_A	Combined thermal resistance of materials in plane of pitched roof (including outside surface resistance) ($m^2 \cdot K \cdot W^{-1}$)
R_a	Thermal resistance of air space ($m^2 \cdot K \cdot W^{-1}$)
R_B	Combined resistance of materials in plane of ceiling (including inside surface resistance) ($m^2 \cdot K \cdot W^{-1}$)
R_b	Thermal resistance of bridged leaf ($m^2 \cdot K \cdot W^{-1}$)
R_{bi}	Thermal resistance of internal blind or curtain ($m^2 \cdot K \cdot W^{-1}$)
R_{bm}	Thermal resistance of mid-pane blind ($m^2 \cdot K \cdot W^{-1}$)
R_{b1}, R_{b2}	Thermal resistances of bridged structures 1, 2 ($m^2 \cdot K \cdot W^{-1}$)
R_f	Thermal resistance of floor ($m^2 \cdot K \cdot W^{-1}$)
R_{fbi}	Thermal resistance of insulating layers incorporated in basement floor ($m^2 \cdot K \cdot W^{-1}$)
R_{fi}	Thermal resistance of floor edge insulation (or foundation) ($m^2 \cdot K \cdot W^{-1}$)
r_g	Thermal resistivity of glass ($m \cdot K \cdot W^{-1}$)
R_h	Thermal resistance of homogeneous leaf ($m^2 \cdot K \cdot W^{-1}$)
R_i'	Additional thermal resistance due to edge insulation (or foundation) ($m^2 \cdot K \cdot W^{-1}$)
R_{ig}	Thermal resistance of insulation between floor and ground ($m^2 \cdot K \cdot W^{-1}$)
R_L	Lower limit of thermal resistance ($m^2 \cdot K \cdot W^{-1}$)
R_m, R_n	Thermal resistances of isotropic layers of sections m, n ($m^2 \cdot K \cdot W^{-1}$)
R_p, R_q	Thermal resistances of isotropic layers of sections p, q ($m^2 \cdot K \cdot W^{-1}$)
R_s	Surface resistance ($m^2 \cdot K \cdot W^{-1}$)
r_s	Average thermal resistivity of window spacer material and sealant ($m \cdot K \cdot W^{-1}$)
R_{se}	External surface resistance ($m^2 \cdot K \cdot W^{-1}$) (formerly R_{so})
$R_{s(p)}$	Surface resistance of non-planar element ($m^2 \cdot K \cdot W^{-1}$)

R_{si} Internal surface resistance ($m^2 \cdot K \cdot W^{-1}$)

R_{s1}, R_{s2} Surface resistances at surfaces 1, 2 ($m^2 \cdot K \cdot W^{-1}$)

R_u Upper limit of thermal resistance ($m^2 \cdot K \cdot W^{-1}$)

R_v Thermal resistance of roof void ($m^2 \cdot K \cdot W^{-1}$)

R_1, R_2 Thermal resistances of components 1, 2 ($m^2 \cdot K \cdot W^{-1}$)

t_a Air temperature (°C)

$\bar{t}_{ao}$ Annual average outside air temperature (°C)

$\bar{t}_{ao(w)}$ Average outside air temperature over the heating season (°C)

t_{ei} Inside environmental temperature (°C)

$\bar{t}_{ei}$ Annual average inside environmental temperature (°C)

$\bar{t}_{ei(w)}$ Average inside environmental temperature over the heating season (°C)

t_r Radiant temperature seen by surface (°C)

$\bar{t}_{ri}$ Mean inside radiant temperature (°C)

T_s Surface temperature (K)

t_s Surface temperature (°C)

t_{si} Inside surface temperature (°C)

U Thermal transmittance ($W \cdot m^{-2} \cdot K^{-1}$)

U_{eu} Equivalent thermal transmittance for heat flow through wall surrounding underfloor space and by ventilation of underfloor space ($W \cdot m^{-2} \cdot K^{-1}$)

U_f Thermal transmittance of (uninsulated) floor ($W \cdot m^{-2} \cdot K^{-1}$)

U_{fg} Thermal transmittance for heat flow through ground ($W \cdot m^{-2} \cdot K^{-1}$)

U_{fi} Thermal transmittance of edge-insulated floor ($W \cdot m^{-2} \cdot K^{-1}$)

U_{fs} Combined thermal transmittance of uninsulated suspended floor structure ($W \cdot m^{-2} \cdot K^{-1}$)

U_{fsi} Thermal transmittance of insulated suspended floor ($W \cdot m^{-2} \cdot K^{-1}$)

U_g Thermal transmittance of glazing ($W \cdot m^{-2} \cdot K^{-1}$)

$U_{gb}{'}$ Thermal transmittance of glazing corrected for mid-pane blind ($W \cdot m^{-2} \cdot K^{-1}$)

$U_{gg}{'}$ Thermal transmittance of glazing corrected for resistivity of glass ($W \cdot m^{-2} \cdot K^{-1}$)

U_{gs} Thermal transmittance of glazing with 12 mm spacer (normal exposure) ($W \cdot m^{-2} \cdot K^{-1}$)

U_r Thermal transmittance of roof ($W \cdot m^{-2} \cdot K^{-1}$)

U_u Thermal transmittance of wall surrounding underfloor space above ground level ($W \cdot m^{-2} \cdot K^{-1}$)

U_w Thermal transmittance of window ($W \cdot m^{-2} \cdot K^{-1}$)

$U_{wb}{'}$ Thermal transmittance of window corrected for internal blind or curtain ($W \cdot m^{-2} \cdot K^{-1}$)

U_{wf} Thermal transmittance of window frame or sash ($W \cdot m^{-2} \cdot K^{-1}$)

v Air velocity at surface ($m \cdot s^{-1}$)

v_w Average wind velocity at 10 m height above ground level ($m \cdot s^{-1}$)

W_i Width of horizontal edge (floor) insulation (m)

Y Thermal admittance ($W \cdot m^{-2} \cdot K^{-1}$)

α Area of ventilation openings per unit perimeter of underfloor space (m)

β Angle of pitch of roof

ε Emissivity of surface

ε_1 Emissivity of exposed surface(s)

ε_2 Emissivity of non-exposed surface(s)

λ Thermal conductivity ($W \cdot m^{-1} \cdot K^{-1}$)

λ_g Thermal conductivity of ground ($W \cdot m^{-1} \cdot K^{-1}$)

λ_m, λ_n Thermal conductivity of materials m, n ($W \cdot m^{-1} \cdot K^{-1}$)

λ_p, λ_q Thermal conductivity of materials p, q ($W \cdot m^{-1} \cdot K^{-1}$)

σ Stefan-Boltzmann constant (5.67×10^{-8}) ($W \cdot m^{-2} \cdot K^{-4}$)

ϕ Time lag associated with decrement factor (h)

ϕ_s Factor related to thermal transmittance of window frame

Ψ Linear thermal transmittance of a thermal bridge ($W \cdot m^{-1} \cdot K^{-1}$)

Ψ_{fi} Factor related to (floor) edge insulation ($W \cdot m^{-1} \cdot K^{-1}$)

Ψ_s Linear thermal transmittance due to window spacer ($W \cdot m^{-1} \cdot K^{-1}$)

ψ Time lag associated with surface factor (h)

ω Time lead associated with thermal admittance (h)

3.3 Heat losses from buildings

3.3.1 General

Heat is lost from buildings by transmission through the building fabric and by ventilation. (For ventilation losses see Section 4: *Infiltration and natural ventilation*.)

This section provides methods for the calculation of the rate of heat loss through individual components of the envelope of a building. In most cases the thermal properties of a building component are represented by its thermal transmittance, U ($W \cdot m^{-2} \cdot K^{-1}$). The U-value multiplied by the area of the component gives the rate of heat loss through the component per unit of temperature difference between inside and outside.

Often it is convenient to characterise the whole building by a transmission heat loss coefficient, H_t, i.e:

$$H_t = \Sigma(A\,U) + \Sigma(L\,\Psi) \qquad (3.1)$$

where H_t is the transmission heat loss coefficent ($W \cdot K^{-1}$), $\Sigma(A\,U)$ is the sum over all the components of the building through which heat flow occurs (i.e. roof, walls, floor, windows) of the product of the area of each component and its U-value ($W \cdot K^{-1}$) and $\Sigma(L\,\Psi)$ is the sum over all thermal bridges of the product of the length of each thermal bridge (m) and its linear thermal transmittance ($W \cdot m^{-1} \cdot K^{-1}$).

Many thermal bridges are taken into account in the calculation of the U-value of the component (see section 3.3.11) and no further allowance is needed. However, Ψ-values can arise at junctions between different components. Although little specific information is available at present, more consideration to this type of thermal bridge may be given in the future.

The transmission heat loss through a component is modified if there is an unheated space between the internal and external environments. One method of allowing for this is given in *BS EN ISO 13789*[12].

3.3.2 Dimensions for heat loss calculations

In the past, the areas used in conjunction with U-values to calculate heat losses have sometimes been based on internal dimensions, as shown by the lower case letters in Figure 3.1. These dimensions omit the areas of walls, floors and ceilings covered by intermediate floors and internal walls, which may be up to 15% of the total area. These losses have been shown to be significant, particularly for well-insulated houses[13]. If measurements are based on internal dimensions, the areas should be increased by an allowance to account for the thickness of internal elements. For dwellings (including flats), an allowance of 15% is appropriate.

A more satisfactory approach is to use the overall internal dimensions measured between finished internal faces of external elements of the building and including the thickness of internal elements, as indicated by the capital letters in Figure 3.1. This is the basis used in current *Building Regulations*[4].

3.3.3 Application of thermal insulation

There are a number of factors that must be considered in both the design and application of thermal insulation. Thermal insulation is most effective when applied as a continuous and even layer, without penetrations or breaks. Penetrations form thermal bridges and breaks permit air flow within and through the insulating layer, both of which reduce its effectiveness.

It is not always possible to achieve the maximum effectiveness of the insulation due to other influences such as structural considerations and weather proofing. This applies particularly where insulation is being added to an existing structure. Therefore, in the design of new buildings, it is essential that thermal insulation is considered at the earliest stages of design.

Where penetrations and breaks in the insulating layer are unavoidable, the effects of the resulting thermal bridges should be investigated. Other deviations from the ideal, such as the effects of gaps or air spaces on the warm side of the insulation layer, may degrade further its performance.

3.3.4 Thermal resistance of materials

The thermal properties of a material are expressed in terms of its thermal resistance. For homogeneous, isotropic materials through which heat is transmitted by conduction only, the thermal resistance is directly proportional to the thickness and is given by:

$$R = d / \lambda \qquad (3.2)$$

where R is the thermal resistance ($\mathrm{m^2 \cdot K \cdot W^{-1}}$), d is the thickness of material (m) and λ is the thermal conductivity ($\mathrm{W \cdot m^{-1} \cdot K^{-1}}$).

In other materials, especially insulating materials, heat may be transmitted by a combination of solid and gaseous conduction, convection and radiation. For such materials,

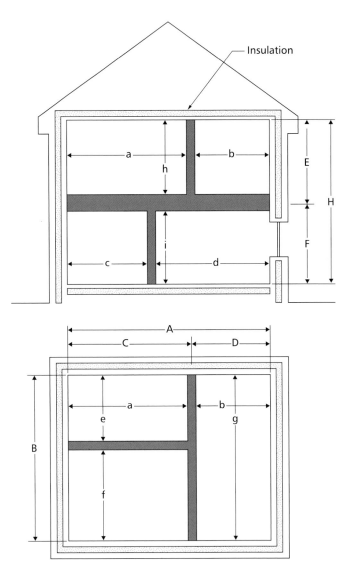

Figure 3.1 Dimensions for heat loss calculations

the thermal properties are not determined solely by the thermal conductivity. However, where materials are thermally homogeneous, an effective thermal conductivity can be ascribed and equation 3.2 may then be applied.

For thermally non-homogeneous materials, the thermal resistance may not be directly proportional to the thickness and equation 3.2 does not apply. This is the case for materials of low density in which the radiant heat transfer is a significant factor. For this reason, some manufacturers, particularly of insulation products, define the thermal properties of these materials by means of thermal resistance (R value) rather than thermal conductivity. The value of thermal resistance applies to a particular thickness of material and cannot be extrapolated for other thicknesses. For a more detailed discussion on thermal resistance, see *BS 874: Part 2: Section 2.1*[1].

3.3.5 Thermal conductivity of masonry materials

For many types of masonry materials, including clay products and various types of aggregate and aerated concrete, the thermal conductivity is related to the bulk density and moisture content. Table 3.1 provides values of

Table 3.1 Thermal conductivity of homogeneous masonry materials at 'standard' moisture content

Material	Dry density (kg·m⁻³)	Thermal conductivity (W·m⁻¹·K⁻¹)		Material	Dry density (kg·m⁻³)	Thermal conductivity (W·m⁻¹·K⁻¹)	
		Protected	Exposed			Protected	Exposed
Brick (fired clay)	1200	0.36	0.50	Pyro-processed	1100	0.39	0.42
	1300	0.40	0.54	colliery material	1200	0.41	0.44
	1400	0.44	0.60	concrete	1300	0.44	0.47
	1500	0.47	0.65		1400	0.46	0.49
	1600	0.52	0.71		1500	0.48	0.52
	1700	0.56	0.77				
	1800	0.61	0.83	Pumice aggregate	500	0.16	0.17
	1900	0.66	0.90	concrete	600	0.18	0.19
	2000	0.70	0.96		700	0.20	0.22
					800	0.24	0.25
Brick	1700	0.77	1.05		900	0.27	0.29
(calcium silicate)	1800	0.89	1.22		1000	0.31	0.34
	1900	1.01	1.38		1100	0.36	0.38
	2000	1.16	1.58		1200	0.40	0.43
	2100	1.32	1.80		1300	0.46	0.49
	2200	1.51	2.06				
				Autoclaved aerated	400	0.12	0.13
Dense aggregate	1700	1.04	1.12	concrete	500	0.15	0.16
concrete	1800	1.13	1.21		600	0.18	0.19
	1900	1.22	1.31		700	0.20	0.22
	2000	1.33	1.43		800	0.24	0.25
	2100	1.46	1.56		900	0.27	0.29
	2200	1.59	1.70				
	2300	1.75	1.87	Other lightweight	600	0.20	0.22
	2400	1.93	2.06	aggregate concrete	700	0.24	0.25
					800	0.28	0.30
Blast furnace	1000	0.19	0.20		900	0.31	0.34
slag concrete	1100	0.24	0.25		1000	0.36	0.38
	1200	0.27	0.29		1100	0.40	0.43
	1300	0.32	0.35		1200	0.46	0.49
	1400	0.38	0.41		1300	0.52	0.55
	1500	0.45	0.48		1400	0.57	0.61
	1600	0.53	0.56		1500	0.63	0.67
	1700	0.60	0.65		1600	0.71	0.76

Note: these data have been derived from the values for the 90% fractile given in *prEN 1745*[14] for the standard moisture contents given in Table 3.2. The value for mortar may be taken as 0.88 W·m⁻¹·K⁻¹ (protected) and 0.94 W·m⁻¹·K⁻¹ (exposed).

Table 3.2 'Standard' moisture contents for masonry

Material	Moisture content	
	Protected	Exposed
Brick (fired clay)	1% (by volume)	5% (by volume)
Brick (calcium silicate)	1% (by volume)	5% (by volume)
Dense aggregate concrete	3% (by volume)	5% (by volume)
Blast furnace slag concrete	3% (by weight)	5% (by weight)
Pumice aggregate concrete	3% (by weight)	5% (by weight)
Other lightweight aggregate concrete	3% (by weight)	5% (by weight)
Autoclaved aerated concrete	3% (by weight)	5% (by weight)

Note: % (by volume) = % (by weight) × density/1000

thermal conductivity for a range of densities at 'standard' values of moisture content, as defined in Table 3.2. 'Protected' includes internal partitions, inner leaves separated from outer leaves by a continuous air space, masonry protected by tile hanging, sheet cladding or other such protection, separated by a continuous air space. 'Exposed' covers rendered or unrendered masonry directly exposed to rain.

Particular masonry products can have thermal conductivities lower than the corresponding values given in Table 3.1, depending on the materials used in manufacture. For such materials, manufacturers may quote thermal conductivity less than those given in Table 3.1. These values should be accepted, and used in place of the tabulated values, provided the tests have been performed in accordance with the requirements laid down in Appendix 3.A2.

If the moisture content of the sample under test differed from the appropriate standard value, a correction should be applied to the measured thermal conductivity using the procedure described in Appendix 3.A1.

3.3.6 Thermal conductivity of materials other than masonry

Appendix 3.A7 gives typical values of thermal conductivity for a variety of materials. In situations where the thermal conductivity of a particular material is critical, e.g. where it provides the bulk of the thermal resistance of a structure, certified test data, obtained in accordance with Appendix 3.A2, should be used. Measured data are also appropriate where the density of the materials to be used, or their working temperatures, are outside the ranges given in the table. Thermal conductivity data for design purposes are also given in *prEN 12524*[15].

3.3.7 Declared and design values

The declared value (of thermal conductivity or thermal resistance) for thermal insulation products is that provided by a manufacturer. It applies under reference conditions of temperature (usually 10°C), moisture content (usually corresponding to equilibrium with an atmosphere of 23°C and 50% RH) and, where relevant, ageing. Declared values are usually based on measurements carried out on the materials concerned.

Design values apply under particular conditions of use and are used in the calculation of thermal performance. In many cases the design value may be taken as equal to the declared value as the design conditions are often similar to those for the declared value. However, in cases where the design conditions are markedly different, thermal conductivity values should be converted before being used in calculations. Conversion coefficients for a range of insulating materials are given in *ISO 10456*[16].

3.3.8 Thermal resistance of air spaces

Heat transfer across an air space is approximately proportional to the difference between the temperatures of the boundary surfaces. However, the thermal resistance depends upon various other factors such as the dimensions of the air space, the direction of heat flow, the emissivities of the inner surfaces and the extent to which the airspace is ventilated.

The thermal resistance of tall, continuous vertical air spaces (i.e. those at angles of 45° or more to the horizontal) increases with the thickness of the air space, up to a thickness of about 25 mm. The thermal resistance is virtually constant for greater thicknesses.

If the air space is not continuous in the horizontal direction but divided into vertical strips or slots, see Figure 3.2, the thermal resistance of the air space also depends upon the breadth of the strip.

Tables 3.3 and 3.4 provide standardised values of thermal resistance for both continuous and divided air spaces. For air spaces of thicknesses greater than 25 mm, the thermal resistance should be taken as 0.18 $m^2 \cdot K \cdot W^{-1}$ if the breadth of the air space is greater than ten times its thickness. Otherwise, the following equation should be used:

$$R_a = \frac{1}{1.25 + 2.32\,[1 + \sqrt{(1 + d_a^2/b_a^2)} - d_a/b_a]} \quad (3.3)$$

where R_a is the thermal resistance of the air space ($m^{-2} \cdot K \cdot W^{-1}$), d_a is the thickness of the air space (m) and b_a is the breadth of the air space (m).

Horizontal air spaces present greater resistance to downward heat flow because downward convection is small. For an air space incorporating multiple layers of aluminium foil insulation, the thermal resistance to downward heat flow can be as high as 2 $m^2 \cdot K \cdot W^{-1}$. Such

Table 3.3 Thermal resistances for continuous air spaces

Air space thickness (mm)	Surface emissivity†	Thermal resistance ($m^2 \cdot K \cdot W^{-1}$) for heat flow in stated direction‡		
		Horizontal	Upward	Downward
5	High	0.11	0.11	0.11
	Low§	0.17	0.17	0.17
≥ 25	High	0.18	0.16	0.19
	Low§	0.44	0.34	0.50

† High emissivity: $\varepsilon > 0.8$; low emissivity: $\varepsilon \le 0.2$
‡ Normal to the surface in the direction of heat flow
§ Assumes that the air space is bounded by one low emissivity surface and one high emissivity surface

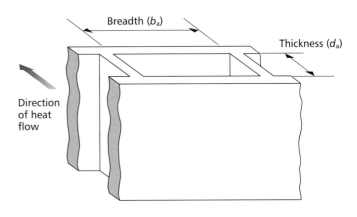

Figure 3.2 Divided vertical air space

Table 3.4 Thermal resistances for divided air spaces for horizontal heat flow

Air space thickness (mm)	Thermal resistance ($m^2 \cdot K \cdot W^{-1}$) for air space of stated breadth (mm)				
	≥ 200	100	50	20	≤ 10
5	0.11	0.11	0.11	0.11	0.12
6	0.12	0.12	0.12	0.13	0.13
7	0.13	0.13	0.13	0.14	0.15
8	0.14	0.14	0.14	0.15	0.16
10	0.15	0.15	0.16	0.17	0.18
12	0.16	0.17	0.17	0.19	0.20
15	0.17	0.18	0.19	0.21	0.23
20	0.18	0.20	0.21	0.24	0.26
25	0.18	0.20	0.21	0.24	0.27

Notes:

(1) Applies to heat flow in horizontal direction only for air spaces of dimensions shown in Figure 3.2.
(2) Calculated in accordance with *BS EN ISO 6946*[17].
(3) Assumes high emissivity at surfaces.

constructions can play an important role in reducing summer heat gains through roofs.

A small inclination of an air space has only a minor effect on the convective heat transfer and therefore little effect on the thermal resistance.

Radiation accounts for about two-thirds of the total heat transfer and most building materials have high emissivities (between 0.9 and 0.95). Therefore, air spaces lined with low emissivity materials, such as aluminium foil, have a higher thermal resistance because radiative heat transfer is reduced. However, unless it is known that the air space is to be lined with such a material, high emissivity should be assumed.

The temperature difference across an air space has little effect on either the radiative or convective heat transfer coefficients. Therefore, no allowance need be made unless the air space resistance forms a major proportion of the total thermal resistance of the structure.

The influence of ventilation on the thermal resistance of air spaces can be estimated from heat transfer theory if the rate and distribution of the air movement is known. This varies according to the prevailing conditions and cannot be determined easily. Therefore, estimates of the thermal resistance for highly ventilated air spaces are necessarily approximate.

Air spaces may be ventilated deliberately, such as loft spaces, or fortuitously as in the case of sheeted constructions with gaps between the sheets. Values for the thermal resistance of highly ventilated air spaces are given in Table 3.5. It should be noted that air infiltration occurs through gaps between tiles or cladding sheets unless precautions are taken to seal the joints. In these cases the thermal resistance of the tiles should be taken as zero. If the surface of the air space is corrugated, as in some cladded

Table 3.5 Thermal resistances for highly ventilated air spaces

Type of air space (minimum thickness 25 mm)	Thermal resistance
Air space between sheeted cladding with unsealed joints, and lining; air space within ventilated flat roof	0.16
Air space between tiles and roofing felt or building paper	0.12
Air space behind tiles on tile-hung wall or roof or profile cladding on wall†	0.12
Air space in cavity wall construction	0.18

† Includes thermal resistance of tiles or cladding

Table 3.6 Thermal resistances for roof spaces (reproduced from *BS EN ISO 6946*[17] by permission of the British Standards Institution)

Item	Description	Thermal resistance ($m^2 \cdot K \cdot W^{-1}$)
1	Tiled roof with no felt, boards or similar	0.06
2	Sheeted roof or tiled roof with felt or boards or similar under the tiles	0.2
3	As 2 but with aluminium cladding or other low emissivity surface at underside of roof	0.3
4	Roof lined with boards and felt	0.3

constructions, the area for convection transfer is about 20% greater but this has a negligible effect on the air space resistance.

Values for the thermal resistance of roof spaces are given in Table 3.6[17]. Note that these values include an allowance for the thermal resistance of the roof construction but do not include the external surface resistance (R_{se}).

3.3.9 Surface resistance

The inside and outside surface resistances are determined by the processes of heat transfer which occur at the boundary between a structural element and the air. Heat is transferred both by radiation interchange with other surfaces and by convective heat transfer at the air/surface interface.

3.3.9.1 Heat transfer by radiation

Heat transfer by radiation is a complex process which depends upon the shape, temperature and emissivity of both the radiating surface and the surface to which it radiates. A detailed description is contained in Guide C3: *Heat transfer*[18]. However, for practical purposes, the heat transfer by radiation is characterised by an emissivity factor, E, and a radiative heat transfer coefficient, h_r.

The emissivity factor depends upon the geometry of the room and the emissivities of the surfaces. However, for a cubical room with one exposed surface, all the internal surfaces having high emissivity, E may be expressed thus (see Appendix 3.A3):

$$E = K \varepsilon \qquad (3.4)$$

where E is the emissivity factor, K is a constant related to room geometry and ε is the emissivity of the surface.

Most common building materials have high emissivities ($\varepsilon > 0.9$). See Appendix 3.A3 for cases of unusual room geometry or for internal surfaces with low emissivities.

The radiative heat transfer coefficient depends upon the absolute temperatures of both the radiating surface and the surface receiving the radiation. However, for ambient temperatures, these are approximately equal and the radiative heat transfer coefficient is given by:

$$h_r = 4 \sigma T_s^3 \qquad (3.5)$$

where h_r is the radiative heat transfer coefficient ($W \cdot m^{-2} \cdot K^{-1}$), σ is the Stefan-Boltzmann constant (5.67×10^{-8}) ($W \cdot m^{-2} \cdot K^{-4}$) and T_s is the surface temperature (K).

Values of the radiative heat transfer coefficient for a range of surface temperatures are given in Table 3.7. It should be noted that, for night time clear skies, the difference between the surface temperature and the 'sky' temperature can be very large, leading to underestimation of h_c in these circumstances. This is particularly important in the prediction of condensation.

Table 3.7 Radiative heat transfer coefficient, h_r

Mean temperature of surfaces (°C)	Radiative heat transfer coefficient, h_r (W·m^{-2}·K^{-1})
–10	4.1
0	4.6
10	5.1
20	5.7

Table 3.8 Convective heat transfer coefficient, h_c

Direction of heat flow	Convective heat transfer coefficient†, h_c (W·m^{-2}·K^{-1})
Horizontal	2.5
Upward	5.0
Downward	0.7

† Assumes still air conditions, i.e. air speed at the surface is not greater than 0.1 m·s^{-1}

3.3.9.2 Heat transfer by convection

Heat transfer by convection is also characterised by a heat transfer coefficient, h_c. This depends upon the temperature difference between the surface and the air, the surface roughness, the air velocity and the direction of heat flow. For still air conditions, values of the convective heat transfer coefficient are given in Table 3.8.

Where significant air movement occurs, heat transfer by convection is more complex and reference should be made to Guide C3: *Heat transfer*[18]. Approximate values may be obtained using the following empirical equation[17] but this should not be used where the air velocity is less than 1 m·s^{-1}.

$$h_c = 4 + 4v \qquad (3.6)$$

where h_c is the convective heat transfer coefficient (W·m^{-2}·K^{-1}) and v is the air velocity at the surface (m·s^{-1}).

3.3.9.3 Internal surface resistance

Appendix 3.A3 shows how the emissivity factor may be combined with the above coefficients to give an internal surface resistance. Because of the complex nature of the heat transfer processes involved, the internal surface resistance is assumed to be independent of surface roughness, temperature differences between radiating surfaces, differences between surface and air temperatures etc. The internal surface resistance is given by:

$$R_{si} = \frac{1}{{}^6/_5 E h_r + h_c} \qquad (3.7)$$

where R_{si} is the internal surface resistance (m^2·K·W^{-1}), E is the emissivity factor, h_r is the radiative heat transfer coefficient (W·m^{-1}·K^{-1}) and h_c is the convective heat transfer coefficient (W·m^{-1}·K^{-1}).

The values for internal surface resistance used in *BS EN ISO 6946*[17] are shown in Table 3.9, which also gives the

Table 3.9 Internal surface resistance, R_{si}

Building element	Direction of heat flow	Surface resistance (m^2·K·W^{-1})	
		BS EN ISO 6946 design value	Traditional UK value
Walls	Horizontal	0.13	0.12
Ceilings or roofs (flat or pitched), floors	Upward	0.10	0.10
Ceilings or floors	Downward	0.17	0.14

'traditional' values still used in the UK for the determination of *U*-values. These values represent a simplification of the heat transfer processes that occur at surfaces.

3.3.9.4 External surface resistance

Appendix 3.A3 also shows how the emissivity factor may be combined with the radiative and convective coefficients to give an external surface resistance. Again, the external surface resistance is assumed independent of surface roughness, temperature differences between radiating surfaces, differences between surface and air temperatures, etc. The external surface resistance is given by:

$$R_{se} = \frac{1}{E h_r + h_c} \qquad (3.8)$$

where R_{se} is the external surface resistance (m^2·K·W^{-1}), E is the emissivity factor, h_r is the radiative heat transfer coefficient (W·m^{-2}·K^{-1}) and h_c is the convective heat transfer coefficient (W·m^{-2}·K^{-1}).

The values for external surface resistance used in *BS EN ISO 6946*[17] are shown in Table 3.10, which also gives the 'traditional' values still used in the UK for the determination of *U*-values. As with the Table 3.9, these values represent a simplification of the heat transfer processes that occur at surfaces.

Table 3.10 External surface resistance, R_{se}

Building element	Direction of heat flow	Surface resistance (m^2·K·W^{-1})			
		BS EN ISO 6946 design value	Traditional UK values for stated conditions of exposure		
			Normal	Sheltered	Exposed
Wall	Horizontal	0.04	0.06	0.08	0.03
Roof	Upward	0.04	0.04	0.07	0.02
Floor	Downward	0.04	0.04	0.07	0.02

The traditional values given correspond to 'normal' conditions of exposure. For well insulated structures, the effect of exposure is small and may be ignored for opaque elements. For glazing, values are given for 'normal', 'sheltered' and 'severe' conditions of exposure. These conditions of exposure are defined thus:

— normal: most suburban and rural buildings, fourth to eighth floors of buildings in city centres

— sheltered: up to third floor of buildings in city centres

— severe: buildings on coastal or hill sites, floors above the fifth in suburban or rural districts, floors above the ninth in city centres.

3.3.9.5 Elements with non-planar surfaces

Finned external elements constructed of masonry (concrete or brickwork), such as the extension of a floor slab to form a balcony, may increase the heat loss compared with the same building element without the fin. The effect of such fins on the total heat loss can be ignored provided that the thermal conductivity of the fin material is not greater than $2 \, W \cdot m^{-1} \cdot K^{-1}$, or external insulation is carried around the fin.

For fins constructed of materials having a thermal conductivity greater than $2 \, W \cdot m^{-1} \cdot K^{-1}$ or where the fin is not insulated, *BS EN ISO 6946*[17] requires the surface resistance (internal or external) to be modified as follows:

$$R_{s(p)} = R_s (A_p / A) \qquad (3.9)$$

where $R_{s(p)}$ is the surface resistance of the non-planar element $(m^2 \cdot K \cdot W^{-1})$, R_s is the surface resistance of the element calculated without the fin $(m^2 \cdot K \cdot W^{-1})$, A_p is the projected area of the fin (m^2) and A is the exposed surface area of the fin (m^2).

The areas A and A_p are illustrated in Figure 3.3.

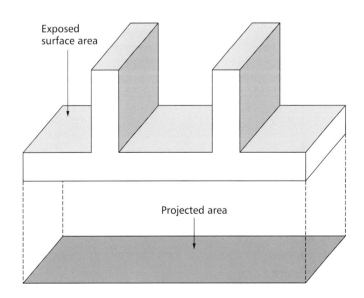

Exposed surface area

Projected area

Figure 3.3 Actual and projected areas for non-planar elements

A method for determining the thermal resistance of the mullions and transoms in aluminium curtain wall framing has been produced by the Council for Aluminium in Building[19]. Guidance on assessing the thermal performance of metal cladding has been published by *BRE*[20].

3.3.10 Thermal transmittance for elements composed of plane homogenous layers

The thermal transmittance of a building element is obtained by combining the thermal resistances of its component parts and the adjacent air layers. Thermal transmittances of simple walls and roofs composed of parallel slabs are obtained by adding the thermal resistances and taking the reciprocal of the sum, thus:

$$U = 1 / (R_{si} + R_1 + R_2 + ... + R_a + R_{se}) \qquad (3.10)$$

where U is the thermal transmittance $(W \cdot m^{-2} \cdot K^{-1})$, R_{si} is the internal surface resistance $(m^2 \cdot K \cdot W^{-1})$, R_1 and R_2 are the thermal resistances of components 1 and 2 $(m^2 \cdot K \cdot W^{-1})$, R_a is the thermal resistance of the air spaces $(m^2 \cdot K \cdot W^{-1})$ and R_{se} is the external surface resistance $(m^2 \cdot K \cdot W^{-1})$.

Example 3.1: Calculation of U-value for structure composed of plane homogeneous layers

An external wall consisting of 105 mm brickwork, 70 mm cavity completely filled with insulation having a thermal conductivity of $0.04 \, W \cdot m^{-1} \cdot K^{-1}$, 100 mm lightweight concrete block finished internally with 13 mm lightweight plaster.

Table 3.11 lists the thicknesses, thermal conductivities and thermal resistances obtained from Appendix 3.A7.

The total thermal resistance is calculated, from which the U-value is then determined. Note that the thermal conductivity of the mortar is taken to be the same as that bulk material for both inner and outer leaves. This is a simplification and is discussed further in section 3.3.11.

Hence:

$$U = 1 / \Sigma R = 0.39 \, W \cdot m^{-2} \cdot K^{-1}$$

Table 3.11 Example 1: thickness, thermal conductivity and thermal resistance of materials

Element	Thickness (mm)	Thermal conductivity $(W \cdot m^{-2} \cdot K^{-1})$	Thermal resistance $(m^2 \cdot K \cdot W^{-1})$
Outer surface	—	—	0.06†
External brickwork	105	0.77	0.136
Cavity insulation	70	0.04	1.75
Blockwork	100	0.19	0.526
Plaster	13	0.16	0.081
Inner surface	—	—	0.12†
			$\Sigma R = 2.673$

† 'Traditional' values used in the UK

3.3.11   Thermal transmittance for elements composed of bridged layers

3.3.11.1   General

In calculating the effect of thermal bridging, the most important factor is whether the thermal bridge is across the entire thickness of the element or limited to bridging of the inner or outer leaf only.

The method of calculation of thermal transmittance given in section 3.3.10 assumes that the direction of heat flow is perpendicular to the plane of the structure. This is true when the layers are of uniform thickness and the thermal conductivity is isotropic along this plane. Dissimilar thermal conductivities and thicknesses mean that heat flows are not unidirectional and thermal bridges are formed.

Rigorous calculation of thermal bridges and their effect on the average U-value requires two- and three-dimensional heat flow analysis. However, for most constructions simple calculation procedures give satisfactory results. Two alternative approaches are suggested:

—   *proportional area method:* the construction is treated as homogeneous leaves penetrated by regularly occurring thermal bridges

—   *combined method:* an average thermal resistance is calculated for the bridged structure.

Note that if the difference between the thermal resistances of the bridged and non-bridged layers is less than 0.1 $W \cdot m^{-1} \cdot K^{-1}$, the effect of thermal bridging is small and may be neglected.

3.3.11.2   Proportional area method

This method is prescribed by Appendix B of *Approved Document L*[5] for determining U-values of structures containing regularly occurring thermal bridges such as mortar joints, timber joists etc. However, it should be noted that *BS EN ISO 6946*[17] adopts the combined method as the basis for determining the thermal transmittance of bridged elements.

Essentially, the proportional area involves the calculation of a weighted average of the thermal transmittances of the bridged and unbridged proportions of the construction. Where the construction comprises two or more leaves separated by cavities, the transmittance of each leaf is calculated separately using half the cavity resistance. The overall transmittance is then determined by taking the reciprocal of the sum of the total resistances for each leaf.

The proportional area method always assumes that heat flow is in one direction, perpendicular to the surfaces of the structure. Consequently, the thermal transmittance of each heat flow path can be calculated separately and then added together in direct proportion to their areas.

Single leaf constructions

For a bridged single leaf construction, see Figure 3.4, the overall U-value is given by:

$$U = \frac{P_m}{R_m} + \frac{P_n}{R_n} \tag{3.11}$$

where U is the thermal transmittance ($W \cdot m^{-2} \cdot K^{-1}$), P_m and P_n are the proportions of the total surface area occupied by elements composed of materials m and n, R_m and R_n are the thermal resistances of isotropic elements composed of materials m and n ($m^2 \cdot K \cdot W^{-1}$).

The thermal resistance of each element is calculated as for a homogenous structure, i.e:

$$R_m = R_{si} + \sum_{j=1}^{j=z} R_{mj} + R_{se} \tag{3.12}$$

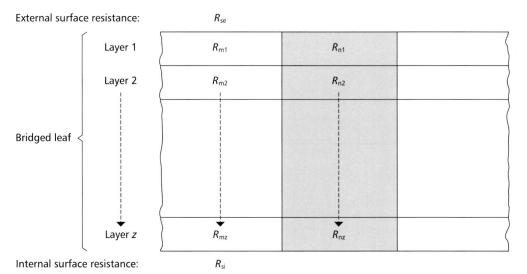

Figure 3.4 Bridged single leaf construction

$$R_n = R_{si} + \sum_{j=1}^{j=z} R_{nj} + R_{se} \tag{3.13}$$

where R_m and R_n are the thermal resistances of isotropic elements composed of materials m_j and n_j (m²·K·W⁻¹), R_{si} is the interior surface resistance (m²·K·W⁻¹), R_{se} is the external surface resistance (m²·K·W⁻¹), R_{mj} is the thermal resistance of layer j composed of material m (m²·K·W⁻¹), R_{nj} is the thermal resistance of layer j composed of material n (m²·K·W⁻¹) and j is an integer taking values from 1 to z where z is the maximum number of layers.

Twin leaf construction, one leaf bridged

For a twin leaf construction where one leaf only is bridged, see Figure 3.5, the overall U-value is given by:

$$U = 1 / (R_h + R_b) \tag{3.14}$$

where U is the thermal transmittance of the construction (W·m⁻²·K⁻¹), R_h is the thermal resistance of the homogeneous leaf (m²·K·W⁻¹) and R_b is the thermal resistance of the bridged leaf (m²·K·W⁻¹).

The boundary between the two leaves is taken to be midway across the air space so that half the air space resistance is added to the thermal resistance of each leaf.

The thermal resistance of the outer (homogeneous) leaf is given by:

$$R_h = {}^1/_2 R_a + R_p + R_{se} \tag{3.15}$$

where R_h is the thermal resistance of the homogeneous leaf (m²·K·W⁻¹), R_a is the thermal resistance of the air space (m²·K·W⁻¹), R_p is the thermal resistance of the element composed of material p (m²·K·W⁻¹), and R_{se} is the external surface resistance (m²·K·W⁻¹).

The thermal resistance of the inner (bridged) leaf is given by:

$$R_b = \frac{1}{(P_m/R_m + P_n/R_n)} \tag{3.16}$$

where R_b is the thermal resistance of the bridged leaf (m²·K·W⁻¹), P_m and P_n are the proportions of the total surface area occupied by elements composed of materials m and n, R_m and R_n are the thermal resistances of elements composed of materials m and n (m²·K·W⁻¹).

R_m and R_n are given by the following equations:

$$R_m = R_{si} + \sum_{j=1}^{j=z} R_{mj} + {}^1/_2 R_a \tag{3.17}$$

$$R_n = R_{si} + \sum_{j=1}^{j=z} R_{nj} + {}^1/_2 R_a \tag{3.18}$$

where R_m and R_n are the thermal resistances of elements composed of materials m and n (m²·K·W⁻¹), R_{si} is the internal surface resistance (m²·K·W⁻¹), R_a is the thermal resistance of the air space (m²·K·W⁻¹), R_{mj} is the thermal resistance of layer j composed of material m (m²·K·W⁻¹), R_{nj} is the thermal resistance of layer j composed of material n (m²·K·W⁻¹) and j is an integer taking values between 1 and z where z is the maximum number of layers.

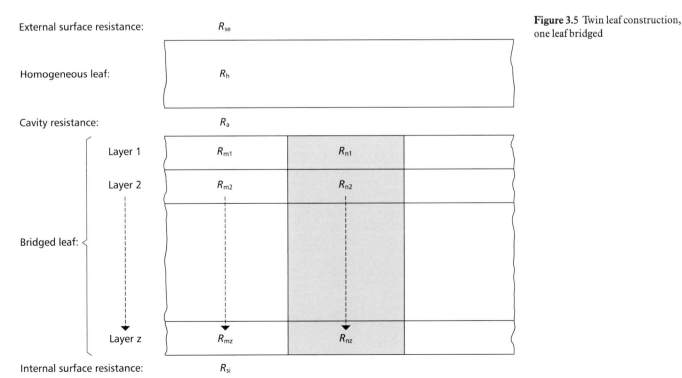

Figure 3.5 Twin leaf construction, one leaf bridged

External surface resistance:	R_{se}	
Homogeneous leaf:	R_h	
Cavity resistance:	R_a	

Layer 1 — R_{m1} — R_{n1}
Layer 2 — R_{m2} — R_{n2}
Bridged leaf:
Layer z — R_{mz} — R_{nz}

Internal surface resistance: R_{si}

Proportion of surface area occupied by material m = P_m
Proportion of surface area occupied by material n = P_n

Example 3.2: Calculation of U-value for cavity wall construction with inner leaf consisting of two bridged layers

Figure 3.6 shows an external wall consisting of 105 mm brickwork, 50 mm cavity, 125 mm concrete blocks (440 mm × 215 mm) bridged by 10 mm mortar joints, 30 mm insulation between timber studs (50 mm × 30 mm) at 600 mm centres, finished internally with 13 mm plasterboard. (Since the thermal conductivities of the brickwork and mortar differ by less than 0.1 $W \cdot m^{-1} \cdot K^{-1}$ the bridging effect of the mortar on the outer leaf is ignored.)

The dimensions and thermal properties of the components of the wall are given in Table 3.12.

(*a*)   Thermal resistance of bridged inner leaf

The inner leaf consists of non-bridged layers (i.e. cavity (inner half), plasterboard, inside surface) and bridged layers (i.e. blockwork bridged by mortar joints and insulation bridged by timber studs). For convenience, the thermal resistances of the unbridged layers can be added together to give a single thermal resistance for the unbridged layers (R_n) as follows:

$$R_n = \tfrac{1}{2}R_a + R_p + R_{si} = 0.29 \ m^2 \cdot K \cdot W^{-1}$$

For the bridged layers, the relative positions of the mortar joints and the timber studs are not known, therefore four different heat flow paths must be considered:

— concrete block–insulation (c–i)

— concrete block–timber (c–t)

— mortar–insulation (m–i)

— mortar–timber (m–t)

The thermal resistance for the non-bridged layers is added to the thermal resistance of the each of the heat flow paths. The total thermal resistances of the heat paths are then combined in parallel, in proportion to their areas.

The thermal resistances of the heat flow paths are as follows.

Concrete block–insulation (c–i) heat flow path:

$$R_{(c-i)} = R_c + R_i + R_n = 2.18 \ m^2 \cdot K \cdot W^{-1}$$

Concrete block–timber (c–t) heat flow path:

$$R_{(c-t)} = R_c + R_t + R_n = 1.64 \ m^2 \cdot K \cdot W^{-1}$$

Mortar–insulation (m–i) heat flow path:

$$R_{(m-i)} = R_m + R_i + R_n = 1.18 \ m^2 \cdot K \cdot W^{-1}$$

Mortar–timber (m–t) heat flow path:

$$R_{(m-t)} = R_m + R_t + R_n = 0.64 \ m^2 \cdot K \cdot W^{-1}$$

The proportions of the facade areas for the flow paths are obtained by multiplying together the proportions of the facade area appropriate to the materials that comprise the flow path.

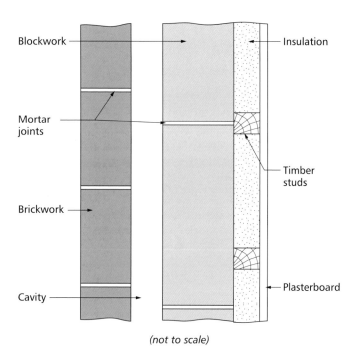

(not to scale)

Figure 3.6 Example 3.2: cavity wall construction, inner leaf consisting of two bridged layers

Table 3.12 Example 3.2: dimensions and thermal properties of materials

Element	Thickness (mm)	Proportion of facade area	Thermal conductivity ($W \cdot m^{-1} \cdot K^{-1}$)	Thermal resistance ($m^2 \cdot K \cdot W^{-1}$)	Symbol
External surface	—	—	—	0.06†	R_{se}
Brickwork	105	1	0.77	0.136	R_b
Cavity (airspace)	—	—	—	0.18	R_a
Concrete blockwork	125	0.934	0.11	1.14	R_c
Mortar (inner leaf)	125	0.066	0.88	0.142	R_m
Insulation	30	0.917	0.04	0.75	R_i
Timber studs	30	0.083	0.14	0.21	R_t
Plasterboard	13	1	0.16	0.081	R_p
Internal surface	—	—	—	0.12†	R_{si}

†'Traditional' values used in the UK

The proportions of the facade areas are as follows.

Concrete block–insulation (c–i) heat flow path:

$$P_{(c-i)} = P_c \times P_i = 0.856$$

Concrete block–timber (c–t) heat flow path:

$$P_{(c-t)} = P_c \times P_t = 0.078$$

Mortar–insulation (m–i) heat flow path:

$$P_{(m-i)} = P_m \times P_i = 0.061$$

Mortar–timber (m–t) heat flow path:

$$P_{(m-t)} = P_c \times P_t = 0.005$$

Using equation 3.16, the thermal resistance of the bridged inner leaf (R_b) is then given by:

$$\frac{1}{R_b} = \frac{P_{(c-i)}}{R_{(c-i)}} + \frac{P_{(c-t)}}{R_{(c-t)}} + \frac{P_{(m-i)}}{R_{(m-i)}} + \frac{P_{(m-t)}}{R_{(m-t)}}$$

$$= (0.856/2.18) + (0.078/1.64)$$

$$+ (0.061/1.18) + (0.005/0.64)$$

$$= 0.500$$

Hence:

$$R_b = 2.0 \ \text{m}^2 \cdot \text{K} \cdot \text{W}^{-1}$$

(b)   Thermal resistance of unbridged outer leaf

The thermal resistance of the unbridged (homogeneous) outer leaf is given by:

$$R_h = R_{se} + R_b + \tfrac{1}{2} R_a = 0.286 \ \text{m}^2 \cdot \text{K} \cdot \text{W}^{-1}$$

(c)   Thermal transmittance of structure

The thermal transmittance of the whole structure is then obtained from equation 3.14:

$$U = \frac{1}{2.0 + 0.286} = 0.44 \ \text{W} \cdot \text{m}^{-2} \cdot \text{K}^{-1}$$

Twin leaf construction, both leaves bridged

Where both leaves are bridged, see Figure 3.7, the overall U-value is given by:

$$U = \frac{1}{R_{b1} + R_{b2}} \tag{3.19}$$

where U is the thermal transmittance of the construction $(\text{W} \cdot \text{m}^{-2} \cdot \text{K}^{-1})$, R_{b1} and R_{b2} are the thermal resistances of bridged leaves 1 and 2 $(\text{m}^2 \cdot \text{K} \cdot \text{W}^{-1})$.

The thermal resistances of the leaves are given by:

$$R_{b1} = \frac{1}{(P_m/R_m + P_n/R_n)} \tag{3.20}$$

$$R_{b2} = \frac{1}{(P_p/R_p + P_q/R_q)} \tag{3.21}$$

where R_{b1} and R_{b2} are the thermal resistances of bridged leaves 1 and 2 $(\text{m}^2 \cdot \text{K} \cdot \text{W}^{-1})$, P_m, P_n, P_p and P_q are the proportions of the total surface area occupied by elements composed of materials m, n, p and q, R_m, R_n, R_p and R_q are the thermal resistances of elements composed of materials m, n, p and q $(\text{m}^2 \cdot \text{K} \cdot \text{W}^{-1})$.

R_m and R_n are given by equations 3.17 and 3.18 and similar equations may be used to determine the thermal resistances of the other bridged leaf.

3.3.11.3   Combined method

The basis of the method is to calculate the upper and lower limits of the thermal resistance of the bridged part of the structure. The lower limit of thermal resistance is that which imposes no resistance to sideways flow of heat and the upper limit is that which imposes an infinite resistance to sideways heat flow. In practice, the heat flow pattern lies between these extremes and the arithmetic mean gives the thermal resistance to a reasonable approximation.

The thermal resistance of the bridged structure is given by:

$$R_b = \tfrac{1}{2}(R_L + R_U) \tag{3.22}$$

where R_b is the thermal resistance of the bridged structure $(\text{m}^2 \cdot \text{K} \cdot \text{W}^{-1})$, R_L is the lower limit of thermal resistance $(\text{m}^2 \cdot \text{K} \cdot \text{W}^{-1})$ and R_U is the upper limit of thermal resistance $(\text{m}^2 \cdot \text{K} \cdot \text{W}^{-1})$.

Structural elements with one bridged layer

Figure 3.8 shows a single leaf composed of material m, bridged repetitively. For simplicity, the leaf is shown bridged by two elements only, composed of materials n and p. The leaf is divided into layers numberered from 1 to z; the bridged layer is shown as layer 2.

(a)   Lower limit

The lower limit of thermal resistance is determined as follows:

$$R_L = R_{se} + R_1 + \frac{A_m + A_n + A_p}{(A_m/R_{m2}) + (A_n/R_{n2}) + (A_p/R_{p2})}$$
$$+ R_3 \cdots + R_z + R_{si} \tag{3.23}$$

where R_L is the lower limit of thermal resistance $(\text{m}^2 \cdot \text{K} \cdot \text{W}^{-1})$, $R_1 \ldots R_z$ are the thermal resistances of (unbridged) layers $1 \ldots z$ $(\text{m}^2 \cdot \text{K} \cdot \text{W}^{-1})$, A_m, A_n and A_p are the areas of elements composed of materials m, n and p (m^2), R_{m2}, R_{n2} and R_{p2} are the thermal resistances of elements composed of materials m, n and p for (bridged) layer 2 $(\text{m}^2 \cdot \text{K} \cdot \text{W}^{-1})$, R_{se} is the external surface resistance $(\text{m}^2 \cdot \text{K} \cdot \text{W}^{-1})$. and R_{si} is the internal surface resistance $(\text{m}^2 \cdot \text{K} \cdot \text{W}^{-1})$.

In terms of proportions of the total surface area:

$$R_L = R_{se} + R_1 + \frac{1}{(P_m/R_{m2}) + (P_n/R_{n2}) + (P_p/R_{p2})}$$
$$+ R_3 + \ldots R_z + R_{si} \tag{3.24}$$

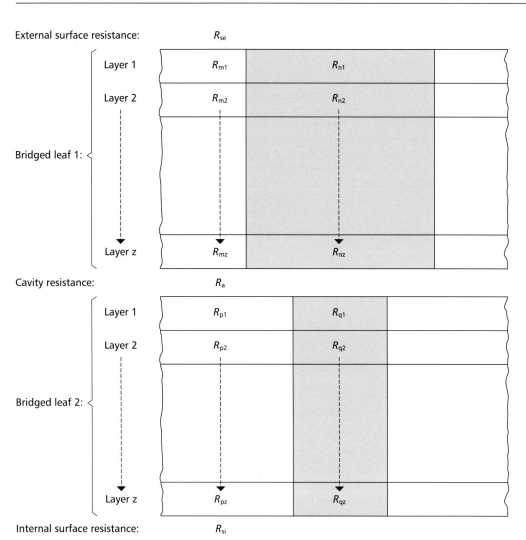

External surface resistance: R_{se}

Layer 1 R_{m1} R_{n1}
Layer 2 R_{m2} R_{n2}

Bridged leaf 1:

Layer z R_{mz} R_{nz}

Cavity resistance: R_{a}

Layer 1 R_{p1} R_{q1}
Layer 2 R_{p2} R_{q2}

Bridged leaf 2:

Layer z R_{pz} R_{qz}

Internal surface resistance: R_{si}

Proportion of surface area occupied by material m $= P_{m}$
Proportion of surface area occupied by material n $= P_{n}$
Proportion of surface area occupied by material p $= P_{p}$
Proportion of surface area occupied by material q $= P_{q}$

Figure 3.7 Twin leaf construction, both leaves bridged

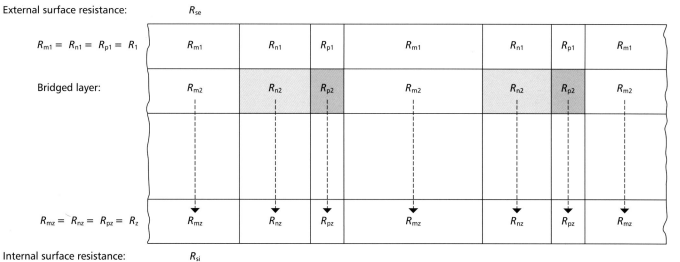

External surface resistance: R_{se}

$R_{m1} = R_{n1} = R_{p1} = R_{1}$ R_{m1} R_{n1} R_{p1} R_{m1} R_{n1} R_{p1} R_{m1}

Bridged layer: R_{m2} R_{n2} R_{p2} R_{m2} R_{n2} R_{p2} R_{m2}

$R_{mz} = R_{nz} = R_{pz} = R_{z}$ R_{mz} R_{nz} R_{pz} R_{mz} R_{nz} R_{pz} R_{mz}

Internal surface resistance: R_{si}

Proportion of surface area occupied by material m $= P_{m}$
Proportion of surface area occupied by material n $= P_{n}$
Proportion of surface area occupied by material p $= P_{p}$

Figure 3.8 Single bridged layer, bridged repetitively by two elements composed of different materials

where P_m, P_n and P_p are the proportions of the total surface area occupied by elements composed of materials m, n and p.

(b)   Upper limit

The upper limit of thermal resistance, R_U, is determined as follows.

$$R_U = (A_m + A_n + A_p) \left(\frac{A_m}{R_{m2} + (R_1 \ldots + R_z) + R_{se} + R_{si}} \right.$$

$$+ \frac{A_n}{R_{n2} + (R_1 \ldots + R_z) + R_{se} + R_{si}}$$

$$\left. + \frac{A_p}{R_{p2} + (R_1 \ldots + R_z) + R_{se} + R_{si}} \right)^{-1} \quad (3.25)$$

where R_U is the upper limit of thermal resistance $(\text{m}^2 \cdot \text{K} \cdot \text{W}^{-1})$, $R_1 \ldots R_z$ are the thermal resistances of (unbridged) layers $1 \ldots z$ etc. $(\text{m}^2 \cdot \text{K} \cdot \text{W}^{-1})$, A_m, A_n and A_p are the areas of elements composed of materials m, n and p (m^2), R_{m2}, R_{n2} and R_{p2} are the thermal resistances of elements composed of materials m, n and p for (bridged) layer 2 $(\text{m}^2 \cdot \text{K} \cdot \text{W}^{-1})$, R_{se} is the external surface resistance $(\text{m}^2 \cdot \text{K} \cdot \text{W}^{-1})$ and R_{si} is the internal surface resistance $(\text{m}^2 \cdot \text{K} \cdot \text{W}^{-1})$.

In terms of proportions of the total surface area:

$$R_U = \left(\frac{P_m}{R_{m2} + (R_1 \ldots + R_z) + R_{se} + R_{si}} \right.$$

$$+ \frac{P_n}{R_{n2} + (R_1 \ldots + R_z) + R_{se} + R_{si}}$$

$$\left. + \frac{P_p}{R_{p2} + (R_1 \ldots + R_z) + R_{se} + R_{si}} \right)^{-1} \quad (3.26)$$

where P_m, P_n and P_p are the proportions of the total surface area occupied by elements composed of materials m, n and p.

The thermal resistance of the bridged element is the average of the upper and lower limiting values, i.e:

$$U = \frac{1}{0.5 (R_L + R_U)} \quad (3.27)$$

Where more than one layer is bridged, the relative positions of the bridging within each bridged layer are not generally known. Each different heat flow path (from internal to external environments) must be considered when calculating the upper limit of thermal resistance. The thermal resistances for each of the paths are combined in parallel, in proportion to their areas. The proportions for each flow path are obtained by multiplying together the proportions appropriate to each material comprising the flow path (cf. example 3.2).

Examples 3.3, 3.4 and 3.5 show the use of the combined method to determine the thermal transmittance of typical bridged constructions.

Example 3.3: Calculation of U-value for masonry wall, inner leaf bridged by mortar joints

See Figure 3.9. The dimensions and thermal properties of the components of the wall are given in Table 3.13. Isothermal planes are taken at the inside air and external air. Since the thermal conductivities of brick and mortar are approximately equal, the outer leaf is regarded as thermally homogenous.

(a)   Mean thermal resistance of bridged structure

The lower limit of thermal resistance is obtained from equation 3.24:

$$R_L = \frac{1}{(0.934 / 1.136) + (0.066 / 0.142)}$$

$$+ 0.136 + 0.18 + 0.081 + 0.06 + 0.12$$

$$= 1.354 \text{ m}^2 \cdot \text{K} \cdot \text{W}^{-1}$$

Table 3.13 Example 3.3: dimensions and thermal properties of materials

Element	Thickness (mm)	Proportion of surface area	Thermal conductivity $(\text{W} \cdot \text{m}^{-1} \cdot \text{K}^{-1})$	Thermal resistance $(\text{m}^2 \cdot \text{K} \cdot \text{W}^{-1})$
Outer surface (R_{se})	—	—	—	0.06†
External brickwork	105	—	0.77	0.136
Cavity	—	—	—	0.18
Blockwork	125	0.934	0.11	1.136
Mortar (inner leaf)	125	0.066	0.88	0.142
Plaster	13	1.0	0.16	0.081
Inner surface (R_{si})	—	—	—	0.12†

†'Traditional' values used in the UK

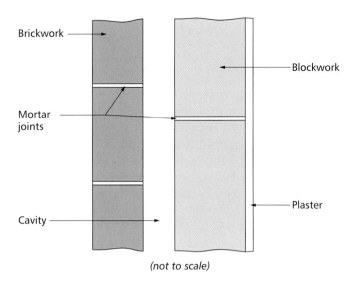

Brickwork

Mortar joints

Cavity

Blockwork

Plaster

(not to scale)

Figure 3.9 Example 3.3: cavity wall construction

The upper limit of thermal resistance is obtained from equation 3.26:

$$R_U = \left(\frac{0.934}{1.136 + 0.136 + 0.18 + 0.081 + 0.06 + 0.12} \right.$$

$$\left. + \frac{0.066}{0.142 + 0.136 + 0.18 + 0.081 + 0.06 + 0.12} \right)^{-1}$$

$$= 1 / (0.5452 + 0.0918)$$

$$= 1.570 \ \text{m}^2 \cdot \text{K} \cdot \text{W}^{-1}$$

Using equation 3.22, these limiting values are averaged to give the thermal resistance of the bridged structure:

$$R_b = 0.5 (1.354 + 1.570) = 1.462 \ \text{m}^2 \cdot \text{K} \cdot \text{W}^{-1}$$

(*b*)   Thermal transmittance of structure

The thermal transmittance of the whole structure is obtained from equation 3.27:

$$U = \frac{1}{0.5 (1.354 + 1.570)} = 0.68 \ \text{W} \cdot \text{m}^{-2} \cdot \text{K}^{-1}$$

For comparison, if the thermal bridging of the inner leaf by the mortar joints is ignored, the thermal resistance is the sum of the thermal resistances given in Table 3.13 minus that of the mortar joints. Hence, $U = 0.58 \ \text{W} \cdot \text{m}^{-2} \cdot \text{K}^{-1}$.

Example 3.4: Calculation of U-value for tile-hung wall

See Figure 3.10. The dimensions and thermal properties of the components of the wall are given in Table 3.14. The inner leaf is bridged by mortar joints. The thermal bridging through the battens need not be taken into account since the difference between the thermal resistance of the battens and that of the cavity is less than $0.1 \ \text{m}^2 \cdot \text{K} \cdot \text{W}^{-1}$. Isothermal planes are taken at the inside air and outside air.

(*a*)   Mean thermal resistance of bridged leaf

The lower limit of thermal resistance is obtained from equation 3.24:

$$R_L = \frac{1}{(0.934 / 1.667) + (0.066 / 0.227)}$$

$$+ 0.12 + 0.081 + 0.06 + 0.12$$

$$= 1.556 \ \text{m}^2 \cdot \text{K} \cdot \text{W}^{-1}$$

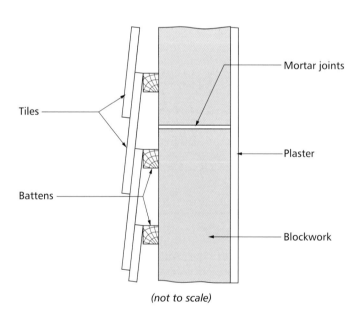

Tiles

Battens

Mortar joints

Plaster

Blockwork

(not to scale)

Figure 3.10 Example 3.4: tile-hung wall

Table 3.14 Example 3.4: dimensions and thermal properties of materials

Element	Thickness (mm)	Proportion of surface area	Thermal conductivity (W·m⁻¹·K⁻¹)	Thermal resistance (m²·K·W⁻¹)
Outer surface	—	—	—	0.06†
Tiles on battens	—	1.0	—	0.12
Blockwork	200	0.934	0.12	1.667
Mortar (inner leaf)	200	0.066	0.88	0.227
Plaster	13	1.0	0.16	0.081
Inner surface	—	—	—	0.12†

†'Traditional' values used in the UK

The upper limit of thermal resistance is obtained from equation 3.26:

$$R_U = \left(\frac{0.934}{1.667 + 0.12 + 0.081 + 0.06 + 0.12} \right.$$
$$\left. + \frac{0.066}{0.227 + 0.12 + 0.081 + 0.06 + 0.12} \right)^{-1}$$
$$= 1 / (0.456 + 0.109) = 1.770 \ \text{m}^2 \cdot \text{K} \cdot \text{W}^{-1}$$

Using equation 3.22, these limiting values are averaged to give the thermal resistance of the bridged structure:

$$R_b = 0.5 (1.556 + 1.770) = 1.663 \ \text{m}^2 \cdot \text{K} \cdot \text{W}^{-1}$$

(b)   Thermal transmittance of structure

The *U*-value for the whole structure is obtained from equation 3.27:

$$U = \frac{1}{0.5 (1.556 + 1.770)} = 0.60 \ \text{W} \cdot \text{m}^{-2} \cdot \text{K}^{-1}$$

For comparison, if the thermal bridging of the inner leaf by the mortar joints is ignored, the thermal resistance is the sum of the thermal resistances given in Table 3.14 excluding that of the mortar joints. Hence, $U = 0.49$ $\text{W} \cdot \text{m}^{-2} \cdot \text{K}^{-1}$.

Example 3.5: Calculation of U-value for timber frame wall

See Figure 3.11. The dimensions and thermal properties of the components of the wall are given in Table 3.15. Thermal bridging takes place at the inner leaf where the timber frame bridges the insulation. Isothermal planes are taken at the inside air and outside air. Since the thermal properties of the brick and mortar are similar, the outer leaf is regarded as homogenous.

The timber frame consists of studs, noggins, top and bottom plates and additional framing around windows and doors. For a typical wall with windows and doors, this represents about 15% of the surface area. (Note that for walls without windows and doors, the frame accounts for

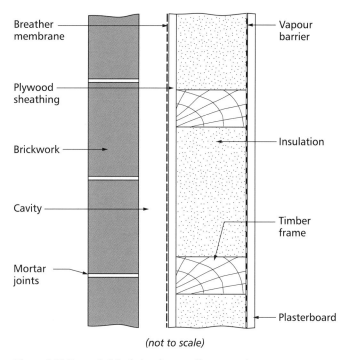

Figure 3.11 Example 3.5: timber frame wall construction

about 10% of the surface area while, for narrow walls with doors and windows, the frame may account for 20% of the surface area.)

(a)   Mean thermal resistance of bridged structure

The lower limit of thermal resistance is obtained from equation 3.24:

$$R_L = \frac{1}{\left(\dfrac{0.85}{1.25 + 0.18} + \dfrac{0.15}{0.685} \right)} + 0.06 + 0.136$$
$$+ 0.18 + 0.071 + 0.063 + 0.12$$
$$= 1.859 \ \text{m}^2 \cdot \text{K} \cdot \text{W}^{-1}$$

The upper limit of thermal resistance is obtained from equation 3.26:

Table 3.15 Example 3.5: dimensions and thermal properties of materials

Element	Thickness (mm)	Proportion of surface area	Thermal conductivity ($\text{W} \cdot \text{m}^{-1} \cdot \text{K}^{-2}$)	Thermal resistance ($\text{m}^2 \cdot \text{K} \cdot \text{W}^{-1}$)
Outer surface	—	—	—	0.06†
External brickwork	105	—	0.77	0.136
Cavity	—	—	—	0.18
Plywood sheathing	10	—	0.14	0.071
Timber frame	89	0.15	0.13	0.685
Insulation between studs	50	0.85	0.04	1.25
Airspace between insulation and sheathing	39	0.85	—	0.18
Vapour barrier	—	—	—	—
Plaster	10	—	0.16	0.063
Inner surface	—	—	—	0.12†

†'Traditional' values used in the UK

Table 3.16 Effect of thermal bridging on U-value of timber frame wall with brick cladding using the combined method

Wall	Proportion of area bridged (%)	U-value (W·m^{-2}·K^{-1}) for stated thickness of timber (mm) and insulation (mm)				
		89 and 25	89 and 50	89 and 89	119 and 119	140 and 140
Centre panel	0	0.70	0.49	0.35	0.28	0.24
Wall with no openings	10	0.70	0.52	0.40	0.32	0.28
Typical wall with openings	15	0.71	0.53	0.42	0.34	0.30
Narrow wall (less than 5 m wide) with openings	20	0.71	0.55	0.45	0.36	0.32

$$R_U = \left(\frac{0.85}{0.06+0.136+0.18+0.071+1.25+0.18+0.063+0.12} \right.$$

$$\left. + \frac{0.15}{0.06+0.136+0.18+0.071+0.685+0.063+0.12} \right)^{-1}$$

$$= 1/(0.4126 + 0.1141) = 1.899 \text{ m}^2 \cdot \text{K} \cdot \text{W}^{-1}$$

Using equation 3.22, these limiting values are averaged to give the thermal resistance of the bridged structure:

$$R_b = 0.5\,(1.859 + 1.899) = 1.879 \text{ m}^2 \cdot \text{K} \cdot \text{W}^{-1}$$

(b)   Thermal transmittance of structure

The thermal transmittance of the whole structure is then obtained from equation 3.27:

$$U = \frac{1}{0.5\,(1.859 + 1.899)} = 0.53 \text{ W} \cdot \text{m}^{-2} \cdot \text{K}^{-1}$$

3.3.11.4   Structural elements consisting of several layers, one or more of which is bridged

For structural elements consisting of several layers in close thermal contact and one or more of the layers is bridged, the isothermal planes will include all the layers. The lower limit is determined by adding together the thermal resistances of the various layers, each being calculated separately using equation 3.24. Determination of the upper limit is more complicated since this requires the division of each layer into isotropic sections, the thermal resistances of which are then added together on an area-weighted basis, as shown in equation 3.26. Appendix 3.A5 shows how this procedure may be applied to the case of a foam-filled masonry block.

3.3.11.5   Effect of bridging on calculated U-value

Examples 3.3, 3.4 and 3.5 above show that in some cases the difference between the upper and lower limiting values is small. For example, in the case of a timber frame wall:

—   lower limit U-value: 0.54 W·m^{-2}·K^{-1}

—   upper limit U-value: 0.53 W·m^{-2}·K^{-1}

— U-value by combined method: 0.53 W·m^{-2}·K^{-1}

In this case, calculation of the U-value using any of the three corresponding values of thermal resistance would give results of acceptable accuracy. Table 3.16 illustrates the calculated effects of thermal bridging on the U-value for a timber frame wall.

3.3.11.6   Correction for wall ties and roof fixings

Where a layer of insulation is penetrated by wall ties or roof fixings, the U-value should be corrected as follows to account for thermal bridging by the ties/fixings.

$$U_c = U + \alpha \lambda_f n_f A_f \tag{3.28}$$

where U_c is the thermal transmittance corrected for thermal bridging by wall ties/roof fixings (W·m^{-2}·K^{-1}), U is the (uncorrected) thermal transmittance of the element (W·m^{-2}·K^{-1}), α is a numerical coefficient (m^{-1}), λ_f is the thermal conductivity of the tie/fixing (W·m^{-1}·K^{-1}), n_f is the number of ties/fixings per unit area (m^{-2}) and A_f is the cross-sectional area of a single tie/fixing (m^2).

Values for α are given in Table 3.17.

No correction is required in the following cases:

—   for wall ties across an empty cavity

—   for wall ties between a masonry leaf and timber studs

—   for wall ties/fixings the thermal conductivity of the tie/fixing is less than 1 W·m^{-1}·K^{-1}.

Where both ends of the tie/fixing are in contact with metal sheets a different procedure must be used. This is set down in *BS EN ISO 10211-1*[21].

Table 3.17 Values of coefficient α for wall ties and roof fixings[17]

Type	α (m^{-1})
Wall tie between masonry leaves	6
Roof fixings	5

3.4   Roofs

3.4.1   Pitched roofs

For simple pitched roofs, the U-value is calculated normal to the plane of the roof. However, if the pitched roof includes a horizontal ceiling and an unheated loft, the U-value is defined with respect to the plane of the ceiling.

For heated lofts, the U-value of the roof is calculated in the normal way. However, in calculating the heat losses, the full surface roof area of the roof must be considered rather than the plan area.

Note that the *Building Regulations*[4] require that roof voids be ventilated. Standardised thermal resistances for loft spaces are given in Table 3.6.

3.4.2 Flat roofs

The thermal transmittance of flat roofs is calculated using the methods given in sections 3.3.10 and 3.3.11

Where components are tapered to achieve a fall, the average thickness may be used in calculating the thermal transmittance of the roof. If the main insulation layer is tapered, the U-value should be calculated at intervals across the roof and the average determined. Alternatively, the method given in Annex C of *BS EN ISO 6946*[17] may be used.

3.5 Ground floors and basements

3.5.1 General

The heat loss through floors in contact with the ground is more complicated than that through above ground components. The heat flow is three-dimensional and the thermal performance is affected by various factors including the size and shape of the floor, the thickness of the surrounding wall and the presence of all-over or edge insulation. However, research has shown that the building dimensions affect the U-values of ground floors only through the ratio of exposed perimeter of the floor to its area[22,23]. This allows the U-value of a ground floor to be readily evaluated for a floor of any size or shape.

The information on ground floors is consistent with *BS EN ISO 13370*[24]. The values of thermal transmittance for floors on clay-type soils are very similar to those given in the previous edition of Guide A3 but the tabular data have been extended to include other soil types. Other changes include a more correct treatment of the effect of thermal insulation of floors, including that of surface resistance, and more realistic values for edge insulation for solid ground floors.

It should be noted that the heat flux density varies over the area of a floor, in general being greatest at the edges and least at the centre. The thermal transmittance of a floor is suitable for calculating the total heat transfer through the floor but cannot be used to obtain the heat flux density at a point on the floor surface nor to calculate the surface temperature of the floor.

3.5.2 Thermal transmittance of solid ground floors

Tables 3.19, 3.20 and 3.21 give U-values for solid ground floors in contact with the earth, calculated using equations 3.28 to 3.31, for the three types of soil in Table 3.18. The tables assume a wall thickness of 0.3 m. The U-values are given as a function of the ratio of exposed perimeter to floor area and the thermal resistance of the floor construction, R_f ($R_f = 0$ for an uninsulated floor). Linear interpolation may be used for values intermediate between those given in the tables.

The U-value of a solid floor in contact with the ground depends on a 'characteristic dimension' of the floor, L_f, and the 'total equivalent thickness', d_{ef}, of the factors that, in combination, restrict the heat flow (i.e. wall thickness, surface resistances, thermal insulation).

The characteristic dimension, see Figure 3.12(a), is defined thus:

$$L_f = \frac{A_{fg}}{0.5\,p_f} \qquad (3.29)$$

where L_f is the characteristic dimension of the floor (m), A_{fg} is the area of floor in contact with the ground (m²) and p_f is the exposed perimeter of the floor (m).

Table 3.18 Thermal conductivity of soils

Soil type	Thermal conductivity, λ_g (W·m⁻¹·K⁻¹)
Clay or silt	1.5
Sand or gravel	2.0
Homogeneous rock	3.5

Table 3.19 U-values for solid ground floors on clay soil ($\lambda_g = 1.5$ W·m⁻¹·K⁻¹)

Ratio p_f/A_f	U-value (W·m⁻²·K⁻¹) for stated thermal resistance, R_f (m²·K·W⁻¹)			
	0	0.5	1.0	2.0
0.05	0.13	0.11	0.10	0.08
0.10	0.22	0.18	0.16	0.13
0.15	0.30	0.24	0.21	0.17
0.20	0.37	0.29	0.25	0.19
0.25	0.44	0.34	0.28	0.22
0.30	0.49	0.38	0.31	0.23
0.35	0.55	0.41	0.34	0.25
0.40	0.60	0.44	0.36	0.26
0.45	0.65	0.47	0.38	0.27
0.50	0.70	0.50	0.40	0.28
0.55	0.74	0.52	0.41	0.28
0.60	0.78	0.55	0.43	0.29
0.65	0.82	0.57	0.44	0.30
0.70	0.86	0.59	0.45	0.30
0.75	0.89	0.61	0.46	0.31
0.80	0.93	0.62	0.47	0.32
0.85	0.96	0.64	0.47	0.32
0.90	0.99	0.65	0.48	0.32
0.95	1.02	0.66	0.49	0.33
1.00	1.05	0.68	0.50	0.33

Table 3.20 U-values for solid ground floors on sand or gravel ($\lambda_g = 2.0\ \mathrm{W \cdot m^{-1} \cdot K^{-1}}$)

Ratio p_f/A_f	U-value ($\mathrm{W \cdot m^{-2} \cdot K^{-1}}$) for stated thermal resistance, R_f ($\mathrm{m^2 \cdot K \cdot W^{-1}}$)			
	0	0.5	1.0	2.0
0.05	0.16	0.14	0.12	0.10
0.10	0.28	0.22	0.19	0.16
0.15	0.38	0.30	0.25	0.20
0.20	0.47	0.36	0.30	0.23
0.25	0.55	0.41	0.33	0.25
0.30	0.63	0.46	0.37	0.26
0.35	0.70	0.50	0.39	0.28
0.40	0.76	0.53	0.42	0.29
0.45	0.82	0.56	0.43	0.30
0.50	0.88	0.59	0.45	0.31
0.55	0.93	0.62	0.47	0.31
0.60	0.98	0.64	0.48	0.32
0.65	1.03	0.66	0.49	0.33
0.70	1.07	0.68	0.50	0.33
0.75	1.12	0.70	0.51	0.34
0.80	1.16	0.72	0.52	0.34
0.85	1.19	0.73	0.53	0.35
0.90	1.23	0.75	0.54	0.35
0.95	1.27	0.76	0.54	0.35
1.00	1.30	0.77	0.55	0.35

Table 3.21 U-values for solid ground floors on homogeneous rock ($\lambda_g = 3.5\ \mathrm{W \cdot m^{-1} \cdot K^{-1}}$)

Ratio p_f/A_f	U-value ($\mathrm{W \cdot m^{-2} \cdot K^{-1}}$) for stated thermal resistance, R_f ($\mathrm{m^2 \cdot K \cdot W^{-1}}$)			
	0	0.5	1.0	2.0
0.05	0.27	0.21	0.18	0.15
0.10	0.45	0.34	0.28	0.22
0.15	0.61	0.43	0.35	0.26
0.20	0.74	0.51	0.40	0.28
0.25	0.86	0.58	0.44	0.30
0.30	0.97	0.63	0.47	0.32
0.35	1.07	0.68	0.50	0.33
0.40	1.16	0.72	0.52	0.34
0.45	1.25	0.75	0.53	0.35
0.50	1.33	0.78	0.55	0.35
0.55	1.40	0.80	0.56	0.36
0.60	1.47	0.82	0.58	0.37
0.65	1.53	0.84	0.59	0.37
0.70	1.59	0.86	0.60	0.37
0.75	1.64	0.87	0.61	0.38
0.80	1.69	0.89	0.62	0.38
0.85	1.74	0.91	0.62	0.38
0.90	1.79	0.92	0.63	0.39
0.95	1.83	0.93	0.64	0.39
1.00	1.87	0.95	0.64	0.39

The total equivalent thickness, see Figure 3.12(b), is given by:

$$d_{ef} = d_w + \lambda_g (R_{si} + R_f + R_{se}) \qquad (3.30)$$

where d_{ef} is the total equivalent thickness of the floor (m), d_w is the thickness of the wall surrounding the ground floor (m), λ_g is the thermal conductivity of the ground ($\mathrm{W \cdot m^{-1} \cdot K^{-1}}$), R_{si} is the inside surface resistance ($\mathrm{m^2 \cdot K \cdot W^{-1}}$), R_{se} is the external surface resistance ($\mathrm{m^2 \cdot K \cdot W^{-1}}$) and R_f is the thermal resistance of the floor ($\mathrm{m^2 \cdot K \cdot W^{-1}}$).

For an infinitely long floor, L_f is the width of the floor and, at the other limiting case of a square floor, L_f is half the length of one side.

R_f includes the thermal resistance of any all-over insulation layers above, below or within the floor slab, and that of any floor covering. The thermal resistance of dense concrete slabs and thin floor coverings may normally be neglected. Hardcore below the slab is assumed to have the same thermal conductivity as the ground and its thermal resistance is therefore not included.

For $d_{ef} < L_f$, as is usually the case, the thermal transmittance is given by:

$$U_f = \frac{2\lambda_g}{\pi L_f + d_{ef}} \log_e [(\pi L_f / d_{ef}) - 1] \qquad (3.31)$$

If $d_{ef} \geq L_f$, as may occur for a small, well-insulated floor:

$$U_f = 1 / (0.457 L_f + d_{ef}) \qquad (3.32)$$

The exposed perimeter, p_f, should be interpreted as the total length of the external wall separating the heated building from the external environment or from an

(a) Plan (not to scale)

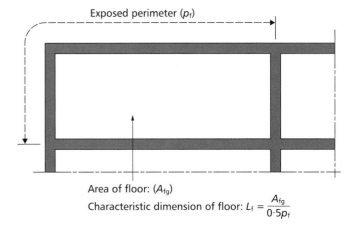

Area of floor: (A_{fg})

Characteristic dimension of floor: $L_f = \dfrac{A_{fg}}{0.5 p_f}$

(b) Section (not to scale)

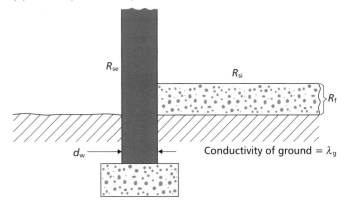

Total equivalent thickness of floor: $d_{ef} = d_w + \lambda_g (R_{si} + R_f + R_{se})$

Figure 3.12 Characteristic dimension and total equivalent thickness of solid ground floor

unheated space outside the insulated fabric. Thus for a complete building p_f is the total perimeter of the building and A_{fg} is its total ground-floor area.

To calculate the heat loss from part of a building (e.g. for each individual dwelling in a row of terraced houses), p_f includes the lengths of external walls separating the heated space from the external environment but excludes the lengths of party walls separating the part under consideration from other spaces heated to a similar internal temperature. In such cases, A_{fg} is the ground-floor area for the part of the building under consideration.

Unheated spaces outside the insulated fabric of the building (e.g. porches, attached garages or storage areas) are excluded when determining p_f and A_{fg}, but the length of the wall between the building and the unheated space must be included in the perimeter. The ground heat losses are assessed as if the unheated spaces were not present.

The thermal conductivity of the ground, λ_g, depends on several factors including density, degree of water saturation, particle size, type of mineral constituting the particles and whether the ground is frozen or unfrozen. Consequently, the thermal properties vary from one location to another and at different depths at any particular location. They may also vary with time due to changes in moisture content or due to freezing and thawing. Table 3.18 gives representative values of λ_g for three broad categories of ground. Clay-type soils are the most prevalent in Britain and should be assumed in the absence of more specific information.

3.5.3 Heat losses through ground floors

Heat losses through ground floors are affected by the large mass of earth in thermal contact with the floor. A full treatment of heat losses through ground floors would need to take account of the steady-state component, related to annual average temperature, and the annual periodic component resulting from the annual cyclical variation of inside and outside temperatures. Such an approach allows the determination of the ground losses for each month of the year, leading to the peak loss for design purposes and the appropriate average over the heating season for energy calculations.

In practice, for the purposes of calculating plant sizes, it has been usual to apply the same temperature difference to all the elements of the structure, including the floor. This tends to overestimate the heat losses through the floor.

For seasonal energy calculations, a more accurate assessment of the ground losses is obtained using the annual average temperature difference between inside and outside, rather than the average difference over the heating season. This is discussed in Appendix 3.A4.

Example 3.7: Calculation of U-value for L-shaped solid ground floor

Figure 3.13 shows a solid ground floor on clay-type soil with surrounding wall of thickness 300 mm.

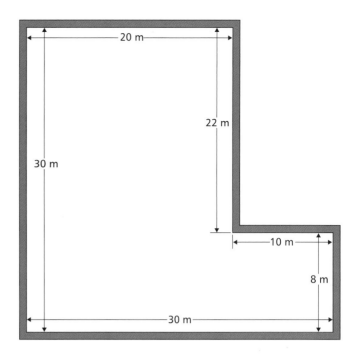

Figure 3.13 Example 3.7: plan of solid ground floor

The length of perimeter of floor is:

$$p_f = 30 + 30 + 20 + 22 + 10 + 8 = 120 \text{ m}$$

The area of the floor in contact with the ground is:

$$A_{fg} = (20 \times 30) + (10 \times 8) = 660 \text{ m}^2$$

Hence:

$$L_f = 660 / (0.5 \times 120) = 11.0 \text{ m}$$

For an uninsulated floor $R_f = 0$. Therefore:

$$d_{ef} = 0.3 + 1.5 (0.14 + 0.04) = 0.57 \text{ m}$$

Since d_{ef} is less than L_f, using equation 3.29:

$$U_f = \frac{2 \times 1.5}{3.142 \times 11.0 + 0.57} \log_e \left(\frac{3.142 \times 11.0}{0.57} + 1 \right)$$

$$= 0.35 \text{ W·m}^{-2}\text{·K}^{-1}$$

Example 3.8: Calculation of the U-value for solid ground floor for semi-detached dwelling with attached unheated garage

The plan is shown in Figure 3.14. The wall thickness is 300 mm, and insulation of thermal resistance 0.7 m²·K·W⁻¹ is applied to the floor.

The exposed perimeter is:

$$p_f = 6 + 8 + 6 = 20 \text{ m}$$

The area of floor in contact with the ground is:

$$A_{fg} = 6 \times 8 = 48 \text{ m}^2$$

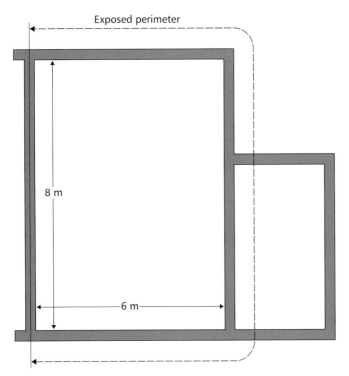

Exposed perimeter = 6+8+6 = 20 m

Figure 3.14 Example 3.8: plan of solid ground floor

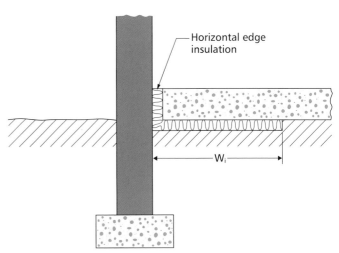

Figure 3.15 Solid ground floor with horizontal edge insulation

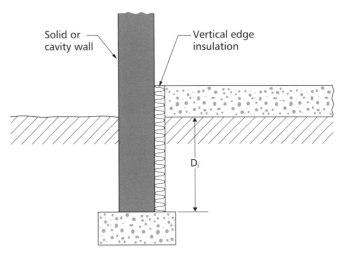

Figure 3.16 Solid ground floor with vertical edge insulation

Hence:

$$L_f = 48 / (0.5 \times 20) = 4.8 \text{ m}$$

$$d_{ef} = 0.3 + 1.5 (0.14 + 0.7 + 0.04) = 1.62 \text{ m}$$

Again, d_{ef} is less than L_f, so using equation 3.30:

$$U_f = \frac{2 \times 1.5}{3.142 \times 4.8 + 1.62} \log_e \left(\frac{3.142 \times 4.8}{1.62} + 1 \right)$$

$$= 0.42 \text{ W·m}^{-2}\text{·K}^{-1}$$

3.5.4 Thermal transmittance of solid ground floors with edge insulation

A slab-on-ground floor may be insulated by means of edge insulation placed either horizontally or vertically round the perimeter of the floor, see Figures 3.15 and 3.16. The following equations are valid provided that no significant thermal bridging is introduced[25].

The U-value of an edge-insulated floor is given by:

$$U_{fi} = U_f + 2 \Psi_{fi} / L_f \qquad (3.33)$$

where U_{fi} is the thermal transmittance of the edge-insulated floor, U_f is the thermal transmittance of the same floor without insulation (W·m^{-2}·K^{-1}), Ψ_{fi} is a factor related to the floor edge insulation (W·m^{-1}·K^{-1}) and L_f is the characteristic dimension of the floor (m), see equation 3.29.

The edge insulation factor Ψ depends on the thermal resistance of the edge insulation, on whether the edge insulation is placed horizontally or vertically and on its width (if horizontal) or depth (if vertical). Low-density foundations, of thermal conductivity less than that of the soil, are treated as vertical edge insulation.

The equations for the determination of the edge factor depend upon the additional equivalent thickness resulting from the edge insulation, d_{ei}' i.e:

$$d_{ei}' = R_i' \lambda_g \qquad (3.34)$$

where d_{ei}' is the additional equivalent thickness of the floor due to edge insulation (m), R_i' is the additional thermal resistance (m^2·K·W^{-1}) due to edge insulation (or foundation) and λ_g is the thermal conductivity of the ground (W·m^{-1}·K^{-1}).

Table 3.22 Edge insulation factor, Ψ_{fi}, for horizontal edge insulation

Soil type	Width of horizontal edge (floor) insulation, W_i (m)	Edge insulation factor, Ψ_{fi} (W·m^{-1}·K^{-1}), for stated additional thermal resistance value, $R_i{'}$ (m^2·K·W^{-1})			
		0.5	1.0	1.5	2.0
Clay/silt	0.50	−0.13	−0.18	−0.21	−0.22
	1.00	−0.20	−0.27	−0.32	−0.34
	1.50	−0.23	−0.33	−0.39	−0.42
Sand/gravel	0.50	−0.17	−0.23	−0.25	−0.27
	1.00	−0.26	−0.35	−0.40	−0.43
	1.50	−0.31	−0.43	−0.50	−0.54
Homogeneous rock	0.50	−0.25	−0.32	−0.35	−0.37
	1.00	−0.41	−0.53	−0.59	−0.62
	1.50	−0.52	−0.68	−0.76	−0.81

$R_i{'}$ is the difference between the thermal resistance of the edge insulation and that of the soil (or slab) it replaces, i.e:

$$R_i{'} = R_{fi} - (d_{fi} / \lambda_g) \tag{3.35}$$

where R_{fi} is the thermal resistance of the floor edge insulation (or foundation) (m^2·K·W^{-1}), d_{fi} is the thickness of the floor edge insulation (or foundation) (m) and λ_g is the thermal conductivity of the ground (W·m^{-1}·K^{-1}).

3.5.4.1 Horizontal edge insulation

For insulation placed horizontally round the perimeter of the floor, see Figure 3.15, the following equation applies:

$$\Psi_{fi} = -\frac{\lambda_g}{\pi} \left[\log_e \left(\frac{W_i}{d_{ef}} + 1 \right) - \log_e \left(\frac{W_i}{d_{ef} + d_{ei}{'}} + 1 \right) \right] \tag{3.36}$$

where Ψ_{fi} is a factor related to the floor edge insulation (W·m^{-1}·K^{-1}), λ_g is the thermal conductivity of the ground (W·m^{-1}·K^{-1}), W_i is the width of the horizontal edge (floor) insulation (m), d_{ef} is the total equivalent thickness of the floor (in the absence of edge insulation) (m) and $d_{ei}{'}$ is the additional equivalent thickness of the floor due to edge insulation (m).

Values of Ψ_{fi} for floors with horizontal edge insulation only are are given in Table 3.22. The wall thickness is taken as 0.3 m.

3.5.4.2 Vertical edge insulation

For insulation placed vertically below ground around the perimeter of the floor, see Figure 3.16, and for foundations of material of lower thermal conductivity than the ground, see Figure 3.17, the following equation applies:

$$\Psi_{fi} = -\frac{\lambda_g}{\pi} \left[\log_e \left(\frac{2D_i}{d_{ef}} + 1 \right) - \log_e \left(\frac{2D_i}{d_{ef} + d_{ei}{'}} + 1 \right) \right] \tag{3.37}$$

where D_i is the depth of the vertical edge (floor) insulation (m), λ_g is the thermal conductivity of the ground (W·m^{-1}·K^{-1}), d_{ef} is the total equivalent thickness of the floor (in the absence of edge insulation) (m) and $d_{ei}{'}$ is the additional equivalent thickness of the floor due to edge insulation (m).

Values of Ψ_{fi} for floors with vertical edge insulation only are are given in Table 3.23. The wall thickness is taken as 0.3 m.

3.5.5 Thermal transmittance of suspended ground floors

A suspended floor is any type of floor not in contact with the ground, e.g. timber or concrete beam-and-block floors, see Figure 3.18.

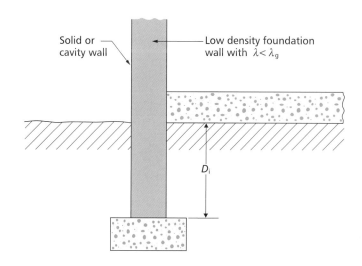

Figure 3.17 Solid ground floor with foundation wall having thermal conductivity less than that of the ground

Table 3.23 Edge insulation factor, Ψ, for vertical edge insulation and for floors with foundation walls having thermal conductivity less than that of the ground

Soil type	Depth of vertical edge (floor) insulation, D_i (m)	Edge insulation factor, Ψ (W·m⁻¹·K⁻¹), for stated additional thermal resistance value, $R_i{}'$ (m²·K·W⁻¹)			
		0.5	1.0	1.5	2.0
Clay/silt	0.25	−0.13	−0.18	−0.21	−0.22
	0.50	−0.20	−0.27	−0.32	−0.34
	0.75	−0.23	−0.33	−0.39	−0.42
	1.00	−0.26	−0.37	−0.43	−0.48
Sand/gravel	0.25	−0.17	−0.23	−0.25	−0.27
	0.50	−0.26	−0.35	−0.40	−0.43
	0.75	−0.31	−0.43	−0.50	−0.54
	1.00	−0.35	−0.49	−0.57	−0.62
Homogeneous rock	0.25	−0.25	−0.32	−0.35	−0.37
	0.50	−0.41	−0.53	−0.59	−0.62
	0.75	−0.52	−0.68	−0.76	−0.81
	1.00	−0.59	−0.79	−0.89	−0.95

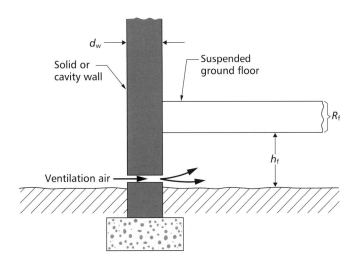

Figure 3.18 Schematic diagram of suspended ground floor

Heat is transferred through a suspended floor to the under floor space, from which it is then transferred to the external environment by three mechanisms:

— through the ground

— through the wall of the under floor space

— by ventilation of the under floor space.

The thermal transmittance, allowing for the combination of these mechanisms, is given by:

$$U_{fs} = [(1 / U_f) + 1 / (U_{fg} + U_{eu})]^{-1} \qquad (3.38)$$

where U_{fs} is the combined thermal transmittance of the uninsulated suspended floor structure (W·m⁻²·K⁻¹), U_f is the thermal transmittance of the (uninsulated) floor, U_{fg} is the thermal transmittance for heat flow through the ground (W·m⁻²·K⁻¹) and U_{eu} is the equivalent thermal transmittance for heat flow through the walls surrounding the under floor space and by ventilation of the under floor space (W·m⁻²·K⁻¹).

U_f may be determined by the methods given in section 3.3, taking the surface resistances on both sides of the floor as 0.14 m²·K·W⁻¹.

The thermal transmittance for heat flow through the ground, U_{fg}, should be calculated as for a solid ground floor, using equation 3.31 or 3.32 as appropriate, but substituting a total equivalent thickness for the ground, d_{eg}, in place of d_{ef}. This equivalent thickness is given by:

$$d_{eg} = d_w + \lambda_g (R_{si} + R_{ig} + R_{se}) \qquad (3.39)$$

where d_{eg} is the total equivalent thickness of the ground (m), d_w is the thickness of wall surrounding the ground floor (m), λ_g is the thermal conductivity of the ground (W·m⁻¹·K⁻¹), R_{si} is the internal surface resistance (m²·K·W⁻¹), R_{ig} is the thermal resistance of the insulation between the floor and the ground (m²·K·W⁻¹) and R_{se} is the external surface resistance (m²·K·W⁻¹).

The general expression for U_{eu} is:

$$U_{eu} = (2 h_f U_u / L_f) + 1450 \, \alpha v_w F_w / L_f \qquad (3.40)$$

Where U_{eu} is the equivalent thermal transmittance for heat flow through the walls surrounding the under floor space and by ventilation of the under floor space (W·m⁻²·K⁻¹), h_f is the height of the floor above external ground level (m), U_u is the thermal transmittance of the walls surrounding the underfloor space above ground level (W·m⁻²·K⁻¹), L_f is the characteristic dimension of the floor (m) (see equation 3.29), α is the area of ventilation openings per unit perimeter of underfloor space (m), v_w is the average wind speed at 10 m height above ground level (m·s⁻¹) and F_w is the wind shielding factor.

If h_f varies around the perimeter of the floor, the average value should be used.

The wind shielding factor relates the wind speed at 10 m height above ground level (assumed unobstructed) to that near ground level, allowing for shielding by adjacent buildings etc. Representative values are as follows:

— sheltered location (city centre): $F_w = 0.02$

— average location (suburban): $F_w = 0.05$

— exposed location (rural): $F_w = 0.10$.

3.5.5.1 Uninsulated suspended floors

Table 3.24 gives U-values for uninsulated suspended floors for the following values of the relevant parameters:

— thermal resistance of floor: $R_f = 0.2 \text{ m}^2 \cdot \text{K} \cdot \text{W}^{-1}$

— ventilation opening: $\alpha = 0.0015$ or 0.003 m

— average wind velocity: $v_w = 3 \text{ m} \cdot \text{s}^{-1}$

— wind shielding factor (average exposure): $F_w = 0.05$

— uninsulated under floor walls: $U_u = 1.7 \text{ W} \cdot \text{m}^{-2} \cdot \text{K}^{-1}$

— height of floor above external ground level: $h_f = 0.5$ m.

Table 3.24 may be used in most cases to obtain the U-value of a suspended floor. However, if the parameters of the actual design differ significantly from the above values, the U-value should be calculated using the equations given above.

3.5.5.2 U-values of insulated suspended floors

For floors having thermal resistances other than 0.2 $\text{m}^2 \cdot \text{K} \cdot \text{W}^{-1}$, the U-value can be obtained from:

$$U_{fsi} = [(1/U_{fs}) - 0.2 + R_f]^{-1} \qquad (3.41)$$

where U_{fsi} is the thermal transmittance of the insulated suspended floor ($\text{W} \cdot \text{m}^{-2} \cdot \text{K}^{-1}$), U_{fs} is the combined thermal transmittance of the uninsulated floor (obtained from Table 3.24) ($\text{W} \cdot \text{m}^{-2} \cdot \text{K}^{-1}$) and R_f is the thermal resistance of the floor ($\text{m}^2 \cdot \text{K} \cdot \text{W}^{-1}$).

Example 3.9: U-value for insulated suspended timber floor

A detached building has a ground floor plan of 9.5 m by 8.2 m with a suspended timber floor consisting of 19 mm chipboard on joists (50 mm by 100 mm at 400 mm centres) with 100 mm of insulation between the joists. The thermal conductivity of the insulation is 0.04 $\text{W} \cdot \text{m}^{-1} \cdot \text{K}^{-1}$ and the thermal conductivity of both the chipboard and the joists is 0.14 $\text{W} \cdot \text{m}^{-1} \cdot \text{K}^{-1}$. The area of the ventilation openings per unit perimeter length is 0.0015 m. The floor is over clay-type soil and of average exposure.

The perimeter is 35.4 m and the plan area of the ground floor is 77.9 m^2. Thus $(p_f/A_{fg}) = 0.45 \text{ m}^{-1}$. From Table 3.24, the U-value for an uninsulated suspended floor of this size is 0.73 $\text{W} \cdot \text{m}^{-2} \cdot \text{K}^{-1}$.

The thermal resistance of the floor is the sum of the thermal resistance of the homogeneous chipboard and the combined thermal resistance of the joists and intervening insulation.

From equation 3.11 the thermal resistance of the insulation, bridged by the joists, is:

$$R_b = [(P_m/R_m) + (P_n/R_n)]^{-1}$$

The proportions of surface area and thermal resistances are:

— insulation: $P_m = (350/400), R_m = (0.1/0.04)$

— joists: $P_n = (50/400), R_n = (0.1/0.14)$

Therefore, the thermal resistance of the floor is:

$$R_f = \frac{0.019}{0.14} + \left(\frac{350}{400} \times \frac{0.04}{0.1} + \frac{50}{400} \times \frac{0.14}{0.1}\right)^{-1}$$

$$= 2.04 \text{ m}^2 \cdot \text{K} \cdot \text{W}^{-1}$$

Table 3.24 U-values for uninsulated suspended floors

Ratio p_f/A_{fg} (m^{-1})	U-value (W·m^{-2}·K^{-1}) for stated soil type and ventilation opening, α (m)					
	Clay/silt		Sand/gravel		Homogeneous rock	
	0.0015	0.003	0.0015	0.003	0.0015	0.003
0.05	0.16	0.17	0.19	0.20	0.27	0.28
0.10	0.27	0.29	0.32	0.33	0.43	0.44
0.15	0.36	0.38	0.42	0.43	0.54	0.55
0.20	0.44	0.46	0.49	0.51	0.63	0.64
0.25	0.50	0.52	0.56	0.58	0.70	0.71
0.30	0.56	0.58	0.62	0.64	0.76	0.77
0.35	0.61	0.63	0.67	0.69	0.81	0.82
0.40	0.65	0.68	0.72	0.74	0.85	0.87
0.45	0.69	0.72	0.76	0.78	0.89	0.91
0.50	0.73	0.76	0.79	0.82	0.92	0.94
0.55	0.76	0.79	0.83	0.85	0.95	0.97
0.60	0.79	0.83	0.86	0.88	0.98	1.00
0.65	0.82	0.85	0.88	0.91	1.00	1.02
0.70	0.85	0.88	0.91	0.94	1.03	1.05
0.75	0.87	0.91	0.93	0.96	1.05	1.07
0.80	0.90	0.93	0.95	0.98	1.06	1.09
0.85	0.92	0.95	0.97	1.00	1.08	1.11
0.90	0.94	0.97	0.99	1.02	1.10	1.12
0.95	0.96	0.99	1.01	1.04	1.11	1.14
1.00	0.98	1.01	1.03	1.06	1.13	1.15

Hence, using equation 3.41:

$$U_{fsi} = [(1/0.73) - 0.2 + 2.04]^{-1} = 0.31 \text{ W·m}^{-2}\text{·K}^{-1}$$

3.5.6 Thermal transmittance of basement floors and walls

Thermal transmittances for basement floors and walls are obtained separately[26]. The U-value for the floor depends upon the ratio of the perimeter of the floor to its area, and on the depth of the basement floor below ground level. The U-value for the walls depends on the depth of the basement and the properties of the materials used in the wall construction.

A U-value may also be defined for the basement as a whole, as follows:

$$U_b = \frac{A_b U_{bf} + h_b p_{bf} U_{bw}}{A_b + h_b p_{bf}} \tag{3.42}$$

where U_b is the average thermal transmittance of the basement (W·m^{-2}·K^{-1}), A_b is the area of the basement floor (m^2), U_{bf} is the thermal transmittance of the basement floor (W·m^{-2}·K^{-1}), h_b is the depth of the basement below ground level (m), p_{bf} is the perimeter of the basement (m) and U_{bw} is the thermal transmittance of the basement wall (W·m^{-2}·K^{-1}). Values of U_{bf} and U_{bw} given in Tables 3.25 and 3.26, respectively.

Sometimes a more precise value may be required, e.g. when comparing thermal transmittances to determine the optimum thickness of insulation. In such cases the more detailed method described in *BS EN ISO 13370*[24] may be used.

The basement floor area, A_b, is measured between the finished internal faces of the walls bounding the basement. The perimeter, p_b, is measured along the finished internal faces, The basement depth, h_b, is measured between the outside ground level and the finished internal surface of the basement floor, see Figure 3.19(a). The depth, h_b, will often be less than the internal height of the basement storey, in which case the U-value obtained by equation 3.42 will apply to the area of basement wall below ground level. Any wall above ground level should be assessed using the methods for walls given in sections 3.3.10 and 3.3.11.

To obtain a U-value for split-level basements and basements on sloping sites the average depth of the basement below ground level should be used, averaged around its perimeter. For the simple case shown in Figure 3.19(b):

$$h_b = (h_{b1} + h_{b2})/2 \tag{3.43}$$

3.5.6.1 Uninsulated basement floors

Table 3.25 gives U-values for uninsulated basement floors in terms of the ratio of basement perimeter to floor area, p_b / A_b, and the depth of the basement, h_b. Linear interpolation may be used to determine intermediate values.

Table 3.25 U-values for uninsulated basement floors

Ratio, p_b/A_b (m^{-1})	U-value of basement floor, U_{bf} (W·m^{-2}·K^{-1}), for stated basement depth, h_b (m)				
	0.5	1.0	1.5	2.0	2.5
0.1	0.20	0.19	0.18	0.17	0.16
0.2	0.34	0.31	0.29	0.27	0.26
0.3	0.44	0.41	0.38	0.35	0.33
0.4	0.53	0.48	0.44	0.41	0.38
0.5	0.61	0.55	0.50	0.46	0.43
0.6	0.68	0.61	0.55	0.50	0.46
0.7	0.74	0.65	0.59	0.53	0.49
0.8	0.79	0.70	0.62	0.56	0.51
0.9	0.84	0.73	0.65	0.58	0.53
1.0	0.89	0.77	0.68	0.60	0.54

Table 3.26 U-values for basement walls

Thermal resistance of basement walls, R_{bw} (m^2·K·W^{-1})	U-value of basement walls, U_{bw} (W·m^{-2}·K^{-1}), for stated basement depth, h_b (m)				
	0.5	1.0	1.5	2.0	2.5
0.2	1.55	1.16	0.95	0.81	0.71
0.5	0.98	0.78	0.66	0.58	0.52
1.0	0.61	0.51	0.45	0.40	0.37
2.0	0.35	0.30	0.27	0.25	0.24
2.5	0.28	0.25	0.23	0.21	0.20

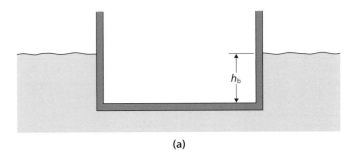

(a)

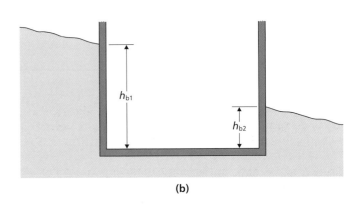

(b)

Figure 3.19 Depth of basement; (a) building on level site, (b) building on sloping site

3.5.6.2   Insulated basement floors

An approximate U-value for insulated basement floors may be obtained by using Table 3.25 to determine the value for an uninsulated basement floor of the same dimensions and modifying the value obtained as follows:

$$U_{bi} = [(1 / U_b) + R_{fbi}]^{-1} \qquad (3.44)$$

where U_{bi} is the thermal transmittance of insulated basement floor ($\text{W·m}^{-2}\text{·K}^{-1}$), U_b is the thermal transmittance of uninsulated basement floor of same dimensions ($\text{W·m}^{-2}\text{·K}^{-1}$) and R_{fbi} is the thermal resistance of the insulation layers incorporated into basement floor ($\text{m}^2\text{·K·W}^{-1}$).

The thermal resistance, R_{fbi}, should not include the thermal resistance of the floor slab or any surface resistances since these are already incorporated into the U-value for the uninsulated basement floor, U_b.

3.5.6.3   Basement walls

Table 3.26 gives U-values for basement walls as a function of the basement depth, h_b, and the thermal resistance of the basement walls, R_{bw}. The inside and outside surface resistances are taken into account in the tabulated U-values and are therefore not to be included when calculating R_{bw}.

If any insulating layers are bridged, e.g. by timber studding or mortar joints in the case of low-density concrete blockwork, the overall thermal resistance should be calculated using the combined method, see section 3.3.11.3.

3.6   Windows

3.6.1   General

The thermal transmittance of windows is made up of three components:

—   glazing (excluding frame or sash)

—   frame or sash

—   spacer between panes (in multiple glazing units)

These components are determined separately as shown in the following sections. The overall U-value of the window is given by:

$$U_w = \frac{A_g U_g + A_{wf} U_{wf} + p_{wf}\, \Psi_s}{A_g + A_{wf}} \qquad (3.45)$$

where U_w is the thermal transmittance of the window ($\text{W·m}^{-2}\text{·K}^{-1}$), A_g is the projected area of the glazing (m^2), A_{wf} is the projected area of the window frame or sash (m^2), U_g is the thermal transmittance of the glazing ($\text{W·m}^{-2}\text{·K}^{-1}$), U_{wf} is the thermal transmittance of the window frame or sash ($\text{W·m}^{-2}\text{·K}^{-1}$), p_{wf} is the length of inner perimeter of the window frame or sash (m) and Ψ_s is the linear thermal transmittance due to the window spacer ($\text{W·m}^{-1}\text{·K}^{-1}$).

The dimensions defined are shown in Figure 3.20.

3.6.2   Glazing (excluding frame or sash)

Tables 3.27 and 3.28 provide U-values for vertical, horizontal and near horizontal sloping glazing combinations for conventional and low-emissivity coated glasses, and for glazing units filled with argon gas. These values were calculated using the method given in BS 6993[2]. A more recent standard, BS EN 673[27], has been published which gives identical values.

Low emissivity coatings are highly transparent in the visual and solar parts of the spectrum but are reflective to radiation with wavelength greater than 5 µm (i.e. far-infrared). To achieve a worthwhile improvement the emissivity must be less than 0.2 and accredited data must be obtained from the manufacturer to confirm that a particular product achieves this performance.

Values have been calculated for the surface resistance values adopted in BS EN ISO 6946[17] and for those corresponding to the conditions of exposure defined in section 3.3.9.4.

For the purposes of the Building Regulations[4], 'vertical' includes glazing up to 20° from the vertical.

The data are given to two decimal places to illustrate the trends, whereas U-values are usually quoted to two significant figures elsewhere in this Guide.

The tabulated values are based on a temperature difference of 15 K between the outer and inner glass surfaces and a mean temperature of 10°C. It is recommended that this basis be used for comparison purposes and in normal building calculations in the UK. For more severe climates, a greater temperature difference and a lower mean temperature may be considered but the quoted values are sufficiently accurate for most cases.

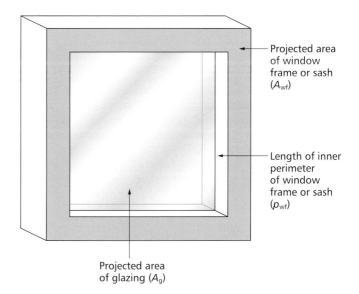

Figure 3.20 Dimensions of window for calculation purposes

Table 3.27 *U*-values for vertical glazing

Type of glazing	Spacing (mm)	*U*-value based on *BS EN ISO 6946* † (W·m^{-2}·K^{-1})	*U*-value (W·m^{-2}·K^{-1}) for stated exposure of panes ‡		
			Sheltered	Normal	Severe
Single	—	5.94	5.00	5.56	6.67
Double	25	2.86	2.62	2.76	3.01
	20	2.84	2.61	2.75	3.00
	16	2.85	2.61	2.76	3.01
	12	2.94	2.69	2.85	3.11
	9	3.11	2.83	3.00	3.30
	6	3.39	3.07	3.27	3.62
Triple	25	1.78	1.69	1.75	1.84
	20	1.79	1.69	1.75	1.85
	16	1.84	1.74	1.80	1.90
	12	1.96	1.84	1.91	2.03
	9	2.11	1.98	2.06	2.19
	6	2.38	2.21	2.31	2.49
Coated double ($\varepsilon = 0.2$)	20	1.85	1.74	1.81	1.91
	16	1.86	1.75	1.82	1.92
	12	2.03	1.90	1.98	2.10
	9	2.31	2.15	2.25	2.41
	6	2.76	2.54	2.67	2.91
Coated double ($\varepsilon = 0.1$)	20	1.60	1.52	1.57	1.65
	16	1.61	1.54	1.58	1.66
	12	1.80	1.71	1.77	1.86
	9	2.11	1.98	2.06	2.20
Coated double (argon-filled; $\varepsilon = 0.2$)	20	1.61	1.53	1.58	1.66
	16	1.60	1.52	1.57	1.65
	12	1.70	1.62	1.67	1.76
	9	1.93	1.82	1.89	2.00
	6	2.31	2.16	2.25	2.42
Coated double (argon-filled; $\varepsilon = 0.1$)	20	1.33	1.28	1.31	1.37
	16	1.33	1.27	1.31	1.36
	12	1.44	1.38	1.42	1.48
	9	1.69	1.61	1.66	1.75
	6	2.12	1.99	2.07	2.21

† Calculated using *BS EN ISO 6946* [17] values of surface resistance, see Tables 3.9 and 3.10
‡ Calculated using 'traditional' values of surface resistance, see Tables 3.9 and 3.10
Notes:
(1) Excludes effect of thermal resistivity of the glass (see equation 3.46).
(2) Insulating effect of low emissivity coatings is independent of which surface within the space is coated

The resistivity of window glass is usually negligible and has been ignored in calculating the tabulated values. However, the resistivity may be taken into to account by means of the following equation:

$$U_{gg}' = [(1 / U_g) + d_g r_g]^{-1} \qquad (3.46)$$

where U_{gg}' is the thermal transmittance of the glazing corrected for the resistivity of glass (W·m^{-2}·K^{-1}), U_g is the thermal transmittance of the glazing (W·m^{-2}·K^{-1}), d_g is the total thickness of the glass panes (m) and r_g is the thermal resistivity of the glass (m·K·W^{-1}).

The thermal resistivity of glass is approximately 1.0 m·K·W^{-1}.

3.6.3 Frames and sashes (excluding glazing)

The *U*-values given in Table 3.29 are based on data given in Norwegian Standard *NS 3031*[28]. These values were obtained either experimentally or by finite element analysis and take account of the fact that the total frame area is greater than the projected area.

3.6.4 Spacer between panes (multiple glazing units)

In multiple glazing units, the thermal transmittance is increased due to thermal bridging at the edges by the metal spacers separating the panes. This can be evaluated in terms of a linear thermal transmittance.

3.6.4.1 Metal spacers

For conventional sealed multiple glazing units, in which a metal internal spacer is roughly level with the frame, the values given in Table 3.30 may be used.

For multiple glazing units in which the internal spacer is not level with the frame, see Figure 3.21, the linear thermal

Table 3.28 U-values for horizontal and roof glazing

Type of glazing	Spacing (mm)	U-value based on BS EN ISO 6946 † ($W \cdot m^{-2} \cdot K^{-1}$)	U-value ($W \cdot m^{-2} \cdot K^{-1}$) for stated exposure of panes ‡		
			Sheltered	Normal	Severe
Single	—	7.75	5.88	7.14	8.33
Double	25	3.57	3.11	3.43	3.69
	20	3.60	3.13	3.46	3.72
	16	3.63	3.16	3.49	3.75
	12	3.67	3.19	3.53	3.79
	9	3.71	3.22	3.56	3.84
	6	3.92	3.38	3.76	4.06
Coated double ($\varepsilon = 0.2$)	20	2.61	2.36	2.54	2.68
	16	2.66	2.40	2.58	2.73
	12	2.72	2.45	2.64	2.79
	9	2.78	2.50	2.70	2.86
	6	3.10	2.75	3.00	3.19
Coated double ($\varepsilon = 0.1$)	20	2.39	2.18	2.33	2.44
	16	2.44	2.22	2.38	2.50
	12	2.51	2.27	2.44	2.57
	9	2.58	2.33	2.50	2.64
Coated double (argon-filled; $\varepsilon = 0.2$)	20	2.20	2.02	2.15	2.25
	16	2.24	2.05	2.19	2.29
	12	2.29	2.09	2.23	2.34
	9	2.34	2.14	2.28	2.39
	6	2.55	2.31	2.48	2.61
Coated double (argon-filled; $\varepsilon = 0.1$)	20	1.94	1.80	1.90	1.97
	16	1.98	1.83	1.94	2.02
	12	2.04	1.88	1.99	2.08
	9	2.10	1.93	2.05	2.14
	6	2.32	2.12	2.26	2.37

† Calculated using BS EN ISO 6946 [17] values of surface resistance, see Tables 3.9 and 3.10
‡ Calculated using 'traditional' values of surface resistance, see Tables 3.9 and 3.10
Notes:
(1) Excludes effect of thermal resistivity of the glass (see equation 3.46).
(2) Insulating effect of low emissivity coatings is independent of which surface within the space is coated

transmittance may be determined from the following equation:

$$\Psi_s = \frac{(U_{gs} / U_g) C d_{gb}}{R_{se} + R_{si} + d_g r_g} + \phi_s \qquad (3.47)$$

where Ψ_s is the linear thermal transmittance due to the window spacer ($W \cdot m^{-1} \cdot K^{-1}$), U_{gs} is the thermal transmittance of the glazing with 12 mm separation (normal exposure) ($W \cdot m^{-2} \cdot K^{-1}$), U_g is the thermal transmittance of the glazing ($W \cdot m^{-2} \cdot K^{-1}$), C is a constant related to the depth of the spacer below the edge of the frame, d_{gb} is the average thickness of the bounding panes (m), R_{se} is the external surface resistance ($m^2 \cdot K \cdot W^{-1}$), R_{si} is the internal surface resistance ($m^2 \cdot K \cdot W^{-1}$), r_g is the thermal resistivity of the glass ($m^2 \cdot K \cdot W^{-1}$), d_g is the total thickness of the glass panes (m) and ϕ_s is a factor related to the thermal transmittance of the frame.

Values of C are given in Table 3.31. The equation assumes that there is no heat transfer from the edge of the glazing to the frame itself. This simple treatment of the thermal bridging is found to give good agreement with measured thermal transmittance and finite element analysis of heat transfer at the edges.

Table 3.29 Thermal transmittances for various types of window frame and sash

Material	Description	U-value ($W \cdot m^{-2} \cdot K^{-1}$)
Wood	Average thickness > 80 mm	1.6
	Average thickness 50–80 mm	2.0
	Average thickness < 50 mm	2.8
Plastic	Without metal reinforcement	2.8
	With metal reinforcement	3.2
Aluminium	Thermal barrier† with thermal path length > 10 mm	3.6
	Thermal barrier† with thermal path length < 10 mm	4.6
Aluminium or steel	Without thermal barrier	7.0

† Thermal barrier must be continuous and totally isolate the interior side of the frame or frame sections from the exterior side.

The factor ϕ_s takes the value 0.1 where the U-value of the frame exceeds 3 $W \cdot m^{-2} \cdot K^{-1}$, to account for the effect of the spacer on the performance of the frame. Where the U-value of the frame is less than 3 $W \cdot m^{-2} \cdot K^{-1}$, ϕ_s is set to zero.

Table 3.30 Linear thermal transmittance for conventional sealed multiple glazing units

Average thickness of bounding panes (mm)	Linear thermal transmittance† ($\mathrm{W \cdot m^{-1} \cdot K^{-1}}$)	Linear thermal transmittance for stated conditions of exposure ($\mathrm{W \cdot m^{-1} \cdot K^{-1}}$)		
		Sheltered	Normal	Severe
4	0.04	0.03	0.04	0.04
6	0.06	0.05	0.05	0.06
10	0.09	0.07	0.08	0.09
12	0.11	0.09	0.10	0.11

† Calculated using *BS EN ISO 6946*[17] values of surface resistance, see Tables 3.9 and 3.10

Table 3.31 Values of constant related to depth of spacer below frame

Depth of spacer below frame (mm)	Constant, C
0	1.6
5	1.2
10	0.9

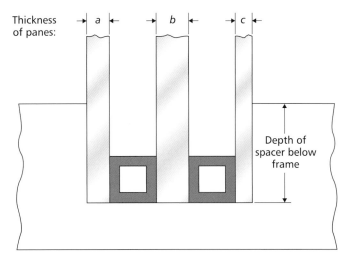

Total thickness of panes: $d_g = a + b + c$

Average thickness of bounding panes: $d_{gb} = \dfrac{a+c}{2}$

Figure 3.21 Cross section through multiple glazing unit

3.6.4.2   Non-metallic spacers

The effect of non-metallic spacers may be taken into account as described above but equation 3.47 must be modified by introducing an additional thermal resistance term to the denominator, i.e:

$$\Psi_s = \frac{(U_{gs}/U_g)\, C\, d_{gb}}{R_{se} + R_{si} + d_g r_g + d_s r_s} + \phi_s \qquad (3.48)$$

where d_s is the thickness of the of the window spacer (m) and r_s is the average thermal resistivity of the window spacer material and sealant ($\mathrm{m \cdot K \cdot W^{-1}}$).

3.6.5   Effect of blinds and curtains

3.6.5.1   Internal blinds and curtains

Internal roller blinds or curtains provide additional insulation due to the air enclosed between the window and the blind. The degree of insulation depends strongly on the level of enclosure achieved[29].

Good levels of air entrapment are almost impossible to achieve with curtains. Roller blinds can achieve effective entrapment provided they run in side channels and are sealed at the top and bottom. With well-sealed blinds, further improvement can be achieved by using a material which has a low emissivity surface protected by layer transparent to infrared radiation.

The thermal transmittance of the window can be corrected for the effect of blinds or curtains, as follows:

$$U_{wb}' = [(1/U_w) + R_{bi}]^{-1} \qquad (3.49)$$

Table 3.32 Thermal resistance of blinds and curtains

Description	Thermal resistance ($\mathrm{m^2 \cdot K \cdot W^{-1}}$)
Conventional roller blind, curtain or venetian blind (vertical slats)	0.05
Closely fitting curtain with pelmet	0.07
Roller blind:	
— bottom only sealed	0.09
— sides only sealed in channels	0.11
— sides and top sealed	0.15
— sides and bottom sealed	0.16
— fully sealed	0.18
Low emissivity roller blind, fully sealed	0.44

where U_{wb}' is the thermal transmittance of the window corrected for an internal blind or curtain ($\mathrm{W \cdot m^{-2} \cdot K^{-1}}$), U_w is the thermal transmittance of the window ($\mathrm{W \cdot m^{-2} \cdot K^{-1}}$), R_{bi} is the thermal resistance of the internal blind or curtain ($\mathrm{m^2 \cdot K \cdot W^{-1}}$).

Values for the thermal resistance of internal blinds and curtains are given in Table 3.32.

3.6.5.2   Mid-pane blinds

Coupled windows are usually fitted with horizontal slatted or roller blinds between the panes. The effect on the insulation of the window with the blind lowered can be estimated by adding the thermal resistance of the blind to that of the glazing, as follows:

$$U_{gb}' = [(1/U_g) + R_{bm}]^{-1} \qquad (3.50)$$

where U_{gb}' is the thermal transmittance of the glazing corrected for a mid-pane blind ($\mathrm{W \cdot m^{-2} \cdot K^{-1}}$), U_g is the thermal transmittance of the glazing ($\mathrm{W \cdot m^{-2} \cdot K^{-1}}$) and R_{bm} is the thermal resistance of the mid-pane blind ($\mathrm{m^2 \cdot K \cdot W^{-1}}$).

Values of thermal resistance for mid-pane blinds are given in Table 3.33.

Table 3.33 Thermal resistance of mid-pane blinds

Description	Thermal resistance ($m^2 \cdot K \cdot W^{-1}$)
Venetian blind:	
— slats horizontal	0.02
— slats vertical	0.07
Roller blind	0.07

Table 3.34 Indicative U-values for conceptual design

Type	Indicative U-value ($W \cdot m^{-2} \cdot K^{-1}$)	
	Glazing only	Window (including frame or sash)
Single	5.7	5.0
Double	2.8	3.0
Double (low emissivity)	2.0	2.3
Triple	2.0	2.3

3.6.6 Indicative *U*-values for conceptual design

At the concept design stage, it is convenient to use indicative U-values for typical window configurations to enable an initial evaluation of the heat losses and energy consumption of the proposed building. Table 3.34 provides values for such purposes.

These values have been calculated using the procedures described in detail in subsequent sections assuming 6 mm glass, a glazed area of 2 m^2 and an internal spacer of 12 mm thickness.

3.6.7 Indicative *U*-values for Building Regulations

Table 3.35, based on Table 2 from *Building Regulations Approved Document L*[5], gives indicative U-values for the purposes of Building Regulations in England and Wales.

3.6.8 *U*-values for typical windows

Tables 3.36 and 3.37 provide U-values for typical windows with ordinary glass and with glasses of emissivity in the range 0.1–0.2 with both air- and argon-filled spaces, these data have been derived from *BS 6993: Part 1*[2]. U-values for triple glazing units may be taken as equal to those for the equivalent double glazing unit with low emissivity coating.

3.6.9 Measurement of thermal transmittance

The thermal transmittance of windows may be determined by direct measurement. This may be necessary where the design of the window is such that the foregoing methods are not applicable or where the manufacturer believes that the performance of the window is better than that predicted[30]. *BS 874: Part 3*[1] (which is likely to be superseded by *prEN 12412: Part 1*[31]) gives a precise methodology for the measurement of the U-values of windows using hot-box techniques.

3.7 Non-steady state thermal characteristics

3.7.1 Admittance procedure

There are several methods available for assessing the non-steady state or dynamic performance of a structure. One of the simplest is the admittance procedure[32] which is described in detail in Section 5: *Thermal response and plant sizing*. The method of calculation of admittances and related parameters is defined in *EN ISO 13786*[33] and a summary is given in Appendix 3.A6

This procedure requires the calculation of three parameters in addition to the thermal transmittance: admittance, surface factor and decrement factor. These parameters depend upon the thickness, thermal conductivity, density

Table 3.35 Indicative U-values for *Building Regulations* (Crown copyright, reproduced by permission of the Controller of Her Majesty's Stationery Office)

Item	Indicative U-value ($W \cdot m^{-2} \cdot K^{-1}$) for single glazing for stated frame type			
	Wood	Metal	Thermal break	PVC-U
Window, single glazed	4.7	5.8	5.3	4.7

	Indicative U-value ($W \cdot m^{-2} \cdot K^{-1}$) for double and triple glazing (sealed) for stated frame type and stated thickness of airgap (mm)							
	Wood		Metal		Thermal break		PVC-U	
	6	12	6	12	6	12	6	12
Window, double glazed	3.3	3.0	4.2	3.8	3.6	3.3	3.3	3.0
Window, double glazed, low-emissivity	2.9	2.4	3.7	3.2	3.1	2.6	2.9	2.4
Window, double glazed, argon-filled	3.1	2.9	4.0	3.7	3.4	3.2	3.1	2.9
Window, double glazed, argon-filled low-emissivity	2.6	2.2	3.4	2.9	2.8	2.4	2.6	2.2
Window, triple glazed	2.6	2.4	3.4	3.2	2.9	2.6	2.6	2.4
Rooflights, double glazed at less than 70° to horizontal	3.6	3.4	4.6	4.4	4.0	3.8	3.6	3.4

Table 3.36 *U*-values for typical windows: single glazed

Frame/sash type	Projected frame area as percentage of total area (%)	*U*-value based on *BS EN ISO 6946* † ($W \cdot m^{-2} \cdot K^{-1}$)	*U*-value ($W \cdot m^{-2} \cdot K$) for stated exposure of panes‡		
			Sheltered	Normal	Severe
Wood; average thickness > 80 mm	10	5.8	4.7	5.2	6.2
	20	5.3	4.3	4.8	5.6
	30	4.9	4.0	4.4	5.1
Wood; average thickness 50–80 mm	10	5.8	4.7	5.2	6.2
	20	5.4	4.4	4.8	5.7
	30	5.0	4.1	4.5	5.3
Wood; average thickness < 55 mm	10	5.9	4.8	5.3	6.3
	20	5.6	4.6	5.0	5.9
	30	5.2	4.3	4.7	5.5
Plastic; no metal reinforcement	10	5.9	4.8	5.3	6.3
	20	5.6	4.6	5.0	5.9
	30	5.2	4.3	4.7	5.5
Plastic; with metal reinforcement	10	6.0	4.9	5.4	6.4
	20	5.7	4.7	5.2	6.0
	30	5.5	4.6	5.0	5.7
Aluminium or steel; no thermal barrier	10	6.3	5.2	5.7	6.7
	20	6.4	5.4	5.8	6.7
	30	6.5	5.6	6.0	6.8
Aluminium; with thermal barrier§ with thermal path length < 10 mm	10	6.1	5.0	5.5	6.5
	20	6.0	5.0	5.4	6.3
	30	5.9	5.0	5.4	6.2
Aluminium; with thermal barrier§ with thermal path length > 10 mm	10	6.0	4.9	5.4	6.4
	20	5.7	4.7	5.2	6.0
	30	5.5	4.6	5.0	5.7

† Calculated using *BS EN ISO 6946*[17] values of surface resistance, see Tables 3.9 and 3.10
‡ Calculated using 'traditional' values of surface resistance, see Tables 3.9 and 3.10
§ Thermal barrier must be continuous and totally isolate the interior side of the frame or frame sections from the exterior side

Table 3.37 *U*-values for typical windows: double glazed

Frame/sash type	Projected frame area as percentage of total area (%)	*U*-value based on *BS EN ISO 6946* † ($W \cdot m^{-2} \cdot K^{-1}$)	*U*-value ($W \cdot m^{-2} \cdot K^{-1}$) for stated exposure of panes		
			Sheltered	Normal	Severe
Wood; average thickness > 80 mm	10	3.1	2.7	2.9	3.2
	20	2.9	2.6	2.7	3.0
	30	2.7	2.5	2.6	2.8
Wood; average thickness 50–80 mm	10	3.1	2.8	2.9	3.2
	20	3.0	2.7	2.8	3.1
	30	2.9	2.6	2.7	2.9
Wood; average thickness < 55 mm	10	3.2	2.9	3.0	3.3
	20	3.1	2.9	3.0	3.2
	30	3.1	2.8	3.0	3.2
Plastic; no metal reinforcement	10	3.2	2.9	3.0	3.3
	20	3.1	2.9	3.0	3.2
	30	3.2	2.8	3.0	3.2
Plastic; with metal reinforcement	10	3.3	2.9	3.1	3.4
	20	3.3	3.0	3.1	3.4
	30	3.3	3.1	3.2	3.4
Aluminium or steel; no thermal barrier	10	3.6	3.3	3.4	3.7
	20	4.0	3.7	3.8	4.1
	30	4.4	4.1	4.2	4.4
Aluminium; with thermal barrier§ with thermal path length < 10 mm	10	3.4	3.1	3.2	3.5
	20	3.6	3.3	3.4	3.7
	30	3.8	3.5	3.6	3.8
Aluminium; with thermal barrier§ with thermal path length > 10 mm	10	3.3	2.9	3.1	3.4
	20	3.3	3.0	3.1	3.4
	30	3.3	3.1	3.1	3.4

† Calculated using *BS EN ISO 6946*[17] values of surface resistance, see Tables 3.9 and 3.10
‡ Calculated using 'traditional' values of surface resistance, see Tables 3.9 and 3.10
§ Thermal barrier must be continuous and totally isolate the interior side of the frame or frame sections from the exterior side

and specific heat capacity of the materials used within the structure and the relative positions of the various elements that make up the construction. Each of these parameters is expressed as an amplitude and an associated time lead/lag.

3.7.1.1 Thermal admittance (Y-value)

The most significant of the three parameters is the admittance. This is the rate of flow of heat between the internal surface of the structure and the environmental temperature in the space, for each degree of deviation of the space temperature about its mean value. The associated time dependency takes the form of a time lead.

For a thin single-layer structure, the admittance is equal in amplitude to the U-value and has a time lead of zero. The amplitude tends towards a limiting value for thicknesses greater than about 100 mm.

For multi-layered structures, the admittance is primarily determined by the characteristics of the materials in the layers nearest to the internal surface. For example, the admittance of a structure comprising heavyweight concrete slabs lined internally with insulation will be close to the value for the insulation alone. However, placing the insulation within the construction, or on the outside surface will have little or no effect on the admittance.

3.7.1.2 Decrement factor (f)

The decrement factor is the ratio of the rate of flow of heat through the structure to the environmental temperature in the space for each degree of deviation in external temperature about its mean value, to the steady state rate of flow of heat (U-value). The associated time dependency takes the form of a time lag.

For thin structures of low thermal capacity, the amplitude of the decrement factor is unity with a time lag of zero. The amplitude decreases and the time lag increases with increasing thickness and/or thermal capacity.

3.7.1.3 Surface factor (F)

The surface factor is the ratio of the variation of heat flow about its mean value readmitted to the space from the surface, to the variation of heat flow about its mean value absorbed by the surface. The associated time dependency takes the form of a time lag.

The amplitude of the surface factor decreases and its time lag increases with increasing thermal conductivity but both are virtually constant with thickness.

3.7.2 Internal structural elements

For internal structural elements, such as floors and partition walls, which are not symmetrical about their mid-plane, the dynamic responses will be different for the two faces and two sets of admittances and surface factors are required. The decrement factor is the same for heat flow in either direction.

Where internal structures divide spaces in which the thermal conditions are identical, the energy transfers can be simplified by combining the admittance and surface factor with the decrement factor to give modified admittance and surface factor respectively.

3.7.3 Effect of thermal bridging

The presence of thermal bridges will affect the overall dynamic performance of a structure. However, since the admittance is mainly determined by the properties of the materials immediately adjacent to the interior spaces of the building, the presence of heat bridges within the structure will have little effect on the overall thermal performance. Therefore, it is only where the bridge material is at or near the surface temperaure that it will affect the dynamic thermal performance. In cases where it is felt necessary to account for the effects of thermal bridges, an area-weighted mean approach, similar to the proportional area method for steady state heat flow, should be used.

References

1   *BS 874: Methods for determining thermal insulating properties: Part 1: 1986: Introduction, definitions and principles of measurement; Part 2: Tests for thermal conductivity and related properties: Section 2.1: 1986: Guarded hot-plate method; Section 2.2: 1988: Unguarded hot-plate method; Part 3: Tests for thermal transmittance and conductance: Section 3.1: 1987: Guarded hot-box method; Section 3.2: 1990: Calibrated hot-box method* (London: British Standards Institution) (dates as indicated)

2   *BS 6993: Thermal and radiometric properties of glazing: Part 1: 1989 (1995): Method for calculation of steady state U-value (thermal transmittance); Part 2: 1990 (1995): Method for direct measurement of U-value (thermal transmittance)* (London: British Standards Institution) (dates as indicated)

3   Clark J A, Yaneske P P and Pinney A A *The harmonisation of thermal properties of building materials* BEPAC Research Report (St Albans: Building Energy Performance Analysis Club) (1990)

4   *Building and Buildings. The Building Regulations 1991* Statutory Instrument 1991 No. 2768 and *Building Regulations (Amendment) Regulations 1994* Statutory Instrument 1994 No 1850 (London: The Stationery Office) (dates as indicated)

5   *The Building Regulations Approved Document L: Conservation of fuel and power* (1995 edition) (London: HMSO) (1995)

6   *BS 8207: 1985 (1995): Code of practice for energy efficiency in buildings* (London: British Standards Institution) (1985)

7   *BS 8211: Energy efficiency in housing; Part 1: 1988 (1995): Code of practice for energy efficient refurbishment of housing* (London: British Standards Institution) (1988)

8   *Building and Buildings. Building Standards (Scotland) Regulations 1990* Statutory Instrument 1990 No. 2179 (S.187) (as amended) (Edinburgh: The Stationery Office) (1990 with subsequent amendments)

9   *Building Standards (Scotland) Regulations Technical Standards for compliance with the Building Standards (Scotland) Regulations 1990 (as amended)* (Edinburgh: The Stationery Office) (1990 with subsequent amendments)

10 *Building Regulations (Northern Ireland) 1994* Statutory Rules of Northern Ireland 1994 No. 243 (Belfast: The Stationery Office) (1994)

11 *The Building Regulations (Northern Ireland) 1994 Technical Booklet F: Conservation of Fuel and Power* (Belfast: The Stationery Office) (1998)

12   *BS EN ISO 13789: Thermal performance of buildings —
        Transmission heat loss coefficient — Calculation Method* (London:
        British Standards Institution) (1999)

13   Siviour J B Areas in heat loss calculations *Building Serv. Eng. Res.
        Technol.* **6** 134 (1985)

14   *prEN 1745: Masonry and masonry materials — Methods for
        determining design thermal values* (Brussels: Comité Européen de
        Normalisation) (available in UK through BSI) (to be published)

15   *prEN 12524: Building materials and products — Hygrothermal
        properties — Tabulated design values* (Brussels: Comité Européen
        de Normalisation) (available in UK through BSI) (to be
        published)

16   *ISO 10456: Building materials and products and products —
        Procedures for determining declared and design thermal values*
        (Geneva: International Standards Organisation) (1997)

17   *BS EN ISO 6946: 1997: Building components and building
        elements. Thermal resistance and thermal transmittance. Calculation
        method.* (London: British Standards Institution) (1997)

18   *Heat transfer* CIBSE Guide section C3 (London: Chartered
        Institution of Building Services Engineers) (1976)

19   *Guide for assessment of the thermal performance of aluminium curtain
        wall framing* (Cheltenham: Council for Aluminium in Building)
        (1996)

20   Ward T I *Metal cladding: assessing thermal performance* BRE
        Information Paper 5/98 (Garston: Building Research
        Establishment) (1998)

21   *BS EN ISO 10211-1: 1996: Thermal bridges in building construction
        — Heat flows and surface temperatures — Part 1: General calculation
        methods* (London: British Standards Institution) (1996)

22   Anderson B R The relationship between the *U*-value of
        uninsulated ground floors and the floor dimensions *Building
        Serv. Eng. Res. Technol.* **12** (3) 103–105 (1991)

23   Anderson B R Calculation of the steady-state heat transfer
        through a slab-on-ground floor *Building and Environment* **26** (4)
        405–415 (1991)

24   *BS EN ISO 13370: 1998: Thermal performance of buildings — Heat
        transfer via the ground — calculation method*s (London: British
        Standards Institution) (1998)

25   Anderson B R The effect of edge insulation on the steady-state
        heat loss through a slab-on-ground floor *Building and
        Environment* **28**(3) 361–367 (1993)

26   Anderson B R *U-values for basements* IP 14/94 (Garston: Building
        Research Establishment) (1994)

27   *BS EN 673: 1998: Glass in building. Determination of thermal
        transmittance (U-value). Calculation method* (London: British
        Standards Institution) (1998)

28   *NS 3031: Thermal insulation — calculation of the energy and power
        element for heating and ventilation in buildings* (Oslo, Norway:
        Norwegian Council for Building Standardisation) (1986)

29   Littler J G F and Ruyssevelt P A Heat reflecting roller blinds
        and methods of edge sealing *Proc. Conf. Windows in Design and
        Maintenance, Gothenberg, Sweden* (1984)

30   Guy A Hot box measurements on coupled windows with and
        without blinds *(internal communication)* (St Helens: Pilkington
        UK Ltd) (May 1984)

31   *prEN 12412-1: Windows, doors and shutters — Determination of
        thermal transmittance by hot box method: Part 1: Windows and doors*
        (Brussels: Comité Européen de Normalisation) (available in UK
        through BSI) (1997)

32   Milbank N O and Harrington-Lynn J Thermal response and the
        admittance procedure *Building Serv. Eng.* **42** 38–51 (1974)

33   *BS EN ISO 13786: 1999: Thermal perfomance of building
        components — Dynamic thermal characteristics — calculation method*
        (London: British Standards Institution) (1999)

Appendix 3.A1: Moisture content of masonry materials

3.A1.1 Standard moisture content

While insulating materials are generally 'air-dry' (i.e. in equilibrium with the internal environment), this is not true for masonry materials in external walls. Research[A1-1] has shown that typical moisture contents of both the inner and outer leaves of external twin-leaf masonry walls are above air-dry values and the thermal conductivities used for calculating U-values should be corrected to take account of the presence of moisture.

The moisture content of the structural elements of occupied buildings varies widely depending upon many factors including climate, type of masonry, thickness of wall, whether or not the wall is rendered, standards of workmanship in construction, local exposure to rain (which varies across the building) etc. Therefore, it is convenient to base U-value calculations on thermal conductivities at standard values of moisture content.

Typical moisture contents for UK conditions are given in Table 3.2 for masonry that is 'protected' or 'exposed'. 'Exposure' refers to the external climate (i.e. solid masonry or the outer leaf of cavity walls without protective cladding). 'Protected' refers to solid masonry or the outer leaf of cavity walls protected by cladding such as tile hanging or weather boarding, and to the inner leaf of cavity walls (whether or not the cavity is filled with an insulating material).

3.A1.2 Correction factors for thermal conductivity

The way in which the thermal conductivity of different materials increases with moisture content is shown in Table 3.38. For maximum accuracy, this variation is given in terms of either percentage by weight or percentage by volume, according to the characteristics of the particular material.

Table 3.38 Correction factors for moisture content

Material	Correction factor
Brick (fired clay)	10% per % (by volume)
Brick (calcium silicate)	10% per % (by volume)
Dense aggregate concrete	4% per % (by volume)
Blast furnace slag concrete	4% per % (by weight)
Pumice aggregate concrete	4% per % (by weight)
Other lightweight aggregate concrete	4% per % (by weight)
Autoclaved aerated concrete	4% per % (by weight)

References (Appendix 3.A1)

A1-1 Arnold P J *Thermal conductivity of masonry materials* BRE CP1/70 (Garston: Building Research Establishment) (1970)

Appendix 3.A2: Thermal conductivity and thermal transmittance testing

With the increasing demand for thermal insulation and the subsequent development of new form of insulation, guidance is required on appropriate methods of determining the thermal performance of these materials.

The thermal conductivity value used in calculations should be representative of material used on site. *EN 1745*[A2-1] sets out a suitable method for determining that this is so, related to the manufactured density range and based on a minimum of three tests. This is an alternative to the use of the tabulated values in Table 3.1.

In the UK, the recommended method of determining the thermal conductivity of of materials is the use of either guarded or unguarded hot plate apparatus as laid down in *BS 874*[A2-2] or the corresponding *BS EN* standards that will in due course supersede *BS 874*. This method, which may be carried out using a comparatively small sample of material, is considered suitable for the majority of available materials. However, correct performance of the test requires considerable expertise, particularly in the preparation of the sample. Therefore, it is recommended that, apart from the standardised values given herein, thermal conductivity values should only be accepted when based on tests performed by a laboratory accredited by the United Kingdom Accreditation Service (UKAS)*.

The thermal transmittance of a complete structure may be determined using apparatus that conforms to *BS EN ISO 8990*[A2-3]. However, where masonry materials are involved, it is not usually possible to replicate the standard moisture contents in a laboratory. Therefore, the results of such tests may not reflect the actual conditions unless suitable analysis has been undertaken to convert the test results to the moisture conditions that will apply in practice.

---

* UKAS, Accreditation House,
  21–47 High Street, Feltham, Middlesex TW13 4UN

References (Appendix 3.A2)

A2-1   *prEN 1745: Masonry and masonry materials — Methods for determining design thermal values* (Brussels: Comité Européen de Normalisation) (available in UK through BSI) (to be published)

A2-2   *BS 874: Methods for determining thermal insulating properties: Part 1: 1986: Introduction, definitions and principles of measurement; Part 2: Tests for thermal conductivity and related properties: Section 2.1: 1986: Guarded hot-plate method; Section 2.2: 1988: Unguarded hot-plate method; Part 3: Tests for thermal transmittance and conductance: Section 3.1: 1987: Guarded hot-box method; Section 3.2: 1990: Calibrated hot-box method* (London: British Standards Institution) (dates as indicated)

A2-3   *BS EN ISO 8990: Thermal Insulation. Detemniation of steady-state thermal Tranmission properties. Calibrated and guarded hot-box* (London: British Standards Institution) (1996)

Appendix 3.A3: Heat transfer at surfaces

3.A3.1   General

Heat is transferred to and from surfaces by radiation interchange with other surfaces and by convective heat transfer at the air/surface interface. This may be represented by:

$$q_s = E h_r (t_r - t_s) + h_c (t_a - t_s) \qquad (3.51)$$

where q_s is the rate of heat transfer to/from the surface (W·m^{-2}), t_r is the radiant temperature experienced by the surface (°C), t_s is the surface temperature (°C), t_a is the air temperature (°C), E is the emissivity factor, h_r is the radiative heat transfer coefficient (W·m^{-2}·K^{-1}) and h_c is the convective heat transfer coefficient (W·m^{-2}·K^{-1}).

This and subsequent equations are valid for heat flow into and out of a surface provided that the sign of q_s is taken as positive if the heat flow is into the surface.

In general, both E and t_r are complicated functions of the geometry and emissivities of the surfaces involved. Usually equation 3.51 is considered in relation to an exposed part of the structure having surface temperature t_s radiating to and from the other surfaces of the enclosure, all of which are assumed to be at the same temperature. Then t_r may be taken as the temperature of these other surfaces.

The emissivity factor E depends on the room geometry and the emissivities of all the surfaces. Where the emissivity of the exposed surfaces is uniform and the emissivity of the non-exposed surfaces is also uniform, but different in value, the emissivity factor is given by:

$$\frac{1}{E A_1} = \frac{1}{A_1} + \frac{1 - \varepsilon_1}{A_1 \varepsilon_1} + \frac{1 - \varepsilon_1}{A_2 \varepsilon_2} \qquad (3.52)$$

where E is the emissivity factor, A_1 is the area of exposed surface(s) (m^2), ε_1 is the emissivity of the exposed surface(s), A_2 is the area of the non-exposed surface(s) (m^2) and ε_2 is the emissivity of the non-exposed surface(s).

For a cubical room with one exposed surface, $A_2 = 5 A_1$, therefore:

$$\frac{1}{E} = 1 + \frac{1 - \varepsilon_1}{\varepsilon_1} + \frac{1 - \varepsilon_2}{5 \varepsilon_2} \qquad (3.53)$$

Hence:

$$E = \varepsilon_1 [1 + \varepsilon_1 (1 - \varepsilon_2)/5 \varepsilon_2]^{-1} \qquad (3.54)$$

For most interior surfaces, the value of ε_2 is high. Taking ε_2 as 0.9 and plotting E as a function of ε_1, it may be demonstrated that E is directly proportional to ε_1 to within 2% for values of ε_1 between 0 and 1.

Hence:

$$E = K \varepsilon_1 \qquad (3.55)$$

where K is a constant related to room geometry.

Note that for the calculation of the conventional values of inside surface resistance given in Table 3.9, K is taken as 1, hence $E = 0.9$.

3.A3.2   Interior surfaces

For practical application at interior surfaces it is convenient to make two modifications to equation 3.51. The first is to use $\bar{t}_{ri}$, the mean temperature of all the surfaces in the enclosure, rather than t_r since this is more easily measured and is more closely related to thermal comfort.

Strictly, $\bar{t}_{ri}$ varies throughout an enclosure dependent on the shape factors for all relevant surfaces at the point chosen. However, at the centre of a cubical room with one exposed wall:

$$6 \bar{t}_{ri} = 5 t_r + t_{si} \qquad (3.56)$$

where t_{ri} is the inside radiant temperature seen by the surface (°C), $\bar{t}_{ri}$ is the mean inside radiant temperature (°C) and t_{si} is the inside surface temperature (°C).

Substituting in equation 3.51, and introducing the subscript 'i' to denote inside temperatures, gives:

$$q_s = {}^6/_5 E h_r (\bar{t}_{ri} - t_{si}) + h_c (t_{ai} - t_{si}) \qquad (3.57)$$

The second modification is to combine radiant and air temperatures into environmental temperature (see Section 5), t_{ei}, defined by the equation:

$$q = (1 / R_{si})(t_{ei} - t_s) \qquad (3.58)$$

where R_{si} is the inside surface resistance (m^2·K·W^{-1}) and t_{ei} is the inside environmental temperature (°C).

This is equivalent to equation 3.57 where:

$$t_{ei} = \frac{{}^6/_5 E h_r}{{}^6/_5 E h_r + h_c} \bar{t}_{ri} + \frac{h_c}{{}^6/_5 E h_r + h_c} t_{ai} \qquad (3.59)$$

and:

$$R_{si} = \frac{1}{{}^6/_5 E h_r + h_c} \qquad (3.60)$$

Thus t_{ei} varies with both t_{ri} and t_{ai}.

3.A3.2   Exterior surfaces

As with interior surfaces, the heat transfer is represented by equation 3.57 by replacing the suffix 'i' by 'o' to denote outside temperatures. However, in this case no enclosure is involved and it is more convenient to retain t_r. The outside environmental temperature is then given by:

$$t_{eo} = \frac{E\,h_r}{E\,h_r + h_c}\,t_{ro} + \frac{h_c}{E\,h_r + h_c}\,t_{ao} \qquad (3.61)$$

and the external surface resistance is given by:

$$R_{se} = \frac{1}{E_{hr} + h_c} \qquad (3.62)$$

For design purposes it is usual to assume that $t_{ro} = t_{ao}$, therefore:

$$t_{eo} = t_{ao} \qquad (3.63)$$

Equation 3.61 can be used to calculate heat losses from roofs, for example, where there is significant radiation to a clear sky, the temperature of which (t_{ro}) is lower than t_{ao}. Note that neither the outside surface resistance nor the U-value is affected by such considerations.

Solar radiation on exterior surfaces has the effect of reducing the heat loss through the component. In appropriate cases this can be allowed for by using the sol-air temperature in place of the external air temperature.

Appendix 3.A4: Seasonal heat losses through ground floors

The U-value of a ground floor (see section 3.5) relates the average heat loss over one year to the average temperature difference over the same period.

The annual variation of external temperature about its mean value gives rise to a similar variation in heat flow but out of phase with the temperature variation[A4-1]. This phase difference is generally between about two weeks and about three months, and is greater for insulated floors than for uninsulated floors.

Measurements have shown[A4-1,A4-2] that when an appreciable phase difference is involved, the average seasonal heat loss is approximately that calculated using the average annual internal and external temperatures, i.e:

$$Q_f = A_f U_f (\bar{t}_{ei} - \bar{t}_{ao}) \tag{3.64}$$

where Q_f is the rate of heat loss through the floor (W), A_f is the area of the floor (m^2), U_f is the thermal transmittance of the floor (W·m^{-2}·K^{-1}), $\bar{t}_{ei}$ is the annual average inside environmental temperature (°C) and $\bar{t}_{ao}$ is the annual average outside air temperature (°C).

With a smaller phase difference, the average seasonal heat loss is given by:

$$Q_f = A_f U_f (\bar{t}_{ei(w)} - \bar{t}_{ao(w)}) \tag{3.65}$$

where $\bar{t}_{ei(w)}$ is the average inside environmental temperature over the heating season (°C), $\bar{t}_{ao(w)}$ is the average outside air temperature over the heating season (°C).

Values of $\bar{t}_{ao}$ and $\bar{t}_{ao(w)}$ for three UK locations are given in Table 3.39.

In general, the actual heat losses, averaged over the heating season will fall between the values indicated by equations 3.64 and 3.65.

Table 3.39 Wintertime average ($\bar{t}_{ao(w)}$) and annual average ($\bar{t}_{ao}$) outside air temperatures

Location	Outside air temperature averaged over stated period (°C)	
	Wintertime†	Annual
London (Heathrow)	7.2	10.8
Manchester (Ringway)	6.3	9.6
Edinburgh (Turnhouse)	5.5	8.6

† October – April inclusive

Notes:
(1) Figures are 20-year means (1976–1995)
(2) Subtract 0.6°C for each 100 m elevation above sea level.

References (Appendix 3.A4)

A4-1   Spooner D C Heat loss measurements through an insulated domestic ground floor *Building Serv. Eng. Res. Technol.* **3**(4) 147–151 (1982)

A4-2   Spooner D C *Private communication*

Appendix 3.A5: Application of the combined method to multiple layer structures

The following example shows how the combined method may be used to determine the thermal resistance of complicated structural elements involving bridged layers.

Example 3.10: Calculation of thermal resistance of foam-filled masonry block

Figure 3.22 shows a hollow masonry block with a single slot, 25 mm thick, closed at one end and filled with expanded polystyrene (EPS) insulation. The thermal conductivities of the masonry and insulation are 0.51 $W \cdot m^{-1} \cdot K^{-1}$ and 0.035 $W \cdot m^{-1} \cdot K^{-1}$ respectively.

Since the thermal resistance is to be calculated for the block alone, rather than as part of a multiple-leaf construction, the surface resistances are not included. Therefore, the isothermal planes are considered to be the inner and outer surfaces of the block.

The block may be considered as consisting of three layers, the outer layers being homogeneous masonry and the middle layer being composed of an EPS slab thermally bridged on three sides by masonry. To simplify the calculation, the outer layers may be rearranged as shown in Figure 3.23. Each layer is divided into sections, each of which is composed of a single material only, as shown.

The areas of the sections, and their proportions of the total area, are:

— section m_1 (masonry): $A_{m1} = 0.0946$ m^2; $P_{m1} = 1$
— section m_2 (masonry): $A_{m2} = 0.0946$ m^2; $P_{m2} = 1$
— section m_3 (masonry): $A_{m3} = 0.0186$ m^2; $P_{m3} = 0.197$
— section n (EPS): $A_n = 0.076$ m^2; $P_n = 0.803$

The thermal resistances are:

— section m_1 (masonry): $R_{m1} = 0.0375/0.51 = 0.0735$ m$^2 \cdot$K$\cdot$W^{-1}
— section m_2 (masonry): $R_{m2} = 0.0375/0.51 = 0.0735$ m$^2 \cdot$K$\cdot$W^{-1}
— section m_3 (masonry): $R_{m3} = 0.025/0.51 = 0.049$ m$^2 \cdot$K$\cdot$W^{-1}
— section n (EPS): $R_n = 0.025/0.035 = 0.714$ m$^2 \cdot$K$\cdot$W^{-1}

(*a*)   Lower limit

Using equation 3.24, the thermal resistance of the bridged layer is added to the thermal resistances of the two unbridged layers:

$$R_L = \frac{1}{(P_n/R_n) + (P_{m3}/R_{m3})} + R_{m1} + R_{m2}$$

$$= \left[\frac{1}{(0.803/0.714) + (0.197/0.049)} \right]$$

$$+ \; 0.0735 + 0.0735$$

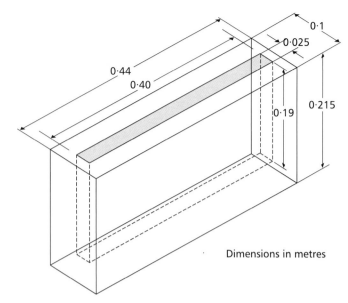

Figure 3.22 Example 3.10; foam-filled masonry block

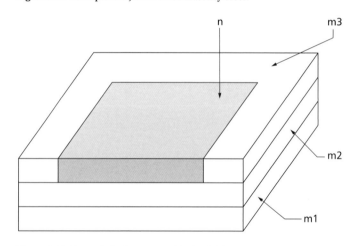

Figure 3.23 Example 3.10; masonry block with layers rearranged

$$= (1/5.145) + 0.0735 + 0.0735$$

$$= 0.341 \; \text{m}^2 \cdot \text{K} \cdot \text{W}^{-1}$$

(*b*)   Upper limit

Using equation 3.26, the thermal resistances of each section are added together on an area-weighted basis:

$$R_U = \frac{1}{\left(\dfrac{P_n}{R_n + R_{m1} + R_{m2}} \right) + \left(\dfrac{P_{m3}}{R_{m3} + R_{m1} + R_{m2}} \right)}$$

$$= \frac{1}{(0.803/0.861) + (0.197/0.196)}$$

$$= 0.516 \; \text{m}^2 \cdot \text{K} \cdot \text{W}^{-1}$$

The thermal resistance of the masonry block is the arithmetic mean of the upper and lower limits, i.e. 0.428 m$^2 \cdot$K$\cdot$W^{-1}.

Appendix 3.A6: Calculation method for admittance, decrement factor and surface factor

The temperature distribution in a homogeneous slab subject to one dimensional heat flow is given by the diffusion equation:

$$\frac{\partial^2 t}{\partial x^2} = \frac{\rho\, c}{\lambda}\, \frac{\partial t}{\partial \theta} \tag{3.66}$$

where t is temperature (°C), x is distance in direction perpendicular to surface of slab (m²), ρ is density (kg·m⁻³), c is specific heat capacity (J·kg⁻¹·K⁻¹), λ is thermal conductivity (W·m⁻¹·K⁻²) and θ is time (s).

For finite slabs and for sinusoidal temperature variations the temperature and energy cycles can be linked by the use of matrix algebra[(A6.1)], i.e:

$$\begin{bmatrix} t_1 \\ q_1 \end{bmatrix} \begin{bmatrix} m_1 & m_2 \\ m_3 & m_1 \end{bmatrix} \begin{bmatrix} t_2 \\ q_2 \end{bmatrix} \tag{3.67}$$

where q is heat flux (W·m⁻²).

For a slab of homogenous material of thickness L (m), the coefficients of the matrix are given by:

$$m_1 = \cosh(p + ip) \tag{3.68}$$

$$m_2 = \frac{L \sinh(p + ip)}{\lambda(p + ip)} \tag{3.69}$$

$$m_3 = \frac{\lambda(p + ip)\sinh(p + ip)}{L} \tag{3.70}$$

For a 24 hour cycle:

$$p = \frac{\pi L^2 \rho\, c}{86400\, \lambda} \tag{3.71}$$

For an air gap, or a surface resistance between a layer and the air, where the diffusivity (i.e. $\lambda / \rho\, c$) is high, the coefficients of the matrix are given by:

$$m_1 = 1 \tag{3.72}$$

$$m_2 = R_a \text{ or } R_s \tag{3.73}$$

$$m_3 = 0 \tag{3.74}$$

Clearly, for a composite wall, the matrices of each of the layers can multiplied together to give the relation between inside and outside, as follows:

$$\begin{bmatrix} t_1 \\ q_1 \end{bmatrix} = \begin{bmatrix} 1 & R_{si} \\ 0 & 1 \end{bmatrix} \begin{bmatrix} m_1 & m_2 \\ m_3 & m_1 \end{bmatrix} \begin{bmatrix} n_1 & n_2 \\ n_3 & n_1 \end{bmatrix} \cdots \begin{bmatrix} 1 & R_{se} \\ 0 & 1 \end{bmatrix} \begin{bmatrix} t_o \\ q_o \end{bmatrix} \tag{3.75}$$

which can be written:

$$\begin{bmatrix} t_1 \\ q_1 \end{bmatrix} = \begin{bmatrix} M_1 & M_2 \\ M_3 & M_4 \end{bmatrix} \begin{bmatrix} t_o \\ q_o \end{bmatrix} \tag{3.76}$$

Note that the components of this matrix will be complex numbers.

The non-steady state parameters are now derived as follows.

Admittance (Y):

$$Y_c = \frac{M_4}{M_2} \tag{3.77}$$

$$Y = |Y_c| \tag{3.78}$$

$$\omega = \frac{12}{\pi} \arctan \frac{\text{Im}(Y_c)}{\text{Re}(Y_c)} \tag{3.79}$$

The arctangent should be evaluated in the range 0 to π radians, thus ω is a time lead.

Decrement factor (f):

$$f_c = \frac{1}{U M_2} \tag{3.80}$$

where U is thermal transmittance (W·m⁻²·K⁻¹).

$$f = |f_c| \tag{3.81}$$

$$\phi = \frac{12}{\pi} \arctan \frac{\text{Im}(f_c)}{\text{Re}(f_c)} \tag{3.82}$$

The arctangent should be evaluated in the range $-\pi$ to 0 radians, thus ϕ is a time lag.

Surface factor (F):

$$F_c = 1 - R_{si} Y_c \tag{3.83}$$

$$F = |F_c| \tag{3.84}$$

$$\psi = \frac{12}{\pi} \arctan \frac{\text{Im}(F_c)}{\text{Re}(F_c)} \tag{3.85}$$

As with decrement factor, the arctangent should be evaluated in the range $-\pi$ to 0 radians, thus ψ is a time lag.

For internal partitions, the decrement factor is combined with the admittance and surface factor, i.e:

$$Y_{ci} = (Y_c - U f_c) = \frac{M_4 - 1}{M_2} \tag{3.86}$$

$$F_{ci} = 1 - R_{si} Y_{ci} \tag{3.87}$$

Equations 3.78, 3.79, 3.84 and 3.85 can then be used as before.

Example 3.11: Non-steady-state properties for a solid external wall

Properties of the wall are as follows:

— thickness, $L = 0.22$ m

— density, $\rho = 1700$ kg·m^{-3}

— thermal conductivity, $\lambda = 0.84$ W·m^{-1}·K^{-1}

— specific heat capacity, $c = 800$ J·kg^{-1}·K^{-1}.

The thermal transmittance is:

$$U = \frac{1}{(0.12 + \dfrac{0.22}{0.84} + 0.06)} = 2.3 \text{ W·m}^{-2}\text{·K}^{-1}.$$

From equation 3.71:

$$p = 1.688$$

For manual calculation, it is convenient to express cosh ($p + ip$) and sinh ($p + ip$) in terms of the functions $\sin p$, $\cos p$ and e^p, i.e:

$$\cosh (p + ip) = {}^1\!/_2 \,[(e^p + e^{-p})\cos p + i(e^p - e^{-p})\sin p]$$
$$(3.88)$$

$$\sinh (p + ip) = {}^1\!/_2 \,[(e^p - e^{-p})\cos p + i(e^p + e^{-p})\sin p]$$
$$(3.89)$$

In the matrix, the coefficient m_1, is given by equation 3.88; m_2 and m_3 are given by:

$$m_2 = \{L\,[(e^p - e^{-p})\cos p + (e^p + e^{-p})\sin p$$
$$- i(e^p - e^{-p})\cos p + i(e^p + e^{-p})\sin p]\}/4\,\lambda p$$
$$(3.90)$$

$$m_3 = \{\,\lambda p\,[(e^p - e^{-p})\cos p + (e^p + e^{-p})\sin p$$
$$+ i(e^p - e^{-p})\cos p + i(e^p + e^{-p})\sin p]\}/4\,\lambda p$$
$$(3.91)$$

Which gives the matrix as follows:

$$\begin{bmatrix} -0.33 + i2.59 & 0.19 + i0.24 \\ -19.9 + i15.9 & -0.33 + i2.59 \end{bmatrix}$$

Performing the matrix multiplication from left to right (which corresponds to inside to outside):

$$\begin{bmatrix} 1 & 0.12 \\ 0 & 1 \end{bmatrix}\begin{bmatrix} -0.33 + i2.59 & 0.19 + i0.24 \\ -19.9 + i15.9 & -0.33 + i2.59 \end{bmatrix}$$

$$= \begin{bmatrix} -2.72 + i4.40 & 0.15 + i0.551 \\ -19.9 + i1.59 & -0.33 + i2.59 \end{bmatrix}$$

Since M_2 and M_4 only are required, it is necessary to evaluate the right-hand column only of the product matrix, i.e:

$$\begin{bmatrix} -2.72 + i4.50 & 0.15 + i0.551 \\ -19.9 + i15.9 & -0.33 + i2.59 \end{bmatrix}\begin{bmatrix} 1 & 0.06 \\ 0 & 1 \end{bmatrix}$$

$$= \begin{bmatrix} * & -0.013 + i0.821 \\ * & -1.52 + i3.54 \end{bmatrix}$$

From equations 3.77, 3.78 and 3.79:

$$Y_c = \frac{-1.52 + i3.54}{-0.013 + i0.821}$$

$$= \frac{(-1.52 + i3.54)(-0.013 - i0.821)}{0.013^2 + 0.821^2}$$

$$= 4.35 + i1.78$$

$$Y = 4.70 \text{ W·m}^{-2}\text{·K}^{-1}$$

$$\omega = 1.48 \text{ h}$$

From equations 3.80, 3.81 and 3.82:

$$f_c = \frac{1}{2.3\,(-0.013 + i0.821)}$$

$$= \frac{-(0.013 + i0.821)}{2.3\,(0.013^2 + 0.821^2)}$$

$$= -0.0084 - i0.530$$

$$f = 0.53$$

$$\phi = -6.0 \text{ h}$$

From equations 3.83, 3.84 and 3.85:

$$F_c = 1 - 0.12\,(4.35 + i1.78) = 0.478 - i0.214$$

$$F = 0.52$$

$$\psi = -1.6 \text{ h}$$

Reference for Appendix 3.A6

1 Pipes L A Matrix analysis of heat transfer problems *J. Franklin Inst.* 623 195–206 (1957)

Appendix 3.A7: Properties of materials

The data tabulated in this appendix have been abstracted, with permission, from the report of a thorough review of existing data sets undertaken by the Building Environmental Performance Analysis Club (BEPAC)[A7.1]. Fourteen data sets were studied, see Table 3.40.

Tables 3.41 to 3.51 contain only a selection of the data given in the BEPAC report, these being regarded as broadly representative of the materials listed. In each case the source of the data is identified by a code which refers to one of the data sets listed in Table 3.40.

Thermal conductivity, density and specific heat capacity data for typical materials are given in Tables 3.41 to 3.44. Table 3.41 refers to impermeable materials, i.e. those which act as a barrier to water in the vapour and/or liquid states, and whose hygrothermal properties do not alter by absorbing water. Table 3.42 includes lightweight insulation materials, such as mineral wools and foamed plastics, which display water vapour permeability, zero hygroscopic water content and an apparent thermal conductivity, and which operate under conditions of air-dry equilibrium normally protected from wetting by rain. Table 3.43 deals with masonry and related materials which are inorganic, porous and may contain significant amounts of water (due to hygroscopic absorption from the air or wetting by rain) which affects their hygrothermal properties and their thermal conductivity in particular. Table 3.44 provides data for organic materials such as wood and wood-based products which are porous and strongly hygroscopic and

which display a highly non-linear water vapour permeability.

Tables 3.45 to 3.47 give absorptivity and emissivity data for impermeable, inorganic porous and hygroscopic materials, respectively.

Tables 3.48 to 3.51 contain vapour resistivity values for a wide variety of materials divided into four categories as for Tables 3.41 to 3.45.

Table 3.40 Sources of data

Data source	Code
ASHRAE, USA	A[A7.2]
BS 5250, UK	BS[A7.3]
CIBSE, UK	C[A7.4]
CSTC, Belgium	T[A7.5]
DOE-2 Program, USA	D[A7.6]
ESP program, UK	E[A7.7]
Eurosol, UK	Eu
France	F[A7.8]
Germany	G[A7.9]
Italy	Y[A7.10]
India	I[A7.11]
Leeds University, UK	L[A7.12,A7.13]
Leuven University, Belgium	B[A7.14]
Netherlands	S[A7.15]

Table 3.41 Thermal conductivity, density and specific heat capacity: impermeable materials

Material	Condition/test (where known)	Source	Thermal conductivity ($W \cdot m^{-1} \cdot K^{-1}$)	Density ($kg \cdot m^{-3}$)	Specific heat ($J \cdot kg^{-1} \cdot K^{-1}$)
Asphalt		C	0.50	1700	1000
		E	1.20	2300	1700
— poured		T	1.20	2100	920
— reflective coat		E	1.20	2300	1700
— roofing, mastic		E	1.15	2330	840
Bitumen					
— composite, flooring		E	0.85	2400	1000
— insulation, all types		T	0.20	1000	1700
Ceramic, glazed		T	1.40	2500	840
Glass					
— cellular sheet		T	0.048	140	840
— foam	At 50°C	I	0.056	130	750
		S	0.052	140	840
— solid (soda-lime)	At 10°C	C	1.05	2500	840
Linoleum		T	0.19	1200	1470
Metals					
— aluminium		T	230	2700	880
— aluminium cladding		D	45	7680	420
— brass		T	110	8500	390
— bronze		T	64	8150	—
— copper		T	384	8600	390
— duraluminium		T	160	2800	580
— iron		T	72	7900	530
— iron, cast		T	56	7500	530
— lead		T	35	11340	130
— stainless steel, 5% Ni		T	29	7850	480
— stainless steel, 20% Ni		T	16	8000	480
— steel		T	45	7800	480
— tin		T	65	7300	240
— zinc		T	113	7000	390
Polyvinylchloride (PVC)		E	0.16	1380	1000
— tiles		T	0.19	1200	1470
Roofing felt		E	0.19	960	840
Rubber		T	0.17	1500	1470
— expanded board, rigid		G	0.032	70	1680
— hard		E	0.15	1200	1000
— tiles		E	0.30	1600	2000

Table 3.42 Thermal conductivity, density and specific heat capacity: non-hygroscopic materials

Material	Condition/test (where known)	Source	Thermal conductivity (W·m⁻¹·K⁻¹)	Density (kg·m⁻³)	Specific heat (J·kg⁻¹·K⁻¹)
Carpet/underlay:					
— with cellular rubber underlay		E	0.10	400	1360
— synthetic		E	0.06	160	2500
Foam:					
— phenol		C	0.040	30	1400
— phenol, rigid		S	0.035	110	1470
— polyisocyanate		S	0.030	45	1470
— polyurethane		T	0.028	30	1470
— polyurethane, freon-filled		S	0.030	45	1470
— polyvinylchloride		S	0.035	37	1470
— urea formaldehyde		C	0.04	10	1400
— urea formaldehyde resin		S	0.054	14	1470
Glass fibre/wool:					
— fibre quilt		C	0.040	12	840
— fibre slab		C	0.035	25	1000
— fibre, strawboard-like		S	0.085	300	2100
— wool	At 10°C	Eu	0.040	10	840
	At 10°C	Eu	0.040	12	840
	At 10°C	Eu	0.037	16	840
	At 10°C	Eu	0.033	24	840
	At 10°C	Eu	0.032	32	840
	At 10°C	Eu	0.03	48	840
	At 10°C	Eu	0.031	80	840
— wool, resin bonded	At 50°C	I	0.036	24	1000
Loose fill/powders:					
— cellulosic insulation		A	0.042	43	1380
— exfoliated vermiculite	At 50°C	I	0.069	260	880
— floor/roof screed		C	0.41	1200	840
— glass, granular cellular		T	0.07	180	840
— gravel		E	0.36	1840	840
— perlite, expanded		A	0.051	100	1090
— polystyrene, moulded beads	At 10°C	A	0.036	16	1210
— roof gravel or slag		D	1.44	880	1680
— sand		I	1.74	2240	840
— stone chippings for roofs		C	0.96	1800	1000
— white dry render		E	0.50	1300	1000
Mineral fibre/wool:					
— fibre blanket, bonded	At 10°C	A	0.042	12	710
	At 10°C	A	0.036	24	710
	At 10°C	A	0.032	48	710
— fibre blanket, metal reinforced	At 37.7°C	A	0.038	140	710
	At 93.3°C	A	0.046	140	710
— fibre board, preformed		D	0.042	240	760
— fibre board, wet felted		A	0.051	290	800
— fibre board, wet moulded		A	0.061	370	590
— fibre board, resin bonded		A	0.042	240	710
— fibre, textile, organic bonded	At 10°C	A	0.043	10	710
— fibre slag, pipe insulation	At 23.8°C	A	0.036	100	710
	At 23.8°C	A	0.048	200	710
	At 93.3°C	A	0.048	100	710
	At 93.3°C	A	0.065	200	710
— wool		S	0.038	140	840
— wool, fibrous		D	0.043	96	840
— wool, resin bonded		I	0.036	99	1000
Miscellaneous materials:					
— acoustic tile		D	0.057	290	1340
— felt sheathing		E	0.19	960	950
— mineral filler for concrete		S	0.13	430	840
— perlite, bitumen bonded		S	0.061	240	840
— perlite, expanded, hard panels		T	0.055	170	840
— perlite, expanded, pure		T	0.046	65	840
— plastic tiles		E	0.50	1050	840
— polyurethane, expanded		D	0.023	24	1590
— polyurethane, unfaced	At 10°C	G	0.023	32	1590

Table 3.42 Thermal conductivity, density and specific heat capacity: non-hygroscopic materials

Material	Condition/test (where known)	Source	Thermal conductivity $(W \cdot m^{-1} \cdot K^{-1})$	Density $(kg \cdot m^{-3})$	Specific heat $(J \cdot kg^{-1} \cdot K^{-1})$
Carpet/underlay:					
— polyurethane board, cellular		A	0.023	24	1590
— polyisocyanurate board		A	0.020	32	920
— polyisocyanurate board,					
— foil-faced, glass-fibre reinforced	At 10°C	A	0.019	32	920
— polystyrene, expanded (EPS)		S	0.035	23	1470
— polystyrene, extruded (EPS)		S	0.027	35	1470
— polyvinylchloride (PVC), expanded		E	0.04	100	750
— vermiculite, expanded, panels		T	0.082	350	840
— vermiculite, expanded, pure		T	0.058	350	840
— silicon		E	0.18	700	1000
Rock wool	At 10°C	Eu	0.037	23	710
	At 10°C	Eu	0.033	60	710
	At 10°C	Eu	0.033	100	710
	At 10°C	Eu	0.034	200	710
— unbonded		I	0.047	92	840
		I	0.043	150	840

Table 3.43 Thermal conductivity, density and specific heat capacity: inorganic, porous materials

Material	Condition/test (where known)	Source	Thermal conductivity $(W \cdot m^{-1} \cdot K^{-1})$	Density $(kg \cdot m^{-3})$	Specific heat $(J \cdot kg^{-1} \cdot K^{-1})$
Asbestos-related materials:					
— asbestos cement		S	1.02	1750	840
— asbestos cement building board		D	0.6	1920	840
— asbestos cement decking		C	0.36	1500	1050
— asbestos cement sheet	Conditioned	C	0.36	700	1050
— asbestos fibre	At 50°C	I	0.06	640	840
— asbestos mill board	At 50°C	I	0.25	1400	840
Brick		D	0.72	1920	840
		D	1.31	2080	921
— aerated		S	0.30	1000	840
— brickwork, inner leaf		C	0.62	1700	800
— brickwork, outer leaf		C	0.84	1700	800
— burned		S	0.75	1300	840
		S	0.85	1500	840
		S	1.00	1700	840
— mud	At 50°C	I	0.75	1730	880
— paviour		E	0.96	2000	840
— reinforced	At 50°C	I	1.10	1920	840
— tile	At 50°C	I	0.8	1890	880
Cement/plaster/mortar:					
— cement		D	0.72	1860	840
— cement blocks, cellular		T	0.33	520	2040
— cement fibreboard, magnesium oxysulphide binder		A	0.082	350	1300
— cement mortar		S	0.72	1650	920
	Dry	T	0.93	1900	840
	Moist	T	1.5	1900	840
— cement/lime plaster		S	0.8	1600	840
— cement panels, wood fibres	Dry	T	0.08	350	1890
	Moist	T	0.12	350	3040
		T	0.12	400	1470
	Dry	T	0.35	1650	840

Table 3.43 Thermal conductivity, density and specific heat capacity: inorganic, porous materials — *continued*

Material	Condition/test (where known)	Source	Thermal conductivity ($W·m^{-1}·K^{-1}$)	Density ($kg·m^{-3}$)	Specific heat ($J·kg^{-1}·K^{-1}$)
— cement plaster		S	0.72	1760	840
		S	1.50	1900	840
— cement plaster, sand aggregate		A	0.72	1860	840
— cement screed		E	1.40	2100	650
— gypsum		E	0.42	1200	840
— gypsum plaster		S	0.51	1120	960
— gypsum plaster, perlite aggregate		A	0.22	720	1340
— gypsum plaster, sand aggregate		A	0.81	1680	840
— gypsum plasterboard		D	0.16	800	840
		S	0.65	1100	840
— gypsum plastering		S	0.80	1300	840
— limestone mortar		T	0.70	1600	840
— plaster		T	0.22	800	840
		T	0.35	950	840
		T	0.52	1200	840
— plaster ceiling tiles		E	0.38	1120	840
— plaster, lightweight aggregate		D	0.23	720	840
— plaster, sand aggregate		D	0.82	1680	840
— plasterboard		C	0.16	950	840
— render, synthetic resin,					
— exterior insulation		T	0.70	1100	900
— rendering	Moisture content 1%	E	1.13	1430	1000
	Moisture content 8%	E	0.79	1330	1000
— vermiculite plaster		E	0.20	720	840
Ceramic/clay tiles:					
— ceramic tiles	Dry	T	1.20	2000	850
— ceramic floor tiles	Dry	T	0.80	1700	850
— clay tiles		E	0.85	1900	840
— clay tile, burnt		S	1.3	2000	840
— clay tile, hollow, 10.2 mm, 1 cell		D	0.52	1120	840
— clay tile, hollow, 20.3 mm, 2 cells		D	0.623	1120	840
— clay tile, hollow, 32.5 mm, 3 cells		D	0.693	1120	840
— clay tile, pavior		D	1.803	1920	840
Concrete blocks/tiles:					
— block, aerated		E	0.24	750	1000
— block, heavyweight, 300 mm		D	1.31	2240	840
— block, lightweight, 150 mm		D	0.66	1760	840
— block, lightweight, 300 mm		D	0.73	1800	840
	Dry	T	0.24	620	840
	Dry	T	0.25	670	840
	Dry	T	0.26	720	840
	Dry	T	0.30	750	840
	Dry	T	0.28	770	840
	Dry	T	0.29	820	840
	Dry	T	0.30	870	840
— block, mediumweight, 150 mm		D	0.77	1900	840
— block, mediumweight, 300 mm		D	0.83	1940	840
	Dry	T	0.31	920	840
	Dry	T	0.32	970	840
	Dry	T	0.35	1050	840
	Dry	T	0.40	1150	840
— block, hollow, heavyweight, 300 mm		D	1.35	1220	840
— block, hollow, lightweight, 150 mm		D	0.48	880	840
— block, hollow, lightweight, 300 mm		D	0.76	780	840

Table 3.43 Thermal conductivity, density and specific heat capacity: inorganic, porous materials — *continued*

Material	Condition/test (where known)	Source	Thermal conductivity ($W \cdot m^{-1} \cdot K^{-1}$)	Density ($kg \cdot m^{-3}$)	Specific heat ($J \cdot kg^{-1} \cdot K^{-1}$)
— block, hollow, mediumweight, 150 mm		D	0.62	1040	840
— block, hollow, mediumweight, 300 mm		D	0.86	930	840
— block, partially filled, heavyweight, 300 mm		D	1.35	1570	840
— block, partially filled, lightweight, 150 mm		D	0.55	1170	840
— block, partially filled, lightweight, 300 mm		D	0.74	1120	840
— block, partially filled, mediumweight, 150 mm		D	0.64	1330	840
— block, partially filled, mediumweight,300 mm		D	0.85	1260	840
— block, perlite-filled, lightweight, 150 mm		D	0.17	910	840
— block, perlite-filled, mediumweight,150mm		D	0.2	1070	840
— block, with perlite, lightweight, 150 mm		D	0.33	1180	840
— block, with perlite,					
— mediumweight, 150 mm		D	0.39	1340	840
— tiles		E	1.10	2100	840
Concrete, cast:					
— aerated		E	0.16	500	840
		S	0.29	850	840
		S	0.42	1200	840
— aerated, cellular		S	0.15	400	840
		S	0.23	700	840
		S	0.70	1000	840
		S	1.20	1300	840
— aerated, cement/lime based		S	0.21	580	840
— cellular		T	0.16	480	840
	At 50°C	I	0.19	700	1050
— cellular bonded		T	0.30	520	2040
— dense		S	1.70	2200	840
— compacted,		S	2.20	2400	840
— dense, reinforced		S	1.90	2300	840
— compacted		S	2.30	2500	840
— expanded clay filling		S	0.26	780	840
		S	0.60	1400	840
— foamed	At 50°C	I	0.07	320	920
	At 50°C	I	0.08	400	920
	At 50°C	I	0.15	700	920
— foam slag		E	0.25	1040	960
— glass reinforced		E	0.90	1950	840
— heavyweight	Dry	T	1.30	2000	840
	Moist	T	1.70	2000	840
— lightweight	Dry	T	0.20	620	840
	Dry	T	0.25	750	840
	Dry	T	0.21	670	840
	Dry	T	0.22	720	840
	Dry	T	0.23	770	840
	Dry	T	0.24	820	840
	Dry	T	0.25	870	840
	Moist	T	0.43	750	840
	Moist	T	0.38	770	840
	Moist	T	0.40	820	840
	Moist	T	0.43	870	840
		S	0.08	200	840
		S	0.12	300	840
		S	0.17	500	840
		S	0.23	700	840
— mediumweight	Dry	T	0.32	1050	840
	Dry	T	0.37	1150	840
	Dry	T	0.59	1350	840
	Dry	T	0.84	1650^{-3}	840$^{-1} \cdot K^{-1}$
	Dry	T	0.37	1050	840
	Dry	T	0.27	920	840

Table 3.43 Thermal conductivity, density and specific heat capacity: inorganic, porous materials — *continued*

Material	Condition/test (where known)	Source	Thermal conductivity (W·m⁻¹·K⁻¹)	Density (kg·m⁻³)	Specific heat (J·kg⁻¹·K⁻¹
	Dry	T	0.29	980	840
	Moist	T	0.59	1050	840
		S	0.50	1000	840
		S	0.80	1300	840
		S	1.20	1600	840
		S	1.40	1900	840
— mediumweight, with lime	At 50°C	I	0.73	1650	880
— no fines		E	0.96	1800	840
— residuals of iron works		S	0.35	1000	840
		S	0.45	1300	840
		S	0.70	1600	840
		S	1.00	1900	840
— roofing slab, aerated		C	0.16	500	840
— vermiculite aggregate		E	0.17	450	840
— very lightweight		T	0.14	370	840
		T	0.15	420	840
		T	0.16	470	840
		T	0.17	520	840
		T	0.18	570	840
		T	0.12	350	840
		T	0.18	600	840
Masonry:					
— block, lightweight		T	0.19	470	840
		T	0.20	520	840
		T	0.22	570	840
		T	0.22	600	840
— block, mediumweight	Dry	T	0.60	1350	840
	Dry	T	0.85	1650	840
	Dry	T	1.30	1800	840
— heavyweight	Dry	T	0.90	1850	840
	Dry	T	0.73	1850	840
	Dry	T	0.79	1950	840
	Dry	T	0.90	2050	840
	Moist	T	0.81	1650	840
— lightweight	Dry	T	0.22	750	840
	Dry	T	0.27	850	840
	Dry	T	0.24	850	840
	Dry	T	0.27	950	840
— mediumweight	Dry	T	0.32	1050	840
	Dry	T	0.54	1300	840
	Dry	T	0.37	1150	840
	Dry	T	0.42	1250	840
	Dry	T	0.45	1350	840
	Dry	T	0.49	1450	840
	Dry	T	0.54	1550	840
— quarry-stones, calcareous	Dry	T	1.40	2200	840
Miscellaneous materials:					
— aggregate	Undried	D	1.8	2240	840
— aggregate (sand, gravel or stone)	Oven dried	A	1.3	2240	920
— building board, tile and lay-in panel		A	0.058	290	590
— calcium silicate brick		S	1.50	2000	840
— granolithic		E	0.87	2085	840
— mud phuska	At 50°C	I	0.52	1620	880
— tile bedding		E	1.40	2100	650
— tile hanging		C	0.84	1900	800
Roofing materials:					
— built-up roofing		D	0.16	1120	1470
— roof tile		C	0.84	1900	800
— tile, terracotta		T	0.81	1700	840
Soil:					
— alluvial clay, 40% sands		I	1.21	1960	840
— black cotton clay, Indore		I	0.61	1680	880
— black cotton clay, Madras		I	0.74	1900	880
— diatomaceous, Kieselguhr or infusorial earth	Moisture content 9%	E	0.09	480	180

Table 3.43 Thermal conductivity, density and specific heat capacity: inorganic, porous materials — *continued*

Material	Condition/test (where known)	Source	Thermal conductivity (W·m^{-1}·K^{-1})	Density (kg·m^{-3})	Specific heat (J·kg^{-1}·K^{-1})
— earth, common		E	1.28	1460	880
— earth, gravel-based		E	0.52	2050	180
Stone:					
— basalt		T	3.49	2880	840
— gneiss		T	3.49	2880	840
— granite		T	3.49	2880	840
— granite, red		E	2.9	2650	900
— hard stone (unspecified)		T	3.49	2880	840
		S	2.9	2750	840
— limestone		E	1.5	2180	720
		S	2.9	2750	840
	At 50°C	I	1.80	2420	840
— marble		S	2.9	2750	840
	Dry	T	2.91	2750	840
	Moist	T	3.49	2750	840
— marble, white		E	2	2500	880
— petit granit (blue stone)	Dry	T	2.91	2700	840
	Moist	T	3.49	2700	840
— porphyry		T	3.49	2880	840
— sandstone		E	1.83	2200	710
		T	3	2150	840
		T	1.3	2150	840
		S	5	2150	840
— sandstone tiles	Dry	T	1.2	2000	840
— slate		D	1.44	1600	1470
	At 50°C	I	1.72	2750	840
— slate shale		T	2.1	2700	840
— white calcareous stone	Firm, moist	T	2.09	2350	840
	Firm, dry	T	1.74	2350	840
	Hard, moist	T	2.68	2550	840
	Hard, dry	T	2.21	2550	840
— tufa, soft	Dry	T	0.35	1300	840
	Moist	T	0.50	1300	1260

Table 3.44 Thermal conductivity, density and specific heat capacity: organic, hygroscopic materials

Material	Condition/test (where known)	Source	Thermal conductivity (W·m^{-1}·K^{-1})	Density (kg·m^{-3})	Specific heat (J·kg^{-1}·K^{-1})
Cardboard/paper:					
— bitumen impregnated paper		E	0.06	1090	1000
— laminated paper		A	0.072	480	1380
Cloth/carpet/felt:					
— bitumen/felt layers		C	0.50	1700	1000
— carpet, simulated wool		E	0.06	200	1360
— carpet, Wilton		E	0.06	190	1360
— felt, semi-rigid, organic	At 37.7°C	A	0.035	48	710
bonded	At 37.7°C	A	0.039	88	710
— jute felt	At 50°C	I	0.042	290	880
— jute fibre	At 50°C	I	0.067	330	1090
— wool felt underlay		E	0.04	160	1360
Cork:		E	0.04	110	1800
— board		E	0.04	160	1890
— expanded		S	0.044	150	1760
— expanded, impregnated		S	0.043	150	1760
— slab		I	0.043	160	960
		I	0.055	300	960
— tiles	Conditioned	E	0.08	530	1800
Grass/straw materials:					
— straw board	At 50°C	I	0.057	310	1300
— straw fibreboard or slab		S	0.10	300	2100
— straw thatch		E	0.07	240	180
Miscellaneous materials:					
— afzelia, minunga, meranti		T	0.29	850	2070

Table 3.44 Thermal conductivity, density and specific heat capacity: organic, hygroscopic materials — *continued*

Material	Condition/test (where known)	Source	Thermal conductivity $(W \cdot m^{-1} \cdot K^{-1})$	Density $(kg \cdot m^{-3})$	Specific heat $(J \cdot kg^{-1} \cdot K^{-1})$
— ebonite, expanded		S	0.035	100	1470
— perlite board, expanded, organic bonded		A	0.052	16	1260
— glass fibre board, organic bonded		A	0.036	100	960
— weatherboard		E	0.14	650	2000
Organic materials and their derivatives:					
— coconut pith insulation board	At 50°C	I	0.06	520	1090
— coir board	At 50°C	I	0.038	97	1000
— flax shive, cement bonded board		S	0.10	520	1470
— flax shive, resin bonded board		S	0.12	500	1880
— rice husk	At 50°C	I	0.051	120	1000
— vegetable fibre sheathing		A	0.055	290	1300
Woods:					
— fir, pine		A	0.12	510	1380
— hardwood (unspecified)		T	0.05	90	2810
	Dry	T	0.17	700	1880
		S	0.23	800	1880
— maple, oak and similar hardwoods		A	0.16	720	1260
— oak, radial		E	0.19	700	2390
— oak, beech, ash, walnut meranti	Moist	T	0.23	650	3050
	Dry	T	0.17	650	2120
— pine, pitch pine	Dry	T	0.17	650	2120
	Moist	T	0.23	650	3050
— red fir, Oregon fir	Dry	T	0.14	520	2280
	Moist	T	0.17	520	3440
— resinous woods (spruce, sylvester pine)	Dry	T	0.12	530	1880
— softwood		D	0.12	510	1380
		E	0.13	630	2760
		S	0.14	550	1880
— timber	At 50°C	I	0.072	480	1680
	At 50°C	I	0.14	720	1680
— timber flooring		C	0.14	650	1200
— willow, North Canadian gaboon		T	0.12	420	2400
— willow, birch, soft beech		T	0.14	520	2280
	Moist	T	0.17	520	3440
Wood derivatives:					
— cellulosic insulation, loose fill		A	0.042	43	1380
— chipboard	At 50°C	I	0.067	430	1260
— chipboard, bonded with PF	Dry	T	0.12	650	2340
	Moist	T	0.25	650	5020
— chipboard, bonded with UF	Dry	T	0.12	630	2260
	Moist	T	0.25	630	5020
— chipboard, bonded with melamine	Dry	T	0.12	630	2260
	Moist	T	0.25	630	5020
— chipboard, perforated	At 50°C	I	0.066	350	1260
— flooring blocks		C	0.14	650	1200
— hardboard		E	0.08	600	2000
		A	0.12	880	1340
		S	0.29	1000	1680
— multiplex, beech	Dry	T	0.15	650	2300
— multiplex, North Canadian gaboon	Dry	T	0.12	450	2300
— multiplex, red fir	Dry	T	0.13	550	2300
	Moist	T	0.21	550	2300
— particle board		I	0.098	750	1300
		A	0.17	1000	1300
		A	0.12	800	1300
— plywood		A	0.12	540	1210
		E	0.15	700	1420

Table 3.44 Thermal conductivity, density and specific heat capacity: organic, hygroscopic materials — *continued*

Material	Condition/test (where known)	Source	Thermal conductivity $(W \cdot m^{-1} \cdot K^{-1})$	Density $(kg \cdot m^{-3})$	Specific heat $(J \cdot kg^{-1} \cdot K^{-1})$
— sawdust	At 50°C	I	0.051	190	1000
— softboard	At 50°C	I	0.047	250	1300
— wallboard	At 50°C	I	0.047	260	1260
— wood chip board, cement bonded		S	0.15	530	1470
— wood fibres, compressed		Y	0.055	320	100
— wood (soft) fibre, loose fill		A	0.043	45	1380
— wood particle panels		T	0.09	300	1880
		T	0.12	500	1880
		T	0.14	700	1880
	Hard	T	0.29	1000	1990
	Soft	T	0.08	250	2520
— wood shingle		D	0.12	510	1260
— woodwool board, cement bonded	At 50°C	I	0.081	400	1130
	At 50°C	I	0.11	670	1130
— woodwool roofing slabs		C	0.10	500	1000
— woodwool, xylolite cement slabs		S	0.11	450	1470
— woodwool		E	0.1	500	1000

Table 3.45 Absorptivity and emissivity: impermeable materials

Material	Condition (where known)	Absorptivity	Emissivity
Aluminium	Polished	0.10–0.40	0.03–0.06
	Dull/rough polish	0.40–0.65	0.18–0.30
	Anodised	—	0.72
Aluminium surfaced roofing		—	0.216
Asphalt	Newly–laid	0.91–0.93	—
	Weathered	0.82–0.89	—
	Block	0.85–0.98	0.90–0.98
Asphalt pavement		0.852–0.928	—
Bitumen/felt roofing		0.86–0.89	0.91
Bitumen pavement		0.86–0.89	0.90–0.98
Brass	Polished	0.30–0.50	0.03–0.05
	Dull	0.40–0.065	0.20–0.30
	Anodised	—	0.59–0.61
Bronze		0.34	—
Copper	Polished	0.18–0.50	0.02–0.05
	Dull	0.40–0.065	0.20–0.30
	Anodised	0.64	0.60
Glass	Normal	*	0.88
	Hemispherical	*	0.84
Iron	Unoxidised	—	0.05
	Bright/polished	0.40–0.65	0.20–0.377
	Oxidised	—	0.736–0.74
	Red rusted	—	0.61–0.65
	Heavily rusted	0.737	0.85–0.94
Iron, cast	Unoxidised/polished	—	0.21–0.24
	Oxidised	—	0.64–0.78
	Strongly oxidised	—	0.95
Iron, galvanised	New	0.64–0.66	0.22–0.28
	Old/very dirty	0.89–0.92	0.89
Lead	Unoxidised	—	0.05–0.075
	Old/oxidised	0.77–0.79	0.28–0.281
Rubber	Hard/glossy	—	0.945
	Grey/rough	—	0.859
Steel	Unoxidised/polished/stainless	0.20	0.074–0.097
	Oxidised	0.20	0.79–0.82
Tin	Highly polished/unoxidised	0.10–0.40	0.043–0.084
Paint			
— aluminium		0.30–0.55	0.27–0.67
— zinc		0.30	0.95
Polyvinylchloride (PVC)		—	0.90–0.92
Tile	Light colour	0.3–0.5	0.85–0.95
Varnish		—	0.80–0.98
Zinc	Polished	0.55	0.045–0.053
	Oxidised	0.05	0.11–0.25

* See manufacturers' data

Table 3.46 Absorptivity and emissivity: inorganic, porous materials

Material	Condition (where known)	Absorptivity	Emissivity
Asbestos:			
— board		—	0.96
— paper		—	0.93–0.94
— cloth		—	0.90
— cement	New	0.61	0.95–0.96
	Very dirty	0.83	0.95–0.96
Brick	Glazed/light	0.25–0.36	0.85–0.95
	Light	0.36–0.62	0.85–0.95
	Dark	0.63–0.89	0.85–0.95
Cement mortar, screed		0.73	0.93
Clay tiles	Red, brown	0.60–0.69	0.85–0.95
	Purple/dark	0.81–0.82	0.85–0.95
Concrete		0.65–0.80	0.85–0.95
— tile		0.65–0.80	0.85–0.95
— block		0.56–0.69	0.94
Plaster		0.30–0.50	0.91
Stone:			
— granite (red)		0.55	0.90–0.93
— limestone		0.33–0.53	0.90–0.93
— marble		0.44–0.592	0.90–0.93
— quartz		—	0.90
— sandstone		0.54–0.76	0.90–0.93
— slate		0.79–0.93	0.85–0.98

Table 3.47 Absorptivity and emissivity: hygroscopic materials

Material	Condition (where known)	Absorptivity	Emissivity
Paper		—	0.091–0.94
— white, bond		0.25–0.28	—
Cloth:			
— cotton, black		0.67–0.98	—
— cotton, deep blue		0.82–0.83	—
— cotton, red		0.562	—
— wool, black		0.75–0.88	—
— felt, black		0.775–0.861	—
— fabric (unspecified)		—	0.89–0.92
Wood:			
— beach		—	0.94
— oak		—	0.89–0.90
— spruce		—	0.82
— walnut		—	0.83

Table 3.48 Vapour resisivity: impermeable materials

Material	Density (kg·m⁻³)	Vapour resistivity (MN·s·g⁻¹)
Asphalt (laid)	—	∞
Bitumen roofing sheets	—	2 000–60 000
Bituminous felt	—	15 000
Glass:		
— brick	—	∞
— cellular	—	∞
— expanded/foamed	—	∞
— sheet/mirror/window	—	∞
Linoleum	1200	9 000
Metals and metal cladding	—	∞
Paint, gloss (vapour resistant)	—	40–200
Plastic, hard	—	45 000
Polyvinylchloride (PVC) sheets on tile	—	800–1300
Rubber	1200–1500	4500
Rubber tiles	1200–1500	∞
Tiles:		
— ceramic	—	500–5000
— glazed ceramic	—	∞

Table 3.49 Vapour resisivity: non-hygroscopic materials

Material	Density (kg·m⁻³)	Vapour resistivity (MN·s·g⁻¹)
Mineral fibre/wool:		
— glass fibre/wool	—	5–7
— mineral fibre/wool	—	5–9
— rock wool	—	6.5–7.5
Phenol formaldehyde	—	19–20
Phenolic (closed cell)	—	150–750
Polyethylene foam	—	20 000
Polystyrene:		
— expanded	—	100–750
— extruded	—	600–1500
— extruded without skin	—	350–400
Polyurethylene foam	—	115–1000
Polyvinylchloride (PVC) foam, rigid	—	40–1300
Urea formaldehyde foam	—	5–20

Table 3.50 Vapour resisivity: inorganic, porous materials

Material	Density (kg·m⁻³)	Vapour resistivity (MN·s·g⁻¹)
Asbestos cement	800	70
Asbestos cement sheet, substitutes	1600–1900	185–1000
Brick:		
— blast furnace slag	1000–2000	350–500
— calcium silicate	<1400	25–50
	>1400	75–125
— dense	>2000	100–250
— heavyweight	>1700	45–70
— lightweight	<1000	25–50
— mediumweight	>1300	23–45
— sand lime	<1400	25–50
	>1500	75–200
Concrete:		
— blocks (lightweight)	—	15–150
— cast	<1000	14–33
	>1000	30–80
	>1900	115–1000
— cellular	450–1300	9–50
— close textured	—	350–750
— expanded clay	500–1000	25–33
	1000–1800	33–75
— foamed steam hardened	400–800	25–50
— insulating	—	23–26
— natural pumice	500–1400	25–75
— no fines	1800	20
— polystyrene, foamed	400	80–100
— porous aggregate	1000–2000	15–50
— porous aggregate (without quartz sand)	—	25–75
— slag and Rhine sand	1500–1700	50–200
Gypsum plasterboard	—	30–60
Plaster/mortar:		
— cement based	1900–2000	75–205
— lime based	1600–1800	45–205
— gypsum	—	30–60
Stone:		
— basalt	—	∞
— bluestone	—	∞
— clay	—	75
— granite	—	150–∞
— limestone, firm	—	350–450
— limestone, soft	—	130–160
— limestone, soft tufa	—	25–50
— marble	—	150–∞
— porphyry	—	∞
— sandstone	—	75–450
— slate	—	150–450
— slatey shale	—	>3000
Tile:		
— clay, ceramic	—	750–1500
— floor tiles, ceramic	—	115
— roof tiles, terracotta	—	180–220

Table 3.51 Vapour resisivity: organic, hygroscopic materials

Material	Density (kg·m⁻³)	Vapour resistivity (MN·s·g⁻¹)
Carpet:		
— normal backing	—	7–20
— foam backed/underlay	—	100–300
Chipboard:	—	230–500
— bonded with melanine	—	300–500
— bonded with PF	—	250–750
— bonded with UF	—	200–700
— cement-bonded	—	19–50
Cork:		
— insulation	—	25–50
— expanded	—	23–50
— expanded, impregnated	—	45–230
— expanded, bitumous binding	—	45–230
Corkboard	—	50–200
Fibreboard:	—	150–375
— bitumen-coated	—	25
— cement-based	—	19–50
— hardwood fibres	—	350
— porous wood fibres	—	25
Hardboard	—	230–1000
Mineral/vegetable fibre insulation	—	5
Multiplex	800	200–2000
— light pine	—	80
— North Canadian gaboon	—	80
— red pine	—	875–250
— triplex	700	200–500
Paper	—	500
Particle board, softwood	—	25
Plywood	—	150–2000
— decking	—	1000–6000
— marine	—	230–375
— sheathing	—	144–1000
Strawboard	—	45–70
Wood:		
— ash	—	200–1850
— balsa	—	45–265
— beech	—	200–1850
— beech, soft	—	90–700
— birch	—	90–700
— fir	—	45–1850
— North Canadian gaboon	—	45–1850
— oak	—	200–1850
— pine	—	45–1850
— pine, Northern red/Oregon	—	90–200
— pine, pitch	—	200–1850
— spruce	—	45–1850
— teak	—	185–1850
— walnut	—	200–1850
— willow	—	45–1850
Wood lath	—	4
Woodwool:		
— slab	—	15–40
— cement slab	—	15–50
— magnesia slab	—	19–50

References for Appendix 3.A7

A7.1   Clark J A, Yanske P P and Pinney A A *The harmonisation of thermal properties of building materials* BEPAC Research Report (Reading: Building Environmental Performance Analysis Club) (1990)

A7.2   *ASHRAE Handbook: Applications* (Atlanta, GA: American Society of Heating, Refrigerating and Air-Conditioning Engineers) (1985)

A7.3   *BS 5250: 1989 (1995): Code of practice for the control of condensation in buildings* (London: British Standards Institution) (1989)

A7.4   *CIBSE Guide A: Design data* and *CIBSE Guide C: Reference data* (London: Chartered Institution of Building Services Engineers) (1986)

A7.5   *NBN B62-002: Thermische geleidbaarheid van de bouwmaterialen/Conductivities thermiques des materiaux de construction* (Brussels: Institut Belge de Normalisation) (1980)

A7.6   *DOE-2 Reference Manual* Report No. LBL-8706 (Berkley CA, USA: Lawrence Berkley Laboratory) (1984)

A7.7   *ESP-r Reference Manual* (Glasgow: Energy Simulation Research Unit/University of Strathclyde) (1989)

A7.8   DTU Regles Th-K77 *Cahiers du CSTB* **1478** November 1977 (Marne La Vallee: Centre Scientific et Technique du Batiment) (1977)

A7.9   *DIN 4108: Warescutz im Hochbau, Warme und feuteschutztechnische Kenwerte* (Berlin: Deutsches Institut fur Normung) (1981)

A7.10   *UNI 7357: Conduttivita termica apparente di materiali* (Milan: Ente Nazionale Italiano di Unificazione) (1974)

A7.11   *IS 3792-1978: Revised guide for heat insulation of non-industrial buildings* (New Delhi: Indian Standards Institution)

A7.12   Tinker J A *Aspects of mix proportioning and moisture content on the thermal conductivity of lightweight aggregate concretes* PhD thesis (Salford: University of Salford) (1985)

A7.13   Tinker J A and O'Rourke A Development of a low thermal conductivity building mortar *Second Europ. Conf. on Architecture, Paris, December 1989* (1990)

A7.14   *IEA Annex XIV: Condensation and Energy 1: Material properties* (Leuven: Laboratorium voor Bouwfysica/Kotholieke Universiteit Leuven) (1991)

A7.15   *Eigenschappen van bouwen isolatiematerialen* Report No. 17 (Rotterdam: Stichting Bouwresearch)

Appendix 3.A8: Thermal properties of typical constructions

Tables 3.54 to 3.60 provide values of thermal transmittance, thermal admittance, decrement factor and surface factor for a range of constructions. The tables are provided to illustrate the thermal properties of typical constructions. For design purposes, values should be calculated for the specific construction under consideration using the methods given in this Guide. The tabulated values have been calculated making certain assumptions about the densities, thermal conductivities and specific heat capacities of the materials involved. These assumed values are given in Tables 3.52 and 3.53.

Representative values for thermal conductivity (λ) have been used in the calculation of U-values for typical constructions. Manufacturers' products may exhibit better thermal properties than those given for the generic types of material listed in Table 3.52. Where such products are likely to be used, U-values may be calculated using thermal conductivity data obtained from tests provided that the data and test methods have been properly accredited, see Appendix 3.A2.

In practice, for some constructions, measurements have indicated U-values greater than those tabulated. One reason for this apparent discrepancy is the effect of thermal bridging which should be taken into account using the methods described in section 3.3.11.

Calculated U-values may also underestimate the actual thermal transmittance due to ventilation within the construction. The effectiveness of thermal insulation depends largely on preventing air movement within the insulating layer. Air flow through gaps and cracks must be avoided, particularly on the warm side of the insulation. Air flow must also be avoided between insulation boards or batts and behind wall linings. Such deficiencies in installation have been shown to add between 0.05 and 0.2 $W \cdot m^{-2} \cdot K^{-1}$ to the nominal U-value of the construction.

The use of unrealistic values for the thermal conductivities of building materials also contibutes to the under-estimation of U-values. Tabulated values are usually based on laboratory measurements using small well-prepared samples. In buildings, the thermal conductivities of the same materials may differ appreciably from the laboratory measurements due to variations in quality during production, storage conditions on site and variations in construction techniques.

The non-steady state thermal properties for ground floors have been calculated by adding an equivalent thickness of earth to the construction and setting the outside surface resistance to zero. The internal surface heat transfer coefficient is calculated for horizontal surfaces with downward heat flow. For floors in contact with the earth and floors exposed to inside air the decrement factor is set to zero since external sol-air fluctuations have no effect in these cases.

Table 3.52 Properties of materials used in calculation of thermal properties of typical constructions

Material	Density (kg·m⁻¹)	Thermal conductivity † (W·m⁻¹·K⁻¹)	Specific heat capacity (J·kg⁻¹·K⁻¹)
Masonry materials:			
— sandstone	2000	1.5	840
— brick (outer leaf)	1700	0.84	800
— brick (inner leaf)	1700	0.62	800
— no–fines concrete	2000	1.13	1000
— concrete block (dense)	2300	1.63	1000
— precast concrete (dense)	2100	1.4	840
— cast concrete	2000	1.13	1000
— lightweight aggregate concrete block	600	0.19	1000
— autoclaved aerated concrete block	700	0.27	1050
autoclaved aerated concrete block	500	0.18	1050
— screed	1200	0.41	840
— ballast (chips or paving slab)	1800	0.96	1000
Surface materials/finishes:			
— external render	1300	0.5	1000
— plaster (dense)	1300	0.5	1000
— plaster (lightweight)	600	0.16	1000
— plasterboard	950	0.16	840
Insulation materials:			
— mineral fibre	30	0.035	1000
— expanded polystyrene (EPS)	25	0.035	1400
— extruded polystyrene	25	0.035	1400
— polyurethane	30	0.025	1400
— urea formaldehyde (UF) foam	10	0.040	1400
— blown fibre	12	0.040	840
Miscellaneous materials:			
— plywood sheathing	530	0.14	1800
— timber studding	650	0.14	1200
— timber battens	650	0.14	1200
— timber decking	650	0.14	1200
— timber flooring	650	0.14	1200
— chipboard	650	0.14	1200
— vinyl floor covering	1200	0.19	1470
— waterproof roof covering	960	0.19	840
— wood blocks	650	0.14	1200
— floor joists	650	0.14	1200

† Note that these are 'traditional' UK values, some of which have been superseded, e.g. masonry materials, see Table 3.1

Table 3.53 Values of surface and airspace resistance used in calculation of thermal properties of typical constructions

Structure	External surface resistance (m²·K·W⁻¹)	Internal surface resistance (m²·K·W⁻¹)	Airspace resistance (m2·K·W⁻¹)
External walls	0.06	0.12	0.18
Party walls and internal partitions	0.12	0.12	0.18
Roofs:			
— pitched	0.04	0.10	0.18
— flat	0.04	0.10	0.16
Internal floors/ceilings	0.12	0.12	0.20

Table 3.54 Thermal properties of typical wall constructions

Construction	Transmittance U (W·m⁻²·K⁻¹)	Admittance		Decrement factor		Surface factor	
		Y (W·m⁻²·K⁻¹)	ω(h)	f	ϕ(h)	F	ψ(h)
1 Stone walls							
(a) 600 mm stone, 50 mm airspace, 25 mm dense plaster on laths	1.23	3.03	1.6	0.03	17	0.68	0.8
(b) 600 mm stone, 50 mm airspace, 25 mm EPS insulation, 12 mm plasterboard on battens	0.65	1.09	2.1	0.02	17	0.89	0.3
2 No-fines concrete walls							
(a) 19 mm render, 220 mm no-fines concrete, 50 mm airspace, 12 mm plasterboard on battens	1.50	2.42	0.9	0.24	9	0.72	0.4
(b) 19 mm render, 220 mm no-fines concrete, 50 mm mineral fibre insulation between battens, 12 mm plasterboard on battens	0.52	0.90	2.9	0.18	9.1	0.92	0.3
(c) 19 mm render, 50 mm mineral fibre insulation between battens, 220 mm no-fines concrete, 50 mm airspace, 12 mm plasterboard on battens	0.48	2.42	0.9	0.08	10	0.72	0.4
3 Solid brick walls							
(a) 220 mm solid brick, 13 mm dense plaster	2.14	4.25	1.4	0.51	6.2	0.55	1.3
(b) 220 mm solid brick, 50 mm airspace, 12 mm plasterboard on battens	1.43	2.32	1.2	0.39	7.1	0.74	0.4
(c) 220 mm solid brick, 50 mm mineral fibre insulation between battens, 12 mm plasterboard on battens	0.51	0.90	2.9	0.29	7.9	0.93	0.3
(d) 19 mm render, 50 mm EPS insulation, 220 mm solid brick, 13 mm dense plaster	0.49	4.29	1.5	0.17	9.9	0.56	1.4
4 Dense concrete walls							
(a) 19 mm render, 200 mm dense concrete block, 13 mm dense plaster	2.73	5.37	0.9	0.36	7	0.41	1.5
(b) 19 mm render, 200 mm dense concrete block, 50 mm airspace, 12 mm plasterboard on battens	1.68	2.49	0.8	0.27	7.5	0.71	0.3
(c) 19 mm render, 200 mm dense concrete block, 25 mm polyurethane insulation, 12 mm plasterboard on battens	0.71	1.04	2.2	0.22	8	0.9	0.3
(d) 19 mm render, 50 mm mineral fibre insulation between battens, 200 mm dense concrete block, 13 mm dense plaster	0.56	5.46	0.9	0.16	8.4	0.39	1.5
5 Precast concrete panel walls							
(a) 80 mm dense concrete, 25 mm EPS insulation, 100 mm dense concrete, 13 mm dense plaster	0.95	5.40	1.6	0.37	7.6	0.49	2.2
(b) 80 mm dense concrete, 25 mm EPS insulation, 100 mm dense concrete, 50 mm airspace, 12 mm plasterboard on battens	0.78	2.56	1.1	0.22	8.5	0.71	0.5
(c) 80 mm dense concrete, 50 mm EPS insulation, 100 mm dense concrete, 12 mm plasterboard	0.55	4.36	1.3	0.29	8.2	0.54	1.3
(d) 19 mm render, 80 mm dense concrete, 50 mm EPS insulation, 100 mm dense concrete, 13 mm dense plaster	0.56	5.48	1.6	0.28	8.9	0.48	2.3
6 Brick/brick cavity walls							
(a) 105 mm brick, 50 mm airspace, 105 mm brick, 13 mm dense plaster	1.47	4.4	1.7	0.44	7.7	0.58	1.6
(b) 105 mm brick, 50 mm airspace, 105 mm brick, 13 mm lightweight plaster	1.36	3.49	1.4	0.40	7.9	0.63	1
(c) 105 mm brick, 50 mm UF foam insulation, 105 mm brick, 13 mm dense plaster	0.57	4.66	1.8	0.32	9.0	0.56	1.8
(d) 105 mm brick, 50 mm blown fibre insulation, 105 mm brick, 13 mm dense plaster	0.57	4.66	1.8	0.32	9.0	0.56	1.8
(e) 105 mm brick, 25 mm EPS insulation, 105 mm brick, 12 mm plasterboard on battens	0.79	3.74	1.5	0.31	8.9	0.61	1.1
7 Brick/dense concrete block cavity walls							
(a) 105 mm brick, 50 mm airspace, 100 mm dense concrete block, 13 mm dense plaster	1.75	5.54	1.2	0.35	7.8	0.43	2
(b) 105 mm brick, 50 mm UF foam insulation, 100 mm dense concrete block, 13 mm dense plaster	0.61	5.74	1.3	0.25	9.0	0.42	2.2
(c) 105 mm brick, 50 mm blown fibre insulation, 100 mm dense concrete block, 13 mm dense plaster	0.61	5.74	1.3	0.25	9	0.42	2.2
(d) 105 mm brick, 50 mm EPS insulation, 100 mm dense concrete block, 13 mm dense plaster	0.55	5.75	1.3	0.25	9.1	0.42	2.2

Table 3.54 Thermal properties of typical wall constructions

Construction	Transmittance U (W·m^{-2}·K^{-1})	Admittance		Decrement factor		Surface factor	
		Y (W·m^{-2}·K^{-1})	ω (h)	f	ϕ (h)	F	ψ (h)
8 Brick/lightweight aggregate concrete block cavity walls							
(a) 105 mm brick, 50 mm airspace, 100 mm lightweight aggregate concrete block, 13 mm dense plaster	0.96	2.74	2.7	0.56	7.1	0.78	1
(b) 105 mm brick, 50 mm UF foam insulation, 100 mm lightweight aggregate concrete block, 13 mm dense plaster	0.47	2.99	2.8	0.44	8.4	0.77	1.2
(c) 105 mm brick, 50 mm blown fibre insulation, 100 mm lightweight aggregate concrete block, 13 mm dense plaster	0.47	2.99	2.8	0.44	8.4	0.77	1.2
(d) 105 mm brick, 100 mm blown fibre insulation, 100 mm lightweight aggregate concrete block, 13 mm dense plaster	0.30	3.06	2.8	0.41	8.9	0.77	1.2
(e) 105 mm brick, 50 mm EPS insulation, 100 mm lightweight aggregate concrete block, 13 mm dense plaster	0.44	3.00	2.8	0.43	8.6	0.77	1.2
(f) 105 mm brick, 25 mm airspace, 25 mm EPS insulation, 100 mm lightweight aggregate concrete block, 13 mm dense plaster	0.57	2.95	2.8	0.46	8.2	0.78	1.2
9 Brick/autoclaved aerated concrete block cavity walls							
(a) 105 mm brick, 50 mm airspace, 100 mm autoclaved aerated concrete block (density 700 kg·m^{-3}), 13 mm lightweight plaster	1.07	2.50	2.1	0.52	7.1	0.76	0.8
(b) 105 mm brick, 50 mm airspace, 150 mm autoclaved aerated concrete block (density 500 kg·m^{-3}), 13 mm lightweight plaster	0.71	2.11	2.4	0.43	8.8	0.81	0.7
(c) 105 mm brick, 25 mm airspace, 25 mm EPS insulation, 150 mm autoclaved aerated concrete block (density 500 kg·m^{-3}), 13 mm lightweight plaster	0.47	2.18	2.3	0.32	10	0.80	0.7
10 Timber frame walls							
(a) 105 mm brick, 50 mm airspace, 19 mm plywood sheathing, 95 mm studding, 13 mm plasterboard	1.13	1.67	1.9	0.69	4.8	0.83	0.4
(b) 105 mm brick, 50 mm airspace, 19 mm plywood sheathing, 95 mm studding, 95 mm mineral fibre insulation between studs, 13 mm plasterboard	0.29	0.86	4.1	0.6	6.15	1	0.4
(c) 105 mm brick, 50 mm airspace, 19 mm plywood sheathing, 140 mm studding, 140 mm mineral fibre insulation between studs, 13 mm plasterboard	0.21	0.86	4.5	0.56	6.7	0.97	0.4
11 Party walls (internal)							
(a) 12 mm plasterboard on battens, 100 mm lightweight aggregate concrete block, 75 mm airspace, 100 mm lightweight aggregate concrete block, 12 mm plasterboard on battens	0.62	2.6	2.5	—	—	0.8	0.9
(b) 13 mm dense plaster, 215 mm brick, 13 mm dense plaster	1.57	4.76	1.8	—	—	0.5	1.8
(c) 13 mm dense plaster, 215 mm dense concrete block, 13 mm dense plaster	2.36	5.81	1.2	—	—	0.4	2.2

Table 3.55 Thermal properties of typical roof constructions

Construction	Transmittance U (W·m^{-2}·K^{-1})	Admittance		Decrement factor		Surface factor	
		Y (W·m^{-2}·K^{-1})	ω(h)	f	ϕ(h)	F	ψ(h)
1 Flat concrete roofs							
(a) Waterproof covering, 75 mm screed, 150 mm cast concrete, 13 mm dense plaster	2.05	5.19	1.1	0.35	7.4	0.45	1.6
(b) Waterproof roof covering, 35 mm polyurethane insulation, vapour control layer, 75 mm screed, 150 mm cast concrete, 13 mm dense plaster	0.53	5.13	1.1	0.17	9.1	0.44	1.5
(c) Waterproof roof covering, 100 mm polyurethane insulation, vapour control layer, 75 mm screed, 150 mm cast concrete, 13 mm dense plaster	0.22	5.13	1.1	0.15	10	0.44	1.5
(d) Waterproof roof covering, 200 mm polyurethane insulation, vapour control layer, 75 mm screed, 150 mm cast concrete, 13 mm dense plaster	0.12	5.13	1.1	0.13	12.3	0.44	1.5
(e) Ballast (chips or paving slab), 50 mm extruded polystyrene insulation, waterproof roof covering, 75 mm screed, 150 mm cast concrete, 13 mm dense plaster	0.51	5.13	1.1	0.17	10	0.4	1.5
(f) Ballast (chips or paving slab), 100 mm extruded polystyrene insulation, waterproof roof covering, 75 mm screed, 150 mm cast concrete, 13 mm dense plaster	0.30	5.13	1.1	0.16	10.5	0.44	1.5
2 Flat timber roofs							
(a) Waterproof roof covering, 19 mm timber decking, ventilated airspace, vapour control layer, 12 mm plasterboard	1.87	1.88	0.8	0.99	0.7	0.78	0.2
(b) Waterproof roof covering, 19 mm timber decking, ventilated airspace, 50 mm mineral fibre insulation, vapour control layer, 12 mm plasterboard	0.51	0.84	3.2	0.99	1	0.94	0.3
(c) Waterproof roof covering, 35 mm polyurethane insulation, vapour control layer, 19 mm timber decking, unventilated airspace, 12 mm plasterboard	0.52	1.42	3.4	0.93	1.9	0.90	0.6
(d) Waterproof roof covering, 100 mm polyurethane insulation, vapour control layer, 19 mm timber decking, unventilated airspace, 12 mm plasterboard	0.22	1.55	4	0.89	2.9	0.92	0.7
(e) Waterproof roof covering, 200 mm polyurethane decking, insulation, vapour control layer, 19 mm timber unventilated airspace, 12 mm plasterboard	0.12	1.61	4	0.76	5.3	0.92	0.7

Table 3.56 Thermal properties of typical internal partitions

Construction	Transmittance U (W·m^{-2}·K^{-1})	Admittance		Decrement factor		Surface factor	
		Y (W·m^{-2}·K^{-1})	ω(h)	f	ϕ(h)	F	ψ(h)
(a) 13 mm lightweight plaster 105 mm brick, 13 mm lightweight plaster	1.75	3.58	2.6	—	—	0.72	1.5
(b) 13 mm lightweight plaster, 100 mm lightweight concrete block, 13 mm lightweight plaster	1.05	2.09	4	—	—	0.90	0.9
(c) 12 mm plasterboard, timber studding, 12 mm plasterboard	1.75	0.69	5.6	—	—	0.99	0.3

Table 3.57 Thermal properties of typical internal floors/ceilings

Construction	Transmittance U (W·m^{-2}·K^{-1})	Admittance		Decrement factor		Surface factor	
		Y (W·m^{-2}·K^{-1})	ω(h)	f	ϕ(h)	F	ψ(h)
(a) 50 mm screed, 150 mm cast concrete, 13 mm dense plaster	2.38	5.09	1.2	—	—	0.45	1.6
(b) 25 mm wood block, 65 mm cast concrete, 50 mm airspace, 12 mm plasterboard ceiling	1.58	2.41	1.2	—	—	0.73	0.5
(c) 19 mm timber flooring or chipboard on 100 mm joists, 12 mm plasterboard ceiling	1.88	1.89	0.8	—	—	0.78	0.2

Table 3.58 Thermal properties of typical floors in contact with the earth

Construction	Transmittance U (W·m⁻²·K⁻¹)	Admittance		Decrement factor		Surface factor	
		Y (W·m⁻²·K⁻¹)	ω(h)	f	ϕ(h)	F	ψ(h)
1 Solid concrete floors							
(a) Vinyl floor covering, 75 mm screed, 150 mm cast concrete	*	3.20	1.4	0	0	0.60	1
(b) 10 mm carpet/underlay, 75 mm screed, 150 mm cast concrete	*	2.34	0.9	0	0	0.69	0.4
(c) Vinyl floor covering, 75 mm screed, 50 mm extruded polystyrene insulation, 150 mm cast concrete	*	3.58	2.5	0	0	0.67	1.8
(d) Vinyl floor covering, 19 mm timber or chipboard, 50 mm extruded polystyrene insulation, 150 mm cast concrete	*	1.68	3.7	0	0	0.89	0.8
2 Suspended timber floors							
(a) Vinyl floor covering, 19 mm timber or chipboard on 100 mm joists, ventilated underfloor cavity	*	3.13	0.5	0	0	0.57	0.3
(b) Vinyl floor covering, 19 mm timber or chipboard on 100 mm joists, 100 mm mineral fibre between joists, ventilated underfloor cavity	*	2.10	4	0	0	0.66	0.1
(c) 10 mm carpet/underlay, 19 mm timber or chipboard on 100 mm joists, ventilated underfloor cavity	*	2.44	0.1	0	0	0.66	0.1
(d) 10 mm carpet/underlay, 19 mm timber or chipboard on 100 mm joists, 100 mm mineral fibre between joists, ventilated underfloor cavity	*	1.15	3.7	0	0	0.92	0.5

* Thermal transmittance of floors depends on upon the size and shape of the floor, see section 3.5.

Table 3.59 Thermal properties of typical floors exposed to outside air below

Construction	Transmittance U (W·m⁻²·K⁻¹)	Admittance		Decrement factor		Surface factor	
		Y (W·m⁻²·K⁻¹)	ω(h)	f	ϕ(h)	F	ψ(h)
(a) Vinyl floor covering, 50 mm screed, 150 mm cast concrete	2.01	3.39	1.2	0.43	6.7	0.57	1
(b) Vinyl floor covering, 50 mm screed, 150 mm cast concrete, 50 mm mineral fibre insulation between battens, 12 mm cementitious building board on underside	0.50	3.43	1.1	0.14	8.6	0.56	0.9
(c) Vinyl floor covering, 50 mm screed, 150 mm cast concrete, 100 mm mineral fibre insulation between battens, 12 mm cementitious building board on underside	0.29	3.43	1.1	0.13	9.0	0.56	0.9
(d) 10 mm carpet/underlay, 50 mm screed, 150 mm cast concrete, 100 mm mineral fibre insulation between battens, 12 mm cementitious building board on underside	0.28	2.48	0.7	0.10	9.1	0.67	0.4
(e) Vinyl floor covering, 19 mm timber or chipboard on 100 mm joists, 12 mm cementitious building board on underside	1.52	1.91	1.8	0.98	1.2	0.77	0.6
(f) Vinyl floor covering, 19 mm timber or chipboard on 100 mm joists, 100 mm mineral fibre insulation between joists, 12 mm cementitious building board on underside	0.30	1.73	4.2	0.95	2.1	0.92	0.9
(g) 10 mm carpet/underlay, 19 mm timber or chipboard on 100 mm joists, 100 mm mineral fibre insulation 12 mm cementitious building board on underside	0.29	1.15	3.8	0.93	2.2	0.92	0.6

Table 3.60 Thermal properties of typical floors exposed to internal air below

Construction	Transmittance U (W·m^{-2}·K^{-1})	Admittance		Decrement factor		Surface factor	
		Y (W·m^{-2}·K^{-1})	ω(h)	f	ϕ(h)	F	ψ(h)
(a) Vinyl floor covering, 50 mm screed, 150 mm cast concrete	1.77	3.78	1.6	—	—	0.56	1.5
(b) Vinyl floor covering, 50 mm screed, 150 mm cast concrete, 50 mm mineral fibre insulation between battens, 12 mm cementitious building board on underside	0.48	3.49	1.1	—	—	0.55	1
(c) Vinyl floor covering, 50 mm screed, 150 mm cast concrete, 100 mm mineral fibre insulation between battens, 12 mm cementitious building board on underside	0.29	3.46	1.1	—	—	0.56	0.9
(d) 10 mm carpet/underlay, 50 mm screed, 150 mm cast concrete, 100 mm mineral fibre insulation between battens, 12 mm cementitious building board on underside	0.28	2.50	0.7	—	—	0.66	0.4
(e) Vinyl floor covering, 19 mm timber or chipboard on 100 mm joists, 12 mm cementitious building board on underside	1.38	1.46	5.1	—	—	0.97	0.8
(f) Vinyl floor covering, 19 mm timber or chipboard on 100 mm joists, 100 mm mineral fibre insulation between joists, 12 mm cementitious building board on underside	0.30	1.78	4.8	—	—	0.95	1
(g) 10 mm carpet/underlay, 19 mm timber or chipboard on 100 mm joists, 100 mm mineral fibre insulation 12 mm cementitious building board on underside	0.29	1.19	4.6	—	—	0.96	0.6

4 Air infiltration and natural ventilation

4.1 Introduction

Air infiltration is the unintentional leakage of air through a building due to imperfections in the structure (mainly cracks around doors, windows or in-fill panels or between cladding sheets) and such other joints or perforations as may exist in the structure. It is closely dependent on the construction, materials, workmanship and condition of the building. Infiltration can represent a significant additional heating or cooling load, and can adversely affect the operation of ventilation systems. Testing to determine the level of air-tightness is recommended, see section 4.5.

Natural ventilation is the airflow through a building resulting from the designed provision of specified routes such as openable windows, ventilators, ducts, shafts, etc.

Both infiltration and natural ventilation depend on the natural forces of gravity and wind, and so will not produce a constant rate of airflow under all conditions. To compensate for the variability of these driving forces some means of control is usually applied to natural ventilation. However, rates of air infiltration cannot be similarly controlled.

Reliance on infiltration as the sole means of ventilation to meet occupancy needs is becoming less acceptable and current Building Regulations[1] places emphasis on the deliberate provision of ventilation.

In the interests of energy economy and of the quality of the indoor environment, the building designer should endeavour to minimise infiltration by making the structure as airtight as possible except for the intended ventilation openings. Appropriate ventilation must then be provided to ensure that the necessary air change rates for a particular building or purpose will be satisfied. Guidance on ventilation for acceptable environmental conditions is given in Section 1: *Environmental criteria for design*.

It is necessary to calculate infiltration and natural ventilation rates for the following purposes:

— to ensure that ventilation is adequate to meet occupancy or other ventilation requirements

— to determine the heat losses or gains arising from infiltration in order to perform heating and cooling load calculations.

The first of these involves calculation procedures for the sizing of openings to ensure that ventilation requirements are met throughout the full range of weather conditions.

For the determination of infiltration heat losses/gains, it is assumed that ventilation requirements are satisfied by alternative means, i.e. by natural or mechanical ventilation, and that the energy implications of this ventilation are additional to those due to infiltration.

The purpose of this section of Guide A is to:

— outline the mechanisms of air infiltration and natural ventilation

— explain how the driving forces may be evaluated

— describe methods for calculating or estimating air infiltration and natural ventilation rates.

Section 4.3 provides general guidance on the theory of airflow through openings and the determination of the driving forces that produce such flow in buildings. Section 4.4 covers alternative methods of predicting air infiltration and natural ventilation rates. These range from the use of empirical data to complex numerical calculation techniques. Section 4.5 considers air-tightness testing.

For detailed information on designing buildings for natural ventilation reference should be made to CIBSE Applications Manual AM10: *Natural ventilation in non-domestic buildings*[2].

4.2 Notation

A	Area of opening (m_2)
A_b	Equivalent area for ventilation by stack effect only (m)
A_w	Equivalent area for ventilation by wind only (m)
A_1, A_2	Area of opening 1, 2 etc. (m^2)
c	Specific heat capacity of air $(J \cdot kg^{-1} \cdot K^{-1})$
C_d	Discharge coefficient
C_j	Flow coefficient for path j
C_p	Wind pressure coefficient
C_{p1}	Wind pressure coefficient on facade 1 of building
C_{p2}	Wind pressure coefficient on facade 2 of building
$C_R(z)$	Roughness coefficient for terrain at height z
C_T	Topography coefficient
g	Acceleration due to gravity $(9.81 \ m \cdot s^{-2})$
h_a	Difference between heights h_1 and h_2 (m)
h_1, h_2	Heights above ground of centres of openings 1 and 2 (m)
$\mathcal{J}_\phi$	Function of angle of window opening ϕ
k	Flow coefficient $(m^3 \cdot s^{-1} \cdot Pa^{-n})$
k_1	Flow coefficient per unit length of crack $(L \cdot s^{-1} \cdot m^{-1} \cdot Pa^{-n})$
L_c	Total length of crack or opening window joint (m)
N	Air change rate (h^{-1})
n	Flow exponent
n_j	Flow exponent for path j
p_i	Inside pressure of building (Pa)
p_{oj}	External pressure due to wind and temperature acting on path j (Pa)
p_w	Surface pressure due to wind (Pa)
Q	Volumetric flow rate through opening $(m^3 \cdot s^{-1})$
Q_b	Volumetric flow rate due to stack effect only $(m^3 \cdot s^{-1})$
Q_c'	Volumetric flow rate through crack $(L \cdot s^{-1})$

Q_t Total volume flow rate $(m^3 \cdot s^{-1})$

q_v Air infiltration heat loss factor per unit room volume $(W \cdot K^{-1} \cdot m^{-3})$

Q_w Volume flow rate due to wind only $(m^3 \cdot s^{-1})$

S Surface area of building (m^2)

t_i Mean inside temperature $(°C)$

$\bar{t}$ Mean of temperature t_i and t_o $(°C)$

t_o Mean outside temperature $(°C)$

v Mean wind speed $(m \cdot s^{-1})$

v_r Mean wind speed at building roof height $(m \cdot s^{-1})$

v_{ref} Reference wind speed measured in open country at datum height of 10 m (m/s)

v_z Mean wind speed at height z $(m \cdot s^{-1})$

z Height above ground level (m)

ΔC_p Difference in wind pressure coefficient

Δp Pressure difference (Pa)

Δt Difference between mean inside and outside temperatures $(°C)$

ε Ratio of areas of openings 1 and 2

θ Wind angle $(°)$

λ Total number of flow paths

ρ Density of air $(kg \cdot m^{-3})$

ϕ Angle of window opening $(°)$

Note: in compound units, the abbreviation 'L' has been used to denote 'litre'.

4.3   Outline of air infiltration and ventilation theory

4.3.1   General

The rate of airflow through a building depends upon the areas and resistances of the various apertures (both intentionally provided and fortuitous) and the pressure difference between one end of the flow path and the other. This pressure difference may be due to the wind or differences in density of the air due to the indoor–outdoor temperature differences (commonly referred to as 'stack effect'), or both.

The effect of wind is to drive air into the building through gaps and openings on the windward side of the building, where the surface pressure is high. The air then passes from one side of the building to the other and exits through apertures on the leeward side, where the pressure is low, see Figure 4.1. The higher the wind speed, the higher will be the air infiltration and natural ventilation rates.

Cool air is denser than warm air. Therefore, in a heated building in winter, gravity (i.e. 'stack effect') causes cold air from outside to enter through low level gaps and openings to displace the warmer internal air, which escapes through gaps and openings at high level, see Figure 4.2. This direction of movement would be reversed in summer if the temperature of the air inside were cooler than that outside.

When both wind and stack effects apply, the magnitude and directions of air infiltration will vary depending on the relative strengths of the two forces and whether they are acting locally in the same or opposite directions, see Figure 4.3.

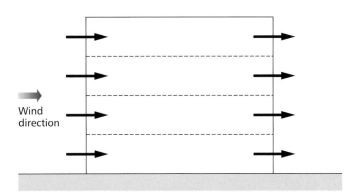

Figure 4.1 Wind driven airflow through a building

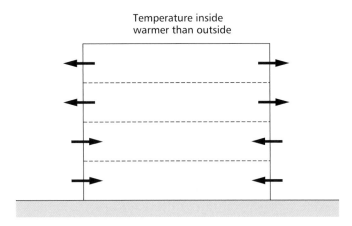

Figure 4.2 Temperature-driven airflow (stack effect) through a building

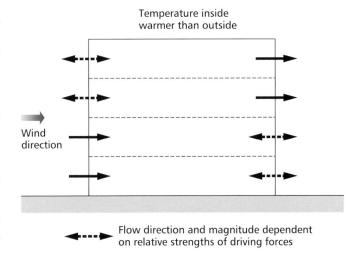

Figure 4.3 Combined wind- and temperature-driven airflow through a building

The routes by which air moves within a building will depend on the presence of such features as corridors, stairwells, lift shafts, flues and mechanical ventilation systems.

4.3.2 Flow through openings

The magnitude of the airflow through an opening is a function of the applied pressure difference across the opening and its length, cross-sectional area and internal geometry. This relationship is described by the empirical power law:

$$Q = k \, (\Delta p)^n \qquad (4.1)$$

where Q is the volumetric flow rate through the opening ($m^3 \cdot s^{-1}$), k is the flow coefficient ($m^3 \cdot s^{-1} \cdot Pa^{-n}$), Δp is the pressure difference across the opening (Pa) and n is the flow exponent.

The flow coefficient (k) is related to the size of opening. The flow exponent (n) characterises the flow regime, its value varying between 0.5 for fully turbulent flow to 1.0 for laminar flow. Typical turbulent flow paths include orifice-type openings such as purpose provided air vents and open windows. Airflow through small, adventitious cracks and gaps tends to be of a more laminar nature, with typical flow exponent values between 0.6 and 0.7.

When considering infiltration through cracks, it is convenient to express the flow coefficient in terms of metre length of crack or opening. Equation 4.1 then becomes:

$$Q_c' = L_c \, k_1 \, (\Delta p)^n \qquad (4.2)$$

where Q_c' is the volumetric flow rate through the crack ($L \cdot s^{-1}$), L_c is the total length of crack or opening (m) and k_1 is the flow coefficient per unit length of opening ($L \cdot s^{-1} \cdot m^{-1} \cdot Pa^{-n}$). Note that, since k_1 is expressed in terms of $L \cdot s^{-1}$, the units for flow rate through the opening are $L \cdot s^{-1}$.

Tables 4.1 and 4.2 give typical values of flow coefficient (k_1) and exponent (n) for a range of door and window types when fully closed[3]. However, in modern buildings, doors and windows may not be the predominant leakage routes so other types of joint or perforation in the building envelope may need to be taken into account. Further data are given in AIVC Technical Note 44[3].

For orifice-type openings such as open windows, equation 4.1 takes the form of the common orifice flow equation:

$$Q = C_d A \, (2 \, \Delta p / \rho)^{0.5} \qquad (4.3)$$

where Q is the volumetric flow rate through the opening ($m^3 \cdot s^{-1}$), C_d is the discharge coefficient, A is the area of the opening (m^2), Δp is the pressure difference across the opening (Pa) and ρ is the density of air ($kg \cdot m^{-3}$).

Thus, the flow characteristics of such openings can be expressed directly in terms of their open area. This greatly simplifies the calculation procedure and forms the basis of the simplified orifice calculations described in section 4.4.3.

Table 4.1 Flow characteristics for doors (per unit length of joint)[3]

Item	Flow coefficient per metre length of joint, k_1 ($L \cdot s^{-1} \cdot m^{-1} \cdot Pa^{-n}$) where $n = 0.6$			Sample size
	Lower quartile	Median	Upper quartile	
External doors (weather stripped):				
— hinged	0.082	0.27	0.84	15
— sliding	—	—	—	0
— revolving (laboratory test)	1.0	1.5	2.0	4
External doors (non-weather stripped):				
— hinged	1.1	1.2	1.4	17
— sliding	—	0.20	—	1
Roller door per m² of surface* (laboratory test)	3.3	5.7	10	2
Internal doors (non-weather stripped)	1.1	1.3	2.0	84
Loft hatches (non-weather stripped)	0.64	0.68	0.75	4

* Flow coefficient expressed in $L \cdot s^{-1} \cdot m^{-2} \cdot Pa^{-n}$

Table 4.2 Flow characteristics for windows (per unit length of joint)[3]

Item	Flow coefficient per metre length of joint, k_1 ($L \cdot s^{-1} \cdot m{-1} \cdot Pa^{-n}$) where $n = 0.6$			Sample size
	Lower quartile	Median quartile	Upper	
Windows (weather stripped):				
— hinged	0.086	0.13	0.41	29
— sliding	0.079	0.15	0.21	19
Windows (non-weather stripped):				
— hinged	0.39	0.74	1.1	42
— sliding	0.18	0.23	0.37	36

The theoretical value of C_d for a sharp-edged opening is 0.61 and it is common practice to refer other openings, for which the airflow is governed by the square root of the pressure difference, to this value. Measurements of flow rate and applied pressure difference are used to calculate an equivalent area assuming a discharge coefficient of 0.61. This approach is particularly useful where the nature of the opening makes it difficult to measure its geometrical area directly, such as in the case of trickle ventilators.

These relationships indicate that with knowledge of the opening characteristics and the pressure drop, the airflow rate can be calculated. Alternatively, calculations can be made of the characteristics of the opening needed to produce the required airflow rate at a predetermined pressure drop.

4.3.3 Driving forces

The forces driving air infiltration and natural ventilation are maintained by the actions of wind and temperature. Unfortunately, the pattern of pressure distribution arising from these parameters is extremely complex and considerable simplification is necessary in any mathematical representation. A brief outline on the calculation of pressure distribution is presented in this section.

4.3.3.1 Wind speed

Within the lower regions of the earth's atmosphere, wind is characterised by random fluctuations in velocity which, when averaged over a fixed period of time yields mean values of speed and direction.

Wind data are provided in Section 2: *External design data*. These consist of summary wind speed and direction data for 21 UK sites and detailed data, consisting of average percentage frequency of wind speed, direction and temperature for three UK sites: London (Heathrow), Manchester (Ringway) and Edinburgh (Turnhouse). Comprehensive data on wind speed and direction in the UK are published by the Meteorological Office[4].

These data are valuable for design purposes such as the calculation of design heat loads, for which the wind speed exceeded for a small proportion of the time, say 10%, may be relevant. Alternatively, for summertime cooling calculations, it may be helpful to know the wind speed likely to prevail for a high proportion, say 80%, of the summer months.

4.3.3.2 Wind pressure calculation

On impinging the surface of a rectangular building, wind deflection induces a positive pressure on the upwind face. The flow then separates at the corners, resulting in negative pressure regions being developed along the sides of the

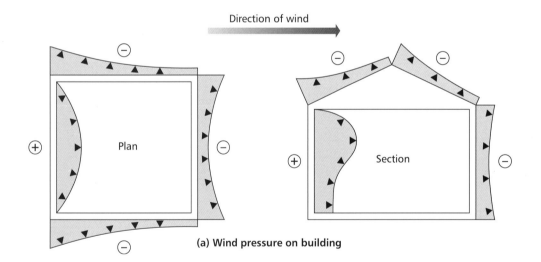

Figure 4.4 Wind pressure; (a) on building, (b) on roof

(a) Wind pressure on building

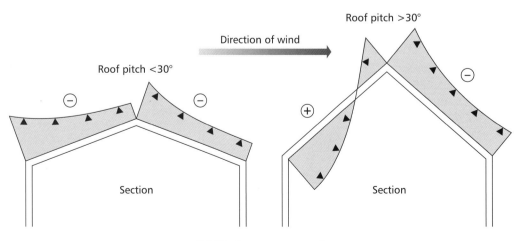

(b) Wind pressure on roof

building, see Figure 4.4(a). A negative pressure distribution is also developed along the rear facing or leeward facade.

The pressure distribution on the roof varies according to pitch, see Figure 4.4(b), the pressure on the upwind face being negative for roof pitches of less than about 30°. For pitches greater than 30°, the pressure on the upwind face is positive.

The magnitude of the wind pressure coefficient at any point for any given wind direction can generally be regarded as independent of the wind speed. Relative to the static pressure of the free wind, the time-averaged pressure acting on any point on the surface of a building may be represented by the following equation:

$$p_w = 0.5 \, \rho \, C_p \, v_z^2 \qquad (4.4)$$

where p_w is the surface pressure due to wind (Pa), ρ is the density of air, C_p is the wind pressure coefficient at a given position on the building surface and v_z is the mean wind velocity at height z (m).

The wind pressure coefficient C_p is a function of wind direction and of spatial position on the building surface. However, accurate evaluation of this parameter is extremely difficult and normally involves wind tunnel tests using a scale model of the building and its surroundings.

In approximate form, the wind pressure coefficient is expressed as a single average value for each face of the building. BS 5925[5] gives average values for buildings of simple shape in exposed locations. However, these data ignore the very significant influence of surrounding obstructions in shielding the building from wind. A synthesis of facade-averaged values for buildings subjected to varying degrees of shelter and wind directions is given in AIVC Applications Guide: *Air Infiltration Calculation Techniques*[6]. A summary of these data for a simple, square-plan building, see Figure 4.5, which may be used for basic design calculations, is given in Table 4.3. The values in the table apply to square plan buildings of heights up to three stories.

Although averaged data provide a useful approximation, their reliability diminishes for high-rise buildings (i.e. greater than four storeys) since the pressure distribution can be significantly dependent on the height of the building. Some test data for high-rise buildings have been published by Bowen[7].

The wind speed (v_z) is always expressed as a value for a given building height (z). Since this term is raised to the power two in the pressure calculation, it is imperative that remote weather station data are corrected for terrain and building height as described in Section 2: *External design data*. The use of unadjusted weather data may result in considerable overestimation of air infiltration or natural ventilation rates.

The procedure for calculating wind pressure at any location on the building surface may be accomplished as follows:

— determine building height

— determine nature of surrounding terrain

— correct meteorological wind speed data according to building height and terrain classification (section 2.8.5)

— determine approximate wind pressure coefficient for each face or for each opening in the building envelope (Table 4.3) or undertake wind tunnel studies if more accurate values of wind pressure coefficient are required.

Example 4.1

Tables 4.4 to 4.6 show the determination of the roof height wind speed and average wind pressure for the front and rear aspects of an 8 m high building located in (a) a 'green field' site in open country and (b) an urban industrial area. The mean wind speed measured at a nearby meteorological station wind speed is 4 m·s⁻¹ (measured in open country at a height of 10 m).

The reference wind speed (v_{ref}) is 4 m·s⁻¹. Values for the roughness (C_R) and topography (C_T) coefficients are obtained as described in section 2.8.5. The wind speed at building height (v_z) is then determined from equation 2.4. The results are shown in Table 4.4.

Values of the average wind pressure coefficient are obtained from Tables 4.3(b) and 4.3(c) for a wind angle of 0° i.e. perpendicular to wall 1, see Table 4.5.

Taking the density of air to be 1.25 kg·m⁻³ (i.e. air at 7.5°C, 60% RH), equation 4.4 is used with the above wind pressure coefficients and the calculated building height wind speeds to give the wind pressure values shown in Table 4.6.

4.3.3.3 Effect of wind turbulence

Turbulent or random fluctuations of the wind can itself influence the rate of infiltration or ventilation particularly when the mean wind speed is low or when the temperature (i.e. stack) effect is minimal.

For example, in the situation shown in Figure 4.7(a), the average wind pressure coefficients at both openings would be equal so that no airflow would be expected across the building. In reality, under turbulent conditions, an exchange of air will occur as inflow and outflow takes place intermittently. However, the turbulent effect need not be considered when estimating infiltration ventilation rates for design wind or temperature conditions, since this will be outweighed by the other driving mechanisms.

Similarly, internal airflow will be generated by turbulence when there is an opening on one side only see Figure 4.7(b). A formula for the quantitative assessment of the ventilation rate under such circumstances is presented in section 4.4.3, Table 4.13(a).

4.3.3.4 Stack effect

Stack effect arises as a result of differences in temperature, and hence air density, between the inside and outside of a building. This produces an imbalance in the pressures of the internal and external air masses, thus creating a vertical pressure gradient.

Table 4.3 Approximate wind pressure coefficients for square-plan building averaged over stated surfaces[6]

(a)   Building in open flat country

Surface	Average wind pressure coefficient, C_p, for stated wind angle θ							
	0	45	90	135	180	225	270	315
Walls:								
— facade 1	0.7	0.35	−0.5	−0.4	−0.2	−0.4	−0.5	−0.35
— facade 2	−0.2	−0.4	−0.5	0.35	0.7	0.35	−0.5	−0.4
— facade 3	−0.5	0.35	0.7	0.35	−0.5	−0.4	−0.2	−0.4
— facade 4	−0.5	−0.4	−0.2	−0.4	−0.5	0.35	0.7	0.35
Roof (front):								
— pitch <10°	−0.8	−0.7	−0.6	−0.5	−0.4	−0.5	−0.6	−0.7
— pitch 11°–30°	−0.4	−0.5	−0.6	−0.5	−0.4	−0.5	−0.6	−0.5
— pitch >30°	0.3	−0.4	−0.6	−0.4	−0.5	−0.4	−0.6	−0.4
Roof (rear):								
— pitch <10°	−0.4	−0.5	−0.6	−0.7	−0.8	−0.7	−0.6	−0.5
— pitch 11°–30°	−0.4	−0.5	−0.6	−0.5	−0.4	−0.5	−0.6	−0.5
— pitch >30°	−0.5	−0.4	−0.6	−0.4	−0.3	−0.4	−0.6	−0.4

(b)   Building in open country with scattered windbreaks

Surface	Average wind pressure coefficient, C_p, for stated wind angle θ							
	0	45	90	135	180	225	270	315
Walls:								
— facade 1	0.4	0.1	−0.3	−0.35	−0.2	−0.35	−0.3	−0.1
— facade 2	−0.2	−0.35	−0.3	0.1	0.4	0.1	−0.3	−0.35
— facade 3	−0.3	0.1	0.4	0.1	−0.3	−0.35	−0.2	−0.35
— facade 4	−0.3	−0.35	−0.2	−0.35	−0.3	0.1	0.4	0.1
Roof (front):								
— pitch <10°	−0.6	−0.5	−0.4	−0.5	−0.6	−0.5	−0.4	−0.5
— pitch 11°–30°	−0.35	−0.45	−0.55	−0.45	−0.35	−0.45	−0.55	−0.45
— pitch >30°	0.3	−0.5	−0.6	−0.5	−0.5	−0.5	−0.6	−0.5
Roof (rear):								
— pitch <10°	−0.6	−0.5	−0.4	−0.5	−0.6	−0.5	−0.4	−0.5
— pitch 11°–30°	−0.35	−0.45	−0.55	−0.45	−0.35	−0.45	−0.55	−0.45
— pitch > 30°	−0.5	−0.5	−0.6	−0.5	−0.3	−0.5	−0.6	−0.5

(c)   Building in urban location

Surface	Average wind pressure coefficient, C_p, for stated wind angle θ							
	0	45	90	135	180	225	270	315
Walls:								
— facade 1	0.2	0.05	−0.25	−0.3	−0.25	−0.3	−0.25	0.05
— facade 2	−0.25	−0.3	−0.25	0.05	0.2	0.05	−0.25	−0.3
— facade 3	−0.25	0.05	0.2	0.05	−0.25	−0.3	−0.25	−0.3
— facade 4	−0.25	−0.3	−0.25	−0.3	−0.25	0.05	0.2	0.05
Roof (front):								
— pitch <10°	−0.5	−0.5	−0.4	−0.4	−0.5	−0.5	−0.4	−0.5
— pitch 11°–30°	−0.3	−0.4	−0.5	−0.4	−0.3	−0.4	−0.5	−0.4
— pitch >30°	0.25	−0.3	−0.5	−0.3	−0.4	−0.3	−0.5	−0.3
Roof (rear):								
— pitch <10°	−0.5	−0.5	−0.4	−0.5	−0.5	−0.5	−0.4	−0.5
— pitch 11°–30°	−0.3	−0.4	−0.5	−0.4	−0.3	−0.4	−0.5	−0.4
— pitch >30°	−0.4	−0.3	−0.5	−0.3	−0.25	−0.3	−0.5	−0.3

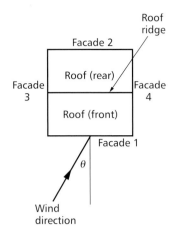

Figure 4.5 Square-plan building used in determination of wind pressure coefficients given in Table 4.3

When the internal temperature is greater than the outside temperature, air enters through openings in the lower part of the building and leaves through openings at a higher level. The flow direction is reversed when the internal air temperature is lower than that of the outside air.

Assuming two vertically displaced openings (see Figure 4.8), one at level h_1 and the other at level h_2, linking air at temperatures t_0 (outside) and t_i (inside), the pressure difference induced by the stack effect is given by:

$$\Delta p = -\rho_0 g\, 273\, (h_2 - h_1)\left(\frac{1}{t_0 + 273} - \frac{1}{t_i + 273}\right) \quad (4.5)$$

Table 4.4 Example 4.1: calculation of wind speed at building height

Site	Terrain category†	C_R†	C_T†	v_{ref} (m·s⁻¹)	v_z (m·s⁻¹)
Open land	II	0.96	1	4.0	3.84
Industrial	III	0.72	1	4.0	2.88

* see section 2.8.5

Table 4.5 Example 4.1: determination of wind pressure coefficients

Surface	Wind pressure coefficient, C_p	
	Open country (with windbreaks)	Industrial (urban)
Facade 1	0.4	0.2
Facade 2	−0.2	−0.25
Roof 1	−0.6	−0.5
Roof 2	−0.6	−0.5

Table 4.6 Example 4.1: calculation of wind pressure

Surface	Wind pressure (Pa)	
	Open country (with windbreaks)	Industrial (urban)
Facade 1	3.7	1.0
Facade 2	−1.8	−1.3
Roof 1	−5.5	−2.6
Roof 2	−5.5	−2.6

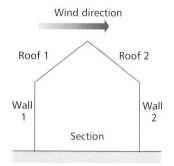

Wind direction

Roof 1   Roof 2

Wall 1   Wall 2

Section

Figure 4.6 Example 4.1: definition of surfaces

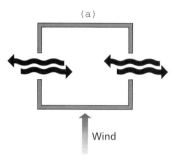

(a)

Wind

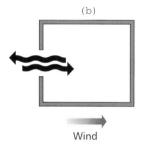

(b)

Wind

Figure 4.7 Effect of turbulent fluctuations of wind; (a) openings on opposite sides of enclosure, (b) openings on one side only

where Δp is the pressure difference (Pa), ρ_o is the density of air at 0°C (kg·m⁻³), g is the acceleration due to gravity (9.81 m·s⁻²), h_1 and h_2 are the heights above ground of openings 1 and 2 (m), t_o is the outside temperature (°C) and t_i is the inside temperature (°C).

For the range of temperatures found in practice, equation 4.5 approximates to:

$$\Delta p = -3455 (h_2 - h_1) \left(\frac{1}{t_o + 273} - \frac{1}{t_i + 273} \right) \quad (4.6)$$

Table 4.7 gives pressure differences, calculated using this expression, for a range of temperature and height differences.

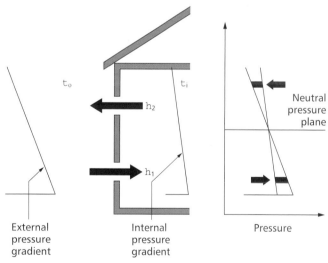

t_o t_i Neutral pressure plane

h_2

h_1

External pressure gradient   Internal pressure gradient   Pressure

Figure 4.8 Stack effect

Table 4.7 Pressure differences due to stack effect

Temperature difference, $(t_i - t_o)$ (K)	Pressure difference (Pa) for stated vertical height difference (m)				
	5	10	20	50	100
−10	2.2	4.3	8.6	22	43
0	0	0	0	0	0
10	−2.2	−4.3	−8.6	−22	−43
20	−4.3	−8.6	−17	−43	−86

Note: minus sign indicates reduction in pressure with height, i.e. flow upwards within the building

Example 4.2

For the building in Example 4.1, assuming openings at heights 1 m and 7 m above ground, the pressure difference created by stack effect for an internal temperature of 20°C and with the outside at 0°C, is:

$$\Delta p = -3455 \times 6 \left[(1/273) - (1/293) \right] = -5.2 \, \text{Pa}$$

Comparing this value with Table 4.6 shows that in this case the pressure difference due to a wind speed of 4 m·s⁻¹ is less than that due to stack effect for both open country and urban sites.

4.3.3.5 Combined wind and stack effects

As illustrated in Figure 4.3, in some parts of a building wind and stack effects may act in the same direction whereas in other parts they may act in opposite directions. The effects are additive in one case and counteractive in the other. The resulting pressures may be calculated accordingly. This is illustrated in Example 4.3.

Example 4.3

For the building considered in Example 4.1, the only additional information required to calculate the local pressures is knowledge of the stack effect neutral plane. The position of the neutral plane is affected by the relative resistances to flow of the openings in the facade. Assuming that similar openings are located in opposite facades at heights of 1 m and 7 m, then the neutral plane will be at mid-height. Therefore, the stack pressure difference calculated above will be divided equally between the upper and lower openings.

The combined pressure distributions at the openings for open country and industrial locations are shown in Table 4.8.

Note that in the industrial location, the impact of the stack effect on the upper windward and lower leeward openings is to reverse the direction of flow compared to that due to wind alone. This is because the pressure changes from positive to negative and vice versa. More complex worked examples are contained in CIBSE Applications Manual AM10[2].

4.4 Estimation methods

4.4.1 General

There are a number of methods available for estimating air infiltration and natural ventilation rates and for determining the area of openings required to provide a specific ventilation rate. The choice ranges from the use of empirical data or standard equations to complex models requiring the use of computer software.

The most appropriate method for a particular application depends on the intended use of the derived data, the complexity of the building and the availability of data relevant to the chosen method. Table 4.9 provides guidance on the appropriateness of each of the methods.

4.4.2 Empirical data for air infiltration

Tables 4.10 and 4.11 give empirical values of the infiltration that may be expected in buildings of typical construction in normal use in winter. They are not necessarily consistent with fresh air requirements, see Section 1: *Environmental criteria for design*.

The data are expressed in two forms:

— air infiltration rate (h⁻¹)

— air infiltration heat loss factor per unit volume of room (W·K⁻¹·m⁻³); for use directly in heat loss calculations.

The air infiltration heat loss factor is obtained as follows:

$$q_v = c \, \rho \, N / 3600 \tag{4.7}$$

where q_v is the air infiltration heat loss factor per unit room volume (W·K⁻¹·m⁻³), c is the specific heat capacity of air (J·kg⁻¹·K⁻¹), N is the air change rate (h⁻¹) and ρ is the density of air (kg·m⁻³).

At room temperatures $(c \, \rho / 3600) \approx \frac{1}{3}$. Therefore, for practical purposes:

$$q_v = N / 3 \tag{4.8}$$

Table 4.8 Example 4.3: calculation of combined wind and stack pressures

Opening	Open country location			Industrial (urban) location		
	Wind pressure	Stack pressure	Combined pressure	Wind pressure	Stack pressure	Combined pressure
Facade 1:						
— upper opening	+3.8	−2.6	+1.2	+1.0	−2.6	−1.6
— lower opening	+3.8	+2.6	+5.0	+1.0	+2.6	+3.6
Facade 2:						
— upper opening	−1.9	−2.6	−0.7	−1.3	−2.6	−3.9
— lower opening	−1.9	+2.6	+4.5	−1.3	+2.6	+1.3

Table 4.9 Summary of estimation methods

Method	Application	Data requirements	Advantages	Disadvantages
Empirical data	Air infiltration rate assessment when little is known about the airflow characteristics of the building	Building type, height and exposure	Easy to use	Does not provide detailed predictions
Standard formulae	Estimation of natural ventilation rates for simple buildings with openings on opposite sides or on one side only	Design wind speed(s) and temperatures, wind pressure coefficients, required ventilation rates or opening areas	Easy to use	Limited to narrow range of building configurations
Theoretical calculation: — single zone model	Estimation of internal airflows for buildings with simple internal layouts	Design wind speed(s) and temperatures, wind pressure coefficients, location, size and flow characteristics of each opening to outside, airflow paths, building volume	Relatively easy to use, predicts magnitude and direction of airflow, calculates internal pressure, changes may be easily accommodated	Requires detailed knowledge of the building
— multi-zone model	Estimation of internal airflows for complex buildings with known characteristics	As above plus internal configuration and its airflow characteristics	As above plus internal pressure distribution	Requires extensive input data and considerable computational effort

The values in Table 4.10 are rates applicable to single rooms or spaces, and are appropriate to the estimation of room heat loads. The load on the central plant will be about half the total of those for the individual rooms because, in multi-room buildings, at any one time only some of the rooms will receive air directly from outside. In others (those on the leeward side for example) air will pass from inside the building to outside. However, this may not apply to some special cases where all the rooms may be exposed to infiltration of air from outside at the same time. (For example, those where all the rooms have openings in at least two opposing external walls).

The air infiltration rates and heat loss factors given in Table 4.10 are appropriate to buildings with average conditions of exposure. However, in view of the many variables involved, they may need to be adjusted according to local exposure conditions. In this context, the following definitions may be used:

— sheltered: up to the third floor of buildings in city centres

— normal: most suburban and country premises; the fourth to eighth floors of buildings in city centres

— severely exposed: buildings on the coasts or exposed on hill sites; floors above the fifth of buildings in suburban or country districts; floors above the ninth of buildings in city centres.

On severely exposed sites, a 50% increase above the tabulated values should be allowed. On sheltered sites, the infiltration rate may be reduced by 33%.

The air change rate in rooms in tall buildings may be significantly higher than the values given in Table 4.10. The design of tall buildings should include barriers against vertical air movement through stairwells and shafts to minimise the stack effect. If this is not done, the balance of internal temperatures can be seriously disturbed.

Allowance must be made in the sizing of heating or cooling plant to meet the needs of both the ventilation air and air infiltration. Where ventilation is achieved by mechanical supply only (or extract only) systems, infiltration (or ex-filtration) is partially inhibited and converted to ventilation airflow. In this case, the plant sizing may be based on the ventilation rate plus an air infiltration rate of 50% or less of the tabulated value, depending on the relative magnitudes of the internal pressure generated by the mechanical system and the natural external pressures. Where ventilation is by a balanced mechanical ventilation system, infiltration is not inhibited and the values given in the table should be applied without modification.

Modern buildings may be more airtight than inferred by these empirical data so, where possible, more rigorous methods of estimating air infiltration rates should be used, see section 4.4.4.

4.4.3 Natural ventilation in simple building layouts

The assumption that ventilation openings can be represented by orifice flow equations (e.g. equation 4.3) enables estimates of ventilation rates using standard formulae for simple building layouts. These layouts and associated formulae are shown in Table 4.12 for a simple building with airflow through opposite sides and in Table 4.13 for a situation with openings in one wall only. Both wind-induced and temperature-induced ventilation are given.

Table 4.10 Empirical values for air infiltration rate and heat loss due to air infiltration for rooms in buildings on normally-exposed sites in winter (tabulated values should be adjusted for local conditions of exposure)

Building type	Air infiltration rate (h^{-1})	Air infiltration heat loss factor $(W \cdot K^{-1} \cdot m^{-3})$	Building type	Air infiltration rate (h^{-1})	Air infiltration heat loss factor $(W \cdot K^{-1} \cdot m^{-3})$
Art galleries and museums	1	0.33	— operating theatres	0.5	0.17
			— storerooms	0.5	0.17
Assembly and lecture halls	0.5	0.17	— wards and patient areas	2	0.67
			— waiting rooms	1	0.33
Banking halls:					
— large (height > 4 m)	1	0.33	Hotels:		
— small (height < 4 m)	1.5	0.5	— bedrooms	1	0.33
			— public rooms	1	0.33
Bars	1	0.33	— corridors	1.5	0.5
			— foyers	1.5	0.5
Canteens and dining rooms	1	0.33			
			Laboratories	1	0.33
Churches and chapels:					
— up to 7000 m³ volume	0.5	0.17	Law courts	1	0.33
— greater than 7000 m³	0.25	0.08			
— vestries	1	0.33	Libraries:		
			— reading rooms (height > 4 m)	0.5	0.17
Dining and banqueting halls	0.5	0.17	— reading rooms (height < 4 m)	0.75	0.25
			— stack rooms	0.5	0.17
Exhibition halls:			— storerooms	0.25	0.08
— large (height > 4 m)	0.5	0.08			
— small (height < 4 m)	0.5	0.17	Offices:		
			— general	1	0.33
Factories — see Table 4.11			— private	1	0.33
			— storerooms	0.5	0.17
Fire stations, ambulance stations:					
— appliance rooms	0.5	0.17	Police stations:		
— watch rooms	0.5	0.17	— cells	5	1.65
— recreation rooms	1	0.33			
			Restaurants, cafes	1	0.33
Houses, flats and hostels:					
— living rooms	1	0.33	Schools, colleges:		
— bedrooms	0.5	0.17	— classrooms	2	0.67
— bed-sitting rooms	1	0.33	— lecture rooms	1	0.33
— bathrooms	2	0.67	— studios	1	0.33
— lavatories, cloakrooms	1.5	0.5			
— service rooms	0.5	0.17	Sports pavilions:		
— staircases, corridors	1.5	0.5	— dressing rooms	1	0.33
— entrance halls, foyers	1.5	0.5			
— public rooms	1	0.33	Swimming pools:		
			— hanging rooms	0.5	0.17
Gymnasia	0.75	0.25	— pool hall	0.5	0.17
Hospitals:			Warehouse:		
— corridors	1	0.33	— working and packing areas	0.5	0.17
— offices	1	0.33	— storage areas	0.25	0.08

Note: this table is provided for the purpose of estimating heat losses; it is not intended for use in the design of mechanical ventilation, air conditioning or warm air heating systems

The values of area (A) used in the formulae should be taken as the minimum cross-sectional area perpendicular to the direction of the airflow passing through the opening. Typical C_p values are given in Table 4.3.

The formulae given in Table 4.12 illustrate a number of general characteristics of natural ventilation, as follows:

— The effective area of a number of openings combined in parallel, across which the same pressure difference is applied, can be obtained by simple addition.

— The effective area of a number of openings combined in series (across which the same pressure difference is applied) can be obtained by adding the inverse squares of the individual areas and taking the inverse of the square root of the total (see Table 4.12(b)).

— When wind is the dominating mechanism the ventilation rate is proportional to wind speed and to the square root of the difference in pressure coefficient. Thus, although ΔC_p may range between 0.1 and 1.0, this will result in a ratio of only about 1 to 3 in the predicted ventilation rates for the same wind speed

— When stack effect is the dominating mechanism the ventilation rate is proportional to the square root of both temperature difference and height between upper and lower openings. When wind and stack effect are of the same order of magnitude their interaction is complicated. However, for the simple case illustrated, the actual rate, to a first approximation, may be taken as equal to the larger of the rates for the two alternative approaches, considered separately. This is shown in Table 4.12(c).

Table 4.11 Empirical values for air infiltration and heat loss due to air infiltration for factories

Construction	Air infiltration rate (h^{-1})	Air infiltration heat loss factor $(W \cdot K^{-1} \cdot m^{-3})$
Multi-storey; brick or concrete construction:		
— lower and intermediate floors	1	0.33
— top floor with flat roof	1	0.33
— top floor with sheeted roof, lined	1.25	0.42
— top floor with sheeted roof, unlined	1.25	0.42
Single storey, non-partitioned; brick or concrete construction:		
— up to 300 m^3 volume	1.5	0.5
— 300 m^3 to 3000 m^3	0.75	0.25
— 3000 m^3 to 10 000 m^3	0.5	0.17
— over 10,000 m^3	0.25	0.08
Curtain wall or sheet construction, lined:		
— up to 300 m^3 volume	1.75	0.58
— 300 m^3 to 3000 m^3	1	0.33
— 3000 m3 to 10 000 m^3	0.75	0.25
— over 10 000 m^3	0.5	0.17
Curtain wall or sheet construction, unlined:		
— up to 300 m^3 volume	2.5	0.75
— 300 m^3 to 3000 m^3	1.5	0.5
— 3000 m^3 to 10 000 m^3	1	0.33
— over 10 000 m^3	0.75	0.25

Note: these values are intended for heat loss calculation purposes only; additional allowances must be made for large doorways and ventilators

Measurements[8,9] have shown that, with normally sized windows, the magnitude of the resulting single-sided ventilation, while smaller than cross-ventilation with similar areas of opening under comparable conditions, can be large enough to contribute to natural cooling. Table 4.13 provides formulae that enable ventilation rates to be calculated for wind and stack effect. It is suggested that calculations be carried out using both formulae and the larger value taken. The formula for wind induced infiltration represents a minimum, which will be enhanced up to threefold for certain wind directions and windows with openings that tend to deflect the impinging wind inwards.

4.4.4 Theoretical calculation method

In principle, the airflow through a building and the ventilation rates of individual spaces within a building can be determined for a given set of weather conditions (i.e. wind speed, wind direction and external air temperature) if the following are known:

— the position and characteristics of all openings through which flow can occur

— a detailed distribution of surface mean pressure coefficients for the wind direction under consideration

— the internal air temperature(s).

Table 4.12 Standard formulae for estimating airflow rates for simple building layouts (openings on opposite sides)

Conditions	Schematic	Equations
(a) Wind only		$Q_w = C_d A_w v_r (\Delta C_p)^{0.5}$ $$\frac{1}{A_w{}^2} = \frac{1}{(A_1 + A_2)^2} + \frac{1}{(A_3 + A_4)^2}$$
(b) Temperature difference only		$$Q_b = C_d A_b \left(\frac{2 \Delta t\, h_a g}{\bar{t} + 273} \right)^{0.5}$$ $$\frac{1}{A_b{}^2} = \frac{1}{(A_1 + A_3)^2} + \frac{1}{(A_2 + A_4)^2}$$
(c) Wind and temperature difference together		$Q_t = Q_b$ for $(v_r / \sqrt{\Delta t}) < 0.26 (A_b/A_w)(h_a/\Delta C_p)^{0.5}$ $Q_t = Q_b$ for $(v_r / \sqrt{\Delta t}) > 0.26 (A_b/A_w)(h_a/\Delta C_p)^{0.5}$

Table 4.13 Standard formulae for estimating airflow rates for simple building layouts (openings on one side only)

Conditions	Schematic	Equations
(a) Wind only		$Q = 0.025\,A\,V_r$
(b) Temperature difference only: two openings		$Q = C_d(A_1 + A_2)\left(\dfrac{\varepsilon\sqrt{2}}{(1+\varepsilon)(1+\varepsilon^2)^{0.5}}\right)\left(\dfrac{\Delta t\,h_a\,g}{\bar{t}+273}\right)^{0.5}$ where $\varepsilon = (A_1/A_2)$
(c) Temperature difference only: one openings		$Q = C_d(A/3)\left(\dfrac{\Delta t\,h_a\,g}{\bar{t}+273}\right)^{0.5}$ If opening light is present: $Q = C_d(A\,\mathcal{J}_\phi/3)\left(\dfrac{\Delta t\,h_a\,g}{\bar{t}+273}\right)^{0.5}$ where $\mathcal{J}_\phi$ given by Figure 4.9

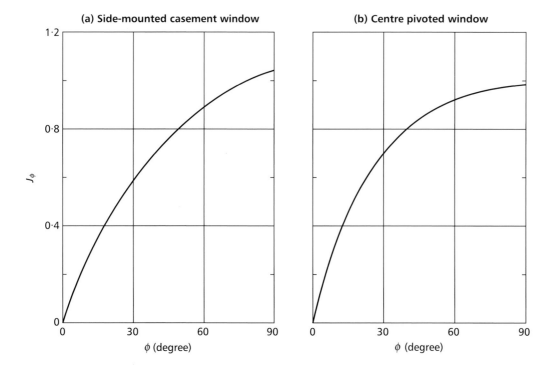

Figure 4.9 Variation of $\mathcal{J}_\phi$ with angle of opening; (a) side-mounted casement window, (b) centre-pivoted windows[10]

In practice, equation 4.1 and its simplified forms are non-linear. Also, because the number of flow paths likely to be present in any but the simplest building will be considerable, full solutions involving the prediction of flow between individual rooms can only be obtained by computer methods. Examples of these techniques are considered in detail in the AIVC Applications Guide: *Air infiltration calculation techniques*[7]. Additionally, predictions are only as accurate as the input data on which they are based and these are often difficult to quantify.

4.4.4.1 Single-zone model

Despite the complexities of flow prediction, the flow equation may be readily solved when the interior of the building is represented as a single enclosed volume. This single cell network approach is a comparatively easy calculation to undertake and provides facilities to:

— incorporate any number of flow paths to and from outside

— take account of combinations of wind, stack and mechanically induced pressures

— identify the magnitude and direction through each of the flow paths

— calculate the internal pressure

— assess the effects of changes to location or characteristics of flow paths

— determine the size of openings required to provide adequate ventilation.

A suitable technique for providing such solutions is described below and an appropriate computer algorithm is given in Appendix 4.A1. The leakage characteristics of the building envelope are first represented by a series of flow paths linking the exterior of the building with the interior, see Figure 4.10.

Ideally, the location, size and flow characteristics of each opening should be defined. In practice this is rarely possible and an approximation or an amalgamation of flow paths is usually necessary. Flow characteristics for typical leakage openings are presented in Tables 4.1 and 4.2; a more comprehensive list is given in AIVC Technical Note 44[3].

Once the flow network has been constructed, equation 4.1 is applied to each opening. Since the magnitude of flow entering the building must be matched by the magnitude of air leaving, a summation of equation 4.1 for all openings must equal zero. Hence:

$$Q = \sum_{j=\lambda}^{1} [C_j (p_{oj} - p_i)^{n_j}] = 0 \qquad (4.9)$$

where λ is the total number of flow paths, C_j is the flow coefficient for path j, p_{oj} is the external pressure due to wind and temperature acting on path j (P_a), p_i is the inside pressure of building (P_a), n_j is the flow exponent of path j.

The external pressures acting on each path are derived directly from the wind and stack pressure equations (i.e. equations 4.4 and 4.5 respectively).

The only remaining unknown in equation 4.9 is the internal pressure, which is determined by iteration. An initial pressure is assumed and is repeatedly adjusted until flow balance is achieved. At this point, infiltration is represented by the sum of the ingress flows. Figure 4.11 illustrates typical infiltration characteristics for the simple network shown in Figure 4.12.

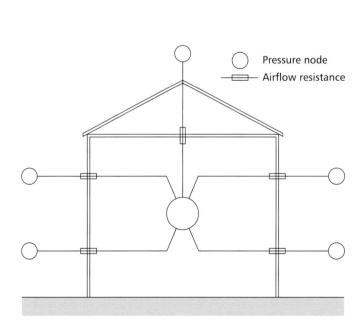

Figure 4.10 Single zone model: simple flow path network

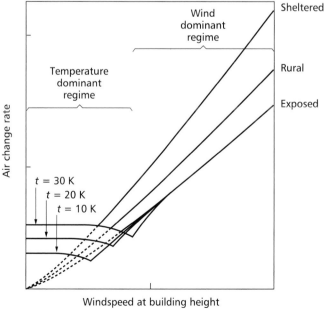

Figure 4.11 Typical infiltration characteristics for a simple flow path network[11]

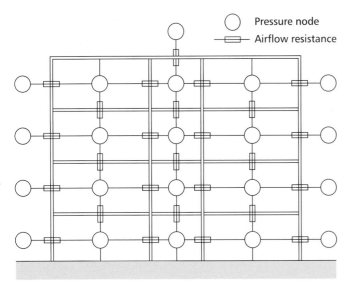

Figure 4.12 Multi-zone model

From this example, it may be deduced that:

—   there is a clearly defined temperature dominant regime at low wind speeds, and a wind dominant regime at higher wind speeds

—   the magnitude of the wind induced infiltration is considerably influenced by the degree of surrounding shielding.

4.4.4.2   Multi-zone model

For buildings with internal divisions that impede the movement of air, it will be necessary to use a multi-zone model that takes account of specific internal airflow paths, see Figure 4.12. In terms of the input data requirements and the output information, single-zone and multi-zone models are similar. However, a multi-zone calculation involves many iterations to produce a solution in which there is a balance of inlet and outlet flows in all of the zones. This adds considerably to the complexity of the numerical method and the computing capacity required for its solution.

The multi-zone approach is capable of predicting air infiltration and ventilation flows in complex buildings provided data are available to numerically define the flow network and the external pressure distribution.

Information on available models is given elsewhere[6].

4.5   Air-tightness testing

4.5.1   Measurement

The rate of air leakage through the fabric of buildings can be measured using an air pressurisation technique. Air is supplied to the building under test at a range of airflow rates, and the resulting pressure differential across the building envelope is measured for each rate of flow. It is recommended that the range of pressure differentials be extended to at least 50 Pa. This pressure is low enough not to cause any damage to the building but high enough to overcome the detrimental effects of moderate wind speeds.

To conduct a test, a fan system is temporarily coupled to a suitable doorway or similar opening in the building envelope. For a large or leaky building, this requires a high capacity fan system. For small buildings, a device known as a 'blower door' may be used. This is an assembly that includes one or more fans, some means of controlling airflow rate and instrumentation for measuring pressures. It is designed to fit into a normal doorframe, with facilities to clamp and seal it in place.

Buildings are tested with all external doors and windows closed, and with all internal doors wedged open. Any natural and mechanical ventilation openings are also sealed with polythene sheet and adhesive tape. Smoke extract fans or vents are left closed but *not* sealed. Other integral openings such as lift shafts are left unsealed.

The measured airflow rates and pressure differentials are related by the equation 4.1.

Air-tightness testing may be accompanied by smoke tests as a means of helping to identify the air leakage routes.

4.5.2   Data processing

The pressure difference across the building envelope versus the measured airflow rate is plotted on a log–log graph. A straight-line relationship will confirm that the test results are as expected and that nothing extraneous, such as a door or window left open, had occurred during the tests.

The airflow test data are further processed to take account of two factors. First, an air density correction is applied. This is determined from the air temperature and barometric pressure at the position of airflow measurement. The second correction factor takes account of any change in the volumetric air flow rate due to differences in the temperature of the supply air and that within the building. During the pressurisation test, outside air passes through the apparatus into the building and mixes with the inside air. If the temperature of the inside air is higher than that of the supply air, the supply air expands so that the volume rate of flow out of the building envelope is slightly greater than the measured airflow rate.

Following these corrections, a regression analysis is carried out on the pressure differentials across the building envelope and the corrected airflow rate in order to calculate the air leakage coefficient (k) and the value of the exponent (n), see equation 4.1. A correlation coefficient is also calculated to indicate the 'closeness of fit' of the measured data to the calculated relationship.

Using the calculated relationship, the airflow rate required to pressurise the building to 50 Pa (Q_{50}) is determined and then normalised with respect to the surface area (S) of the building to yield values for the quotient (Q_{50} / S) (($m^3 \cdot h^{-1}) \cdot m^{-2}$). This gives an air leakage value that may be compared with specified standards or with air leakage rates for other buildings. Other reference pressures may be used, as well as air leakage rates expressed in air changes per hour, for example.

References

1   *Building Regulations 1991 Approved Document F: Ventilation* (London: The Stationery Office) (1995)

2   *Applications Manual AM10: Natural ventilation in non-domestic buildings* (London : Chartered Institution of Building Services Engineers) (1997)

3   Orme M, Liddament M W and Wilson A *An analysis and summary of AIVC's numerical database* AIVC Technical Note 44 (Coventry: Air Infiltration and Ventilation Centre) (1994)

4   Caton P G F *Maps of hourly mean wind speed over the United Kingdom 1956–1973* Meteorological Office Climatology Memorandum 79 (Bracknell: Meteorological Office) (1976)

5   *BS 5925: 1991: Code of practice for ventilation principles and designing for natural ventilation* (London : British Standards Institution) (1991)

6   Liddament M W *Air infiltration calculation techniques — an application guide* (Coventry: Air Infiltration and Ventilation Centre) (1986)7   Bowen A J *A wind tunnel investigation using simple models to obtain mean surface wind pressure coefficients for air infiltration estimates* Report LTR LA 20N (Canada: National Aeronautical Establishment) (1976)

8   Warren P R Ventilation through openings on one wall only *Proc. UNESCO International Seminar on Heat Transfer in Buildings, Dubrovnik 1977* 5 (1977)

9   Walker R R and White M K Single sided natural ventilation: how deep an office? *Building Serv. Eng. Res. Technol.* **13**(4), 231–236 (1992)

10   *Principles of natural ventilation* BRE Digest 210 (Garston: Building Research Establishment) (1978)

11   Liddament M W *A guide to energy efficient ventilation* (Coventry: Air Infiltration and Ventilation Centre) (1996)

Appendix 4.A1: Air infiltration development algorithm (AIDA)

4.A1.1   Introduction

This algorithm was developed by the Air Infiltration and Ventilation Centre (AIVC)* and is reproduced here by kind permission of the AIVC. The CIBSE cannot take responsibility for its accuracy. Any queries regarding the algorithm or its use should be referred to the AIVC.

AIDA is a basic infiltration and ventilation calculation procedure intended for the calculation of air change rates in single zone enclosures. It also resolves flow rates for any number of user-defined openings and calculates wind and stack pressures. The program is easy to use and provides an accurate solution to the flow balance equation. As its name suggests, this is a development algorithm that may be adapted to suit individual needs. It uses concepts outlined in chapter 12 of the AIVC *Guide to energy efficient ventilation*[11].

4.A1.2   Program operation

AIDA is written in BASIC and a full listing is given in section 4.A1.4. Initiation of the code will be machine dependent but in the BASIC environment will normally be achieved by using the 'RUN' command. Once the response 'Welcome to AIDA' appears on the screen, the 'EXE' or 'ENTER' key is pressed sequentially in response to each input question (identified by '?').

Data entry is self-explicit. The order of data entry for each flow path is as follows:

— building volume (m³)
— number of flowpaths
— height of flow path (m)
— flow coefficient (m³·s⁻¹ at 1 Pa)
— wind pressure coefficient.

Once the flow path data have been entered, the following items of climatic data are requested:

— outdoor temperature (°C)
— internal temperature (°C)
— wind speed at building height (m·s⁻¹)

On completion of data entry, the computer responds with the message 'Calculation in progress'. After iteration is completed, the infiltration rate is displayed. The air change rate and request for further climatic data are automatically displayed; breakout of the program may be achieved using 'CONTROL BREAK'. At the end of a session, the most recent data remain in store and can be recovered using the 'PRINT' command followed by the variable name, e.g:

* Air Infiltration and Ventilation Centre, University of Warwick Science Park, Sovereign Court, Sir William Lyons Road, Coventry CV4 7EZ, UK.

— 'PRINT Q' displays the infiltration rate
— 'PRINT F(2)' displays flow path 2.

Care must be taken when entering data since there is no error trapping and no editing facility. It will be necessary to restart the program if an error is made.

As a demonstration algorithm, the input/output routines are rudimentary and may be adapted to suit individual requirements.

4.A1.3   Solution technique

The flow balance equation is solved by iteration using a combination of 'bisection' and 'addition'. An internal pressure, known to be substantially negative with respect to the true pressure, is selected as a starting condition. For most applications, a value of –100 Pa should be satisfactory and is introduced automatically at line 320. Successive iterations improve the internal pressure value until a flow balance within 0.0001 m²·s⁻¹ is achieved. The flow balance criterion is established in line 450. An understanding of the technique may be gleaned from an analysis of lines 320 to 470 of the program. While the approach adopted is not necessarily the most numerically efficient, it is extremely robust and should not fail under normal circumstances over a wide range of flow conditions and leakage characteristics.

4.A1.4   Program listing and variable names

```
20    PRINT "Welcome to AIDA"
30    PRINT "Air Infiltration Development Algorithm"
40    PRINT "M Liddament - AIVC Guide to
      Ventilation 1995"
50    DIM H(50), C(50), N(50), P(50), T(50), W(50),
      S(50), F(50)
55    PRINT:PRINT:PRINT
60    D=1.29:REM Air density at 0 deg C
70    PRINT "Enter building data: "
80    INPUT "Building volume (m3) = ";V
85    PRINT:PRINT:PRINT
90    PRINT "Enter flow path data: "
100   INPUT "Number of flow paths = ";L
110   FOR J=1 TO L
115   PRINT:PRINT:PRINT
120       PRINT "Height (m) (Path ";J;") = ";
          :INPUT H(J)
130       PRINT "Flow coef (Path ";J;") = ";
          :INPUT C(J)
140       PRINT "Flow exp (Path ";J;") = ";
          :INPUT N(J)
150       PRINT "Pres coef (Path ";J;") = ";:INPUT
          P(J)
160   NEXT J
```

```
170    PRINT "Enter climatic data:"
175    PRINT:PRINT:PRINT
180    INPUT "Ext temp (deg C) = " ;E
190    INPUT "Int temp (deg C) = " ;I
200    INPUT "Wind spd (bldg ht) (m/s) = " ;U
210    REM   Pressure calculation
220    FOR J=1 TO L
230            REM Wind pressure calculation
240            W(J)=.5*D*P(J)*U*U
250            REM Stack pressure calculation
260            S(J)=-3455*H(J)*(1/(E+273)-1/(I+273))
270            REM Total pressure
280            T(J)=W(J)+S(J)
290    NEXT J
300    REM Calculate infiltration
305    CLS: PRINT:PRINT:PRINT
310            PRINT "Calculation in progress"
320    R=-100
330    X=50
340    Y=0
350    B=0
360    R=R+X
370    FOR J=1 TO L
380            Y=Y+1
390            O=T(J)-R
400            IF O=0 THEN F(J)=0; GOTO 430
410            F(J)=C(J)*ABS(O) ^ N(J))*O/ABS(O)
420            B+B+F(J)
430    NEXT J
440    IF B<0 THEN R+R-X: X=X/2: GOTO 350
450    IF B<.0001 THEN GOTO 470
460    GOTO 350
470    Q=0
480    FOR J=1 TO L
490            IF F(J)>0 THEN Q=Q+F(J)
500    NEXT J
505    PRINT:PRINT:PRINT
520    PRINT "Infiltration rate (m³/s) = ";Q
530    A=Q*3600/V
540    PRINT "Air change rate (ach) = ";A
545    PRINT:PRINT:PRINT
550    GOTO 170
```

The names of variables are as follows:

A	Air change rate (h^{-1})
B	Flow balance
C(J)	Flow coefficient for path J
D	Air density ($kg \cdot m^{-3}$)
E	External temperature (°C)
F(J)	Calculated flow rate for flow path J ($m^3 \cdot s^{-1}$)
H(J)	Height of flow path J (m)
I	Internal temperature (°C)
J	Flow path number
L	Total number of flow paths
N(J)	Flow exponent for flow path J
O	Pressure difference across flow path (Pa)
P(J)	Wind pressure coefficient for flow path J
Q	Infiltration rate ($m^3 \cdot s^{-1}$)
R	Internal pressure (Pa)
S(J)	Stack-induced pressure for flow path J (Pa)
T(J)	Total external pressure on flow path J (Pa)
U	Wind speed at building height ($m \cdot s{-1}$)
V	Volume of building enclosure (m^3)
W(J)	Wind-induced pressure (Pa)
X	Iteration pressure step (Pa)
Y	Iteration counter

5 Thermal response and plant sizing

5.1 Introduction

This section presents design information for the calculation of heating loads, cooling loads and heating plant capacity. The heating and cooling requirements are determined by:

— design internal and external temperatures

— design internal and external humidities

— thermal characteristics of the building

— ventilation rate

— type of system

— building usage patterns.

This section gives the background to steady-state and dynamic calculation techniques which can be used for sizing plant when the above conditions are known. At the time of publication (September 1999) there is considerable international debate on the preferred methods for load calculation and a draft European Standard which sets down compliance tests is under development. In the meantime guidance is given on the various methods currently available. Data and guidance are provided on the calculation of steady-state heat losses, determination of summertime temperatures for naturally and mechanically ventilated buildings and the determination of peak space cooling loads. Reference data are provided where available and definitions of commonly used indices and parameters are also given.

In using this Guide, it is important to understand the distinction between comfort temperature, the various air and surface temperatures which determine the rate of heat transfer to and from the building, and the temperatures sensed by the detectors employed to control the heating, air conditioning and ventilation systems. For design and calculation purposes these are often combined together and treated as a single index temperature.

The assumed thermal properties of the building, its construction and pattern of use as represented by the calculation techniques are likely to differ from those found in reality. Therefore some discrepancies between predicted and measured performance must be expected.

In order to rationalise the presentation of the calculations, it has been necessary to re-define some of the numerical factors. This must be borne in mind when comparing this edition with earlier editions of the Guide.

5.2 Notation

5.2.1 Symbols

Some of the quantities in this Guide occur in three forms: the instantaneous value, which is denoted by the appropriate letter (e.g. X). The 24-hour mean or steady-state value, denoted by $\bar{X}$; and the instantaneous variation about the mean value, denoted by $\tilde{X}$. Where time lags occur, the variation symbol may be given a subscript to indicate the time at which it occurs, e.g. $\tilde{X}_\theta$ is the value of $\tilde{X}$ at time θ. Peak values are indicated by a caret mark ($^\wedge$) above the symbol (e.g. $\hat{I}$). Symbols that appear only in the appendices are omitted here and are defined in the appendices in which they occur.

A_h	Projected area of heat emitter (m^2)
A_n	Area of surface n (m^2)
c	Specific heat capacity of air (J·kg^{-1}·K^{-1})
C_v	Ventilation conductance (W·K^{-1})
f	Decrement factor
F	Surface factor
F_{au}	Room conduction factor with respect to air node*
F_{ay}	Room admittance factor with respect to air node*
F_{cu}	Room conduction factor with respect to dry resultant temperature*
F_{cy}	Room admittance factor with respect to dry resultant temperature*
f_r	Thermal response factor
F_{1cu}, F_{2cu}	Factors related to characteristics of heat source with respect to dry resultant temperature*
F_3	Correction factor for intermittent heating
H	Hours of plant operation including preheat (h)
h_c	Convective heat transfer coefficient (W·m^{-2}·K^{-1})
h_r	Radiative heat transfer coefficient of a black body (W·m^{-2}·K^{-1})
h_{so}	Outside heat transfer coefficient (W·m^{-2}·K^{-1})
I_l	Re-radiation loss (W·m^{-2})
I_t	Total solar irradiance (W·m^{-2})
$\dot{m}_a$	Mass flow rate of air (kg·s^{-1})
N	Number of air changes per hour (h^{-1})
Q_{av}	Heat gain from ventilation (W)
Q_b	Cooling load (W)
Q_{bl}	Back loss (W)
Q_c	Internal heat gain (W)
Q_f	Fabric heat gain (W)
Q_{fa}	Fabric gain to the air node (W)
Q_i	Plant size for intermittent operation (W)
Q_k	Total sensible cooling load to the air node (W)
q_s	Short wave heat flow (W·m^{-2})
q_{cn}	Instantaneous heat gain from internal heat source n (W)
Q_{sa}	Solar heat gain to the air node (W)
Q_{sc}	Solar cooling load (W)
Q_{se}	Solar heat gain to the environmental node (W)
Q_t	Total heat loss (W)
Q_{ta}	Total gains to the air node (W)

Q_{te}	Total gains to the environmental node (W)
R	Radiant fraction of the heat source
R_{si}	Thermal resistance between the inside of a surface and the environmental temperature ($m^2 \cdot K \cdot W^{-1}$)
$\tilde{S}_a$	Cyclic solar gain factor at air node
$\bar{S}_a$	Mean solar gain factor at air node
S_c	Shading coefficient
$\tilde{S}_e$	Cyclic solar gain factor at environmental node
$\bar{S}_e$	Mean solar gain factor at environmental node
$\tilde{S}_{eh}$	Cyclic solar gain factor at environmental node for heavyweight building
$\tilde{S}_{el}$	Cyclic solar gain factor at environmental node for lightweight building
t_a	Air temperature (°C)
t_{ai}	Inside air temperature (°C)
t_{ao}	Outside air temperature (°C)
t_c	Dry resultant temperature at centre of room (°C)
t_e	Heat transfer temperature (°C)
t_{ei}	Environmental temperature (°C)
t_{eo}	Sol-air temperature (°C)
t_h	Temperature of heat emitter (°C)
t_m	Mean surface temperature (°C)
t_r	Mean radiant temperature (°C)
t_s	Temperature of surface (°C)
U_n	Thermal transmittance of material n ($W \cdot m^{-2} \cdot K^{-1}$)
U''	Thermal transmittance modified for heat loss through internal partitions ($W \cdot m^{-2} \cdot K^{-1}$)
V	Room volume (m^3)
Y	Thermal admittance ($W \cdot m^{-2} \cdot K^{-1}$)
α	Surface absorption co-efficient
θ	Time (h)
θ_{cn}	Duration of internal heat source n (h).
ρ	Density of air ($kg \cdot m^{-3}$)
ΣA	Sum of room surface areas, unless otherwise indicated (m^2)
$\Sigma (A\,U)$	Sum of the products of surface area and corresponding thermal transmittance over surfaces through which heat flow occurs ($W \cdot K^{-1}$)
$\Sigma (A\,Y)$	Sum of the products of surface area and corresponding thermal admittance over all surfaces ($W \cdot K^{-1}$)
ϕ	Time lag associated with decrement factor (h)
φ	Time lag associated with surface factor (h)
ω	Time lead associated with admittance (h)

* Note that the definitions of these factors differ from those adopted in earlier editions of Guide A.

5.2.2 Definitions

Air node

The hypothetical point in space at which all convective heat transfer is assumed to take place.

Air temperature (t_a)

The temperature registered by a dry thermometer, shielded from radiation, suspended in the air.

Black body

A body which absorbs all incident radiation at all wavelengths (i.e. emissivity = 1). A black body is also an ideal radiator.

Table 5.1 Surface convective heat transfer coefficient, h_c

Surface	Direction of heat flow	Surface coefficient, h_c ($W \cdot m^{-2} \cdot K^{-1}$)
Floor	Upwards	4.3
	Downwards	1.5
Wall	Horizontal	3.0
Ceiling	Upwards	4.3
	Downwards	1.5

Convective heat transfer coefficient (h_c)

The coefficient relating the exchange of heat between a surface and the surrounding air. The value of h_c will depend upon the nature of the airflow over the surface (natural or forced) and the temperature of that surface. For design purposes, standard values are used, see Table 5.1. Heat flow from surfaces is defined such that a positive heat flow is one that flows from a hot body to a cold body. For example, upward heat flow from a warm floor would be positive, as would upward heat flow into a cold ceiling.

The convective heat transfer coefficient depends on the dimensions, slope, roughness of the surface, surface temperature, and the local air temperature and air velocity. Detailed thermal models may make use of coefficients based on correlations between these variables[1,2]. The values given in Table 5.1 are for buoyancy driven flow. No simple figures are available for forced convection but an average value of 3 $W \cdot m^{-2} \cdot K^{-1}$ may be considered typical.

Decrement factor (f)

The variation in the rate of heat flow through the structure due to variations in external heat transfer temperature from its mean value with the environmental temperature held constant, divided by the steady-state transmittance.

Dry resultant temperature (t_c)

The dry resultant temperature[3] is the temperature registered by a thermometer at the centre of an externally blackened sphere 150 mm diameter, being a function of air temperature, mean radiant temperatures and velocity. It is used as an index temperature for comfort[4] where the air velocities are low.

For the purposes of this Guide, the following simplified expression is used which assumes the air velocity to be 0.1 $m \cdot s^{-1}$:

$$t_c = 0.5\,t_{ai} + 0.5\,t_r \tag{5.1}$$

where t_c is the dry resultant temperature (°C), t_{ai} is the inside air temperature at the same point (°C) and t_r is the mean radiant temperature (°C).

Environmental node

The hypothetical point in a room from which radiant and convective heat is exchanged to the room surfaces. It has a temperature equal to the environmental temperature.

Environmental temperature (t_{ei})

A hypothetical temperature that determines rate of heat flow into a room surface by convection from the room and radiation from surrounding surfaces and other radiant sources. It is the temperature at the environmental node.

G-value

See *total solar energy transmittance*.

Grey body

A body which absorbs the same fraction of incident radiation at all wavelengths (i.e. assumes that emissivity is independent of wavelength). A grey body is often used to simplify the problems of predicting radiant energy exchange between surfaces.

Heat transfer temperature (t_e)

A temperature calculated to give a rate of heat transfer to a surface equivalent to that from a combination of radiation and convection. For example, the rate of heat flow to a surface can be expressed as:

$$q_s = h_c(t_a - t_s) + q_r \qquad (5.2)$$

or:

$$h_c(t_e - t_s) = h_c(t_a - t_s) + q_r \qquad (5.3)$$

$$t_e = t_a + q_r / h_c \qquad (5.4)$$

where q_s is the rate of heat flow into the surface (W·m^{-2}), h_c is the convective heat transfer coefficient (W·m^{-2}·K^{-1}), t_a is the air temperature (°C), t_s is the surface temperature (°C), q_r is the net rate of radiant heat flow into the surface (W·m^{-2}), t_e is the heat transfer temperature (°C).

Inside air temperature (t_{ai})

The average air temperature in an enclosed space.

Inside surface temperature (t_s)

The temperature of the surface immediately adjacent to an air space. It is the driving temperature for both the convective and radiant energy transfers within the building and can be directly measured by means of a suitable contact thermometer. The temperature varies across the surface and is affected by corners, changes in construction, air movement etc. For most heat transfer calculations a single temperature is assumed for each surface.

Long-wave radiation

Radiation from a 'low temperature' source (i.e. less than, say, 500°C), e.g. walls, heating radiators. Long-wave radiation exchange depends on the temperatures of the emitter and receiver.

Mean radiant temperature (t_r)

The mean radiant temperature is a function of the respective areas, shapes and surface temperatures of the enclosing elements as viewed from a point. For a point at the centre of a cubical room with all surfaces having an emissivity of 1 and where there are no other radiant sources, the mean radiant temperature is the same as the mean surface temperature (t_m). Determination of precise values is complex due to the effect of surface view factors (see also

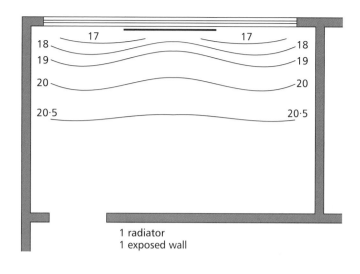

Figure 5.1 Mean radiant temperatures across a room (plan view)

1 radiator
1 exposed wall

Appendix 5.A1). The mean radiant temperature varies from point to point within a space. Figure 5.1 shows a computer prediction of mean radiant temperature for a specific situation in which a radiator is placed adjacent to a cold surface to minimise the variation of radiant temperature.

Mean surface temperature (t_m)

The mean surface temperature is determined by totalling the products of the areas and temperatures of the surrounding surfaces and dividing this total by the sum of the areas, i.e.:

$$t_m = \frac{\Sigma(A t_s)}{\Sigma(A)} \qquad (5.5)$$

Method

The way in which a model is implemented.

Model

A mathematical representation of reality.

Outside air temperature (t_{ao})

The average temperature of the air surrounding the building.

Overheating criteria

Criteria used to assess the performance of naturally and mechanically ventilated buildings during periods of hot weather. Design criteria can vary in complexity from the number of hours for which a particular temperature is exceeded to a sophisticated comfort prediction. (See also 5.6.3.4 and 5.8.4.1.)

Radiant heat transfer coefficient (h_r)

The coefficient relating the exchange of long-wave radiation between surfaces. It is a function of the geometrical arrangement of the bodies and their temperatures. For simplified techniques a constant value of $5.7 \ W \cdot m^{-2} \cdot K^{-1}$ is used (corresponding to a temperature of 20 °C and an emissivity of 1).

Radiant temperature

The apparent radiant temperature of a surface as measured by a suitable radiant thermometer. The measured temperature varies depending on the position of the thermometer to the surface. For a surface forming part of a black body (i.e. with emissivity = 1) the radiant temperature measured will equal the actual surface temperature. For a surface forming part of a grey body (i.e. with emissivity less than 1) the radiant temperature measured is a function of the temperature of the surface, the emissivity of the surface and radiation from the surroundings reflected from the surface.

Shading coefficient (S_c)

The ratio of the instantaneous heat gain at normal incidence transmitted by a particular glass/blind combination to that transmitted by a reference glass, usually 3 or 4 mm thick clear glass, see 5.6.3.3.

Short-wave radiation

Radiation from a high temperature source, e.g. the sun, electric lights. Short-wave radiation exchange does not depend upon the temperature of the receiving surface.

Sol-air temperature (t_{eo})

The hypothetical temperature that determines the rate of heat flow into an external surface by convection from the surrounding air, short-wave solar radiation and radiative exchange to the surrounding (other buildings, ground and sky), see Section 2: *External design data*.

Surface factor (F)

The ratio of the variation of radiant heat flow about its mean value readmitted to the space from the surface, to the variation of heat flow about its mean value incident upon the surface.

Thermal admittance (Y-value)

The rate of flow of heat between the internal surfaces of the structure and the environmental temperature in the space, for each degree of deviation of that temperature about its mean value.

Thermal transmittance (U-value)

The thermal transmission through unit area of a given structure, divided by the difference between the effective ambient temperature on either side of the structure under steady state conditions.

Total solar energy transmittance (G-value)

The sum of the direct solar transmittance and the heat transferred by radiation and convection into the space[5]. It is generally applied to glazing combinations.

5.3 Background to calculation methods

5.3.1 Steady-state methods

Steady-state methods are used to calculate heat losses for the purposes of sizing space emitters and boiler plant. Over the last 35 years, the Institution has recommended only two methods for the calculation of the rate of heat loss from a space. These methods are based on (*a*) air temperature and (*b*) environmental temperature. These methods do not take account of gains due to solar radiation or internal sources. The main differences between them are the ways in which the heat transfer mechanisms of convection and radiation are dealt with, see below.

5.3.1.1 Air temperature method

The rate of heat loss through a wall is balanced by the convective gain from the room air to that surface and long-wave radiant interchange between room surfaces. Both processes are complex so any practical calculation technique needs to introduce approximations. The approximation made in the 1959 IHVE Guide[6] was that all heat transfer occurred between the surface and the air temperature. This approximation is acceptable for well-insulated spaces but will generally lead to under-estimation for radiant heating systems and over-estimation for fully convective heating systems.

5.3.1.2 Environmental temperature method

The deficiencies of the 1959 approach were partly addressed in the 1970 IHVE Guide[7] by the introduction of the concept of environmental temperature. (Note that the only difference between the 1970 method and that given in the 1986 Guide is in the replacement of the environmental temperature by the dry resultant temperature as the design temperature.) The intention was to combine the effects of radiant and convective heat transfer within a single air temperature index. While the method gives a fairly accurate representation of heat losses[8] the presentation of the theory has been questioned[9]. The main problem occurs in the representation of long-wave radiant heat transfer between room surfaces. A complete representation of this process is given in Appendix 5.A1. Simplifications may take the form of approximations to the view factors, or, as chosen by the 1970 IHVE Guide[7], reduction of the radiant exchange to that between a single surface and an enclosure at some mean radiant temperature. An alternative proposal by Davies[10] (the 'Two Star Method') uses exact view factor values for a room having six surfaces. In practice, there is little difference between heat losses calculated by that method and those calculated using the 1970 IHVE Guide[7] method. The Two Star Method suffered the disadvantage that it was impractical to do the calculation by hand but the widespread availability of computers now makes this method viable.

5.3.2 Choice of steady-state method

The approach adopted in this Guide is to accept the differences between methods and allow the engineer to use professional judgement to select the appropriate method for a particular application. A reference model is proposed, based upon an equation set developed by an accurate representation of the long-wave radiant exchange between surfaces. This is intended to serve as a benchmark against which the effect of approximations may be assessed. Two levels of simplification are then offered: (1) the approximation to radiant exchange developed by Davies[10] and (2) a manual calculation method based on that given in the 1986 CIBSE Guide[11].

5.3.3 Dynamic methods

For design purposes a dynamic model is required to determine:

— summertime overheating

— cooling loads

— pre-heat requirements.

The admittance procedure[12] offers a simple way to achieve these requirements. The procedure assumes that all internal and external load fluctuations can be represented by the sum of a steady-state component and a sine wave with a period of 24 hours. Implicit within this assumption is that steady cyclic conditions are achieved; i.e. a single day repeated for subsequent days until all long-term transients have died away. The method does not represent the effects of rapid load changes nor long term storage. Therefore it is not suitable as a means of calculating the performance of buildings with a large thermal capacity or the effects of rapid changes in load. Nonetheless it is considered suitable for use at an early stage of design and as a means of predicting the limiting state. There is also some evidence that, for naturally ventilated buildings, the peak temperatures predicted by the admittance procedure are close to those which actually occur[13]. This method may also be used as a manual check on the results from computer modelling. For these reasons the admittance method is currently retained.

True dynamic modelling can only be carried out by means of computer models. These models are capable of producing a realistic prediction of the performance of buildings and systems. However, the accuracy of all such models is open to question since, in common with all numerical representations of real systems, there are many approximations including those made by the user. The effect of any particular approximation will depend upon circumstances. An idea of the potential performance of dynamic models may be obtained from the results of a validation exercise[14]. Careful examination of the results of this exercise shows that:

— current models are quite good but no model gets everything right

— models that predict energy well may not be as good at predicting summertime temperatures.

The latter point applies equally to steady-state models. Similarly, the considerations of heat flow within rooms for steady-state models apply also to dynamic models. This Guide does not recommend any particular detailed dynamic model. The features that are required and some ways in which the results of dynamic models may be checked are discussed in Appendices 5.A7 and 5.A8.

The main difference between detailed dynamic models and the admittance procedure is the way in which the fabric storage and solar gains are represented. Dynamic models use particular numerical techniques to approximate and then solve the heat conduction equation whereas the admittance procedure uses an exact solution to the equation but approximates the boundary conditions. While harmonic analysis can be extended beyond the admittance method, all current detailed thermal models are based on either:

(*a*)   response factors[15,16] (as defined in the USA) or transfer coefficients[17]

(*b*)   finite differences[18] (i.e. numerical solution of the heat conduction equation).

In general, (*a*) is favoured in the USA and (*b*) is favoured in Europe. In practice there is little to choose between them. Descriptions of the basic techniques used in numerical solutions are available in many textbooks; Clarke[19] presents a detailed description of one approach to the problem.

5.4 Introduction to calculation methods

This section presents recommended calculation techniques of varying complexity that can be used to determine:

— steady-state heat loss from a building

— plant capacity necessary to ensure comfort conditions are reached at the start of occupancy when a building is intermittently heated

— peak temperatures where there is no mechanical cooling (summertime temperatures)

— maximum room cooling loads.

Four steady-state and three dynamic techniques are described, see Figures 5.2 and 5.3. Previous editions of Guide A recommended the use of a single method of calculation[11]. This edition takes a different approach. It describes the fundamentals of building physics and describes how these can be applied in practice, using sensible approximations where necessary, to a range of problems of varying complexity. It also makes recommendations to enable the user to select the appropriate calculation procedure or technique to meet the complexity of the design. Examples are provided which may be used to assess the performance of any selected technique.

The widespread availability of powerful computers has resulted in the possibility of accounting for many parameters that had to be excluded from previous methods. For example, it is no longer necessary to make simple approximations of the distribution of radiant energy within a space and it is now practicable to calculate conditions in a room for every hour of the year. The environmental temperature model assumes a simple radiant field. In the admittance procedure, the dynamic response of a space was reduced to the fundamental daily frequency. Both of these methods were developed to overcome the difficulties of performing complex calculations within a realistic time period and at an acceptable cost.

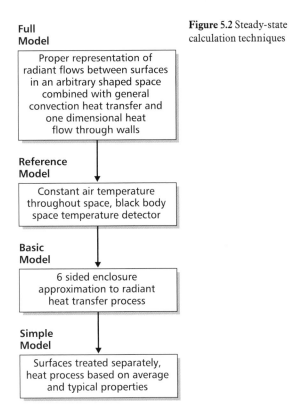

Figure 5.2 Steady-state calculation techniques

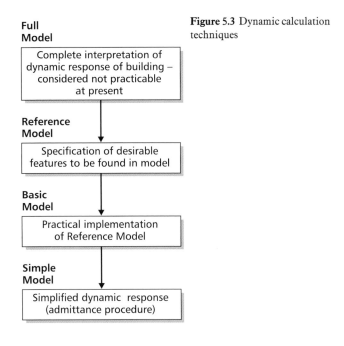

Figure 5.3 Dynamic calculation techniques

The need for a simple, rapid assessment method is still considered relevant and therefore manual methods are included. These are intended also to enable order of magnitude checks on the predictions made by more sophisticated methods. While it would be unreasonable to expect the same result to be obtained from any two methods under all conditions (this also applies to any two computer programs), similar results should be obtained under certain limiting conditions.

It is important to understand that simplified calculation techniques are not necessarily applicable to special cases (e.g. buildings with very large glazed areas). In such cases, it is recommended that any method claimed to be suitable be checked against example calculations, see 5.5.1.1 and Appendix 5.A3. This will not guarantee that the method is suitable for the particular case but should indicate a level of confidence.

All heating and cooling load calculation methods assume a design temperature, see Section 1: *Environmental criteria for design*. That temperature may be a comfort temperature such as the dry resultant temperature. Comfort temperatures are a function of air temperature, radiant temperature and air speed. The last of these can often be assumed (and should be selected) to lie within a range where it has little effect upon the comfort index. In many cases the assumption that there is no variation in the spatial distribution of air temperature is reasonable. Radiant temperature depends upon surface temperatures and the distance between the room surfaces, the observer and the radiant component of the heat emitter. It is unrealistic to assume the radiant temperature to be constant within a space (see Figure 5.1). For practical purposes it is necessary to define a fixed location for the observer, which is implicit within the assumptions contained in the calculation method. It is also accepted that, for analytical purposes,

calculations of comfort conditions throughout the space may need to be performed. A method has been suggested by Fanger[20] and a practical application has been demonstrated by Holmes and Connor[21].

Whatever the calculation technique, reliable data for the following will be required:

— thermal properties of materials

— internal design conditions

— outside air requirement (indoor air quality)

— internal gains

— external design conditions.

5.4.1 Properties of materials

5.4.1.1 Opaque components

The principal fundamental properties are as follows:

— density

— specific heat capacity

— thermal conductivity and resistance

— vapour resistivity

— absorptivity

— emissivity.

Derived properties are as follows:

— thermal transmittance (U-values)

— thermal admittance (Y-values)

— decrement factors

— surface factors.

Typical values of the above properties for a range of opaque fabrics and building structures are given in Section 3: *Thermal properties of building structures*, along with a description of the calculation procedure for thermal transmittance.

The use of standard thermal properties, in particular the overall conductance of a material (*U*-value) may be related to a specific calculation method. The *U*-values given in Section 3 are derived on the basis of an internal surface resistance to heat flow that is consistent with the theory for steady-state heat transfer, see Appendix 5.A2 (standard external coefficients are also used). While such values are accepted as standard for the purposes of Building Regulations[22] in England and Wales, care should be taken when using other calculation methods to ensure that the surface heat transfer coefficients are appropriate to the method.

5.4.1.2 Glazing

The principal fundamental properties are:

— solar transmittance

— solar absorptance

— solar reflectance

— light transmittance.

Additional derived properties are solar gain factors.

Solar gain factors for generic glass and blind combinations are given in 5.6.3.3, Table 5.7. The method used to calculate the tabulated solar gain factors is described in Appendix 5.A4. This appendix also gives the values of the transmission (T), absorption (A) and radiation (R) components (for thermal short-wave radiation) and emissivities (for thermal long-wave radiation) used in calculating the solar gain factors.

5.4.2 Internal design conditions

The selection of appropriate internal design conditions is covered in Section 1: *Environmental criteria for design*, which also contains information related to air quality.

5.4.3 Ventilation rates

Table 5.2 suggests daily mean ventilation rates that might be obtained under certain conditions. The 'closed window' values assume that suitable means are taken to achieve acceptable ventilation rates.

Information on ventilation rates for use in predicting the performance of naturally ventilated buildings is contained in Section 4: *Infiltration and natural ventilation* and CIBSE Applications Manual AM10[23].

5.4.4 Internal heat gains

Data for the calculation of internal heat gains are given in Section 6: *Internal heat gains* and in BSRIA Technical Note TN8/92[24]. It is important that appropriate values for these parameters are agreed with the client.

5.4.5 External design conditions

The following external design criteria are required in order to determine the plant capacity:

— winter design dry and wet bulb temperatures

— summer design dry and wet bulb temperatures

— solar irradiation

— long-wave radiation loss

— sol-air temperatures

— wind speed and direction.

Summary data for the UK and elsewhere are given in Section 2: *External design data*. More extensive data are contained in CIBSE Guide: *Weather and solar data*[25].

While heat loss and cooling load calculations are based on specific design conditions, energy and overheating predictions require either a complete year of hourly weather data, or a statistically reduced version, e.g. degree-days, mean values etc. It is essential to agree the choice of external design conditions with the client.

5.4.5.1 Winter heating design criteria

For heated and naturally ventilated buildings the external design dry bulb conditions given in Section 2 should be used. Where mechanical ventilation and/or air-conditioning are used the fresh air plants need to be sized using a lower temperature than that for the fabric heat loss calculation. This is because the air plant responds virtually instantaneously, whereas the heat transfer through the fabric will incur a time delay due to fabric storage. The selection of a suitable design temperature will depend on the pattern of occupation for the building and the acceptable design risk.

Table 5.2 Effective mean ventilation rates for openable windows

Location of openable windows	Usage of windows		Effective mean ventilation rate	
	Day	Night	Air changes (h^{-1})	Ventilation loss ($W \cdot m^{-2} \cdot K$)
One side of building only	Closed	Closed	1	0.3
	Open	Closed	3	1.0
	Open	Open	10	3.3
More than one side of building	Closed	Closed	2	0.6
	Open	Closed	10	3.3
	Open	Open	30	10.0

The approach adopted in Section 2: *External design data* is to base the design temperature for the room emitters on either 24-hour or 48-hour mean outside air temperatures. This allows for the effect of thermal storage, i.e. the 24-hour mean for buildings for which the thermal response factor, f_r, is less than 4 and the 48-hour mean for $f_r \geq 4$. For sizing fresh air coils, in which the storage effect is non-existent, the design temperature should be based on hourly recorded temperatures. The external design temperature is the temperature below which the outside air temperature is not expected to fall on more than some specified number of occasions over, say, a 20-year period. Suitable data for eight UK locations are given in Section 2. The acceptable number of occasions, and hence the design temperature, should be agreed with the client.

5.4.5.2   Winter humidification

For naturally or mechanically ventilated buildings, providing minimum fresh air requirements without humidification in cold dry winter conditions could mean that the relative humidity (RH) in the room may fall to a level that could have a detrimental effect on health[26,27], see Section 1: *Environmental criteria for design*.

5.4.5.3   Summer design criteria

The maximum demand of an air conditioning system will depend on peak coincident zone loads. However, depending on the type of system, the peak external design dry and wet bulb temperatures will also have a significant influence on the installed plant capacity. System effects are considered in Guide B3: *Ventilation and air conditioning (systems, equipment and control)*[28].

External design data are contained in Section 2: *External design data*. Detailed thermal models usually require hourly meteorological data and so it is necessary to devise methods to select suitable sets of measured data. Guidance on such methods is contained in CIBSE Guide: *Weather and solar data*[25].

Note that various sets of climatic data are available which contain hourly values of the relevant parameters for a complete year. The datasets are often called Example Weather Years (EWYs), e.g. CIBSE Example Weather Years[29,30], or Test Reference Years (TRYs). In most cases the data have been selected as representative of typical years and so are not suitable for plant sizing purposes. Some may contain sequences of extreme data but most EWYs and TRYs are intended only for energy calculations or the prediction of building performance under average conditions.

5.5   Steady-state models

For the purposes of plant sizing, three practicable steady-state models are considered, all of which are simplifications of what is referred to as the Full Model, see Figure 5.2. The basis of the models is given in Appendix 5.A1. Although intended for the purpose of calculating steady-state heat losses they are also suitable as components of dynamic models. The three practicable models, two of which are computer based, are:

—   Reference (steady-state) Model (computer-based)

—   Basic (steady-state) Model (computer-based)

—   Simple (steady-state) Model (for manual calculation).

It is important to understand that, even with the most complex models, simplifications are introduced such as:

—   planar surfaces

—   isothermal surfaces

—   one-dimensional heat flow, i.e. corner effects are ignored

—   surfaces are assumed to be smooth

—   internal surface heat transfer coefficients are assumed not to vary over a surface and, probably, not to vary with temperature

—   thermal properties are constant

—   space air temperatures are uniform

—   infiltration rates are notional

—   heat loss is independent of the emitter location.

The Full Model allows for both variable air temperatures throughout the space and complex long-wave radiation transfer between room surfaces. The main simplifications that result in the three practicable models, see Figure 5.2, are shown in Table 5.3.

In all cases, any radiant heat input from an emitter is assumed to be distributed uniformly over the room surfaces while the convective input enters an air node directly.

All models contain a representation of the space temperature detector. However, because the location of the device cannot be specified at the design stage and it is usually not practical to model a detector in any detail, a

Table 5.3 Comparison of steady-state models

Model	Main simplifications	Main applications	Usual means of implementation
Reference	Uniform air temperature throughout the space	Surface temperature prediction Standard for comparison of models	Computer program
Basic	As for Reference Model with single-node radiant model	Design calculations	Computer program
Simple	As for Basic Model with combined radiant/convective heat transfer model	Design calculations	Manual calculation or computer program

'generic' sensor is used. Such a sensor detects both the air temperature and a mean radiant temperature related to the surface temperatures and the radiant heat input, see Appendix 5.A1.

5.5.1 Applicability of steady-state models

5.5.1.1 Differences between models

The major difference between the models is the way in which long-wave radiant exchange is represented. Numerical differences will depend upon the characteristics of the space, i.e. shape and surface emissivity. The practical significance depends upon the application. While it is not possible to provide a general statement regarding differences, the examples given in Appendix 5.A3 provide some guidance. These are examples of heat loss and surface temperature calculations using dry resultant as the design temperature. With reference to Appendix 5.A3, and assuming the Reference Model to be a 'truth' model, the following observations emerge:

— the Simple Model should not be used where emissivities are significantly less than 0.9

— the Simple Model will usually underestimate the heat loss

— the Basic Model gives an accurate value of heat loss for simple rooms

— the accuracy of the Basic Model declines as the complexity of the space increases

— for practical purposes the ratio of the radiant to the convective components of the emitter output does not affect the differences between the models

— where accurate surface temperatures are required it is necessary to use the Reference Model.

These observations are intended to assist the engineer in the selection of a model for a particular application.

5.5.1.2 Use of computers

Both the Basic and Reference Models are intended for use within a computer program. In order to conform with this Guide any computer program must reproduce the heat losses (to within, say, ± 2%) and surface temperatures (to within, say, ± 0.05 K) calculated in Appendix 5.A3. In the case of programs based upon the Reference Model it is also essential that the view factors for long-wave radiation exchange given in Appendix 5.A3 be reproduced.

Manual models allow the user to check the output from any computer program.

5.5.2 Basic and Reference (steady-state) Models

Appendix 5.A1 provides algorithms describing the Basic and Reference Models. The application of these models is practicable only by means of a computer program. These models are not constrained to design to a particular temperature index and can easily be extended to take account of non-uniform distributions of radiant heat over the room surfaces, surfaces with fixed temperatures and non-standard heat transfer coefficients. However, in common with all calculations based on conditions that differ from the norm, any such differences should be reported with the calculation results, together with the reasons for adopting 'non-standard' values.

5.5.3 Simple (steady-state) Model

This section gives the pertinent equations and a numerical example to illustrate their use in calculating the steady-state heat loss using dry resultant temperature. A detailed explanation of the model is given in Appendix 5.A1.

The total heat loss is the sum of the fabric and ventilation losses, i.e.:

$$Q_t = [F_{1cu} \Sigma (A\, U) + F_{2cu}\, C_v]\,(t_c - t_{ao}) \tag{5.6}$$

where Q_t is the total heat loss (W), F_{1cu} and F_{2cu} are factors related to characteristics of the heat source with respect to dry resultant temperature, $\Sigma (A\, U)$ is sum of the products of surface area and corresponding thermal transmittance over surfaces through which heat flow occurs (W·K^{-1}), C_v is the ventilation conductance (W·K^{-1}), t_c is the dry resultant temperature at centre of room (°C) and t_{ao} is the outside air temperature (°C).

The ventilation conductance is given by:

$$C_v = N\, V / 3 \tag{5.7}$$

where N is the number of room air changes for air entering the space at the outside air temperature (h^{-1}) and V is the room volume (m^3).

Where the fabric loss term contains heat loss through internal partitions, a modified U-value should be used:

$$U' = \frac{U\,(t_c - t_c')}{(t_c - t_{ao})} \tag{5.8}$$

where U' is the thermal transmittance modified for heat loss through internal partitions (W·m^{-2}·K^{-1}) and t_c' is the dry resultant temperature on the opposite side of partition through which heat flow occurs (°C).

F_{1cu} and F_{2cu} are calculated as follows (see Appendix 5.A2, equations 5.169 and 5.170):

$$F_{1cu} = \frac{3\,(C_v + 6\,\Sigma A)}{\Sigma (A\, U) + 18\,\Sigma A + 1.5\,R\,[3\,C_v - \Sigma (A\, U)]} \tag{5.9}$$

$$F_{2cu} = \frac{\Sigma (A\, U) + 18\,\Sigma A}{\Sigma (A\, U) + 18\,\Sigma A + 1.5\,R\,[3\,C_v - \Sigma (A\, U)]} \tag{5.10}$$

where R is the radiant fraction of the heat source, A is the total area through which heat flow occurs (m^2) and $\Sigma (A\, U)$ is the sum of the products of surface area and corresponding thermal transmittance over surfaces through which heat flow occurs (W·K^{-1}). Typical values for R are given in Table 5.4

Table 5.4 Typical proportions of radiant (R) and convective heat from heat emitters

Emitter type	Proportion of emitted radiation	
	Convective	Radiative (R)
Forced warm air heaters	1.0	0
Natural convectors and convector radiators	0.9	0.1
Multi column radiators	0.8	0.2
Double and treble panel radiators, double column radiators	0.7	0.3
Single column radiators, floor warming systems, block storage heaters	0.5	0.5
Vertical and ceiling panel heaters	0.33	0.67
High temperature radiant systems	0.1	0.9

Table 5.5 Example 5.1: surface areas and U-values

Surface	Area, A (m²)	U-value (W·m⁻²·K⁻¹)	($A \times U$) (W·K⁻¹)
Floor	112.5	0.45	50.6
Roof	112.5	0.3	33.8
External walls	171.0	0.5	85.5
Glazing	48.0	3.3	158.4
Doors	6.0	2.9	17.4
$\Sigma A = 450.0$		$\Sigma(A\,U) = 345.7$	

The corresponding air and mean surface temperatures are given by:

$$t_{ai} = \frac{Q_t(1-1.5R) + C_v t_{ao} + 6\Sigma A t_c}{C_v + 6\Sigma A} \quad (5.11)$$

$$t_m = 2t_c - t_{ai} \quad (5.12)$$

where t_{ai} is the inside air temperature (°C), t_m is the mean surface temperature (°C), t_{ao} is the outside air temperature (°C) and t_c is the dry resultant temperature at the centre of the space (°C).

Note that the constants contained in the above equations assume standard heat transfer coefficients and emissivity values, i.e. $h_c = 3$ W·m⁻²·K⁻¹, $h_r = 5.7$ W·m⁻²·K⁻¹, $\varepsilon = 0.9$.

Example 5.1: Calculation of steady-state design heat losses using the Simple Model

A small factory, see Figure 5.4, is to be heated to a dry resultant temperature of 19°C. The site is subject to 'normal' conditions of exposure. Surface areas and the corresponding U-values are given in Table 5.5. A ventilation rate of 0.5 air changes per hour is assumed. The external design temperature is –1°C. It is required to determine the total heat loss and the inside air and mean radiant temperatures under steady-state design conditions when heated by (a) forced circulation warm air heaters and (b) high temperature radiant strip heaters.

(a)   Heating by forced circulation warm air heaters

Step 1: ventilation conductance (C_v)

Volume of building (V) = 562.5 m³ and ventilation rate (N) = 0.5 h⁻¹, therefore using equation 5.7:

$$C_v = (0.5 \times 562.5)/3 = 93.75 \text{ W·K}^{-1}$$

Step 2: factors related to characteristics of heat source (F_{1cu}, F_{2cu})

From Table 5.4, for a forced warm air heater, $R = 0$. Therefore, from equation 5.9:

$$F_{1cu} = \frac{3[93.75 + (6\times450)]}{345.7 + (18\times450)} = 0.99$$

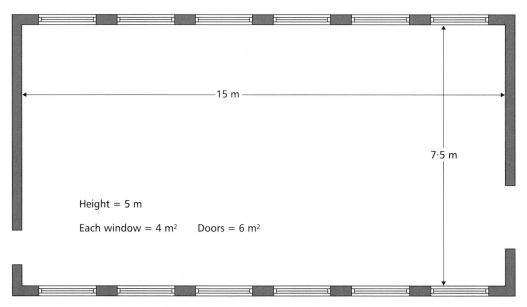

Figure 5.4 Example 5.1: Small factory building

15 m

7·5 m

Height = 5 m

Each window = 4 m²   Doors = 6 m²

and from equation 5.10:

$$F_{2cu} = \frac{345.7 + (18 \times 450)}{345.7 + (18 \times 450)} = 1$$

Step 3: total heat loss (Q_t)

From equation 5.6:

$$Q_t = [(0.99 \times 345.7) + (1 \times 93.75)](19 + 1)$$

$$= 8.72 \text{ kW}$$

Step 4: inside air temperature (t_{ai})

From equation 5.11:

$$t_{ai} = \frac{(8.72 \times 10^3) + [93.75 \times (-1)] + (6 \times 450 \times 19)}{93.75 + (6 \times 450)}$$

$$= 21.45 \,^{\circ}\text{C}$$

Step 5: mean surface temperature (t_m)

From equation 5.12:

$$t_m = (2 \times 19) - 21.45 = 16.55^{\circ}\text{C}$$

(b)　Heating by radiant strips

Step 1: ventilation conductance (C_v)

As for (a) above.

Step 2: factors related to characteristics of heat source (F_{1cu}, F_{2cu})

From Table 5.4, for radiant strip heater, $R = 0.9$. Therefore, from equations 5.9 and 5.10, respectively:

$$F_{1cu} = 3 \, [93.75 + (6 \times 450)]/[345.7 + (18 \times 450)$$
$$+ \{1.5 \times 0.9 \, [(3 \times 93.75) - 345.7]\}]$$
$$= 1.00$$

$$F_{2cu} = 345.7 + (18 \times 450)/[345.7 + (18 \times 450)$$
$$+ \{1.5 \times 0.9 \, [(3 \times 93.75) - 345.7]\}]$$
$$= 1.01$$

Step 3: total heat loss (Q_t)

From equation 5.6:

$$Q_t = [(1 \times 345.7) + (1.01 \times 93.75)](19 + 1)$$
$$= 8.81 \text{ kW}$$

Step 4: inside air temperature (t_{ai})

From equation 5.11:

$$t_{ai} = \{(8.81 \times 10^3) \, [1 - (1.5 \times 0.9)] + [93.75 \times (-1)]$$
$$+ (6 \times 450 \times 19)\}/\{93.75 + (6 \times 450)\}$$
$$= 17.23 \,^{\circ}\text{C}$$

Step 5: mean surface temperature (t_m)

From equation 5.12:

$$t_m = (2 \times 19) - 17.23 = 20.77^{\circ}\text{C}$$

Example 5.1 illustrates how the method may be used to compare different types of heating system and to determine whether they can achieve the design comfort criteria. For example, a large difference between the air and radiant temperatures may lead to discomfort.

5.6　Dynamic models

The objective of the thermal dynamic model is to provide a means for calculating:

—　peak summertime temperature

—　peak space cooling loads

—　excess heating capacity necessary for morning pre-heat.

The specification of the dynamic model is similar to that of the steady-state model in that a number of levels of simplification are adopted, see Figure 5.3. The full dynamic model will not be described since it is considered impracticable for the purposes of routine design calculations. Also, the treatment of dynamic models differs from that for steady-state models in that, with the exception of the Simple (dynamic) Model, no particular method is recommended. Instead, guidance is given on the features necessary for a model to meet the requirements of Guide A. Guidance on the selection of a suitable model is given in CIBSE Applications Manual AM11: *Building energy and environmental modelling*[31].

At the core of the dynamic model is the representation of the storage of heat within the building fabric; how this is achieved is not important except that the non-steady heat conduction equation must be solved correctly. There is no general analytical method available for the solution of this equation and so numerical methods must be used. Therefore practicable dynamic models invariably require computer programs for their solution.

A fabric storage model alone is not sufficient to define a dynamic model; it is essential that the heat flows into and out of the structure are correctly represented. To this end the dynamic model will include representations of:

—　internal room surface heat balance

—　non-steady-state fabric conduction

—　characteristics of the emitter

—　internal solar distribution

—　temporal distribution of internal heat gains

—　temporal variation of the external climate

—　external solar radiation.

It is also important that the model meets certain criteria in order to demonstrate that it is valid for the intended purpose. The development of validation methods is still at an early stage and a number of approaches have been explored[14,32]. There is no simple way for the user to ensure that a particular model is suitable for the intended purpose. The situation for the Simple (dynamic) Model is different because the theoretical basis is clear and it can be used as a manual method for simple cases. It may also be used to check the validity of more complex dynamic models. The issue of validity is dealt with in more detail in Applications Manual AM11[31].

The models presented here are intended only for assessing the effects of sensible heat gains. In some climates moisture is absorbed within the building fabric and its contents, which can significantly affect the loads on the system. Whilst there have been some attempts to derive simple models of the processes involved[33], this is a complex issue[34–37] and as yet there is no consensus on any particular analytical method.

5.6.1 Reference (dynamic) Model

In order to satisfy the requirements of the Reference (dynamic) Model, the features described in Appendix 5.A7 must be incorporated. The specification given in Appendix 5.A7 is not exhaustive but contains sufficient detail to allow the engineer to assess the level of a particular model. While it may be that at present there is no computer program available to match these requirements exactly, they are relevant in that they set a target that will ultimately be achieved.

5.6.2 Basic (dynamic) Model

The requirements of the Reference (dynamic) Model may be relaxed, often with little loss in accuracy, to produce the Basic (dynamic) Model. While it is not easy to provide detailed guidance on the effect of simplifications, the results of an international validation exercise offer some general guidance[14]. That study identified three areas of importance:

— the need to represent correctly the proportions of radiant and convective heat from room emitters

— the need to represent surface heat transfer coefficients

— the need to make a realistic determination of the internal distribution of solar radiation.

Whatever the model selected it is important to ascertain that it is suitable for the intended purpose. One way to do this is to carry out simple check tests. This is of particular importance when the analysis is to be applied to special cases. The two examples contained in Appendix 5.A8 indicate the types of test that should be carried out. The first enables a check to be made on the ability of the model to take account of thermal storage and the other checks its applicability to highly glazed spaces.

5.6.3 Simple (dynamic) Model (admittance procedure)

This model is intended for application at an early stage in the design process. The objective is to enable the designer to make rapid assessments of:

— probability of overheating

— space cooling loads

— pre-heat requirement.

The basis for the model and its implementation are given below. It is important to realise that predictions made using the Simple (dynamic) Model will differ from those obtained by means of the Reference Model. However, the Simple Model can be used to provide order-of-magnitude checks on the validity of computer predictions.

The Simple (dynamic) Model is based on the following assumptions:

— all dynamics can be represented by the response to a sine wave with a period of 24 hours

— heat interchange between room surfaces follows the heat transfer assumptions given for the Simple (steady-state) Model, see Appendix 5.A1.5

— a uniform distribution of transmitted short-wave solar radiation over room surfaces.

The dynamic response may therefore be represented by means of the admittance method as described by Milbank and Harrington-Lynn[12], the method is given further justification by Davies[38]. The properties of the glazing are calculated using methods described in Appendix 5.A4. The theoretical basis for applications of the admittance method is covered elsewhere[39,40].

The parameters used by the model to characterise the performance of a space are as follows:

— thermal response

— admittance, decrement factor and surface factor

— solar gain factor.

These parameters are considered in the following sections, along with the equations necessary for the calculation of space temperatures and cooling loads. The derivation of admittance and its related factors is given in Section A3, *Thermal properties of building structures*, Appendix 3.A8.

The Simple (dynamic) Model may be implemented as either a manual calculation or a computer program. The manual calculation is a further simplification of the method involving the use of constants to represent the time-varying processes. The description of the application of the method given in the following sections is for the manual calculation method. Computer-based versions will follow the same general procedure but with adjustments, as follows:

— actual, rather than standardised, values for the admittance and surface factor of each surface, and their associated time delays

— solar transmission and absorption, and shading, calculated for each hour of the day (see Appendix 5.A4)

— internal gains divided into radiant and convective components.

5.6.3.1 Thermal response ('thermal weight')

Conventionally, buildings are classified as having either a slow or a fast response to heat transfer[41].

The response of a space to thermal input depends upon:

— type of thermal input

— surface finishes

— thermal properties of the construction

— thickness of the construction

— furnishings within the space.

The heat input to the surfaces will be in the form of either short-wave radiation (solar radiation and energy from electric lights) or a combination of long-wave radiation (from surfaces and other emitters) and convective exchange with the air. The way in which a surface responds to short-wave radiation is different to that for other inputs, and is characterised by the surface factor (see 5.6.3.2). This depends on the short-wave absorption coefficient, the surface heat transfer coefficient and the thermal properties of the structure. The physical process involved is that short-wave radiation is absorbed at the surface which, after a delay due to thermal storage, causes the temperature of that surface to rise. Heat is then transferred to the space in the form of long-wave radiation and convection. The effect is to raise the internal heat transfer (i.e. environmental) temperature.

The response of a space to changes in environmental temperature is characterised by the admittance of the surfaces (see 5.6.3.2) which depends upon the long-wave emissivity, the surface heat transfer coefficient and the thermal properties of the structure.

There are therefore two time delays associated with the thermal response of the space, one which applies to short-wave radiation and the other due to surface-to-surface and surface-to-air heat exchanges. Thus, it is possible for a space to be lightweight in terms of its response to solar radiation but heavyweight in terms of the change in temperature arising from other sources of heat input.

For the Simple (dynamic) Model, the definition of thermal response to short-wave radiation is as follows:

— fast: surface factor = 0.8 with a delay of 1 hour

— slow: surface factor = 0.5 with a delay of 2 hours

Response to the changes in the environmental temperature is characterised by the response factor, f_r, given by:

$$f_r = \frac{\Sigma (A\, Y) + C_v}{\Sigma (A\, U) + C_v} \qquad (5.13)$$

where f_r is the response factor, $\Sigma (A\, Y)$ is the sum of the products of surface areas and their corresponding thermal admittances (W·K^{-1}), $\Sigma (A\, U)$ is the sum of the products of surface area and corresponding thermal transmittance over surfaces through which heat flow occurs (W·K^{-1}). C_v is the ventilation conductance (W·K^{-1}), see equation 5.7.

Structures with a high thermal response factor (> 4) are referred to as slow response buildings, i.e. 'heavyweight' structures, and those with a low thermal response factor (≤ 4) as fast response buildings, i.e. 'lightweight' structures. Note that these definitions are only approximations to the thermal behavior of actual buildings. Since the thermal response factor partly depends on the ventilation rate, a building having a nominally slow thermal response may, if the rate of ventilation is high, have a low thermal response factor. Table 5.6 gives nominal building classifications and corresponding response factors. These classifications should be regarded as giving only a general indication of expected performance.

The response factor as defined in equation 5.13 should not be confused with that used (mainly in the USA) to describe the dynamic characteristics of walls.

5.6.3.2 Parameters associated with the response of surfaces

Values of the following parameters for a wide range of constructions are given in Section A3: *Thermal properties of building structures*.

Thermal admittance (Y-value)

The most significant parameter is the admittance. This is the rate of flow of heat between the internal surfaces of the structure and the environmental temperature in the space, for each degree of deviation of that temperature about its mean value. The associated time dependency takes the form of a time lead denoted by ω.

Table 5.6 Thermal response

Thermal response	Typical features of construction	Response factor, f_r	Response to short-wave radiation		Time lead for admittance, $\omega(h)$
			Average surface factor, F	Time delay, $\phi(h)$	
Slow	Masonry external walls and Internal partitions, bare solid floors and ceilings	> 4	0.5	2	1
Fast	Lightweight external cladding, de-mountable partitions, suspended ceilings, solid floors with carpet or wood block finish or suspended floors	≤ 4	0.8	1	0

For thin structures of low thermal capacity, the admittance is equal in amplitude to the U-value and has a time lead of zero. In the case of an exciting frequency with a period of 24 hours the amplitude tends towards a limiting value for thicknesses greater than about 100 mm.

For multi-layered structures, the admittance is primarily determined by the characteristics of the materials in the layers nearest to the internal surface. For example, the admittance of a heavy concrete slab construction lined internally with insulation will be close to the value for the insulation alone, whereas placing the insulation within the construction, or on the outside surface, will result in an admittance that differs little from that for the uninsulated slab.

Decrement factor (f)

The decrement factor is the ratio of the rate of heat flow through the structure, due to variations in the external heat transfer temperature from its mean value with the environmental temperature held constant, to the steady-state conduction. The associated time dependency takes the form of a time lag denoted by ϕ.

For thin structures of low thermal capacity, the amplitude of the decrement factor is unity and the time lag zero. The amplitude decreases and the time lag increases with increasing thermal capacity.

Surface factor (F)

The surface factor is the ratio of the variation of radiant heat flow (from short-wave sources) about its mean value readmitted to the space from the surface, to the variation of heat flow about its mean value incident upon the surface. The associated time dependency takes the form of a time lag denoted by φ.

The amplitude of the surface factor decreases and its time lag increases with increasing thermal conductivity but both are virtually constant with thickness.

For the Simple (dynamic) Model, the only short-wave gain considered is that from the sun; gains from other sources are treated as long-wave gains.

5.6.3.3 Parameters associated with solar gain

The thermal load on a space due to solar irradiation depends upon the radiation transmitted by and absorbed within the glazing system. The amount of radiation transmitted and absorbed is a function of the intensity of the incident radiation and the angle of incidence between the solar beam and the glazing. Therefore, for an accurate determination of this load, it is necessary to calculate the gain occurring at various times of the day. A computer-based method is required to achieve this cost effectively. However, if the objective is to determine either the maximum space temperature or the maximum cooling load, the transmission and absorption characteristics calculated at the time of peak solar irradiation are often the most significant. The Simple (dynamic) Model is based on these assumptions.

The response of a space to solar radiation transmitted and absorbed in the glazing system is characterised by two parameters, see Appendix 5.A4:

— mean solar gain factor

— alternating solar gain factor.

These are further divided into factors relating the gain to the environmental node and to the room air. The latter is used only where internal blinds are fitted. This is because increased convection from blinds significantly changes the proportions of long-wave and convective heat from the surface. The factors are defined as follows:

$$\bar{S}_a = \frac{\text{Mean solar gain at air node per m}^2 \text{ of glazing}}{\text{Mean solar intensity incident on glazed facade}} \qquad (5.14)$$

$$\bar{S}_e = \frac{\text{Mean solar gain at environmental node per m}^2 \text{ of glazing}}{\text{Mean solar intensity incident on glazed facade}} \qquad (5.15)$$

$$\widetilde{S}_a = \frac{\text{Instantaneous cyclic solar gain at air node per m}^2 \text{ of glazing}}{\text{Instantaneous cyclic solar intensity incident on glazed facade}} \qquad (5.16)$$

$$\widetilde{S}_e = \frac{\text{Instantaneous cyclic solar gain at environmental node per m}^2 \text{ of glazing}}{\text{Instantaneous cyclic solar intensity incident on glazed facade}} \qquad (5.17)$$

In the absence of shading devices, the alternating gain usually lags the solar intensity by between zero and two hours, the duration of the lag depending on the surface factors for the internal surfaces. High surface factors (e.g. 0.8) give rise to delays of about one hour, low surface factors (e.g. 0.5) give rise to delays of about two hours.

Typical values of the above factors for various glazing configurations are given in Table 5.7. The transmission (T), absorption (A) and reflection (R) components (for thermal short-wave radiation) and emissivities (for thermal long-wave radiation) for generic glass and blind types used in calculating the solar gain factors are given in Appendix 5.A4, Table 5.44.

Glazing manufacturers do not usually provide values of these solar factors for their products. More commonly, one or more of the following are provided:

— properties at normal incidence (see Appendix 5.A4)

— shading coefficients

— total solar energy transmittance ('G-value').

Only the first of these can be used to calculate solar gain factors. However, shading coefficients and G-values can be derived from fundamental properties and so it is possible to obtain the corresponding solar gain factors by a process of iteration. Shading coefficients and G-values are defined in 5.2.2.

Table 5.7 Solar gain factors and shading coefficients for generic glazing/blind combinations

Description (inside to outside)	Solar gain factor at environmental node†			Solar gain factor at air node		Shading coefficient (S_c)	
						Short-wave	Long-wave
	$\overline{S}_e$	$\widetilde{S}_{el}$	$\widetilde{S}_{eh}$	$\overline{S}_a$	$\widetilde{S}_a$		
Single glazing/blind combinations:							
— clear glass	0.75	0.66	0.50	—	—	0.90	0.06
— reflecting glass	0.51	0.45	0.35	—	—	0.49	0.11
— absorbing glass	0.55	0.50	0.42	—	—	0.53	0.19
— reflecting slats/clear	0.30	0.25	0.22	0.08	0.08	—	—
— absorbing slats/clear	0.42	0.41	0.40	0.18	0.18	—	—
— roller blind/clear	0.36	0.31	0.25	0.06	0.06	—	—
— 'generic' blind/clear	0.34	0.32	0.29	0.11	0.11	—	—
Double glazing/blind combinations:							
— clear/clear	0.61	0.56	0.44	—	—	0.70	0.12
— clear/reflecting	0.40	0.36	0.29	—	—	0.39	0.11
— clear/absorbing	0.40	0.38	0.31	—	—	0.41	0.15
— reflecting/clear	0.48	0.45	0.38	—	—	0.39	0.21
— absorbing/clear	0.54	0.53	0.47	—	—	0.41	0.32
— low emissivity/clear	0.56	0.51	0.41	—	—	0.56	0.15
— low emissivity/reflecting	0.36	0.33	0.27	—	—	0.32	0.11
— low emissivity/absorbing	0.34	0.32	0.27	—	—	0.33	0.14
— reflecting slats/clear/clear	0.26	0.23	0.20	0.13	0.13	—	—
— Absorbing slats/clear/clear	0.34	0.35	0.35	0.20	0.21	—	—
— roller blind/clear/clear	0.30	0.27	0.22	0.10	0.10	—	—
— clear/roller blind/clear	0.33	0.29	0.24	—	—	0.28	0.11
— 'generic' blind/clear/clear	0.28	0.28	0.26	0.14	0.15	—	—
— clear/'generic' blind/clear	0.29	0.28	0.26	—	—	0.15	0.21
Triple glazing:							
— clear/clear/clear	0.51	0.48	0.40	—	—	0.55	0.17
— clear/clear/absorbing	0.32	0.31	0.27	—	—	0.33	0.15
— clear/clear/reflecting	0.34	0.31	0.26	—	—	0.31	0.12
— clear/low emissivity/clear	0.49	0.46	0.38	—	—	0.45	0.20

† For $\widetilde{S}_e$, subscripts 'l' and 'h' denote lightweight and heavyweight buildings, respectively

Note: shading coefficients for windows with slatted blind or windows with inner blind are not given since these not compatible with the properties of plain glass

Shading coefficients are calculated as follows:

$$S_c = \frac{\text{Solar gain through subject glass and blind at direct normal incidence}}{\text{Solar gain through reference glass at direct normal incidence}} \quad (5.18)$$

where the solar gain through the reference glass at normal incidence is 0.87.

Solar gain in this case can be considered to mean the short-wave or the long-wave component, or the total of both components. Therefore, the shading coefficient can take three forms, as follows:

— short-wave shading coefficient: the solar direct transmittance divided by 0.87

— long-wave shading coefficient: the fraction of the solar absorptance that is re-radiated and contributes to the total transmittance, divided by 0.87

— total shading coefficient: the solar transmittance divided by 0.87.

Values of shading coefficients for short-wave and long-wave radiation are given in Table 5.7. When values of shading coefficient are quoted it is important to know the basis on which they were calculated, see Appendix 5.A4.4.

5.6.3.4 Calculation of overheating risk

The risk of overheating is usually based on the probability of a particular specified space temperature (in this case the dry resultant temperature) being exceeded for a specified period of time. The result is dependent upon the climatic data selected for the analysis.

The principles of the method and the relevant equations are given below, along with a numerical example.

The data required are as follows:

— climatic data: see Section 2: *External design data* and CIBSE Guide: *Weather and solar data*[25]

— surface areas of internal and external structural elements

— construction details of internal and external structural elements

— thermal transmittances (*U*-values) of internal and external structural elements: see Section 3: *Thermal properties of building structures*

— thermal admittances (*Y*-values) of internal and external structural elements: see Section 3: *Thermal properties of building structures*

— surface areas of glazing

— solar gain factors

— shading details

— internal heat gains due to occupants, electric lighting, IT and other sources: see Section 6: *Internal heat gains*

— ventilation rate and profile: empirical values for naturally ventilated buildings are given in Table 5.2.

Table 5.8 shows how the various sources of heat gain contribute to the internal temperature.

Using the Simple (dynamic) Model, the following need to be determined in order to calculate the peak internal space temperature:

— mean heat gains from all sources

— mean internal dry resultant temperature

— swing (deviation), mean-to-peak, in heat gains from all sources

— swing (deviation), mean-to-peak, in dry resultant temperature.

These calculations are described in the following sections and illustrated by means of a numerical example. For complex situations (e.g. the ventilation rate varies over 24 hours or there is shading) manual calculations are unlikely to be practicable. This is because it is necessary to determine, for example, the shaded area for each hour of the day so that the mean can be established.

Mean heat gains

(a)   Solar heat gains

Solar gains through glazing consist of solar radiation which is absorbed in the glazing and transmitted to the environmental node and also the transmitted solar radiation which is absorbed at the internal surfaces of the room and appears at the environmental node.

The mean solar heat gain to the internal environmental node is given by:

$$\bar{Q}_{se} = \bar{S}_e \bar{I}_t A_g \tag{5.19}$$

where $\bar{Q}_{se}$ is the mean solar heat gain to the environmental node (W), $\bar{S}_e$ is the mean solar gain factor at the environmental node, $\bar{I}_t$ is the mean total solar irradiance (W·m^{-2}) and A_g is the area of glazing (m^2).

For the case of internal shading (i.e. blinds), part of the solar gain will enter the air node and part will enter the environmental node.

Mean solar heat gain to the air node is given by:

$$\bar{Q}_{sa} = \bar{S}_a \bar{I}_t A_g \tag{5.20}$$

where $\bar{Q}_{sa}$ is the mean solar heat gain to the air node (W) and $\bar{S}_a$ is the mean solar gain factor at the air node.

Table 5.8 Sources of heat gain and their influence on internal temperature

Source of gain	Mechanism for transfer of heat gain	Means of converting gain at source to heat gain in the space			Node at which gain acts	Means of converting gain at source to temperature rise in the space		
		Modifier		Delay (h)		Modifier		Overall delay† (h)
		Mean	Swing			Mean	Swing	
Solar radiation	Direct transmission	Unmodified	Surface factor	1 or 2	Environmental	Unmodified	Admittance	0 or 1
	Absorption by glazing	Unmodified	Unmodified	0	Environmental	Unmodified	Admittance	0 or 1
	Absorption by internal shades	Unmodified	Unmodified	0	Air	Unmodified	Unmodified	0
	Absorption by opaque fabric	U-value	Decrement factor	0 – 24	Environmental	Unmodified	Admittance	0 – 24
Outside air	Conduction through opaque fabric	U-value	Decrement factor	0 – 24	Environmental	Unmodified	Admittance	0 – 24
	Infiltration/ ventilation	Ventilation conductance	Ventilation conductance	0	Air	Unmodified	Unmodified	0
Occupants, business machines, sundry equipment, heating/cooling emitters	Radiation‡	Unmodified	Unmodified	0	Environmental (1.5 × radiant component)	Unmodified	Admittance	0 or 1
	Convection‡	Unmodified	Unmodified	0	Air (convective component minus 0.5 × radiant component)	Unmodified	Unmodified	0

† Time between occurrence of source of gain and rise of temperature in the space
‡ Radiative and convective proportions depend on characteristics of the source
Note: 'Unmodified' means that the Simple (dynamic) Model uses the value of the gain at its source

(b) Internal heat gains

The mean heat gain from internal sources such as occupants, lighting, computers etc. is calculated by multiplying each individual load by its duration, summing over all sources and averaging the total over 24 hours. It is assumed that all the internal gains are to the environmental node. Hence:

$$\bar{Q}_c = \frac{\Sigma\,(q_{cn}\,\theta_{cn})}{24} \tag{5.21}$$

where $\bar{Q}_c$ is the mean internal heat gain (W), q_{cn} is the instantaneous heat gain from internal heat source n (W) and θ_{cn} is the duration of internal heat source n (h).

(c) Mean structural heat gain

The mean gain due to transmission through the fabric is calculated by summing the mean gains through the external opaque and glazed surfaces:

$$\bar{Q}_f = \Sigma\,(A\,U)\,\bar{t}_{eo} \tag{5.22}$$

where $\bar{Q}_f$ is the mean fabric heat gain (W), $\Sigma\,(A\,U)$ is the sum of the products of surface area and corresponding thermal transmittance over surfaces through which heat flow occurs (W·K⁻¹) and t_{eo} is the mean sol-air temperature (°C) (see Section 2: *External design data*).

Note that, for glazing, t_{ao} is used in equation 5.22 rather than t_{eo}, because the effect of solar radiation is included in the solar heat gain, see *(a)* above.

(d) Total gain to the environmental node

The total gain to the environmental node is given by:

$$\bar{Q}_{te} = \bar{Q}_{se} + \bar{Q}_c + \bar{Q}_f \tag{5.23}$$

where $\bar{Q}_{te}$ is the mean total gain to the environmental node (W), $\bar{Q}_{se}$ is the mean solar heat gain to the environmental node (W), $\bar{Q}_c$ is the mean internal heat gain (W) and $\bar{Q}_f$ is the mean fabric heat gain (W).

(e) Total gain to the air node

The total gain to the air node is given by:

$$\bar{Q}_{ta} = \bar{Q}_{sa} + C_v\,\bar{t}_{ao} \tag{5.24}$$

where $\bar{Q}_{ta}$ is the mean total gain to the air node (W), Q_{sa} is the mean solar heat gain to the air node (W), C_v is the ventilation loss (W·K⁻¹) and $\bar{t}_{ao}$ is the mean outside air temperature (°C).

Mean internal dry resultant temperature

For a fixed ventilation rate the mean dry resultant temperature is given by (see Appendix 5.A2, equation 5.191):

$$\bar{t}_c = \frac{\bar{Q}_{ta} + F_{cu}\,\bar{Q}_{te}}{C_v + F_{cu}\,\Sigma\,(A\,U)} \tag{5.25}$$

where $\bar{t}_c$ is the mean dry resultant temperature at centre of room (°C), $\bar{Q}_{ta}$ is the 24-hour mean total gains at the air node (W), $\bar{Q}_{te}$ is the 24-hour mean total gains at the environmental node (W), F_{cu} is the room conduction correction factor with respect to dry resultant temperature, C_v is the ventilation loss (W·K⁻¹) and $\Sigma\,(A\,U)$ is the sum of the products of surface area and corresponding thermal transmittance over surfaces through which heat flow occurs (W·K⁻¹).

Using standard heat transfer coefficients and emissivity values (i.e. $h_c = 3$ W·m⁻²·K⁻¹, $h_r = 5.7$ W·m⁻²·K⁻¹, $\varepsilon = 0.9$), F_{cu} is given by (see Appendix 5.A2, equation 5.162):

$$F_{cu} = \frac{3\,(C_v + 6\,\Sigma A)}{\Sigma\,(A\,U) + 18\,\Sigma A} \tag{5.26}$$

Table 5.2 suggests values of the daily mean ventilation rates that might be obtained under certain conditions. Information on ventilation rates for use in predicting the performance of naturally ventilated buildings is contained in Section 4: *Infiltration and natural ventilation* and CIBSE Applications Manual AM10[23]. If the ventilation varies throughout the day then the solution is complex. One approach to the solution is given by Harrington-Lynn[39].

Swing (deviation), mean-to-peak, in heat gains

The variations in heat input due to solar radiation, outside air temperature and internal gains must be determined separately and summed to give the total swing in heat input.

Rooms with south or west facing external walls will usually experience a peak temperature in the early or late afternoon when high solar irradiance coincides with high outside temperatures. North facing rooms with little solar radiation will experience the peak indoor temperature in the afternoon due to the warmth of the ventilation air. East facing rooms will experience a peak temperature in the morning or afternoon dependant on the window size, amount of natural ventilation and the internal gains.

The thermal response of the building must be assessed, see 5.6.3.1, to determine whether the building has a fast or slow response since this determines the time at which heat stored in the structure will be re-transmitted into the space. The time of day at which the maximum indoor temperature is likely to occur must be established.

Swing in solar heat input

Tables of solar radiation data are contained in Section 2: *External design data*.

The swing in solar gain to the environmental node is given by:

$$\tilde{Q}_{se} = \tilde{S}_e\,A_g\,(\hat{I}_t - \bar{I}_t) \tag{5.27}$$

and, where internal blinds are present, that to the air node by:

$$\tilde{Q}_{sa} = \tilde{S}_a\,A_g\,(\hat{I}_t - \bar{I}_t) \tag{5.28}$$

where $\tilde{Q}_{se}$ and $\tilde{Q}_{sa}$ are the swings in solar gain to environmental and air nodes respectively (W), $\tilde{S}_e$ and $\tilde{S}_a$ are the cyclic solar gain factors at the environmental and air nodes respectively, A_g is the area of glazing (m²), $\hat{I}_t$ is the peak total solar irradiance (W·m⁻²) and $\bar{I}_t$ is the mean total solar irradiance (W·m⁻²).

There will be a time delay between the occurrence of the gain and the consequent increase in space temperature due to the admittance of the room surfaces. This delay is 1 hour for spaces having a 'slow' response and zero for 'fast' response spaces. The time at which the peak space temperature occurs is called the 'peak hour'.

To demonstrate the calculation technique, it is assumed here that the peak internal temperature is the result of the incidence of solar radiation on the facade. The same techniques may be used to determine the internal temperature at other times.

Swing in structural heat gain

The peak temperature will generally be determined by the peak solar irradiance as this is often the largest heat input, however the outside sol-air temperature will contribute to the peak load. The swing in sol-air temperature is modified in amplitude and experiences a time delay. These factors are described in terms of the decrement factor (f) and an associated time lag (ϕ). Values of decrement factor and its time lag are given in Section 3: *Thermal properties of building structures*.

The swing in the sol-air temperature is given by:

$$\tilde{t}_{eo} = (t_{eo} - \bar{t}_{eo}) \tag{5.29}$$

where $\tilde{t}_{eo}$ is the swing in sol-air temperature (K), t_{eo} is the sol-air temperature (°C) at time $(\theta - \phi)$, θ is the time of day at which the peak space temperature occurs (i.e. the 'peak hour'), ϕ is the time lag associated with decrement factor (h) and $\bar{t}_{eo}$ is the mean sol-air temperature (°C).

The swing in effective heat input due to fabric heat gain is given by:

$$\tilde{Q}_f = \sum_n f_n A_n U_n \tilde{t}_{eo} + \sum_n f_{gn} A_{gn} U_{gn} \tilde{t}_{ao} \tag{5.30}$$

where $\tilde{Q}_f$ is the swing in fabric heat gain (W), f_n is the decrement factor for (opaque) surface n, A_n is the area of (opaque) surface n (m²), U_n is the thermal transmittance of (opaque) surface n (W·m⁻²·K⁻¹), $\tilde{t}_{eo}$ is the swing in sol-air temperature (K), f_{gn} is the decrement factor for glazed surface n, A_{gn} the area of glazed surface n (m²), U_{gn} is the thermal transmittance of glazed surface n (W·m⁻²·K⁻¹), $\tilde{t}_{ao}$ is the swing in outside air temperature (K) at time θ.

For glazing, the decrement factor (f) is unity and the time delay for t_{ao} (ϕ) is zero; the outside air temperature and the sol-air temperature are calculated with the incident solar radiation set to zero.

Design values of sol-air temperature (t_{eo}) for three locations within the UK are given in Section 2: *External design data*.

Swing in internal heat gain

At the assumed time of peak load:

$$\tilde{Q}_c = \hat{Q}_c - \bar{Q}_c \tag{5.31}$$

where $\tilde{Q}_c$ is the swing in internal heat gain (W), $\hat{Q}_c$ is the peak internal heat gain (W) and $\bar{Q}_c$ is the mean internal heat gain (W). The peak internal heat gain is taken as the sum of all internal gains within the space.

Swing in heat gain from ventilation

The swing in heat gain is given by:

$$\tilde{Q}_{av} = C_v \tilde{t}_{ao} \tag{5.32}$$

where $\tilde{Q}_{av}$ is the swing in heat gain due to ventilation (W), C_v is the ventilation conductance (W·K⁻¹) and $\tilde{t}_{ao}$ is the swing in outside air temperature (K).

The swing in outside air temperature is given by the difference between the outdoor air temperature at the peak hour and the mean outdoor air temperature, i.e:

$$\tilde{t}_{ao} = t_{ao} - \bar{t}_{ao} \tag{5.33}$$

where t_{ao} is the outside air temperature at the peak hour (°C) and $\bar{t}_{ao}$ is the mean outside air temperature (°C).

Total swing in heat gain

The total swing in heat gain to the environmental node is given by:

$$\tilde{Q}_{te} = \tilde{Q}_{se} + \tilde{Q}_f + \tilde{Q}_c \tag{5.34}$$

where $\tilde{Q}_{te}$ is the total swing in heat gain to the environmental node (W), $\tilde{Q}_{se}$ is the swing in solar heat gain to the environmental node (W), $\tilde{Q}_f$ is the swing in fabric heat gain (W) and $\tilde{Q}_c$ is the swing in internal heat gain (W).

The total swing in heat gain to the air node is given by:

$$\tilde{Q}_{ta} = \tilde{Q}_{sa} + \tilde{Q}_{av} \tag{5.35}$$

where $\tilde{Q}_{ta}$ is the total swing in heat gain to the air node (W), $\tilde{Q}_{sa}$ is the swing in solar heat gain to the air node (W), $\tilde{Q}_{av}$ is the swing in heat gain due to ventilation (W).

Swing, mean-to-peak in internal dry resultant temperature

The swing in dry resultant temperature is determined from the following equation (see Appendix 5.A2, equation 5.192):

$$\tilde{t}_c = \frac{\tilde{Q}_{ta} + F_{cy} \tilde{Q}_{te\theta}}{C_v + F_{cy} \Sigma (A\,Y)} \tag{5.36}$$

where $\tilde{t}_c$ is the swing in dry resultant temperature at the peak hour (K), $\tilde{Q}_{ta}$ is the total swing in heat gain to the air node at the peak hour (W), $\tilde{Q}_{te\theta}$ is the total swing in heat gain to the environmental node at time θ (W), F_{cy} is the room admittance factor with respect to dry resultant temperature and $\Sigma (A\,Y)$ is the sum of the products of surface areas and their corresponding thermal admittances (W·K⁻¹).

Using standard heat transfer coefficients and emissivity values (i.e. $h_c = 3$ W·m^{-2}·K^{-1}, $h_r = 5.7$ W·m^{-2}·K^{-1}, $\varepsilon = 0.9$), F_{cy} is given by (see Appendix 5.A2, equation 5.180):

$$F_{cy} = \frac{3(C_v + 6\Sigma A)}{\Sigma(A\,Y) + 18\Sigma A} \qquad (5.37)$$

Peak dry resultant temperature

The peak dry resultant temperature is given by:

$$\hat{t}_c = \bar{t}_c + \tilde{t}_c \qquad (5.38)$$

where $\hat{t}_c$ is the peak dry resultant temperature (°C), $\bar{t}_c$ the mean dry resultant temperature (°C) and $\tilde{t}_c$ is the swing in dry resultant temperature (K).

Example 5.2: Determination of overheating risk using the Simple (dynamic) Model

Figure 5.5 shows a single office module. It is situated on an intermediate floor, facing south, in a building located in SE England. It is assumed that the peak dry resultant temperature will occur during a sunny period in August. It is required to determine the peak dry resultant temperature in order to assess the risk of overheating. Constructional and occupancy details are given in Table 5.9. Surface areas, thermal transmittances and admittances are given in Table 5.10.

The calculation is based on the following assumptions:

— the dry resultant temperature in adjoining rooms is equal to that for the module under consideration and hence heat flow occurs only through the outside window–wall

— the window will be open during the day and closed at night

— the thermal transmittance of the window frame is equal to that of the glass

— there are no internal blinds, therefore the solar gain to the air node is zero (i.e. $\bar{S}_a = 0$)

Step 1: solar gain through glazing ($\bar{Q}_{se}$)

From Section 2: *External design data*, Table 2.24, the mean total solar irradiance (i.e. beam plus diffuse) for south facing surfaces in August is 177 W·m^{-2}. There are no internal blinds therefore all solar gains are to the environmental node. The window frame occupies 10% of window area, hence glazed area is $(7 \times 0.9) = 6.3$ m^2. Hence, from equation 5.19 and Table 5.7, the mean solar gain is:

$$\bar{Q}_{se} = 0.61 \times 177 \times 6.3 = 680.21 \text{ W}$$

Step 2: internal gains ($\bar{Q}_c$)

From equation 5.21:

Table 5.9 Example 5.2: constructional and occupancy details

Item	Details
External wall (opaque)	105 mm outer brickwork; 75 mm mineral fibre insulation; 105 mm inner brickwork; 13 mm lightweight plaster
Internal partition wall	100 mm lightweight concrete block; 25 mm air gap; 100 mm lightweight concrete block; 13 mm lightweight plaster each side
Internal floor/ceiling	25 mm wood block flooring; 65 mm cast concrete; 25 mm air gap; 25 mm glass fibre quilt; 16 mm plasterboard ceiling
Window	Double glazed; aluminium frame with thermal break occupying 10% of window area
Lighting	10 W·m^{-2} of floor area; in use 0700–0900 h and 1700–1900 h
Occupancy	Occupied 0900–1700 h by 2 persons; 80 W sensible heat output per person
Electrical equipment	IT equipment generating 10 W·m^{-2}; in use 0900–1700 h

Table 5.10 Example 5.2: surface areas, U-values and Y-values

Surface†	Area (m^2)	U value (W·m^2·K^{-1})	$(A \times U)$ (W·K^{-1})	Y value (W·m^2·K^{-1})	$(A \times Y)$ (W·K^{-1})	Decrement factor	Time lag (h)
External wall (opaque)	5	0.37	1.85	3.7	18.5	0.26	10
Internal partitions	42	0.61	—	2.5	105.0	—	—
Floor	20	0.71	—	3.3	66.0	—	—
Ceiling	20	0.71	—	1.4	28.0	—	—
Windows	7‡	3.3	23.1	3.3	23.1	1	0
	$\Sigma A = 94$		$\Sigma(A\,U) = 25.0$		$\Sigma(A\,Y) = 240.60$		

† Including internal partitions if present; $\Sigma(A\,U)$ is calculated over surfaces through which heat flow occurs
‡ Window frame occupies 10% of window area; hence glazed area (for assessment of solar gain) $= 7 \times 0.9 = 6.3$ m^2

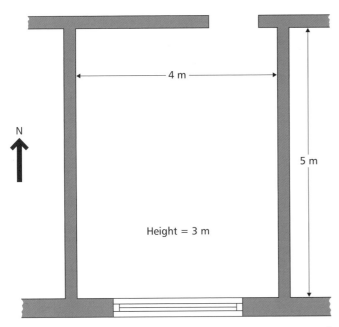

Figure 5.5 Example 5.2: south-facing office module; module volume = 60 m³

$$\bar{Q}_c = \{[10 \times 20 \times (2 + 2)] + (10 \times 20 \times 8)$$
$$+ (2 \times 80 \times 8)\}/24$$
$$= 153.33 \text{ W}$$

Step 3: fabric heat gains ($\bar{Q}_f$)

From Section 2, Table 2.28(*h*), mean sol-air temperature (dark, south-facing surface) is 26.9°C and mean air temperature is 19.8°C. Therefore, using equation 5.22, for both opaque and glazed (including frame) areas of south-facing façade:

$$\bar{Q}_f = (5 \times 0.37 \times 26.9) + (7 \times 3.3 \times 19.8) = 507.15 \text{ W}$$

Step 4: total gains to environmental node ($\bar{Q}_{te}$)

From equation 5.23:

$$\bar{Q}_{te} = 680.21 + 153.33 + 507.15 = 1340.69 \text{ W}$$

From equation 5.7 and Table 5.2, for a room volume of 60 m³:

$$C_v = (3 \times 60)/3 = 60 \text{ W·K}^{-1}$$

Step 5: total gains to air node ($\bar{Q}_{ta}$)

From equation 5.24:

$$\bar{Q}_{ta} = 60 \times 19.8 = 1188.0 \text{ W}$$

Step 6: mean dry resultant temperature ($\bar{t}_c$)

From equation 5.13, the response factor for the room is:

$$f_r = \frac{240.6 + 60}{25.0 + 60} = 3.5$$

Hence from Table 5.6 the structure may be regarded as having a fast thermal response (i.e. thermally 'lightweight').

The room conductance correction factor is calculated using equation 5.26, hence:

$$F_{cu} = \frac{3 [60 + (6 \times 94)]}{25 + (18 \times 94)} = 1.09$$

Therefore, from equation 5.25:

$$\bar{t}_c = \frac{1188.0 + (1.09 \times 1340.69)}{60 + (1.09 \times 25)} = 30.37 \text{ K}$$

Step 7: swing in solar gain ($\tilde{Q}_{se}$)

For a thermally lightweight structure, Table 5.7 gives the cyclic solar gain factor ($\tilde{S}_{el}$) as 0.56. Section 2, Table 2.24 indicates a mean total solar irradiance of 177 W·m⁻² (see step 1) and peak solar irradiance (i.e. beam plus diffuse) of 603 W·m⁻², occurring at 1130 h. Therefore, from equation 5.27, the swing in solar gain is:

$$\tilde{Q}_{se} = 0.56 \times 6.3 \times (603 - 177) = 1502.93 \text{ W}$$

Step 8: swing in structural gain ($\tilde{Q}_f$):

The swing in structural gain is obtained from equation 5.30. For a thermally lightweight (i.e. fast response) building the time lag due to the thermal response of the building is zero. Hence the time at which the peak space temperature occurs (i.e. the 'peak hour' for solar radiation) is 1130 h. (Note that, for a building with a slow response, the peak hour would occur one hour later, i.e. 1230 h. The swing in the sol-air temperature ($\tilde{t}_{eo}$) is determined by subtracting the mean sol-air temperature from the sol-air temperature at a time preceding the peak hour by the value of the time lag associated with the decrement factor of the structure. For this example, the peak hour is 1130 h and the time lag for the structure is 10 h; hence the sol-air temperature at 0130 (i.e. 10 h earlier) is required, thus the sol-air temperature for hour-ending 0200 h is used.

Section 2, Table 2.28, gives the mean sol-air temperature (for a dark, south-facing surface) as 26.9 °C and the sol-air temperature at hour-ending 0200 h as 12.4 °C. The outside air temperature, t_{ao}, at hour-ending 1200 h is 23.9 °C. Therefore the swing in structural gain is:

$$\tilde{Q}_f = (0.26 \times 5 \times 0.37) (12.4 - 26.9)$$
$$+ (1 \times 3.3 \times 7) (23.9 - 19.8)$$
$$= 87.74 \text{ W}$$

Step 9: swing in internal gain ($\tilde{Q}_c$)

From equation 5.31:

$$\tilde{Q}_c = [(2 \times 80) + (10 \times 20)] - 153.33 = 206.67 \text{ W}$$

Step 10: swing in ventilation heat gain ($\tilde{Q}_{av}$)

From equation 5.32:

$$\tilde{Q}_{av} = 60 \times (23.9 - 19.8) = 246.0 \text{ W}$$

Step 11: total swing in heat gain to environmental node ($\tilde{Q}_{te}$)

From equation 5.34:

$$\tilde{Q}_{te} = 1502.93 + 87.74 + 206.67 = 1797.34 \text{ W}$$

Step 12: total swing in heat gain to air node ($\tilde{Q}_{ta}$)

From equation 5.35:

$$\tilde{Q}_{ta} = 0 + 246.0 = 246.0 \text{ W}$$

Step 13: mean-to-peak swing in internal dry resultant temperature ($\tilde{t}_{c1130}$)

From equation 5.37:

$$F_{cy} = \frac{3 \, [60 + (6 \times 94)]}{240.6 + (18 \times 94)} = 0.97$$

Therefore, using equation 5.36, the swing in internal dry resultant temperature (at 1130 h) is:

$$\tilde{t}_{c1130} = \frac{246.0 + (0.97 \times 1797.34)}{60 + (0.97 \times 240.6)} = 6.78 \text{ K}$$

Step 14: peak internal dry resultant temperature ($\hat{t}_c$)

From equation 5.38:

$$\hat{t}_c = 30.37 + 6.78 = 37.2 \text{ °C}$$

Clearly this temperature is high for an office space and some form of shading and/or cooling may be required.

5.6.3.5 Air conditioning cooling load calculation

The cooling load is equal to the sum of the mean and alternating components as determined from Appendix 5.A2, equations 5.153 to 5.188, depending on the characteristics of the emitter and the control temperature. This section describes how the calculation is performed for a convective cooling system (i.e. radiant component is zero).

The total sensible cooling load (Q_k) is given by:

$$Q_k = \bar{Q}_a + \tilde{Q}_a + Q_{sg} + Q_v \qquad (5.39)$$

where Q_k is total sensible cooling load to the air node (W), $\bar{Q}_a$ is the mean convective cooling load (W), $\tilde{Q}_a$ is the alternating component of the convective cooling load (W), Q_{sg} is the cooling load due to windows and blinds (W) and Q_v is the cooling load due to infiltration (W).

To calculate the mean ($\bar{Q}_a$) and alternating ($\tilde{Q}_a$) components for convective cooling and control on dry resultant temperature, equations 5.163 and 5.179 apply (see Appendix 5.A2). For convenience, these may be written as follows:

$$\bar{Q}_a = \bar{Q}_{fa} + F_{cu} \, 1.5 \sum \bar{Q}_{rad} + \sum \bar{Q}_{con} - 0.5 \sum \bar{Q}_{rad} \qquad (5.40)$$

$$\tilde{Q}_a = \tilde{Q}_{fa} + F_{cy} \, 1.5 \sum \tilde{Q}_{rad} + \sum \tilde{Q}_{con} - 0.5 \, \tilde{Q}_{rad} \qquad (5.41)$$

where $\bar{Q}_a$ is the mean convective cooling load (W), $\bar{Q}_{fa}$ is mean fabric gain to the air node (W), F_{cu} is the room conduction factor with respect to dry resultant temperature, $\bar{Q}_{rad}$ is the daily mean radiant gain (W), $\bar{Q}_{con}$ is the daily mean convective gain (W), $\tilde{Q}_a$ is the alternating component of the convective cooling load (W), $\tilde{Q}_{fa}$ is alternating component of the fabric gain to the air node (W), F_{cy} is the room admittance factor with respect to dry resultant temperature, $\tilde{Q}_{rad}$ is the alternating component of the radiant gain (W) and $\tilde{Q}_{con}$ is the alternating component of the convective gain (W).

The cooling load due to infiltration (Q_v) is given by:

$$Q_v = C_v \, (t_{ao\theta} - t_c) \qquad (5.42)$$

where Q_v is the cooling load due to infiltration (W), C_v is the ventilation conductance (W·K^{-1}), $t_{ao\theta}$ the outside air temperature at time θ (°C) and t_c is the dry resultant temperature (°C).

For control on air temperature, the above equations may be used by substituting for t_c, F_{cu} and F_{cy}, as follows:

— t_c is replaced by the inside air temperature, t_{ai} (°C)

— F_{cu} is replaced by the room conduction factor with respect to air temperature, F_{au}

— F_{cy} is replaced by the room admittance factor with respect to air temperature, F_{ay}.

Corrections can be applied to deal with fluctuations in the control temperature, see 5.8.4.4. For 'comfort air conditioning', it is recommended that dry resultant temperature be taken as the control temperature. It should be noted that most temperature detectors measure something other than dry resultant. However, it may be assumed that the set point will be adjusted to provide comfortable working conditions equivalent to the design dry resultant temperature.

Note that the procedure presented here assumes that, for intermittent operation, it is unnecessary to correct for gains other than solar gain. This is a simplification required to enable manual calculation. For a more accurate assessment of cooling loads, the correction given in 5.8.4.3 should be applied.

Thus assessment of the sensible cooling load falls into four stages, as follows:

— cooling load due to solar gain through windows and blinds, Q_{sg}

— cooling load due to conduction through fabric (i.e. opaque surfaces), Q_{fa}

— cooling load due to internal gains, Q_{rad} and Q_{con}

— infiltration load, Q_v.

The following sections give the principles and basis of these stages of the calculation, along with a numerical example. The use of psychrometric charts and the interaction of sensible and latent cooling loads which are required to size the plant are dealt with in Guide B3: *Air conditioning systems and equipment*[28].

Cooling loads through windows and blinds (Q_{sg})

To simplify the assessment of solar gain, tables of solar cooling loads (Tables 5.18 to 5.23) have been calculated for various generic glass types, see Table 5.7. The method used to determine the tabulated values of cooling load is given in Appendix 5.A6. The basis of the tables is as follows:

— constant internal temperature held by plant operating 10 hours per day (0730–1730 sun time)

— sunny spell of 4–5 days duration

— climatic data from Section 2: *External design data*.

The data in the tables apply to 'fast response' (i.e. light-weight) buildings, see Table 5.6. The characteristics of such buildings are:

— average surface factor ≈ 0.8

— de-mountable partitioning

— suspended ceilings

— solid floor (with carpet or wood-block finish) or suspended floor.

Correction factors are given for buildings of heavyweight construction (i.e. 'slow response' buildings), the characteristics of which are:

— average surface factor ≈ 0.5

— solid internal walls and partitions

— solid floors and ceilings.

Surface factors for typical constructions are given in Section 3: *Thermal properties of building structures*. It should be noted that the cooling load required to maintain constant air temperature will generally be about 10–15% less than that required to maintain constant dry resultant temperature due to radiation from the surfaces. The data listed should be applied to the problem as follows.

In order to maintain constant dry resultant temperature, for the UK, the cooling load may be read directly from Tables 5.18 to 5.23. (For worldwide locations, values may be obtained from the tables provided on the CD-ROM that accompanies this Guide.) For glasses other than 6 mm clear glass and for buildings of heavyweight construction, the tabulated values must be modified using the factors at the foot of each table. Interpolation is permitted where factors appropriate to the particular design situation are not given.

In order to maintain constant internal air temperature, the procedure follows that for constant dry resultant temperature but the tabulated values must be modified by an additional factor, related to the thermal response of the building. Values are given at the foot of the tables of cooling loads (Tables 5.18 to 5.23).

Cooling load due to conduction (Q_{fa})

If the dry resultant temperature is held constant, the heat gain to the air node is given by the following equation (see Appendix 5.A2, equation 5.161):

$$\bar{Q}_{fa} = F_{cu} \sum (A\,U)(\bar{t}_{eo} - \bar{t}_c) \qquad (5.43)$$

where $\bar{Q}_{fa}$ is the mean fabric gain to the air node (W), F_{cu} is the room conduction factor with respect to dry resultant temperature, see equation 5.26, A is the area of the surface through which heat flow occurs (m²), U is the thermal transmittance of the surface (W·m⁻²·K⁻¹), $\bar{t}_{eo}$ is the mean sol-air temperature (°C) and $\bar{t}_c$ is the mean dry resultant temperature (°C).

The method for calculating sol-air temperatures, along with tabulated values for three UK locations, is given in Section 2: *External design data*.

The cyclic variation about the mean is given by:

$$\tilde{Q}_{fa} = F_{cy} \sum (A\,U)f\,\tilde{t}_{eo(\theta-\phi)} \qquad (5.44)$$

where $\tilde{Q}_{fa}$ is the swing in fabric gain to the air node (W), F_{cy} is the room admittance factor with respect to dry resultant temperature, see equation 5.37, f is the decrement factor and $\tilde{t}_{eo(\theta-\phi)}$ is the swing in sol-air temperature at time $(\theta-\phi)$ where ϕ is the time lag associated with decrement factor (h).

If the air temperature is held constant the factors F_{cu} and F_{cy} are replaced by the dimensionless factors F_{au} and F_{ay}, respectively and the dry resultant temperature (t_c) is replaced by the inside air temperature (t_{ai}).

For standard values of heat transfer coefficients and emissivity (h_c = 3 W·m⁻²·K⁻¹, h_r = 5.7 W·m⁻²·K⁻¹, ε = 0.9), F_{au} and F_{ay} are given by (see Appendix 5.A2, equations 5.165 and 5.182):

$$F_{au} = \frac{4.5 \sum A}{4.5 \sum A + \sum (A\,U)} \qquad (5.45)$$

$$F_{ay} = \frac{4.5 \sum A}{4.5 \sum A + \sum (A\,Y)} \qquad (5.46)$$

where F_{au} is the room conduction factor with respect to the air node and F_{ay} is the room admittance factor with respect to the air node.

Where the building fabric is glass, the above calculation procedure may be used provided that the sol-air temperature, see Section 2: *External design data*, is calculated with the incident radiation set to zero. This is to ensure that only long-wave losses to the surroundings are considered. The decrement factor must be set to unity with time lag ϕ set to 0.

Cooling load due to internal gains (Q_{rad}, Q_{con})

Internal gains will usually comprise both radiant and convective components which must be converted to the equivalent loads at the air and environmental nodes, as follows:

— load at air node = $\sum Q_{con} - 0.5 \sum Q_{rad}$

— load at environmental node = $1.5 \sum Q_{rad}$

There is little information on the relative proportions of the radiant and convective components of internal heat gains

Table 5.11 Relative proportions of radiant and convective components of heat gains for some items of office equipment

Source of heat gains	Proportion of emitted radiation (%)	
	Convective	Radiative
Personal computer and monitor	76	24
Photocopier	86	14
Laser printer	78	22

but Table 5.11 provides some guidance for typical office equipment, adapted from published data by Wilkins et. al.[42] and Hosni et. al.[43]. The proportions for heat gains from people may be taken to be 50% convective and 50% radiant.

To maintain constant dry resultant temperature, the cooling load due to internal gains is the load at the environmental node multiplied by the factors F_{cu} and F_{cy} for the mean and cyclic components, respectively. The load at the air node is added directly to the cooling load. Where cooling to maintain a constant air temperature is required, F_{cu} and F_{cy} are replaced by F_{au} and F_{ay} respectively.

Cooling load due to air infiltration (Q_v)

When the dry resultant temperature is used as the control temperature, the load due to infiltration is given by equation 5.42.

When the air temperature is held constant, the heat gain at the air node due to air infiltration is given by:

$$Q_v = C_v (t_{ao\theta} - t_{ai}) \qquad (5.47)$$

where Q_v is the cooling load due to infiltration (W), C_v is the ventilation conductance (W), see equation 5.7, $t_{ao\theta}$ is the outside air temperature at time θ (°C) and t_{ai} is the inside air temperature (°C).

Cooling load due to outdoor air supply

The outdoor air supply is generally dealt with by a central air handling plant that regulates the temperature and humidity of the air supplied to the space. This air is used to control the temperature and humidity within the space. Hence account must be taken of the latent and sensible loads, see Guide B3: *Air conditioning (systems and equipment)*. These are direct loads at the air node.

Example 5.3: Calculation of air conditioning cooling load using the Simple (dynamic) Model

For this example, the single office module used for Example 5.2, see page 5-19, is situated on the top floor, facing south. The building is located in SE England. Constructional and occupancy details are given in Table 5.12; surface areas and their corresponding thermal transmittances and admittances are given in Table 5.13. It is required to determine the sensible cooling load to be extracted at the air point at 1230 h in September for a convective system controlled on (a) dry resultant temperature and (b) air temperature.

The calculation is based on the following assumptions:

— building has slow response

— external walls are light in colour; roof is dark in colour

— air conditioning operates for 10 hours per day

— air infiltration rate is equivalent to 1 air change per hour

— control temperature for room is 21°C

— set point temperature for adjoining rooms is 21°C.

(a) Control on dry resultant temperature

Step 1: response factor (f_r)

From equation 5.7, ventilation conductance due to infiltration is:

$$C_v = (1 \times 60)/3 = 20 \ \text{W·K}^{-1}$$

Hence, from equation 5.13:

$$f_r = \frac{225.8 + 20}{24.16 + 20} = 5.57$$

Table 5.12 Example 5.3: constructional and occupancy details

Item	Details
External wall (opaque)	105 mm outer brickwork; 75 mm mineral fibre insulation; 105 mm inner brickwork; 13 mm lightweight plaster
Internal partition wall	100 mm lightweight concrete block; 25 mm air gap; 100 mm lightweight concrete block; 13 mm lightweight plaster each side
Internal floor/ceiling	25 mm wood block flooring; 65 mm cast concrete; 25 mm air gap; 25 mm glass fibre quilt; 16 mm plasterboard ceiling
Roof	19 mm asphalt, 13 mm fibreboard, 25 mm air gap, 75 mm glass fibre quilt, 10 mm plasterboard
Window/blind	Double glazed; aluminium frame with thermal break occupying 10% of window area; fitted with external blind
Occupancy	0900–1700 h by 1 person; 80 W sensible heat output (40 W convective, 40 W radiant)
Internal heat gains	90 W (50 W convective, 40 W radiant) during occupied hours

Table 5.13 Example 5.3: surface areas, thermal transmittances and admittances

Surface†	Area (m²)	U value (W·m⁻²·K⁻¹)	$(A \times U)$ (W·K⁻¹)	Y value (W·m²·K⁻¹)	$(A \times Y)$ (W·K⁻¹)	Decrement factor	Time lag (h)
External wall (opaque)	8	0.37	2.96	3.7	29.6	0.26	10
Internal partition wall	42	0.61	—	2.5	105	—	—
Internal floor	20	—	—	3.2	64	—	—
Roof	20	0.4	8	0.7	14	0.99	1
Windows	4‡	3.3	13.2	3.3	13.2	1	0
$\Sigma A = 94$			$\Sigma (A\,U) = 24.16$		$\Sigma (A\,Y) = 225.8$		

† Including internal partitions if present; $\Sigma (A\,U)$ is calculated over surfaces through which heat flow occurs

‡ Window frame occupies 10% of window area; hence glazed area (for assessment of solar gain) = $4 \times 0.9 = 3.6$ m²

Step 2: solar gain through glazing (Q_{sg})

From Table 5.21, the cooling load for a fast-response building in SE England with south facing glazing with intermittent blinds is 303 W·m⁻² at 1230 h in September. Applying the correction factor appropriate to a 'slow-response' building with double glazing and an external blind, and multiplying by glazed area:

$$Q_{sg} = 0.61 \times 303 \times 3.6 = 665.39 \text{ W}$$

Step 3: mean fabric gain at air node $(\bar{Q}_{fa})$

Factors F_{cu}, and F_{cy} are determined from equations 5.26 and 5.37 respectively:

$$F_{cu} = \frac{3\,[20 + (6 \times 94)]}{24.16 + (18 \times 94)} = 1.021$$

$$F_{cy} = \frac{3\,[20 + (6 \times 94)]}{225.8 + (18 \times 94)} = 0.914$$

The mean sol-air and air temperatures are obtained from Section 2, Table 2.28(i):

— opaque wall (south facing, light): $\bar{t}_{eo} = 19.2\,°C$

— roof (dark): $\bar{t}_{eo} = 19.9\,°C$

— window: $\bar{t}_{ao} = 15.4\,°C$

Equation 5.43 is then used to determine the mean gains for a mean dry resultant temperature of 21°C.

For (opaque) wall:

$$(\bar{Q}_{fa})_{wall} = 1.021 \times 8 \times 0.37 \times (19.2 - 21.0)$$
$$= -5.44 \text{ W}$$

For roof:

$$(\bar{Q}_{fa})_{roof} = 1.021 \times 20 \times 0.4 \times (19.9 - 21.0)$$
$$= -8.98 \text{ W}$$

For window:

$$(\bar{Q}_{fa})_{win} = 1.021 \times 4 \times 3.3 \times (15.4 - 21.0)$$
$$= -75.47 \text{ W}$$

Hence total mean conduction gain at the air point is:

$$\bar{Q}_{fa} = -5.44 - 8.98 - 75.47 = -89.89 \text{ W}$$

Step 4: cyclic conduction gain at air node $(\tilde{Q}_{fa})$

The sol-air and air temperatures are obtained from Section 2, Table 2.28(i) for times of the day corresponding to 1230 h minus the time lag appropriate to the decrement factor for the surface. Subtracting the mean temperatures from these values, see equations 5.29 and 5.33, gives the swing in the sol-air and air temperatures respectively.

For walls (i.e. t_{eo} for hour-ending 0300 h):

$$\tilde{t}_{eo} = 7.7 - 19.2 = -11.5\,°C$$

For roof (i.e. t_{eo} for hour-ending 1200 h):

$$\tilde{t}_{eo} = 38.5 - 19.9 = 18.6\,°C$$

For window (i.e. t_{ao} for hour-ending 1300 h):

$$\tilde{t}_{ao} = 20.4 - 15.4 = 5.0\,°C$$

Equation 5.44 is used to determine the cyclic conduction gains at the air node.

For (opaque) walls:

$$(\tilde{Q}_{fa})_{wall} = 0.914 \times 8 \times 0.37 \times 0.26 \times (-11.5)$$
$$= -8.09 \text{ W}$$

For roof:

$$(\tilde{Q}_{fa})_{roof} = 0.914 \times 20 \times 0.4 \times 0.99 \times 18.6 = 134.64 \text{ W}$$

For window:

$$(\tilde{Q}_{fa})_{win} = 0.914 \times 4 \times 3.3 \times 1 \times 5.0 = 60.32 \text{ W}$$

Hence total cyclic conduction gain at the air node:

$$\tilde{Q}_{fa} = -8.09 + 134.64 + 60.32 = 186.87 \text{ W}$$

Step 5: internal gains (Q_{con}, Q_{rad})

The convective and radiant components of the mean internal gain for 8-hour occupancy are as follows:

$$\bar{Q}_{con} = (50 + 40) \times (8/24) = 30.0 \text{ W}$$

$$\bar{Q}_{rad} = (40 + 40) \times (8/24) = 26.67 \text{ W}$$

Hence convective and radiant components of the swing in internal gain (i.e. value at the calculation hour minus mean value) are as follows:

$$\tilde{Q}_{con} = 90 - 30 = 60 \text{ W}$$

$$\tilde{Q}_{rad} = 80 - 26.67 = 53.33 \text{ W}$$

Step 6: infiltration gain (Q_v)

From equation 5.42:

$$Q_v = 20(20.4 - 21.0) = -12.0 \text{ W}$$

Step 7: total sensible cooling load (Q_k)

The components of the total sensible cooling load are $\bar{Q}_a$, $\tilde{Q}_a$, Q_{sg} and Q_v, see equation 5.39.

$\bar{Q}_a$ is determined using equation 5.40, i.e:

$$\bar{Q}_a = (-89.89) + (1.021 \times 1.5 \times 26.67)$$
$$+ 30 - (0.5 \times 26.67)$$
$$= -32.38 \text{ W}$$

$\tilde{Q}_a$ is determined using equation 5.41, i.e:

$$\tilde{Q}_a = 186.87 + (0.914 \times 1.5 \times 53.33)$$
$$+ 60 - (0.5 \times 53.33)$$
$$= 293.32 \text{ W}$$

Q_{sg} and Q_v are calculated above, see steps 2 and 6, i.e:

$$Q_{sg} = 665.39 \text{ W}$$

$$Q_v = -12.0 \text{ W}$$

Hence, from equation 5.39:

$$Q_k = (-32.38) + 293.32 + 665.39 + (-12.0)$$
$$= 914.3 \text{ W}$$

(b)   Control on air temperature

Step 1: response factor (f_r)

As for (a) above.

Step 2: solar gain through glazing (Q_{sg})

As for (a) above but an additional factor must be included for control at the air node. From Table 5.21, the value appropriate to a 'slow-response' building with double glazing and external blind is 0.85.

Hence:

$$Q_{sg} = 0.85 \times 0.61 \times 303 \times 3.6 = 565.58 \text{ W}$$

Step 3: mean conduction gain at air node ($\bar{Q}_{fa}$)

Factors F_{au} and F_{ay} are determined from equations 5.45 and 5.46 respectively:

$$F_{au} = \frac{4.5 \times 94}{(4.5 \times 94) + 24.16} = 0.95$$

$$F_{ay} = \frac{4.5 \times 94}{(4.5 \times 94) + 225.8} = 0.65$$

The mean sol-air and air temperatures are as (a) above.

Substituting F_{au} for F_{cu} in equation 5.43, the mean gains to the air node may be determined for a mean inside air temperature of 21°C.

For (opaque) walls:

$$(\bar{Q}_{fa})_{wall} = 0.95 \times 8 \times 0.37 \times (19.2 - 21.0) = -5.06 \text{ W}$$

For roof:

$$(\bar{Q}_{fa})_{roof} = 0.95 \times 20 \times 0.4 \times (19.9 - 21.0) = -8.36 \text{ W}$$

For window:

$$(\bar{Q}_{fa})_{win} = 0.95 \times 4 \times 3.3 \times (15.4 - 21.0) = -70.22 \text{ W}$$

Hence total mean conduction gain at the air node is:

$$\bar{Q}_{fa} = -5.06 - 8.36 - 70.22 = -83.64 \text{ W}$$

Step 4: cyclic conduction gain at air node ($\tilde{Q}_{fa}$)

The swings in sol-air and air temperatures are as for (a) above.

Substituting F_{ay} for F_{cy} in equation 5.44, the cyclic gains to the air node may be determined for a mean inside air temperature of 21°C.

For (opaque) walls:

$$(\tilde{Q}_{fa})_{wall} = 0.65 \times 8 \times 0.37 \times 0.26 \times (-11.5) = -5.75 \text{ W}$$

For roof:

$$(\tilde{Q}_{fa})_{roof} = 0.65 \times 20 \times 0.4 \times 0.99 \times 18.6 = 95.75 \text{ W}$$

For window:

$$(\tilde{Q}_{fa})_{win} = 0.65 \times 4 \times 3.3 \times 1 \times 5.0 = 42.90 \text{ W}$$

Hence total cyclic conduction gain at the air node:

$$\tilde{Q}_{fa} = -5.75 + 95.75 + 42.90 = 132.90 \text{ W}$$

Step 5: internal gains at air and environmental nodes:

As for (a) above, i.e:

$$\bar{Q}_{con} = 30.0 \text{ W}$$

$$\bar{Q}_{rad} = 26.67 \text{ W}$$

$$\tilde{Q}_{con} = 60.0 \text{ W}$$

$$\tilde{Q}_{rad} = 53.33 \text{ W}$$

Step 6: infiltration gain (Q_v) From equation 5.47:

$$Q_v = -12\,\text{W}$$

Step 7: total sensible cooling load (Q_k)

The components of the total sensible cooling load are $\bar{Q}_a$, $\tilde{Q}_a$, Q_{sg} and Q_v, see equation 5.39.

$\bar{Q}_a$ is determined using equation 5.40, i.e:

$$\bar{Q}_a = (-83.64) + (0.95 \times 1.5 \times 26.67) + 30.0$$
$$- (0.5 \times 26.67)$$
$$= -28.97\,\text{W}$$

$\tilde{Q}_a$ is determined using equation 5.41, i.e:

$$\tilde{Q}_a = 132.9 + (0.65 \times 1.5 \times 53.33) + 60.0$$
$$- (0.5 \times 53.33)$$
$$= 218.23\,\text{W}$$

Q_{sg} and Q_v are calculated above, see steps 2 and 6, i.e:

$$Q_{sg} = 565.58\,\text{W}$$

$$Q_v = -12.0\,\text{W}$$

Hence, from equation 5.39:

$$Q_k = (-28.97) + 218.23 + 565.58 + (-12.0)$$
$$= 742.8\,\text{W}$$

5.7 Assessment of energy consumption

5.7.1 General

Energy prediction methods may be either manual or computer based. Any manual method can be developed into a computer program and it may be desirable to do so if the objective is to speed up the search for a satisfactory design solution. Computer methods are essential where it is not cost effective to carry out a manual calculation. The advantage of manual methods is their transparency, which also indicates their limitations. It is important to realise that computer methods also have limitations. It is also necessary to understand that modelling unoccupied test cells is very different to modelling real buildings.

A study of comparisons between predictions and measurements of energy use in occupied buildings[44] has indicated that cooling and energy savings are more difficult to predict than heating consumption and that errors of up to ±20% are possible. This error band includes the effect of input errors, which is an important aspect of computer modelling. (Inappropriate assumptions regarding patterns of use are input errors.) The error band was approximately halved when input errors were corrected.

When selecting a calculation method, the requirements of BS 8207[45] for energy prediction procedures should be considered. These are as follows:

— required environmental conditions and periods of use

— climatic conditions

— thermal transmittance of each part of the enclosure of the building

— thermal response of the main constructional elements of the building

— air change rate

— effects of glazing on lighting

— effects of incidental gains (e.g. occupants, lighting, solar gain)

— effects of shading

— effects of controls on the main energy-using services

— efficiency of the equipment.

The procedure should also permit the calculation of the interaction of these and any other relevant factors.

BS 8207[45] imposes considerable demands on the calculation method. In particular, though not explicitly excluded, manual methods are unlikely to be able to meet all of the stated requirements. The engineer will need to apply experience when assessing the suitability of a particular method.

5.7.2 Manual methods

With the exception of those based on experience, all energy assessment methods involve averaging of the building and climatic parameters that are assumed to affect energy consumption. Manual methods average over periods from one day to one year whereas computer based methods usually average on an hourly basis (though much shorter times are possible). An alternative to calculating over a specific period is to sort the climatic data into representative groups or 'bins' and analyse the performance of the building and system for each bin[46]. At some stage the number of bins become too large to allow manual analysis and a computer program is required.

CIBSE Building Energy Code 1[47] is an example of a manual method for the prediction of space heating demands. While not intended for predicting the energy consumption of buildings in use, the Code enables comparative assessments to be made at an early stage of the design.

When applying manual methods, it is essential to be aware of the effects of assumptions contained within the method. A simple example of where errors may occur is when the space heating energy is determined from mean external and internal temperatures over the heating season, without setting a limit on the usefulness of internal gains. For well-insulated buildings, this can lead to an apparent space heating energy requirement of zero, which is unlikely to be the case in reality.

5.7.3 Computer based methods

The advantage of computer based techniques is that they remove the need for long term averaging and can therefore take account of most system effects. However, a significant disadvantage is that assumptions made in the calculation procedure are often hidden from the user. This is particularly important in cases where the computer is being used to implement what is basically a manual method.

Many computer methods use detailed thermal models that, in most cases, will meet the requirements of the Basic (dynamic) Model. Proper use of these methods requires the preparation of a significant quantity of input data. Furthermore, the accuracy of the predictions depends on the quality of the input data, particularly with regard to the specification of occupancy patterns and details of operating and control schedules for the plant. The correct use of computer based methods is considered in detail in CIBSE Applications Manual AM11[31].

5.8 Application of calculation methods

5.8.1 General

This section describes the general application of the calculation methods. Examples of the manual methods are given in 5.5.3 (heat loss), 5.6.3.4 (summertime overheating) and 5.6.3.5 (cooling load).

Guidance on the application of software based methods is given in CIBSE Application Manual AM11[31].

Where it is the intention to size equipment it is first necessary to select the design conditions. In the case of heating, these will usually be the external air dry bulb temperature and the internal dry resultant temperature. The system may also be required to be able to raise the internal temperature from some minimum temperature to the design condition within a specified time.

Cooling systems design will require the specification of design values for the following:

— external dry bulb temperature

— external wet bulb temperature (possibly)

— solar irradiance

— internal dry resultant temperature

— internal relative humidity (possibly)

— internal heat gains.

The selection of appropriate internal design conditions is considered in Section 1: *Environmental criteria for design*. The selection of external design conditions is considered briefly in 5.4.5 and in greater detail in Section 2: *External design data*.

5.8.1.1 Building/room dimensions

The theory presented herein assumes one-dimensional heat flow. In reality two- and three-dimensional flow occurs. It is common practice to account for the deviation from one-dimensional heat flow through walls by measuring surface dimensions between the mid-points of the walls. However, dimensions obtained in this way produce an incorrect value for room volume. Furthermore, they are not appropriate where the surface effects of long-wave radiant and convective heat flows and solar absorption need to be considered. Therefore it is recommended that measurements should be taken between internal wall surfaces. Deviation from one-dimensional heat flow may be taken into account by modifying the thermal conductivity value for the wall.

Consistency of surface dimensions is of particular importance when using software packages.

5.8.1.2 Safety margins

Calculation of heating and cooling capacities in this Guide do not incorporate safety margins except where specifically stated (e.g. section 5.8.3.3, equation 5.50) and it is incumbent upon the designer to assess the plant margin required.

5.8.2 Design conditions

Guidance on the selection of internal design conditions is given in Section 1: *Environmental design criteria*.

The choice of the external design conditions will depend on the application. When sizing heating systems it is normally sufficient to consider steady-state conditions with an allowance for intermittent operation. However, for the purposes of summertime temperature and cooling load calculations, it is essential to take account of the building dynamics and hence non-steady climatic conditions. Climatic data are given in Section 2: *External design data*. These data are intended for use with the Simple (dynamic) Model and are not appropriate for applications where long-term storage effects are to be investigated. In such cases it will be necessary to use the Basic or Reference Model together with hourly sequences of measured data.

Comfort depends upon many factors but it is practicable to design to satisfy only a single parameter, dry resultant temperature. It is the responsibility of the engineer to ensure that the system installed does not introduce discomfort by, for example, high air velocities, asymmetric radiation fields, excessive air–surface temperature differences and low or high relative humidity. While the Reference (steady-state) Model will yield the most accurate estimate of surface temperatures, both the Simple and Basic (steady-state) Models should be adequate for judging if there is a potential problem with surface temperatures. An assessment of unacceptable velocities can be made using computational fluid dynamics (CFD). However simple empirical methods[48,49] may be used to identify problem areas.

5.8.3 Heating system design

This section considers the calculation of the overall heating capacity for a building or zone on the assumption that heat will be supplied from a central plant. It is however recognised that there will be circumstances when local heat sources are more appropriate; in such cases each zone must be considered separately. The selection of heating plant is considered in Guide B1[50].

The following calculation sequence is recommended:

— determine room heat emitter sizes (section 5.8.3.1)

— apply corrections for local effects (section 5.8.3.2)

— apply corrections for intermittent operation (section 5.8.3.3)

— assess heat losses from the distribution system, where appropriate (section 5.8.3.4)

— assess diversity factor for central plant, where appropriate (section 5.8.3.5)

— select central plant, see Guide B1[50].

There will be circumstances in which a different approach will be required and it is often necessary for the designer to devise a suitable strategy.

Guidance is also provided for the following applications:

— storage systems (section 5.8.3.6)

— highly radiant systems (section 5.8.3.7)

— selective systems (section 5.8.3.8).

5.8.3.1 Sizing room emitters

It is usual to exclude from the calculation heat gains from sources other than the emitter and its associated distribution system because, in most cases, plant will be operated at times when the building is unoccupied. However, where it is certain that heating will be operating continuously (over 24 hours) and heat sources such as electric lighting and occupants will be available at all times, the steady-state heat requirement can be reduced by deducting the continuous loads from the calculated heat loss. In such cases, it must be made clear to the client that if the internal gains be removed or reduced, or the plant operated intermittently, then the internal design temperature will not be achieved.

The type of heating system can have a significant effect on the calculated design load therefore it is essential to use appropriate values for the heat transfer correction factors F_{1cu} and F_{2cu} when calculating the steady-state heat requirements. An example of this calculation is given in section 5.5.3.

5.8.3.2 Local effects

The size of the emitter will be affected by its position within the space and the characteristics of the space. Three important effects are:

— back losses from radiators

— stratification

— presence of furniture

— direct radiation incident on occupants.

There will also be cases where the airflow pattern generated by the emitter, or due to features of the space, will be important. For example, a radiator placed at the back of a heated space, away from the window, will induce air movement whereby cool air close to the window will fall and be drawn across the room at floor level to replace warm air rising from the radiator. The temperature gradient produced and the increased air movement at floor level may exacerbate feelings of discomfort experienced by the occupants. The position of warm air inlets is also important, a high-level inlet causing a larger temperature gradient than that produced by a low-level inlet.

A detailed assessment of these effects requires the combination of the Reference (dynamic) Model and computational fluid dynamics (CFD).

Back losses

For the theoretical models, it is assumed that emitters and sources of internal gains are free standing within a space and therefore their total energy output enters the space. For energy sources embedded in or fixed to the surfaces surrounding a space, it is necessary to introduce a correction for the additional heat losses which occur due to part of the surface being exposed to the temperature of the emitter rather than the internal environmental temperature in the room. This is referred to as the back loss.

For wall mounted radiators, the back loss is given by:

$$Q_{bl} = A_h U (t_h - t_{ei}) \qquad (5.48)$$

where Q_{bl} is the back loss (W), A_h is the projected area of the emitter (m²), U is the thermal transmittance of the exposed wall to which the emitter is fixed (W·m⁻²·K⁻¹), t_h is the surface temperature of the heat emitter (°C) and t_{ei} is the environmental temperature in the space (°C).

Other sources of back loss can be corrected for in a similar way.

Stratification

For heat loss calculations a uniform temperature is assumed throughout the height of the heated space. Some heating systems cause vertical temperature gradients across the space, which can lead to increased heat losses, particularly through the roof, see Figure 5.6.

Temperature gradients also depend on the height of the space. An accurate assessment of the effect on the heat loss due to space height requires calculation of the airflow pattern within the space, for which computational fluid dynamics may be required. However, some allowance can be made for the increase in fabric losses using Table 5.14. The table provides percentage increases in fabric loss for various systems and for heated spaces of various heights. This percentage increase applies to the fabric loss only, not to the total heat loss. The increase in air losses should be based directly on the estimated difference in temperature between the bulk air in the space (as given by the heat loss calculation, see 5.5.3, equation 5.11) and that at the point where the air leaves the space, multiplied by the ventilation conductance, C_v.

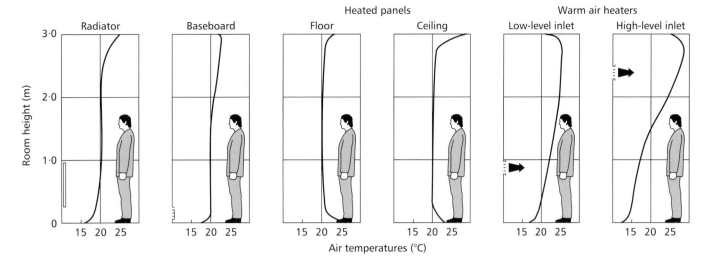

Figure 5.6 Vertical air temperature gradients[51]

Table 5.14 Allowances for height of heated space

Type of heating system	Percentage increase (%) in fabric loss for heated space of stated height (m)		
	5 m	5–10 m	>10 m
Mainly radiant:			
— warm floor	0	0	0
— warm ceiling	0	0–5	†
— medium and high temperature downward radiation from high level	0	0	0–5
Mainly convective:			
— natural warm air convection	0	0–5	†
— forced warm air; cross flow at low level	0–5	5–15	15–30
— forced warm air; downward from high level	0–5	5–10	15–20
— medium and high temperature cross radiation from intermediate level	0	0–5	5–10

† System not appropriate to this application

Note: most conventional 'radiators' may be regarded as mainly convective

Furnishings

If emitters are located behind furnishings much of the space will be denied radiant heat from the emitter. While the heat absorbed by the furnishings will eventually enter the space, often it will not be available during pre-heating, prior to occupancy. In such cases the emitter should be sized as though the output were 100% convective. When selecting an emitter for such situations it will be necessary to ignore any radiant component of the output. For example, to meet a space heating demand of 1400 W using an emitter having an output which is nominally 70% convective and 30% radiant, if the emitter is positioned such that none of the radiant component will enter the space directly, its installed capacity should be increased to 2000 W (i.e. 1400 / 0.7).

Direct radiation

The effect of radiation exchange (hot or cold) on occupants is not included in the calculation method. This is because it is necessary to know both the temperature of the emitter and the view factor between the occupant and the emitter. Fanger[20] gives a method by which the effect may be assessed, see Section 1: *Environmental criteria for design*. The effect may be taken into account by adjusting the design temperature.

5.8.3.3 Intermittent operation

Intermittent heating is where the plant is switched off at the end of a period of building occupancy and turned on again at maximum output prior to the next period of occupancy in order to return the building to design conditions. Intermittent heating is the most common form of operation for heating plant in the UK. There are two main types of intermittent operation. 'Normal' intermittent operation is where the output of the heating system is reduced when the building is unoccupied or when the occupants are sleeping. 'Highly' intermittent operation is where a building is occupied for short periods only and therefore must be brought up to temperature rapidly, just prior to use. With highly insulated buildings, there may be a case to minimise overall costs by using smaller plant operating continuously. This will require an estimate of the likely savings in capital costs and the increase in running costs over the life of the heating plant. Dynamic modelling will usually to required to perform such an estimate.

Normal intermittent operation

The degree to which the plant output can be reduced will depend upon:

— building type and purpose

— level of insulation

— external temperature.

The building type will influence the level to which temperatures can be allowed to fall, e.g. the minimum temperature for bedrooms will differ from that for the storage of works of art.

The possibility of damage to the fabric due to condensation and structural movement caused by fluctuating temperatures must also be considered. In situations where the minimum temperature is critical, it must be determined by discussion with the client. Otherwise a temperature of 10°C is suggested as a general minimum.

If it is required to raise the internal temperature from the overnight minimum temperature to the required level for occupancy within a reasonable period, it will be necessary to install plant with a capacity greater than the steady-state design capacity. The excess capacity will depend upon:

— required heat up time

— dynamic characteristics of the boiler plant and distribution network

— thermal storage characteristics of the building.

Modern building control systems usually include software that determines the preheat time automatically from an assessment of previous building performance[52] (i.e. 'adaptive optimum start') and therefore an accurate determination of the design preheat time is not essential.

However, it is essential that a rational approach be used to determine the necessary excess capacity to ensure that the plant selected is economic and energy efficient. Plants with rapid response are most suitable for intermittent use in order to minimise the preheat time and energy losses due to the storage of thermal energy within the heating system. It has also been demonstrated that, provided means are taken properly to control multiple boiler installations, the energy consumption for an intermittently operated system is not very sensitive to excess capacity[53]. Thus an accurate determination of excess capacity is not warranted and equation 5.49, based on admittance theory, is adequate for most applications.

Exceptions are:

— highly intermittent operation (i.e. short occupation periods such as assembly halls, churches etc.)

— systems with a long time constant (e.g. underfloor heating).

Therefore, with the above exceptions, the intermittent or peak heating load can be calculated as follows:

$$Q_i = F_3 Q_t \qquad (5.49)$$

where Q_i is the plant size for intermittent operation (W), F_3 is a correction factor for intermittent heating and Q_t the total heat loss (W).

F_3 is based on the thermal response factor and the total hours of plant operation, including preheat but neglecting the time for the system to reach its operating conditions, and is given by the following equation, see Appendix 5.A5:

$$F_3 = \frac{24 f_r}{H f_r + (24 - H)} \qquad (5.50)$$

where H is the hours of plant operation (including preheat) (h) and f_r the thermal response factor (see equation 5.13).

If the calculated value of F_3 is less than 1.2, it is suggested that its value be taken as 1.2 to ensure that the customary safety margin of 20% is maintained. However, designers may choose to use other values. The value chosen may be justified by building simulation using the thermal Reference or Basic (dynamic) Models.

Large values for F_3 indicate that consideration should be given to extending the operating period or operating continuously, rather than greatly oversizing the plant capacity. Example 5.4 illustrates the calculation of plant size for intermittent operation.

Equation 5.50 is based on heating to the internal environmental temperature with an emitter that has the same radiation/convection ratio (i.e. 2:1) as in the definition of the environmental node. It can be expected that the excess capacity will be underestimated for a system that is 100% radiant and overestimated for an all-air system. There is a further safety margin in that no account is taken of a minimum internal temperature (for protection of the fabric) in the derivation of the excess capacity.

For greater accuracy in assessing the excess capacity a dynamic simulation model should be used, which will enable a proper assessment of the system performance to be undertaken. The minimum requirements for such a model are that it must:

— meet the requirements of the thermal Basic (dynamic) Model

— represent the characteristics of the space heat emitter

— be capable of representing time delays associated with the boiler and distribution system (the latter may be particularly important where there are significant transportation delays)

— model the characteristics of an optimum start system.

Sizing of the emitters and the size of the central plant relative to the emitters must be considered. This may not require physically re-sizing the heating system. A degree of effective over-sizing can be achieved during the pre-heat period by:

— operating the central plant to provide an elevated flow temperature

— reduction of the ventilation rate by window closure or control of the mechanical ventilation

— reduction of fabric transmittance by the use of window shutters or curtains

— increased emitter output due to initial low building temperatures.

Example 5.4: Correction of heating plant capacity for intermittent heating

For the small factory considered in Example 5.1, see page 5-19, it is required to determine the effect of intermittent operation of the heating plant. The heating plant is assumed to operate for 8 hours with a preheat time of 3 hours. Surface areas and their corresponding thermal transmittances and admittances are given in Table 5.15.

Step 1: ventilation conductance (C_v)

From Example 5.1, $C_v = 93.75$ W·K^{-1}

Step 2: thermal response factor (f_r)

From equation 5.13:

$$f_r = \frac{1438.1 + 93.75}{345.7 + 93.75} = 3.49$$

Step 3: correction factor for intermittent heating (F_3)

From equation 5.50:

$$F_3 = \frac{24 \times 3.49}{(11 \times 3.49) + (24 - 11)} = 1.63$$

Step 4: plant capacity for intermittent operation (Q_i)

From Example 5.1, the total heat loss for the system types considered were as follows:

— warm air system: $Q_t = 8.72$ kW

— radiant strip: $Q_t = 8.81$ kW

Hence, using equation 5.49, excluding distribution and back losses and ignoring internal heat gains, the calculated plant capacity for intermittent operation is as follows.

For warm air system:

$$Q_i = 1.63 \times 8.72 = 14.21 \text{ kW}$$

For radiant strip:

$$Q_i = 1.63 \times 8.81 = 14.36 \text{ kW}$$

Highly intermittent operation

Where a building is used for very short periods (e.g. a meeting hall), the steady-state heat loss is inappropriate for the purposes of plant sizing and it is necessary to consider the way in which the heat is absorbed by the fabric. In the terms of the Simple (dynamic) Model this is represented by the admittance of the structure, in which case the heat output required from the room appliance is given by:

$$Q_i = [F_{1cy} \Sigma (A \, Y) + C_v F_{2cy}] (t_c - t_{ao}) \qquad (5.51)$$

where Q_i is the plant size for intermittent operation (W), F_{1cy} and F_{2cy} are factors related to the characteristics of the heat source, $\Sigma (A \, Y)$ is the sum of the products of surface areas and the corresponding thermal admittances (W·K^{-1}), C_v is ventilation conductance (W·K^{-1}), t_c is the dry resultant temperature (°C) and t_{ao} is the outside air temperature (°C).

C_v is given by equation 5.7. F_{1cy} and F_{2cy} are given by (see Appendix 5.A2, equations 5.184 and 5.185):

$$F_{1cy} = \frac{3 (C_v + 6 \Sigma A)}{\Sigma (A \, Y) + 18 \Sigma A + 1.5 R [3 C_v - \Sigma (A \, Y)]} \qquad (5.52)$$

$$F_{2cy} = \frac{\Sigma (A \, Y) + 18 \Sigma A}{\Sigma (A \, Y) + 18 \Sigma A + 1.5 R [3 C_v - \Sigma (A \, Y)]} \qquad (5.53)$$

where R is the radiant fraction of the heat source.

Dynamic thermal properties such as thermal admittance are functions of the frequency of the driving force for heat transfer. Therefore, for highly intermittent operation, the numerical value of the thermal admittance (Y) should be based on the actual hours of plant operation rather than the standard (24-hour) cycle. Table 5.16 shows the relationship between the thermal admittance and the hours of plant operation for surfaces with fast and slow thermal responses. The multiplying factors are the ratios of thermal admittance to 'standard' Y-values for an excitation period of 24 hours. The tabulated data are provided for general guidance and interpolation between the values is permitted.

The derivation of thermal admittance given in Section 3, Appendix 3.A8, allows the use of variable cycle times.

Table 5.15 Example 5.4: surfaces areas, thermal transmittances and admittances

Surface*	Area, A (m²)	U value (W·m⁻²·K⁻¹)	(A × U) (W·K⁻¹)	Y value (W·m⁻²·K⁻¹)	(A × Y) (W·K⁻¹)
Floor	112.5	0.45	50.6	5.2	585.0
Roof	112.5	0.3	33.8	0.7	78.8
External walls	171.0	0.5	85.5	3.5	598.5
Glazing	48.0	3.3	158.4	3.3	158.4
Doors	6.0	2.9	17.4	2.9	17.4
	$\Sigma A = 450.0$		$\Sigma (A U) = 345.7$		$\Sigma (A \, Y) = 1438.1$

* Including internal partitions if present; $\Sigma (A U)$ is calculated over surfaces through which heat flow occurs

Table 5.16 Multiplying factors to relate thermal admittance to daily hours of plant operation

Daily hours of plant operation	Multiplying factor for stated nominal thermal response*	
	Slow	Fast
12	1.0	1.0
6	1.1	2.0
4	1.2	2.8
3	1.2	3.5
2	1.2	4.7
1	1.3	6.5

* See Table 5.6

5.8.3.4 Heat loss from the distribution system

Heat losses from the distribution system may be determined from the data for heat loss from pipes contained in Guide C3: *Heat transfer*[54].

5.8.3.5 Diversity factor for central plant

In estimating the required duty of the central plant for a building, it should be noted that the total net infiltration of outdoor air is about half the sum of the rates for the separate rooms. This is because at any one time, infiltration of outdoor air takes place only on the windward part of the building, the flow in the remainder being outwards, see Section 4: *Infiltration and natural ventilation*.

In practice, for intermittent heating, the preheat periods for all the rooms in a building will generally be coincident. In this case, the central plant rating is the sum of the heat demands for the individual rooms, modified to account for the net infiltration. For continuously heated buildings, some diversity can be expected between the room heating loads and Table 5.17 suggests some values. When mechanical ventilation is combined with heating, the heating plant and the ventilation plant may have different hours of use and the peak loads on the respective plants may often occur at different times.

The central plant may also be required to provide hot water for domestic and/or process purposes. These loads may have to be added to the net heating load to determine the necessary plant duty. However, careful design may avoid the occurrence of simultaneous peaks and, for large installations, boiler curves may indicate whether reductions in the boiler rating can be made[55]. In many cases, little or no extra capacity may be needed for hot water supply, the demand being met by diverting capacity from the heating circuits for short periods.

5.8.3.6 Storage systems

It may be financially advantageous to supply heat outside of normal hours and to store it within the fabric of the building or in water based storage systems. Such systems are generally used only when cheap off-peak electrical power is available. However any fuel can be used where cheap tariffs occur at certain times.

Table 5.17 Diversity factors for central plant (continuous heating)

Space or buildings served by plant	Diversity factor
Single space	1.0
Single building or zone, central control	0.9
Single building, individual room control	0.8
Group of buildings, similar type and use	0.8
Group of buildings, dissimilar uses†	0.7

† Applies to group and district heating schemes where there is substantial heat storage in the distribution mains, whether

Two types of storage system are described below. In both cases energy will generally be supplied to the store at night, during the times of cheap fuel tariffs. Under design conditions, the storage and charge must be equal to the 24 hour demand.

The input rating for both systems can be calculated using the following equation, where the mean heat requirement and mean heat losses are expressed in joules:

$$Q = \frac{\left(\begin{array}{c} \text{Mean heat requirement (J)} \\ + \\ \text{Mean heat losses (J)} \end{array}\right)}{3600\, \theta_r} \tag{5.54}$$

where Q is input rating of plant (W) and θ_r is the recharge time for the system (h).

The losses may be determined from the mean storage temperature or the mean space temperature and the level of insulation. Where the storage vessel is also the space heat emitter the losses may be considered as useful heat. Such systems differ widely and the designer must assess each individually. Often this will require the use of a dynamic model.

Uncontrolled storage systems (continuous heating)

In these cases, heat is dissipated continuously throughout 24 hours (e.g. uncontrolled floor or block heating) and no intermittent heating factors should be applied.

The daily storage and charge (in joules) is given by the mean heat required (in watts) multiplied by (24 × 3600). The mean heat requirement is equal to the steady-state heat loss calculated at the estimated mean internal temperature, which will usually be the design internal temperature.

With these systems the highest room temperature is likely to be at the end of the recharging period and the lowest will occur just prior to recharging, at the end of the usage period. This temperature swing will depend on the thermal properties of the building and those of the appliance but should be limited to 3 K or less for acceptability. The individual room units should be sized according to the method described for continuous heating.

With floor heating systems the floor surface temperature should conform to the comfort criteria set down in Section 1: *Environmental criteria for design*.

Controlled storage systems

In cases where heat dissipation takes place only during the hours of use (e.g. controlled block heating or electrically heated water with thermal storage), the design rate of emission should be calculated as for conventional intermittent systems with the total storage capacity based on the mean internal temperature. This may be calculated as follows[56]:

$$\bar{t}_i = \frac{(Hf_r)(t_r - \bar{t}_o)}{Hf_r + (24 - H)} + \bar{t}_o \qquad (5.55)$$

where $\bar{t}_i$ is the 24-hour mean daily internal temperature (°C), H is the daily heating period including pre-heating (h), f_r is the thermal response factor (see equation 5.13), t_r is the internal design temperature (°C) and $\bar{t}_o$ is the 24-hour mean daily outside temperature (°C).

The 24-hour mean daily outside temperature ($\bar{t}_o$) is assumed to equal the design outside temperature.

A review of the environmental benefits of thermal storage systems is given in CIBSE Research Report RR06: *Environmental benefits of thermal storage*[57].

5.8.3.7 Radiant heating systems

High temperature radiant systems are generally chosen for local heating or for situations where very intermittent heating is required. In either case the standard heat loss calculations are not appropriate for evaluating the total output for the purposes of equipment selection. For these systems it is essential to determine the distribution of radiant energy within the space. To do this it is necessary to obtain a radiant polar diagram for the emitter.

Medium and low temperature radiant systems can be sized using the usual heat loss calculation methods. For these cases, the total panel area is determined by dividing the net heat requirement by the emission per unit area of panel.

The distribution of hot surfaces needs to be considered to ensure a reasonable degree of uniformity over the working plane[58,59]. Generally, low and medium temperature panels should be placed near the exposed walls of the space. A single panel should not normally be placed in the centre of the ceiling as this could produce a temperature peak in the middle of the working zone. The panel area and temperature should be checked in relation to the mounting height in order to ensure comfort.

Limiting factors for the design of these systems are given in Section 1: *Environmental criteria for design* and Fanger[20] gives a method by which system performance can be assessed.

5.8.3.8 Selective systems

Systems of this type are used in situations where all the spaces in the building do not require heating at the same time. This is often the case in dwellings where demands for heat in the living spaces and the bedrooms do not coincide. The individual appliances must be sized as described above

according to heat losses, gains and intermittency of operation. The central plant should be capable of meeting the peak simultaneous output of the units. The units can usually be operated intermittently.

5.8.4 Cooling system design

This section describes the calculation sequence to assess if a building needs cooling and, if so, to determine the room cooling load and the maximum system demand. As with heating systems there will be situations for which central plant is not appropriate and local cooling devices will be used.

The recommended calculation sequence is as follows:

— assess risk of overheating (section 5.8.4.1)

— determine room cooling load (section 5.8.4.2)

— apply corrections for intermittent plant operation, if appropriate (section 5.8.4.3)

— apply corrections for fluctuations in control temperature, if appropriate (section 5.8.4.4)

— assess the diversity factor for the central plant, if appropriate (section 5.8.4.5)

— assess the heat gains/losses to the distribution system, if appropriate (section 5.8.4.6).

The calculations described herein are for a fully convective cooling system. However, this is not always the case and guidance is given in 5.8.5 on passive cold (i.e. chilled) surfaces and multi-mode systems such as mechanical ventilation and chilled beams. The application of ice storage systems is covered in CIBSE Technical Memoranda TM18: *Ice storage*[60].

5.8.4.1 Assessment of overheating risk

This assessment should be carried out to determine if cooling is required. The method of assessment of overheating risk will differ according to the model chosen. In the case of the Basic and Simple (dynamic) Models, a period of hot days should be analysed with the intention of identifying a number of hours where each critical space is above a specified limit temperature. That limit temperature may be a single value or a function of the outside air temperature. The selection of suitable weather data and the overheating criteria must be agreed between the client and the designer; some guidance for overheating is given in Section 1: *Environmental criteria for design*. Climatic data for the UK are given in CIBSE Guide: *Weather and solar data*[25].

The prediction of hours of overheating, i.e. the hours for which a specified temperature will be exceeded, is very sensitive to the method of assessment[14,31].

Equations for the calculation of overheating risk and a numerical example using the Simple (dynamic) Model are given in 5.6.3.4.

If it is found that overheating is likely to occur an assessment should be made to establish whether it can be reduced to an acceptable level by changes to the building fabric, increasing the natural ventilation, or by other means.

The assessment of overheating risk for naturally ventilated buildings requires knowledge of the likely air change rates. Modern buildings are usually well sealed and infiltration rates may be as low as 0.25 air changes per hour. This is much lower than that required for acceptable air quality. It is expected that, in practice, a minimum ventilation rate of about 1 air change per hour will be achieved either by trickle ventilators or by windows 'cracked' open. Although ventilation rates greater than 10 air changes per hour can be achieved by cross ventilation etc., they can cause discomfort. Furthermore, the effectiveness of ventilation as a cooling medium is reduced as the air change rate increases.

5.8.4.2 Room cooling load calculation

Once it has been established that air conditioning is necessary then the maximum room cooling loads need to be determined in order to obtain the plant size. Equations for calculating the cooling load and a numerical example using the Simple (dynamic) Model are given in section 5.6.3.5.

Note that the cooling loads calculated using the methods described in section 5.6.3.5 do not include latent cooling which depends on the type of system selected. System effects are considered in Guide B3: *Ventilation and air conditioning (systems, equipment and control)*[28].

5.8.4.3 Corrections for intermittent plant operation

Generally the air conditioning plant is operated intermittently and the plant size can, in principle, be calculated directly[40]. However, if the infiltration ventilation rate is constant or small, then the increase in load ΔQ_k in going from continuous to intermittent operation can be calculated more simply[40] as follows:

$$\Delta Q_k = \frac{24 \left[F_{cy} \Sigma (A\,Y) - F_{cu} \Sigma (A\,U) \right] \bar{Q}_b}{(24 - n)\, F_{cu} \Sigma (A\,U) + n\, F_{cy} \Sigma (A\,Y) + 24\, c\, \rho\, v} \quad (5.56)$$

where ΔQ_k is the increase in cooling load (W), F_{cy} is the room admittance factor with respect to dry resultant temperature, F_{cu} is the room conduction factor with respect to dry resultant temperature, $\bar{Q}_b$ is the 24 hour mean of the continuous load which would otherwise have occurred during the off period (W), n is the hours of plant operation (h), c is the specific heat capacity of air (J·kg^{-1}·K^{-1}), ρ is the density of air (kg·m^{-3}), v is the natural ventilation rate (m^3·s^{-1}), $\Sigma (A\,U)$ is the sum of the products of surface area and corresponding thermal transmittance over surfaces through which heat flow occurs (W·K^{-1}) and $\Sigma (A\,Y)$ is the sum of the products of surface areas and their corresponding thermal admittances (W·K^{-1}).

This correction must be added to cooling loads calculated on the basis of continuous plant operation. Alternatively, when the load in the 'off' period is small:

$$\Delta Q_k = \bar{Q}_b \quad (5.57)$$

The cooling loads due to solar gain given in Tables 5.18 to 5.23 allow for intermittent operation. In temperate climates the effect of ignoring intermittency for fabric, internal and infiltration loads is not usually significant as their overnight values constitute only a small fraction of the peak load.

5.8.4.4 Corrections for fluctuations in control temperature

If the controlled temperature in the space is allowed to rise at the time of peak load then the room sensible load can be reduced.

For a rise in the dry resultant temperature (Δt_c), the reduction in cooling load is approximately given by the following equation (see Appendix 5.A2, equation 5.189):

$$\Delta Q_k = \left[c\,\rho\,v_m + F_{cy} \Sigma (A\,Y) \right] \Delta t_c \quad (5.58)$$

where ΔQ_k is the change in plant output (W), c is the specific heat capacity of air (J·kg^{-1}·K^{-1}), ρ is the density of air (kg·m^3), v_m is the total ventilation (i.e. mechanical plus infiltration) rate (m^3·s^{-1}), F_{cy} is the room admittance factor with respect to dry resultant temperature, $\Sigma (A\,Y)$ is the sum of the products of surface areas and their corresponding thermal admittances (W·K^{-1}) and Δt_c is the rise in dry resultant temperature (K). F_{cy} is given by equation 5.37.

For a rise in the internal air temperature (Δt_{ai}), the reduction in cooling load is approximately given by the following (see Appendix 5.A2, equation 5.190):

$$\Delta Q_k = \left[c\,\rho\,v_m + F_{ay} \Sigma (A\,Y) \right] \Delta t_{ai} \quad (5.59)$$

where F_{ay} is the room admittance factor with respect to the air node, $\Sigma (A\,Y)$ is the sum of the products of surface areas and their corresponding thermal admittances (W·K^{-1}) and Δt_{ai} is the rise in internal air temperature (K). F_{ay} is given by equation 5.46.

5.8.4.5 Diversity factor for central plant

In most cases the peak load for each space (i.e. room) will depend on the time of day. An east facing space will probably have a maximum heat gain at 1000 hours while that for a west facing space may occur at 1700 hours. The maximum space cooling demand is therefore determined by summing the individual space demands for each hour of the day and selecting the peak hourly demand.

How this demand is satisfied will depend on the type of system, see Guide B3: *Ventilation and air conditioning (systems, equipment and control)*[28]. It is also important to recognise that the maximum load on the central plant may arise from the fresh air load rather than the peak coincident space cooling loads.

The sizing of plant for thermal storage systems using ice is covered in CIBSE Technical Memoranda TM18: *Ice storage*[60] and a review of the environmental benefits of storage systems may be found in CIBSE Research Report RR06: *Environmental benefits of thermal storage*[57].

5.8.4.6 Heat gain/loss to the distribution system

Cooling will be distributed from a central plant directly in the form of air to room terminals or indirectly as water or refrigerant to devices such as fan coil units, induction units or chilled ceilings. Heat gains to air and water based systems can be determined by methods described in Guide C3: *Heat transfer*[54]. The effect of heat gains to refrigeration distribution systems should be discussed with the equipment manufacturer.

5.8.5 Special applications

The majority of the design work carried out by building services engineers is associated with 'conventional' spaces, i.e. rectilinear (often approximately cubical) rooms with walls composed of brick, concrete and insulation about 200 mm in thickness and with glazed areas of the order of 20–60% of the facade area. Occupancy is usually at least 8 hours with levels of internal gains appropriate to office spaces (see Section 6: *Internal heat gains*).

However, situations will arise which deviate significantly from the norm such as highly glazed atria and buildings with high thermal mass being operated intermittently. The designer may also be expected to cope with emitters having unusual characteristics. The following sections offer some guidance on calculation techniques appropriate in such cases, i.e:

— atria (section 5.8.5.1)

— intermittent operation of buildings with high thermal mass (section 5.8.5.2)

— surface cooling and heating systems (section 5.8.5.3)

— natural convection cooling systems (section 5.8.5.4).

5.8.5.1 Atria

The distinctive features of atria are their height, large areas of glazing, and the possible requirement for local temperature control. Heat transfer by radiation is particularly important together with the need to take temperature gradients into consideration. Steady-state heat loss calculations should be made using the Reference Model. Dynamic models will generally require the capability to predict the distribution of short-wave radiation within the space together with the direct transmission of radiation from the space, either to outside or to adjacent spaces. Computational fluid dynamics may be helpful in predicting temperature gradients, however it is often sufficient to assume a linear gradient within the space.

5.8.5.2 Spaces with high thermal mass

To predict the long-term effects of thermal mass a detailed thermal model, e.g. Basic (dynamic) Model, will be required. Appendix 5.A8 suggests means to ensure that the model takes proper account of the thermal storage.

5.8.5.3 Surface heating and cooling

These systems usually comprise either (*a*) a heated/cooled plate or matrix in direct contact with the space, e.g. a chilled ceiling, or (*b*) ducts or pipes embodied within the structure. In both cases the steady-state performance will require the use of the Reference or Basic Model, adapted to take account of the constant temperature surfaces; the

algorithms contained in Appendix 5.A1 demonstrate how this may be achieved. The Simple (dynamic) Model can be used to give an approximate duty for a chilled ceiling. Manufacturers' data will indicate the proportions of radiant and convective heating. The calculation method given in Appendix 5.A2 may then be used.

The performance of systems using ducts or pipes embodied within the fabric can generally be assessed using the Basic (dynamic) Model. However, provided care is taken to assess the effect of the fabric on surface temperatures, peak cooling duty may be estimated using the Simple (dynamic) Model.

In all cases it is essential to take account of losses from the heating or cooling medium to the surrounding structure.

The fresh air supply may be by means of a conventional ceiling or wall mounted diffuser, or a floor level displacement or swirl diffuser. When determining the peak cooling load it may be assumed that, for both cases, the air is well mixed within the space.

5.8.5.4 Natural convective cooling systems ('chilled beams')

These systems comprise a finned tube element mounted at ceiling level. They cause a downward flowing plume of cooled air. It is usual to supply fresh air at floor level using a displacement terminal. For the purposes of calculating peak loads, such systems may be regarded as 100% convective and the air in the space assumed to be fully mixed. Therefore the Simple (dynamic) Model may be applied.

5.8.6 Airflow models

5.8.6.1 General

The performance of heating and cooling units is not determined solely by capacity load calculations. Some types of unit, e.g. downward projecting warm air diffusers and displacement airflow terminals, also depend on the airflow patterns within the space. The way in which the air moves through a building may also influence summertime overheating. For example, where an atrium is used to induce air flow through the surrounding offices, it is possible for warm air from the atrium to flow into the upper offices[61]. The prediction of airflow patterns cannot therefore always be separated from the calculation of the thermal performance of buildings.

There are four main approaches for quantifying airflow patterns:

— design guides

— zonal air flow models

— field airflow models using computational fluid dynamics (CFD)

— analogue models.

Examples of the first of these approaches are CIBSE Applications Manual AM10: *Natural ventilation in non-domestic buildings*[23] and BSRIA Application Guide:

Designing variable volume systems for room air movement[49]. Zonal and field airflow models are described briefly in the following sections. Detailed descriptions of air flow models are given by Awbi[62]. Excluding wind tunnels, the most common analogue model uses salt solutions and pure water to provide an inverted representation of the difference in density between the air inside and outside a building[63], thereby simulating buoyancy driven flow. The method requires significant laboratory facilities and expert application.

5.8.6.2   Zonal airflow models

The bulk movement of air within a building can be predicted using computer programs. Originally, such programs were popular for predicting infiltration rates but they are now often combined with dynamic thermal models to predict the performance of buildings where ventilation strategies are considered to be important. The analysis usually considers the movement of air as driven by forces due to both buoyancy and wind. Resistance to airflow is treated in a similar way to that for flow through an orifice.

A significant difficulty in applying these models is obtaining values for the pressure coefficients required to determine the wind pressures on the building. These can be obtained from wind tunnels tests, CFD simulations or tables[64]. However, the accuracy of the coefficients obtained by these methods should be treated with caution. The validity of computational methods is an area of ongoing research.

Examples of the application of zonal air flow models are given in CIBSE Applications Manual AM10: *Natural ventilation in non-domestic buildings*[23].

5.8.6.3   Computational fluid dynamics (CFD)

The objective of CFD is to provide a numerical solution to the equations governing the flow of fluids. The nature of fluid flow requires calculations to be made at a very large number of positions within the space under consideration. The result of the calculations is a detailed picture (both quantitative and qualitative) of the air movement and temperatures within the space.

At present, CFD is expensive due to need to use very fast computers with large amounts of memory to obtain results within realistic timescales. Expert knowledge is required to make the many assumptions necessary in describing the problem, such as the choice of computational grid, boundary conditions and turbulence model, and to ensure that the results obtained are interpreted correctly. There are also difficulties associated in obtaining a converged solution (the solution involves iteration). Mathematical convergence can be a problem, particularly with buoyancy driven airflow.

Notwithstanding the difficulties and expense, CFD is a useful tool to obtain insight to areas where information is otherwise unavailable. It is not, however, an everyday design tool nor is it necessary for most conventional spaces.

5.9   Solar cooling load tables

Tables 5.18 to 5.23 provide solar cooling loads for three UK regions: SE England (Bracknell, 51°33′N), NW England (Manchester/Aughton: 53°33′N) and NE Scotland (lowlands) (Edinburgh/ Mylnefield, 56°00′N). These tables are based on measured irradiances that were not exceeded on more than $2^1/_2$% of occasions during the period 1976–1995. Similar tables for latitudes from 0–60°N and 0–60°S, based on theoretical predictions of irradiance, are given on the computer disk which accompanies this publication. The calculation method used to produce the tabulated values is described in Appendix 5.A6. The tables may be used in order to assess the plant loads at an early stage in the design.

Tables 5.18 to 5.20 are for buildings without shading and Tables 5.21 to 5.23 for buildings with intermittent shading. The tabulated values apply to 'lightweight' buildings (i.e. those with a fast response to solar radiation) with single clear glass and assume that control of the cooling system will be based on the dry resultant temperature. Multiplying factors are given at the foot of each table to adjust the tabulated cooling loads for application to buildings having a slow response to solar radiation and for other types of glazing. The glazing types should be regarded as generic, see Appendix 5.A4. The term 'blind' refers to a generic shading device having a transmission coefficient of 0.2 and a reflectivity of 0.4. An additional factor is given to enable the values to be adjusted for situations where the cooling system will be controlled at the air node.

Table 5.18 Solar cooling loads for fast-response building with single clear glazing: **SE England, unshaded**

Date	Orient-ation	Solar cooling load at stated sun time (W·m⁻²)											Orient-ation
		0730	0830	0930	1030	1130	1230	1330	1430	1530	1630	1730	
Jan 29	N	6	12	20	29	36	40	40	37	29	19	11	N
	NE	9	29	26	32	37	41	41	38	29	20	12	NE
	E	28	103	201	229	171	77	61	54	45	35	28	E
	SE	61	148	292	408	452	406	316	193	96	69	60	SE
	S	77	128	233	366	476	514	507	422	299	190	111	S
	SW	51	57	70	109	218	327	404	402	328	228	117	SW
	W	20	26	34	43	50	63	86	167	191	157	78	W
	NW	7	13	20	30	37	41	41	38	33	26	27	NW
	Horiz.	29	43	76	133	182	206	203	168	115	67	40	Horiz.
Feb 26	N	16	24	36	49	57	62	60	55	46	34	22	E
	NE	49	78	60	58	60	65	63	59	49	37	25	NE
	E	100	203	277	281	211	107	90	79	70	57	45	E
	SE	126	236	361	446	472	427	325	203	106	89	75	SE
	S	110	163	269	388	484	533	522	473	389	267	155	S
	SW	74	83	99	127	229	350	434	476	468	380	241	SW
	W	45	53	65	78	86	101	125	230	305	298	209	W
	NW	22	30	42	55	63	68	69	86	62	68	83	NW
	Horiz.	61	93	155	226	282	313	306	274	221	150	86	Horiz.
Mar 29	N	38	50	64	74	83	86	86	81	72	60	47	N
	NE	160	181	135	83	97	98	98	93	84	72	58	NE
	E	252	355	400	361	261	147	133	120	111	99	84	E
	SE	231	353	456	498	483	426	319	196	142	121	105	SE
	S	109	176	283	384	457	505	497	454	377	270	161	S
	SW	104	118	135	162	224	347	443	501	514	467	358	SW
	W	87	101	115	126	135	150	175	293	389	420	370	W
	NW	55	69	83	93	102	105	106	104	97	154	193	NW
	Horiz.	134	206	292	365	417	449	443	413	358	282	195	Horiz.
Apr 28	N	70	87	95	103	110	115	116	110	103	93	86	N
	NE	322	308	236	143	146	143	143	137	131	120	106	NE
	E	439	501	510	430	314	192	179	167	160	149	136	E
	SE	331	433	511	515	487	413	301	186	169	149	135	SE
	S	115	157	255	346	418	457	455	409	339	236	142	S
	SW	133	149	162	184	212	330	437	503	535	505	434	SW
	W	138	154	167	176	184	199	226	351	465	518	513	W
	NW	104	120	133	142	149	154	155	159	167	258	325	NW
	Horiz.	251	342	437	499	548	572	570	540	496	417	329	Horiz.
May 29	N	118	121	126	131	137	140	139	135	130	123	120	N
	NE	382	362	290	190	174	166	165	161	155	146	134	NE
	E	475	519	518	450	329	208	194	184	179	169	157	E
	SE	321	408	471	485	448	367	258	167	166	152	140	SE
	S	110	129	201	289	355	388	384	345	274	182	116	S
	SW	142	156	168	183	193	290	393	465	497	477	420	SW
	W	170	184	196	204	210	223	247	371	484	544	554	W
	NW	142	156	168	176	182	185	185	197	221	321	394	NW
	Horiz.	326	417	507	578	615	625	621	605	564	492	407	Horiz.
Jun 21	N	144	139	142	147	151	154	154	151	147	144	143	N
	NE	440	413	320	211	190	180	181	178	173	165	154	NE
	E	533	579	550	469	343	220	207	199	195	186	176	E
	SE	345	437	482	487	446	363	253	168	171	159	148	SE
	S	111	123	191	276	342	376	374	331	261	174	116	S
	SW	147	159	170	182	190	282	389	460	492	476	424	SW
	W	185	197	207	215	220	232	257	382	497	561	578	W
	NW	160	172	182	190	195	198	199	214	244	347	424	NW
	Horiz.	365	463	545	609	642	650	648	629	590	521	439	Horiz.
Jul 4	N	126	126	130	136	142	146	146	141	136	130	127	N
	NE	394	372	294	196	179	171	171	166	161	152	139	NE
	E	480	525	509	437	323	210	196	187	182	172	160	E
	SE	314	400	450	458	422	346	244	162	162	149	136	SE
	S	102	118	184	265	328	359	360	320	253	168	108	S
	SW	135	149	160	174	184	272	372	438	467	453	401	SW
	W	168	182	192	202	209	221	245	360	467	529	542	W
	NW	144	157	168	177	183	187	188	200	226	322	394	NW
	Horiz.	329	420	503	565	599	606	608	590	551	487	407	Horiz.

Table continues

Table 5.18 Solar cooling loads for fast-response building with single clear glazing: **SE England, unshaded** — *continued*

Date	Orient-ation	Solar cooling load at stated sun time (W·m⁻²)											Orient-ation
		0730	0830	0930	1030	1130	1230	1330	1430	1530	1630	1730	
Aug 4	N	81	92	99	107	113	117	117	115	106	97	91	N
	NE	316	314	244	153	148	143	144	141	132	123	109	NE
	E	414	486	487	420	309	189	176	167	159	149	135	E
	SE	302	406	471	484	459	378	270	173	160	144	130	SE
	S	107	137	223	311	382	410	405	367	298	203	122	S
	SW	125	139	152	170	189	294	393	460	490	452	372	SW
	W	134	148	161	170	176	189	215	334	440	480	454	W
	NW	105	120	132	141	147	150	152	161	171	257	303	NW
	Horiz.	261	354	442	509	557	567	560	539	498	417	325	Horiz.
Sep 4	N	43	55	65	78	86	88	87	82	74	64	54	N
	NE	241	244	167	97	109	107	106	101	93	83	70	NE
	E	365	462	465	394	277	159	144	132	124	114	101	E
	SE	304	433	508	521	482	410	310	189	147	129	116	SE
	S	106	175	283	379	439	470	478	439	362	257	151	S
	SW	110	124	138	165	215	329	436	502	520	481	375	SW
	W	99	112	124	137	146	158	183	306	408	450	404	W
	NW	65	78	91	103	111	113	113	112	109	181	225	NW
	Horiz.	171	258	345	413	453	471	477	451	398	321	230	Horiz.
Oct 4	N	19	30	42	52	59	64	64	61	53	40	28	N
	NE	91	132	87	66	67	71	70	68	59	47	35	NE
	E	172	324	381	351	236	119	103	94	86	73	61	E
	SE	183	348	472	535	504	415	315	200	115	104	89	SE
	S	120	194	315	435	499	507	499	460	383	266	165	S
	SW	79	90	105	124	222	332	419	470	473	395	285	SW
	W	54	64	76	86	94	109	134	243	324	325	266	W
	NW	28	38	50	61	68	73	73	72	74	90	117	NW
	Horiz.	82	136	216	293	337	347	342	316	264	188	120	Horiz.
Nov 4	N	7	13	22	32	38	42	43	39	31	21	13	N
	NE	12	43	34	37	40	44	44	41	33	23	14	NE
	E	37	153	279	288	196	85	70	61	53	43	35	E
	SE	73	203	391	501	507	447	328	204	105	81	70	SE
	S	89	158	295	439	527	566	527	457	352	235	132	S
	SW	58	64	79	117	233	356	421	438	395	298	151	SW
	W	25	31	40	50	56	69	95	187	235	214	110	W
	NW	8	14	23	33	39	44	44	41	37	35	37	NW
	Horiz.	36	55	105	173	223	247	234	200	147	90	50	Horiz.
Dec 4	N	4	5	12	21	28	32	32	27	20	11	4	N
	NE	5	6	23	23	28	32	32	27	20	11	5	NE
	E	17	26	139	209	156	63	48	39	32	23	17	E
	SE	50	62	219	395	448	403	306	191	92	57	50	SE
	S	70	79	190	362	478	518	495	429	314	159	70	S
	SW	48	49	62	109	221	329	392	405	342	179	48	SW
	W	16	16	24	32	40	50	73	154	185	112	16	W
	NW	5	5	13	21	28	32	32	27	23	22	5	NW
	Horiz.	20	22	45	96	143	164	158	129	84	39	20	Horiz.

Glazing configuration (inside to outside)	Correction factor for stated building response		Glazing configuration (inside to outside)	Correction factor for stated building response	
	Fast	Slow		Fast	Slow
Clear	1.00	0.89	Clear/clear/absorbing	0.46	0.39
Absorbing	0.74	0.64			
Reflecting	0.67	0.59	Low-E/clear	0.81	0.69
			Low-E/reflecting	0.52	0.44
Clear/clear	0.83	0.71	Low-E/absorbing	0.55	0.47
Clear/reflecting	0.53	0.46			
Clear/absorbing	0.56	0.47	Low-E/clear/clear	0.70	0.59
			Low-E/clear/reflecting	0.44	0.38
Clear/clear/clear	0.71	0.60	Low-E/clear/absorbing	0.46	0.39
Clear/clear/reflecting	0.44	0.38			
Air node correction factor	0.86	0.83			

Table 5.19 Solar cooling loads for fast-response building with single clear glazing: **NW England, unshaded**

Date	Orientation	Solar cooling load at stated sun time (W·m⁻²)											Orientation
		0730	0830	0930	1030	1130	1230	1330	1430	1530	1630	1730	
Jan 29	N	6	11	18	28	35	39	40	35	27	16	10	N
	NE	9	27	37	31	36	40	41	36	28	18	11	NE
	E	24	80	152	189	156	71	58	48	40	30	24	E
	SE	53	119	224	338	406	370	298	184	88	60	53	SE
	S	70	110	188	310	430	471	477	407	284	172	100	S
	SW	48	53	65	101	204	304	383	389	313	203	105	SW
	W	19	24	31	41	48	60	84	160	181	140	68	W
	NW	7	12	19	29	36	40	41	36	33	39	24	NW
	Horiz.	25	36	61	108	156	178	179	148	101	57	34	Horiz
Feb 26	N	16	23	36	47	53	57	58	52	45	34	21	N
	NE	51	85	61	56	56	61	62	55	48	38	25	NE
	E	103	208	301	301	213	104	89	77	70	60	46	E
	SE	131	245	395	485	492	440	337	205	112	94	78	SE
	S	115	175	293	420	508	552	539	468	405	282	163	S
	SW	75	83	101	130	237	359	444	465	483	396	236	SW
	W	44	52	65	76	82	97	122	223	310	307	202	W
	NW	21	28	42	53	58	62	63	58	60	68	86	NW
	Horiz.	59	88	153	222	270	296	291	252	212	145	82	Horiz.
Mar 29	N	39	52	63	76	88	88	88	82	74	63	48	N
	NE	151	170	127	81	101	98	98	92	85	73	57	NE
	E	239	335	385	365	269	148	133	119	111	100	84	E
	SE	222	338	446	513	502	421	324	202	145	123	105	SE
	S	111	178	284	400	480	498	498	449	375	262	159	S
	SW	101	115	130	161	234	344	438	486	495	426	319	SW
	W	82	96	108	121	134	146	170	280	368	378	322	W
	NW	53	67	79	92	104	104	104	100	94	142	170	NW
	Horiz.	130	196	276	357	413	422	421	388	339	261	181	Horiz.
Apr 28	N	72	90	98	109	116	118	118	114	107	98	91	N
	NE	299	296	222	142	148	143	143	140	132	123	110	NE
	E	409	485	482	418	308	192	179	168	160	151	138	E
	SE	317	428	493	509	479	417	316	198	173	153	140	E
	S	121	167	265	357	423	466	477	425	351	247	154	SE
	SW	132	148	163	189	222	336	448	504	528	485	405	S
	W	133	149	163	173	181	195	219	342	448	486	466	SW
	NW	101	118	131	142	149	151	151	156	158	242	296	NW
	Horiz.	244	334	416	481	522	549	561	524	478	400	317	Horiz.
May 29	N	124	128	132	139	144	148	150	146	140	135	138	N
	NE	402	382	289	190	181	175	177	173	166	159	152	NE
	E	503	560	532	459	339	217	207	197	190	183	176	E
	SE	346	446	494	506	472	393	284	185	180	165	158	SE
	S	122	142	223	316	384	420	421	379	305	210	13	S9
	SW	148	161	173	190	204	310	418	490	519	495	418	SW
	W	170	183	194	203	209	222	249	374	488	547	530	W
	NW	142	155	167	175	181	184	187	199	215	315	378	NW
	Horiz.	342	436	514	580	619	633	635	614	573	502	413	Horiz.
Jun 21	N	136	139	144	149	155	158	157	151	145	141	144	N
	NE	416	391	307	206	195	186	185	179	172	165	156	NE
	E	508	554	535	462	343	225	212	200	193	186	177	E
	SE	336	428	480	490	455	379	268	175	172	159	151	SE
	S	115	134	210	296	365	400	395	351	281	192	125	S
	SW	147	162	175	190	201	300	401	467	503	496	434	SW
	W	180	194	207	214	221	234	257	376	492	568	576	W
	NW	153	168	181	188	194	198	198	208	229	336	415	NW
	Horiz.	356	450	531	593	631	644	638	615	583	525	441	Horiz.
Jul 4	N	135	137	141	148	155	158	155	150	141	135	137	N
	NE	412	386	298	202	192	183	180	176	167	158	150	NE
	E	506	553	527	457	338	223	208	197	188	180	171	E
	SE	337	429	476	488	448	377	270	174	167	154	146	SE
	S	116	134	210	298	361	398	402	359	285	191	122	S
	SW	150	163	175	193	205	303	409	478	512	496	431	SW
	W	186	199	211	220	227	240	261	385	500	568	573	W
	NW	159	172	184	193	199	202	200	211	228	333	410	NW
	Horiz.	351	442	520	584	614	631	638	617	580	513	427	Horiz.

Table continues

Table 5.19 Solar cooling loads for fast-response building with single clear glazing: **NW England, unshaded** — *continued*

Date	Orient-ation	Solar cooling load at stated sun time (W·m⁻²)											Orient-ation
		0730	0830	0930	1030	1130	1230	1330	1430	1530	1630	1730	
Aug 4	N	81	95	103	112	116	121	121	116	109	99	96	N
	NE	312	319	231	151	149	146	147	142	135	124	114	NE
	E	413	505	464	403	305	192	180	168	160	150	140	E
	SE	306	426	457	471	459	391	286	180	164	145	135	SE
	S	112	146	233	318	393	430	425	389	313	214	134	S
	SW	130	145	160	181	204	313	411	479	497	456	392	SW
	W	140	155	169	178	183	198	223	341	440	477	472	W
	NW	111	126	139	149	153	157	159	164	171	251	313	NW
	Horiz.	261	359	425	484	539	559	554	535	486	407	331	Horiz.
Sep 4	N	46	58	71	83	89	93	92	87	77	68	58	N
	NE	216	217	154	96	109	109	108	103	93	84	72	NE
	E	327	409	415	384	282	160	144	131	122	112	100	E
	SE	280	393	462	515	506	434	318	200	150	131	117	SE
	S	112	177	279	389	471	505	487	457	383	273	161	S
	SW	114	127	144	174	230	353	442	514	538	492	370	SW
	W	101	114	128	140	147	163	186	309	415	455	391	W
	NW	67	80	95	106	113	117	116	114	108	178	218	NW
	Horiz.	167	242	320	399	454	475	461	442	393	318	227	Horiz.
Oct 4	N	20	30	42	55	63	66	67	61	52	40	28	N
	NE	78	110	77	67	68	71	72	66	57	45	34	NE
	E	143	261	311	293	210	114	100	88	79	67	55	E
	SE	155	284	388	444	435	391	306	189	107	94	80	SE
	S	110	169	272	373	439	479	481	420	357	243	152	S
	SW	74	85	100	122	212	320	404	429	437	355	254	SW
	W	50	60	72	85	94	107	131	223	298	290	234	W
	NW	27	37	49	62	70	74	74	70	71	82	105	NW
	Horiz.	74	118	183	248	291	315	317	281	237	168	109	Horiz.
Nov 4	N	7	14	23	33	41	44	45	41	31	21	13	N
	NE	11	39	33	38	42	45	46	42	32	22	14	NE
	E	30	116	210	226	159	80	66	57	47	37	29	E
	SE	60	157	295	388	390	387	308	190	93	69	59	SE
	S	76	131	233	348	412	490	493	424	316	205	115	S
	SW	53	60	74	108	200	317	398	410	357	260	132	SW
	W	23	30	39	49	57	69	93	177	212	185	95	W
	NW	8	15	24	34	42	45	46	42	36	32	34	NW
	Horiz.	31	49	87	139	176	209	209	178	127	77	44	Horiz.
Dec 4	N	4	4	10	18	25	28	27	24	17	10	4	N
	NE	4	6	21	20	25	28	27	24	17	10	4	NE
	E	14	22	110	170	134	56	40	34	27	20	14	E
	SE	43	52	177	324	386	356	277	168	80	50	43	SE
	S	60	68	159	300	414	458	448	373	263	134	60	S
	SW	42	42	53	94	194	291	355	351	284	147	42	SW
	W	13	14	20	27	34	44	64	132	153	90	13	W
	NW	4	5	11	18	25	28	27	24	19	20	4	NW
	Horiz.	16	18	36	72	112	132	128	103	65	32	16	Horiz.

Glazing configuration (inside to outside)	Correction factor for stated building response		Glazing configuration (inside to outside)	Correction factor for stated building response	
	Fast	Slow		Fast	Slow
Clear	1.00	0.89	Clear/clear/absorbing	0.46	0.39
Absorbing	0.75	0.64			
Reflecting	0.67	0.58	Low-E/clear	0.81	0.69
			Low-E/reflecting	0.52	0.45
Clear/clear	0.83	0.72	Low-E/absorbing	0.55	0.47
Clear/reflecting	0.53	0.46			
Clear/absorbing	0.56	0.48	Low-E/clear/clear	0.70	0.60
			Low-E/clear/reflecting	0.44	0.38
Clear/clear/clear	0.71	0.60	Low-E/clear/absorbing	0.46	0.39
Clear/clear/reflecting	0.44	0.38			
Air node correction factor	0.86	0.83			

Table 5.20 Solar cooling loads for fast-response building with single clear glazing: **NE Scotland (lowlands), unshaded**

Date	Orient-ation	Solar cooling load at stated sun time (W·m⁻²)											Orient-ation
		0730	0830	0930	1030	1130	1230	1330	1430	1530	1630	1730	
Jan 29	N	4	8	12	21	27	34	34	26	18	11	7	N
	NE	6	14	25	23	28	34	35	27	18	11	8	NE
	E	19	38	147	216	160	69	52	40	31	24	20	E
	SE	53	74	225	399	451	415	325	206	89	59	54	SE
	S	74	91	193	363	481	533	528	480	341	171	81	S
	SW	52	55	65	108	222	340	421	459	381	202	62	SW
	W	18	21	26	35	41	56	83	176	210	131	27	W
	NW	5	8	13	22	28	34	35	27	21	22	12	NW
	Horiz.	21	28	46	94	137	163	162	134	84	40	26	Horiz.
Feb 26	N	12	18	28	38	43	47	47	43	37	27	16	N
	NE	43	72	51	46	47	50	50	46	40	30	19	NE
	E	96	193	302	308	216	95	77	69	62	52	42	E
	SE	128	235	406	513	533	463	349	221	110	90	77	SE
	S	115	171	301	444	550	585	568	526	405	265	151	S
	SW	73	80	96	127	246	373	462	519	476	360	204	SW
	W	39	45	55	65	71	83	112	228	296	271	167	W
	NW	16	22	33	42	48	51	51	48	48	54	68	NW
	Horiz.	50	73	132	200	251	271	265	241	184	119	67	Horiz.
Mar 29	N	41	53	64	75	83	87	87	83	73	63	51	N
	NE	117	134	120	95	92	95	95	90	81	70	57	NE
	E	182	255	362	344	239	139	125	113	103	93	80	E
	SE	179	268	426	490	453	412	317	205	124	118	102	SE
	S	110	166	283	393	444	494	490	461	360	261	160	S
	SW	100	113	128	143	228	344	431	492	463	413	305	SW
	W	81	94	107	118	126	142	166	277	340	361	303	W
	NW	54	67	80	91	98	103	103	101	106	133	162	NW
	Horiz.	123	175	259	329	360	390	387	369	306	244	174	Horiz.
Apr 28	N	70	85	92	101	106	109	109	105	99	91	83	N
	NE	257	268	205	124	133	131	130	126	120	112	100	NE
	E	356	451	486	414	303	180	166	155	149	140	128	E
	SE	289	411	512	526	507	436	324	201	167	148	136	SE
	S	126	175	283	380	457	498	498	457	372	256	160	S
	SW	135	148	160	186	229	352	461	531	543	480	411	SW
	W	133	146	157	166	172	186	212	341	446	470	465	W
	NW	100	113	124	133	139	142	141	143	143	222	285	NW
	Horiz.	233	316	408	467	516	538	539	516	463	379	306	Horiz.
May 29	N	120	125	129	136	141	143	141	140	139	164	126	N
	NE	418	381	276	176	175	169	167	166	162	153	142	NE
	E	533	580	540	462	336	214	198	192	187	179	168	E
	SE	370	471	514	525	489	410	298	189	178	161	150	SE
	S	125	151	244	339	410	446	449	402	320	224	138	S
	SW	150	162	173	191	213	326	437	505	521	507	445	SW
	W	175	187	197	204	210	223	245	373	480	550	561	W
	NW	146	158	168	175	181	183	182	191	203	302	383	NW
	Horiz.	350	440	511	572	608	622	629	602	549	491	412	Horiz.
Jun 21	N	140	143	144	151	154	158	157	154	151	144	144	N
	NE	416	391	293	190	182	178	178	175	171	163	152	NE
	E	518	576	548	469	343	219	207	198	194	186	176	E
	SE	353	456	507	519	485	401	288	184	178	163	152	SE
	S	125	145	231	327	399	431	429	389	308	212	133	S
	SW	160	171	181	198	214	324	430	505	524	511	470	SW
	W	203	214	224	231	235	249	272	399	508	581	620	W
	NW	175	187	196	203	207	210	211	220	237	340	437	NW
	Horiz.	370	463	539	600	639	645	642	626	578	519	454	Horiz.
Jul 4	N	132	137	139	147	152	154	153	151	145	138	138	N
	NE	411	376	284	191	188	182	180	178	173	164	154	NE
	E	512	550	521	446	337	222	209	200	195	186	176	E
	SE	351	439	484	490	467	394	289	187	178	162	152	SE
	S	126	148	231	318	389	424	427	385	310	216	136	S
	SW	153	165	176	195	213	317	421	489	513	500	436	SW
	W	181	193	203	211	217	230	252	373	482	552	557	W
	NW	154	166	176	184	189	192	191	201	214	313	390	NW
	Horiz.	356	438	508	560	603	618	622	602	560	503	423	Horiz.

Table continues

Table 5.20 Solar cooling loads for fast-response building with single clear glazing: **NE Scotland (lowlands), unshaded** — *continued*

Date	Orient-ation	Solar cooling load at stated sun time (W·m⁻²)											Orient-ation
		0730	0830	0930	1030	1130	1230	1330	1430	1530	1630	1730	
Aug 4	N	88	101	107	116	122	126	124	121	115	107	100	N
	NE	306	299	227	150	155	153	150	147	141	133	120	NE
	E	406	474	470	408	309	198	184	173	167	159	146	E
	SE	310	414	475	489	474	396	307	198	175	156	143	SE
	S	126	164	257	344	417	436	451	408	323	232	150	S
	SW	128	141	154	178	208	314	417	474	466	426	367	SW
	W	125	138	150	159	165	181	202	316	393	424	418	W
	NW	101	113	125	135	140	144	143	147	151	222	272	NW
	Horiz.	265	347	420	476	522	526	541	515	455	388	321	Horiz.
Sep 4	N	50	62	73	82	89	92	94	90	81	71	60	N
	NE	210	209	152	92	106	107	108	105	96	86	73	NE
	E	319	398	439	389	271	158	145	134	125	115	102	E
	SE	277	388	495	535	493	430	312	205	155	135	120	SE
	S	113	184	299	406	462	497	456	410	359	246	152	S
	SW	104	117	133	160	224	339	403	442	473	392	284	SW
	W	88	102	114	124	132	146	169	268	358	354	291	W
	NW	62	76	88	98	105	108	110	108	101	148	169	NW
	Horiz.	162	231	315	382	415	436	409	380	348	272	199	Horiz.
Oct 4	N	19	29	41	50	57	61	61	57	50	39	28	N
	NE	81	117	78	63	63	66	67	63	56	45	33	NE
	E	154	293	354	323	221	113	97	87	80	70	58	E
	SE	169	322	447	504	482	436	305	196	115	101	87	SE
	S	116	186	308	419	485	534	469	417	358	231	149	S
	SW	72	82	98	120	224	344	388	415	426	314	224	SW
	W	46	56	68	77	85	98	120	210	284	252	201	W
	NW	25	35	47	57	64	67	68	64	66	74	92	NW
	Horiz.	70	115	183	245	284	311	283	255	218	151	100	Horiz.
Nov 4	N	6	12	19	29	38	40	38	33	26	17	10	N
	NE	10	33	29	33	39	41	39	34	27	18	11	NE
	E	32	121	240	274	181	80	62	52	45	36	30	E
	SE	65	167	341	484	463	399	306	190	98	70	63	SE
	S	81	138	263	425	486	504	486	417	335	204	115	S
	SW	52	58	72	114	225	322	387	396	374	253	123	SW
	W	21	27	34	44	54	64	85	166	217	177	85	W
	NW	7	12	20	30	39	41	39	34	31	27	27	NW
	Horiz.	27	41	74	133	171	186	178	149	110	62	36	Horiz.
Dec 4	N	3	3	8	13	19	24	24	18	12	6	3	N
	NE	3	3	8	14	20	24	24	19	12	7	3	NE
	E	13	19	96	155	138	53	36	28	21	16	13	E
	SE	46	55	167	304	422	396	326	203	87	56	46	SE
	S	67	74	157	289	456	514	537	473	284	147	67	S
	SW	48	49	64	103	212	326	425	448	308	159	48	SW
	W	14	14	19	24	31	41	69	157	161	90	14	W
	NW	3	3	8	13	20	24	24	19	13	8	3	NW
	Horiz.	13	14	27	53	93	115	117	92	49	23	13	Horiz.

Glazing configuration (inside to outside)	Correction factor for stated building response		Glazing configuration (inside to outside)	Correction factor for stated building response	
	Fast	Slow		Fast	Slow
Clear	1.00	0.90	Clear/clear/absorbing	0.46	0.39
Absorbing	0.74	0.64			
Reflecting	0.67	0.59	Low-E/clear	0.81	0.69
			Low-E/reflecting	0.52	0.45
Clear/clear	0.83	0.72	Low-E/absorbing	0.55	0.47
Clear/reflecting	0.53	0.46			
Clear/absorbing	0.56	0.47	Low-E/clear/clear	0.70	0.60
			Low-E/clear/reflecting	0.44	0.38
Clear/clear/clear	0.70	0.60	Low-E/clear/absorbing	0.46	0.39
Clear/clear/reflecting	0.44	0.38			
Air node correction factor	0.86	0.83			

Table 5.21 Solar cooling loads for fast-response building with single clear glazing: **SE England, intermittent shading**

Date	Orient-ation	Solar cooling load at stated sun time (W·m⁻²)											Orient-ation
		0730	0830	0930	1030	1130	1230	1330	1430	1530	1630	1730	
Jan 29	N	6	11	18	26	33	37	37	35	27	18	11	N
	NE	7	27	24	30	34	38	38	36	28	19	12	NE
	E	11	164	149	131	41	62	47	40	33	24	16	E
	SE	22	210	238	287	276	225	74	155	62	36	27	SE
	S	29	71	305	281	324	331	291	214	74	142	67	S
	SW	18	22	31	140	183	245	263	228	165	54	83	SW
	W	16	21	28	36	43	52	67	234	50	148	74	W
	NW	7	11	18	27	34	38	38	36	31	24	27	NW
	Horiz.	20	31	60	113	248	142	55	153	104	59	32	Horiz.
Feb 26	N	15	22	33	45	52	57	56	52	44	33	21	N
	NE	42	72	56	53	55	60	59	55	47	35	24	NE
	E	73	287	191	161	55	87	71	61	53	42	31	E
	SE	77	321	271	304	291	234	80	162	68	53	39	SE
	S	48	180	210	283	328	335	310	261	186	67	98	S
	SW	33	41	54	71	301	262	301	308	267	181	64	SW
	W	25	33	43	55	63	74	181	189	204	161	56	W
	NW	20	28	39	51	58	63	62	82	55	61	79	NW
	Horiz.	34	60	117	297	200	204	188	157	59	122	61	Horiz.
Mar 29	N	34	46	58	68	76	79	80	76	68	57	45	N
	NE	144	167	129	76	90	90	91	86	78	68	55	NE
	E	216	262	256	202	77	118	105	93	85	74	61	E
	SE	297	271	315	318	290	228	83	147	94	75	60	SE
	S	47	201	214	271	311	318	297	253	187	68	106	S
	SW	58	71	85	105	282	267	316	337	319	258	99	SW
	W	45	58	71	81	89	100	222	230	268	252	188	W
	NW	51	64	77	87	95	98	99	98	83	138	180	NW
	Horiz.	76	240	211	252	280	285	270	238	191	74	142	Horiz.
Apr 28	N	64	80	87	95	101	106	107	102	96	86	80	N
	NE	223	189	85	121	124	121	122	117	111	101	90	NE
	E	325	347	312	242	104	150	139	127	121	111	99	E
	SE	261	322	341	331	292	224	93	138	122	103	91	SE
	S	59	177	194	248	284	293	271	230	166	62	92	S
	SW	68	83	95	112	238	249	304	335	329	291	216	SW
	W	74	89	101	109	115	127	258	269	320	332	285	W
	NW	72	87	99	107	114	118	119	122	209	206	214	NW
	Horiz.	264	244	294	332	355	362	347	321	274	215	94	Horiz.
May 29	N	109	111	116	121	126	129	129	125	120	114	109N	N
	NE	263	227	107	163	148	140	139	135	130	122	111	NE
	E	344	355	325	255	116	163	150	140	136	127	116	E
	SE	251	301	323	310	265	197	88	122	122	109	98	SE
	S	70	80	253	217	248	254	236	195	74	143	79	S
	SW	80	93	104	117	205	222	280	312	310	280	223	SW
	W	96	109	120	128	133	141	269	280	334	354	330	W
	NW	92	105	116	123	129	132	132	139	260	243	266	NW
	Horiz.	349	293	347	382	396	398	390	368	324	269	124	Horiz.
Jun 21	N	134	128	131	135	140	142	143	140	136	133	129	N
	NE	303	255	124	182	161	152	152	150	146	138	129	NE
	E	388	385	343	268	128	173	160	153	149	142	132	E
	SE	272	314	328	311	264	195	90	123	127	116	107	SE
	S	74	77	239	209	240	248	229	187	73	137	79	S
	SW	85	97	106	117	198	220	277	309	309	283	229	SW
	W	107	119	128	136	140	148	276	289	345	369	350	W
	NW	106	117	127	134	139	141	142	152	284	264	291	NW
	Horiz.	251	311	360	391	404	406	397	375	334	280	218	Horiz.
Jul 4	N	117	116	120	125	131	135	135	131	126	121	115	N
	NE	272	233	113	169	153	144	145	140	136	128	116	NE
	E	350	354	319	251	119	165	153	144	139	131	120	E
	SE	250	294	310	296	253	107	204	122	123	111	100	SE
	S	66	74	231	201	230	238	220	181	69	132	73	S
	SW	80	92	102	115	114	328	267	296	297	271	219	SW
	W	96	109	119	127	133	142	265	271	325	346	327	W
	NW	94	107	117	125	131	135	135	142	265	245	269	NW
	Horiz.	355	294	342	373	385	389	382	360	321	269	126	Horiz.

Table continues

Table 5.21 Solar cooling loads for fast-response building with single clear glazing: **SE England, intermittent shading** — *continued*

Date	Orient-ation	Solar cooling load at stated sun time (W·m^{-2})											Orient-ation
		0730	0830	0930	1030	1130	1230	1330	1430	1530	1630	1730	
Aug 4	N	74	85	91	99	104	108	108	106	99	91	84	N
	NE	225	193	88	130	126	121	122	120	112	104	91	NE
	E	314	332	303	238	104	148	135	127	120	111	99	E
	SE	244	298	320	313	270	203	86	127	116	101	88	SE
	S	64	84	281	233	262	267	249	210	79	160	83	S
	SW	67	81	92	108	212	224	278	309	299	253	187	SW
	W	75	88	99	108	113	122	248	257	300	298	254	W
	NW	75	88	100	108	114	117	118	125	216	197	201	NW
	Horiz.	278	250	301	340	356	357	346	323	276	214	96	Horiz.
Sep 4	N	39	51	60	71	79	81	81	76	69	60	51	N
	NE	180	77	158	87	100	97	97	93	86	77	66	NE
	E	294	318	288	219	88	127	113	102	95	86	75	E
	SE	252	317	341	326	285	224	88	140	101	83	71	SE
	S	46	203	213	263	291	303	288	244	179	65	99	S
	SW	51	63	75	96	250	248	304	328	315	257	180	SW
	W	52	64	75	87	95	103	226	240	284	272	220	W
	NW	45	57	68	80	88	90	90	89	77	236	148	NW
	Horiz.	105	305	244	278	296	305	295	264	217	87	171	Horiz.
Oct 4	N	18	27	38	47	54	59	59	57	50	38	27	N
	NE	78	122	82	60	61	65	65	63	56	44	33	NE
	E	261	240	242	183	60	90	75	67	60	48	37	E
	SE	248	273	333	334	286	221	76	151	67	57	44	SE
	S	55	227	244	302	319	318	299	256	184	67	107	S
	SW	38	47	60	68	285	251	295	310	274	207	75	SW
	W	32	41	52	62	68	79	190	201	220	194	70	W
	NW	26	35	46	56	63	68	68	67	66	80	111	NW
	Horiz.	44	92	279	209	223	224	211	182	68	150	87	Horiz.
Nov 4	N	6	12	20	29	35	39	40	37	30	21	13	N
	NE	8	40	32	34	36	40	41	38	31	22	14	NE
	E	14	241	194	155	48	67	53	45	38	28	20	E
	SE	25	296	302	330	306	238	78	160	65	42	32	SE
	S	27	183	238	312	352	342	302	238	161	58	76	S
	SW	20	26	35	147	198	257	281	265	212	70	114	SW
	W	12	18	26	35	41	49	147	149	152	51	98	W
	NW	8	13	21	30	36	40	41	38	34	31	37	NW
	Horiz.	22	37	82	238	163	163	61	178	129	76	37	Horiz.
Dec 4	N	4	4	11	19	25	29	30	25	19	11	4	N
	NE	5	5	22	21	26	29	30	25	19	11	5	NE
	E	10	10	211	122	38	53	39	30	24	16	10	E
	SE	16	92	213	279	271	217	142	44	57	23	16	SE
	S	24	24	262	279	325	324	290	223	74	114	24	S
	SW	18	18	26	145	187	241	263	240	78	149	18	SW
	W	12	12	18	26	33	40	55	222	46	108	12	W
	NW	5	5	11	19	26	29	30	25	21	22	5	NW
	Horiz.	20	20	39	86	131	153	149	123	82	39	20	Horiz.

Glazing configuration (inside to outside)	Correction factor for stated building response		Glazing configuration (inside to outside)	Correction factor for stated building response	
	Fast	Slow		Fast	Slow
Clear/blind	0.73	0.81	Clear/clear/reflecting/blind	0.30	0.33
Absorbing/blind	0.52	0.55	Clear/clear/blind/absorbing	0.39	0.39
Reflecting/blind	0.50	0.53	Clear/clear/absorbing/blind	0.32	0.34
Clear/blind/clear	0.69	0.72	Low-E/clear/blind	0.56	0.58
Clear/clear/blind	0.57	0.61	Low-E/reflecting/blind	0.39	0.39
Clear/blind/reflecting	0.47	0.48	Low-E/absorbing/blind	0.39	0.41
Clear/reflecting/blind	0.37	0.38	Low-E/clear/blind/clear	0.55	0.57
Clear/blind/absorbing	0.50	0.51	Low-E/clear/clear/blind	0.48	0.55
Clear/absorbing/blind	0.38	0.40	Low-E/clear/blind/reflecting	0.37	0.38
Clear/clear/blind/clear	0.56	0.58	Low-E/clear/reflecting/blind	0.32	0.35
Clear/clear/clear/blind	0.47	0.51	Low-E/clear/blind/absorbing	0.39	0.39
Clear/clear/blind/reflecting	0.37	0.38	Low-E/clear/absorbing/blind	0.35	0.37

Table continues

Table 5.21 Solar cooling loads for fast-response building with single clear galzing: **SE England, intermittent shading** — *continued*

Glazing configuration (inside to outside)	Correction factor for stated building response		Glazing configuration (inside to outside)	Correction factor for stated building response	
	Fast	Slow		Fast	Slow
Blind/clear	1.00	1.03	Blind/low-E/clear	0.92	0.92
Blind/reflecting	0.69	0.71	Blind/low-E/reflecting	0.59	0.60
Blind/absorbing	0.75	0.76	Blind/low-E/absorbing	0.63	0.62
Blind/clear/clear	0.95	0.94	Blind/low-E/clear/clear	0.84	0.83
Blind/clear/reflecting	0.62	0.62	Blind/low-E/clear/reflecting	0.53	0.53
Blind/clear/absorbing	0.66	0.66	Blind/low-E/clear/absorbing	0.55	0.55
Blind/clear/clear/clear	0.86	0.86			
Blind/clear/clear/reflecting	0.55	0.55			
Blind/clear/clear/absorbing	0.57	0.56			
Air node correction factor:					
— internal blind	0.91	0.89			
— mid pane blind	0.87	0.83			
— external blind	0.88	0.85			

Table 5.22 Solar cooling loads for fast-response building with single clear glazing: **NW England, intermittent shading**

Date	Orient-ation	Solar cooling load at stated sun time (W·m⁻²)											Orient-ation
		0730	0830	0930	1030	1130	1230	1330	1430	1530	1630	1730	
Jan 29	N	6	10	16	25	32	36	37	33	25	16	10	N
	NE	7	23	35	28	33	37	38	34	26	17	11	NE
	E	15	65	218	48	145	64	51	42	35	26	20	E
	SE	19	159	191	252	251	211	69	150	58	32	24	SE
	S	25	60	243	249	295	309	279	205	69	127	59	S
	SW	23	27	34	61	281	237	259	225	76	174	80	SW
	W	18	22	28	37	45	53	69	144	170	135	67	W
	NW	7	11	17	26	33	37	38	34	29	37	23	NW
	Horiz.	23	33	54	97	144	164	168	141	97	55	33	Horiz.
Feb 26	N	14	20	33	43	48	52	54	48	42	33	21	N
	NE	43	78	56	52	52	56	57	52	45	36	24	NE
	E	75	301	205	166	56	84	70	58	52	43	31	E
	SE	103	215	293	318	297	238	79	158	68	51	36	SE
	S	50	198	229	299	341	347	309	267	196	70	104	S
	SW	30	37	52	149	197	266	293	310	275	178	60	SW
	W	25	31	43	54	59	69	175	189	210	159	54	W
	NW	19	26	38	49	54	58	59	54	53	60	83	NW
	Horiz.	37	61	119	294	193	198	178	68	184	123	61	Horiz.
Mar 29	N	35	47	57	69	81	81	82	76	69	59	46	N
	NE	136	157	120	73	93	91	91	86	79	69	54	NE
	E	327	247	252	205	75	116	102	89	82	72	58	E
	SE	282	262	319	331	291	230	84	152	97	77	60	SE
	S	49	202	221	286	312	317	295	251	182	66	103	S
	SW	56	69	82	103	294	265	309	326	296	231	90	SW
	W	56	69	80	92	104	112	230	233	258	234	94	W
	NW	49	62	73	85	97	97	97	94	81	128	159	NW
	Horiz.	79	232	208	254	271	273	258	229	89	210	135	Horiz.
Apr 28	N	65	82	90	100	107	109	109	106	100	91	85	N
	NE	222	105	209	130	137	131	131	129	122	114	103	NE
	E	313	330	301	237	103	151	139	129	122	113	103	E
	SE	256	312	335	326	291	233	97	149	126	107	96	SE
	S	70	107	332	259	295	312	290	245	93	196	109	S
	SW	70	85	97	119	254	258	309	334	319	274	200	SW
	W	79	95	107	117	124	133	262	268	310	311	262	W
	NW	75	90	102	113	120	121	121	125	118	312	197	NW
	Horiz.	262	238	287	322	345	358	344	315	268	112	242	Horiz.
May 29	N	114	118	121	128	133	136	139	135	129	124	127	N
	NE	280	234	114	163	155	148	150	147	141	135	129	NE
	E	372	373	335	264	124	171	162	153	146	140	134	E
	SE	275	320	338	326	283	216	97	137	133	120	113	SE
	S	78	89	280	236	269	278	260	217	84	166	98	S
	SW	84	96	106	121	221	238	296	327	324	282	225	SW
	W	99	110	121	129	134	143	276	285	340	345	319	W
	NW	95	107	118	126	131	134	137	145	255	237	259	NW
	Horiz.	370	302	351	385	401	406	398	374	332	274	129	Horiz.
Jun 21	N	126	128	133	137	142	146	146	140	134	131	131	N
	NE	282	239	117	171	160	151	151	145	139	133	125	NE
	E	371	374	337	267	129	178	166	155	149	142	134	E
	SE	265	311	328	315	273	206	93	129	128	116	108	SE
	S	75	84	262	224	256	263	242	201	79	151	86	S
	SW	83	97	109	122	215	228	282	314	320	291	234	SW
	W	104	118	129	137	142	151	276	286	349	370	349	W
	NW	102	115	127	134	140	143	143	148	268	258	286	NW
	Horiz.	244	303	351	383	399	401	389	369	335	283	222	Horiz.
Jul 4	N	125	126	130	136	143	146	143	140	131	125	124	N
	NE	285	240	120	173	164	155	153	149	141	133	125	NE
	E	370	370	333	263	127	177	162	153	144	136	129	E
	SE	266	309	326	311	270	206	93	129	124	111	103	SE
	S	76	84	264	222	254	265	247	204	79	150	83	S
	SW	86	98	109	124	218	233	289	321	323	289	234	SW
	W	109	121	132	140	146	155	280	291	350	368	351	W
	NW	106	118	129	138	144	147	144	151	263	255	287	NW
	Horiz.	366	294	342	371	387	396	388	366	326	271	212	Horiz.

Table continues

Table 5.22 Solar cooling loads for fast-response building with single clear glazing: **NW England, intermittent shading — *continued***

Date	Orient-ation	Solar cooling load at stated sun time (W·m⁻²)											Orient-ation
		0730	0830	0930	1030	1130	1230	1330	1430	1530	1630	1730	
Aug 4	N	74	87	94	103	107	111	112	108	102	92	89	N
	NE	231	107	210	131	130	127	128	123	117	108	99	NE
	E	325	326	289	233	104	150	140	128	122	112	104	E
	SE	256	297	310	310	277	214	90	134	120	102	93	SE
	S	66	92	291	239	274	280	263	221	83	169	93	S
	SW	70	84	97	114	230	236	291	315	300	263	202	SW
	W	78	92	104	114	117	128	254	258	297	305	272	W
	NW	75	89	102	111	114	119	120	123	122	315	210	NW
	Horiz.	283	245	287	327	351	353	344	317	269	217	99	Horiz.
Sep 4	N	42	53	65	76	82	86	85	81	72	64	55	N
	NE	161	71	145	87	99	100	99	95	86	77	67	NE
	E	261	282	272	219	87	129	115	103	94	86	75	E
	SE	228	285	327	336	302	233	89	151	103	85	73	SE
	S	49	200	215	279	314	313	297	257	190	69	106	S
	SW	54	66	80	103	273	256	310	339	325	256	179	SW
	W	54	65	79	90	96	108	231	244	289	267	215	W
	NW	59	71	84	96	102	106	105	104	89	184	75	NW
	Horiz.	103	280	232	277	300	298	287	261	215	87	169	Horiz.
Oct 4	N	18	27	38	50	57	61	62	57	49	38	27	N
	NE	68	102	72	62	63	66	67	62	54	43	32	NE
	E	213	195	201	159	53	88	76	64	57	45	35	E
	SE	204	224	275	283	262	214	73	145	65	54	41	SE
	S	51	194	208	261	295	307	278	238	170	61	99	S
	SW	35	45	58	70	275	244	273	286	249	184	68	SW
	W	33	43	53	65	73	83	98	313	202	175	67	W
	NW	25	34	45	57	65	68	69	65	64	73	100	NW
	Horiz.	40	79	233	178	200	207	190	163	61	134	78	Horiz.
Nov 4	N	7	13	21	30	38	41	42	38	29	20	13	N
	NE	8	36	31	35	39	42	43	39	30	21	14	NE
	E	15	183	153	55	143	68	55	46	37	29	21	E
	SE	21	223	232	253	254	219	72	154	61	37	28	SE
	S	29	75	302	247	300	320	290	224	78	158	72	S
	SW	21	28	37	63	275	242	267	245	189	64	101	SW
	W	15	21	29	38	46	54	70	248	136	48	87	W
	NW	8	14	22	31	39	42	43	39	33	29	33	NW
	Horiz.	25	40	74	124	158	280	60	166	118	71	39	Horiz.
Dec 4	N	4	4	9	16	22	26	25	22	16	10	4	N
	NE	4	4	19	18	23	26	25	23	17	10	4	NE
	E	10	10	170	41	125	50	35	29	23	17	10	E
	SE	19	19	267	242	242	201	65	139	55	26	19	SE
	S	21	21	215	239	285	292	256	189	62	95	21	S
	SW	18	18	25	56	270	221	234	204	68	123	18	SW
	W	13	13	18	25	32	38	51	119	146	89	13	W
	NW	4	4	10	16	23	26	25	23	18	20	4	NW
	Horiz.	16	16	31	65	103	122	121	99	63	31	16	Horiz.

Glazing configuration (inside to outside)	Correction factor for stated building response		Glazing configuration (inside to outside)	Correction factor for stated building response	
	Fast	Slow		Fast	Slow
Clear/blind	0.78	0.85	Clear/clear/reflecting/blind	0.32	0.38
Absorbing/blind	0.54	0.59	Clear/clear/blind/absorbing	0.39	0.42
Reflecting/blind	0.53	0.57	Clear/clear/absorbing/blind	0.34	0.39
Clear/blind/clear	0.70	0.74	Low-E/clear/blind	0.58	0.64
Clear/clear/blind	0.59	0.64	Low-E/reflecting/blind	0.38	0.43
Clear/blind/reflecting	0.47	0.50	Low-E/absorbing/blind	0.40	0.48
Clear/reflecting/blind	0.38	0.43	Low-E/clear/blind/clear	0.56	0.60
Clear/blind/absorbing	0.50	0.52	Low-E/clear/clear/blind	0.51	0.62
Clear/absorbing/blind	0.40	0.44	Low-E/clear/blind/reflecting	0.37	0.40
Clear/clear/blind/clear	0.56	0.61	Low-E/clear/reflecting/blind	0.33	0.41
Clear/clear/clear/blind	0.50	0.56	Low-E/clear/blind/absorbing	0.40	0.42
Clear/clear/blind/reflecting	0.37	0.40	Low-E/clear/absorbing/blind	0.38	0.42

Table continues

Table 5.22 Solar cooling loads for fast-response building with single clear glazing: **NW England, intermittent shading** — *continued*

Glazing configuration (inside to outside)	Correction factor for stated building response		Glazing configuration (inside to outside)	Correction factor for stated building response	
	Fast	Slow		Fast	Slow
Blind/clear	1.00	1.04	Blind/low-E/clear	0.92	0.92
Blind/reflecting	0.68	0.71	Blind/low-E/reflecting	0.59	0.60
Blind/absorbing	0.74	0.75	Blind/low-E/absorbing	0.62	0.63
Blind/clear/clear	0.94	0.95	Blind/low-E/clear/clear	0.83	0.83
Blind/clear/reflecting	0.61	0.62	Blind/low-E/clear/reflecting	0.53	0.53
Blind/clear/absorbing	0.66	0.66	Blind/low-E/clear/absorbing	0.55	0.54
Blind/clear/clear/clear	0.85	0.85			
Blind/clear/clear/reflecting	0.54	0.55			
Blind/clear/clear/absorbing	0.57	0.56			
Air node correction factor:					
— internal blind	0.91	0.88			
— mid-pane blind	0.87	0.83			
— external blind	0.88	0.85			

Table 5.23 Solar cooling loads for fast-response building with single clear glazing: **NE Scotland (lowlands), intermittent shading**

Date	Orient-ation	Solar cooling load at stated sun time (W·m⁻²)											Orient-ation
		0730	0830	0930	1030	1130	1230	1330	1430	1530	1630	1730	
Jan 29	N	4	7	11	19	25	31	32	25	17	10	7	N
	NE	5	12	24	21	25	31	33	26	18	11	7	NE
	E	10	20	221	125	39	58	43	31	23	17	13	E
	SE	16	106	216	280	277	228	154	48	53	23	19	SE
	S	26	34	262	279	331	341	321	246	81	123	34	S
	SW	17	19	24	137	187	253	292	266	163	48	26	SW
	W	11	13	17	25	31	42	138	140	49	123	19	W
	NW	5	7	11	20	25	31	33	26	19	22	11	NW
	Horiz.	20	26	40	85	126	151	153	128	82	39	25	Horiz.
Feb 26	N	11	16	26	35	40	43	43	40	35	26	16	N
	NE	36	66	47	42	43	46	46	43	38	28	19	NE
	E	68	287	208	169	55	75	59	50	45	36	26	E
	SE	73	328	307	342	315	248	164	57	65	46	34	SE
	S	48	191	240	323	364	363	343	278	185	66	89	S
	SW	31	36	48	152	208	278	327	321	258	87	159	SW
	W	24	29	38	47	52	61	173	187	193	68	149	W
	NW	15	20	30	39	44	47	48	45	43	48	65	NW
	Horiz.	30	48	102	268	177	179	168	63	160	99	48	Horiz.
Mar 29	N	38	48	59	69	76	81	81	77	69	59	48	N
	NE	106	122	113	88	84	88	88	84	75	66	55	NE
	E	241	220	238	185	67	111	98	86	78	69	57	E
	SE	127	374	311	306	281	229	85	163	83	78	64	SE
	S	50	191	220	266	303	312	301	246	179	66	106	S
	SW	57	68	83	87	290	261	312	312	283	221	86	SW
	W	57	68	80	90	97	110	229	219	244	222	89	W
	NW	50	62	74	84	91	96	96	94	94	120	151	NW
	Horiz.	79	125	327	227	250	255	248	214	85	200	134	Horiz.
Apr 28	N	64	78	84	92	98	101	101	98	92	85	78	N
	NE	198	95	193	113	122	120	119	116	111	104	93	NE
	E	289	330	305	239	104	147	134	123	117	110	100	E
	SE	239	316	345	341	305	239	97	151	119	100	90	SE
	S	65	199	214	272	309	319	301	254	180	68	105	S
	SW	72	84	94	113	265	266	324	347	320	276	200	SW
	W	80	93	103	111	116	127	255	268	302	308	257	W
	NW	75	87	97	105	111	114	113	115	106	289	189	NW
	Horiz.	153	368	280	317	339	346	336	307	255	202	94	Horiz.
May 29	N	111	116	118	125	130	133	131	129	126	155	116	N
	NE	285	229	113	150	149	144	142	141	137	130	120	NE
	E	389	382	338	264	126	168	154	147	144	136	126	E
	SE	291	334	350	337	294	225	100	140	130	115	105	SE
	S	78	94	306	252	285	296	276	228	88	177	95	S
	SW	85	96	105	120	234	250	308	330	328	298	231	SW
	W	102	114	123	130	135	144	268	281	339	362	328	W
	NW	99	110	119	126	131	134	132	138	235	238	259	NW
	Horiz.	253	306	351	382	398	406	395	364	326	276	134	Horiz.
Jun 21	N	129	132	133	139	142	145	145	143	140	134	131	N
	NE	283	233	114	155	148	144	144	141	138	131	121	NE
	E	384	385	344	269	131	172	161	152	149	142	133	E
	SE	281	329	346	335	289	219	99	136	131	117	107	SE
	S	81	91	290	245	277	284	266	220	86	167	91	S
	SW	92	102	111	125	228	246	306	332	330	310	257	SW
	W	113	123	132	139	142	152	278	291	349	386	378	W
	NW	110	120	129	136	139	143	143	148	254	262	303	NW
	Horiz.	255	311	357	390	403	404	397	370	332	289	234	Horiz.
Jul 4	N	122	126	128	136	140	143	142	140	135	127	126	N
	NE	275	225	113	157	154	148	147	145	140	132	123	NE
	E	372	368	327	262	130	176	164	155	151	143	134	E
	SE	274	315	329	321	283	219	99	141	133	117	109	SE
	S	82	94	287	239	272	282	264	221	87	172	94	S
	SW	88	100	109	125	231	242	297	324	325	293	231	SW
	W	108	119	128	136	141	150	273	283	341	360	333	W
	NW	105	116	126	134	138	141	140	146	247	244	269	NW
	Horiz.	255	306	346	379	397	403	395	371	336	286	140	Horiz.

Table continues

Table 5.23 Solar cooling loads for fast-response building with single clear glazing: **NE Scotland (lowlands), intermittent shading** — *continued*

Date	Orient-ation	Solar cooling load at stated sun time (W·m⁻²)											Orient-ation
		0730	0830	0930	1030	1130	1230	1330	1430	1530	1630	1730	
Aug 4	N	80	93	98	107	112	117	115	112	107	99	93	N
	NE	220	105	207	130	135	133	131	129	124	116	105	NE
	E	308	323	294	236	107	157	144	133	128	121	109	E
	SE	250	303	323	322	282	225	97	151	129	111	100	SE
	S	77	107	322	257	281	294	279	229	88	183	106	S
	SW	83	95	106	125	253	252	303	312	291	259	107	SW
	W	94	106	117	125	131	143	264	255	287	296	129	W
	NW	90	101	112	121	126	131	129	132	128	303	99	NW
	Horiz.	289	246	288	324	336	346	338	304	259	114	248	Horiz.
Sep 4	N	46	57	66	75	82	85	87	84	76	67	57	N
	NE	191	193	145	83	98	99	100	97	89	80	69	NE
	E	252	292	280	215	85	128	116	105	97	88	76	E
	SE	224	300	345	334	298	229	88	156	108	89	75	SE
	S	55	220	233	283	314	302	271	240	89	190	102	S
	SW	62	74	88	107	287	250	282	309	278	208	83	SW
	W	67	80	91	100	107	118	132	369	250	219	93	W
	NW	58	70	82	91	98	101	102	102	89	134	157	NW
	Horiz.	107	280	231	261	280	272	252	232	95	219	150	Horiz.
Oct 4	N	18	26	37	46	53	56	57	53	47	37	27	N
	NE	70	109	73	58	58	61	62	58	52	42	32	NE
	E	233	222	223	170	56	86	71	62	56	46	35	E
	SE	225	257	313	316	293	221	74	148	69	56	43	SE
	S	57	224	239	294	336	314	275	240	88	174	96	S
	SW	38	46	61	71	304	245	267	282	230	82	18	SW
	W	34	43	54	63	70	79	94	301	184	71	184	W
	NW	24	32	43	53	59	62	63	60	60	66	87	NW
	Horiz.	42	81	238	178	201	194	175	67	186	123	75	Horiz.
Nov 4	N	6	10	17	26	35	37	36	31	25	16	10	N
	NE	7	30	27	30	36	38	37	32	25	17	11	NE
	E	12	194	180	144	44	64	47	38	31	23	17	E
	SE	23	244	285	308	274	218	72	150	61	35	27	SE
	S	27	160	231	295	318	315	279	227	79	151	66	S
	SW	18	23	31	146	182	235	254	249	187	59	89	SW
	W	17	21	28	37	46	53	66	243	55	167	80	W
	NW	7	11	18	27	35	38	36	32	28	24	27	NW
	Horiz.	25	36	65	121	158	173	167	141	106	61	36	Horiz.
Dec 4	N	3	3	7	11	18	22	22	18	11	6	3	N
	NE	3	3	7	13	18	22	22	18	12	6	3	NE
	E	10	10	102	37	129	48	31	24	18	13	10	E
	SE	17	17	240	250	265	229	157	49	57	27	17	SE
	S	23	23	198	253	317	343	322	217	67	102	23	S
	SW	18	18	28	135	182	256	293	231	71	128	18	SW
	W	8	8	12	16	22	29	120	112	37	84	8	W
	NW	3	3	7	12	18	22	22	18	13	7	3	NW
	Horiz.	13	13	24	47	85	106	110	89	48	23	13	Horiz.

Glazing configuration (inside to outside)	Correction factor for stated building response		Glazing configuration (inside to outside)	Correction factor for stated building response	
	Fast	Slow		Fast	Slow
Clear/blind	0.79	0.94	Clear/clear/reflecting/blind	0.32	0.35
Absorbing/blind	0.53	0.56	Clear/clear/blind/absorbing	0.40	0.41
Reflecting/blind	0.51	0.52	Clear/clear/absorbing/blind	0.34	0.36
Clear/blind/clear	0.70	0.73	Low-E/clear/blind	0.59	0.64
Clear/clear/blind	0.62	0.72	Low-E/reflecting/blind	0.37	0.40
Clear/blind/reflecting	0.47	0.49	Low-E/absorbing/blind	0.40	0.44
Clear/reflecting/blind	0.38	0.40	Low-E/clear/blind/clear	0.56	0.59
Clear/blind/absorbing	0.50	0.52	Low-E/clear/clear/blind	0.51	0.62
Clear/absorbing/blind	0.40	0.43	Low-E/clear/blind/reflecting	0.37	0.39
Clear/clear/blind/clear	0.57	0.58	Low-E/clear/reflecting/blind	0.34	0.39
Clear/clear/clear/blind	0.51	0.56	Low-E/clear/blind/absorbing	0.40	0.40
Clear/clear/blind/reflecting	0.37	0.39	Low-E/clear/absorbing/blind	0.38	0.40

Table continues

Table 5.23 Solar cooling loads for fast-response building with single clear glazing: **NE Scotland (lowlands), intermittent shading** — *continued*

Glazing configuration (inside to outside)	Correction factor for stated building response		Glazing configuration (inside to outside)	Correction factor for stated building response	
	Fast	Slow		Fast	Slow
Blind/clear	1.00	1.04	Blind/low-E/clear	0.92	0.92
Blind/reflecting	0.68	0.71	Blind/low-E/reflecting	0.59	0.60
Blind/absorbing	0.74	0.75	Blind/low-E/absorbing	0.63	0.63
Blind/clear/clear	0.94	0.95	Blind/low-E/clear/clear	0.84	0.84
Blind/clear/reflecting	0.62	0.62	Blind/low-E/clear/reflecting	0.53	0.53
Blind/clear/absorbing	0.66	0.66	Blind/low-E/clear/absorbing	0.55	0.55
Blind/clear/clear/clear	0.86	0.86			
Blind/clear/clear/reflecting	0.55	0.55			
Blind/clear/clear/absorbing	0.57	0.57			
Air node correction factor:					
— internal blind	0.91	0.88			
— mid-pane blind	0.87	0.83			
— external blind	0.88	0.85			

References

1 Almadari F and Hammond G P Improved data correlations for buoyancy driven convection in rooms *Building Serv. Eng. Res. Technol.* **4**(3) 106–112 (1980)

2 Hatton A and Awbi H B Convective heat transfer in rooms *Proc. Building Simulation '95, August 1995, Wisconsin, USA* (1995)

3 *BS 5643:1984: Glossary of refrigeration, heating, ventilating and air conditioning terms* (London: British Standards Institution) (1984)

4 *Environmental criteria for design* CIBSE Guide A1 (London: Chartered Institution of Building Services Engineers) (1986) (out of print)

5 *prEN 410 Glass in buildings: Determination of luminous and solar characteristics of glazing* (draft) (Brussels: Comité Européen de Normalisation) (available in UK through BSI) (October 1994)

6 *A Guide to Current Practice* (London: Institution of Heating and Ventilating Engineers) (1959) (out of print)

7 *Design Data* IHVE Guide A (London: Institution of Heating and Ventilating Engineers) (1970) (out of print)

8 Holmes M J Heat loss from rooms: comparison of determination methods *Building Serv. Eng. Res. Technol.* **9**(2) 69-78 (1988)

9 Davies M G Flaws in the environmental temperature model *Building Serv. Eng. Res. Technol.* **13**(4) 209–215 (1992)

10 Davies M G The basis for a room global temperature *Phil. Trans. Roy. Soc. A.* **339** 153–191 (1992)

11 *Thermal response of buildings* CIBSE Guide A5 (London: Chartered Institution of Building Services Engineers) (1986) (out of print)

12 Milbank N O and Harrington-Lynn J Thermal response and the admittance procedure *Building Serv. Eng.* **42** 38–51 (May 1974)

13 *Passive and hybrid solar commercial buildings: Advanced Case Studies Seminar, April 1991* (Harwell: Energy Technology Support Unit) (1991)

14 Lomas K J et. al. Empirical validation of thermal building simulation programs using test room data *IEA Energy conservation in buildings and community systems programme Annex 21* (Leicester: De Montfort University/International Energy Agency) (September 1994)

15 Mitalas G P and Stephenson D G Room thermal response factors *ASHRAE Trans.* **73** 2.1–2.10 (1967)

16 Stephenson D G and Mitalas G P Calculation of heat conduction transfer functions for multi-layer slabs *ASHRAE Trans.* **77** 117–126 (1971)

17 *Non-residential cooling and heating load calculations* ASHRAE Handbook: Fundamentals chapter 28 (Atlanta GA, USA: American Society of Heating Refrigerating and Air-conditioning Engineers) (1997)

18 Krief K *Principals of Heat Transfer* (New York: Harper and Row) (1976)

19 Clarke J A *Energy simulation in building design* (Bristol: Adam Hilger) (1985)

20 Fanger P O *Thermal Comfort* (Copenhagen: Danish Technical Press) (1970)

21 Holmes M J and Connor P A ROOM: A method to predict thermal comfort at any point in a space *Proc. CIBSE Nat. Conf., Canterbury, 1991* (London: Chartered Institution of Building Services Engineers) (1991)

22 *Building Regulations Approved Document L: Conservation of fuel and power* (London: The Stationery Office) (1995)

23 *Natural ventilation in non-domestic buildings* CIBSE Applications Manual AM10 (London: Chartered Institution of Building Services Engineers) (1997)

24 Pascoe C and Hejab M *Small power loads* BSRIA Technical Note TN8/92 (Bracknell: Building Services Research and Information Association) (1992)

25 *Weather and solar data* CIBSE Guide (London: Chartered Institution of Building Services Engineers) (to be published)

26 *Healthy workplaces* CIBSE Guidance Note GN2 (London: Chartered Institution of Building Services Engineers) (1993)

27 *Health and Safety (Display Screen Equipment) Regulations 1992* (London: Stationery Office) (1992)

28 *Ventilation and air conditioning (systems, equipment and control)* CIBSE Guide B3 (London: Chartered Institution of Building Services Engineers) (1986)

29 Holmes M J and Hitchen E R An Example Weather Year for the calculation of energy demand in buildings *Building Serv. Eng.* **45** 186–189 (1978)

30 *Passive solar design studies: Provision of weather data* ETSU Passive Solar Programme: UK Meteorological Data — Example Weather Years (Harwell: Energy Technology Support Unit) (1991)

31   *Building energy and environmental modelling* CIBSE Applications Manual AM11 (London: Chartered Institution of Building Services Engineers) (1998)

32   Judkoff R and Neymark J *Building Energy Simulation Test (BESTEST) and diagnostic method* Report NREL/TP-472-6231 (Golden, CO: US National Renewable Energy Laboratory) (1994)

33   Jones R   Modelling water vapour conditions in buildings *Building Serv. Eng. Res. Technol.* **14**(3) 99–106 (1993)

34   Cunningham M J Modelling of moisture transfer in structures 1: A description of a finite difference model *Building and Environment* **25**(1) 55–61 (1990)

35   Huang C L D Multi-phase moisture transfer in porous media subjected to temperature gradient *Int. J. Heat Mass Transfer* **22** 1293–1307 (1973)

36   Luikov A V Systems of differential equations of heat and mass transfer in capillary porous bodies (review) *Int. J. Heat Mass Transfer* **18** 1–14 (1975)

37   Philip J R and DeVries D R Moisture movement in porous media under temperature gradients *Trans. Am. Geophysical Union* **38**(2) 222–232 (1957)

38   Davies M G The thermal response of an enclosure to periodic excitation: the CIBSE approach *Building and Environment* **29**(2) 217–235 (1994)

39   Harrington-Lynn J The admittance procedure: variable ventilation *Building Serv. Eng.* **42** 199–200 (November 1974)

40   Harrington-Lynn J The admittance procedure: intermittent plant operation *Building Serv. Eng.* **42** 219–221 (December 1974)

41   *Estimating plant capacity* CIBSE Guide A9 (London: Chartered Institution of Building Services Engineers) (1986) (out of print)

42   Wilkins C K, Kosonen R and Laine T An analysis of office equipment load factors *ASHRAE J.* **33**(9) 38–44 (1991)

43   Hosni M H, Jones B W, Sipes J M and Xu Y Total heat gain and the split between radiant and convective heat gain from office and laboratory equipment in buildings *ASHRAE Trans.* **104**(1A) 356–365 (1998)

44   Wagner B S Comparisons of predicted and measured energy use in occupied buildings. *ASHRAE Trans.* **90**(2B) 232–253 (June 1984)

45   *BS 8207: 1985: Code of practice for energy efficiency in buildings* (London: British Standards Institution) (1985)

46   Knebel D E Simplified energy analysis using the modified BIN method (Atlanta GA: American Society of Heating, Refrigerating and Air-conditioning Engineers) (1983)

47   *Energy demands and targets for heated and ventilated buildings* CIBSE Building Energy Code 1 (London: Chartered Institution of Building Services Engineers) (1999)

48   Jackman P J *Air movement in rooms with ceiling mounted diffusers* HVRA Laboratory Report 81 (Bracknell: Building Services Research and Information Association) (1973)

49   Holmes M J *Designing variable volume systems for a room air movement* BSRIA Application Guide AG1/74 (Bracknell: Building Services Research and Information Association) (1974)

50   *Heating* CIBSE Guide B1 (London: Chartered Institution of Building Services Engineers) (1986)

51   Martin P L and Oughton D R *Faber and Kell's Heating and air conditioning of buildings* (London: Butterworth/Heinemann) (1989)

52   Birtles A B and John R W A new optimum start algorithm *Building Serv. Eng. Res. Technol.* **6**(3) 117–122 (1985)

53   Adams S and Holmes M J *System simulation: A study of the effects of boiler oversize and heating controls on the energy consumption of a heating system* BSRIA Project Report 15/111 (Bracknell: Building Services Research and Information Association) (1978)

54   *Heat transfer* CIBSE Guide C3 (London: Chartered Institution of Building Services Engineers) (1986)

55   Jamieson H C The Mechanical Services at Shell Centre *J. Inst. Heating Ventilating Eng.* **31** 1–35 1963 (1963)

56   Harrington-Lynn J Derivation of equations for intermittent heating used in CIBSE Building Energy Code Part 2a *Building Serv. Eng. Res. Technol.* **19**(4) (1998)

57   *Thermal storage: environmental benefits* CIBSE Research Report RR06 (London: Chartered Institution of Building Services Engineers) (May 1997)

58   *Space heating by medium temperature radiant panels* HVRA Laboratory Report 36 (Bracknell: Building Services Research and Information Association) (1966)

59   *Siting of medium temperature radiant heating strip panels in long rooms* HVRA Laboratory Report 40 (Bracknell: Building Services Research and Information Association) (1967)

60   *Ice storage* CIBSE Technical Memoranda TM18 (London: Chartered Institution of Building Services Engineers) (1994)

61   Holmes M J Design for ventilation *Proc. 6th AIC Conf., Ventilation strategies and measurement techniques, Netherlands 16–19 September 1985* (1985)

62   Awbi H B *Ventilation of buildings* (London: E & F N Spon) (1991)

63   Linden P F, Lane Serff G F and Smeed D A Emptying filling boxes: the fluid mechanics of natural ventilation *J. Fluid Mech.* **212** 309–335 (1990)

64   Liddament M W *Air infiltration calculation techniques: an application guide* (Coventry: Air Infiltration and Ventilation Centre) (1986)

Appendix 5.A1: Derivation of steady-state thermal models

5.A1.1 Notation

Symbols used in this appendix are as follows.

A_n	Area of surface n (m^2)
a, b	Linearising constants
b_n	Radiant heat transfer coefficient (W·m^{-2}·K^{-1})
c_p	Specific heat capacity of air (J·kg^{-1}·K^{-1})
C_v	Ventilation conductance (W·K^{-1})
E_{bn}	Black body radiation from surface n (W·m^{-2})
F_a	fraction of air temperature detected by sensor (0.5 for a dry resultant temperature sensor)
$F_{m,n}$	View factor from surface m to surface n
h_a	Heat transfer coefficient between air and environmental nodes (W·m^{-2}·K^{-1})
H_c	Thermal transmittance due to convection (W·K^{-1})
h_c	Convective heat transfer coefficient (W·m^{-2}·K^{-1})
h_{cn}	Convective heat transfer coefficient for surface n (W·m^{-2}·K^{-1})
H_r	Thermal transmittance due to radiation (W·K^{-1})
h_r	Radiative heat transfer coefficient (W·m^{-2}·K^{-1})
$\mathcal{J}_n$	Radiosity of surface n (W·m^{-2})
L_n	Long-wave radiant heat flux incident on surface n (W·m^{-2})
m	Integer denoting particular surface
$\dot{m}_a$	Mass flow rate of air (kg·s^{-1})
N	Total number of surfaces
N_v	Number of room air changes (h^{-1})
n	Integer denoting particular surface
Q_a	convective energy from emitter (W)
Q_f	Fabric heat gain (W)
Q_{ln}	Long-wave energy incident on surface n from sources other than room surfaces (W)
Q_r	radiant energy from emitter (W)
q_n	Radiant heat flow from surface n (W·m^{-2})
Q_t	Total heat loss (W)
R	Radiant fraction of source from source
R_{sin}	Thermal resistance between inner face of surface n and environmental temperature (m^2·K·W^{-1})
R_{sn}	Thermal resistance of surface n (m^2·K·W^{-1})
t_{ai}	Inside air temperature (°C)
t_{ain}	Air temperature for convective heat exchange with surface n (°C)
t_c	Dry resultant temperature at centre of room (°C)
$t_c{'}$	Dry resultant temperature on far side of internal partition through which heat flow occurs (°C)
t_{ei}	Environmental temperature (°C)
t_o	External heat transfer temperature (°C)
t_{on}	External heat transfer temperature for surface n (°C)
t_r	Mean radiant temperature (°C)
t_s	Surface temperature (°C)
t_{sn}	Surface temperature of surface n (°C)
t^*	Radiant-star temperature (°C)
U_n	Thermal transmittance for material of which surface n is composed (W·m^{-2}·K^{-1})
$U_n{'}$	Thermal transmittance between inner face of surface n and heat transfer temperature on outer face of surface n (W·m^{-2}·K^{-1})
U_p	Thermal transmittance modified for heat flow through internal partition (W·m^{-2}·K^{-1})
V	Room volume (m^3)
α	Surface absorption coefficient
ε_n	emissivity of surface n

5.A1.2 Full Model

The rate of loss of heat from a space through the building fabric can be expressed as:

$$Q_f = \sum_{n=1}^{N} A_n (t_{sn} - t_{on}) / R_{sn} \qquad (5.60)$$

The rate of heat flow through a wall is equal to that into the wall, thus the fabric heat loss can also be expressed as:

$$Q_f = \sum_{n=1}^{N} [A_n (t_{ain} - t_{sn}) h_{cn} - q_n] \qquad (5.61)$$

Note that q_n is positive for heat flows leaving the surface.

The first term inside the square brackets represents the rate of convection of heat from the room air to the surface and the second term is the rate of radiant heat flow into the surface. This radiant term represents the exchange of long-wave radiation between the surface and all other surfaces within the room. (The calculation of steady-state loss ignores short-wave radiation.) The exchange of long-wave radiation can be seen as analogous to the reflection of light from a diffuse source, i.e. there are an infinite number of reflections of radiation between the surfaces.

The rate of radiant heat flow into the surface is the difference between that incident (L_n) upon the surface and that leaving the surface ($\mathcal{J}_n$) that is:

$$q_n = A_n (\mathcal{J}_n - L_n) \qquad (5.62)$$

Now the rate at which radiant energy leaves a surface may be expressed as:

$$\mathcal{J}_n = (1 - \varepsilon_n) L_n + \varepsilon_n E_{bn} \qquad (5.63)$$

Thus:

$$q_n = A_n (E_{bn} - \mathcal{J}_n) \varepsilon_n / (1 - \varepsilon_n) \qquad (5.64)$$

The radiation incident upon the surface is the sum of that received from other surfaces and that from radiant heating sources. Radiation from another surface depends upon the view factor between that surface and the subject surface (n) and the rate at which radiation leaves that surface (i.e. the radiosity).

Thus the radiation incident upon surface n is:

$$A_n L_n = \sum_{m=1}^{N} (\mathcal{J}_m A_m F_{m,n}) - Q_{ln} \qquad (5.65)$$

However:

$$A_n F_{n,m} = A_m F_{m,n} \qquad (5.66)$$

Therefore:

$$A_n L_n = \sum_{m=1}^{N} (\mathcal{J}_m A_n F_{n,m}) - Q_{ln} \qquad (5.67)$$

This represents a set of simultaneous equations (one for each surface), that when solved give the amount of radiation leaving each surface ($\mathcal{J}_n$). Simultaneous solution means that the infinite number of reflections of radiation is accounted for automatically.

In order to solve equation 5.67 it is first necessary to substitute for L_n by combining equations 5.64 and 5.67. Assuming that $F_{n,m}$ is zero (i.e. that is all surfaces are planar), this results in the following equation set:

$$\mathcal{J}_n / (1 - \varepsilon_n) - \sum_{1}^{N} F_{n,m} \mathcal{J}_m \ldots \qquad (5.68)$$

$$= \varepsilon_n E_{bn} / (1 - \varepsilon_n) + Q_{ln} / A_n$$

This relationship is converted into a heat loss model by linearising the black body emissive power and introducing the steady state surface heat balance. Thus:

$$E_{bn} = a + b\, t_{sn} \qquad (5.69)$$

where a and b are constants.

From equation 5.60, for a single surface (n):

$$Q_f = A_n (t_{sn} - t_{on}) U_n' \qquad (5.70)$$

Therefore, equating 5.70 and 5.61 to eliminate Q_f gives:

$$-q_n + t_{ain} h_{cn} + U_n' t_{on} = t_{sn} (h_{cn} + U_n') \qquad (5.71)$$

U_n' is the transmittance between the surface temperature t_{sn} and the outside temperature t_{on}, i.e. the heat transfer temperature on the other side surface n, given by:

$$U_n' = U_n / (1 - U_n R_{sin}) \qquad (5.72)$$

R_{sin} is the standard value of the inner surface resistance used to calculate the standard U-value (see Section 3: *Thermal properties of building structures*) for surface n, U_n. Since U_n' is also dependent on the external surface heat transfer coefficient, i.e. the surface coefficient appropriate to the 'other' side of surface, it may be necessary to include a correction for exposure.

Substitution of equations 5.69 and 5.71 into equation 5.68 gives the following set of equations (5.73), which represent both radiant interchange between surfaces and the conduction of heat through room surfaces:

Equation 5.73 places no restrictions on the air temperature distribution within the space. A means of obtaining air temperatures would be to combine the solution of the above with computational fluid dynamics. Alternatively, some rules could be assigned to the distribution of air temperature throughout the space[A1.1].

5.A1.3 Reference Model

The Reference Model is developed by adding convective heat transfer and control sensor models to the Full Model and making some assumptions about the distribution of the radiant component of heat from the emitter.

The Full Model contains an arbitrary model of the convective heat transfer process. The Reference Model assumes a fully mixed space, i.e. the dry bulb temperature of the air does not vary from point to point within the space. Thus in equation 5.73 all values of t_{ain} are equal to the inside air temperature t_{ai} and the convective heat balance is then given by:

$$-\sum_{n=1}^{N} h_{cn} A_n t_{sn} + t_{ai} (\dot{m}_a c_p + \sum_{n=1}^{N} h_{cn} A_n)$$

$$= Q_t (1 - R) + t_{ao} \dot{m}_a c_p \qquad (5.75)$$

The model is completed by the introduction of the control temperature t_c, for example the dry resultant temperature which at low air speeds is the average of the air and mean radiant temperatures. The mean radiant temperature 'seen' by a sensor may be considered to be the equivalent temperature for radiant heat exchange between the sensor and its surroundings. It therefore depends upon:

— surface temperature

— surface emissivity

— emissivity of the sensor

— view factor between the surfaces and the sensor

— radiation from a heat emitter incident on the sensor.

Thus, the mean radiant temperature varies throughout the space. It is possible to model the sensor as an additional room surface. However, for the purposes of design calculations, the sensor is deemed to be located at a position where the proportion of long-wave radiation received from each surface is directly proportional to the ratio of the area of the surface to the total room area. Furthermore, the sensor is also assumed to have an emissivity of unity (i.e. a black body). Thus the design mean radiant temperature is:

$$(h_{cn} + U_n' + \varepsilon_n h_{rn})(t_{sn} / \varepsilon_n) - \sum_{m=1}^{N} (F_{n,m} / \varepsilon_m)[(h_{cm} + U_m')(1 - \varepsilon_m) + h_r \varepsilon_m] t_{sm} - (h_{cn} t_{ain} / \varepsilon_n) + \sum_{m=1}^{N} (F_{n,m} / \varepsilon_m)[h_{cm}(1 - \varepsilon_m) t_{aim}]$$

$$= (t_{on} U_n' / \varepsilon_n) - \sum_{m=1}^{N} (F_{n,m} / \varepsilon_m)[U_m'(1 - \varepsilon_m) t_{om}] + Q_{ln} / A_n \qquad (5.73)$$

where:

$$h_{rn} = \varepsilon_n b_n \qquad (5.74)$$

$$t_r = \frac{\sum \varepsilon_n t_{sn} A_n}{\sum A_n} + \frac{R Q_t}{h_r \sum A_n} \quad (5.76)$$

Note that h_r is calculated for an emissivity of unity.

The control temperature is given by:

$$t_c = F_a t_{ai} + (1 - F_a) t_r \quad (5.77)$$

where $F_a = 0.5$ if the sensed parameter is the dry resultant temperature.

Assuming that any radiant heat input is uniformly distributed over each surface, and is equal to $(Q_t R / \sum A)$, the Reference Model may be represented by the equation set:

$$A X = C \quad (5.78)$$

where A, X and C are matrices, defined as follows.

Matrix A:

(a)   Surface heat balance equations

Terms $A(n,n)$ for $n = 1$ to $n = $ total number of room surfaces:

$$A(n,n) = (h_{cn} + U_n' + h_r \varepsilon_n) / \varepsilon_n \quad (5.79)$$

Terms $A(n,m)$ where $n \neq m$, for $n = 1$ to $n = $ total number of room surfaces and for $m = 1$ to $m = $ total number of room surfaces:

$$A(n,m) = -F_{n,m} [(h_{cm} + U_m')(1 - \varepsilon_m) \\ + h_r \varepsilon_m)] / \varepsilon_m \quad (5.80)$$

Terms $A(n,m)$ for $n = 1$ to $n = $ total number of room surfaces and for $m = $ total number of room surfaces + 1:

$$A(n,m) = (-h_{cn} / \varepsilon_n) + \sum_{i=1}^{N} h_{ci} F_{n,i} (1 - \varepsilon_n) / \varepsilon_i \quad (5.81)$$

Terms $A(n,m)$ for $n = 1$ to $n = $ total number of room surfaces and for m = total number of room surfaces + 2:

$$A(n,m) = -R / \sum A \quad (5.82)$$

(b)   Control sensor heat balance equations

Terms $A(n,n)$ for $n = $ total number of room surfaces + 1:

$$A(n,n) = F_a \quad (5.83)$$

where F_a is the fraction of the air temperature detected by the sensor. ($F_a = 0.5$ for a dry resultant temperature sensor.)

Terms $A(n,m)$ for $n = $ total number of room surfaces + 1 and for $m = 1$ to $m = $ total number of room surfaces:

$$A(n,m) = \varepsilon_n (1 - F_a) A_n / \sum A \quad (5.84)$$

Terms $A(n,m)$ for $n = $ total number of room surfaces + 1 and for $m = $ total number of room surfaces + 2:

$$A(n,m) = R (1 - F_a) / (h_r \sum A) \quad (5.85)$$

(c)   Convection heat balance

Terms $A(n,n)$ for $n = $ total number of room surfaces + 2:

$$A(n,n) = (R - 1) / \sum A \quad (5.86)$$

Terms $A(n,m)$ for $n = $ total number of room surfaces + 2 and for $m = 1$ to $m = $ total number of room surfaces:

$$A(n,m) = -h_{cn} A_n / \sum A \quad (5.87)$$

Terms $A(n,m)$ for n = total number of room surfaces + 2 and for $m = $ total number of room surfaces + 1:

$$A(n,m) = [C_v + \sum (A_n h_{cn})] / \sum A \quad (5.88)$$

Vector C:

Terms $C(n)$ for $n = 1$ to $n = $ the total number of room surfaces:

$$C(n) = (t_{on} U_n' / \varepsilon_n) \\ - \sum_{i=1}^{N} [F_{n,i} U_n' t_{oi} (1 - \varepsilon_i) / \varepsilon_i] \quad (5.89)$$

Terms $C(n)$ for $n = $ total number of room surfaces + 1:

$$C(n) = t_c \quad (5.90)$$

Terms $C(n)$ for $n = $ total number of room surfaces + 2:

$$C(n) = t_{ao} C_v / \sum A \quad (5.91)$$

Solution vector X:

Terms $X(n)$ for $n = 1$ to $n = $ total number of room surfaces provide the temperatures for each surface.

Term $X(n)$ for $n = $ total number of room surfaces + 1 provides the room air temperature.

Term $X(n)$ for $n = $ total number of room surfaces + 2 provides the emitter output (i.e. sum of convective and radiant outputs).

The ventilation transmittance is represented by the conventional term C_v, see equation 5.7. If it is necessary to take account of air flows from a number of sources, that term in matrix A should be replaced by the summation $\sum (\dot{m}_a c_p)_i$ where the summation covers all sources i.

In vector C, the term $(t_{ao} C_v / \sum A)$ is then replaced by $[\sum (t_i \dot{m}_{ai} c_{pi}) / \sum A]$ where t_i is the temperature of air from source i.

View factors are not easy to calculate and while some standard relationships are given in Guide C3[A1.2] these will not cover many applications. Figure 5.7 and the following algorithm enables view factors to be determined for rectangular rooms[A1.3].

(a)   Two parallel room surfaces

Radiation shape factor (F_{1-2}) between parallel surfaces 1 and 2 separated by a distance G, see Figure 5.7(a), is given by:

$$2\pi(b_1-a_1)(d_1-c_1)F_{1\text{-}2} =$$

$$\{[P(b_2-b_1)+P(a_2-a_1)]\times[Q(c_2-c_1)+Q(d_2-d_1)$$

$$-Q(c_2-d_1)-Q(d_2-c_1)]\}$$

$$+\{[P(b_2-a_1)+P(a_2-b_1)]\times[Q(c_2-d_1)$$

$$+Q(d_2-c_1)-Q(c_2-c_1)-Q(d_2-d_1)]\} \qquad (5.92)$$

P and Q are functions; expanding equation 5.92 gives products of the form $P(b_2-b_1)Q(c_2-c_1)$, given by:

$$P(Z_1)Q(Z_2)=Z_1W\tan^{-1}(Z_1/W)$$
$$+Z_2V\tan^{-1}(Z_2/V)-(G^2/2)\ln[(W^2+Z_1^2)/W^2)] \qquad (5.93)$$

where Z_1 and Z_2 are generalised variables, e.g. $Z_1=(b_2-b_1)$ and $Z_2=(c_2-c_1)$, and:

$$V^2=G^2+Z_1^2 \qquad (5.94)$$

$$W^2=G^2+Z_2^2 \qquad (5.95)$$

(b)   Two perpendicular room surfaces

Radiation shape factor $(F_{1\text{-}2})$ between perpendicular surfaces 1 and 2, see Figure 5.7(a), is given by:

$$2\pi(b_1-a_1)(d_1-c_1)F_{1\text{-}2}=\{[R(b_2-b_1)+R(a_2-a_1)]$$

$$\times[S(c_2-c_1)+S(d_2-d_1)-S(c_2-d_1)-S(d_2-c_1)]\}$$

$$+\{[R(b_2-a_1)+R(a_2-b_1)]\times[S(c_2-d_1)$$

$$+S(d_2-c_1)-S(c_2-c_1)-S(d_2-d_1)]\} \qquad (5.96)$$

R and S are functions; expanding equation 5.96 gives products of the form $R(b_2-b_1)S(c_2-c_1)$, given by:

$$R(Z_1)S(Y_2-Y_1)=TZ_1\tan^{-1}(Z_1/T)$$
$$+\tfrac{1}{4}(Z_1^2-T^2)\ln(T^2+Z_1^2) \qquad (5.97)$$

where Z_1 and (Y_2-Y_1) are generalised variables, as above, and:

$$T^2=Y_2^2+Y_1^2 \qquad (5.98)$$

These equations when combined with view factor algebra will satisfy the majority of needs. The relevant view factor algebra is as follows.

For conservation of energy:

$$\sum_{m=1}^{M}F_{n,m}=1.0 \qquad (5.99)$$

where the summation is over all surfaces comprising the enclosure.

For reciprocity:

$$A_nF_{n,m}=A_mF_{m,n} \qquad (5.100)$$

If surface m is constructed from a number of sub-surfaces, e.g. windows, doors, wall, then:

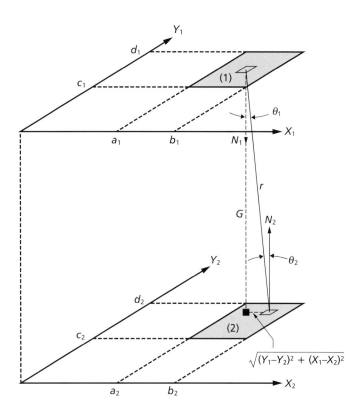

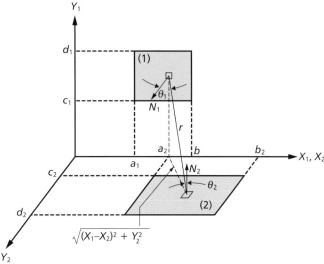

Figure 5.7 View factors for radiation heat exchange; (a) between two parallel room surfaces, (b) between two perpendicular room surfaces

$$A_nF_{n,m}=A_nF_{n,m1}+A_nF_{n,m2}+\ldots\ldots \qquad (5.101)$$

where surface m is made up from sub-surfaces $m1, m2$ etc.

For cases where non-rectangular or concealed surfaces are involved or where rooms are not orthogonal, numerical techniques will be necessary for calculating view factors. These methods usually make use of contour integration[A1.4] although statistically based methods have also been used[A1.5]. The application of these methods is outside of the scope of this Guide.

5.A1.4   Basic Model

The Reference Model considered the heat transfer process within a room from the view of direct surface-to-surface radiant heat flows, surface-to-air convection and surface-to-outside conduction. The surface-to-surface radiant flow is the most difficult of these processes to model. An alternative approach is to assume that just as all convective heat input must first increase the air temperature, i.e. enters the 'air temperature node' so all radiant heat enters at the 'radiant temperature node' (t^*). Heat then flows into each room surface by means of a heat transfer coefficient that is adjusted to take account of the multiple reflections of radiation between surfaces. Davies[A1.6] has shown that it is possible to make a very close approximation to the exact equivalent of the radiosity matrix used in the Reference Model for a six-sided enclosure.

In such a case the radiant heat transfer coefficient is equal to the product ($E^*_n h_r$) where:

$$E^*_n = \varepsilon_n / (1 - \varepsilon_n + \beta_n \varepsilon_n) \tag{5.102}$$

where β_n is given by the regression equation:

$$\beta_n = 1 - f_n [1 - 3.53 (f_n - 0.5) - 5.04 (f_n^2 - 0.25)] \tag{5.103}$$

where:

$$f_n = A_n / \Sigma A \tag{5.104}$$

The standard error for the regression is 0.0068 and the exact value of β_n for a cube is $5/6$.

While the terms β_n are specific to a six-sided enclosure, they can often be used in most design applications. Introducing this close approximation to the radiant exchange process, greatly simplifies matrix A at the minor expense of the introduction of a new temperature t^*, as follows:

$$(\sum_{n=1}^{N} h_{cn} A_n + \dot{m}_a c_p) t_{ai} - \sum_{n=1}^{N} h_{cn} A_n t_{sn} = Q_a + t_{ao} \dot{m}_a c_p \tag{5.105}$$

$$\sum_{n=1}^{N} h^*_r E^*_n A_n t^* - \sum_{n=1}^{N} h^*_r E^*_n A_n t_{sn} = Q_n + Q_r \tag{5.106}$$

where Q_a is the convective output from an emitter (W) and Q_r is the radiant output (W).

For each surface n:

$$-A_n h_{cn} t_{ai} - A_n E^*_n h_r t^* + (h_{cn} + E^*_n h_r + U'_n) A_n t_{sn}$$
$$= Q_n + t_{on} A_n U'_n \tag{5.107}$$

where Q_n is a heat input to surface n (W), e.g. the absorbed solar radiation incident upon the surface. For the purposes of a heat loss model, all Q_n are set to zero.

The Basic Model is given by the equation set represented by the matrix equation:

$$A^* X^* = C^* \tag{5.108}$$

where A^*, X^* and C^* are matrices, defined as follows.

Matrix A^*:

(a)   Surface heat balance

Terms $A^*(n,n)$ for $n = 1$ to $n = $ total number of room surfaces:

$$A^*(n,n) = (h_{cn} + U'_n + E^*_n h_r) \tag{5.109}$$

Terms $A^*(n,m)$ where $n \neq $ m, for $n = 1$ to $n = $ total number of room surfaces and for $m = 1$ to $m = $ total number of room surfaces:

$$A^*(n,m) = 0 \tag{5.110}$$

Terms $A^*(n,m)$ for $n = 1$ to $n = $ total number of room surfaces and for $m = $ total number of room surfaces + 1:

$$A^*(n,m) = -h_{cn} \tag{5.111}$$

Terms $A^*(n,m)$ for $n = 1$ to $n = $ total number of room surfaces and for $m = $ total number of room surfaces + 2:

$$A^*(n,m) = 0 \tag{5.112}$$

Terms $A^*(n,m)$ for $n = 1$ to $n = $ total number of room surfaces and for $m = $ total number of room surfaces + 3:

$$A^*(n,m) = -E^*_n h_r \tag{5.113}$$

(b)   Control sensor heat balance

Terms $A^*(n,n)$ for $n = $ total number of room surfaces + 1:

$$A^*(n,n) = F_a \tag{5.114}$$

Terms $A^*(n,m)$ for $n = $ total number of room surfaces + 1 and for $m = 1$ to $m = $ total number of room surfaces:

$$A^*(n,m) = \varepsilon_n (1 - F_a) A_n / \Sigma A \tag{5.115}$$

Terms $A^*(n,m)$ for $n = $ total number of room surfaces + 1 and for $m = $ total number of room surfaces + 2:

$$A^*(n,m) = R (1 - F_a) / (h_r \Sigma A) \tag{5.116}$$

Terms $A^*(n,m)$ for $n = $ total number of room surfaces + 1 and for $m = $ total number of room surfaces + 3:

$$A^*(n,m) = 0 \tag{5.117}$$

(c)   Convection heat balance

Terms $A^*(n,m)$ for $n = $ total number of room surfaces + 2 and for $m = 1$ to $m = $ total number of room surfaces:

$$A^*(n,m) = -h_{cn} A_n / \Sigma A \tag{5.118}$$

Terms $A^*(n,m)$ for $n = $ total number of room surfaces + 2 and for $m = $ total number of room surfaces + 1:

$$A^*(n,m) = [C_v + \Sigma (A_n h_{cn})] / \Sigma A \tag{5.119}$$

Terms $A^*(n,m)$ for $n = $ total number of room surfaces + 2 and for $m = $ total number of room surfaces + 2:

$$A^*(n,m) = (R - 1) / \Sigma A \tag{5.120}$$

Terms $A^*(n,m)$ for n = total number of room surfaces + 2 and for m = total number of room surfaces + 3:

$$A^*(n,m) = 0 \qquad (5.121)$$

(d)   Radiant heat balance

Terms $A^*(n,n)$ for n = total number of room surfaces + 3:

$$A^*(n,n) = \Sigma E^*_n h_r A_n / \Sigma A \qquad (5.122)$$

Terms $A^*(n,m)$ for n = total number of room surfaces + 3 and for m = 1 to m = total number of room surfaces:

$$A^*(n,m) = -E^*_n h_r A_n / \Sigma A \qquad (5.123)$$

Terms $A^*(n,m)$ for n = total number of room surfaces + 3 and for m = total number of room surfaces + 1:

$$A^*(n,m) = 0 \qquad (5.124)$$

Terms $A^*(n,m)$ for n = total number of room surfaces + 3 and for m = total number of room surfaces + 2:

$$A^*(n,m) = -R / \Sigma A \qquad (5.125)$$

Vector C^*:

Terms $C^*(n)$ for n = 1 to n = the total number of room surfaces:

$$C^*(n) = t_{on} U'_n \qquad (5.126)$$

Terms $C^*(n)$ for n = total number of room surfaces + 1:

$$C^*(n) = t_c \qquad (5.127)$$

Terms $C^*(n)$ for n = total number of room surfaces + 2:

$$C^*(n) = t_{ao} C_v / \Sigma A \qquad (5.128)$$

Terms $C^*(n)$ for n = total number of room surfaces + 3:

$$C^*(n) = 0 \qquad (5.129)$$

Solution vector X^*:

Terms $X^*(n)$ for n = 1 to n = total number of room surfaces provide the temperature of each surface.

Term $X^*(n)$ for n = total number of room surfaces + 1 provides the room air temperature.

Term $X^*(n)$ for n = total number of room surfaces + 2 provides the total heat input.

Term $X^*(n)$ for n = total number of room surfaces + 3 provides the radiant-star temperature (t^*), which is *not* the radiant temperature.

The ventilation transmittance is represented by the conventional term C_v, see equation 5.7. If it is necessary to take account of air flows from a number of sources, that term in matrix A^* should be replaced by the summation $\Sigma (\dot{m}_a c_p)_i$ where the summation covers all sources i.

In vector C^*, the term $(t_{ao} C_v / \Sigma A)$ is then replaced by

$[\Sigma (t_i \dot{m}_{ai} c_{pi}) / \Sigma A]$ where t_i is the temperature of air from source i.

5.A1.5   Simple Model

If the radiant exchange between surfaces can be treated separately, the surface heat balance equations are decoupled and the need for matrix manipulation is removed. This leads to a manual calculation procedure.

One means of achieving this approximation is to assume that, with the exception of the subject surface, all surface temperatures are known. In this case, the heat balance on the subject surface is described by the surface heat balance equations given for the Basic Model, see equation 5.107. Hence:

$$t_s (h_c + U' + E^* h_r) - h_c t_{ai} - E^* h_r t^* = t_o U' \qquad (5.130)$$

Rearranging equation 5.130 gives the fabric heat loss:

$$U' (t_s - t_o) = h_c (t_{ai} - t_s) + h_r E^* (t^* - t_s) \qquad (5.131)$$

It then remains to determine a value for E^*. A simple method should use parameters that are independent of the shape of the enclosure. The simplest assumption is that the subject surface has an area equivalent to one sixth of that of the enclosure of which it forms a part. Therefore, from equation 5.102, with $f_n = {}^1/_6$ (see equation 5.104) and $\beta_n = {}^5/_6$ (see equation 5.103):

$$E^* = \frac{\varepsilon}{(1 - \varepsilon + {}^5/_6 \varepsilon)} \qquad (5.132)$$

Now for $\varepsilon \approx 1, E^* \approx {}^6/_5 \varepsilon$, hence:

$$q_f = h_c (t_{ai} - t_s) + {}^6/_5 \varepsilon h_r (t^* - t_s) \qquad (5.133)$$

Equation 5.133 may be summed for all surfaces to give the total fabric loss, that is:

$$Q_f = h_c \Sigma A (t_{ai} - t_m) + {}^6/_5 \varepsilon h_r \Sigma A (t^* - t_m) \qquad (5.134)$$

where it is assumed that h_c and h_r are constants and that:

$$t_m = \Sigma A t_s / \Sigma A \qquad (5.135)$$

The heat input to a space comprises a radiant and convective component. From equation 5.106, the radiant component is:

$$Q_r = {}^6/_5 \varepsilon h_r \Sigma A (t^* - t_m) \qquad (5.136)$$

The convective components associated with the fabric heat loss is:

$$Q_c = h_c \Sigma A (t_{ai} - t_m) \qquad (5.137)$$

Equations 5.134, 5.136 and 5.137 can be expressed in analogue form by the network shown in Figure 5.8, where:

$$H_c = h_c \Sigma A \qquad (5.138)$$

and:

$$H_r = {}^6/_5 \varepsilon h_r \Sigma A \qquad (5.139)$$

Figure 5.8 shows a radiant input Q_r acting at the radiant star node t^*, being lost by conduction Q_f from t_s and by ventilation Q_v from t_{ai}. This network may be transformed exactly into that shown in Figure 5.9 where the rad-air node t_{ra} is located on the convective transmittance H_c, dividing it into two components: $X = H_c (H_c + H_r)/H_r$ and $Y = (H_c + H_r)$. An augmented flow, $Q_r (1 + H_c / H_r)$ acts at t_{ra} and the excess, $Q_r (H_c / H_r)$ is withdrawn from t_{ai}. Components X and Y can be considered, in effect, in parallel[A1.6]. The physically significant quantities, i.e. the observable temperatures t_s and t_{ai}, and the heat flows from them, Q_f and Q_v, can be considered the same in both cases.

There is a further transmittance, $[(H_c + H_r) H_c / H_r]$, between t_{ra} and t_{ai}. The rad-air temperature, t_{ra}, is related to the two generating temperatures by the following equation:

$$t_{ra} = \frac{H_c\, t_{ai}}{H_c + H_r} + \frac{H_r\, t^*}{H_c + H_r} \tag{5.140}$$

If the mean surface temperature, t_m, is taken as an approximation for t^*, then $t_{ra} \approx t_{ei}$. Hence:

$$t_{ei} = \frac{H_c\, t_{ai}}{H_c + H_r} + \frac{H_r\, t_m}{H_c + H_r} \tag{5.141}$$

It is appropriate to standardise the heat transfer coefficients as follows:

$h_c = 3.0\ \text{W·m}^{-2}\text{·K}^{-1}$ (an average figure)

$h_r = 5.7\ \text{W·m}^{-2}\text{·K}^{-1}$ (for temperatures $\approx 20\ ^\circ\text{C}$)

$H_r / \Sigma A = 6.0\ \text{W·m}^{-2}\text{·K}^{-1}$ (for $\varepsilon = 0.9$)

$H_c / \Sigma A = 3.0\ \text{W·m}^{-2}\text{·K}^{-1}$

Also,

$H_a / \Sigma A = (H_r + H_c) H_c / H_r = 4.5\ \text{W·m}^{-2}\text{·K}^{-1}$

So,

$h_a = 4.5\ \text{W·m}^{-2}\text{·K}^{-1}$

Therefore, it follows from equation 5.141 that:

$$t_{ei} = \tfrac{1}{3} t_{ai} + \tfrac{2}{3} t_m \tag{5.142}$$

That is, the effective radiant heat input is 1.5 times the actual input, with the excess (50%) of radiant input subtracted from the convective component of the heat input. A further implication is that a heat source that is effectively directly linked to the environmental temperature has the characteristics of $\tfrac{2}{3}$ radiation and $\tfrac{1}{3}$ convection.

It is accepted that a number of approximations are embodied in this relationship. However empirical testing over a number of years has not revealed any serious deficiencies in practice and, as such, it is therefore accepted as the basis of the CIBSE simple heat loss model, which is developed as follows.

The heat loss due to the fabric is defined as:

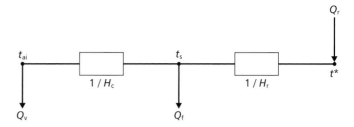

Figure 5.8 Simplified heat flow network

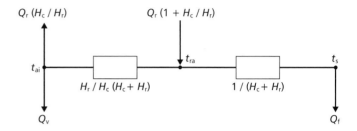

Figure 5.9 Equivalent heat flow network

$$Q_f = \sum_{n=1}^{N} A_n U_n (t_{ei} - t_{on}) \tag{5.143}$$

Where the fabric term contains heat loss through internal partitions, a modified U-value should be used:

$$U_p = \frac{U (t_c - t_c')}{(t_c - t_{ao})} \tag{5.144}$$

This correction is based on the internal design dry resultant temperature (t_c) and therefore is not exact. However, the dry resultant is usually very close to the heat loss temperature (t_{ei}) which means that any error is small in what is already a second order correction. This approximation makes it unnecessary to determine the value of the environmental temperature in adjacent spaces.

The heat loss due to infiltration and/or ventilation by outdoor air is:

$$Q_v = \frac{c_p\, \rho\, N_v\, V}{3600} (t_{ai} - t_{ao}) \tag{5.145}$$

For practical purposes $(c_p\, \rho / 3600) = \tfrac{1}{3}$, therefore $C_v = N_v V/3$.

Hence:

$$Q_v = C_v (t_{ai} - t_{ao}) \tag{5.146}$$

Ventilation rates must include infiltration, natural ventilation due to open windows and, where appropriate, mechanical ventilation. Guidance on ventilation requirements and design allowances for infiltration are given in Section 1: *Environmental criteria for design* and Section 4: *Infiltration and natural ventilation*, respectively.

The total heat loss is the sum of the fabric and infiltration losses:

$$Q_t = \sum_{n=1}^{N} A_n U_n (t_{ei} - t_{on}) + C_v (t_{ai} - t_{ao}) \qquad (5.147)$$

For winter heating design conditions it is conventional to assume that the outside heat transfer temperature (t_{on}) equals the outside air temperature (t_{ao}), therefore:

$$Q_t = \sum_{n=1}^{N} A_n U_n (t_{ei} - t_{ao}) + C_v (t_{ai} - t_{ao}) \qquad (5.148)$$

In order to relate the heat loss to the design dry resultant temperature, it is necessary to eliminate t_{ai} and t_{ei}. This is achieved by introducing factors F_{1cu} and F_{2cu}, as follows (see Appendix 5.A2, equations 5.169 and 5.170):

$$F_{1cu} = \frac{3.0 (C_v + 6.0 \Sigma A)}{\Sigma (A U) + 18.0 \Sigma A + 1.5 R [3.0 C_v - \Sigma (A U)]} \qquad (5.149)$$

$$F_{2cu} = \frac{\Sigma (A U) + 18.0 \Sigma A}{\Sigma (A U) + 18.0 \Sigma A + 1.5 R [3.0 C_v - \Sigma (A U)]} \qquad (5.150)$$

Therefore the Simple Model is:

$$Q_t = (F_{1cu} \sum_{n=1}^{N} A_n U_n + F_{2cu} C_v)(t_c - t_{ao}) \qquad (5.151)$$

and the corresponding air temperature is calculated using the following equation (see Appendix 5.A2.4, equation 5.172):

$$\bar{t}_{ai} = \frac{\bar{Q}_t (1 - 1.5 R) + C_v \bar{t}_{ao} + 6.0 \Sigma A \bar{t}_c}{C_v + 6.0 \Sigma A} \qquad (5.152)$$

References for Appendix 5.A1

A1.1   Gagneau S, Nataf J M and Wurtz E An illustration of automatic generation of zonal models *Proc. Int. Building Performance Simulation Association.Conf., Prague, Czech Republic* **2** 437–444 (1997)

A1.2   *Heat transfer* CIBSE Guide C3 (London: Chartered Institution of Building ServicesEngineers) (1986)

A1.3   *Energy calculation procedures to determine heating and cooling loads for computer analysis* (Atlanta GA: American Society of Heating Refrigerating and Air-conditioning Engineers) (1976)

A1.4   Walton G N *Algorithms for calculating radiation view factors between plane convex polygons with obstructions* NBSIR 86-3463 (Washington DC: US Department of Commerce) (October 1986)

A1.5   Malalasekera W M G and James E H Thermal radiation in a room: numerical evaluation *Building Serv. Eng. Res. Technol.* **14**(4) 159-168 (1993)

A1.6   Davies M G An idealised model for room radiant exchange *Building and Environment* **25**(4), 375–378 (1990)

Appendix 5.A2: Equations for determination of sensible heating and cooling loads

5.A2.1 Introduction

The Simple (dynamic) Model is based on the assumption that all loads and heat flows comprise a daily mean (or steady-state) value and an alternating component (i.e. swing, or deviation from the mean). The total load (or temperature) is the sum of these two components. Thus the calculation of the space load requires the evaluation of each. The space load comprises the following elements:

— solar gain through glazing

— internally generated heat

— conduction through walls and glazing

— air infiltration.

The first of these is treated separately, see Appendix 5.A4.

Internally generated heat gains are calculated from design conditions. For the purposes of the Simple Model a single design level is assumed constant during the occupied hours. Thus the mean level is the sum of the gain over the occupied hours divided by 24, the number of hours in a day. The swing is the difference between the design load during the occupied hours and the daily mean value. These two elements must be divided into convective and radiant components. The model also assumes that heat is added (or removed) at two nodes, the air node and the environmental node. In the case of radiant gains 150% of that gain is realised at the environmental node (a hypothetical heat transfer node) with the excess 50% removed at the air node, see Appendix 5.A1, section 5.A1.5. The whole of the convective gain is realised at the air node.

Conduction and infiltration gains are discussed in the following sections where the mean and alternating components are handled separately. Furthermore, it is recognised that the design intent may be to cool to either a specific dry resultant or air temperature therefore calculations for both cases are given.

For the purposes of this appendix, emitter output is taken as positive for heating and negative for cooling. When applying the equations, they are presented such that both heating and cooling loads are expressed as positive values. This also necessitates the use of a single symbol (Q_p) for the emitter output. When applied, cooling is distinguished from heating by replacing Q_p by Q_k in the case of cooling load.

5.A2.2 Notation

Symbols used in this appendix are as follows. Some of the quantities occur in three forms: the instantaneous value, which is denoted by the appropriate letter (e.g. X). The 24-hour mean or steady-state value, denoted by $\bar{X}$; and the instantaneous variation about the mean value, denoted by $\tilde{X}$. Where appropriate, the variation symbol is given a subscript to indicate the time at which it occurs, e.g. $\tilde{X}_\theta$ is the value of $\tilde{X}$ at time θ.

A	Surface area (m^2)
C_v	Ventilation conductance ($W \cdot K^{-1}$)
F_{au}	Room conduction factor with respect to air node *
F_{ay}	Room admittance factor with respect to air node *
F_{cu}	Room conduction factor with respect to dry resultant temperature
F_{cy}	Room admittance factor with respect to dry resultant temperature
F_{1au}, F_{2au}	Conduction factors related to characteristics of heat source with respect to air temperature
F_{1cu}, F_{2cu}	Conduction factors related to characteristics of heat source with respect to dry resultant temperature
F_{1ay}, F_{2ay}	Admittance factors related to characteristics of heat source with respect to air temperature
F_{1cy}, F_{2cy}	Admittance factors related to characteristics of heat source with respect to dry resultant temperature
h_a	Heat transfer coefficient between air and environmental nodes ($W \cdot m^{-2} \cdot K^{-1}$)
h_c	Convective heat transfer coefficient ($W \cdot m^{-2} \cdot K^{-1}$)
h_r	Radiative heat transfer coefficient of a black body ($W \cdot m^{-2} \cdot K^{-1}$)
Q_a	Heat flow to the air node (W)
Q_e	Heat flow to the environmental node (W)
Q_k	Cooling Load (W)
Q_p	Emitter output (W)
Q_{pa}	Emitter output supplied to the air node (W)
Q_{pe}	Emitter output supplied to the environmental node (W)
R	Radiant fraction of the heat source
t_{ai}	Inside air temperature (°C)
t_{ao}	Outside air temperature (°C)
t_c	Dry resultant temperature at centre of room (°C)
t_{ei}	Environmental temperature (°C)
t_{eo}	Sol-air temperature (°C)
t_m	Surface temperature (°C)
t_r	Radiant temperature (°C)
U	Thermal transmittance ($W \cdot m^{-2} \cdot K^{-1}$)
v_m	Total ventilation (mechanical plus infiltration) rate ($m^3 \cdot s^{-1}$)
Y	Thermal admittance ($W \cdot m^{-2} \cdot K^{-1}$)
θ	Time (h)
ΣA	Sum of room surface areas, unless otherwise indicated (m^2)
$\Sigma (AU)$	Sum of the products of surface area and corresponding thermal transmittance over surfaces through which heat flow occurs ($W \cdot K^{-1}$)
$\Sigma (AY)$	Sum of the products of surface area and corresponding thermal admittance over all surfaces ($W \cdot K^{-1}$)
$\Sigma \bar{Q}_{con}$	Sum of daily mean convective heat gains (W)
$\Sigma \bar{Q}_{rad}$	Sum of daily mean radiant heat gains (W)

* Note that the definitions of these factors differ from those adopted in earlier editions of Guide A.

5.A2.3 Calculation of the steady-state load

The Simple (steady-state) Model assumes that heat enters the space at two points: the air node and a hypothetical node called the environmental temperature node. For a convective heat input, the heat flow into these nodes may be written as (see also Appendix 5.A1, section 5.A1.5):

Heat flow to air node:

$$\bar{Q}_a = C_v(\bar{t}_{ai} - \bar{t}_{ao}) - h_c \sum A (\bar{t}_m - \bar{t}_{ai}) \qquad (5.153)$$

Heat flow to environmental node:

$$\bar{Q}_e = \sum(A\,U)(\bar{t}_{ei} - \bar{t}_{eo}) + h_a \sum A (\bar{t}_{ei} - \bar{t}_{ai}) \qquad (5.154)$$

The method also defines the following relationships:

(a)   Environmental temperature:

$$\bar{t}_{ei} = \tfrac{1}{3}\,\bar{t}_{ai} + \tfrac{2}{3}\,\bar{t}_m \qquad (5.155)$$

(b)   Dry resultant temperature

$$\bar{t}_c = \tfrac{1}{2}\bar{t}_{ai} + \tfrac{1}{2}\bar{t}_m \qquad (5.156)$$

The definition of environmental temperature follows from the introduction of standard heat transfer coefficients (see Appendix 5.A1, section 5.A1.5). It is therefore rational to use the same coefficients in the following derivation. That is:

$$h_c = 3.0 \text{ W·m}^{-2}\text{·K}^{-1}$$

$$\tfrac{6}{5}\,\varepsilon\,h_r = 6.0 \text{ W·m}^{-2}\text{·K}^{-1}$$

$$h_a = 4.5 \text{ W·m}^{-2}\text{·K}^{-1}$$

Now, all gains to the space have been expressed in terms of gain to the air and environmental temperature nodes. Therefore to calculate the heating or cooling load to maintain to a specific dry resultant temperature it is necessary to eliminate $\bar{t}_{ei}$ and $\bar{t}_{ai}$ from equations 5.153 and 5.154, while for a specific air temperature, $\bar{t}_{ei}$ and $\bar{t}_c$ are not required. Rearranging equation 5.156 and substituting into equation 5.155 provides the following relationships that can be used to eliminate the unwanted variables:

$$\bar{t}_m = 2\bar{t}_c - \bar{t}_{ai} \qquad (5.157)$$

$$\bar{t}_{ai} = 4\bar{t}_c - 3\bar{t}_{ei} \qquad (5.158)$$

Substituting for t_m and replacing the heat transfer coefficients with the standard numerical values given above, equation 5.153 gives:

$$\bar{t}_{ai} = \frac{\bar{Q}_a + C_v\bar{t}_{ao} + 6.0\sum A\,\bar{t}_c}{C_v + 6.0\sum A} \qquad (5.159)$$

Similarly, equation 5.154 gives:

$$\bar{t}_{ei} = \frac{\bar{Q}_e + \sum(A\,U)\bar{t}_{eo} + 18.0\sum A\,\bar{t}_c}{\sum(A\,U) + 18.0\sum A} \qquad (5.160)$$

5.A2.3.1 Convective heating/cooling source for control on dry resultant temperature

Equations 5.159 and 5.160 together with equation 5.158 can be manipulated to give the convective heat input ($\bar{Q}_a$) for control at a specific dry resultant temperature as:

$$\bar{Q}_a = C_v(\bar{t}_c - \bar{t}_{ao}) + F_{cu}[\sum(A\,U)(\bar{t}_c - \bar{t}_{eo}) - \bar{Q}_e] \qquad (5.161)$$

where:

$$F_{cu} = \frac{3.0\,(C_v + 6.0\sum A)}{\sum(A\,U) + 18.0\sum A} \qquad (5.162)$$

The steady-state, or mean, load for control of dry resultant temperature is calculated by including solar gains, occupancy gains and equipment and lighting gains in equation 5.161. These gains comprise both radiant and convective components. In the case of radiant gains, 150% is released as a gain to the environmental node and 50% as a gain to the convective node, see Appendix 5.A1, section 5.A1.5. Thus the mean convective cooling load is:

$$\bar{Q}_a = C_v\,(\bar{t}_c - \bar{t}_{ao}) + F_{cu}[\sum(A\,U)(\bar{t}_c - \bar{t}_{eo}) \\ - \bar{Q}_e - 1.5\sum\bar{Q}_{rad}] - \sum\bar{Q}_{con} + 0.5\sum\bar{Q}_{rad} \qquad (5.163)$$

where $\sum\bar{Q}_{rad}$ and $\sum\bar{Q}_{con}$ are the sums of the daily mean radiant and convective gains, respectively (cooling loads are negative).

The extension of this calculation to cover a combination of convective and radiant heating or cooling sources is given below, see section 5.A2.3.3.

Note that in equation 5.163 and elsewhere, the short-wave radiant component of lighting, i.e. the visible light, is assumed to form part of the long-wave radiant component.

5.A2.3.2 Convective heating/cooling source for control on air temperature

In this case, equation 5.158 is used to provide a value for $\bar{t}_c$ in equations 5.159 and 5.160, thus:

$$\bar{Q}_a = C_v(\bar{t}_{ai} - \bar{t}_{ao}) + F_{au}[\sum(A\,U)(\bar{t}_{ai} - \bar{t}_{eo}) \\ - \bar{Q}_e - 1.5\sum\bar{Q}_{rad}] - \sum\bar{Q}_{con} + 0.5\sum\bar{Q}_{rad} \qquad (5.164)$$

where:

$$F_{au} = \frac{4.5\sum A}{\sum(A\,U) + 4.5\sum A} \qquad (5.165)$$

The calculation then follows that for control of the dry resultant temperature, see section 5.A2.3.1.

5.A2.3.3 Combined convective and radiant heating/cooling sources for control on dry resultant temperature

If the emitter output is Q_p with a radiant fraction of R (where $R = 1.0$ for a 100% radiant load), then the heat supplied to the air node (Q_{pa}) is:

$$Q_{pa} = Q_p(1-R) - 0.5\,Q_p R = Q_p(1-1.5\,R) \quad (5.166)$$

and the heat supplied to the environmental node (Q_{pe}) is:

$$Q_p = 1.5\,Q_p R \quad (5.167)$$

From equation 5.163, by replacing $\bar{Q}_a$ and $\bar{Q}_e$ by $\bar{Q}_{pa}$ and $\bar{Q}_{pe}$, respectively, and substituting from equations 5.166 and 5.167, the daily mean, or steady-state, load is:

$$\bar{Q}_p = F_{1cu}\,[\Sigma\,(A\,U)\,(\bar{t}_c - \bar{t}_{eo}) - 1.5\,\Sigma\,\bar{Q}_{rad}]$$
$$+ F_{2cu}\,[C_v(\bar{t}_c - \bar{t}_{ao}) - \Sigma\,\bar{Q}_{con} + 0.5\,\Sigma\,\bar{Q}_{rad}]$$
$$(5.168)$$

where:

$$F_{1cu} = \frac{3.0\,(C_v + 6.0\,\Sigma A)}{\Sigma\,(A\,U) + 18.0\,\Sigma A + 1.5\,R\,[3.0\,C_v - \Sigma\,(A\,U)]}$$
$$(5.169)$$

$$F_{2cu} = \frac{\Sigma\,(A\,U) + 18.0\,\Sigma A}{\Sigma\,(A\,U) + 18.0\,\Sigma A + 1.5\,R\,[3.0\,C_v - \Sigma\,(A\,U)]}$$
$$(5.170)$$

For the purposes of calculation of the steady-state design heat loss (where all internal gains are ignored), equation 5.168 reduces to:

$$\bar{Q}_p = [F_{1cu}\,\Sigma\,(A\,U) + F_{2cu}\,C_v]\,(\bar{t}_c - \bar{t}_{ao}) \quad (5.171)$$

where it is assumed that $\bar{t}_{eo}$ and $\bar{t}_{ao}$ are equal.

The corresponding air temperature, t_{ai}, is obtained by substituting Q_{pa} for Q_a in equation 5.159 and then replacing Q_{pa} by Q_p using equation 5.166, hence:

$$t_{ai} = \frac{Q_p(1-1.5\,R) + C_v t_{ao} + 6.0\,\Sigma A\,t_c}{C_v + 6.0\,\Sigma A} \quad (5.172)$$

5.A2.3.4 Combined convective and radiant heating/cooling sources for control on air temperature

In this case, the emitter load relationships given by equations 5.166 and 5.167 are substituted into equation 5.164 to give:

$$\bar{Q}_p = F_{1au}\,[\Sigma\,(A\,U)\,(\bar{t}_{ai} - \bar{t}_{eo}) - 1.5\,\Sigma\,\bar{Q}_{rad}]$$
$$+ F_{2au}\,[C_v(\bar{t}_{ai} - \bar{t}_{ao}) - \Sigma\,\bar{Q}_{con} + 0.5\,\Sigma\,\bar{Q}_{rad}]$$
$$(5.173)$$

where:

$$F_{1au} = \frac{4.5\,\Sigma A}{(1-1.5\,R)\,\Sigma\,(A\,U) + 4.5\,\Sigma A} \quad (5.174)$$

$$F_{2au} = \frac{\Sigma\,(A\,U) + 4.5\,\Sigma A}{(1-1.5\,R)\,\Sigma\,(A\,U) + 4.5\,\Sigma A} \quad (5.175)$$

For the purposes of calculation of the steady-state design heat loss, equation 5.173 reduces to:

$$\bar{Q}_p = [F_{1au}\,\Sigma\,(A\,U) + F_{2au}\,C_v]\,(\bar{t}_c - \bar{t}_{ao}) \quad (5.176)$$

5.A2.4 Alternating component of cooling load

5.A2.4.1 Convective cooling for control on dry resultant temperature

This may be derived in a similar way to that for the mean cooling loads. However, in this case the fabric heat load is dependent on the thermal admittance of the surfaces. Thus the heat flow to the air node is:

$$\tilde{Q}_{a\theta} = C_v\,\tilde{t}_{ai\theta} - h_c\,\Sigma A\,(\tilde{t}_{m\theta} - \tilde{t}_{ai\theta}) \quad (5.177)$$

Note: equation 5.177 assumes that changes in the ventilation load due to fluctuations in external temperature are taken into account separately.

Heat flow to the environmental node is:

$$\tilde{Q}_{e\theta} = \Sigma\,(A\,Y)\,\tilde{t}_{ei\theta} + h_a\,\Sigma A\,(\tilde{t}_{ei\theta} - \tilde{t}_{ai\theta}) + \Sigma\,(A f U \tilde{t}_{eo}) \quad (5.178)$$

Note: it is assumed that phase differences are not significant.

Thus the alternating component of the cooling load for control to the dry resultant temperature is:

$$\tilde{Q}_{a\theta} = C_v\,\tilde{t}_{c\theta} + F_{cy}\,[\Sigma\,(A\,Y)\,\tilde{t}_{c\theta} + \Sigma\,(A f U \tilde{t}_{eo})$$
$$- 1.5\,\tilde{Q}_{rad}] - \Sigma\,\tilde{Q}_{con} + 0.5\,\tilde{Q}_{rad} \quad (5.179)$$

where:

$$F_{cy} = \frac{3.0\,(C_v + 6.0\,\Sigma A)}{\Sigma\,(A\,Y) + 18.0\,\Sigma A} \quad (5.180)$$

Note: $\tilde{t}_{c\theta} = 0$ for 24-hour plant operation.

5.A2.4.2 Convective cooling for control on air temperature

The alternating component of the cooling load for control to the air temperature is:

$$\tilde{Q}_{a\theta} = C_v\,\tilde{t}_{a\theta} + F_{ay}\,[\Sigma\,(A\,Y)\,\tilde{t}_{a\theta} - \tilde{Q}_{e\theta} - 1.5\,\Sigma\,\tilde{Q}_{rad}]$$
$$- \Sigma\,\tilde{Q}_{con} + 0.5\,\tilde{Q}_{rad} \quad (5.181)$$

where:

$$F_{ay} = \frac{4.5\,\Sigma A}{\Sigma\,(A\,Y) + 4.5\,\Sigma A} \quad (5.182)$$

Note: $\tilde{t}_{a\theta} = 0$ for 24-hour plant operation.

5.A2.4.3 Combined convective and radiant cooling for control on dry resultant temperature

The emitter load relationships given in section 5.A2.3.3 can also be applied to the alternating component of the emitter load. In this case substitution of equations 5.166 and 5.167 into equation 5.171 gives:

$$\tilde{Q}_{p\theta} = F_{1cy}[\Sigma(AY)\,\tilde{t}_{c\theta} + \Sigma AfU\,\tilde{t}_{eo} - 1.5\,\Sigma\tilde{Q}_{rad}]$$
$$+ F_{2cy}[C_v\,\tilde{t}_{c\theta} - \Sigma\tilde{Q}_{con} + 0.5\,\Sigma\tilde{Q}_{rad}] \qquad (5.183)$$

where:

$$F_{1cy} = \frac{3.0\,(C_v + 6.0\,\Sigma A)}{\Sigma(AY) + 18.0\,\Sigma A + 1.5\,R\,[3.0\,C_v - \Sigma(AY)]} \qquad (5.184)$$

$$F_{2cy} = \frac{\Sigma(AY) + 18.0\,\Sigma A}{\Sigma(AY) + 18.0\,\Sigma A + 1.5\,R\,[3.0\,C_v - \Sigma(AY)]} \qquad (5.185)$$

Note: $\tilde{t}_{c\theta} = 0$ for 24-hour plant operation.

5.A2.4.4   Combined convective and radiant cooling for control on air temperature

Substitution of equations 5.166 and 5.167 into equation 5.181 gives:

$$\tilde{Q}_{p\theta} = F_{1ay}[\Sigma(AY)\,\tilde{t}_{a\theta} + \Sigma AfU\,\tilde{t}_{eo} - 1.5\,\Sigma\tilde{Q}_{rad}]$$
$$+ F_{2ay}[C_v\,\tilde{t}_{a\theta} - \Sigma\tilde{Q}_{con} + 0.5\,\Sigma\tilde{Q}_{rad}] \qquad (5.186)$$

where:

$$F_{1ay} = \frac{4.5\,\Sigma A}{(1 - 1.5\,R)\,\Sigma(AY) + 4.5\,\Sigma A} \qquad (5.187)$$

$$F_{2ay} = \frac{\Sigma(AY) + 4.5\,\Sigma A}{(1 - 1.5\,R)\,\Sigma(AY) + 4.5\,\Sigma A} \qquad (5.188)$$

Note: $\tilde{t}_{a\theta} = 0$ for 24-hour plant operation.

5.A2.5   Effect of allowing room temperature to rise above set point

The peak cooling capacity can be reduced if the room temperature is allowed to rise above the set point for a period sufficiently short that the effect on the mean temperature is small (e.g. 2 hours at the time of peak load). Because the mean is not changed, the reduction may be calculated from the alternating component of the gain, i.e. from either equation 5.179 or equation 5.181. Thus for control on the dry resultant temperature, the change in load becomes:

$$\Delta Q_k = [c\,\rho\,v_m + F_{cy}\,\Sigma(AY)]\,\Delta t_c \qquad (5.189)$$

For control on the air temperature:

$$\Delta Q_k = [c\,\rho\,v_m + F_{ay}\,\Sigma(AY)]\,\Delta t_{ai} \qquad (5.190)$$

where ΔQ_k is the change in cooling load resulting from a small change in temperature (Δt), c is the specific heat capacity of air ($J\cdot kg^{-1}\cdot K^{-1}$), ρ is the density of air ($kg\cdot m^{-3}$), v_m is the total ventilation (mechanical plus infiltration) rate ($m^3\cdot s^{-1}$) F_{cy} is the room admittance factor with respect to dry resultant temperatures, F_{ay} is the room admittance factor with respect to the air node, $\Sigma(AY)$ is the sum of the products of surface areas and their corresponding thermal admittances ($W\cdot K^{-1}$), Δt_c is the rise in dry resultant temperature (K) and Δt_{ai} is the rise in internal air temperature (K).

5.A2.6   Summertime temperatures

The Simple (dynamic) Model may be used to assess peak temperatures when there is no heating or cooling. The method used is essentially the inverse of the cooling load calculation. However, further simplifications are introduced to enable rapid hand checks on designs.

The intent of the calculation is to obtain the peak dry resultant temperature, which is achieved using a transposition of equations 5.160 and 5.161. Thus from equation 5.161 the daily mean dry resultant temperature is:

$$\bar{t}_c = \frac{C_v\,\bar{t}_{ao} + F_{cu}\,\Sigma(AU)\,\bar{t}_{eo} + F_{cu}\bar{Q}_e + \bar{Q}_a}{C_v + F_{cu}\,\Sigma(AU)} \qquad (5.191)$$

where:

$$\bar{Q}_a = \Sigma\bar{Q}_{con}$$

Note that for glazed surfaces, $\bar{t}_{eo} = \bar{t}_{ao}$.

The alternating dry resultant temperature follows from equation 5.183:

$$\tilde{t}_{c\theta} = \frac{\bar{Q}_{a\theta} + F_{cy}\bar{Q}_{e\theta}}{C_v + F_{cy}\,\Sigma(AY)} \qquad (5.192)$$

where:

$$\bar{Q}_{a\theta} = \Sigma\bar{Q}_{con}$$

Equation 5.192 is based on the ventilation rate remaining constant throughout the day. An assessment of the effect of a varying ventilation rate is given by Harrington-Lynn[A2.1].

Reference for Appendix 5.A2

A2.1   Harrington-Lynn J *The admittance procedure: variable ventilation Building Serv. Engineer* **42** 99–200 (November 1974)

Appendix 5.A3: Comparison of thermal steady-state models

This appendix contains a number of example calculations intended to demonstrate differences between the three methods described for the calculation of design heat losses. These examples will assist building services engineers in assessing the suitability of the methods for a particular application and enable software designers to demonstrate that the results obtained from computer programs are consistent with the methods described in this Guide.

The example calculations are as follows:

— a cubic enclosure with uniform U-value but variable internal emissivity.

— a cubic enclosure with variable U-value but constant emissivity (i.e. 0.9)

— a typical room, with typical U-values and surface emissivity

— a non-typical application; in this case an atrium

— an example of applying the calculation methods to multiple surfaces.

In each case, the following are calculated:

— heat losses for various generic system types

— surface temperatures

— radiation view factors.

Example A3.1: Cubic enclosure; uniform U-values, varying emissivities

See Figure 5.10 and Tables 5.24 to 5.27. This example demonstrates a weakness of the Simple Model when emissivities differ from 0.9. It offers a means of checking that a computer program can account for variable emissivity.

Dry resultant temperature: 21°C
Outside air temperature: –1°C
Infiltration rate: 0.5 h^{-1}

Table 5.24 Example A3.1: surface data

Surface number	Area (m^2)	U-value (W·m^{-2}·K^{-1})	Emissivity of surface, ε_n	Convective heat transfer coefficient, h_c	Inside surface resistance, R_{si} (m^2·K·W^{-1})	Temperature on outer side of surface (°C)
1	100	1.00	1.00	3.00	0.12	–1.0
2	100	1.00	1.00	3.00	0.12	–1.0
3	100	1.00	0.8	3.00	0.12	–1.0
4	100	1.00	0.6	3.00	0.12	–1.0
5	100	1.00	0.4	3.00	0.12	–1.0
6	100	1.00	0.2	3.00	0.12	–1.0

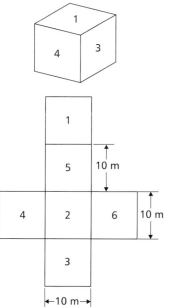

Figure 5.10 Examples A3.1 and A3.2: geometry for cubic enclosure

Table 5.25 Example A3.1: heat loss

Emitter characteristics (% convective)	Component of heat loss	Heat loss using Reference Model (W)	Percentage difference using stated model	
			Basic Model	Simple Model
100	Fabric	14556.0	0.0	−14.1
	Ventilation	4906.0	0.0	−13.5
	Total	19461.0	0.0	−13.9
70	Fabric	14999.0	0.0	−14.0
	Ventilation	4513.0	0.0	−13.3
	Total	19512.0	0.0	−13.8
50	Fabric	15296.0	0.0	−13.9
	Ventilation	4250.0	0.0	−13.2
	Total	19547.0	0.0	−13.7
30	Fabric	15594.0	0.0	−13.8
	Ventilation	3987.0	0.0	−13.0
	Total	19581.0	0.0	−13.7

Table 5.26 Example A3.1: surface temperatures

Emitter characteristics (% convective)	Surface number	Surface temperature using Reference Model (°C)	Difference in calculated surface temperature using stated model (K)	
			Basic Model	Simple Model
100	1	20.35	0	+3.01
	2	20.35	0	+3.01
	3	20.35	0	+3.01
	4	20.35	0	+3.01
	5	20.35	0	+3.01
	6	20.35	0	+3.01
70	1	21.7	0	+3.77
	2	21.7	0	+3.77
	3	21.39	0	+3.46
	4	20.99	−0.01	+3.06
	5	20.47	0	+2.54
	6	19.73	0	+2.00
50	1	22.61	0	+4.29
	2	22.61	0	+4.29
	3	22.09	0	+3.77
	4	21.43	0	+3.11
	5	20.54	−0.01	+2.22
	6	19.32	0	+1.00
30	1	23.52	0	+4.81
	2	23.52	0	+4.81
	3	22.79	0	+4.08
	4	21.86	0	+3.15
	5	20.62	−0.01	+1.91
	6	18.90	−0.01	+0.19

Table 5.27 Example A3.1 radiation view factors

Surface number	View factor for stated surface as viewed from surface indicated in first column					
	1	2	3	4	5	6
1	0	0.2000	0.2000	0.2000	0.2000	0.2000
2	0.2000	0	0.2000	0.2000	0.2000	0.2000
3	0.2000	0.2000	0	0.2000	0.2000	0.2000
4	0.2000	0.2000	0.2000	0	0.2000	0.2000
5	0.2000	0.2000	0.2000	0.2000	0	0.2000
6	0.2000	0.2000	0.2000	0.2000	0.2000	0

Example A3.2: Cubic enclosure; varying U-values, uniform emissivities

See Figure 5.10 and Tables 5.28 to 5.31. This example demonstrates the order of magnitude of uncertainties resulting from applying the Simple Model and offers a means of checking that a computer program can account for variable *U*-values. The emissivity of all surfaces is taken as 0.9.

Dry resultant temperature: 21°C
Outside air temperature: –1°C
Infiltration rate: 0.5 h^{-1}

Table 5.28 Example A3.2: surface data

Surface number	Area (m^2)	U-value (W·m^{-2}·K^{-1})	Emissivity of surface, ε_n	Convective heat transfer coefficient, h_c	Inside surface resistance, R_{si} (m^2·K·W^{-1})	Temperature on outer side of surface (°C)
1	100	2.5	0.9	4.3	0.1	–1.0
2	100	0.25	0.9	1.5	0.14	–1.0
3	100	2.0	0.9	3.0	0.12	–1.0
4	100	1.5	0.9	3.0	0.12	–1.0
5	100	1.0	0.9	3.0	0.12	–1.0
6	100	0.5	0.9	3.0	0.12	–1.0

Table 5.29 Example A3.2: heat loss

Emitter characteristics (% convective)	Component of heat loss	Heat loss using Reference Model (W)	Percentage difference using stated model	
			Basic Model	Simple Model
100	Fabric	16872.0	0.0	–5.7
	Ventilation	4583.0	0.0	–3.9
	Total	21455.0	0.0	–5.3
70	Fabric	18242.0	0.0	–4.8
	Ventilation	3558.0	0.0	–2.8
	Total	21800.0	0.0	–4.4
50	Fabric	17846.0	0.0	–5.0
	Ventilation	3854.0	0.0	–3.1
	Total	21700.0	0.0	–4.7
30	Fabric	17454.0	0.0	–5.3
	Ventilation	4147.0	0.0	–3.5
	Total	21601.0	0.0	–5.0

Table 5.30 Example A3.2: surface temperatures

Emitter characteristics (% convective)	Surface number	Surface temperature using Reference Model (°C)	Difference in calculated surface temperature using stated model (K)	
			Basic Model	Simple Model
100	1	15.70	+0.01	+1.3
	2	18.41	−0.01	−0.4
	3	15.50	+0.01	+0.90
	4	16.72	0.0	+0.89
	5	17.92	−0.01	+0.86
	6	19.12	−0.01	+0.82
70	1	16.45	+0.01	+0.64
	2	21.94	−0.02	+1.31
	3	17.07	+0.01	+1.03
	4	18.40	0.0	+1.02
	5	19.72	−0.01	+0.99
	6	21.03	−0.02	+0.96
50	1	16.23	+0.01	+0.63
	2	20.92	−0.02	+0.82
	3	16.61	+0.01	+0.99
	4	17.92	+0.01	+0.99
	5	19.20	−0.01	+0.96
	6	20.48	−0.01	+0.93
30	1	16.02	+0.01	+1.03
	2	19.90	−0.02	+0.32
	3	16.17	+0.01	+0.96
	4	17.43	0.0	+0.94
	5	18.69	0.0	+0.92
	6	19.93	−0.02	+0.88

Table 5.31 Example A3.2: radiation view factors

Surface number	View factor for stated surface as viewed from surface indicated in first column					
	1	2	3	4	5	6
1	0	0.2000	0.2000	0.2000	0.2000	0.2000
2	0.2000	0	0.2000	0.2000	0.2000	0.2000
3	0.2000	0.2000	0	0.2000	0.2000	0.2000
4	0.2000	0.2000	0.2000	0	0.2000	0.2000
5	0.2000	0.2000	0.2000	0.2000	0	0.2000
6	0.2000	0.2000	0.2000	0.2000	0.2000	0

Example A3.3: Typical room; varying U-values, uniform emissivities

See Figure 5.11 and Tables 5.32 to 5.35. This example indicates the uncertainties likely to occur in a typical design situation.

Dry resultant temperature: 21°C
Outside air temperature: –1°C
Infiltration rate: 1.0 h⁻¹

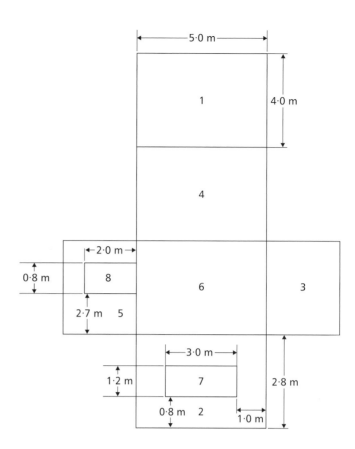

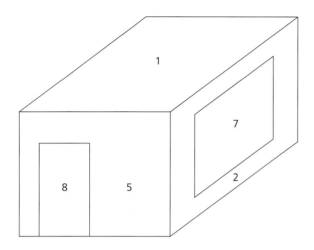

Figure 5.11 Example A3.3: geometry for typical room

Table 5.32 Example A3.3: surface data

Surface number	Area (m²)	U-value (W·m⁻²·K⁻¹)	Emissivity of surface, ε_n	Convective heat transfer coefficient, h_c	Inside surface resistance, R_{si} (m²·K·W⁻¹)	Temperature on outer side of surface (°C)
1	20.0	0.4	0.9	4.3	0.1	–1.0
2	10.4	0.6	0.9	3.0	0.12	–1.0
3	11.2	2.5	0.9	3.0	0.12	18.0
4	14.0	2.5	0.9	3.0	0.12	18.0
5	9.6	0.6	0.9	3.0	0.12	–1.0
6	20.0	0.2	0.9	1.5	0.14	–1.0
7	3.6	3.0	0.9	3.0	0.12	–1.0
8	1.6	2.0	0.9	3.0	0.12	–1.0

Table 5.33 Example A3.3: heat loss

Emitter characteristics (% convective)	Component of heat loss	Heat loss using Reference Model (W)	Percentage difference using stated model	
			Basic Model	Simple Model
100	Fabric	1068.0	+0.2	–6.7
	Ventilation	486.0	0.0	–4.9
	Total	1536.0	+0.1	–6.2
60	Fabric	1124.0	–1.0	–9.2
	Ventilation	437.0	0.0	–4.7
	Total	1560.0	–0.1	–7.9

Table 5.34 Example A3.3: surface temperatures

Emitter characteristics (% convective)	Surface number	Surface temperature using Reference Model (°C)	Difference in calculated surface temperature using stated model (K)	
			Basic Model	Simple Model
100	1	20.83	−0.02	+1.3
	2	20.05	+0.12	+2.20
	3	20.46	0.0	+0.42
	4	20.41	−0.05	+0.37
	5	19.93	+0.01	+1.08
	6	20.29	−0.02	+0.5
	7	13.09	+0.04	+0.4
	8	15.87	+0.04	+0.62
60	1	21.12	−0.06	+1.09
	2	20.57	+0.17	+1.24
	3	20.86	+0.02	+0.77
	4	20.81	−0.04	+0.72
	5	20.45	+0.06	+1.12
	6	21.24	−0.1	+0.95
	7	13.38	+0.1	+0.36
	8	16.23	+0.12	+0.58

Table 5.35 Example A3.3: radiation view factors

Surface number	View factor for stated surface as viewed from surface indicated in first column							
	1	2	3	4	5	6	7	8
1	0	0.1358	0.1458	0.1849	0.1289	0.3387	0.0491	0.0169
2	0.2611	0	0.1544	0.1690	0.1449	0.2611	0	0.0095
3	0.2604	0.1434	0	0.1845	0.0943	0.2604	0.0411	0.0159
4	0.2641	0.1255	0.1476	0	0.1158	0.2641	0.0511	0.0318
5	0.2686	0.1570	0.1101	0.1689	0	0.2525	0.0429	0
6	0.3387	0.1358	0.1458	0.1849	0.1212	0	0.0491	0.0246
7	0.2727	0	0.1279	0.1986	0.1143	0.2727	0	0.0136
8	0.2107	0.0616	0.1116	0.2782	0	0.3073	0.0306	0

Example A3.4: Atrium; varying U-values, varying emissivities

See Figure 5.12 and Tables 5.36 to 5.39. This example illustrates a non-typical application, in this case an atrium. It is intended mainly to assist in comparing computer programs.

Dry resultant temperature: 21°C
Outside air temperature: −1°C
Infiltration rate: 0.1 h⁻¹

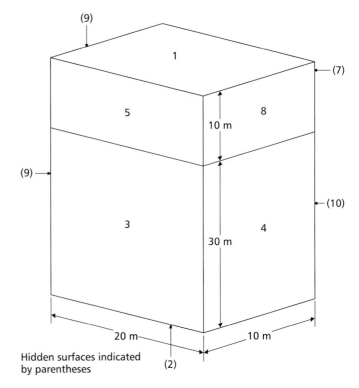

Figure 5.12 Example A3.4: geometry for atrium

Table 5.36 Example A3.4: surface data

Surface number	Area (m²)	U-value (W·m^{-2}·K^{-1})	Emissivity of surface, ε_n	Convective heat transfer coefficient, h_c	Inside surface resistance, R_{si} (m²·K·W^{-1})	Temperature on outer side of surface (°C)
1	200.0	3.0	0.8	4.3	0.1	−4.0
2	200.0	0.7	0.9	1.5	0.14	−1.0
3	600.0	2.0	0.9	3.0	0.12	21.0
4	300.0	2.0	0.9	3.0	0.12	21.0
5	200.0	2.0	0.8	3.0	0.12	21.0
6	100.0	3.0	0.8	3.0	0.12	−1.0
7	200.0	3.0	0.8	3.0	0.12	−1.0
8	100.0	3.0	0.8	3.0	0.12	−1.0
9	300.0	0.45	0.9	3.0	0.12	−1.0
10	600.0	0.45	0.9	3.0	0.12	−1.0

Table 5.37 Example A3.4: heat loss

Emitter characteristics (% convective)	Component of heat loss	Heat loss using Reference Model (W)	Percentage difference using stated model	
			Basic Model	Simple Model
100	Fabric	52181.0	+4.2	−2.4
	Ventilation	6976.0	+0.7	−4.4
	Total	59160.0	+3.8	−2.6
50	Fabric	55732.0	+4.1	−5.0
	Ventilation	6288.0	+0.3	−4.5
	Total	62020.0	+3.7	−4.9

Table 5.38 Example A3.4: surface temperatures

Emitter characteristics (% convective)	Surface number	Surface temperature using Reference Model (°C)	Difference in calculated surface temperature using stated model (K)	
			Basic Model	Simple Model
100	1	12.68	−1.07	−0.02
	2	19.43	−1.04	+1.5
	3	21.75	+0.59	+0.75
	4	21.83	+0.54	+0.83
	5	19.53	−1.92	−1.47
	6	11.86	−1.17	−0.57
	7	12.0	−1.09	−0.43
	8	11.84	−1.19	−0.59
	9	20.89	+0.68	+2.03
	10	21.06	+0.93	+2.2
50	1	12.85	−1.03	−0.51
	2	20.95	+1.11	+2.26
	3	22.48	+0.5	+1.48
	4	22.55	+0.58	+1.55
	5	20.04	−1.93	−0.96
	6	12.29	−1.15	−0.68
	7	12.42	−1.1	−0.55
	8	12.27	−1.17	−0.7
	9	21.78	+0.73	+2.13
	10	21.94	+0.18	+2.29

Table 5.39 Example A3.4: radiation view factors

Surface	View factor for stated surface as viewed from surface indicated in first column									
	1	2	3	4	5	6	7	8	9	10
1	0	0.0362	0.0740	0.0509	0.2406	0.1164	0.2406	0.1164	0.0509	0.0740
2	0.0362	0	0.3081	0.1617	0.0065	0.0056	0.0065	0.0056	0.1617	0.3081
3	0.0247	0.1027	0	0.1595	0	0.0121	0.0539	0.0121	0.1595	0.4756
4	0.0339	0.1078	0.3190	0	0.0242	0.0255	0.0242	0	0.1464	0.3190
5	0.2406	0.0065	0	0.0362	0	0.1164	0.2859	0.1164	0.0362	0.1617
6	0.2329	0.0112	0.0725	0.0766	0.2329	0	0.2329	0.0686	0	0.0725
7	0.2406	0.0065	0.1617	0.0362	0.2859	0.1164	0	0.1164	0.0362	0
8	0.2329	0.0112	0.0725	0	0.2329	0.0686	0.2329	0	0.0766	0.0725
9	0.0339	0.1078	0.3190	0.1464	0.0242	0	0.0242	0.0255	0	0.3190
10	0.0247	0.1027	0.4756	0.1595	0.0539	0.0121	0	0.0121	0.1595	0

Example A3.5: Enclosure with multiple surfaces; varying U-values, uniform emissivities

See Figure 5.13 and Tables 5.40 to 5.43. In this example, the calculation methods are applied to multiple surfaces. It is intended to assist in checking computer programs to determine the accuracy with which surface temperatures are calculated.

Dry resultant temperature: 21°C
Outside air temperature: –1°C
Infiltration rate: $1.0\ \text{h}^{-1}$

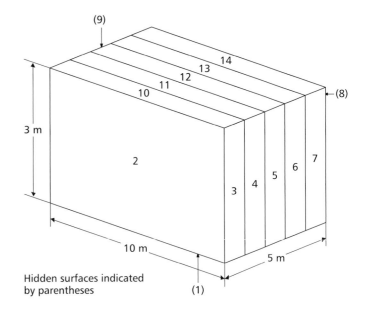

Figure 5.13 Example A3.5: geometry for enclosure with multiple surfaces

Table 5.40 Example A3.5: surface data

Surface number	Area (m²)	U-value (W·m⁻²·K⁻¹)	Emissivity of surface, ε_n	Convective heat transfer coefficient, h_c	Inside surface resistance, R_{si} (m²·K·W⁻¹)	Temperature on outer side of surface (°C)
1	50.0	1.0	0.8	1.5	0.14	–1.0
2	30.0	5.6	0.8	3.0	0.12	–1.0
3	3.0	1.0	0.8	3.0	0.12	–1.0
4	3.0	1.0	0.8	3.0	0.12	–1.0
5	3.0	1.0	0.8	3.0	0.12	–1.0
6	3.0	1.0	0.8	3.0	0.12	–1.0
7	3.0	1.0	0.8	3.0	0.12	–1.0
8	30.0	1.0	0.8	3.0	0.12	–1.0
9	15.0	1.0	0.8	3.0	0.12	–1.0
10	10.0	1.0	0.8	4.3	0.10	–1.0
11	10.0	1.0	0.8	4.3	0.10	–1.0
12	10.0	1.0	0.8	4.3	0.10	–1.0
13	10.0	1.0	0.8	4.3	0.10	–1.0
14	10.0	1.0	0.8	4.3	0.10	–1.0

Table 5.41 Example A3.5: heat loss

Emitter characteristics (% convective)	Component of heat loss	Heat loss using Reference Model (W)	Percentage difference using stated model	
			Basic Model	Simple Model
100	Fabric	7074.0	–0.2	–6.9
	Ventilation	1506.0	+0.1	–7.8
	Total	8579.0	–0.2	–7.1
50	Fabric	7728.0	+0.1	–7.8
	Ventilation	1233.0	–0.1	–7.5
	Total	8961.0	0	–7.7

Table 5.42 Example A3.5: surface temperatures

Emitter characteristics (% convective)	Surface number	Surface temperature using Reference Model (°C)	Difference in calculated surface temperature using stated model (K)	
			Basic Model	Simple Model
100	1	16.24	+0.27	−0.02
	2	6.07	+0.02	+0.49
	3	17.29	−0.99	+0.62
	4	18.00	−0.28	+1.33
	5	18.39	+0.11	+0.72
	6	18.64	+0.36	+1.97
	7	18.80	+0.52	+2.14
	8	18.24	+0.10	+1.58
	9	18.22	−0.01	+1.56
	10	18.58	−1.12	+1.52
	11	19.19	−0.51	+2.12
	12	19.59	−0.11	+2.52
	13	19.85	+0.15	+2.79
	14	20.06	+0.36	+2.99
50	1	19.17	−0.20	+1.49
	2	6.70	+0.00	+0.57
	3	18.89	−0.85	+0.76
	4	19.67	−0.07	+1.55
	5	20.10	+0.36	+1.98
	6	20.37	+0.63	+2.24
	7	20.53	+0.80	+2.41
	8	19.93	+0.04	+1.81
	9	19.91	+0.12	+1.79
	10	19.38	−0.93	+0.83
	11	20.08	−0.23	+1.53
	12	20.53	+0.21	+1.97
	13	20.81	+0.49	+2.25
	14	20.98	+0.67	+2.43

Table 5.43 Example A3.5: radiation view factors

Surface number	View factor for stated surface as viewed from surface indicated in first column													
	1	2	3	4	5	6	7	8	9	10	11	12	13	14
1	0	0.1867	0.0155	0.0188	0.0196	0.0188	0.0155	0.1867	0.0083	0.0783	0.0957	0.1019	0.0957	0.0783
2	0.3112	0	0.0359	0.0220	0.0151	0.0109	0.0082	0.1934	0.0921	0.1311	0.0803	0.0490	0.0307	0.0211
3	0.2585	0.3593	0	0	0	0	0	0.0821	0.0416	0.1361	0.0652	0.0304	0.0168	0.0101
4	0.3136	0.2198	0	0	0	0	0	0.1092	0.0438	0.0652	0.1361	0.0652	0.0304	0.0168
5	0.3272	0.1505	0	0	0	0	0	0.1505	0.0445	0.0304	0.0652	0.1361	0.0652	0.0304
6	0.3136	0.1092	0	0	0	0	0	0.2198	0.0438	0.0168	0.0304	0.0652	0.1361	0.0652
7	0.2585	0.0821	0	0	0	0	0	0.3593	0.0416	0.0101	0.0168	0.0304	0.0652	0.1361
8	0.3112	0.1934	0.0082	0.0109	0.0151	0.0220	0.0359	0	0.0921	0.0200	0.0307	0.0409	0.0803	0.1311
9	0.2943	0.1842	0.0083	0.0088	0.0089	0.0088	0.0083	0.1842	0	0.0517	0.0627	0.0654	0.0627	0.0517
10	0.3916	0.3934	0.0408	0.0196	0.0091	0.0050	0.0030	0.0600	0.0776	0	0	0	0	0
11	0.4786	0.2409	0.0196	0.0408	0.0196	0.0091	0.0050	0.0921	0.0941	0	0	0	0	0
12	0.5094	0.1471	0.0091	0.0196	0.0408	0.0196	0.0091	0.1471	0.0982	0	0	0	0	0
13	0.4786	0.0921	0.0050	0.0091	0.0196	0.0408	0.0196	0.2409	0.0941	0	0	0	0	0
14	0.3916	0.0600	0.0030	0.0050	0.0091	0.0196	0.0408	0.3934	0.0776	0	0	0	0	0

Appendix 5.A4: Derivation of solar gain factors

5.A4.1 Introduction

This appendix describes the method used to determine the mean and alternating solar gain factors given in Table 5.7. While these factors are applicable only to the CIBSE Simple (dynamic) Model (i.e. the admittance procedure), much of what follows is general in nature and therefore also appropriate to more complex thermal models.

The cooling load due to solar radiation has three components:

(a) *Direct gain:* radiation transmitted through the glazing system falls upon the room surfaces and contents where it is both reflected and absorbed. The majority of the reflected radiation is absorbed by the surfaces but some passes out through the windows. For normal rooms this retransmitted radiation is small and can be ignored for the purposes of design calculations. Absorbed radiation increases the temperature of the surfaces and so becomes a room load through both convection and radiation. There is a time delay between the incidence of the direct solar gain and the corresponding room gain because thermal storage occurs within the room fabric. In terms of the Simple (dynamic) Model, this process is represented by the surface factor with the load being realised at the environmental node.

(b) *Indirect gain:* radiation is absorbed within the elements of the glazing system resulting in an increase in the temperature of those elements. Therefore there is a heat gain to the room due to the difference between the inner surface temperature of the glazing, the room surfaces and the room air. For the Simple (dynamic) Model, in the absence of an internal blind, this gain is realised at the environmental node.

(c) Where internal blinds are fitted, the possibility for air to circulate around the blind results in an increase in the rate of convective heat transfer from the blind surface. In terms of the Simple (dynamic) Model, this is expressed as an additional gain to the air node.

The calculation of transmitted and absorbed radiation provides the basis for the calculation of room cooling loads. However, this is too laborious for manual calculation and some simplification is necessary. This is achieved by the introduction of a 'solar gain factor' which is the ratio of the gain to the external radiation producing the gain.

The room load at a given time is due to the combined effect of the three components described above. That is, the room load at time t consists of:

(a)   load due to direct gain at time $(t - \text{delay})$, plus

(b)   load due to indirect gain at time t, plus

(c)   load due to additional gain at air node at time t.

The appropriate solar gain factor could be obtained by normalising the room load by the external irradiance at time t. However, the direct gain is due to external radiation incident at some time (t_o) before t and should therefore be normalised by the external radiation at time t_o. Therefore, it is suggested that three solar gain factors are required:

—   A 'short-wave' factor based on the ratio between the direct room load at time t and the external irradiance at time t_o

—   A 'long-wave' factor based on the ratio between the indirect room load at time t and the external irradiance at time t

—   An 'air node' factor based on the ratio between the additional air gain load at time t and the external irradiance at time t.

The use of a separate air node factor is justified by the theoretical approach used in the Simple Model where a distinction is made between the different sources of heat gains. While theoretically justifiable, the use of three factors (two of which are based on external conditions at a different time to the third) cannot be considered simple. Furthermore, solar gain factors defined in this way are not constants but vary hour-by-hour and thus can only be used to predict conditions at a particular time. (More strictly, at a single angle of incidence between the solar beam and the glazing.) However, for most types of glass the transmission and absorption properties are almost independent of the angle of incidence up to an angle of about 45 degrees. It is unlikely that peak loads will occur at high angles of incidence and so that effect can be ignored.

Figure 5.14 shows the transmitted short-wave and indirect gain to a space for a particular glazing type, (without an internal blind) together with the associated external irradiance. The Simple Model is based on the response of a space to the 24-hour mean (see Figure 5.15) and the deviation from that mean (i.e. the swing), see Figure 5.16. In the Simple (dynamic) Model, the solar loads that act at the environmental node within the space are equal to the sum of the mean and alternating gains. In the case of direct (short-wave) transmission, the alternating gain is the swing multiplied by the appropriate surface factor and delayed by the corresponding time delay. The indirect gain acts directly at the environmental node. Figure 5.17 shows these components of the gain to the environmental node for a space with an average surface factor of 0.5 and a time delay of 2 hours. The total solar gain to the environmental node (i.e. sum of mean and swings) is given in Figure 5.18.

The Simple (dynamic) Model is based on the response to a mean and the deviation from that mean; the solar gain factor must be consistent with that model.

The mean solar gain factor is the sum of the daily average values of the transmitted gain, divided by the daily average level of the incident irradiation.

In theory, the alternating component should comprise the three factors described above. However, for the practical purpose of the calculation of peak gain, the short-wave and long-wave components are combined. Thus, two alternating factors are defined:

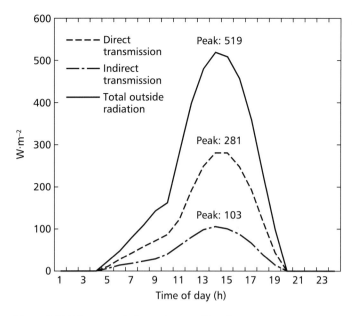

Figure 5.14 Solar transmission and external irradiance

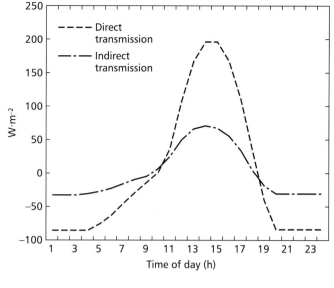

Figure 5.16 Swing in solar transmission

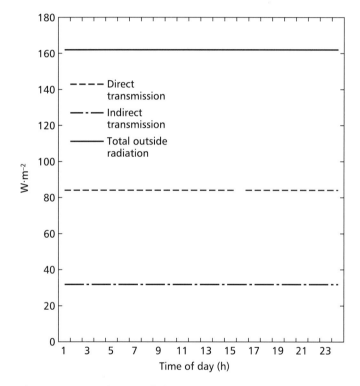

Figure 5.15 Mean solar transmission and external irradiance

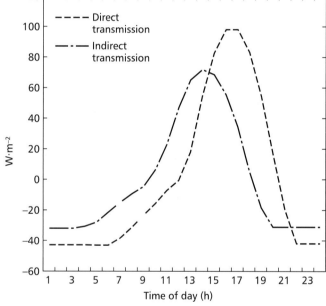

Figure 5.17 Solar gains; swing in gains

— *alternating solar gain factor:* the swing in solar load due to the sum of direct transmission and indirect gain from the surface of the glazing, divided by the swing in the external incident irradiation

— *alternating air node factor:* the swing in the additional air node load, divided by the swing in the external incident irradiation.

In the case of the air node factor, the swing in irradiation is calculated at the same time as that used to determine the swing in the corresponding gain. In the case of the alternating solar gain factor, there is a time delay associated with the directly transmitted component. Modern glazing systems are usually designed to minimise transmission and so a pragmatic decision must be taken to normalise the alternating solar gain factor by the swing at the time of the

gain to the space. Figure 5.19 shows the variation of alternating solar gain factor throughout the day. Therefore, there is no single value which is representative of all hours of the day. CIBSE solar gain factors are calculated to be representative of conditions around the time of peak gain.

5.A4.2 Notation

Symbols used in this appendix are as follows.

a Fraction of incident energy absorbed by thickness L (mm) of glass

A Absorption coefficient

A' Absorption coefficient for double glazing

A'' Absorption coefficient for triple glazing

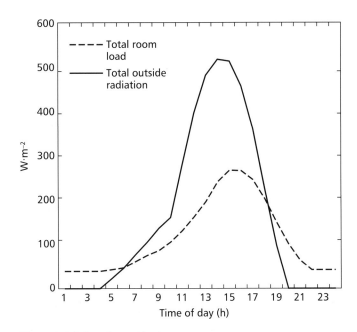

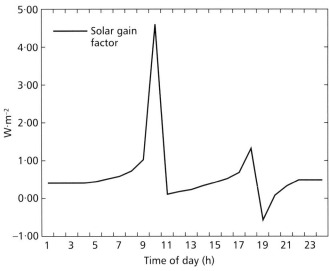

Figure 5.19 Alternating solar gain factor

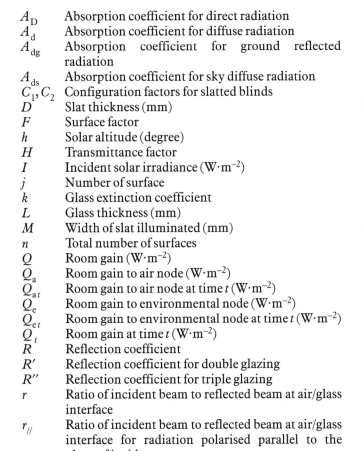

Figure 5.18 Solar gains; total gains

A_D	Absorption coefficient for direct radiation
A_d	Absorption coefficient for diffuse radiation
A_{dg}	Absorption coefficient for ground reflected radiation
A_{ds}	Absorption coefficient for sky diffuse radiation
C_1, C_2	Configuration factors for slatted blinds
D	Slat thickness (mm)
F	Surface factor
h	Solar altitude (degree)
H	Transmittance factor
I	Incident solar irradiance (W·m^{-2})
j	Number of surface
k	Glass extinction coefficient
L	Glass thickness (mm)
M	Width of slat illuminated (mm)
n	Total number of surfaces
Q	Room gain (W·m^{-2})
Q_a	Room gain to air node (W·m^{-2})
Q_{at}	Room gain to air node at time t (W·m^{-2})
Q_e	Room gain to environmental node (W·m^{-2})
Q_{et}	Room gain to environmental node at time t (W·m^{-2})
Q_t	Room gain at time t (W·m^{-2})
R	Reflection coefficient
R'	Reflection coefficient for double glazing
R''	Reflection coefficient for triple glazing
r	Ratio of incident beam to reflected beam at air/glass interface
$r_{//}$	Ratio of incident beam to reflected beam at air/glass interface for radiation polarised parallel to the plane of incidence
$r_\perp$	Ratio of incident beam to reflected beam at air/glass interface for radiation polarised perpendicular to the plane of incidence
R_D	Reflection coefficient for direct radiation
R_d	Reflection coefficient for diffuse radiation
R_{dg}	Reflection coefficient for ground reflected radiation
R_{ds}	Reflection coefficient for sky diffuse radiation
R_{se}	External surface resistance (W·m^{-2}·K^{-1})
R_{si}	Internal surface resistance (W·m^{-2}·K^{-1})
T	Transmission coefficient
T'	Transmission coefficient for double glazing
T''	Transmission coefficient for triple glazing

T_D	Transmission coefficient for direct radiation
T_d	Transmission coefficient for diffuse radiation
T_{dg}	Transmission coefficient for ground reflected radiation
T_{ds}	Transmission coefficient for sky diffuse radiation
T_n	Transmission coefficient at normal incidence
t	Time (h)
W	Slat width (m)
α	Absorptivity (thermal short-wave radiation)
β	Profile angle (degree)
γ	Wall azimuth (degree)
γ_s	Wall–solar azimuth (degree)
θ_i	Angle of incidence (degree)
θ_r	Angle of refraction (degree)
μ	Refractive index of glass ($= 1.52$)
σ_v	Vertical shadow angle (degree)
ϕ	Solar azimuth (degree)
ψ	Slat angle (degree)
ω	Time lag associated with surface factor (h)

Where required additional subscripts 'A', 'R' and 'T' indicate gains due to absorbed, reflected and transmitted components of radiation, respectively.

5.A4.3   Response of room to solar radiation

Short-wave solar radiation incident upon a window will be reflected, absorbed in the glazing elements or directly transmitted into the space beyond the window. The absorbed radiation will increase the temperature of the glazing and is therefore both a long-wave radiant heat gain and a convective gain to the space. In terms of the Simple (dynamic) Model these gains are considered to enter the model at the environmental node. If internal blinds are present, there will be an increase in the convective portion of the gain which enters the model at the air node. Transmitted radiation must be absorbed at the room surfaces before it can become a heat gain to the space. With the exception of any short-wave radiation that passes directly out of the space by transmission through glazed surfaces, all the radiation entering the space is absorbed at the room surfaces or within the furnishings.

Once absorbed, the radiation warms the surfaces and, after a time delay, enters the space at the environmental node by means of convection and radiation.

For the purposes of the Simple (dynamic) Model, the room gain is divided into a 24-hour mean component and an hourly cyclic component.

For any given source:

$$\bar{Q} = (1/24) \sum_{t=1}^{t=24} Q_t \qquad (5.193)$$

and:

$$\tilde{Q}_t = Q_t - \bar{Q} \qquad (5.194)$$

In the case of the Simple (dynamic) Model the gain will be either to the environmental node only or to both the environmental and air nodes. The gain to the environmental node from transmitted radiation is:

$$Q_{eTt} = \bar{Q}_{eT} + F \tilde{Q}_{eT\,(t-\omega)} \qquad (5.195)$$

$$\tilde{Q}_{eTt} = Q_{eTt} - \bar{Q}_{eT} \qquad (5.196)$$

$$\bar{Q}_{eT} = (1/24) \sum_{t=1}^{t=24} Q_{eTt} \qquad (5.197)$$

$$Q_{eTt} = T I_t \qquad (5.198)$$

where Q_{eTt} is the overall gain to the environmental node from transmitted radiation at time t. However, in practice, direct and diffuse transmitted radiation must be treated separately.

The gain to the environmental node due to conduction and radiation from the inner surface of the glazing is:

$$Q_{eAt} = \sum_{j=1}^{j=n} (H_{ej} A_j I_t) \qquad (5.199)$$

where A is the component of the radiation absorbed by the glass, subscript j denotes the number of the glazing element and n is the total number of glazing elements within the window system.

Thus the total gain to the environmental node is:

$$Q_{et} = Q_{eTt} + Q_{eAt} \qquad (5.200)$$

Additionally, if there is an internal blind, the gain to the air node is:

$$Q_{aAt} = \sum_{j=1}^{j=n} (H_{aj} A_j I_t) \qquad (5.201)$$

Thus the total gain to the air node is:

$$Q_{at} = Q_{aAt} \qquad (5.202)$$

To simplify the calculation of these gains, solar gain factors are used. These are the ratios of the components of the gain to the incident solar radiation. The room load has both steady state and cyclic components and the space gains are to the environmental and, possibly, the air nodes. Additionally, the surface factor depends on the response time of the space. To calculate the solar gain factors, typical values are taken, as follows:

— for slow response space: $F = 0.5$; time delay = 2 h

— for a fast response space: $F = 0.8$; time delay = 1 h

The solar gain factors are as follows:

$$\bar{S}_e = \bar{Q}_e / \bar{I} \qquad (5.203)$$

$$\tilde{S}_{et} = \tilde{Q}_{et} / \tilde{I}_t \qquad (5.204)$$

$$\bar{S}_a = \bar{Q}_a / \bar{I} \qquad (5.205)$$

$$\tilde{S}_{at} = \tilde{Q}_{at} / \tilde{I}_t \qquad (5.206)$$

Solar gain factors for generic glass and blind combinations are given in Table 5.7. These have been calculated using banded solar radiation data for Kew (1959–1968)[A4.1] incident on a south-west facing vertical window (see Section 2: *External design data*). The transmission (T), absorption (A) and reflection (R) components (for thermal short-wave radiation) and emissivities (for thermal long-wave radiation) for the generic glass and blind types used in calculating the solar gain factors are given in Table 5.44.

Effectively, solar gain factors can only be calculated by means of a computer program. The following sections describe the basis of the calculation procedure.

5.A4.3.1 Transmission, absorption and reflection for direct solar radiation

Clear glass

For clear glass the transmission, absorption and reflection values (TAR) can be derived theoretically[A4.2].

The angle of refraction is obtained from the angle of incidence using Snell's Law:

$$\theta_r = \arcsin (\sin \theta_i / \mu) \qquad (5.207)$$

The reflected beams for radiation polarised parallel to and perpendicular to the plane of incidence are determined using Fresnel's formula:

$$r_{//} = \frac{\tan^2 (\theta_i - \theta_r)}{\tan^2 (\theta_i + \theta_r)} \qquad (5.208)$$

$$r_\perp = \frac{\sin^2 (\theta_i - \theta_r)}{\sin^2 (\theta_i + \theta_r)} \qquad (5.209)$$

As the angle of incidence approaches 0 (i.e. normal incidence):

$$\tan \theta_i \rightarrow \sin \theta_i \rightarrow \theta_i \qquad (5.210)$$

hence:

$$r_{//} \rightarrow r_\perp \rightarrow \frac{(\mu - 1)^2}{(\mu + 1)^2} \qquad (5.211)$$

This is a useful result as it enables the calculation of the extinction coefficient (k) if the transmission at normal incidence (T_n) is known. The extinction coefficient is a non-linear function of the glass thickness (L) and is related to the transmission coefficient by:

$$T_n = \frac{(1-r)^2 \exp(-kL)}{1 - r^2 \exp(-2kL)} \qquad (5.212)$$

For the beam polarised parallel to the plane of incidence, the fraction of incident energy absorbed for each beam is calculated as follows:

$$a_{//} = 1 - \exp(-kL / \cos \theta_r) \qquad (5.213)$$

and similarly for the perpendicularly polarised beam.

The transmitted, absorbed and reflected coefficients are calculated separately for each beam (i.e. parallel and perpendicularly polarised) and the average taken to give the overall coefficients. For the beam polarised parallel to the plane of incidence:

$$T_{D//} = \frac{(1-r)^2 (1-a_{//})}{1 - r^2 (1-a_{//})^2} \qquad (5.214)$$

$$A_{D//} = \frac{a_{//} (1-r) [1 + r(1-a_{//})]}{1 - r^2 (1-a_{//})^2} \qquad (5.215)$$

$$R_{D//} = \frac{r(1-r)^2 (1-a_{//})}{1 - r^2 (1-a_{//})} + r \qquad (5.216)$$

and similarly for the perpendicularly polarised beam.

Therefore:

$$T_D = {}^1\!/_2 (T_{D//} + T_{D\perp}) \qquad (5.217)$$

and similarly for the absorption and reflection coefficients.

Note that since the transmitted, absorbed and reflected components add up to unity, only two need be calculated, the third being obtained by subtraction.

Reflecting and other glasses

The characteristics of such glasses differ from those for plain glass and therefore must be obtained from the manufacturers. If the characteristics are supplied as a graph of TAR coefficients against angle of incidence, the appropriate values can be read-off directly or by curve-fitting techniques.

Slatted blinds

The analysis is the same for both horizontal and vertical slatted blinds. Radiation may be transmitted into a room by the following paths[A4.3].

— *direct:* i.e. passes through the blind without touching any surface; may be zero

— *reflected* (1): i.e. passes through the blind after one reflection from the slat surface which is directly irradiated by the sun

— *reflected* (2): i.e. passes through the blind after undergoing any number of reflections, the final reflection being from the slat surface opposite the one directly illuminated by the sun

— *reflected* (3): i.e. passes through the blind after undergoing any number of reflections, the final reflection being from the one directly illuminated by the sun.

In order to calculate these components, up to five configuration factors are required, each of which depends on the blind geometry. The number of factors needed depends on whether all or only part of the slat is illuminated.

The amount of a slat that is illuminated (i.e. not shaded by the slat above it) depends on the geometry of the blind and the 'profile angle'.

The profile angle (β) is the angle that the direct radiation beam makes with the blind in a vertical plane perpendicular to the plane of the window. For horizontal slatted blinds on a vertical window, the profile angle is the vertical shadow angle:

$$\beta = \sigma_v = \arctan(\tan h \sec \gamma_s) \qquad (5.218)$$

For vertical slatted blinds on a vertical window, the profile angle is the wall–solar azimuth:

$$\beta = \gamma_s = \phi - \gamma \qquad (5.219)$$

In the following analysis, it is assumed that the radiation is incident on the upper surface of the slat. The width of slat that is illuminated is calculated from:

$$M = \min\left(W, \frac{D \cos \beta}{\sin(\beta + \psi)}\right) \qquad (5.220)$$

The configuration factors are calculated as follows.

Radiation that is reflected by the lower slat and passes into the room when the whole width is illuminated (C_1):

$$C_1 = {}^1\!/_2 \{1 + (D/W) - [1 + (D^2/W^2) + (2D \sin \psi / W)]^{1/2}\} \qquad (5.221)$$

Radiation that is reflected by the lower slat and intercepted by the upper slat when the whole width is illuminated (C_2):

$$C_2 = {}^1\!/_2 \{[1 + (D^2/W^2) + (2D \sin \psi / W)]^{1/2} + [1 + (D^2/W^2) - (2D \sin \psi / W)]^{1/2} - (2D/W)\} \qquad (5.222)$$

Radiation reflected by the upper slat which passes into the room (C_3):

$$C_3 = {}^1\!/_2 \{[1 + (D/W) - [1 + (D^2/W^2) - (2D \sin \psi / W)]^{1/2}\} \qquad (5.223)$$

Radiation reflected by the lower slat, which passes into the room when the lower slat is partially shaded (C_4):

$$C_4 = \tfrac{1}{2}(1 + \{[(W-M)^2/M^2] + (D^2/M^2) + [2(W-M)D\sin\psi/M^2]\}^{1/2}$$
$$- [(W^2/M^2) + (D^2/M^2) + (2WD\sin\psi/M^2)]^{1/2}) \qquad (5.224)$$

Radiation reflected by the lower slat, which is intercepted by the upper slat when the lower slat is partially shaded (C_5):

$$C_5 = \tfrac{1}{2}([(W^2/M^2) + (D^2/M^2) + (2DW\sin\psi/M^2)]^{1/2} - (D/M)$$
$$+ [1 + (D^2/M^2) - (2D\sin\psi/M)]^{1/2}$$
$$- \{[(W-M)^2/M^2] + (D^2/M^2) + [2(W-M)D\sin\psi/M^2]\}^{1/2}) \qquad (5.225)$$

If the whole of the lower slat is illuminated and some radiation may pass directly into the room, the TAR coefficients for the blind are calculated from:

$$T_D = 1 - \left(\frac{W\sin(\phi+\psi)}{D\cos\phi}\right)$$
$$\times\left(1 - C_1(1-a) - \frac{C_2(1-a)^2 - [C_3 + C_1 C_2(1-a)]}{1 - C_2^2(1-a)^2]}\right) \qquad (5.226)$$

$$A_D = a\, W\sin(\phi+\psi)/D\cos\phi[1 - C_2(1-a)] \qquad (5.227)$$

$$R_D = 1 - A_D - T_D \qquad (5.228)$$

Where part of the lower slat is shaded by the slat above:

$$T_D = C_4(1-a) + \{C_5(1-a)^2 \times [C_3 + C_1 C_2(1-a)]/[1 - C_2^2(1-a)^2]\} \qquad (5.229)$$

$$A_D = a(1 + \{[C_5(1-a)]/[1 - C_2(1-a)]\}) \qquad (5.230)$$

$$R_D = 1 - A_D - T_D \qquad (5.231)$$

Roller blinds

The properties for roller blinds are not well defined. It is generally sufficient to assume that the TAR coefficients are independent of the angle of incidence and take the values at normal incidence supplied by the manufacturers.

5.A4.3.2 Transmission, absorption and reflection for sky diffuse and ground reflected radiation

Transmission, absorption and reflection coefficients for glasses and blinds are calculated by considering the direct properties over a range of angles appropriate to the radiation. For glass, the TAR values for sky diffuse and ground reflected radiation are the same since glass has symmetrical properties. The characteristics for roller blinds can be assumed to be the same for direct and diffuse radiation. However, slatted blinds are highly asymmetrical so the two sources of diffuse radiation must be calculated separately.

Glasses

The standard properties are calculated on the assumption that the glass is exposed to a hemispherical source of uniform radiance therefore the transmission and absorption angles are from 0° to 90°. Mathematically, the expressions for TAR could be integrated over this range, i.e:

$$T_d = \int_0^{90} T_D(\theta_i)\sin(2\theta_i)\,d\theta_i \qquad (5.232)$$

In practice the direct properties are summed for angles of incidence from 2.5° to 87.5° at intervals of 5°, i.e:

$$T_d = \sum_{\theta=2.5}^{\theta=87.5}\{T_{D\theta}[\sin^2(\theta_i+2.5) - \sin^2(\theta_i-2.5)]\} \qquad (5.233)$$

A_d is calculated similarly and R_d is obtained by subtraction from unity, see equation 5.228.

Slatted blinds

The direct properties are summed for profile angles from 5° to 85° at intervals of 10° for sky diffuse radiation. For ground reflected radiation, they are summed from –85° to –5° at intervals of 10° taking into account the configuration factor of the hemispherical radiating source bounded by profile angles of $(\beta+5)°$ and $(\beta–5)°$[(A4.4)]. Thus, for sky diffuse radiation:

$$T_{ds} = \sum_{\beta=5}^{\beta=85}\{T_{D\beta}[\sin(\beta+5) - \sin(\beta-5)]\} \qquad (5.234)$$

For ground reflected radiation:

$$T_{dg} = \sum_{\beta=-5}^{\beta=-85}\{T_{D\beta}[\sin(\beta+5) - \sin(\beta-5)]\} \qquad (5.235)$$

A_{ds} and A_{dg} are calculated similarly and R_{ds} and R_{dg} are obtained by subtraction from unity, see equation 5.228.

5.A4.3.3 Properties of glass and blind combinations

The properties of multiple layer windows can be calculated from the properties of the individual components. There are many glass types and many permutations; the method of calculation is demonstrated in the following for double and triple glazing using generic glass and blind types.

In the same way that the properties of a single sheet of glass are calculated from the fundamental properties of the glass and an infinite number of inter-reflections at both glass/air interfaces, the properties of multiple glazing are calculated by considering the inter-reflections between the

Table 5.44 Transmission, absorption and reflection components and emissivities for generic glass and blind combinations

Description	Proportion of short-wave radiation			Emissivity
	Transmitted	Absorbed	Reflected	
Glass:				
— plain	0.78	0.15	0.07	0.84
— reflecting	0.43	0.29	0.28	0.84
— absorbing	0.46	0.49	0.05	0.84
— low emissivity	0.62	0.33	0.20	0.84/0.12*
Slatted blind†				
— reflecting	0.0	0.40	0.80	0.80
— absorbing	0.0	0.80	0.10	0.80
Roller blind	0.40	0.10	0.50	0.80
'Generic' blind	0.20	0.40	0.40	0.80

* Values for untreated and treated surfaces, respectively

† Properties apply to slats

component layers[A4.2,A4.5]. These calculations are performed for both direct and diffuse radiation. However, if the window incorporates a blind, the radiation reflected by or transmitted through it is assumed to be diffuse whatever the nature of the source. This is because the slat surfaces are assumed to be diffusing rather than specular reflectors[A4.3].

The following equations are derived from Figure 5.20 where all layers are symmetrical, i.e. both surfaces of the layer have the same reflection and the specularity of the radiation is not changed by the layer. If any of the layers are asymmetrical, the equations become more complicated since they have to include the reflection of both surfaces of the layer. If any of the layers is a diffusing slatted blind, then the direct radiation equations need to include the diffuse properties of the elements for radiation that has been reflected by the blind(s). Examples for some of these situations are given elsewhere[A4.2].

Double glazing

TAR coefficients for double glazing, denoted by prime ('), are as follows:

$$T' = (T_o T_i)/(1 - R_o R_i) \qquad (5.236)$$

$$A_o' = A_o + [(T_o A_o R_i)/(1 - R_o R_i)] \qquad (5.237)$$

$$A_i' = (T_o A_i)/(1 - R_o R_i) \qquad (5.238)$$

$$R' = 1 - T' - A_o' - A_i' \qquad (5.239)$$

where subscript 'o' denotes the outer glazing element and subscript 'i' denotes the inner glazing element.

Triple glazing

TAR coefficients for triple glazing, denoted by double prime ("), are as follows:

$$T'' = \frac{T_o T_c T_i}{(1 - R_o R_c)(1 - R_c R_i) - T_c^2 R_o R_i} \qquad (5.240)$$

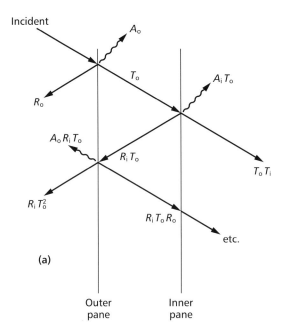

(a)

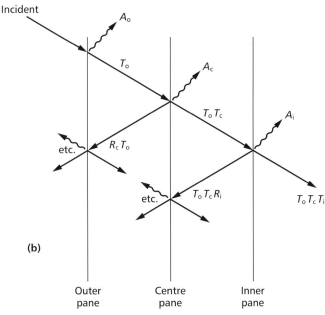

(b)

Figure 5.20 Transmitted, absorbed and reflected radiation; (a) double glazing, (b) triple glazing

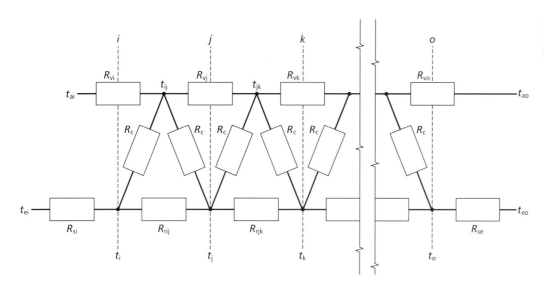

$$A_o'' = A_o + \frac{T_o A_o R_c}{1 - R_o R_c}$$

$$+ \frac{T_o T_c^2 A_o R_i}{(1 - R_o R_c)(1 - R_c R_i) - T_c^2 R_o R_i} \quad (5.241)$$

$$A_c'' = \frac{T_o A_c (1 - R_c R_i + T_c R_i)}{(1 - R_o R_c)(1 - R_c R_i) - T_c^2 R_o R_i} \quad (5.242)$$

$$A_i'' = \frac{T_o T_c A_i}{(1 - R_o R_c)(1 - R_c R_i) - T_c^2 R_o R_i} \quad (5.243)$$

$$R'' = 1 - T'' - A_o'' - A_c'' - A_i'' \quad (5.244)$$

where subscript 'o' denotes the outer glazing element, subscript 'c' denotes the central glazing element and subscript 'i' denotes the inner glazing element.

The heat gain to the environmental node due to conduction and radiation from the inner surface of the glazing is given by equation 5.199. If there is an internal blind, the additional heat gain to the air node is given by equation 5.201. In these equations, the transmittance factors (H) depend on the values taken for the thermal resistances (i.e. the radiant and convective heat transfer coefficients) of the layers of the window. They are calculated by considering the thermal resistance network for the window. Figure 5.21 shows the general thermal resistance network for a multiple-layer window.

The properties of the glazing systems are calculated using the following standard thermal resistances and heat transfer coefficients:

— thermal resistance between inner surface of window and environmental point (i.e. inside thermal resistance): $R_{si} = 0.12 \text{ m}^2 \cdot \text{K} \cdot \text{W}^{-1}$

— thermal resistance between outer surface of window and sol-air temperature (i.e. outside thermal resistance): $R_{se} = 0.06 \text{ m}^2 \cdot \text{K} \cdot \text{W}^{-1}$

— convective resistance between a window layer and the air: $R_c = 0.33 \text{ m}^2 \cdot \text{K} \cdot \text{W}^{-1}$ (for vertical window, corresponding to $h_c = 3 \text{ W} \cdot \text{m}^2 \cdot \text{K} \cdot \text{W}^{-1}$)

— radiative resistance between two layers (j, k) of window:

$$(R_r)_{j,k} = (\varepsilon_j + \varepsilon_k - \varepsilon_j \varepsilon_k) / (h_r \varepsilon_j \varepsilon_k) \quad (5.245)$$

(if both layers have an emissivity of 0.84 and $h_r = 5.7 \text{ W} \cdot \text{m}^{-2} \cdot \text{K}^{-1}$; $(R_r)_{j,k} = 0.24 \text{ m}^2 \cdot \text{K} \cdot \text{W}^{-1}$)

— ventilation resistance across window layer between adjacent air spaces: $R_v = 0 \text{ m}^2 \text{K} \cdot \text{W}^{-1}$ if the layer is a blind; $R_v = \infty$ if the layer is glass.

Example A4.1: Triple glazing without blinds

Figure 5.22 shows the network for triple glazing and Figure 5.23 shows the simplified network resulting from evaluation of the parallel resistances.

The total resistance of the network is:

$$\Sigma (R) = R_{si} + R_{ic} + R_{co} + R_{se} =$$
$$= 0.12 + 0.18 + 0.18 + 0.06$$
$$= 0.54 \text{ m}^2 \cdot \text{K} \cdot \text{W}^{-1}$$

where R_{ic} is the thermal resistance between inner and central elements of the glazing ($\text{m}^2 \cdot \text{K} \cdot \text{W}^{-1}$) and R_{co} is the thermal resistance between central and outer elements of the glazing ($\text{m}^2 \cdot \text{K} \cdot \text{W}^{-1}$).

The transmittance factors for the inner, central and outer elements of the glazing can be shown to be:

$$H_{ei} = (R_{ic} + R_{co} + R_{se}) / \Sigma R$$
$$= (0.18 + 0.18 + 0.06) / 0.54 = 0.78$$

$$H_{ec} = (R_{co} + R_{se}) / \Sigma R = (0.18 + 0.06) / 0.54 = 0.44$$

$$H_{eo} = R_{se} / \Sigma R = 0.06 / 0.54 = 0.11$$

From equation 5.199, the cyclic component of the convective and long-wave radiant gain from the glazing to the environmental node is calculated as follows:

$$\tilde{H}_e A = H_{ei} \tilde{A}_i + H_{ec} \tilde{A}_c + H_{eo} \tilde{A}_o$$

Table 5.45 Example A4.1: components of radiation

Time (h)	Solar irradiance (W·m⁻²)	Radiation absorbed/transmitted by glazing system (W·m⁻²)				Gains to space (W·m⁻²)		
		Radiation absorbed by inner, central and outer glazing elements			Directly transmitted radiation, T	Cyclic component of absorbed radiation, (H_eA)	Cyclic component of transmitted radiation for lightweight (L) and heavyweight (H) buildings	
		A_i	A_c	A_o			$\tilde{T}_L$	$\tilde{T}_H$
1200	442	35	58	89	133	37	—	—
1300	531	46	71	104	189	53	54	—
1400	572	52	77	108	223	60	99	34
1500	563	52	75	105	229	59	126	62
1600	504	47	67	94	205	50	131	79
Mean:	179	15	24	34	65	26	—	—

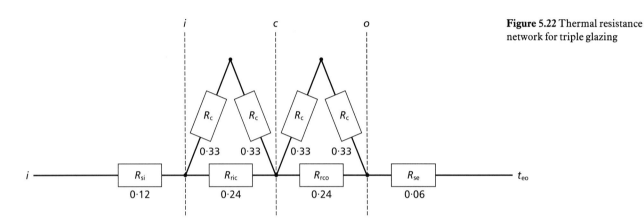

Figure 5.22 Thermal resistance network for triple glazing

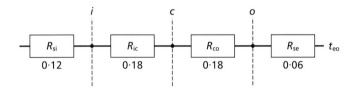

Figure 5.23 Simplified thermal resistance network for triple glazing

Table 5.45 summarises the steps in the calculation of the solar gain to the space by means of an example. The calculation was carried out as follows.

For 1200 h:

$$\tilde{H}_e A = 0.78\,(35-15) + 0.44\,(58-24)$$
$$+ 0.11\,(89-34) = 36.6$$

The gain at other times is calculated similarly. The mean gain is calculated using the mean, rather than the cyclic, absorption values.

The cyclic component of the directly transmitted short-wave radiation is attenuated by the surface factor (F) which is appropriate to the thermal weight of the building and corresponding time delay, see Table 5.6.

For a lightweight building, $F = 0.8$ and the time delay is 1 hour, i.e:

$$\tilde{T}_L = 0.8 \times (T_{t+1} - \bar{T})$$

and for a heavyweight building, $F = 0.5$ and the time delay is 2 hours, i.e:

$$\tilde{T}_H = 0.5 \times (T_{t+2} - \bar{T})$$

where subscript 'L' denotes thermally lightweight building and subscript 'H' denotes thermally heavyweight building.

The mean solar gain factor is given by:

$$\bar{S}_e = \frac{\text{mean transmitted radiation plus mean absorbed radiation}}{\text{daily mean incident radiation}}$$

Hence:

$$\bar{S}_e = (65 + 26)/179 = 0.51$$

The cyclic solar gain factors are calculated using the gains appropriate to a time one or two hours after the time of peak radiation, depending on the thermal weight of the structure, i.e:

$$\tilde{S}_e = \frac{\text{total swing in gain to space}}{\text{swing in external gain}}$$

Peak solar irradiance occurs at 1400 h; hence, for a thermally lightweight structure (i.e. 1 hour delay):

$$\tilde{S}_{eL} = (126 + 59)/(563 - 179) = 0.48$$

and for a thermally heavyweight structure (i.e. 2 hour delay):

$$\tilde{S}_{eH} = (79 + 50)/(504 - 179) = 0.4$$

Example A4.2: Single glazing with internal absorbing blind

Figure 5.24 shows the network for single glazing with an internal blind and Figure 5.25 shows the simplified network resulting from evaluation of the parallel resistances.

In this case, there are transmittance factors to both the air and environmental nodes, which are calculated as follows:

$$R_{ix} = R_{rio} + [(R_c R_{se})/(R_c + R_{se})]$$
$$= 0.23 + [(0.33 \times 0.06)/(0.33 + 0.06)] = 0.28$$

$$H_{ei} = \frac{R_c R_{ix}/(R_c + R_{ix})}{R_{si} + [(R_c R_{ix})/(R_c + R_{ix})]}$$

$$= \frac{(0.33 \times 0.28)/(0.33 + 0.28)}{0.12 + [(0.33 \times 0.28)/(0.33 + 0.28)]} = 0.56$$

$$H_{ai} = \frac{R_{si} R_{ix}/(R_{si} + R_{ix})}{R_c + [(R_{si} R_{ix})/(R_{si} + R_{ix})]}$$
$$+ \left(\frac{R_{si} R_c/(R_{si} + R_c)}{R_{ix} + [(R_{si} R_c)/(R_{si} + R_c)]} \right)$$
$$\times \left(\frac{R_{se}}{R_{se} + R_c} \right) = 0.24$$

$$R_{ox} = R_{rio} + [(R_c R_{si})/(R_c + R_{si})] = 0.32$$

$$H_{eo} = \frac{R_c R_{se}/(R_c + R_{se})}{R_{ox} + (R_c R_{se})/(R_c + R_{se})} \times \frac{R_c}{(R_c + R_{si})} = 0.10$$

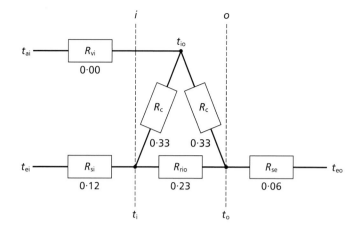

Figure 5.24 Thermal resistance network for single glazing with internal blind

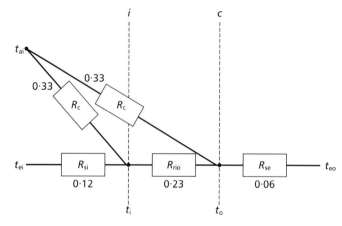

Figure 5.25 Simplified thermal resistance network for single glazing with internal blind

$$H_{ao} = \frac{R_{se} R_{ox}/(R_{se} + R_{ox})}{R_c + [(R_{se} R_{ox})/(R_{se} + R_{ox})]}$$
$$+ \left(\frac{R_{se} R_c/(R_{se} + R_c)}{R_{ox} + [(R_{se} R_c)/(R_{se} + R_c)]} \right)$$
$$\times \left(\frac{R_{si}}{R_c + R_{si}} \right) = 0.17$$

Table 5.46 Example A4.2: components of radiation

Time (h)	Solar irradiance (W·m⁻²)	Radiation absorbed/transmitted by glazing system (W·m⁻²)			Gains to space (W·m⁻²)			
		Radiation absorbed by inner, and outer glazing elements		Directly transmitted radiation, T	Cyclic components of absorbed radiation		Cyclic components of transmitted radiation for lightweight (L) and heavyweight (H) buildings	
		A_i	A_o		$(H_e A)$	$(H_a A)$	$\tilde{T}_L$	$\tilde{T}_H$
1200	442	116	146	47	45	53	—	—
1300	531	151	178	52	68	67	22	—
1400	572	171	191	54	81	74	26	14
1500	563	173	186	51	81	73	28	17
1600	504	157	167	45	70	66	26	18
Mean:	179	51	58	19	34	22	—	—

Table 5.46 summarises the steps in the calculation of the solar gain to the space.

The cyclic component of the convective and long-wave radiant gain from the glazing to the environmental node is calculated as for triple glazing, see Example A4.1, i.e:

$$\tilde{H}_e A = H_{ei}\tilde{A}_i + H_{ec}\tilde{A}_c + H_{eo}\tilde{A}_o$$

The instantaneous component of the convective and long-wave radiant gain from the glazing to the air node is calculated as follows:

$$H_a A = H_{ai}A_i + H_{ao}A_o$$

Hence, for 1200 h:

$$H_a A = (0.24 \times 116) + (0.17 \times 146) = 52.66$$

The gain at other times is calculated similarly, see Table 5.46. The mean gain is calculated using the mean, rather than the cyclic, absorption values.

The cyclic component of the directly transmitted short-wave radiation and attenuated by the surface factor (F) appropriate to the thermal weight of the building and delayed by a time corresponding to the thermal weight, see Table 5.6.

For a lightweight building, $F = 0.8$ and the time delay is 1 hour, i.e:

$$\tilde{T}_L = 0.8 \times (T_{t+1} - \bar{T})$$

and for a heavyweight building, $F = 0.5$ and the time delay is 2 hours, i.e:

$$\tilde{T}_H = 0.5 \times (T_{t+2} - \bar{T})$$

where subscript 'L' denotes thermally lightweight building and subscript 'H' denotes thermally heavyweight building.

As for example A4.1, the mean solar gain factor at the environmental node is given by:

$$\bar{S}_e = \frac{\text{mean transmitted radiation plus mean absorbed radiation}}{\text{daily mean incident radiation}}$$

Hence:

$$\bar{S}_e = (19 + 34)/179 = 0.3$$

Again, as for example A4.1, the cyclic solar gain factors at the environmental node are calculated using the gains appropriate to a time depending on the thermal weight of the structure, i.e:

$$\tilde{S}_e = \frac{\text{total swing in gain to space}}{\text{swing in external gain}}$$

Peak solar irradiance occurs at 1400 h; hence, for a thermally lightweight structure (i.e. 1 hour delay):

$$\tilde{S}_{eL} = (28 + 81)/(563 - 179) = 0.28$$

and for a thermally heavyweight structure (i.e. 2 hour delay):

$$\tilde{S}_{eH} = (18 + 70)/(504 - 179) = 0.27$$

The mean solar gain factor at the air node is given by:

$$\bar{S}_a = \frac{\text{mean gain to air node}}{\text{mean incident radiation}}$$

Hence:

$$\bar{S}_a = 22/179 = 0.12$$

The cyclic solar gain factor at the air node is given by:

$$\tilde{S}_a = \frac{\text{total swing in gain to air node}}{\text{swing in external gain}}$$

There is no time delay associated with the air node, hence:

$$\tilde{S}_a = 74/(572 - 179) = 0.19$$

5.A4.4   Shading coefficients

In addition to solar gain factors, Table 5.7 also gives the short-wave and long-wave shading coefficients (S_c). These correspond to the direct and indirect transmission to the space for direct radiation at normal incidence, divided by 0.87 (i.e. the transmission coefficient of nominal 4 mm plain glass at normal incidence). However, it should be noted that the room gains, and hence the solar gain factors, depend on the direct and diffuse components of the incident radiation and the angle of incidence of the direct radiation.

References for Appendix 5.A4

A4.1   *Weather and solar data* CIBSE Guide A2 (London: Chartered Institution of Building Services Engineers) (1986)

A4.2   Jones R H L Solar radiation through windows —theory and equations *Building Serv. Eng. Res. Technol.* **1**(2) 83–91 (1980)

A4.3   Parmelee G V and Vild D J Design data for slat-type sun shades for use in load estimating *ASHVE Trans.* **59** 1403–1434 (1953)

A4.4   Nicol J F Radiation transmission characteristics of louver systems *Building Science* **1** 167–182 (1966)

A4.5   Mitalas G P and Stephenson D G *Absorption and transmission of thermal radiation by single and double glazed windows* Research Paper No. 173 (National Research Council of Canada, Division of Building Research) (1962)

A4.6   Parmelee G V and Aubele W W The shading of sunlit glass *ASHVE Trans.* **58** 377–395 (1952)

Appendix 5.A5: Derivation of factor for intermittent heating

The symbols used in this appendix are defined in section 5.2.1.

Equation 5.49 defines the factor for intermittent heating, F_3, as follows:

$$F_3 = Q_i / Q_t \qquad (5.246)$$

where Q_i is the installed capacity for intermittent operation (W) and Q_t is the total heat loss (W).

Assuming that the installed capacity is that required to raise the space temperature from the daily mean space temperature $(\bar{t}_i)$ to the internal design temperature (t_i) then, for a design day where the mean outside temperature $(\bar{t}_o)$ is equal to the design outside temperature:

$$F_3 = \frac{[\Sigma(A\,U) + C_v]\,(\bar{t}_i - \bar{t}_o) + [\Sigma(A\,Y) + C_v]\,(t_i - \bar{t}_i)}{[\Sigma(A\,U) + C_v]\,(t_i - \bar{t}_o)} \qquad (5.247)$$

Assuming the ventilation rate is constant and equal to the design value:

$$F_3 = \frac{\bar{t}_i - \bar{t}_o}{t_i - \bar{t}_o} + \frac{[\Sigma(A\,Y) + C_v]\,(t_i - \bar{t}_i)}{[\Sigma(A\,U) + C_v]\,(t_i - \bar{t}_o)} \qquad (5.248)$$

$$= \frac{\bar{t}_i - \bar{t}_o}{t_i - \bar{t}_o} + f_r \frac{(t_i - \bar{t}_i)}{(t_i - \bar{t}_o)} \qquad (5.249)$$

where f_r is the response factor (see equation 5.13).

It has been shown that[A5.1]:

$$\frac{\bar{t}_i - \bar{t}_o}{t_i - \bar{t}_o} = \frac{H f_r}{H f_r + (24 - H)} \qquad (5.250)$$

where H is hours of plant operation including preheat (h).

Therefore, subtracting both sides from t_i and rearranging gives:

$$\frac{t_i - \bar{t}_i}{t_i - \bar{t}_o} = 1 - \frac{H f_r}{H f_r + (24 - H)} \qquad (5.251)$$

Substituting equations 5.251 and 5.250 into equation 5.249 gives:

$$F_3 = \frac{24 f_r}{H f_r + (24 - H)} \qquad (5.252)$$

Reference for Appendix 5.A5

A5.1   Harrington-Lynn J Derivation of equations for intermittent heating used in CIBSE Building Energy Code Part 2a *Building Serv. Eng. Res. Technol.* **19**(4) (1998)

Appendix 5.A6: Algorithm for tabulated solar cooling loads

(1)   Determine incident solar radiation

See CIBSE Guide: *Weather and solar data*, section 2.7.2.2 or 2.7.2.3.

(2)   Determine radiation absorbed and transmitted by window

For each hour of the day, calculate the angle of incidence between the solar beam and the window; combine with the direct and diffuse incident radiation, using the methods given in Appendix 5.A4, to determine the radiation transmitted and absorbed by each glazing element of the window.

(3)   Calculate gains to environmental node

For each hour of the day, calculate the long-wave and convective gains to environmental node from the window using the methods given in Appendix 5.A4.

(4)   Determine swing in gains

Determine the response time for the space and then calculate the mean and deviation from the mean (swing) of the gains to environmental node and, if internal blinds are present, the additional gains to the air node for each hour of the day.

(5)   Determine solar cooling load

For 24-hour operation, to maintain constant dry resultant temperature, solar cooling load is given by:

$$Q_{sc\theta} = \bar{Q}_{se} F_{cu} + \tilde{Q}_{se\theta} F_{cy} + Q_{sa\theta} \qquad (5.253)$$

where θ is time of day. Note that $Q_{sa\theta}$ will be zero in the absence of internal shading.

To maintain constant air temperature, the solar cooling is given by:

$$Q_{sc\theta} = \bar{Q}_{se} F_{au} + \tilde{Q}_{se\theta} F_{ay} + Q_{sa\theta} \qquad (2.254)$$

(6)   Correct for intermittent operation (if required)

If the plant is to be operated intermittently, a correction, given by equation 5.56 (see section 5.8.4.3) is added to the solar cooling load. For the tables of solar cooling load given in this Guide, the loads during the plant 'off' time were summed outside the hours of operation (i.e. between 1530 h and 0730 h).

(7)   Correction factors to cooling load tables

For each orientation, determine the maximum cooling load and the hour during which it occurs. Divide this peak cooling load by the cooling load calculated for the reference glazing for the same hour, month and orientation. Average the correction factor for all orientations and months.

(8)   Correction factors $F_{cu}, F_{cy}, F_{au}, F_{ay}$

For Tables 5.18 to 5.23, values of parameters used for calculating the above correction factors were as follows:

—   module location: intermediate floor with one exposed surface

—   module dimensions: $(4.8 \times 4.8 \times 2.7)$ m

—   glazed percentage: 40% of external wall

—   properties of surfaces of module: see Table 5.47.

For both cases (i.e. fast and slow thermal response), a relatively well-sealed facade was assumed, with an infiltration rate of 0.25 h^{-1}.

(9)   Glazing properties

As given in Appendix 5.A4, Table 5.44.

(10)   Shading

For Tables 5.21 to 5.23, generic shading device having 20% transmission and 40% reflection was assumed, see Appendix 5.A4, Table 5.44. The shading device was assumed to operate when direct radiation on the façade was greater than 200 W·m^{-2}.

Table 5.47 Properties of surfaces for module used for determination of cooling load tables

Surface	Slow thermal response				Fast thermal response			
	U-value (W·m^{-2}·K^{-1})	Y-value (W·m^{-2}·K^{-1})	Surface factor, F	Time lag Ψ(h)	U-value (W·m^{-2}·K^{-1})	Y-value (W·m^{-2}·K^{-1})	Surface factor, F	Time lag Ψ(h)
Glass	3.0	3.0	—	—	3.0	3.0	—	—
Wall	0.45	5.5	0.5	2	0.45	2	0.8	1

Appendix 5.A7: Specification for Reference (dynamic) Model

In order to satisfy the requirements of the Reference (dynamic) Model, the features indicated below should be incorporated. This specification is not exhaustive but gives sufficient detail to provide a basis for assessing computer models.

5.A7.1 Analytical method

Calculations should be carried out for time increments not exceeding one hour using appropriate time sequences of climatic data, internal load patterns and required control set points. These may be hourly average values or, if the calculation requires a time increment of less than one hour, measured data corresponding to the time increment should be used or values may be interpolated from hourly data.

5.A7.2 Climatic data

Data for the following parameters are required at time increments not exceeding one hour:

— dry bulb temperature

— moisture content (or equivalent)

— solar irradiation, comprising direct, sky diffuse, ground reflected (taking account of site factors), sky temperature (or other parameter appropriate to the determination of long-wave radiation from external surfaces)

— wind speed

— wind direction.

The effect on the convective heat transfer coefficient of wind speed and direction should be taken into account.

The solar component should include long-wave radiation transfer to the sky and surroundings.

The conversion of solar irradiance data measured at a particular orientation and slope into values for other orientations and slopes should be achieved using the methods described in CIBSE Guide: *Weather and solar data*[A7.1].

Solar altitude and azimuth should be determined using the methods contained in CIBSE Guide: *Weather and solar data*[A7.1].

The conversion of measured climatic data into the form required by the calculation procedure should be achieved using the relationships given in CIBSE Guide C1: *Properties of humid air*[A7.2].

5.A7.3 Properties of opaque fabric

The following properties should be represented:

— thermal resistance

— thermal capacitance

— surface emissivity (at boundaries and internal cavities)

— surface absorption coefficient for short-wave radiation

— convective and radiant heat transfer characteristics within cavities.

The dynamic response of opaque components may be determined using finite difference techniques or by response factors; other methods may be used provided that it may be demonstrated that they can achieve equal precision[A7.3].

5.A7.4 Glazing

The following properties should be represented:

— thermal resistance

— solar absorption

— solar transmission

— surface emissivity

— convective and radiant heat transfer characteristics within internal cavities.

The performance of glazing systems should be based on the values of solar altitude and azimuth calculated at the solar time corresponding to the time for which the calculation is being performed. This may differ due to longitude and/or the effect of local adjustments for daylight saving.

The performance of glazing systems must take account of reflections between the elements comprising the system.

Separate calculations must be made for shaded and unshaded areas of glazed surfaces.

5.A7.5 Shading

Shading devices may consist of purpose built overhangs, side fins adjacent to or part of a window or moveable devices such as blinds, shutters or curtains.

The shading effect should be calculated for time increments not exceeding one hour using values of solar altitude and azimuth at the appropriate solar time. Where shading devices may be adjusted or controlled the effect of such features should be represented.

The model should take account of the effect of shading on glazing performance, as follows:

— in the case of purpose built shades, the determination of the amount and location of shade falling on the glazing; reflected radiation from the shades should also be considered

— for blinds and curtains, the absorbed and transmitted radiation to be calculated, if appropriate, as a function of slat angle; the interaction between glazing elements and blinds due to reflection of radiation from blinds must be represented.

Other obstacles to radiation such as shading by adjacent buildings and other site features should also be included, as should self-shading by the building under analysis.

5.A7.6   Internal long-wave radiation

Long-wave radiant heat transfer between surfaces and convective heat transfer between room air and room surfaces should be modelled using the fundamental heat balance described in Appendix 5.A1.

Long-wave interchange between sources of internal heat gain and room surfaces must be modelled. The location of heat emitters should be taken into account.

5.A7.7   Internal short-wave radiation (direct solar gain)

The distribution of short-wave energy should be determined by calculation of the amount of direct and diffuse transmitted solar radiation incident upon each room surface. If a surface transmits short-wave radiation the quantity transmitted must be calculated using the same methods as for the transmission of solar radiation into the building. Reflections of short-wave radiation should be modelled.

The solar distribution must be calculated at the same frequency as that for the climatic data.

5.A7.8   Room air model

Convective heat gains may be assumed to enter directly into the air. The convective heat balance should include a representation of the thermal capacity of the room air.

Under some circumstances it may be appropriate to increase the heat storage capacity of the air artificially to take account of furnishings. However, there is little guidance available on when this is necessary.

The convective heat transfer coefficient at room surfaces should be calculated as a function of surface and air temperatures; suitable correlations are given by Alamdari[A7.4] and Hatton[A7.5]. It is not considered practicable at present to include the influence of room air movement patterns.

5.A7.9   Infiltration and ventilation

The needs of design models and simulation models differ in that, for design purposes, it is usual to specify the value of infiltration whereas simulation techniques require this parameter to be calculated. Furthermore, ventilation to remove excess heat gain is an essential factor in the calculation of overheating risk. One way to determine ventilation rates is by means of a zonal airflow model. See Section 4: *Infiltration and natural ventilation* for guidance on the calculation of natural ventilation rates. The program supplier should provide details of the method used and be able to justify the assumptions made in the model.

References for Appendix 5.A7

A7.1   *Weather and solar data* CIBSE Guide (London: Chartered Institution of Building Services Engineers) (to be published)

A7.2   *Properties of humid air* CIBSE Guide C1 (London: Chartered Institution of Building Services Engineers) (1986)

A7.3   *Building energy and environmental modelling* CIBSE Applications Manual AM11 (London: Chartered Institution of Building Services Engineers) (1998)

A7.4   Almadari F and Hammond G P Improved data correlations for buoyancy driven convection in rooms *Building Serv. Eng. Res. Technol.* **4**(3) 106–112 (1980)

A7.5   Hatton A and Awbi H B Convective heat transfer in rooms *Proc. Building Simulation '95, August 1995, Wisconsin, USA* (1995)

Appendix 5.A8: Tests for assessing computer software

The tests described below suggest the type of questions that might be asked of a vendor of computer software. While the results shown here were obtained using particular software and are intended for guidance only; they are not compliance tests and should not be treated as such.

5.A8.1 Thermal mass test

5.A8.1.1 Climate parameters

Climate parameters are as follows:

— solar irradiation: set to zero

— long-wave radiation loss: not calculated

— effect of wind speed on external convection heat transfer coefficient: not considered

— external dry bulb for preconditioning and month 1: sine wave with period of 24 hours; mean: 10°C; maximum: 15°C; minimum: 5°C

— external dry bulb for preconditioning and month 2: constant at –1°C.

5.A8.1.2 Building data

Four test cases are considered, each being a thermally isolated cube, with surfaces constructed of following materials:

(1) 1 mm plasterboard

(2) 100 mm concrete

(3) 250 mm concrete

(4) 500 mm concrete.

Infiltration and/or ventilation are set to zero. There is no heating or cooling plant.

5.A8.1.3 Results

The results comprise outside and inside air temperatures, see Figure 5.26. The effect of thermal storage by the walls is clearly shown. It will be noted that all internal temperatures decay to a constant temperature of –1°C, indicating a heat balance.

5.A8.2 Solar distribution test

This test is intended to demonstrate the way in which direct solar irradiation is distributed over the internal surfaces. Accurate solar distribution is necessary in highly glazed spaces because direct transmission from the space will often significantly decrease the heat gain to that space while increasing the gain to adjacent spaces.

5.A8.2.1 Building and climate parameters

The input data are as follows:

— climate: clear sky

— building: glass cube with one vertical wall facing due south.

5.A8.2.2 Results

Table 5.48 shows the results for latitude 50°N. They comprise the fraction of solar irradiation transmitted by a particular surface which falls upon the remaining surfaces.

Table 5.48 Results of solar distribution test (south facade)

Time of day	Percentage of solar radiation transmitted through south facade falling on stated internal surface (%)					
	Roof	S	E	N	W	Floor
0800	0.00	0.00	0.00	0.00	0.65	0.35
0900	0.00	0.00	0.00	0.00	0.48	0.52
1000	0.00	0.00	0.00	0.00	0.30	0.70
1100	0.00	0.00	0.00	0.00	0.14	0.86
1200	0.00	0.00	0.00	0.00	0.00	1.00
1300	0.00	0.00	0.14	0.00	0.00	0.86
1400	0.00	0.00	0.30	0.00	0.00	0.70
1500	0.00	0.00	0.48	0.00	0.00	0.52
1600	0.00	0.00	0.65	0.00	0.00	0.35

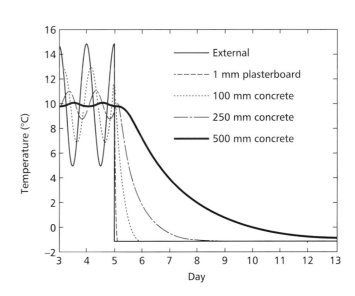

Figure 5.26 Results of thermal mass test

6 Internal heat gains

6.1 Introduction

Internal heat gain is the sensible and latent heat emitted within an internal space by the following sources:

— human and animal bodies

— lighting

— computers and office equipment

— electric motors

— cooking appliances and other domestic equipment.

In the design of air conditioning systems, the internal heat gain may contribute a significant part of the total cooling load and it is therefore important that all such gains be included. However, the plant must also be capable of operating satisfactorily at part load. Over-estimating internal heat gains may result in over-sizing of plant leading to higher capital costs of plant, poor part load performance and increased running costs.

The following section provides information on heat emission from various sources which will enable designers to estimate the internal heat gains. A diversity factor will need to be applied in instances where a number of similar heat sources exist but do not operate simultaneously. Guidance is given on likely heat gains where equipment and occupant details are not known.

It must be emphasised that the data contained herein are typical only. Equipment gains, particularly the radiant component, vary significantly with type, manufacturer and technology. Care should be taken in estimating the gains from equipment associated with information technology (IT) since data for such equipment become outdated very quickly due to technological advances. The designer should use specific information for all sources of internal heat gains where such information is available.

The proportions of convective/conductive and radiant gains are provided where known. For most equipment there will be a radiant gain due to the case temperature of the equipment being higher than the mean radiant temperature for the room. The radiant heat gain is first absorbed by the room surfaces before being re-emitted to produce a reduced cooling load some time later, see Section 5: *Thermal response and plant sizing*. All convective heat gains result in an instantaneous cooling load at the air point. If the case temperature is known the radiant heat gain can be approximated using the following equation:

$$Q = A_c \, \sigma \varepsilon \, (T_c^4 - T_r^4) \tag{6.1}$$

where Q is the radiant heat gain (W), A_c is the case area (m²), σ is the Stefan-Boltzmann constant (5.67×10^{-8} W·m⁻²·K⁻⁴), ε is the emissivity of the surface, T_c is the case temperature (K) and T_m is the mean radiant temperature (K).

6.2 Human and animal bodies

6.2.1 Human bodies

The emission of heat from a human body in relation to the surrounding indoor climate is discussed in Section 1: *Environmental criteria for design*. Table 6.1 provides representative heat emissions (sensible and latent) from an average adult male in different states of activity and for different indoor dry bulb temperatures. The figures in parenthesis are adjusted heat emissions based on normal percentages of men, women and children for the applications listed. The typical occupancy density for each application is also given, but specific assessments should be applied where such data are available. Where the actual occupancy density and the proportions of men, women and children are known, the appropriate heat output for an average adult male should be used, corrected for women and children by multiplying it by a factor of 0.85 for women and 0.75 for children.

The latent heat gain from a human body results in an instantaneous addition to the cooling load, whereas the sensible heat gain is not all directly convected. Of the sensible heat emission, between 20 and 60%[1] can be radiant depending on type of clothing, activity, dry resultant temperature and air velocity.

6.2.2 Animal bodies

The sensible and latent heat emissions from the bodies of a variety of animals of average mass are listed in Table 6.2.

In the absence of experimental results, an approximation to the basal metabolic rate (BMR) from an animal may be established using the expression:

$$h = 3.2 \, m^{0.75} \tag{6.2}$$

where h is the basal metabolic rate (W) and m is the mass of the animal (kg).

The basal metabolic rate is the rate at which heat is emitted from a body at rest in a warm environment. The equation should be modified to take account of any physical activity.

6.3 Lighting

6.3.1 General

All the electrical energy used by a lamp is ultimately released as heat. The energy is emitted by means of conduction, convection or radiation. When the light is switched on the luminaire itself absorbs some of the heat

Table 6.1 Heat emission (W) from an adult male body (of surface area 2 m²) and average heat emission per person for a mixture of men, women and children typical of the stated application

Activity	Typical application	Occupancy density (m²/person)	Total, sensible and latent heat emission (W) for stated application and dry bulb temperature (C) for adult male (and average for mixture of men, women and children)										
			Total	15		20		22		24		26	
				Sensible	Latent	Sensible	Latent	Sensible	Latent	Sensible	Latent	Sensible	Latent
Seated, inactive	Theatre, cinema matinee	0.75–1.0$^{(2,3)}$	115 (100)	100 (87)	15 (13)	90 (78)	25 (22)	80 (70)	35 (30)	75 (65)	40 (35)	65 (57)	50 (43)
Seated, inactive	Theatre, cinema evening	0.75–1.0$^{(2,3)}$	115 (105)	100 (91)	15 (14)	90 (82)	25 (23)	80 (73)	35 (32)	75 (68)	40 (37)	65 (59)	50 (46)
Seated, light work	Restaurant	1.0–2.0$^{(2,3)}$	140 (126)	110 (99)	30 (27)	100 (90)	40 (36)	90 (81)	50 (45)	80 (72)	60 (54)	70 (63)	70 (63)
Seated, moderate work	Office	8–39$^{(4-6)}$, 14$^{(4,7)}$*	140 (130)	110 (102)	30 (28)	100 (93)	40 (37)	90 (84)	50 (46)	80 (74)	60 (56)	70 (65)	70 (65)
Standing, light work, walking	Department store	1.7–4.3$^{(2,3)}$	160 (141)	120 (106)	40 (35)	110 (97)	50 (44)	100 (88)	60 (53)	85 (75)	75 (66)	75 (66)	85 (75)
Standing, light work, walking	Bank	—	160 (142)	120 (107)	40 (35)	110 (98)	50 (44)	100 (89)	60 (53)	85 (76)	75 (66)	75 (66)	85 (76)
Light bench work	Factory	—	235 (209)	150 (133)	85 (76)	130 (116)	105 (93)	115 (102)	120 (107)	100 (89)	135 (121)	80 (71)	155 (138)
Medium bench work	Factory	—	265 (249)	160 (150)	105 (99)	140 (132)	125 (117)	125 (117)	140 (132)	105 (99)	160 (150)	90 (85)	175 (164)
Heavy work	Factory	—	440 (440)	220 (220)	220 (220)	190 (190)	250 (250)	165 (165)	275 (275)	135 (135)	305 (305)	105 (105)	335 (335)
Moderate dancing	Dance hall	0.5–1.0	265 (249)	160 (150)	105 (99)	140 (132)	125 (117)	125 (117)	140 (132)	105 (99)	160 (150)	90 (85)	175 (164)

* Recommended

Notes:

(1) Figures in parenthesis are adjusted heat gains based on normal percentage of men, women and children for the applications listed. This is based on the heat gain for women and children of 85% and 75% respectively of that of an adult male.

(2) For restaurant serving hot meals add 10 W sensible and 10 W latent for food per individual.

Table 6.2 Sensible and latent heat emissions from animal bodies at normal body temperature

Creature	Average body weight	Rectal temperature (°C)	BMR (W)	Typical occupancy per 10 m² floor area	Estimated heat emission* (W)	
					Sensible	Latent
Mouse	0.02	36.5	0.175	2000	0.5	0.3
Hamster	0.12	36.9	0.483	1350	1.6	0.4
Rat	0.30	37.3	1.32	485	3.7	1.2
Guinea pig	0.41	39.1	1.7	400	4.6	2.2
Rabbit	2.6	39.4	5.6	32	8.5	2.5
Cat	3.0	38.6	7.35	16	11	3.8
Monkey	4.2	38.8	10	16	24	14
Dog	16	38.9	26	5	40	13
Goat	36	39.2	41	5	62	21
Sheep	45	38.8	56	5	81	29
Pig	250	39.3	210	1.5	317	106
Pigeon	0.27	43.3	1.35	400	2.2	0.5
Chicken	2.0	41.4	5.6	195	9.2	1.8

* Based on a 24-hour average; during periods of high activity the heat production may be double that of the estimated 24-hour average

emitted by the lamp. Some of this heat may then be transmitted to the building structure, depending on the manner in which the luminaire is mounted. The radiant energy emitted (both visible and invisible) from a lamp will result in a heat gain to the space only after it has been absorbed by the room surfaces. This storage effect results in a time lag before the heat appears as a part of the cooling load.

In determining the internal heat gains due to artificial lighting the following must be known:

— total electrical input power

— fraction of heat emitted which enters the space

— radiant, convective and conductive components.

Both the total electrical input power and the distribution of the heat output will vary with manufacturer. In particular, the optical properties of the luminaire can affect greatly the radiant/convective proportion emitted by the lamp. All figures quoted in the following section are typical. Manufacturers' data should be used where possible.

6.3.2   Total electrical input power

The total electrical power input to the lighting installation must be known. For lamps with associated control gear, it is important to add the power dissipated by the control gear to that dissipated by the lamp. The control gear power loss is likely to be about 10% of the lamp rating for electronic ballast and about 20% for conventional ballast[8].

Case studies carried out on a number of offices built or refurbished between 1977 and 1983 found that the lighting loads were between 10 and 32 W·m⁻² for a maintained illuminance levels of 150–800 lux[5]. Surveys carried out on newer buildings found that the lighting loads were in the range 8–18 W·m⁻² for a maintained illuminance levels of 350–500 lux[6].

Where the actual installed power is not known reference should be made to Table 6.3, which provides target ranges of installed power density per 100 lux (maintained illuminance) for general lighting installations. For new

installations, the actual installed power should be towards the lower end of the recommended range. Most existing installations are likely to be at the higher end of the range. The ranges, which apply to general lighting installations using a conventional layout, are classified according to application, area, room surface reflectance, room index, luminaire maintenance categories, light source type and wattage used.

6.3.3   Fraction of emitted heat entering the space

The proportion of heat entering the space depends upon the type and location of the light fittings.

Where the lamp or luminaire is suspended from the ceiling or wall-mounted, or where uplighters or desk lamps are used, all the heat input will appear as an internal heat gain.

Where recessed or surface-mounted luminaires are installed below a false ceiling, some of the total input power will result in a heat gain to the ceiling void. An accurate assessment of the distribution of energy from particular types of luminaire should be obtained from the manufacturer. In the absence of manufacturers' data, Table 6.4 provides an indication of the energy distribution for various arrangements of fluorescent lamp luminaires, based on laboratory measurements.

For air handling luminaires, up to 80% of the total input power can be removed by the air stream, leaving only 20% to enter the space as heat gain. The specific manufacturer should be contacted for actual test data. Heat taken away from a luminaire through a ceiling plenum, or directly from the luminaire itself, will not form part of the room sensible heat gain but may still constitute part of the total refrigeration load.

Table 6.3 Target ranges of installed power density per 100 lux maintained illuminance for general lighting installations[9]

Lamp type	Wattage range used to calculate target ranges (W)	Luminaire maintenance categories*	Power density range at working plane (W·m⁻² per 100 lux) for stated room index		
			1	2.5	5
(a) High bay industrial (reflectances: ceiling 0.5–0.3, wall 0.5–0.3, floor 0.2–0.1)					
Metal halide:					
— clear or coated	250–400	B, C, E	2.6–4.5	2.1–3.6	2.0–3.4
High pressure mercury:					
— coated	250–00	B, C, E	4.2–6.2	3.5–5.1	3.3–4.8
High pressure sodium:					
— improved colour	250–400	B, C, E	2.4–3.6	2.0–2.9	1.9–2.8
— standard or high efficiency	250–1000	B, C, E	1.4–2.7	1.2–2.2	1.1–2.1
(b) Industrial (reflectances: ceiling 0.7–0.3, wall 0.5, floor 0.2)					
Fluorescent:					
— triphosphor	32–100	B, C, E	2.5–4.9	1.9–3.5	1.6–2.9
— halophosphate	32–100	B, C, E	3.2–6.3	2.4–4.5	2.1–3.7
Metal halide:					
— clear or coated	150–400	B, C, E	2.9–6.8	2.3–4.4	2.1–3.9
High pressure mercury:					
— coated	125–400	B, C, E	4.8–9.4	3.7–6.1	3.5–5.5
High pressure sodium:					
— improved colour	150–400	B, C, E	2.7–5.5	2.1–3.5	2.0–3.2
— standard or high efficiency	100–400	B, C, E	1.8–4.7	1.3–3.0	1.3–2.7
(c) Commercial (reflectances: ceiling 0.7–0.5, wall 0.5, floor 0.2)					
Fluorescent:					
— triphosphor	32–100	A, B, C, D, E	2.7–5.4	2.2–4.2	2.1–3.7
— halophosphate	32–100	A, B, C, D, E	3.4–7.0	2.8–5.4	2.6–4.8
— compact	36–55	A, B, C, D, E	3.3–6.4	2.8–4.9	2.6–4.4
Metal halide:					
— clear or coated	150–400	B, C	4.4–7.1	3.6–5.7	3.4–5.3
High pressure mercury:					
— coated	125–400	B, C	6.6–9.9	5.4–7.9	5.1–7.3
High pressure sodium:					
— improved colour	150–400	B, C	3.8–5.8	3.1–4.6	2.9–4.3
— standard or high efficiency	100–400	B, C	2.4–4.9	2.0–3.9	1.9–3.6

* See CIBSE *Code for Interior Lighting*[9] section 3.3.2 and Table 4.5

Notes:

(1) The above figures assume design to good current practice and existing installations may exceed the ranges given.

(2) Room index = (length × width) / [(length + width) × height of luminaire above working plane].

(3) Maintenance categories[9] : A = bare lamp batten; B = open top reflector (ventilation, self-cleaning); C = closed top reflector (unventilated); D = enclosed (IP2X); E = dust proof (IP5X); F = indirect uplighter.

(4) Heat output for tungsten lamps: opal sphere 50–60 W·m⁻² (300 lux); halogen uplighters 30–50 W·m⁻² (300 lux).

6.3.4 Radiant, convective and conductive components

Little information exists on the proportions of radiant, convective and conducted heat gain from lighting. Lamps radiate in both the visible and invisible wavebands and there will be a net gain of infrared radiation from the lamp and luminaire due to their radiant temperature being above the room mean radiant temperature. Table 6.5 provides approximate data for different lamp types and shows that a substantial proportion of the energy dissipated by all sources is emitted as radiant heat. Radiant heat can cause discomfort to the occupants. It is mainly detected by the occupants on the forehead and the backs of the hands as these parts are more sensitive to radiant heat than other parts of the body. The optics and body design of the luminaire can reduce substantially the radiant component and, for the purposes of determining room cooling load, it may be sufficient to assume that the heat is purely convective.

Table 6.5 Energy dissipation in lamps[10]

Lamp type	Heat output (%)		
	Radiant	Conducted/ convected*	Total
Fluorescent	30	70	100
Filament (tungsten)	85	15	100
High pressure mercury/ sodium, metal halide	50	50	100
Low pressure sodium	43	57	100

* The power loss of ballasts should be added to the conducted/convected heat.

Table 6.4 Measured energy distribution for fluorescent fittings having four 70W lamps[8]

Type of fitting		Energy distribution (%)	
Mounting	Description	Upwards	Downwards
Recessed			
	Open	38	62
	Louvre	45	55
	Prismatic or opal diffuser	53	47
Surface			
	Open	12	88
	Enclosed prismatic or opal	22	78
	Enclosed prismatic on metal spine	6	94

6.4 Computers and office equipment

6.4.1 General

Computers and office equipment will result in heat gains to the room equal to the total power input. Many client organisations refer to power demand in terms of watts per square metre ($W \cdot m^{-2}$) of net usable floor area. Such measures must be considered carefully as there are a number of factors which can affect the value. For example, the net usable floor area will include access space, meeting rooms and managers' offices, all of which may have very low power requirements. If there are many such areas this will inflate the allowance for the remainder of the floor, resulting in oversizing.

Furthermore, a value expressed in $W \cdot m^{-2}$ will be influenced by the occupation density. If the occupation density is high then the required power demand per unit of floor area is likely to be higher than that for a less densely occupied building. Furthermore, occupation densities themselves vary widely. Occupation densities in commercial office buildings are known to vary from 8 m^2 per person to 39 m^2 per person[4-6] and recent surveys have concluded that services demand calculations should be based on 14 m^2 net area per person[4,7]. Many offices built in 1980s were designed to meet a perceived market need and to ensure that the building could accommodate the forecast growth in the use of information technology (IT). Typical values used in the City of London and nearby have been 25–40 $W \cdot m^{-2}$[11]. Developments in IT have since reduced the heat output of office equipment that can result in over-specification of small power loads and hence heat gains.

Over-specification of small power loads can affect air conditioning systems in three ways:

— occupier comfort may suffer due to the air conditioning system being required to operate below its peak performance

— increased running costs due to the need to run the air conditioning system continuously below its peak efficiency

— increased capital costs resulting from the size and cost of chillers, air handling plant, ductwork etc.

To ensure flexibility in the use of a building and provide scope for expansion, the capacity of the power distribution system may be considerably higher than that required to cope with present demands. However, in estimating the heat gains for the purposes of calculating cooling loads, it should not be assumed that this capacity will be fully utilised nor that it will be utilised throughout the building. Each area should be considered individually.

Surveys carried out on a small number of buildings have shown[6] that the small power loads were between 7 and 16 $W \cdot m^{-2}$ with occasional 'pockets' of higher loads of up to 25 $W \cdot m^{-2}$. Recent recommendations have concluded that a cooling load of 15 $W \cdot m^{-2}$ is adequate to cope with small power consumption for all but the most intensive user needs[7,11-13]. Specialist high-load areas should be calculated separately and treated by dedicated or supplementary systems.

To assess the power demands for IT equipment in a particular building the following must be taken into account[14]:

— individual machine loads

— diversity factors (i.e. work function and usage diversity)

— shared machines

— future trends.

These issues are considered below.

6.4.2 Individual machine loads

Electronic equipment manufacturers are often unable to provide accurate average power demand values. The name-

Table 6.6 Worst case power demands for individual IT equipment [14]

Item	Worst case power demand (W)	Worst case nameplate ratio (%)
Personal computers with display screen/file servers	187 (116)*	70 (46)*
Mini/mainframe computer workstations	160	60
Laser printers	150 (98)*	20 (15)*
Dot matrix printers:		
— nameplate rating 100–120 W	54	45
— nameplate rating 120–220 W	67	31
Plotters:		
— electrostatic, monochrome (A4–A0)	300	60
— electrostatic, colour (A4–A0)	850	75
— thermal, colour A4	400	51
— thermal, colour A0	750	56
— pen plotter	200	43
Fax machine	38	25
Electronic typewriters	38	40
Modems	20	—
Paper drills (punches)	110	44
Microfiche viewers	150	50
Overhead projector	300	99
Slide projector	350	100

* Figures in brackets represent typical averages

Note: Nameplate ratio (%) =
(average power demand / nameplate rating) × 100

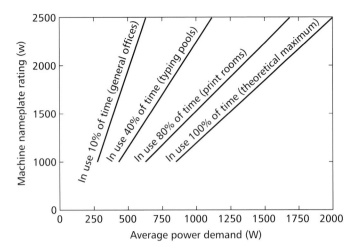

Figure 6.1 Average power demands for photocopiers [14]

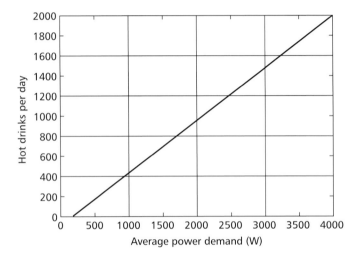

Figure 6.2 Average power demands for vending machines [14]

plate ratings on many machines indicate peak values which are approached only briefly on start-up and bear no relationship to the actual current drawn. Applying the rated consumption with no adjustment would lead to over-design of the air conditioning system.

The average power demands for office machines remain relatively constant for some equipment while for other equipment the load is highly variable.

6.4.2.1 Constant load machines

Electronic machines that perform tasks that involve minimal movement of working parts have virtually constant power demands except for short-term peaks, such as when personal computer (PC) disk drives are accessed or when laser printers are actually printing. As these peaks occur for only a short time, their effect on the average power demand over an extended period is negligible.

Table 6.6 shows the estimated average and worst case values based on site testing of different machines over a period of one working day (8 hours). Peak and mean values are shown for personal computers and laser printers since a large number of these machines were tested. For all other equipment, where the sample size was below 20 machines, the highest value measured has been assumed as a worse case maximum.

6.4.2.2 Variable load machines

The average power demands of photocopiers and vending machines are very dependent on the mode of operation. For such machines, different circuits and components are

activated during different activities and therefore the power demand is constantly changing. Approximations can be made, provided that some information is available concerning their intended method of operation.

For photocopiers, the power demand of a typical machine at idle is approximately 20% of the nameplate rating while the working power demand when printing is approximately 80% of the nameplate rating. For most general purpose machines, the time spent printing is usually less than 10% of the total time for which the machine is switched on. Figure 6.1 shows the average power demands for photocopiers based on different applications and times in use [14].

For machines dispensing hot drinks, the average power demand is proportional to the number of cups dispensed. Assuming an average cup size of 0.2 litres containing a hot drink at 80°C, the energy consumed per cup is approximately 60 kJ, which, if averaged over an 8-hour working day, is equivalent to 2 W per cup. There will also be a heat gain due to the power demand of the machine itself. Figure 6.2 shows the approximate average power demands for vending machines based on the number of hot drinks dispensed per day [14].

Table 6.7 Diversity factors for computer usage in different work functions[14].

Job function	Computer users (%)			Non-users (%)
	Continuous	Intermittent	Overall	
Managers/executives	45	45	90	10
Admin/support staff:				
— secretaries and typists	100	0	100	0
— receptionists, filing clerks, personal assistants, librarians	52	33	85	15
Engineering:				
— quantity and building surveyors	23	51	74	26
— buyers, sales engineers, estimators	75	12	87	13
— design engineers, architects, project managers	57	32	89	11
— draughtsmen, tracers, CAD operators	49	47	96	4
— researchers/specialist consultants	96	4	100	0
Accountancy/insurance:				
— accounts clerks and book-keepers	45	38	83	17
— accountants	100	0	100	0
— insurance consultants	75	25	100	0
Computing:				
— programmers and systems analysts	100	0	100	0
— hardware/software support	67	33	100	0

Notes:

(1) Continuous users use a computer all of the time; intermittent users use a computer occasionally; non-users never need to use a computer.

(2) No allowance is made for intermittent users who leave their computer permanently switched on.

Note that the total heat gain from such machines may not all be liberated within the space surrounding the machine. Hot drinks may be taken to other areas of the building resulting in a uniform dissipation of the heat.

6.4.3 Diversity factors

Diversity factors should be applied to the number of office machines to account for (*a*) the number of persons using them (i.e. the 'work function') and (*b*) the amount of time for which the machines are in use (i.e. the 'usage diversity'). These factors are obtained as follows.

6.4.3.1 Work function

The number of computers in an office and their degree of usage will vary depending on the work function for which they are used. For example, managers and directors may seldom need to use a computer whereas typists and secretaries may use their machines continuously. Table 6.7 provides diversity factors for computer usage in different work functions[14].

6.4.3.2 Usage diversity

For any group of office machines there will be times when some will be switched off. The number in use will vary depending on the nature of the machine and its role within the office.

For convenience, machines such as printers, photocopiers, fax machines and network-linked computers (where log-on/off procedures may be time consuming) are often left switched on for the whole working day. Personal computers used intermittently may or may not be switched off when not in use.

It is usually appropriate to allow a factor for usage diversity of computer terminals. An allowance can be calculated by estimating the percentage of time for which each machine will be switched on; i.e. a usage ratio for each machine. This will be established with greater reliability if the job function is known. For example, the computers in a typing pool are likely to be switched on virtually 100% of the time. However, computers used by salespersons may frequently be switched off when the salesperson is away from the office, resulting in a usage ratio of 60% or even 40%.

Once a usage ratio has been established for each machine, the number of machines in use simultaneously at any moment may be predicted by multiplying the total number of machines by the diversity factor given in Figure 6.3.

For small groups of computers (i.e. less than 20) it is likely that all the machines will be in use simultaneously for at least some of the time.

6.4.4 Shared machines

In the absence of firm data concerning the number of machines in an office, it is possible to derive an estimate based on the 'worst case' number of people sharing individual machines. If the number of persons in the area is known, it will then be possible to estimate the likely number of machines.

Table 6.8 shows typical numbers of persons per machine. It can be seen that current worst case is one person per computer. In offices involved in computer intensive work, such as dealing rooms and CAD offices, it is possible that each occupant will have more than one computer each. However, such situations are unusual and should be considered as special cases.

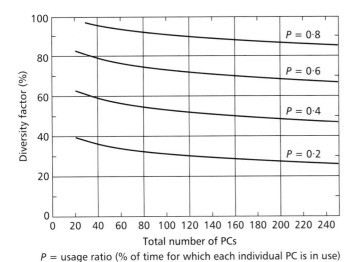

P = usage ratio (% of time for which each individual PC is in use)

Figure 6.3 Usage diversity factors for groups of personal computers[14]

Table 6.8 Worst case numbers of persons sharing individual machines[14]

Machine	Persons per machine
Personal computers	1
File servers	20
Laser printers	3
Photocopiers	20
Fax machines	20
Modems	20

6.4.5   Future trends of office equipment development and use

Office equipment is constantly changing in terms of technology and use, therefore the design engineer may wish to account for the future trends[12,14,15]. The trends identifiable at the time of publication (mid-1999) are as follows:

—   Development of more powerful computers will keep the number of computers at present levels (i.e. 1 per person).

—   Usage of PCs is expected to grow so that most office workers will use a PC for 80–90% of the time.

—   Fax machines may increase to one per five workers (though fax attachments for PCs may make stand-alone fax machines redundant).

—   Photocopier density may drop to one per 50 workers as electronic data storage and transfer reduces the need for hard copies and faster, more compact printers become available.

—   Building owners/operators will make employees more aware of energy conservation and encourage or insist that equipment is switched off when not in use.

—   Building occupiers will become more aware of the power consumption of office equipment when selecting makes/models[16].

—   Manufacturers will produce more energy efficient PCs and office equipment in response to legislation requiring or recommending energy-saving features[16]. This will reduce power demands for office equipment.

—   Better use of office space through increased use of (a) shared work spaces ('hot desking'), (b) 'telecommuting' to combine office- and home-based work and (c) IT systems to allow people to work away from the office. This may increase the amount of electronic equipment in use and also increase the diversity factors for computer usage.

—   The number of modems in offices will increase as datalinks become more essential. However, modems are often incorporated into PCs and do not increase power consumption substantially.

6.4.6   Computer rooms

Computer rooms may have very large heat gains from computer equipment, therefore the air conditioning design should be based on actual installed power. No diversity should be applied. The air conditioning designer should contact the IT/UPS equipment suppliers and the client to obtain the heat output from the computer room equipment and for information on likely future expansion. For preliminary design purposes, the heat rejected from a UPS system may be taken as 45–60 W per UPS kVA rating above 40 kVA[17].

For preliminary design purposes only, a heat gain of between 450 and 900 W·m⁻² may be assumed for the whole computer room.

6.4.7   Radiation, convection and conduction components

The electrical consumption of office equipment gives the total heat dissipated but it is also useful to know how that heat is transferred to the space. Heat that is convected or conducted is an instantaneous gain whereas that which is radiated is absorbed by the building mass and dissipated over time. Little information is available on the radiant, conductive and convective components of heat gain from office equipment. Table 6.9 provides an indication of the likely breakdown of heat gains for a computer, monitor and laser printer. These figures should be used with caution since they were obtained from tests of a single computer, two monitors and one laser printer.

Table 6.9 Components of heat gain dissipated from office equipment[18]

Device	Heat gain component (%)	
	Convective/conductive	Radiant
Desktop computer	86	14
Monitor	65	35
Laser printer	67	33

6.4.8 Examples of assessment of small power loads[14]

6.4.8.1 Example 1: Office building

Proposed office building having 2000m^2 of net usable floor area; open plan layout, housing 140 staff consisting of engineers, draughtsmen, managers and secretarial/support staff. The client provides nameplate ratings for standardised office equipment as shown, but with the exception of the plotters, the precise numbers of machines is not known.

Nameplate ratings:

— Personal computers: 200 W

— File servers: 370 W

— Laser printers: 850 W

— Photocopiers: 1250 W

— Fax machines: 85 W

— Plotters (monochrome, A4–A0): 3 × 300 W

— Modems: 20 W

Coffee machines will be provided and it is assumed that each person will consume an average of 3 cups per day. It is assumed that photocopiers are used for general office purposes, i.e. in use for not more than 10% of the working day.

From Table 6.7 and the client's breakdown of staff, the proportions of overall and intermittent computer users is determined as follows.

From Table 6.10 it is estimated that 94% of the staff will be computer users, i.e. 133 of 140 staff, 31% of which will be intermittent users (i.e. 41). For these users, a usage ratio of 0.4 is assumed (i.e. each computer will be used 40% of the time). A diversity factor may then be obtained from Figure 6.3. For 41 computers with a usage factor of 0.4, Figure 6.3 indicates a diversity factor of 60%.

Therefore the number of intermittently used computers is equivalent to 24 computers in continuous use (i.e. 60% of 41).

The total number of computers likely to be switched on simultaneously is (133 − 41) + 24 = 116.

The numbers of other items of equipment can be estimated from the values given in Table 6.8. In the case of printers, modems and file servers, the number of machines is related to the number of personal computers. Based on these values, the following numbers of machines are predicted:

— file servers: 7

— laser printers: 44

— photocopiers: 7

— fax machines: 7

— modems: 7

The average power demand in the building may then be estimated as shown in Table 6.11. The total power demand equates to 212 W per person or 15 W·m^{-2}.

In consideration of future trends in computer usage, it is appropriate to make some allowance for increased usage of computers by increasing the usage ratio to, say, 0.8. From Figure 6.3 this would increase the diversity factor to about 95% and hence the number of intermittently used computers likely to be switched on will increase from 24 to 39. This could result in an additional heat output of 2.1 kW. Allowing for this trend increases the total small power load to 227 W per person or 16 W·m^{-2}. Allowances for future trends should be agreed with the client.

Table 6.10 Example 1: proportions of overall and intermittent computer users

Job function	% of total staff	% of overall users (from Table 6.7)	Total % of overall users	% of intermittent users (from Table 6.7)	Total % of intermittent users
Managers	10	90	9	45	5
Secretaries	25	100	25	0	0
Support staff	5	85	4	33	2
Engineers	30	89	27	32	10
Draughtsmen	30	96	29	47	14
Total: (%)	100		94		31

Table 6.11 Example 1: calculation of total power demand

Item	Number	Nameplate rating (W)	Nameplate ratio (Table 6.6)	Power demand (W)
Personal computers	116	200	0.7	16 240
File servers	7	370	0.7	1813
Laser printers	44	850	0.2	7480
Fax machines	7	85	0.25	148
Modems	7	20	1	140
Plotters	3	300	0.6	540
Photocopiers	7	325*	—	2275
Coffee machines	420 hot drinks	—	—	1000
			Total:	29 636

* See Figure 6.1

6.4.8.2 Example 2: Speculative office development

Consider a speculative air-conditioned office development of 6000 m². Worst case occupation density is 14 m² per person; maximum number of occupants is 430. Potential tenants will have different office equipment requirements.

Table 6.6 provides estimates for the worst case maximum power demands of different office equipment. In addition, it is assumed that each person will consume at most 3 cups of coffee per day, i.e. a maximum of 1290 cups per day.

Table 6.8 indicates the worst case number of people per machine. For 430 occupants the maximum number of machines is:

— PCs: 430

— file servers: 22

— laser printers: 143

— photocopiers: 22

— fax machines: 22

— modems: 22

Photocopiers are assumed to be of average size (i.e. 1250 W nameplate rating) and used for general office purposes (i.e. in use not more than 10% of the time). From Figure 6.1, the average power demand is 325 W.

As a worst case, the future occupants may each need to use a computer continuously. Therefore, no allowance should be made for usage diversity or for nameplate ratio. Hence, individual machine loads are as shown in Table 6.12. This equates to 272 W per person or 19.5 W·m⁻².

This calculation incorporates a number of worst case situations that, in reality, are unlikely to occur simultaneously. The example therefore demonstrates a theoretical maximum which is unlikely to be encountered in practice. Although individual offices may achieve loads of this order, it is unlikely to be repeated across an entire floor of a building. The designer would need to consult the developer before applying diversity factors to the above estimates.

6.5 Electric motors

6.5.1 General

For situations where the motor and the motor driven equipment are both situated within the space (e.g. machinery in a workshop), the heat output is given by:

$$\Phi_g = P_a / \eta_t \tag{6.3}$$

where Φ_g is the rate of heat gain to the space (W), P_a is the power at the equipment shaft (W) and η_t is the overall efficiency of transmission. The overall efficiency of transmission (η_t) is the product of the motor efficiency (η_m) and the drive efficiency (η_d).

For situations where the motor is situated within the space but the driven equipment is situated elsewhere:

$$\Phi_g = P_a \left[(1/\eta_t) - 1 \right] \tag{6.4}$$

For motor driven equipment situated within, or related to the space (e.g. fans) but with the motor situated outside the space:

$$\Phi_g = P_a \tag{6.5}$$

For precise details of efficiencies, which will vary with motor type, speed, performance and the character of the drive, reference should be made to manufacturers' data. For preliminary system design, in the absence of such data, reference may be made to Tables 6.13 and 6.14.

'High efficiency' motors are designed to minimise the inherent losses of the motor by using more copper in the stator and low-loss steel in the rotor. The improvement in efficiency is greatest at part-load, see Figure 6.4[19], particularly for loads below 50%.

6.5.2 Escalator motors

It may be assumed that all the input power to the escalator motor will be converted to heat (ignoring the potential energy gained by ascending passengers). However, the motor will normally run at less than the motor rating and guidance should be sought from the manufacturer.

Table 6.12 Example 2: calculation of total power demand

Item	Number	Nameplate rating (W)	Nameplate ratio (Table 6.6)	Power demand (W)
Personal computers	430	187	1	80 410
File servers	22	187	1	4114
Laser printers	143	150	1	21 450
Photocopiers	22	325*	—	7150
Fax machines	22	38	1	836
Modems	22	20	1	440
Coffee machines	1290 hot drinks	—	—	2650
			Total:	117 050

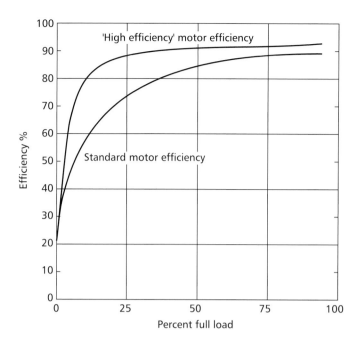

Figure 6.4 Comparison of efficiencies of standard and 'high efficiency' motors[19]

Table 6.13 Average efficiencies for electric motors

Motor output rating	Average motor efficiencies, η_m (%)			
	DC motors	AC motors		
		Single phase	Two-phase	Three-phase
0.75	76	65	73	74
3.75	83	78	84	85
7.50	86	81	87	88
15	88	83	88	90
38	90	85	91	91
56	92	86	92	92

Table 6.14 Average drive efficiencies

Drive	Drive efficiency, η_d (%)
Plain bearings	95–98
Roller bearings	98
Ball bearings	99
Vee-belts	96–98
Spur gears	93
Bevel gears	92

6.5.3 Lift motors

It may be assumed that all the input power to the lift motor will be dissipated as heat within the lift motor room. The motor will not work continuously, nor at constant load. Table 6.15 may be used for preliminary systems design, in the absence of manufacturer's data.

6.6 Cooking appliances[1]

6.6.1 General

Heat gain estimates for cooking appliances are subjective due to the variety of appliances, applications, time in use and types of installation. In estimating appliance loads, the probability of simultaneous use and operation for different appliances located in the same area must be considered.

To estimate heat gains from cooking appliances the actual energy input rating supplied by manufacturers should be used, suitably modified by appropriate usage factors, efficiencies or other judgmental factors. When preliminary assessment is required prior to the establishment of detailed design, Appendix 6.A1 provides typical data[1] for a wide range of appliances. Such preliminary assessments should be checked once manufacturers' information is available.

6.6.2 Hooded appliances

Laboratory tests of hooded cooking appliances have indicated that the heat gains from effective hooded cooking appliances is primarily radiant, and that latent and convective heat are exhausted and do not enter the space[20].

The radiant heat gain from hooded cooking appliances varies from 15 to 45% of the actual energy consumption of the appliance[22–23]. This may be expressed as a radiation factor, F_r, which depends on the appliance type and the fuel used by the appliance. The rate of heat gain to the space, Φ_h, is obtained by multiplying the average rate of energy consumption for the appliance by the radiation factor. The average rate of energy consumption for the appliance is obtained from the manufacturer's rated energy input, Φ_i, by applying a usage factor, F_u. Therefore:

$$\Phi_h = F_r (F_u \times \Phi_i) \qquad (6.6)$$

Table 6.15 Measured average power consumption of passenger lift motors

Drive type	Speed ($m \cdot s^{-1}$)	Number of passengers									
		8		10		13		16		21	
		Motor rating (kW)	Average power (kW)	Motor rating (kW)	Average power (kW)	Motor rating (kW)	Average power (kW)	Motor rating (kW)	Average power (kW)	Motor rating (kW)	Average power (kW)
Geared variable	1.0	10	2.4	10	2.4	2.4	10	12	2.9	15	3.6
voltage	1.6	15	3.6	15	3.6	15	3.6	17.6	4.2	22	5.3
Geared variable	1.0	5.5	1.0	7.5	1.3	9.5	1.6	11	1.8	15	2.4
frequency	1.6	9.5	1.6	11	1.8	13	2.2	18.5	3.0	22	3.6
Gearless static	2.5	—	—	—	—	—	3.8	—	4.2	—	5.2
direct drive	4.0	—	—	—	—	—	6.7	—	7.6	—	8.6

Table 6.16 Useage and radiation factors for hooded cooking appliances[1]

Appliance	Usage and radiation factors for appliances using stated fuel			
	Electrical appliance		Gas appliances	
	Usage factor (F_u)	Radiation factor (F_r)	Usage factor (F_u)	Radiation factor (F_r)
Griddle	0.16	0.45	0.25	0.25
Fryer	0.06	0.43	0.07	0.35
Convection oven	0.42	0.17	0.42	0.20
Charbroiler	0.83	0.29	0.62	0.18
Open top range, without oven	0.34	0.46	0.34	0.17
Hot-top range:				
— without oven	0.79	0.47	—	—
— with oven	0.59	0.48	—	—
Steam cooker	0.13	0.30	—	—

where (Φ_h is the rate of sensible heat gain to the space from a hooded appliance (W), Φ_i is the manufacturer's input rating or nameplate rating (W), F_r is the radiant factor and F_u is the usage factor.

Values for F_r and F_u for the main types of cooking equipment are given in Table 6.16.

The usage factor, F_u, is the ratio of the standby or idle energy input to manufacturer's input rating. For appliances with a hood not listed in Table 6.16, typical values are 0.5 for types of equipment which cycle or require a constant temperature to be maintained, 0.4 for refrigerators and freezers and 1.0 for all other types of equipment.

The radiation factor, F_r, is the ratio of maximum room heat gain to the idle energy input of a hooded appliance. An average value is 0.32.

6.6.3 Appliances without hoods

For cooking appliances not installed under an extract hood nor connected directly to an exhaust duct, a usage factor of 0.5 should be assumed, regardless of the type of energy or fuel used by the appliance. On average, 34% of the total heat gain may be asssumed to be latent and 66% sensible heat[1].

For the purposes of estimating cooling loads, appliances served by hoods which are not exhausted to outside should be treated as appliances without hoods.

6.7 Hospital and laboratory equipment

Hospital and laboratory equipment can be major sources of heat gain in conditioned spaces. As this equipment is highly specialised, heat outputs for the specific pieces of equipment intended to occupy the space should be obtained from manufacturer. Care must be taken in evaluating the probability and duration of simultaneous usage when components are concentrated in one area.

For laboratories, the heat gains from equipment will vary widely according to the type of laboratory and the equipment likely to be installed and specific data should be obtained from the equipment suppliers. Heat gains of 50 to

200 W·m^{-2}[24] are common for laboratories with high concentrations of equipment.

References

1   *Non-residential Cooling and Heating Load Calculations* ASHRAE Fundamentals Handbook 1997 chapter 28 (ISBN 1 883413 45 1) (Atlanta GA: American Society of Heating, Refrigerating and Air-conditioning Engineers) (1997)

2   Jones W P *Air Conditioning Applications and Design* (ISBN 0 713134 23 2) (London: Edward Arnold) (1996)

3   Pavey N and Crampton P *Rules of Thumb UK/Italy* BSRIA Technical Note TN19/95 (ISBN 0 86022 421) (Bracknell: Buildings Services Research and Information Association)

4   Katsikakis D and Laing A *Assessment of Occupational Density Levels in Commercial Office Buildings* (London: Stanhope Properties) (1993)

5   *Energy Efficiency in Offices* Good Practice Case Studies Nos. 1/14/15/16/17/18/19/20/21/62 (Garston: Building Research Energy Conservation Support Unit) (various dates)

6   Probe 1: Tanfield House *Building Serv., CIBSE J.* **17**(9) 38–41 September 1995; Probe 2: 1 Aldermary Square *Building Serv., CIBSE J.* **17**(12) 29–33 December 1995; Probe 3: C&G Chief Office *Building Serv., CIBSE J.* **18**(2) 31–34 February 1996; Probe 4: Queens Building *Building Serv., CIBSE J.* **18**(4) 35–38 April 1996; Probe 5: Cable and Wireless College *Building Serv., CIBSE J.* **18**(6) 35–39 June 1996; Probe 6: Woodhouse Medical Centre *Building Serv., CIBSE J.* **18**(8) 35–38 August 1996; Probe 7: Gardner House *Building Serv., CIBSE J.* **18**(10) 39–43 October 1996

7   *Best practice in the specification for offices* (ISBN 0 9524131 2 4) (Reading: British Council for Offices) (1997)

8   Bedocs L and Hewitt H Lighting and the thermal environment *J. Inst. Heating and Ventilating Eng.* 37 217–231 (January 1970)

9   *CIBSE Code for Interior Lighting* (ISBN 0 900953 64 0) (London: Chartered Institution of Building Services Engineers) (1994)

10   *LIF Lamp Guide* (London: Lighting Industry Federation) (1994)

11   LoPinto A, Farnfield T and Eames J *An assessment of Small Power Loads for Commercial Office* Buildings (London: Stanhope Properties) (1993)

12   *Cost Model 'Offices of the Future' Procurement* (London: Davis Langdon & Everest) (1996)

13   Parsloe C J *Over-engineering in building services – an international comparison of design and installation methods* BSRIA Technical

Note TR21/95 (ISBN 086022 423 6) (Bracknell: Buildings Services Research and Information Association) (1995)

14   Parsloe C and Hejab M *Small power loads* BSRIA Technical Note TN8/92 (ISBN 086022 340 X) (Bracknell: Buildings Services Research and Information Association) (1992)

15   Bray P Energy waste in the office *The Resource* **1**(5) 8–10 (July/August 1993)

16   *Managing energy use* Good Practice Guide 118 (Garston: Building Research Energy Conservation Unit) (1996)

17   *Guide to uninterruptible power supply systems* (Harrow: Merlin Gerin) (1997)

18   Wilkins C K, Kosonen R and Laine T An analysis of office equipment load factors *ASHRAE J.* **33**(9) 38–44 (September 1991)

19   *Energy efficiency in buildings* CIBSE Guide F (London: Chartered Institution of Building Services Engineers) (1998)

20   Marn W L *Commercial gas kitchen ventilation studies* Research Bulletin No. 90 (Cleveland OH: Gas Association Laboratories) (March 1962)

21   Talbert S G, Canigan L J and Eibling J A An experimental study of ventilation requirements of commercial electric kitchens *ASHRAE Trans.* **73**(1) 34 (1973)

22   Gordon E B, Horton D J and Parvin F A Development and application of a standard test method for the performance of exhaust hoods with commercial cooking appliances *ASHRAE Trans.* **100**(2) 988–999 (1994)

23   Smith V A, Swierczyna R T and Claar C N Application and enhancement of the standard test method for the performance of commercial kitchen ventilation systems *ASHRAE Trans.* **101**(2) (1995)

24   *Laboratory Systems* ASHRAE Applications Handbook 1995 chapter 13 (ISBN 1 883413 23 0) (Atlanta GA: American Society of Heating, Refrigerating and Air-conditioning Engineers) (1995)

Appendix 6.A1: Rate of heat gain from restaurant/cooking equipment

The following table is reproduced from *ASHRAE Fundamentals Handbook 1997*[1] by kind permission of the American Society of Heating, Refrigerating and Air Conditioning Engineers.

Table 6.17 Typical rates of heat gain from restaurant and cooking equipment[1]

Appliance	Size	Energy rate (W)		Rate of heat gain (W)			
		Rated	Standby	Without hood			With hood
				Sensible	Latent	Total	Latent
(a) Electric, no hood required							
Barbeque (pit), per kg of food capacity	36–136 kg	88	—	57	31	88	27
Barbeque (pressurised), per kg food capacity	20 kg	210	—	71	35	106	33
Blender, per litre of capacity	1.0–3.8 litre	480	—	310	160	470	150
Braising pan, per lire of capacity	102–133 litre	110	—	55	29	84	40
Cabinet, large, hot (holding)	0.46–0.49 m³	2080	—	180	100	280	85
Cabinet, large, hot (serving)	1.06–1.15 m³	2000	—	180	90	270	82
Cabinet, large (proofing)	0.45–0.48 m³	2030	—	180	90	270	82
Cabinet, small, hot (holding)	0.09–0.18 m³	900	—	80	40	120	37
Cabinet, very hot, (holding)	0.49 m³	6150	—	550	280	830	250
Can opener		170	—	170	0	170	0
Coffee brewer	12 cup/2 burners	1660	—	1100	560	1660	530
Coffee heater, per boiling burner	1–2 burners	670	—	440	230	670	210
Coffee heater, per warming burner	1–2 burners	100	—	66	34	100	32
Coffee/hot water boiling urn, per litre of capacity	11 litre	120	—	79	41	120	38
Coffee brewing urn (large), per litre of capacity	22–38 litre	660	—	440	220	660	210
Coffee brewing urn (small), per litre of capacity	10 litre	420	—	280	140	420	130
Cutter (large)	460 mm bowl	750	—	750	0	750	0
Cutter (small)	360 mm bowl	370	—	370	0	370	0
Cutter and mixer (large)	28–45 litre	3730	—	3730	0	3730	0
Dishwasher (hood type, chemical sanitising), per 100 dishes/h	950–2000 dish/h	380	—	50	110	160	50
Dishwasher (hood type, chemical sanitising), per 100 dishes/h	950–2000 dish/h	380	—	56	123	179	56
Dishwasher (conveyor type, chemical sanitising) per 100 dishes/h	5000–9000 dish/h	340	—	41	97	138	44
Dishwasher (conveyor type, water sanitising) per 100 dishes/h	5000–9000 dish/h	340	—	44	108	152	50
Display case (refrigerated), per m³ of interior	0.17–1.9 m³	1590	—	640	0	640	0
Dough roller (large)	2 rollers	1610	—	1610	0	1610	0
Dough roller (small)	1 roller	460	—	460	0	460	0
Egg cooker	12 eggs	1800	—	850	570	1420	460
Food processor	2.3 litre	520	—	520	0	520	0
Food warmer (infrared bulb), per lamp	1–6 bulbs	250	—	250	0	250	250
Food warmer (shelf type), per m² of surface	0.28–0.84 m³	2930	—	2330	600	2930	820
Food warmer (infrared tube), per metre length	1.0–2.1 m	950	—	950	0	950	950
Food warmer (well type), per m³ of well	20–70 litre	37 400	—	12 400	6360	18 760	6000
Freezer (large)	2.07 m³	1340	—	540	0	540	0
Freezer (small)	0.51 m³	810	—	320	0	320	0
Griddle/grill (large), per m² of cooking surface	0.43–1.1 m²	29 000	—	1940	1080	3020	1080
Griddle/grill (small), per m² of cooking surface	0.20–0.42 m²	26 200	—	1720	970	2690	940
Hot dog boiler	48–56 hot dogs	1160	—	100	50	150	48
Hot plate (double burner, high speed)		4900	—	2290	1590	3880	1830
Hot plate (double burner, stockpot)		4000	—	1870	1300	3170	1490
Hot plate (single burner, high speed)		2800	—	1310	910	2220	1040
Hot water run (large), per litre of capacity	53 litre	130	—	50	16	66	21
Hot water run (small), per litre of capacity	7.6 litre	2.30	—	87	30	117	37
Ice maker (large)	100 kg/day	1090	—	2730	0	2730	0
Ice maker (small)	50 kg/day	750	—	1880	0	1880	0
Microwave oven (heavy duty, commercial)	20 litre	2630	—	2630	0	2630	0
Microwave oven (residential type)	30 litre	600–1400	—	600–1400	0	600–1400	0
Mixer (large), per litre of capacity	77 litre	29	—	29	0	29	0
Mixer (small), per litre of capacity	11–72 litre	15	—	15	0	15	0
Press cooker (hamburger)	300 patties/h	2200	—	1450	750	2200	700
Refrigerator (large), per m³ of interior space	0.71–2.1 m³	780	—	310	0	310	0
Refrigerator (small) per m³ of interior space	0.17–0.71 m³	1730	—	690	0	690	0
Rotisserie	300 burgers/h	3200	—	2110	1090	3200	1020
Serving cart (hot), per m³ of well	50–90 litre	21 200	—	7060	3530	10 590	3390
Serving drawer (large)	252–336 rolls	1100	—	140	10	150	45
Serving drawer (small)	84–168 rolls	800	—	100	10	110	33
Skillet (tilting), per litre of capacity	45–125 litre	180	—	90	50	140	66
Slicer, per square metre of slicing carriage	0.06–0.09 m²	2150	—	2150	0	2150	680

Table continues

Table 6.17 Typical rates of heat gain from restaurant and cooking equipment[1] – *continued*

Appliance	Size	Energy rate (W)		Rate of heat gain (W)			
				Without hood			With hood
		Rated	Standby	Sensible	Latent	Total	Latent
Soup cooker, per litre of well	7–11 litre	130	—	45	24	69	21
Steam cooker, per m³ of compartment	30–60 litre	214 000	—	17 000	10 900	27 900	8120
Steam kettle (large), per litre of capacity	76–300 litre	95	—	7	5	12	4
Steam kettle (small), per litre of capacity	23–45 litre	260	—	21	14	35	10
Syrup warmer, per litre of capacity	11 litre	87	—	29	16	45	14
Toaster (bun toasts on one side only)	1400 buns/h	1500	—	800	710	1510	480
Toaster (large conveyor)	720 slices/h	3200	—	850	750	1600	510
Toaster (small conveyor)	360 slices/h	2100	—	560	490	1050	340
Toaster (large pop-up)	10 slice	5300	—	2810	2490	5300	1700
Toaster (small pop-up)	4 slice	2470	—	1310	1160	2470	790
Waffle iron	0.05 m²	1640	—	700	940	1640	520
(b) Electric, exhaust hood required							
Broiler (conveyor infrared), per m² of cooking area/minute	0.19–9.5 m²	60 800	—	—	—	—	12 100
Broiler (single deck infrared), per m² of broiling area	0.24–0.91 m²	34 200	—	—	—	—	6780
Charbroiler, per linear metre of cooking surface	0.6–2.4 m	10 600	8900	—	—	—	2700
Fryer (deep fat)	15–23 kg oil	14 000	850	—	—	—	350
Fryer (pressurised), per kg of fat capacity	6–15 kg	1010	—	—	—	—	38
Griddle, per metre length of cooking surface	0.6–2.4 m	18 800	3000	—	—	—	1350
Oven (full-size convection)		12 000	5000	—	—	—	850
Oven (large deck baking with 15.2 m³ decks) per m³ of oven space	0.43–1.3 m³	17 300	—	—	—	—	710
Oven (roasting), per m³ of oven space	0.22–0.66 m³	28 300	—	—	—	—	1170
Oven (small convention), per m³ of oven space	0.04–0.15 m³	107 000	—	—	—	—	1520
Oven (small deck baking with 7.7 m³ decks), per m³ of oven space	0.22–0.66 m³	28 700	—	—	—	—	1170
Open range (top), per 2 element section	2–10 elements	4100	1350	—	—	—	620
Range (hot top/fry top), per m² of cooking surface	0.36–0.74 m²	22 900	—	—	—	—	8500
Range (oven section), per m³ of space	0.12–0.32 m³	40 600	—	—	—	—	1660
(c) Gas, no hood required							
Broiler, per m² of broiling area	0.25	46 600	190*	16 800	9030	25 830	3840
Cheese melter, per m² of cooking surface	0.23–0.47	32 500	190*	11 600	3400	15 000	2680
Dishwasher (hood type), chemical sanitising), per 100 dish/h	950–2000 dish/h	510	190*	150	59	209	67
Dishwasher (hood type, water sanitising), per 100 dish/h	950–2000 dish/h	510	190*	170	64	234	73
Dishwasher (conveyor type, chemical sanitising), per 100 dish/h	5000–9000 dish/h	400	190*	97	21	118	38
Dishwasher (conveyor type, water sanitising), per 100 dish/h	5000–9000 dish/h	400	190*	110	23	133	41
Griddle/grill (large), per m² of cooking surface	0.43–1.1 m²	53 600	1040	3600	1930	5530	1450
Griddle/grill (small), per m² of cooking surface	0.23–0.42 m²	45 400	1040	3050	1610	4660	1260
Hot plate	2 burners	5630	390*	3430	1020	4450	1000
Oven (pizza), per m² of hearth	0.59–1.2 m²	14 900	190*	1970	690	2660	270
(d) Gas, exhaust hood required							
Braising pan, per litre of capacity	102–133 litre	3050	190*	—	—	—	750
Broiler, per m² of broiling area	0.34–0.36 m³	68 900	1660	—	—	—	5690
Broiler (large conveyor, infrared), per m² of cooking area/minute	0.19–9.5 m²	162 000	6270	—	—	—	16 900
Broiler (standard infrared), per m² of broiling area	0.22–0.87 m²	61 300	1660	—	—	—	5040
Charbroiler (large), per metre length of cooking area	0.6–2.4 m	34 600	21 000	—	—	—	3650
Fryer (deep fat)	15–23 kg	23 500	1640	—	—	—	560
Oven (bake deck), per m³ of oven space	0.15–0.46 m³	79 400	190*	—	—	—	1450
Griddle, per metre length of cooling surface	0.6–2.4 m	24 000	6060	—	—	—	1540
Oven (full-size convection)		20 500	8600	—	—	—	1670
Oven (pizza), per m² of oven hearth	0.86–2.4 m²	22 800	190*	—	—	—	410
Oven (roasting), per m³ of oven space	0.26–0.79 m³	44 500	190*	—	—	—	800
Oven (twin bake deck), per m³ of oven space	0.31–0.61 m³	45 400	190*	—	—	—	810
Range (burners), per 2 burner section	2–10 burners	9840	390	—	—	—	1930
Range (hot top or fry top), per m² of cooking surface	0.26–0.74 m³	37 200	1040	—	—	—	10 700
Range (large stock pot)	3 burners	29 300	580	—	—	—	5740

* Standby input rating is for entire appliance regardless of size

Table continues

Table 6.17 Typical rates of heat gain from restaurant and cooking equipment[1] – *continued*

Appliance	Size	Energy rate (W)		Rate of heat gain (W)			
		Rated	Standby	Without hood			With hood
				Sensible	Latent	Total	Latent
Range (small stock pot)	2 burners	11 700	390	—	—	—	2290
Range top, open burner (per 2 element section)	2–6 elements	11 700	4000	—	—	—	640
(e) Steam							
Compartment steamer, per kg of food capacity/h	21–204 kg	180	—	14	9	23	7
Dishwasher (hood type, chemical sanitising), per 100 dish/h	950–2000 dish/h	920	—	260	110	370	120
Dishwasher (conveyor, water sanitising), per 100 dish/h	950–2000 dish/h	920	—	290	120	410	130
Dishwasher (conveyor, chemical sanitising), per 100 dish/h	5000–9000 dish/h	350	—	41	97	138	44
Dishwasher (conveyor, water sanitising), per 100 dish/h	5000–9000 dish/h	350	—	44	108	152	50
Steam kettle, per litre of capacity	12–30 litre	160	—	12	8	20	6

7 Moisture transfer and condensation

7.1 Introduction

Moisture can cause serious problems in buildings. In the majority of cases, these can be solved or ameliorated by considering the sources of the moisture and its behaviour. This section of Guide A gives procedures for the control of moisture content, methods for condensation prediction and guidelines on how to avoid or minimise the problems. Some of the basic physics of moisture movement and psychrometrics are also discussed. Industrial drying, moisture conditioning and swimming pool design are not considered in this section.

7.2 Notation

c_p Specific heat capacity at constant pressure $(J \cdot kg^{-1} \cdot K^{-1})$

c_{pa} Specific heat capacity at constant pressure for air $(J \cdot kg^{-1} \cdot K^{-1})$

d Thickness (m)

G Vapour resistance $(N \cdot s \cdot kg^{-1})$

G_i Vapour resistance of layer i $(N \cdot s \cdot kg^{-1})$

g Moisture content $(kg \cdot kg^{-1})$

g_a Moisture content of air $(kg \cdot kg^{-1})$

g_d Design room moisture content $(kg \cdot kg^{-1})$

g_e External moisture content (assumed constant) $(kg \cdot kg^{-1})$

g_{max} Maximum moisture content to avoid condensation $(kg \cdot kg^{-1})$

g_θ Room moisture content at time θ after plant 'off' $(kg \cdot kg^{-1})$

g_s Supply air moisture content $(kg \cdot kg^{-1})$

h Specific enthalpy (sensible or latent) of room air per kilogram of dry air $(kJ \cdot kg^{-1})$

h_a Specific enthalpy (sensible or latent) of supply air per kilogram of dry air $(kJ \cdot kg^{-1})$

h_c Convective heat transfer coefficient $(W \cdot m^{-2} \cdot K^{-1})$

h_o Initial specific enthalpy (sensible or latent) of room air per kilogram of dry air $(kJ \cdot kg^{-1})$

k_m Surface mass transfer coefficient $(m \cdot s^{-1})$

l_e Specific latent heat of evaporation $(J \cdot kg^{-1})$

N Room air change rate (h^{-1})

n Number of layers in an element

p Pressure (Pa)

p_s Saturation vapour pressure (Pa)

p_{ss} Saturation vapour pressure at surface temperature (Pa)

p_v Vapour pressure (Pa)

p_{va} Vapour pressure of water vapour in air (Pa)

p_{vj} Vapour pressure of interface j (Pa)

q_m Mass flow rate per unit area $(kg \cdot m^{-2} \cdot s^{-1})$

q_{mj} Mass flow rate per unit area through sub-construction j $(kg \cdot m^{-2} \cdot s^{-1})$

q_{mw} Mass flow rate per unit area of moisture (condensation if positive, evaporation if negative) $(kg \cdot m^{-2} \cdot s^{-1})$

q_v Volume flow rate $(m^3 \cdot s)$

R Molar gas constant $(J \cdot mol^{-1} \cdot K^{-1})$

r Vapour resistivity $(N \cdot s \cdot kg^{-1} \cdot m^{-1})$

R_t Thermal resistance $(m^2 \cdot K \cdot W^{-1})$

R_{ti} Thermal resistance of layer i $(m^2 \cdot K \cdot W^{-1})$

R_w Molar gas constant for 1 kg of water $(J \cdot K^{-1})$

T Temperature (K)

t Temperature (°C)

t_j Temperature at interface j (°C)

V Volume (m^3)

v Number of moles (gram-molecules) of gas (mol)

Δh_θ Change of specific enthalpy of room air over time period θ $(J \cdot kg^{-1})$

Δp_v Vapour pressure difference (Pa)

θ Time (h)

ρ_a Density of air $(kg \cdot m^3)$

ϕ_h Heat flow rate $(W \cdot m^{-2})$

ϕ_l Latent heat flow rate $(W \cdot m^{-2})$

7.3 Sources of moisture

In order to select the internal design conditions for condensation calculations, it is necessary to have some idea of the moisture content or vapour pressure of the air in a building. This will largely be determined by the sources of moisture in the building. There is little information available on rates of moisture production. Table 7.1 gives estimates for the amounts of moisture produced by various sources.

BS 5250[1] suggests a typical daily moisture production rate of 7 kg for a five person family but clothes washing and the use of moisture-producing (i.e. non-electric) room heaters can increase this to 20 kg. The instantaneous moisture production will vary with the activities, e.g. a maximum will usually occur during cooking and clothes washing.

Industrial buildings present special problems due to the rate of production of moisture by some processes. The engineer should discuss the proposed use of the building with the client to enable any likely problems to be anticipated. For example, in the textiles industry it is estimated that about half a kilogram of water vapour is produced for each kilogram of wool that is scoured, dyed and washed.

Animal houses need special consideration since chickens produce about 0.003 kg·h⁻¹ (per bird) of moisture, sheep produce about 0.04 kg·h⁻¹ (per animal) and pigs about 0.15 kg·h⁻¹ (per animal).

Table 7.1 Sources of moisture within buildings

Source	Moisture produced
Combustion in room heaters/cookers without flues:	
— paraffin	0.1 kg·h⁻¹·kW⁻¹
— natural gas	0.16 kg·h⁻¹·kW⁻¹
— butane	0.12 kg·h⁻¹·kW⁻¹
— propane	0.13 kg·h⁻¹·kW⁻¹
Household activities:	
— cooking (3 meals)	0.9–3.0 kg·day⁻¹
— dish washing (3 meals)	0.15–0.45 kg·day⁻¹
— clothes washing	0.5–1.8 kg·day⁻¹
— clothes drying (indoors)	5–14 kg·day⁻¹
— baths/showers	0.75–1.5 kg·day⁻¹
— floor washing	1–1.5 kg per 10 m⁻²
— indoor plants	Up to 0.8 kg·day⁻¹
Perspiration and respiration of building occupants	0.04–0.1 kg·h⁻¹·person⁻¹
Direct penetration of rain, groundwater or moist ambient air	Variable
'Drying-out' of water used in construction of building (e.g. medium sized office building)	4000 kg·year⁻¹

Table 7.2 Equilibrium moisture content of materials[2]

Material	Density (kg·m⁻³)	Moisture content at 50% saturation of ambient air (% by mass)
Brick	1600	0.5
Concrete	2300	1
Plaster:		
— lime sand	1750	1
— cement sand	2000	1
Cork	95	1
Glasswool slab	120	0.5
Mineral wool	—	0
Slag wool	—	0
Strawboard	—	10
Woodwool/cement slab	360	10

Note: for newly constructed buildings, moisture contents will be higher than stated until 'drying-out' is completed

Table 7.3 Pore radius for hygroscopic equilibrium

Radius of curvature of pore (nm)	Saturation of ambient air for equilibrium (%)
2.1	60
5	80
10	90
100	99

7.4 Moisture content of materials

Most materials will take up water when exposed to moist air, the equilibrium quantity depending on the nature of the material, its pore structure and the moisture saturation of the air. This phenomenon is important when assessing the thermal conductivity of building and insulating materials, see Section 3: *Thermal properties of building structures*, Appendix 3.A1. Equilibrium moisture contents for various materials are given in Table 7.2.

The moisture absorption is largely though not solely due to capillary forces. The vapour pressure over a concave surface is less than that over a plane surface. Water will condense on any surface having a radius of curvature such that the corresponding vapour pressure is less than that in the ambient air. If the radius is sufficiently small, condensation will occur from unsaturated atmospheres. Table 7.3 shows the saturation of an air/water vapour mixture that is in equilibrium with a concave surface.

If the saturation is greater than that given in Table 7.3, water will condense on the surface. For example, a dry material containing pores of radius 2.1 nm will take up water from an atmosphere that is 60% saturated and these, and any smaller pores, will become filled with water. This process can contribute to the movement of water vapour through building materials. If the opposite face of the material is exposed to an atmosphere that is 40% saturated, moisture will evaporate from the pore menisci and a state of dynamic equilibrium is set up whereby water condenses at one side, moves under capillary forces through the material to the other side and there evaporates. This transfer mechanism should not be confused with interstitial condensation.

7.5 Mechanisms of moisture movement

7.5.1 Surface moisture transfer

The moisture mass transfer rate at a surface is derived from Fick's diffusion law[3] which can be written as:

$$q_{mw} = (p_{va} - p_{ss}) k_m / R_w T \qquad (7.1)$$

where q_{mw} is the mass flow rate per unit area of moisture (condensation if positive, evaporation if negative) (kg·m⁻²·s⁻¹), p_{va} is the vapour pressure of the water vapour in the air (Pa), p_{ss} is the saturation vapour pressure at the surface temperature (Pa), k_m is the surface mass transfer coefficient (m·s⁻¹), R_w is the molar gas constant for water (= 461) (J·kg⁻¹·K⁻¹) and T is the temperature (K).

Mass transfer is analogous to heat transfer and the surface mass transfer coefficient is numerically related to the convective heat transfer coefficient by the Lewis relation[3]:

$$k_m = h_c / \rho_a c_{pa} \qquad (7.2)$$

where k_m is the surface mass transfer coefficient (m·s⁻¹), h_c is the convective heat transfer coefficient (W·m⁻²·K⁻¹), ρ_a is the density of air (kg·m⁻³) and c_{pa} is the specific heat capacity of air (J·kg⁻¹·K⁻¹).

Values of the convective heat transfer coefficient can be derived from the appropriate expressions given in CIBSE

Table 7.4 Values of convective heat transfer and surface mass transfer coefficients

Direction of heat flow	Convective heat transfer coefficient h_c (W·m^{-2}·K^{-1})	Surface mass transfer coefficient, k_m (m·s^{-1})
Downward	1.5	1.25×10^{-3}
Horizontal	3.0	2.5×10^{-3}
Upward	4.3	3.6×10^{-3}

Guide C3: *Heat transfer*[4]. Some common values are given in Table 7.4.

7.5.2 Diffusion

Diffusion is the movement of molecules from a place at which they are present in a high concentration to one in which they are present in a low concentration.

Most solid materials permit the diffusion of water vapour to some extent and, whenever there is a difference in the vapour pressure across the material, a movement of water takes place. This is analogous to the flow of heat through a material when subjected to a temperature difference and this similarity is exploited in the calculation methods described.

Under steady state conditions, the rate of mass transfer per unit area through an element of a given material is given by:

$$q_m = \Delta p_v / G \qquad (7.3)$$

where q_m is the mass flow rate per unit area (kg·m^{-2}·s^{-1}), Δp_v is the vapour pressure difference (Pa) and G is the vapour resistance (N·s·kg^{-1}).

The vapour resistance of an element of a given material is defined by:

$$G = r\,d \qquad (7.4)$$

where r is the vapour resistivity (N·s·kg^{-1}·m^{-1}) and d is the thickness of the element (m).

Vapour resistivity data for a wide range of materials are given in Section 3: *Thermal properties of building structures*, Appendix 3.A7.

Table 7.5 gives an indication of the likely resistivities of fibrous and open-celled materials and may be used in the absence of data for specific materials. Table 7.5 also gives a value for the vapour resistivity of air spaces within composite structures.

Vapour barriers are usually thin materials and it is more convenient to classify them by their vapour resistance than by their thickness and vapour resistivity. Table 7.6 gives approximate values of the vapour resistances of vapour barriers. It should be noted that these values apply to undamaged vapour barriers only and the presence of any perforations may reduce the vapour resistance considerably. For this reason, perfect vapour barriers are rarely achieved on site.

Table 7.5 Approximate values of vapour resistivity for fibrous or open-celled materials and for air spaces within structures

Density (kg·m^{-3})	Vapour resistivity (GN·s·kg^{-1}·m^{-1})
Air space	5
600	20
800	30
1000	40
1500	100
2000	220
2500	520

Table 7.6 Vapour resistance of films

Material	Thickness (mm)	Vapour resistance (GN·s·kg^{-1})
Polythene film	0.05	125
	0.1	200
	0.15	350
Mylar film	0.025	25
Gloss paint (average)	—	8
Interior paint	—	3
Varnish (phenolic, epoxy, polyurethane)	0.05	5
Roofing felt	—	4–100
Kraft paper:		
— single	—	0.2
— double	—	0.35
Building paper:		
— plain	—	5
— foil-backed	—	> 4000
Aluminium foil	—	> 4000

7.5.3 Air movement

Moisture is transferred by air movement through gaps at the junctions of (and, sometimes, cracks in) elements of the construction. In a typical masonry wall with windows or other openings, the mass flow of moisture due to air movement through such gaps can be as much as an order of magnitude greater than that produced by diffusion.

Depending on the relative internal and external pressures and wind forces, movement will be inwards or outwards. This mechanism is important in the consideration of the mean conditions to which a construction is subjected over a period of time.

7.6 Outside and inside design conditions

7.6.1 UK climate

Inside and outside conditions are chosen to suit the purpose of the analysis, bearing in mind that the simpler calculation methods assume steady state conditions. Usually the purpose is to determine either the long term build-up of condensation within the thickness of a construction or the short term rate of condensation on one of its exposed surfaces. Relatively less extreme conditions will be more appropriate for the former purpose and relatively more extreme for the latter.

Design conditions are generally taken as the average of those that pertain for a 60-day period. *BS 5250*[1] suggests the following for the UK in winter:

— outdoors: 5 °C, 95% RH

— indoors (dry–moist occupancy): 15 °C, 65% RH

— indoors (moist–wet occupancy): 15 °C , 85% RH.

However, severe exposure may require some amendment to these conditions. In particular, surfaces of roofs, especially metal roofs, can fall to temperatures some way below the air temperature due to night-time radiation loss. In winter, this can exacerbate condensation problems and the following conditions are given in *BS 6229*[5]:

— outdoors (winter): –5 °C, 90% RH

— outdoors (summer): 18 °C, 65% RH

— indoors (offices): 20 °C, 40% RH.

BS 6229[5] also suggests the quantities of condensate that will be retained without liquid flow by fibrous and non-fibrous insulating materials.

For the analysis of condensation on windows and any constructions of very low thermal mass, the conditions used in the calculation of heat losses from the building will normally be appropriate.

7.6.2 Other locations

The indoor conditions are dependent on the type of building and its purpose. For climates other than that of the UK, the design conditions should be based on local weather data. For example, tropical climates may have the following conditions:

— winter: 8 °C, 60% RH

— summer: 32 °C, 90% RH.

Conditions such as these mean that condensation can occur in the summer due to the outside moisture condensing as it moves through the building fabric towards the inside; the reverse of the situation in the UK.

7.6.3 Other factors

The internal conditions used in calculations should allow for any moisture gains, humidification or dehumidification.

Where elements of building construction can resist some temporary, but not permanent, interstitial condensation, it may be appropriate to analyse conditions of short term extremes in longer periods of less extreme conditions, e.g:

— winter extreme: –5 °C, 90% RH for 3 days

— winter mean: 5 °C, 90% RH for 10 days.

Similarly, it may be necessary to analyse daytime and night-time internal conditions in case that condensation occurs only when the building cools down.

7.7 Condensation

7.7.1 Psychrometry of condensation of water vapour

The vapour pressures and temperatures at which water and air are in equilibrium are uniquely related by the saturation or steam line, which applies whether the water vapour is present on its own or mixed with air. The equilibrium condition can be thought of in two ways:

(a) when the temperature of the air equals the saturation temperature corresponding to the partial pressure of the water vapour in the mixture

(b) when the partial pressure of the water vapour equals the saturation pressure corresponding to the temperature of the mixture.

The first is useful when considering surface or superficial condensation on surfaces cooler than the room or ambient air. The second is more appropriate when considering internal or interstitial condensation within a building construction through which water vapour is moving under the influence of a difference between internal and external partial pressures.

The conventional psychrometric relationships are given in Guide C1: *Properties of humid air*[6]. Note that, to an extremely good approximation, the vapour pressure of water vapour in air at a given total pressure with a constant moisture content is the same at all dry bulb temperatures. Also, to a moderately good approximation, the vapour pressure of water vapour in air is proportional to the moisture content. For example, a calculated value at 0.01 kg·kg^{-1}, based on an accurate value at 0.001 kg·kg^{-1}, will be within 1.5% of the accurate value. The latter approximation simplifies certain calculations significantly, particularly when dynamic situations are being considered.

7.7.2 Surface condensation

Surface condensation occurs when moist air is in contact with a surface that is below the dew-point temperature of the air. The dew-point temperature can be calculated or obtained from the psychrometric tables given in Guide C1: *Properties of humid air*[6]. Condensation does not occur if the surface temperature is above the dew-point temperature and, under these conditions, any surface moisture evaporates. Note that, however, mould growth can occur with a surface relative humidity of 80% and corrosion can occur with a surface relative humidity of 60%.

A flowchart for the prediction of surface condensation is given in Figure 7.1. This provides a rational approach by reducing the problem to one of finding the dew-point and surface temperatures[7]. However, interstitial condensation is not covered by this flowchart and this should be investigated using the methods described in the following sections.

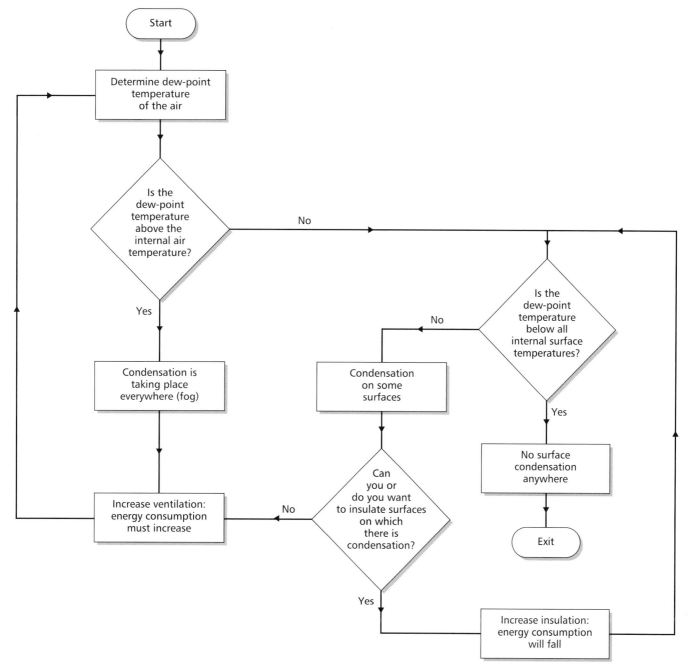

Figure 7.1 Flowchart for prediction of surface condensation

7.7.3 Interstitial condensation

A building element will have a temperature gradient and a vapour pressure gradient across it due to the differing conditions on either side. In some cases these gradients may be zero but more usually, particularly for external elements, they are non-zero. Intermediate values of vapour pressure and temperature can be calculated inside the structure. Interstitial condensation, i.e. free liquid water, will result if the calculated vapour pressure at any point is greater than the saturated vapour pressure corresponding to the calculated temperature at that point.

In multi-layer constructions, it is usually sufficiently accurate to calculate the saturation vapour pressure (SVP) at each interface and to assume a linear relationship between them. In fact, a plot of SVP against distance, or cumulative vapour resistance, droops slightly between falling values. In a monolithic construction, such as a solid brick wall or a cold store wall, the occurrence of interstitial condensation

may not be demonstrated by simple analysis, particularly at extreme conditions (see Figure 7.2).

A simple check can be made by dividing monolithic constructions into three or four arbitrary layers and proceeding in the same way as for constructions in which the layers are composed of different materials.

7.7.4 Condensation calculation

For a multi-layer construction, the thickness, thermal conductivity and vapour resistivity of each layer is required. From these, the thermal resistance and vapour resistance can be calculated. In the case of a vapour barrier, the vapour resistance is normally provided and the thickness and thermal resistance are taken as zero.

Additionally, the surface thermal resistances must be known, although the surface vapour resistances are usually

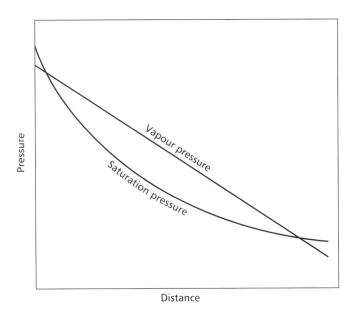

Figure 7.2 Comparison of vapour pressure and saturation pressure lines in a homogeneous material

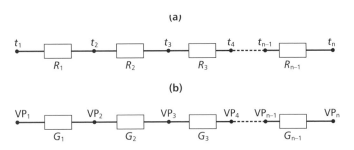

Figure 7.3 Representation of a typical construction as a series of (a) temperatures and thermal resistances and (b) vapour pressures and vapour resistances

taken as zero since they are very much smaller than the vapour resistances of the individual layers. The construction can now be represented as a number of resistances in series with fixed points, either temperatures or vapour pressures, at each end, see Figure 7.3.

It is assumed that the heat flow or moisture flow through the construction is also the flow through each layer. Then, the temperature or vapour pressure at each node (i.e. interface between two layers), can then be calculated from:

$$t_j = t_1 + [(t_n - t_1) \overset{(j-i)}{\underset{i=1}{\sum}} R_{ti} \, / \, \overset{n}{\underset{i=1}{\sum}} R_{ti}] \tag{7.5}$$

$$p_{vj} = p_{v1} + [(p_{vn} - p_{v1}) \overset{(j-i)}{\underset{i=1}{\sum}} G_i \, / \, \overset{n}{\underset{i=1}{\sum}} G_i] \tag{7.6}$$

where t_j is the temperature of interface j (°C), R_{ti} is thermal resistance of layer i (m^2·K·W^{-1}), p_{vj} is the vapour pressure of interface j (Pa) and G_i is the vapour resistance of layer i (N·s·kg^{-1}).

At each node, the saturation vapour pressure corresponding to the calculated temperature is either calculated or obtained from the tables given in Guide C1: *Properties of*

humid air[6]. Provided that at each node the saturation pressure is not less than the vapour pressure, there will be no interstitial condensation.

The flow of heat or moisture through the structure can be calculated from:

$$\phi_h = (t_1 - t_n) / \overset{n}{\underset{i=1}{\sum}} R_{ti} \tag{7.7}$$

$$q_m = (p_{v1} - p_{vn}) / \overset{n}{\underset{i=1}{\sum}} G_i \tag{7.8}$$

where ϕ_h is the heat flow rate (W·m^{-2}) and q_m is the mass flow rate per unit area (kg·m^{-2}·s^{-1}).

It is impossible for the saturation pressure to be less than the vapour pressure. Therefore, if the saturation pressure at any node, or nodes, is less than the calculated vapour pressure, that node is assumed to be saturated and is considered as another fixed point for the moisture calculations. The construction is then divided into two sub-constructions and the calculations repeated for each sub-construction until none of the sub-constructions has any interstitial condensation.

A computer algorithm for the prediction of interstitial condensation is given in Appendix 7.A1.

Example 7.1

The wall shown in Figure 7.4 has the properties shown in Table 7.7 giving the resistance paths and fixed points shown in Figure 7.5.

Taking inside conditions of 21°C at 60% RH (vapour pressure = 1490 Pa) and outside conditions of 10°C at 80% RH (vapour pressure = 981 Pa), the temperatures, saturation vapour pressures and vapour pressures are given in Table 7.8. In this instance, none of the saturation pressures is less than the corresponding vapour pressure so there is no interstitial condensation.

If the outside conditions are 5°C at 90% RH then the conditions are as shown in Table 7.9 and there is clearly a problem on the inside surface of the outer brick leaf. In this case, the moisture calculations must be repeated with the construction split into two subdivisions, giving the resistances and fixed potentials shown in Figure 7.6. The calculations, see Table 7.10, show that there are no further saturated nodes so the amount of condensation can then be determined.

The rate of condensation is the difference between the moisture flowing from the inside to the node and the moisture flowing from the node to the outside. From equation 7.8:

$$q_{m1} = (1490 - 930) / [(0.6 + 3.0 + 0.45) \times 10^9]$$
$$= 138 \times 10^{-9} \text{ kg·m}^{-2}\text{·s}^{-1}$$

$$q_{m2} = (930 - 784) / (5.25 \times 10^9)$$
$$= 28 \times 10^{-9} \text{ kg·m}^{-2}\text{·s}^{-1}$$

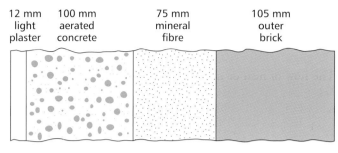

Figure 7.4 Example 7.1: construction of typical wall

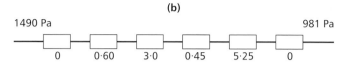

Figure 7.5 Example 7.1: thermal and vapour resistances and fixed points for wall construction shown in Figure 7.4

Table 7.7 Example 7.1: properties of typical wall

Element	Thickness (mm)	Thermal conductivity (W·m⁻¹·K⁻¹)	Vapour resistivity (GN·s·kg⁻¹·m⁻¹)	Thermal resistance (m²·K·W⁻¹)	Vapour resistance (GN·s·kg⁻¹)
Internal surface	—	—	—	0.12	0
Lightweight plaster	12	0.16	50.0	0.075	0.60
Aerated concrete	100	0.16	30.0	0.625	3.0
Mineral fibre	75	0.035	6.0	2.14	0.45
Outer brick	105	0.84	50.0	0.125	5.25
External surface	—	—	—	0.06	0

Table 7.8 Example 7.1: temperature and vapour pressure distribution

Surface or node	Location of node (between stated elements)	Temperature (°C)	Vapour pressure (Pa)	Saturation vapour pressure (Pa)
Inside	—	21.0	1490	2484
Node 1	Inside surface/plaster	20.6	1490	2421
Node 2	Plaster/concrete	20.3	1458	2382
Node 3	Concrete/insulation	18.1	1293	2079
Node 4	Insulation/outer brick	10.6	1269	1281
Node 5	Outer brick/external surface	10.2	981	1244
External surface	—	10.0	981	1226

Table 7.9 Example 7.1: temperature and vapour pressure distribution with interstitial condensation present

Surface or node	Location of node (between stated elements)	Temperature (°C)	Vapour pressure (Pa)	Saturation vapour pressure (Pa)
Inside	—	21.0	1490	2484
Node 1	Inside surface/plaster	20.4	1490	2393
Node 2	Plaster/concrete	20.0	1444	2337
Node 3	Concrete/insulation	16.8	1217	1915
Node 4	Insulation/outer brick	5.9	1183	930
Node 5	Outer brick/external surface	5.3	784	890
External surface	—	5.0	784	871

Table 7.10 Example 7.1: temperature and vapour pressure distribution in sub-constructions

Surface or node	Location of node (between stated elements)	Temperature (°C)	Vapour pressure (Pa)	Saturation vapour pressure (Pa)
Sub-construction (a):				
Inside	—	21.0	1490	2484
Node 1	Inside surface/plaster	20.4	1490	2393
Node 2	Plaster/concrete	20.0	1407	2337
Node 3	Concrete/insulation	16.8	992	1915
Node 4	(fixed point)	5.9	930	930
Sub-construction (b):				
Node 4	(fixed point)	5.9	930	930
Node 5	Outer brick/external surface	5.3	784	890
External surface	—	5.0	784	871

Table 7.11 Example 7.1: temperature and vapour pressure distribution in sub-constructions for evaporation

Surface or node	Location of node (between stated elements)	Temperature (°C)	Vapour pressure (Pa)	Saturation vapour pressure (Pa)
Sub-construction (a):				
Inside	—	21.0	1490	2484
Node 1	Inside surface/plaster	20.9	1490	2467
Node 2	Plaster/concrete	20.8	1578	2456
Node 3	Concrete/insulation	20.2	2018	2367
Node 4	(fixed point)	18.2	2084	2084
Sub-construction (b):				
Node 4	(fixed point)	18.2	2084	2084
Node 5	Outer brick/external surface	18.1	1340	2096
External surface	—	18.0	1340	2061

Table 7.12 Example 7.1: temperature and vapour pressure distribution for structure with vapour barrier

Surface or node	Location of node (between stated elements)	Temperature (°C)	Vapour pressure (Pa)	Saturation vapour pressure (Pa)
Inside	—	21.0	1490	2484
Node 1	Inside surface/plaster	20.4	1490	2393
Node 2	Plaster/concrete	20.0	1488	2337
Node 3	Concrete/vapour barrier	16.8	1478	1915
Node 4	Vapour barrier/insulation	16.8	803	1915
Node 5	Insulation/outer brick	5.9	802	930
Node 6	Outer brick/external surface	5.3	784	890
External surface	—	5.0	784	871

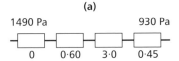

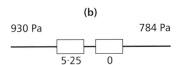

Figure 7.6 Example 7.1: vapour resistances and fixed points for sub-construction

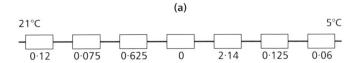

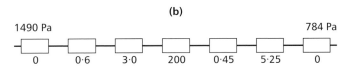

Figure 7.7 Example 7.1: thermal and vapour resistances and fixed points for structure with vapour barrier

$$q_m = q_{m1} - q_{m2} = 110 \times 10^{-9} \text{ kg·m}^{-2}\text{·s}^{-1}$$

$$= 0.4 \text{ g·m}^{-2}\text{·h}^{-1}$$

Having calculated the amount of condensation, the designer can choose to try to prevent it from occurring or to allow it to evaporate in warmer weather. The calculation of evaporation is the same as the calculation of interstitial condensation. The nodes where condensation occurred, together with the inside and outside, are taken as fixed points and the construction is subdivided accordingly.

The temperatures and vapour pressures are calculated at each node and the moisture flow to and from the condensation nodes is calculated. So long as the total flow to a condensation node is negative, i.e. evaporation, and its magnitude is greater than that of the condensation, there should be no net annual accumulation of moisture. Table 7.11 shows the temperature and vapour pressure distributions.

From equation 7.8:

$$q_{m1} = (1490 - 2084)/[(0.6 + 3.0 + 0.45) \times 10^9]$$

$$= -147 \times 10^{-9} \text{ kg·m}^{-2}\text{·s}^{-1}$$

$$q_{m2} = (2084 - 1340)/(5.25 \times 10^{-9})$$

$$= 142 \times 10^{-9} \text{ kg·m}^{-2}\text{·s}^{-1}$$

$$q_m = q_{m1} - q_{m2} = -289 \times 10^{-9} \text{ kg·m}^{-2}\text{·s}^{-1}$$

$$= -1.0 \text{ g·m}^{-2}\text{·h}^{-1}$$

The evaporation rate is significantly greater than the condensation rate so over the year there should be no net moisture gain.

In this case, prevention could be achieved by inserting a vapour barrier between the aerated slab and the insulation. Using medium polythene with a vapour resistance of 200 GN·s·kg^{-1} as the vapour barrier, the resistance networks are modified as shown in Figure 7.7 and the temperatures and

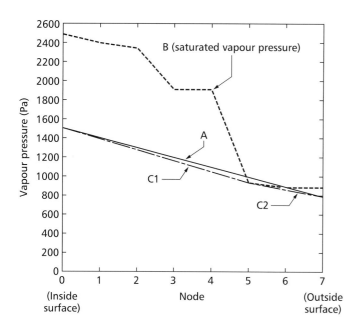

Figure 7.8 Example 7.1: graphical solution of condensation

vapour pressures are shown in Table 7.12. In this case there is no interstitial condensation.

After the initial calculations, it is possible to perform the subsequent analysis graphically. This requires a plot of the vapour pressure and saturation vapour pressure against the cumulative vapour resistance through the construction, see Figure 7.8. It may be found helpful to indicate where the actual layers in the construction occur, as shown.

The initial vapour pressure line is drawn as a straight line between the inner surface and outer surface conditions (line A). The saturation vapour pressure line is then plotted through the inner and outer surface conditions and the conditions at each node (line B). If the two lines cross, condensation is indicated.

A corrected vapour pressure line is then obtained by joining the inner surface vapour pressure point to the first node on the saturation vapour pressure line that lies under the original vapour pressure line (line C1). This point is then joined to the next saturation point that lies under the original vapour pressure line or, if there is not such a point, to the vapour pressure at the outer surface condition (line C2).

7.8 Control of condensation

7.8.1 Condensation assessment

The assessment of whether condensation control will be necessary requires the designer's judgement on whether the construction can cope with condensation. Factors that affect the decision are:

— condensation rate

— time for which condensation occurs

— amount of condensate that can be retained without flow occurring

— effect of liquid water on properties of the materials contained in the structure

— effect of liquid water on the potential for organic growth

— whether liquid water can be drained away.

7.8.2 Vapour barriers

Vapour barriers are used to control the rate of diffusion of water vapour, and therefore the vapour pressure, through a construction at potentially awkward locations. The optimum location for a vapour barrier depends on constructional and user-based factors but it should be as close as is possible to the warmer and moister side of the construction, i.e. the side from which the moisture is diffusing. Where the vapour gradient (and therefore the vapour pressure) can change due to variations in temperature and/or humidity on one or both sides of the wall, it may be appropriate to locate the vapour barrier towards the centre of the wall.

Roof finishes in cold constructions and patent glazing wall claddings may be the most efficient vapour resistance elements of a construction. In the UK climate, there will be interstitial condensation at these elements in winter if there is an internal moisture gain or maintained internal relative humidity. Wall claddings can be drained and roof membranes relieved with elements such as screed drying breathers, but in many cases it will be more appropriate to redesign the construction. It will be almost impossible to install a significantly more vapour resistive layer on the inside of the construction because of the difficulties in maintaining continuity at junctions of surfaces and at penetrations by fixings and services.

It may be best to omit a vapour barrier if it is difficult to locate it in a position where it does not become the condensation plane. This approach is successful where the materials of construction of the element are sufficiently vapour resistive to ensure that the net movement of moisture does not cause humidification or dehumidification problems in the internal spaces.

7.8.3 Effect of air movement

Air movement in a space has the obvious effect of introducing air at the supply condition and removing air at the room condition so this can often reduce the moisture content of a space. However, air movement can cause draughts and can also change the temperature of a space, which may not be desirable. Reducing the temperature reduces the dew-point temperature, which may increase the risk of surface condensation while maintaining the temperature may require increased energy consumption.

Controlled air movement in voids or cavities can be used to prevent interstitial condensation. The air supplied to the cavity can be used to absorb moisture diffusing from the high vapour pressure side and so reduce the vapour pressure in the void or cavity and the moisture transfer into the rest of the construction. Air supplied at the temperature of the cavity that would occur if it were not ventilated, will not change the thermal characteristics of the wall.

Uncontrolled air movement through gaps in a construction will transfer moisture at rates which are orders of magnitude greater than that of diffusion, particularly where there are vapour barriers which are bypassed.

Some assessment of the steady state ventilation rate required can be made from the following equation:

$$q_v = \phi_l / (g_{max} - g_a) \rho_a l_e \qquad (7.9)$$

where q_v is the volume flow rate ($m^3 \cdot s^{-1}$), ϕ_l is the latent heat flow rate ($W \cdot m^{-2}$), g_{max} is the maximum moisture content to avoid condensation ($kg \cdot kg^{-1}$), g_a is the moisture content of air ($kg \cdot kg^{-1}$), l_e is the specific latent heat of evaporation ($J \cdot kg^{-1}$) and ρ_a is the density of air ($kg \cdot m^{-3}$).

7.9 Non-steady state calculations

7.9.1 General

There are two areas where variable state, as opposed to steady state, calculations should be considered:

— moisture flow through a material layer

— moisture content of a ventilated space.

The former could be approached by adopting a 'moisture admittance' concept since moisture transfer and heat transfer through a material can be described by similar equations. However, the variation of vapour pressure encountered in reality is not sinusoidal. Internally, it is more likely to tend exponentially to some upper or lower limit while externally, the changes can vary rapidly or remain reasonably constant depending on the weather. Finite element/difference methods are being developed to allow for these difficulties.

Both these and any 'moisture admittance' method would need to be based on a moisture transfer property analogous to thermal diffusivity. However, the moisture transfer properties of materials are not known with the same confidence as are their thermal properties and, at present, this reduces the benefits that would be gained from such analysis. The justification for the development of these methods is that it has already been shown that the moisture transfer time constants differ considerably from the corresponding thermal time constants and, as would be expected, are not necessarily proportional to them.

For the analysis of moisture in ventilated spaces, if the moisture generation or ventilation is intermittent, steady state calculation techniques are inadequate and a non-steady state method must be used.

Equations can be written directly in terms of the conditions of the supply air, the initial space air and the latent gains, but these are complicated. It is simpler to write equations in terms of enthalpy and solve for either sensible or latent heat flow. The dry bulb temperature and moisture content (or saturation) can then be evaluated. A suitable enthalpy equation[8] is given below but it is essential to evaluate the sensible heat gain or loss and the latent heat gain or loss separately.

$$h = (h_a + \Delta h_\theta)(1 - e^{(-N\theta)}) + h_o e^{(-N\theta)} \qquad (7.10)$$

where h is the specific enthalpy (sensible or latent) of room air ($kJ \cdot kg^{-1}$), h_a is the specific enthalpy (sensible or latent) of supply air ($kJ \cdot kg^{-1}$), h_o is the initial specific enthalpy (sensible or latent) of room air ($kJ \cdot kg^{-1}$), Δh_θ is the change of specific enthalpy of room air over time θ ($kJ \cdot kg^{-1}$), N is the room air change rate (h^{-1}) and θ is time (h).

7.9.2 Variation of room moisture content with intermittent plant operation

An example of where transient calculations are of interest is where air conditioning plant is operated intermittently. If the plant is turned off at night, the difference between the inside and outside moisture contents will vary according to the following relationship[8]:

$$(g_\theta - g_e) / (g_d - g_e) = e^{(-N\theta)} \qquad (7.11)$$

where g_θ is the room moisture at time θ after plant 'off' ($kg \cdot kg^{-1}$), g_e is the external moisture content (assumed constant) ($kg \cdot kg^{-1}$), g_d is the room design moisture content ($kg \cdot kg^{-1}$), N is the room air change rate for outside air (h^{-1}) and θ is time (h).

For example, if $N = 0.25$ air changes per hour, the difference between the room and outside will be 50% of the design difference after 2.8 hours, 10% after 9.2 hours and 5% after 12 hours.

Example 7.2

Consider a fan coil system with treated primary air. Dehumidification is by primary air, the fan coil chilled water flow temperature is equal to the room dew-point temperature plus 0.5 K. How soon can chilled water be circulated through the coils, assuming a suitable pre-occupancy ventilation period?

If $g_e = 1.3\, g_d$ and the difference between internal and external moisture content is 10% of the design value, then:

$$(g_\theta - 1.3\, g_d) / (g_d - 1.3\, g_d) = 0.1$$

Hence:

$$g_\theta = 1.27\, g_d$$

This condition becomes the initial condition when the primary air is first circulated, so that at two air changes per hour, the time to pull down the room moisture content to the design value is obtained from equation 7.11, thus:

$$\theta = -0.5 \log_n [(g_d - g_s) / (1.27\, g_d - g_s)]$$

where g_s is the supply moisture content ($kg \cdot kg^{-1}$).

Taking $g_s = 0.8\, g_d$:

$$\theta = 0.43\ h;\ i.e.\ about\ 26\ minutes$$

References

1   *BS 5250: 1989 (1995): Code of practice for control of condensation in buildings* (London: British Standards Institution) (1995)

2   Johansson C H Moisture transmission and moisture distribution in building materials *Technical Translation 189* (Ottawa: National Research Council)

3   Billington N S *Building Physics: Heat* (London: Pergamon Press) (1967)

4   *Heat transfer* CIBSE Guide C3 (London: Chartered Institution of Building Services Engineers) (1976)

5   *BS 6229: 1982: Code of practice for flat roofs with continuously supported coverings* (London: British Standards Institution) (1982)

6   *Properties of humid air* CIBSE Guide C1 (London: Chartered Institution of Building Services Engineers) (1975)

7   Fitzgerald D Avoiding condensation in buildings *Heating and Air Conditioning* 55 10 (October 1985)

8   Letherman K M Room air moisture content: Dynamic effects of ventilation vapour generation *Building Services Eng.* **9**(2) 49–53 (1988)

Appendix 7.A1: Algorithm for interstitial condensation

Enter the details of each layer of the wall (thickness, vapour resistivity, thermal conductivity) and the surface thermal and vapour resistances. Calculate the thermal and vapour resistances of each layer, together with the cumulative resistances, starting from the inside.

Data:
— internal surface thermal resistance   RSIN
— internal surface vapour resistance   GSIN
— number of layers in wall   NLAY

Calculation:
— cumulative thermal resistance at internal surface (interface 1)   RCUM(1)
   RCUM(1)=RSIN
— cumulative vapour resistance at internal surface (interface 1)   GCUM(1)
   GCUM(1)=GSIN

Data:
— thickness of layer N   THIK(N)
— thermal conductivity of layer N   COND(N)
— vapour resistivity of layer N   DIFF(N)

Calculation:
— thermal resistance of layer N   RLAY(N)
   RLAY(N)=THIK(N)/COND(N)
— vapour resistance of layer N   GLAY(N)
   GLAY(N)=THIK(N)* DIFF(N)
— cumulative thermal resistance up to and including layer N   RCUM(N+1)
   RCUM(N+1)=RCUM(N)+RLAY(N)
— cumulative vapour resistance up to and including layer N   GCUM(N+1)
   GCUM(N+1)=GCUM(N)+GLAY(N)

Data:
— outside thermal resistance   ROUT
— outside vapour resistance   GOUT

Calculation:
— cumulative thermal resistance to outside air   RCUM(NLAY+2)
   RCUM(NLAY+2)=RCUM(NLAY+1)+ROUT
— cumulative vapour resistance to outside air   GCUM(NLAY+2)
   GCUM(NLAY+2)=GCUM(NLAY+1)+GOUT

Enter the inside and outside design conditions (air temperatures and relative humidities) and calculate the inside and outside vapour pressures. Calculate the temperature distribution through the wall and the corresponding saturation vapour pressures at each interface. Check for surface condensation.

Data:
— inside air temperature   TIN
— inside relative humidity   RHIN
— outside air temperature   TOUT
— outside relative humidity   RHOUT
— inside saturation vapour pressure   SVPIN
— outside saturation vapour pressure   SVPOUT

Calculation:
— inside vapour pressure   VP(1)
   VP(1)=SVPIN*RHIN/100
— outside vapour pressure   VP(1)
   VP(NLAY+1)=SVPOUT*RHIN/100
— heat flow through wall   HEAT
   HEAT=(TIN-TOUT)/RCUM(NLAY+2)
— temperature at interface N   TEMP(N)
   TEMP(N)=TIN-RCUM(N)*HEAT

— saturation vapour pressure at each interface   SVP(N)
   IF TEMP(N)>=0 THEN SVP(N)=33.59051-
   8.2*LOG10(273.15+TEMP(N))+
   (0.0024804*(273.15+TEMP(N)))-
   3142.31/(273.15+TEMP(N))
   IF TEMP(N)<0 THEN SVP(N)=12.5380997-
   (2663.91/(273.15+TEMP(N)))
— check for surface condensation
   IF VP(1)≥ SVP(1) THEN
   (surface condensation occurs)

Enter the data appropriate to the inner and outer interfaces for the construction. Initially these will be 1 and NLAY+1. Starting from the inside, calculate the vapour pressure at each interface and compare this with the saturation vapour pressure. If the vapour pressure is not greater than the saturation vapour pressure, there is no condensation. If the vapour pressure is greater than the saturation vapour pressure, then condensation occurs. In this case, the condition at the interface must be changed to the saturation vapour pressure and the wall, or section of wall, divided into two sub-sections: from the inner interface to the condensation point and from the condensation point to the outer interface. Repeat above procedure for each section.

Because the calculation can be repeated for a section of the wall before it has been completed for the whole wall, it provides an opportunity to use recursion if programmed in a language which permits this approach.

Data:
— inner interface   NIN
— outer interface   NOUT

Calculation:
— moisture flow between inner interface and outer interface   WFLO
   WFLO=(VP(NIN)-VP(NOUT))/(GCUM(NOUT)-GCUM(NIN))
— vapour pressure at interface N   VP(N)
   VP(N)=(VP(NIN)-((GCUM(N)-GCUM(NIN))*WFLO
   IF VP(N)<=SVP(N) THEN (carry on to next surface)
   IF VP(N)>SVP(N) THEN VP(N)=SVP(N)
— repeat calculation for sub-sections of wall

Calculate the condensation at each interface by taking the difference between the moisture flow to and from each interface. Ignore inner surface when doing this.

Calculation:
— flow to interface N   FLO1
   FLO1=(VP(N-1)-VP(N))/(GCUM(N)-GCUM(N-1))
— flow from interface N   FLO2
   FLO2=(VP(N)-VP(N+1))/(GCUM(N+1)-GCUM(N))
— condensation at interface N   DRIP(N)
   DRIP(N)=FLO1-FLO2
   END

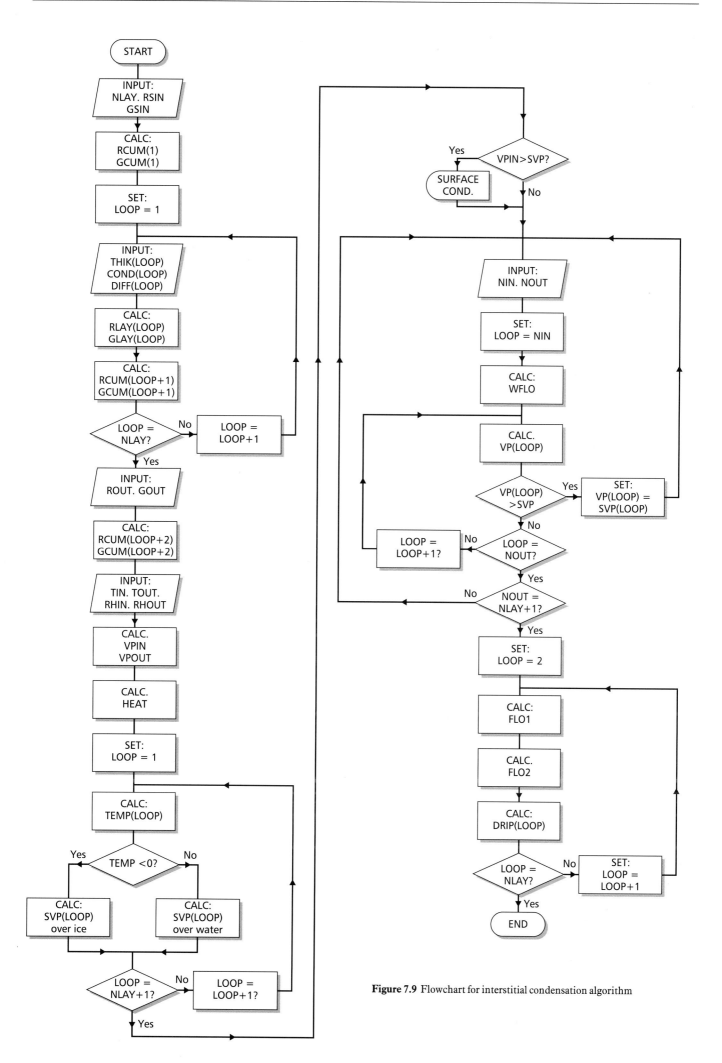

Figure 7.9 Flowchart for interstitial condensation algorithm

Index